A MARVEL COMICS EVENT

# CIVIL WAR

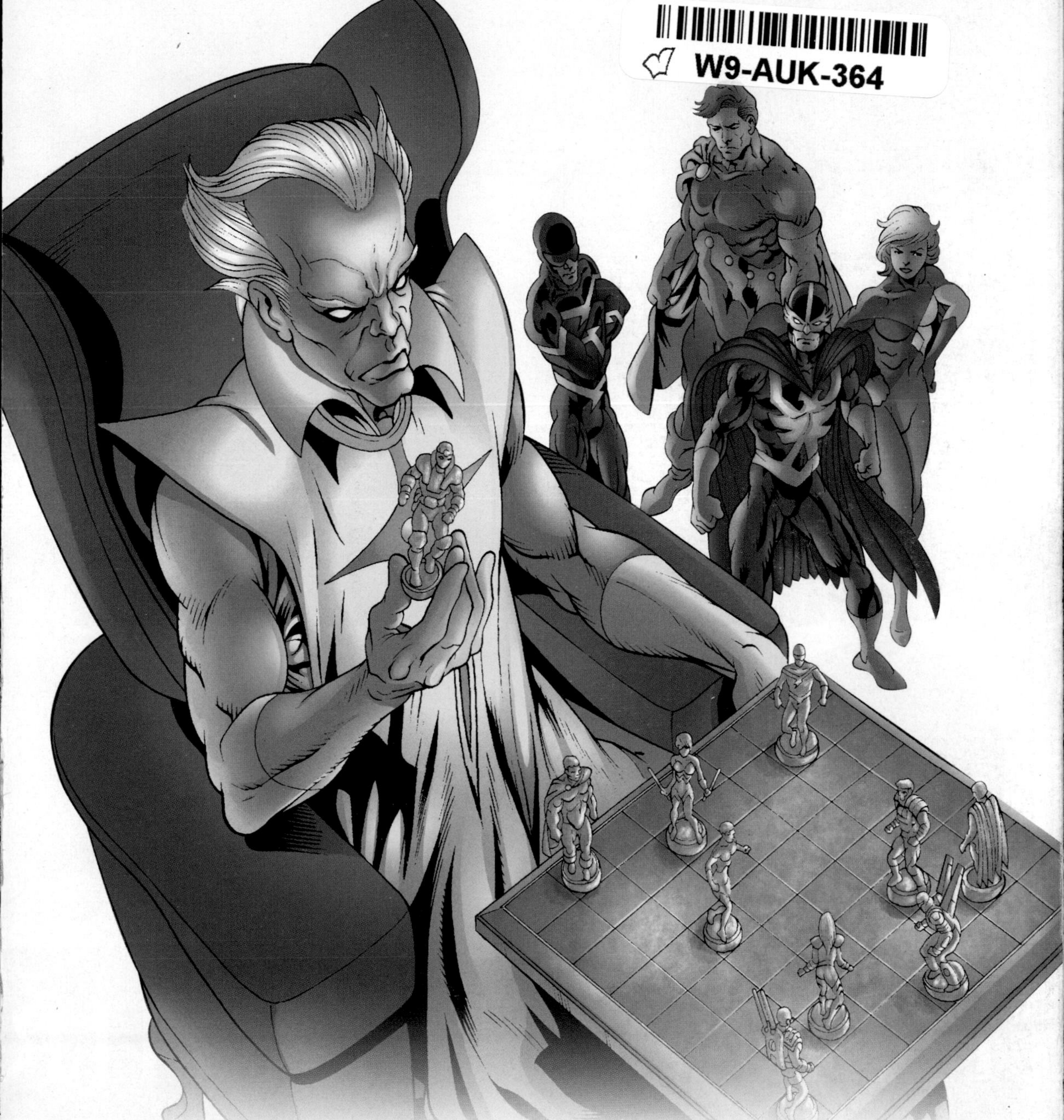



# HEROES FOR HIRE
# THUNDERBOLTS

A

# MARVEL COMICS

## PRESENTATION

# CIVIL
# HEROES FOR HIR

**CIVIL WAR: HEROES FOR HIRE/THUNDEBOLTS.** Contains material originally published in magazine form as HEROES FOR HIRE #1-5 and THUNDERBOLTS #101-105. First printing 2016. ISBN# 978-0-7851-9566-5. Published by MARVEL WORLDWIDE, INC., a subsidiary of MARVEL ENTERTAINMENT, LLC. OFFICE OF PUBLICATION: 135 West 50th Street, New York, NY 10020. Copyright © 2016 MARVEL No similarity between any of the names, characters, persons, and/or institutions in this magazine with those of any living or dead person or institution is intended, and any such similarity which may exist is purely coincidental. **Printed in the U.S.A.** ALAN FINE, President, Marvel Entertainment; DAN BUCKLEY, President, TV, Publishing & Brand Management; JOE QUESADA, Chief Creative Officer; TOM BREVOORT, SVP of Publishing; DAVID BOGART, SVP of Business Affairs & Operations, Publishing & Partnership; C.B. CEBULSKI, VP of Brand Management & Development, Asia; DAVID GABRIEL, SVP of Sales & Marketing, Publishing; JEFF YOUNGQUIST, VP of Production & Special Projects; DAN CARR, Executive Director of Publishing Technology; ALEX MORALES, Director of Publishing Operations; SUSAN CRESPI, Production Manager; STAN LEE, Chairman Emeritus. For information regarding advertising in Marvel Comics or on Marvel.com, please contact Vit DeBellis, Integrated Sales Manager, at vdebellis@marvel.com. For Marvel subscription inquiries, please call 888-511-5480. **Manufactured between 2/3/2016 and 3/7/2016 by R.R. DONNELLEY, INC., SALEM, VA, USA.**

10 9 8 7 6 5 4 3 2 1

**THUNDERBOLTS #101-103**
WRITER
FABIAN NICIEZA

PENCILERS
TOM GRUMMETT
WITH DAVE ROSS (#101)

INKERS
GARY ERSKINE
WITH CAM SMITH (#101)

COLORISTS
SOTOCOLOR'S J. BROWN
WITH A. STREET (#101)

LETTERERS
RS & COMICRAFT'S
ALBERT DESCHESNE

COVER ART
TOM GRUMMETT,
GARY ERSKINE &
CHRIS SOTOMAYOR

EDITOR
MOLLY LAZER

CONSULTING EDITOR
TOM BREVOORT

**HEROES FOR HIRE #1-5**
WRITERS
JUSTIN GRAY &
JIMMY PALMIOTTI

PENCILERS
BILLY TUCCI (#1-4) &
FRANCIS PORTELA (#2-5)

INKERS
TOM PALMER (#1-4) &
TERRY PALLOT (#4-5)

COLORISTS
MARTE GRACIA (#1-2) &
BRAD ANDERSON (#2-5)

LETTERER
ARTMONKEYS'
DAVE LANPHEAR

COVER ART
BILLY TUCCI &
MARK SPARACIO

ASSISTANT EDITOR
NATE COSBY

EDITOR
MARK PANICCIA

COLLECTION EDITOR
JENNIFER GRÜNWALD

ASSOCIATE EDITOR
SARAH BRUNSTAD

ASSOCIATE MANAGING EDITOR
ALEX STARBUCK

EDITOR, SPECIAL PROJECTS
MARK D. BEAZLEY

VP, PRODUCTION &
SPECIAL PROJECTS
JEFF YOUNGQUIST

SVP PRINT, SALES & MARKETING
DAVID GABRIEL

EDITOR IN CHIEF
AXEL ALONSO

CHIEF CREATIVE OFFICER
JOE QUESADA

PUBLISHER
DAN BUCKLEY

EXECUTIVE PRODUCER
ALAN FINE

# WAR
## /THUNDERBOLTS

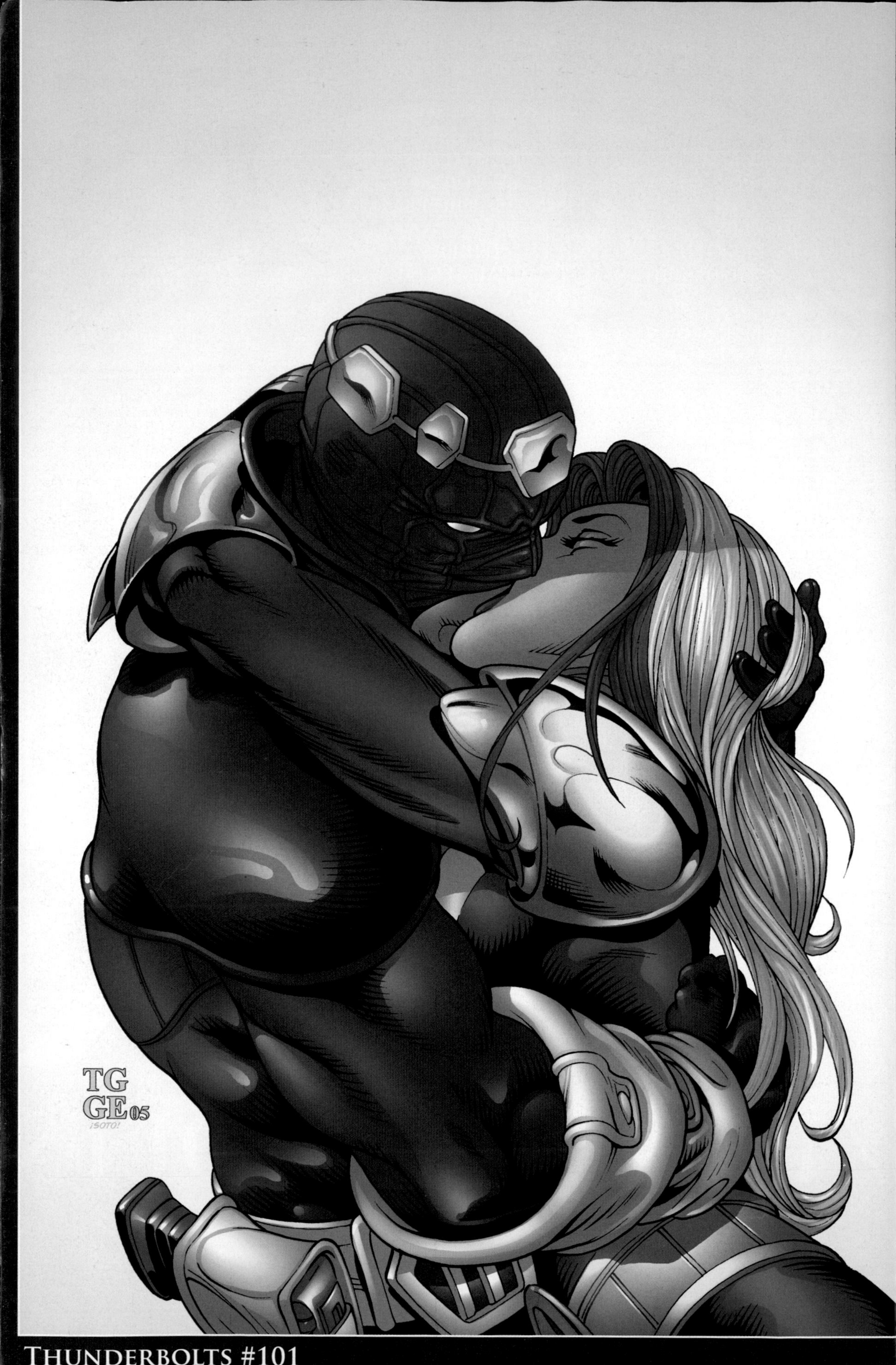
TG
GE05
¡SOTO!

THUNDERBOLTS #101

THEY WERE THE MASTERS OF EVIL. THEY WERE SUPER-VILLAINS. THEY HAD A PLAN. THEY PRETENDED TO BE HEROES. SLOWLY, THEY REALIZED THEY REALLY WANTED TO BE HEROES. SOME HAVE FAILED. SOME HAVE SUCCEEDED. MOST ARE STILL TRYING...

BARON HELMUT ZEMO

MELISSA GOLD
SONGBIRD

ABE JENKINS
M.A.C.H. IV

P. NORBERT EBERSOL
FIXER

IT DOESN'T ALWAYS GO THE WAY WE PLANNED. THE WAY WE WANT. IT'S GETTING TO THE POINT WHERE I ALMOST DON'T WANT TO BOTHER ASKING WHY ANYMORE. IN ORDER TO SAVE THE UNIVERSE, WE HAD TO KILL ONE OF OUR TEAMMATES. RIDICULOUS. *GENIS-VELL* WAS ONCE KNOWN AS *LEGACY*, THEN HE ACCEPTED HIS FATHER'S MANTLE, CALLING HIMSELF *CAPTAIN MARVEL*. THEN, FEELING HE'D FAILED LIVING UP TO THAT, HE CHANGED HIS NAME TO *PHOTON*.

I THINK HE DID THAT BECAUSE A PART OF HIM *KNEW* HE WAS GOING TO HAVE TO DIE AND HE DIDN'T WANT TO FAIL AGAIN AS CAPTAIN MARVEL. I WAS TEAM LEADER, AND I AGREED WITH THE DECISION TO KILL HIM BECAUSE HE'D BECOME LIKE SOME WALKING *HOLE* IN *TIME* AND *SPACE* AND THOSE HOLES WERE *SPREADING*. EVENTUALLY, THEY WOULD HAVE SWALLOWED UP ALL OF EXISTENCE.

SO WITH GENIS BURIED, WE'VE DONE WHAT WE ALWAYS DO: WE'VE MOVED ON (ACTUALLY, SINCE HIS BODY WAS BISECTED AND SPREAD ACROSS TIME AND SPACE, THERE WASN'T MUCH TO BURY).

DR. CHEN LU
THE RADIOACTIVE MAN

*ZEMO* HAD GATHERED A GROUP OF FORMER T-BOLTS TO KILL PHOTON. HE WAS RESPONSIBLE FOR THE PROBLEMS GENIS WAS HAVING AND WANTED TO SOLVE THE MATTER--AND TAKE THE RESPONSIBILITY OUT OF OUR HANDS.

ERIK JOSTEN
ATLAS

AFTER THE FIGHT, THERE WERE SOME LOOSE ENDS. OUR OLD TEAMMATE, *MOONSTONE*, WHO HAD ATTACKED US, TURNED OUT TO STILL BE IN A *VEGETATIVE STATE* (PUPPET STRINGS PULLED COURTESY OF ZEMO'S CONTROL OVER HER TWIN ALIEN GEMSTONES).

AND *BLACKOUT*, WHO WE *KNEW* HAD *DIED* BATTLING THE *AVENGERS* YEARS AGO, TURNED OUT TO HAVE BEEN DEAD ALL ALONG. HIS CORPSE HAD BEEN SUCKED INTO THE DARKFORCE DIMENSION, WHICH SEEMS TO CALL BACK ITS OWN, AND THAT PROVED TO BE THE HIDING PLACE FOR ATLAS'S BROTHER, THE *SMUGGLER*, WHO HAD BEEN LOST IN BATTLE OVER A YEAR AGO.

DONNIE GILL
BLIZZARD

CONRAD JOSTEN
SMUGGLER

OH, YEAH, *MAN-KILLER* PULLED A DISAPPEARING ACT LIKE SHE ALWAYS DOES WHEN IT'S TIME TO MAKE HARD CHOICES.

SO THAT LEAVES US WITH *TEN THUNDERBOLTS*, EVERY SINGLE ONE OF THEM AFRAID TO ASK THE HARDEST QUESTION: *AFTER EVERYTHING THAT'S HAPPENED, WHY ARE WE DOING THIS?*

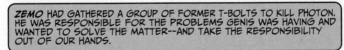

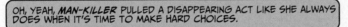

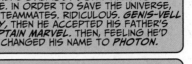

JANICE OLIVIA YANIZESKI
JOYSTICK

ANDREAS STRUCKER
SWORDSMAN

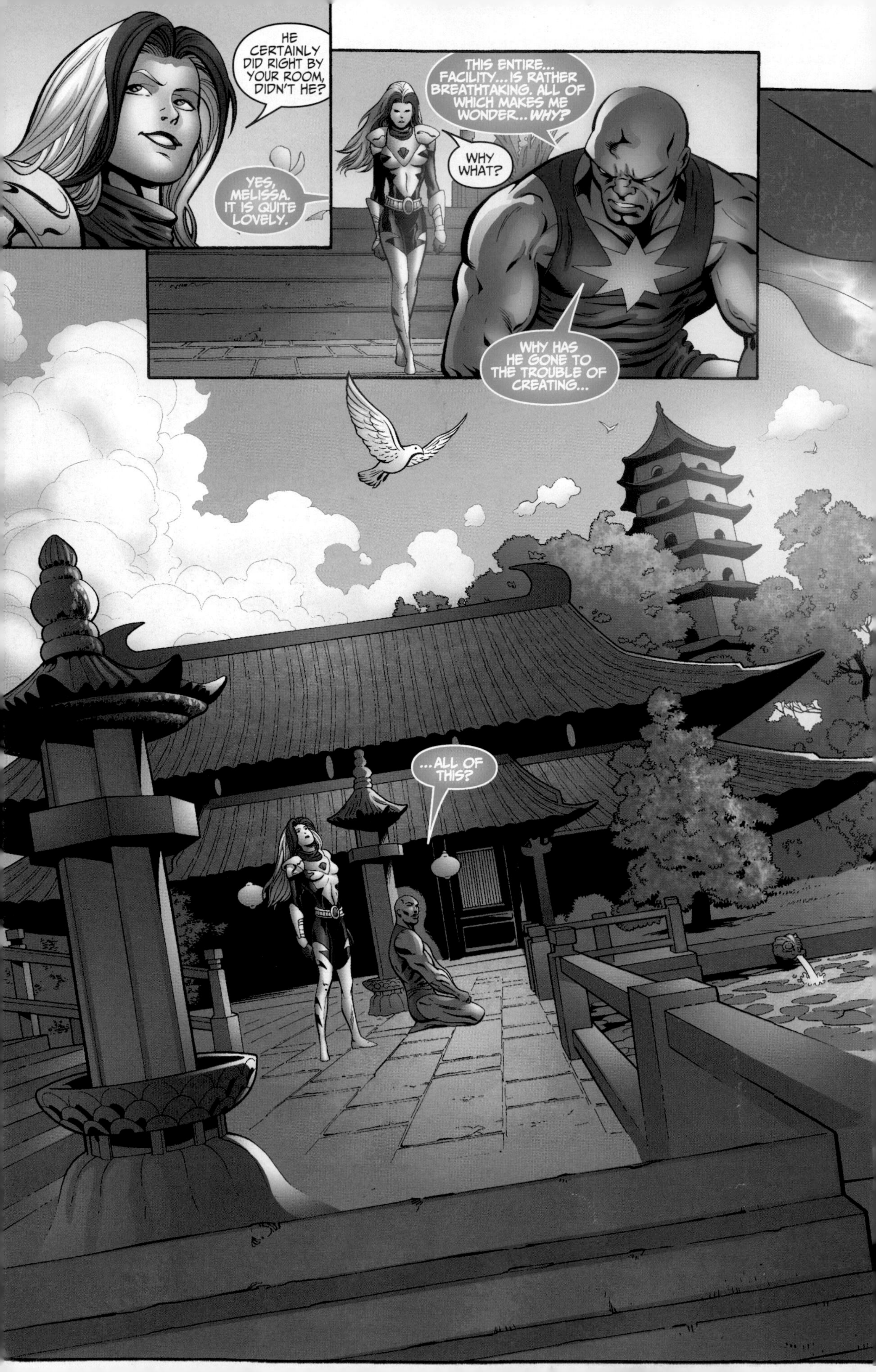
HE CERTAINLY DID RIGHT BY YOUR ROOM, DIDN'T HE?
YES, MELISSA. IT IS QUITE LOVELY.
THIS ENTIRE... FACILITY... IS RATHER BREATHTAKING. ALL OF WHICH MAKES ME WONDER... WHY?
WHY WHAT?
WHY HAS HE GONE TO THE TROUBLE OF CREATING...
...ALL OF THIS?

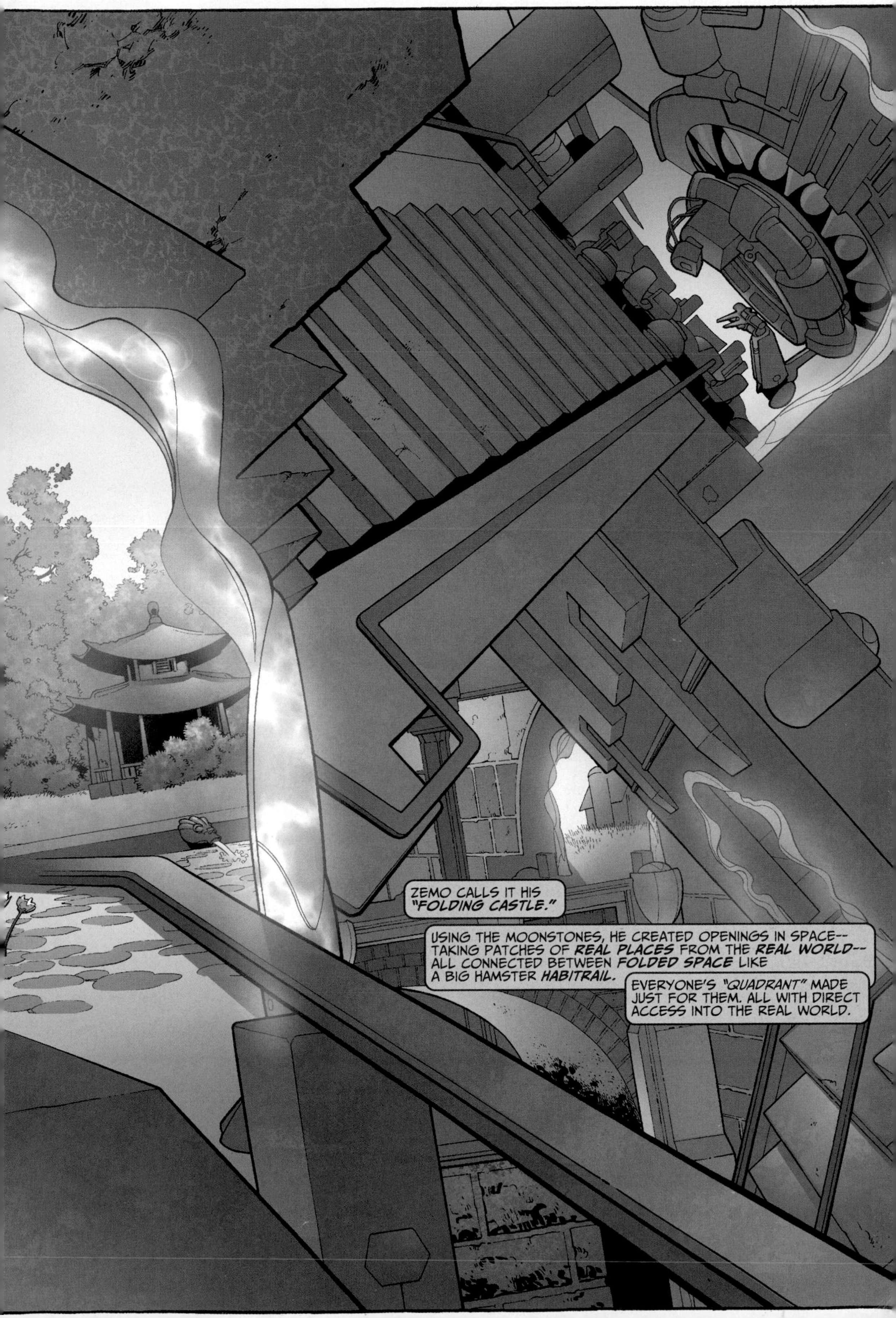
ZEMO CALLS IT HIS "FOLDING CASTLE."
USING THE MOONSTONES, HE CREATED OPENINGS IN SPACE-- TAKING PATCHES OF REAL PLACES FROM THE REAL WORLD-- ALL CONNECTED BETWEEN FOLDED SPACE LIKE A BIG HAMSTER HABITRAIL.
EVERYONE'S "QUADRANT" MADE JUST FOR THEM. ALL WITH DIRECT ACCESS INTO THE REAL WORLD.

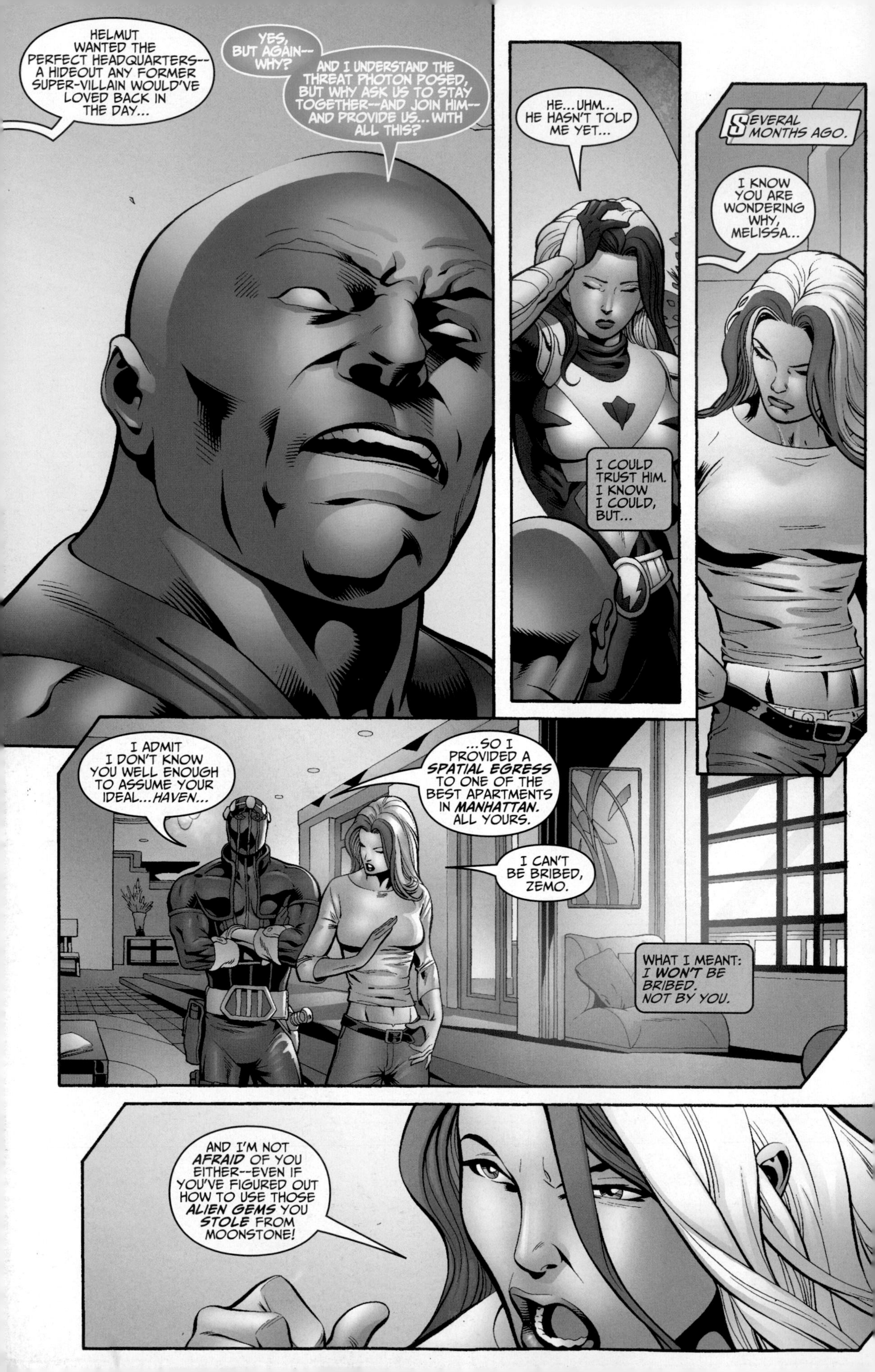

HELMUT WANTED THE PERFECT HEADQUARTERS-- A HIDEOUT ANY FORMER SUPER-VILLAIN WOULD'VE LOVED BACK IN THE DAY...
YES, BUT AGAIN-- WHY?
AND I UNDERSTAND THE THREAT PHOTON POSED, BUT WHY ASK US TO STAY TOGETHER--AND JOIN HIM-- AND PROVIDE US... WITH ALL THIS?
HE... UHM... HE HASN'T TOLD ME YET...
I COULD TRUST HIM. I KNOW I COULD, BUT...
SEVERAL MONTHS AGO.
I KNOW YOU ARE WONDERING WHY, MELISSA...
I ADMIT I DON'T KNOW YOU WELL ENOUGH TO ASSUME YOUR IDEAL...HAVEN...
...SO I PROVIDED A SPATIAL EGRESS TO ONE OF THE BEST APARTMENTS IN MANHATTAN. ALL YOURS.
I CAN'T BE BRIBED, ZEMO.
WHAT I MEANT: I WON'T BE BRIBED. NOT BY YOU.
AND I'M NOT AFRAID OF YOU EITHER--EVEN IF YOU'VE FIGURED OUT HOW TO USE THOSE ALIEN GEMS YOU STOLE FROM MOONSTONE!

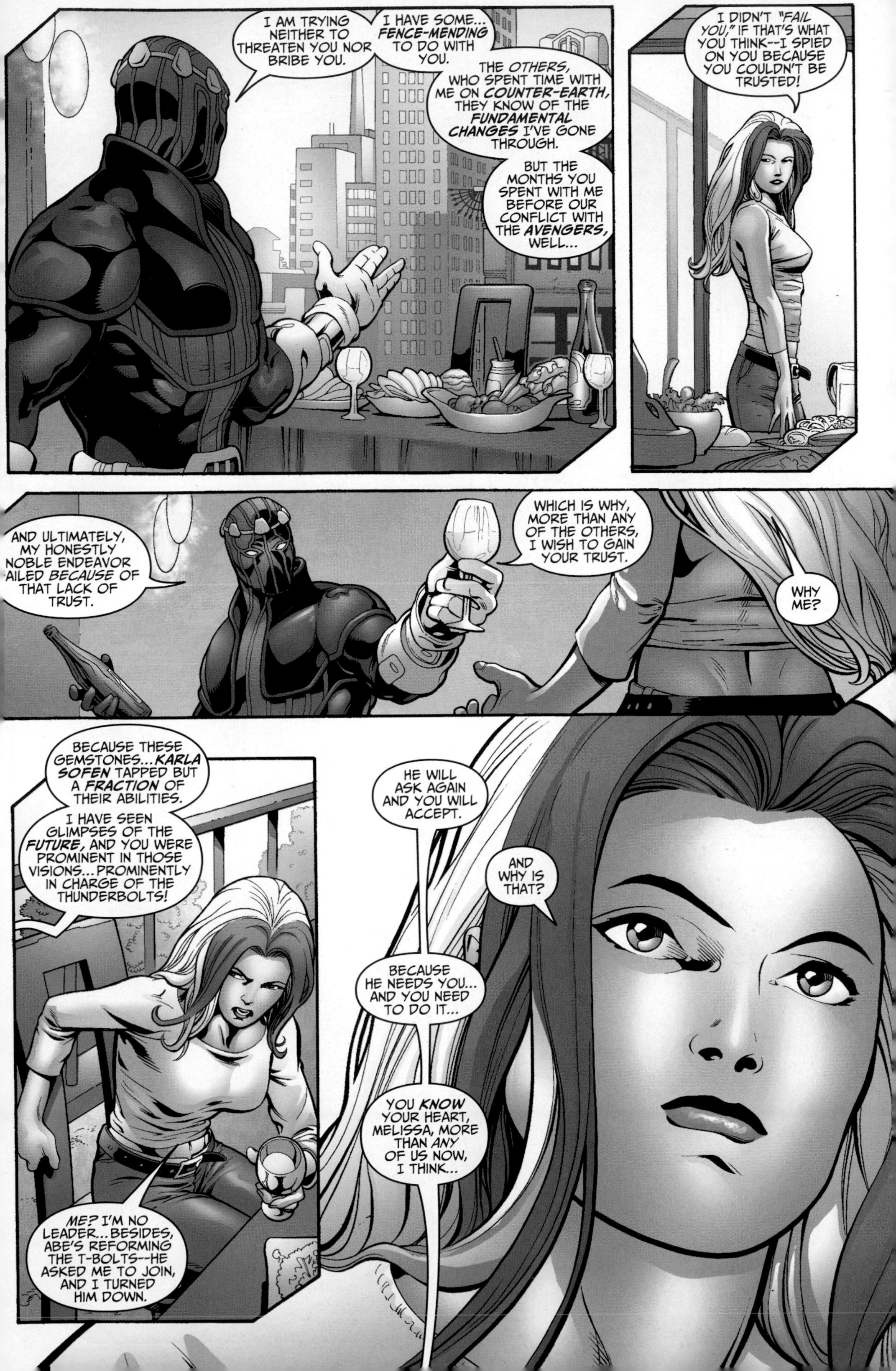
I AM TRYING NEITHER TO THREATEN YOU NOR BRIBE YOU.
I HAVE SOME... FENCE-MENDING TO DO WITH YOU.
THE OTHERS, WHO SPENT TIME WITH ME ON COUNTER-EARTH, THEY KNOW OF THE FUNDAMENTAL CHANGES I'VE GONE THROUGH.
BUT THE MONTHS YOU SPENT WITH ME BEFORE OUR CONFLICT WITH THE AVENGERS, WELL...
I DIDN'T "FAIL YOU," IF THAT'S WHAT YOU THINK--I SPIED ON YOU BECAUSE YOU COULDN'T BE TRUSTED!
AND ULTIMATELY, MY HONESTLY NOBLE ENDEAVOR AILED BECAUSE OF THAT LACK OF TRUST.
WHICH IS WHY, MORE THAN ANY OF THE OTHERS, I WISH TO GAIN YOUR TRUST.
WHY ME?
BECAUSE THESE GEMSTONES... KARLA SOFEN TAPPED BUT A FRACTION OF THEIR ABILITIES.
I HAVE SEEN GLIMPSES OF THE FUTURE, AND YOU WERE PROMINENT IN THOSE VISIONS... PROMINENTLY IN CHARGE OF THE THUNDERBOLTS!
ME? I'M NO LEADER... BESIDES, ABE'S REFORMING THE T-BOLTS--HE ASKED ME TO JOIN, AND I TURNED HIM DOWN.
HE WILL ASK AGAIN AND YOU WILL ACCEPT.
AND WHY IS THAT?
BECAUSE HE NEEDS YOU... AND YOU NEED TO DO IT...
YOU KNOW YOUR HEART, MELISSA, MORE THAN ANY OF US NOW, I THINK...

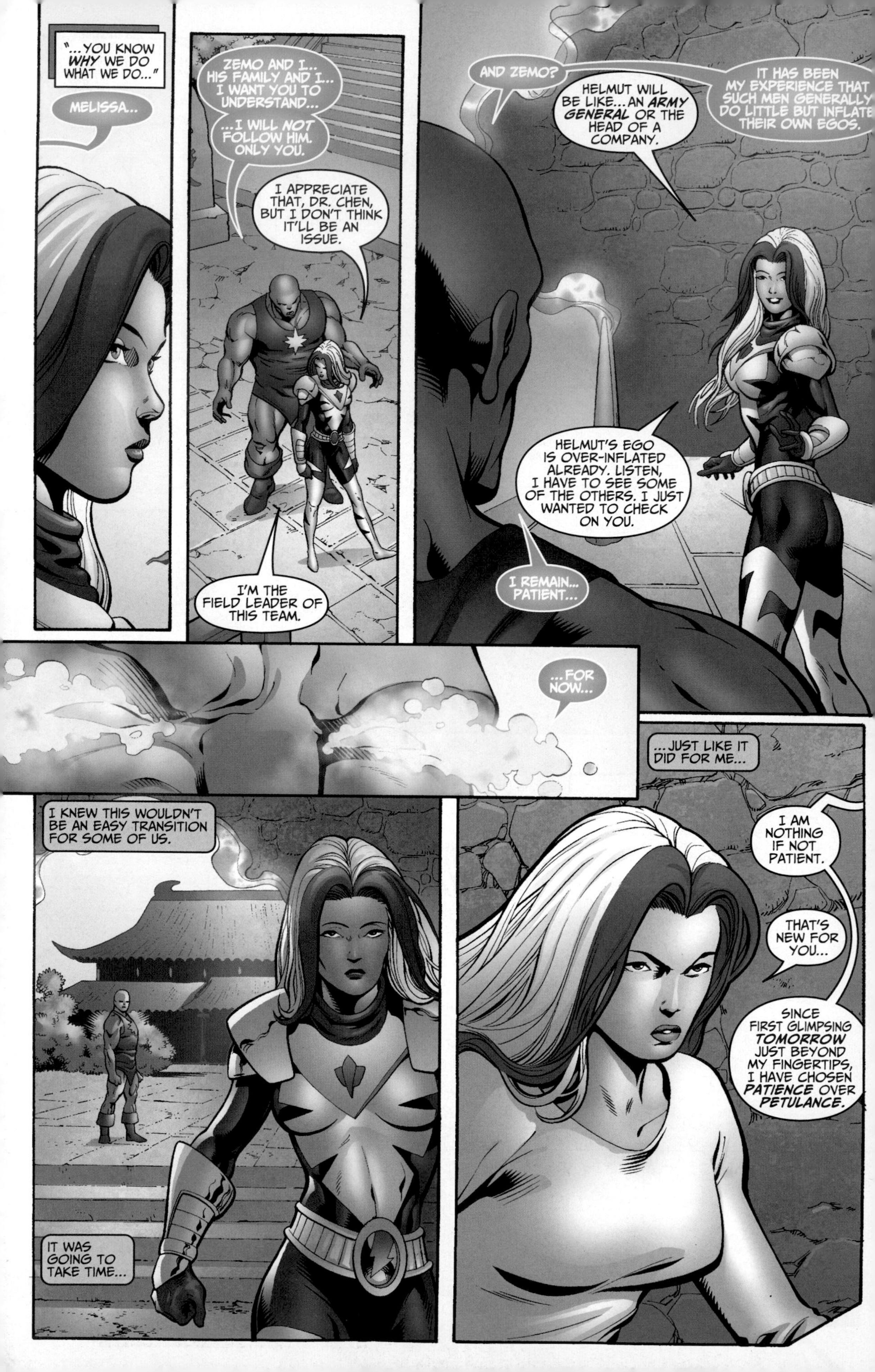
"...YOU KNOW *WHY* WE DO WHAT WE DO..."
MELISSA..
ZEMO AND I... HIS FAMILY AND I... I WANT YOU TO UNDERSTAND...
...I WILL *NOT* FOLLOW HIM. ONLY YOU.
I APPRECIATE THAT, DR. CHEN, BUT I DON'T THINK IT'LL BE AN ISSUE.
I'M THE FIELD LEADER OF THIS TEAM.
AND ZEMO?
HELMUT WILL BE LIKE...AN *ARMY GENERAL* OR THE HEAD OF A COMPANY.
IT HAS BEEN MY EXPERIENCE THAT SUCH MEN GENERALLY DO LITTLE BUT INFLATE THEIR OWN EGOS.
HELMUT'S EGO IS OVER-INFLATED ALREADY. LISTEN, I HAVE TO SEE SOME OF THE OTHERS. I JUST WANTED TO CHECK ON YOU.
I REMAIN... PATIENT...
...FOR NOW...
I KNEW THIS WOULDN'T BE AN EASY TRANSITION FOR SOME OF US.
IT WAS GOING TO TAKE TIME...
...JUST LIKE IT DID FOR ME...
I AM NOTHING IF NOT PATIENT.
THAT'S NEW FOR YOU...
SINCE FIRST GLIMPSING *TOMORROW* JUST BEYOND MY FINGERTIPS, I HAVE CHOSEN *PATIENCE* OVER *PETULANCE*.

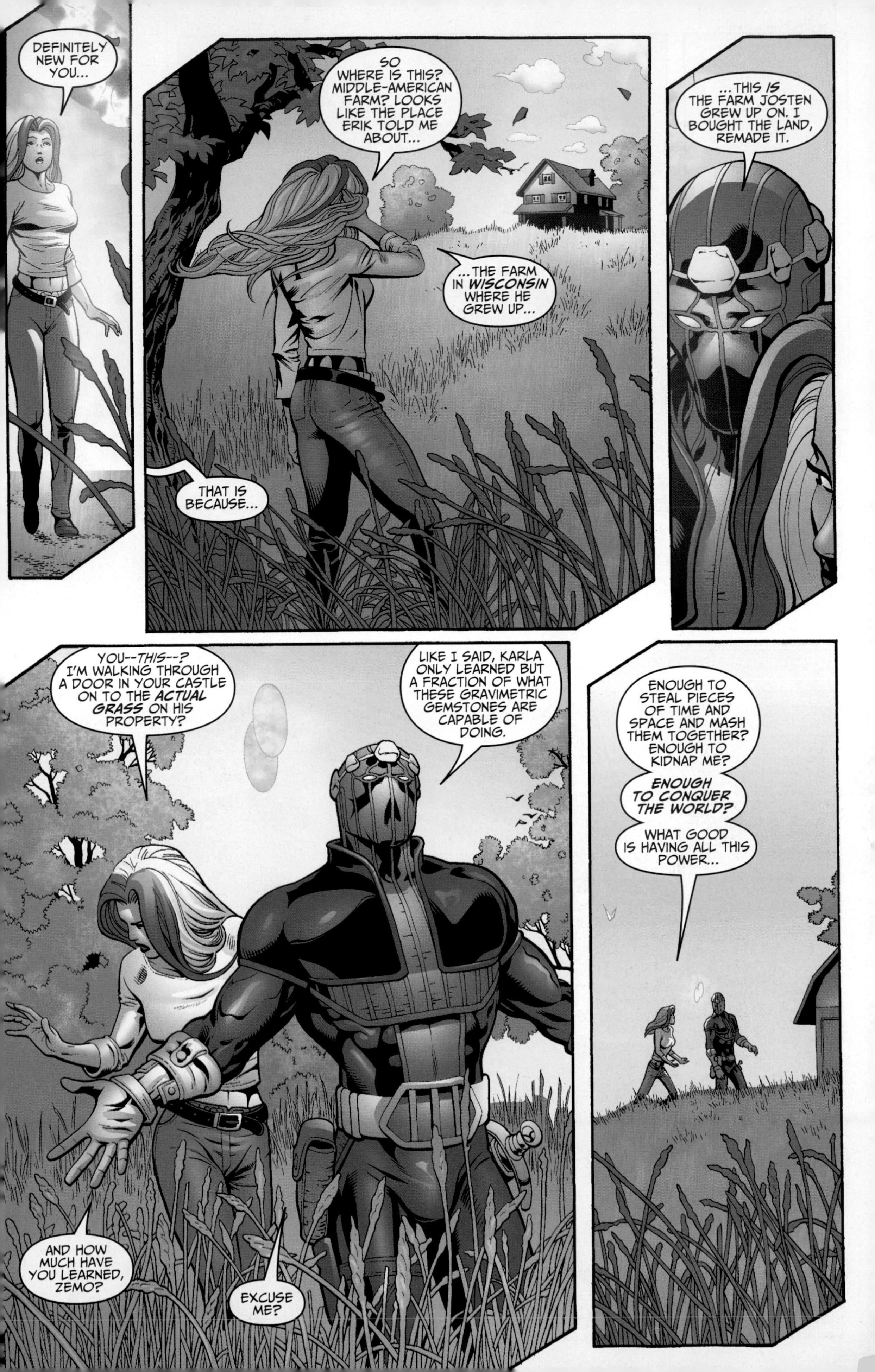
DEFINITELY NEW FOR YOU...
SO WHERE IS THIS? MIDDLE-AMERICAN FARM? LOOKS LIKE THE PLACE ERIK TOLD ME ABOUT...
...THE FARM IN WISCONSIN WHERE HE GREW UP...
THAT IS BECAUSE...
...THIS IS THE FARM JOSTEN GREW UP ON. I BOUGHT THE LAND, REMADE IT.
YOU--THIS--? I'M WALKING THROUGH A DOOR IN YOUR CASTLE ON TO THE ACTUAL GRASS ON HIS PROPERTY?
LIKE I SAID, KARLA ONLY LEARNED BUT A FRACTION OF WHAT THESE GRAVIMETRIC GEMSTONES ARE CAPABLE OF DOING.
AND HOW MUCH HAVE YOU LEARNED, ZEMO?
EXCUSE ME?
ENOUGH TO STEAL PIECES OF TIME AND SPACE AND MASH THEM TOGETHER? ENOUGH TO KIDNAP ME?
ENOUGH TO CONQUER THE WORLD?
WHAT GOOD IS HAVING ALL THIS POWER...

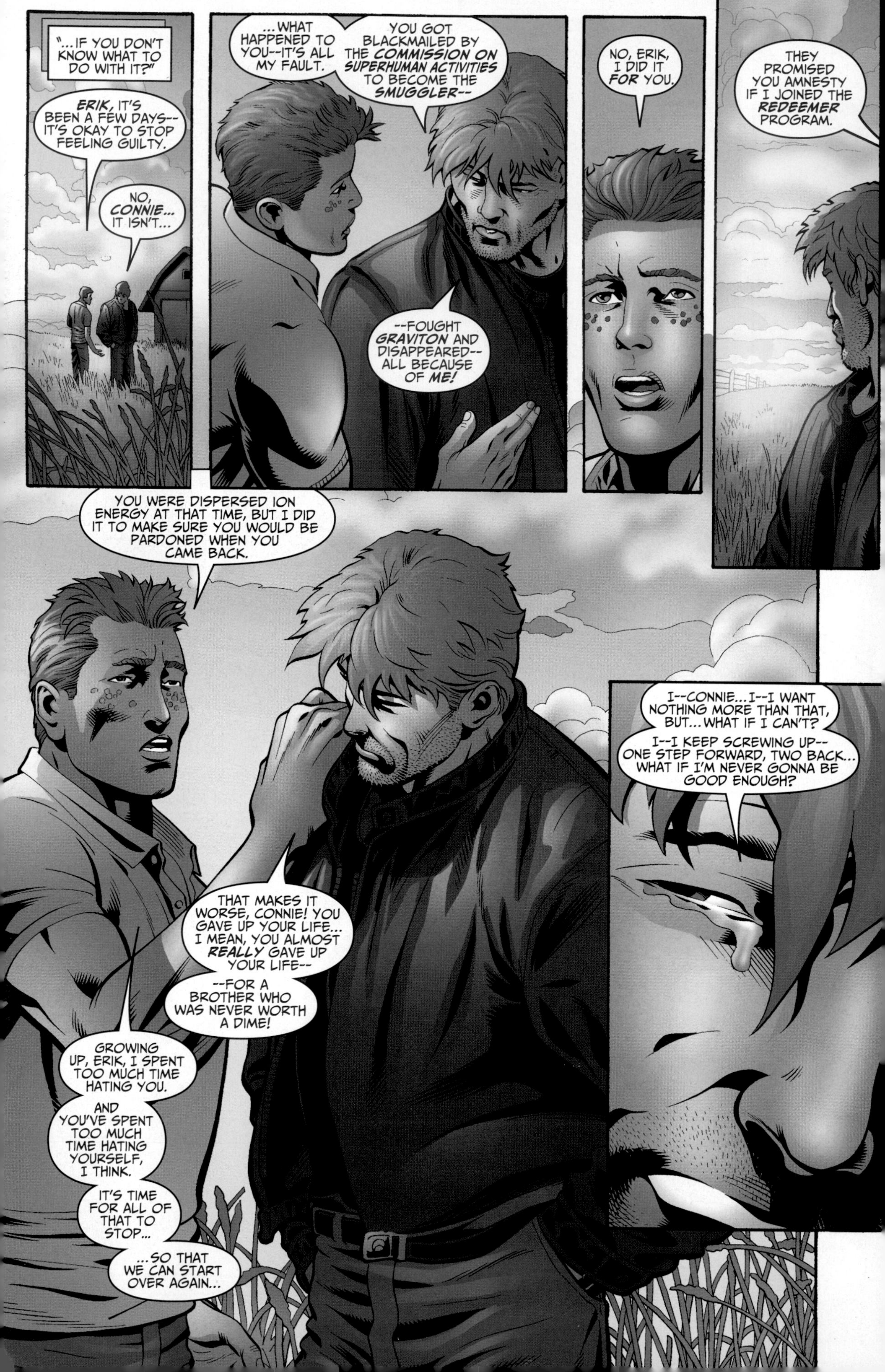
"...IF YOU DON'T KNOW WHAT TO DO WITH IT?"
ERIK, IT'S BEEN A FEW DAYS-- IT'S OKAY TO STOP FEELING GUILTY.
NO, CONNIE... IT ISN'T...
...WHAT HAPPENED TO YOU--IT'S ALL MY FAULT.
YOU GOT BLACKMAILED BY THE COMMISSION ON SUPERHUMAN ACTIVITIES TO BECOME THE SMUGGLER--
--FOUGHT GRAVITON AND DISAPPEARED-- ALL BECAUSE OF ME!
NO, ERIK, I DID IT FOR YOU.
THEY PROMISED YOU AMNESTY IF I JOINED THE REDEEMER PROGRAM.
YOU WERE DISPERSED ION ENERGY AT THAT TIME, BUT I DID IT TO MAKE SURE YOU WOULD BE PARDONED WHEN YOU CAME BACK.
THAT MAKES IT WORSE, CONNIE! YOU GAVE UP YOUR LIFE... I MEAN, YOU ALMOST REALLY GAVE UP YOUR LIFE--
--FOR A BROTHER WHO WAS NEVER WORTH A DIME!
GROWING UP, ERIK, I SPENT TOO MUCH TIME HATING YOU.
AND YOU'VE SPENT TOO MUCH TIME HATING YOURSELF, I THINK.
IT'S TIME FOR ALL OF THAT TO STOP...
...SO THAT WE CAN START OVER AGAIN...
I--CONNIE... I--I WANT NOTHING MORE THAN THAT, BUT... WHAT IF I CAN'T?
I--I KEEP SCREWING UP-- ONE STEP FORWARD, TWO BACK... WHAT IF I'M NEVER GONNA BE GOOD ENOUGH?

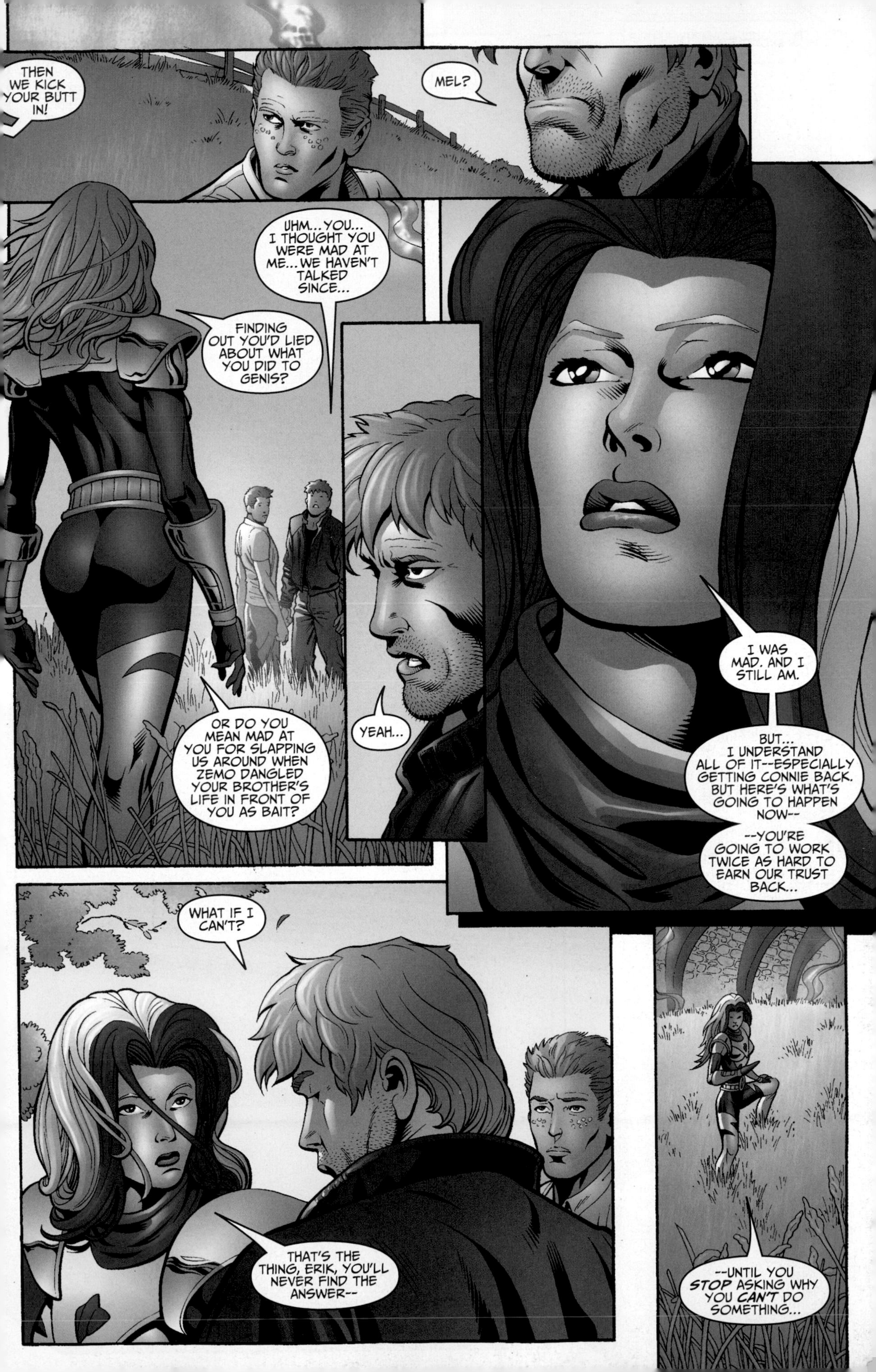
THEN WE KICK YOUR BUTT IN!
MEL?
UHM...YOU... I THOUGHT YOU WERE MAD AT ME...WE HAVEN'T TALKED SINCE...
FINDING OUT YOU'D LIED ABOUT WHAT YOU DID TO GENIS?
OR DO YOU MEAN MAD AT YOU FOR SLAPPING US AROUND WHEN ZEMO DANGLED YOUR BROTHER'S LIFE IN FRONT OF YOU AS BAIT?
YEAH...
I WAS MAD. AND I STILL AM.
BUT... I UNDERSTAND ALL OF IT--ESPECIALLY GETTING CONNIE BACK. BUT HERE'S WHAT'S GOING TO HAPPEN NOW--
--YOU'RE GOING TO WORK TWICE AS HARD TO EARN OUR TRUST BACK...
WHAT IF I CAN'T?
THAT'S THE THING, ERIK, YOU'LL NEVER FIND THE ANSWER--
--UNTIL YOU STOP ASKING WHY YOU CAN'T DO SOMETHING...

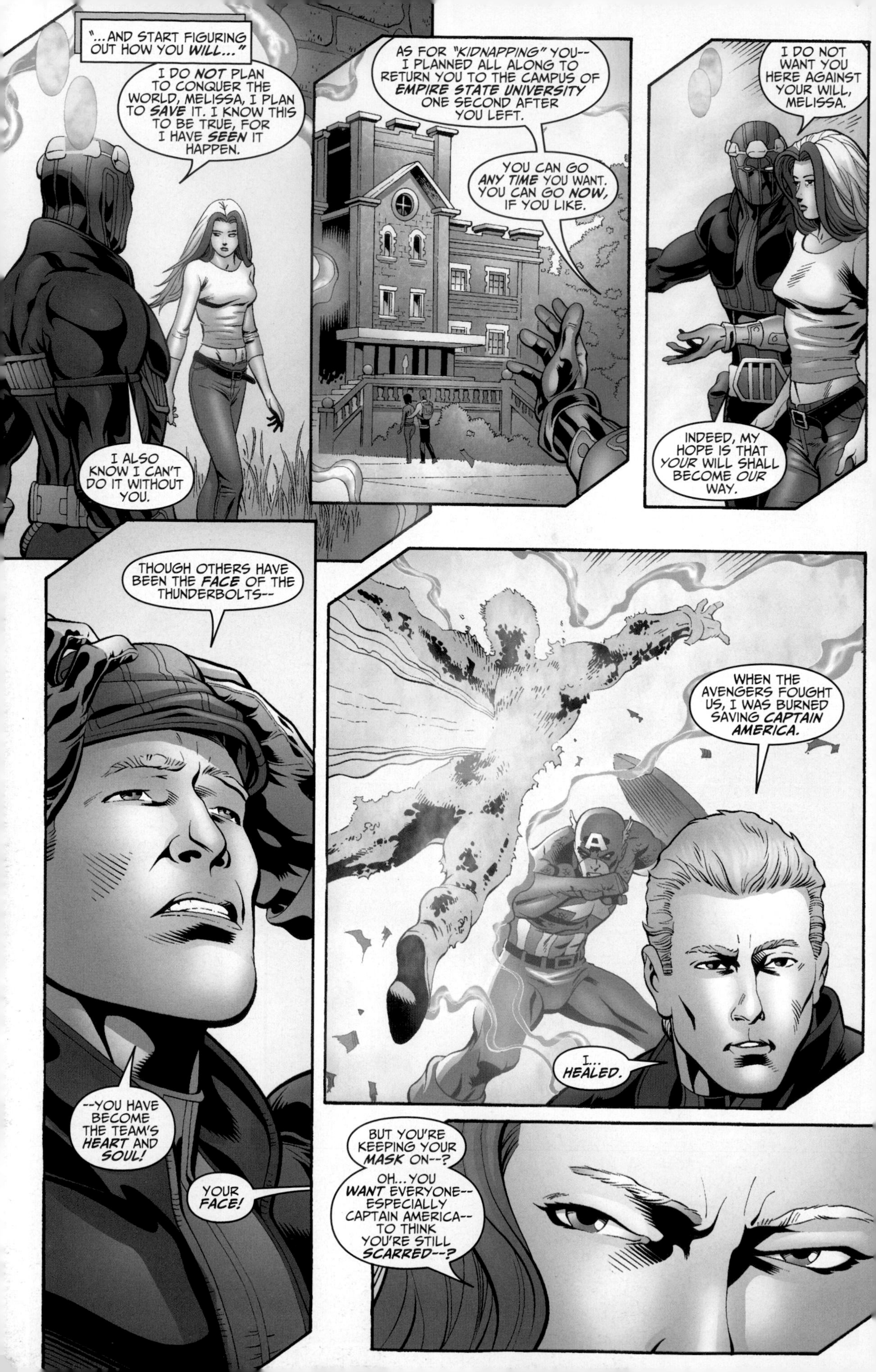
"...AND START FIGURING OUT HOW YOU WILL..."
I DO NOT PLAN TO CONQUER THE WORLD, MELISSA, I PLAN TO SAVE IT. I KNOW THIS TO BE TRUE, FOR I HAVE SEEN IT HAPPEN.
I ALSO KNOW I CAN'T DO IT WITHOUT YOU.
AS FOR "KIDNAPPING" YOU-- I PLANNED ALL ALONG TO RETURN YOU TO THE CAMPUS OF EMPIRE STATE UNIVERSITY ONE SECOND AFTER YOU LEFT.
YOU CAN GO ANY TIME YOU WANT. YOU CAN GO NOW, IF YOU LIKE.
I DO NOT WANT YOU HERE AGAINST YOUR WILL, MELISSA.
INDEED, MY HOPE IS THAT YOUR WILL SHALL BECOME OUR WAY.
THOUGH OTHERS HAVE BEEN THE FACE OF THE THUNDERBOLTS--
--YOU HAVE BECOME THE TEAM'S HEART AND SOUL!
YOUR FACE!
WHEN THE AVENGERS FOUGHT US, I WAS BURNED SAVING CAPTAIN AMERICA.
I... HEALED.
BUT YOU'RE KEEPING YOUR MASK ON--?
OH... YOU WANT EVERYONE-- ESPECIALLY CAPTAIN AMERICA-- TO THINK YOU'RE STILL SCARRED--?

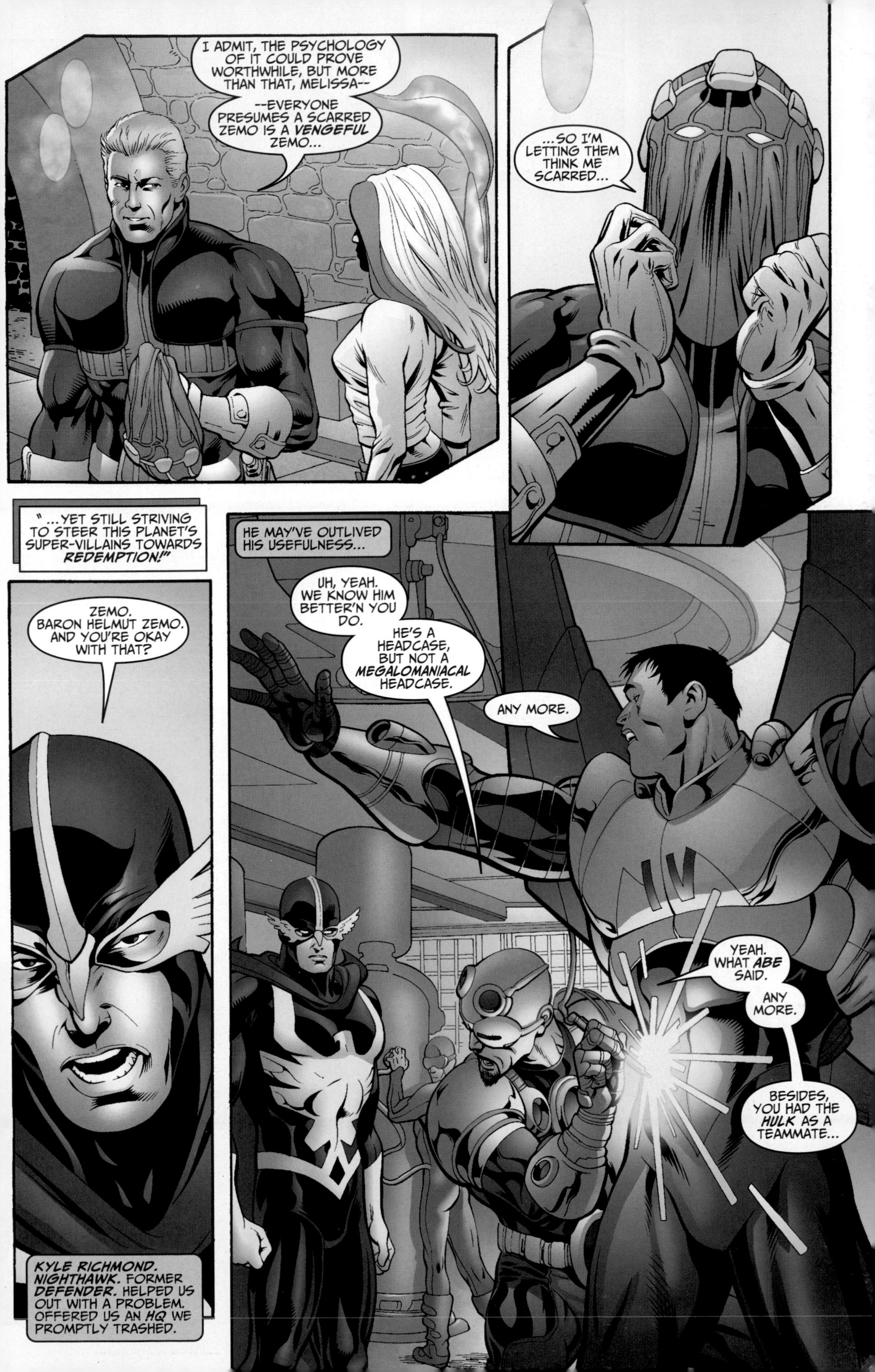
I ADMIT, THE PSYCHOLOGY OF IT COULD PROVE WORTHWHILE, BUT MORE THAN THAT, MELISSA--
--EVERYONE PRESUMES A SCARRED ZEMO IS A *VENGEFUL* ZEMO...
...SO I'M LETTING THEM THINK ME SCARRED...
"...YET STILL STRIVING TO STEER THIS PLANET'S SUPER-VILLAINS TOWARDS *REDEMPTION!*"
ZEMO. BARON HELMUT ZEMO. AND YOU'RE OKAY WITH THAT?
*KYLE RICHMOND. NIGHTHAWK.* FORMER *DEFENDER.* HELPED US OUT WITH A PROBLEM. OFFERED US AN *HQ* WE PROMPTLY TRASHED.
HE MAY'VE OUTLIVED HIS USEFULNESS...
UH, YEAH. WE KNOW HIM BETTER'N YOU DO.
HE'S A HEADCASE, BUT NOT A *MEGALOMANIACAL* HEADCASE.
ANY MORE.
YEAH. WHAT *ABE* SAID.
ANY MORE.
BESIDES, YOU HAD THE *HULK* AS A TEAMMATE...

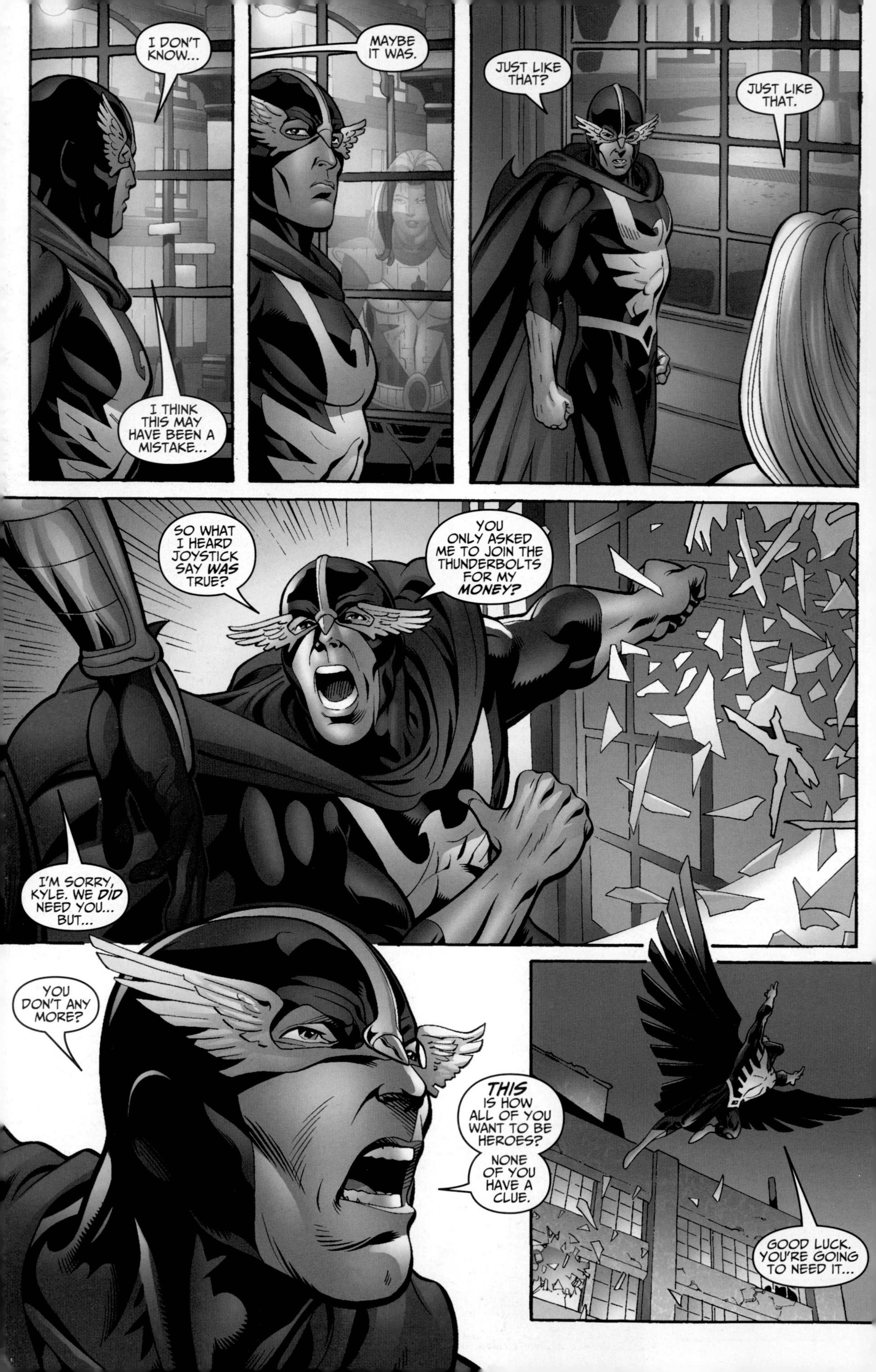
I DON'T KNOW...
I THINK THIS MAY HAVE BEEN A MISTAKE...
MAYBE IT WAS.
JUST LIKE THAT?
JUST LIKE THAT.
SO WHAT I HEARD JOYSTICK SAY WAS TRUE?
YOU ONLY ASKED ME TO JOIN THE THUNDERBOLTS FOR MY MONEY?
I'M SORRY, KYLE. WE DID NEED YOU... BUT...
YOU DON'T ANY MORE?
THIS IS HOW ALL OF YOU WANT TO BE HEROES?
NONE OF YOU HAVE A CLUE.
GOOD LUCK. YOU'RE GOING TO NEED IT...

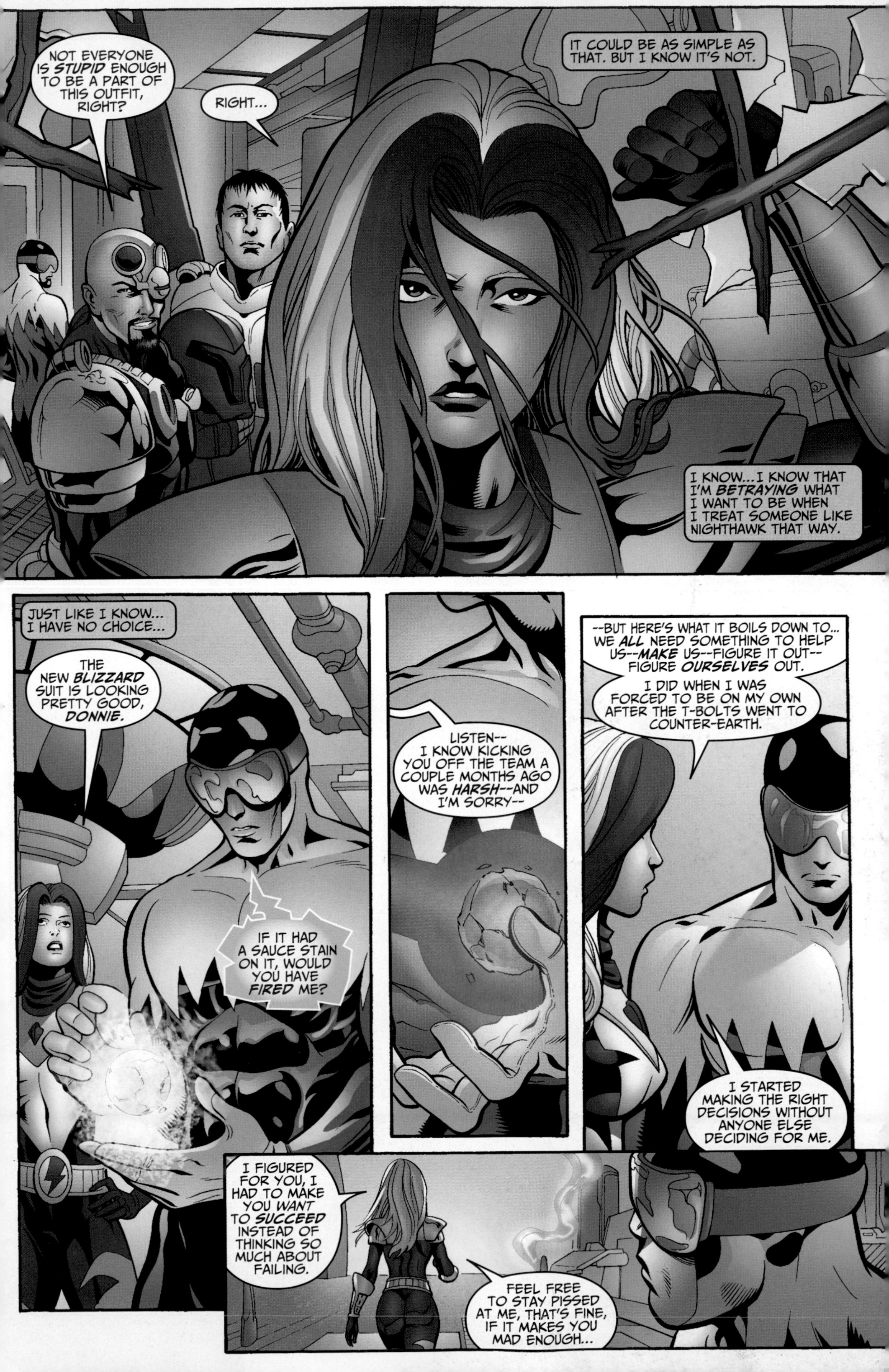
NOT EVERYONE IS STUPID ENOUGH TO BE A PART OF THIS OUTFIT, RIGHT?
RIGHT...
IT COULD BE AS SIMPLE AS THAT. BUT I KNOW IT'S NOT.
I KNOW...I KNOW THAT I'M BETRAYING WHAT I WANT TO BE WHEN I TREAT SOMEONE LIKE NIGHTHAWK THAT WAY.
JUST LIKE I KNOW... I HAVE NO CHOICE...
THE NEW BLIZZARD SUIT IS LOOKING PRETTY GOOD, DONNIE.
IF IT HAD A SAUCE STAIN ON IT, WOULD YOU HAVE FIRED ME?
LISTEN-- I KNOW KICKING YOU OFF THE TEAM A COUPLE MONTHS AGO WAS HARSH--AND I'M SORRY--
--BUT HERE'S WHAT IT BOILS DOWN TO... WE ALL NEED SOMETHING TO HELP US--MAKE US--FIGURE IT OUT-- FIGURE OURSELVES OUT.
I DID WHEN I WAS FORCED TO BE ON MY OWN AFTER THE T-BOLTS WENT TO COUNTER-EARTH.
I STARTED MAKING THE RIGHT DECISIONS WITHOUT ANYONE ELSE DECIDING FOR ME.
I FIGURED FOR YOU, I HAD TO MAKE YOU WANT TO SUCCEED INSTEAD OF THINKING SO MUCH ABOUT FAILING.
FEEL FREE TO STAY PISSED AT ME, THAT'S FINE, IF IT MAKES YOU MAD ENOUGH...

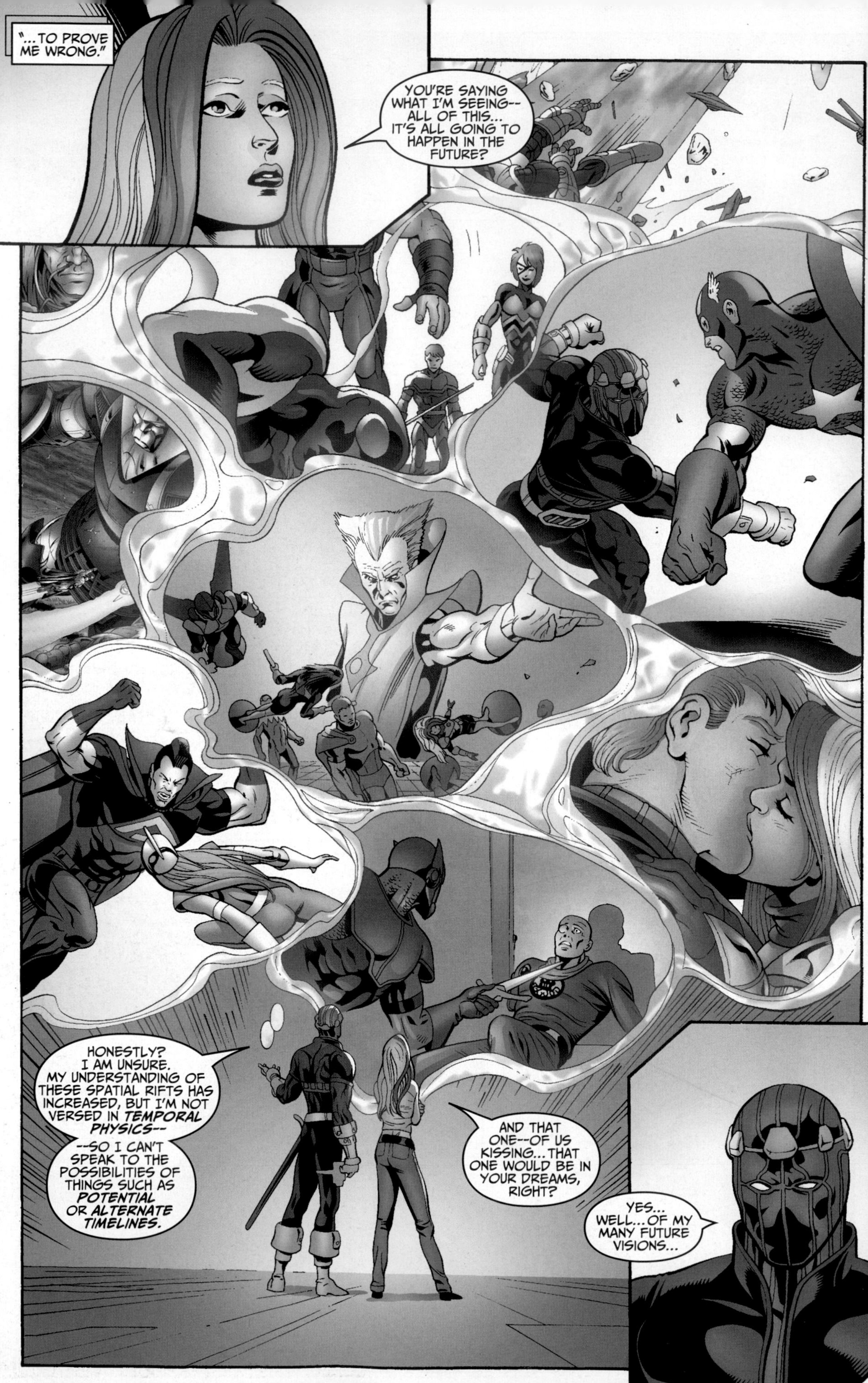
"...TO PROVE ME WRONG."
YOU'RE SAYING WHAT I'M SEEING-- ALL OF THIS... IT'S ALL GOING TO HAPPEN IN THE FUTURE?
HONESTLY? I AM UNSURE. MY UNDERSTANDING OF THESE SPATIAL RIFTS HAS INCREASED, BUT I'M NOT VERSED IN *TEMPORAL PHYSICS*--
--SO I CAN'T SPEAK TO THE POSSIBILITIES OF THINGS SUCH AS *POTENTIAL* OR *ALTERNATE TIMELINES.*
AND THAT ONE--OF US KISSING...THAT ONE WOULD BE IN YOUR DREAMS, RIGHT?
YES... WELL...OF MY MANY FUTURE VISIONS...

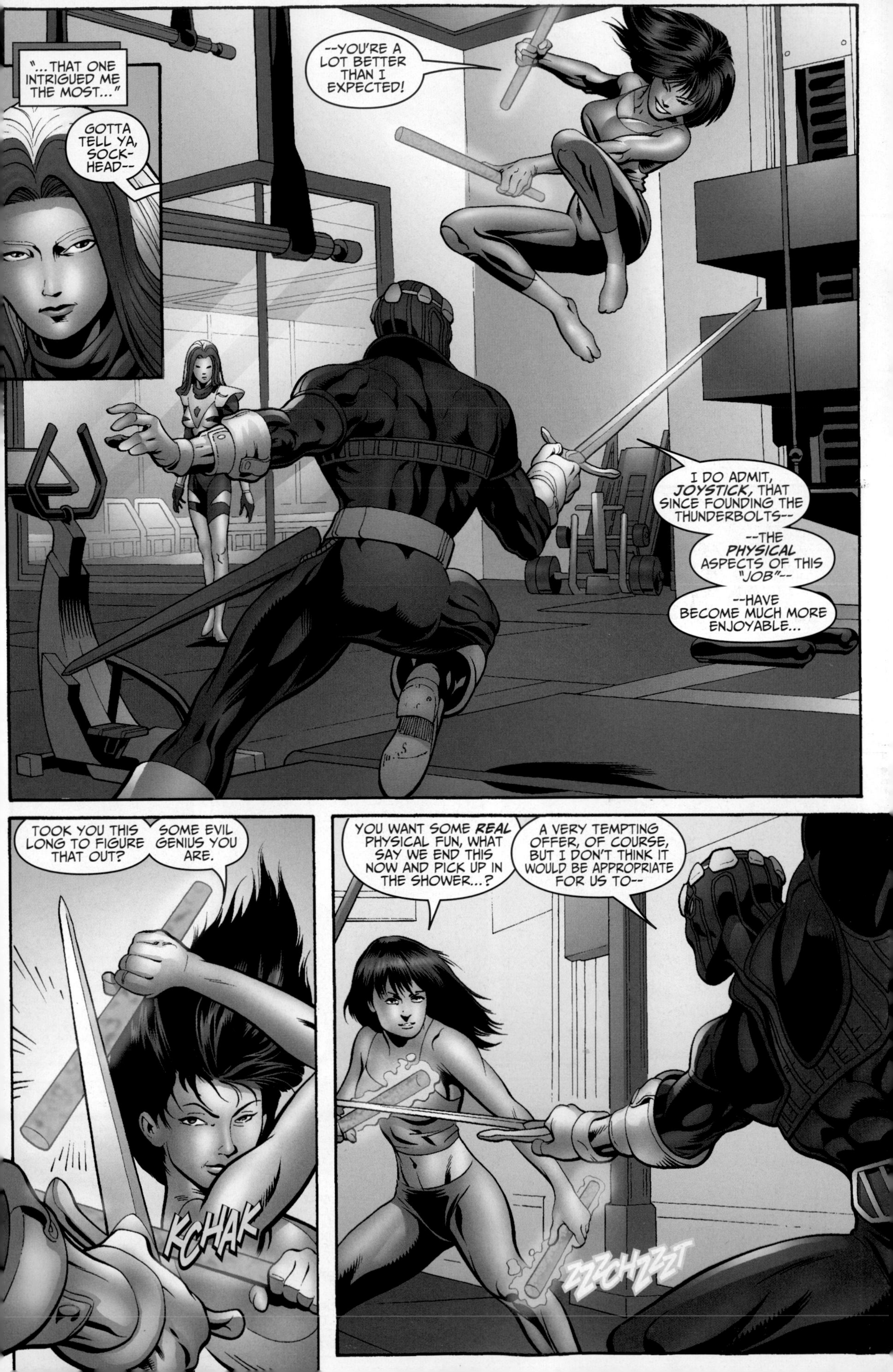
"...THAT ONE INTRIGUED ME THE MOST..."
GOTTA TELL YA, SOCK-HEAD--
--YOU'RE A LOT BETTER THAN I EXPECTED!
I DO ADMIT, JOYSTICK, THAT SINCE FOUNDING THE THUNDERBOLTS--
--THE PHYSICAL ASPECTS OF THIS "JOB"--
--HAVE BECOME MUCH MORE ENJOYABLE...
TOOK YOU THIS LONG TO FIGURE THAT OUT?
SOME EVIL GENIUS YOU ARE.
KCHAK
YOU WANT SOME REAL PHYSICAL FUN, WHAT SAY WE END THIS NOW AND PICK UP IN THE SHOWER...?
A VERY TEMPTING OFFER, OF COURSE, BUT I DON'T THINK IT WOULD BE APPROPRIATE FOR US TO--
ZZZCHZZZT

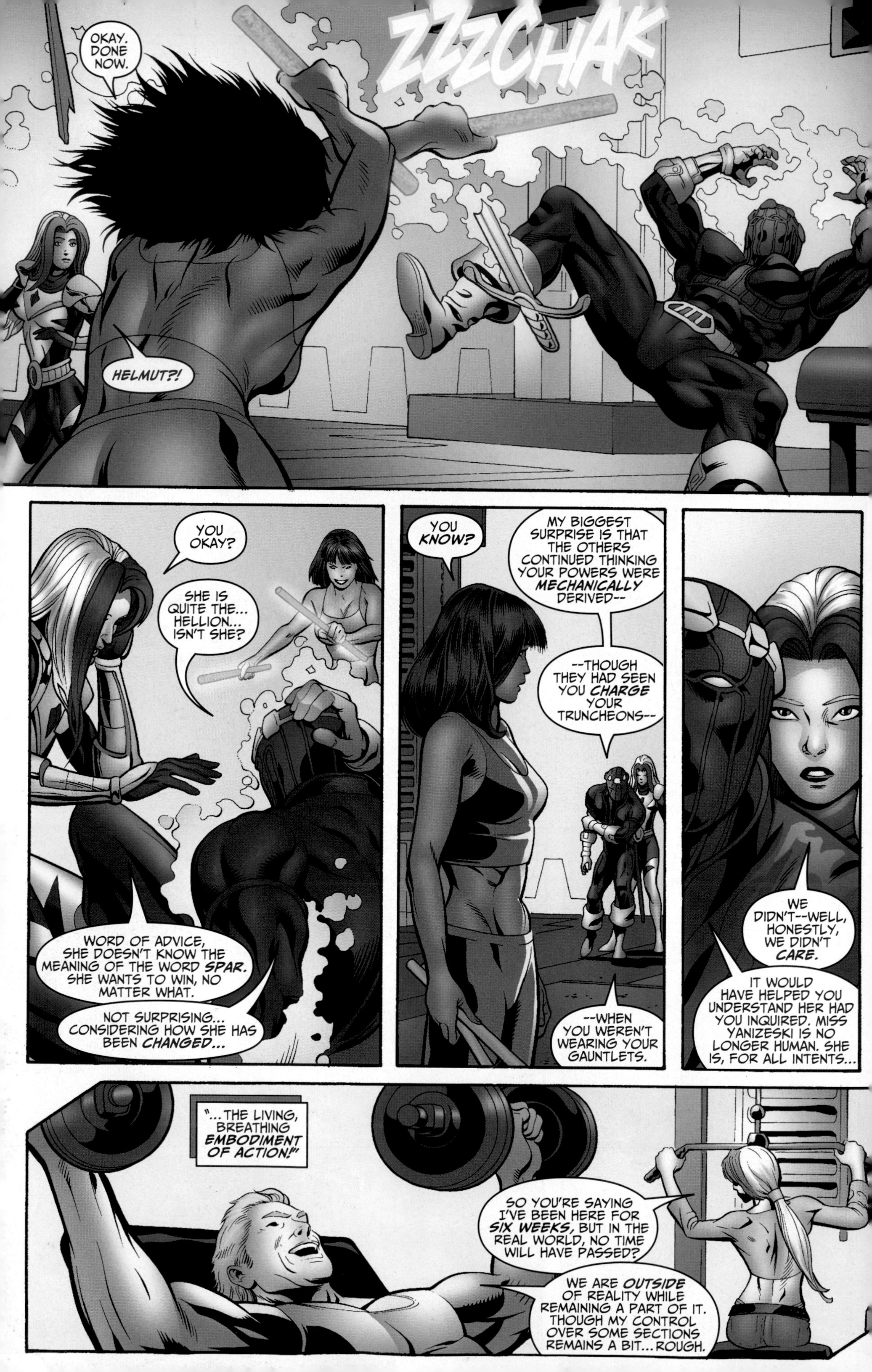
ZZZCHAK
OKAY. DONE NOW.
HELMUT?!
YOU OKAY?
SHE IS QUITE THE... HELLION... ISN'T SHE?
WORD OF ADVICE, SHE DOESN'T KNOW THE MEANING OF THE WORD SPAR. SHE WANTS TO WIN, NO MATTER WHAT.
NOT SURPRISING... CONSIDERING HOW SHE HAS BEEN CHANGED...
YOU KNOW?
MY BIGGEST SURPRISE IS THAT THE OTHERS CONTINUED THINKING YOUR POWERS WERE MECHANICALLY DERIVED--
--THOUGH THEY HAD SEEN YOU CHARGE YOUR TRUNCHEONS--
--WHEN YOU WEREN'T WEARING YOUR GAUNTLETS.
WE DIDN'T--WELL, HONESTLY, WE DIDN'T CARE.
IT WOULD HAVE HELPED YOU UNDERSTAND HER HAD YOU INQUIRED. MISS YANIZESKI IS NO LONGER HUMAN. SHE IS, FOR ALL INTENTS...
"...THE LIVING, BREATHING EMBODIMENT OF ACTION!"
SO YOU'RE SAYING I'VE BEEN HERE FOR SIX WEEKS, BUT IN THE REAL WORLD, NO TIME WILL HAVE PASSED?
WE ARE OUTSIDE OF REALITY WHILE REMAINING A PART OF IT. THOUGH MY CONTROL OVER SOME SECTIONS REMAINS A BIT... ROUGH.

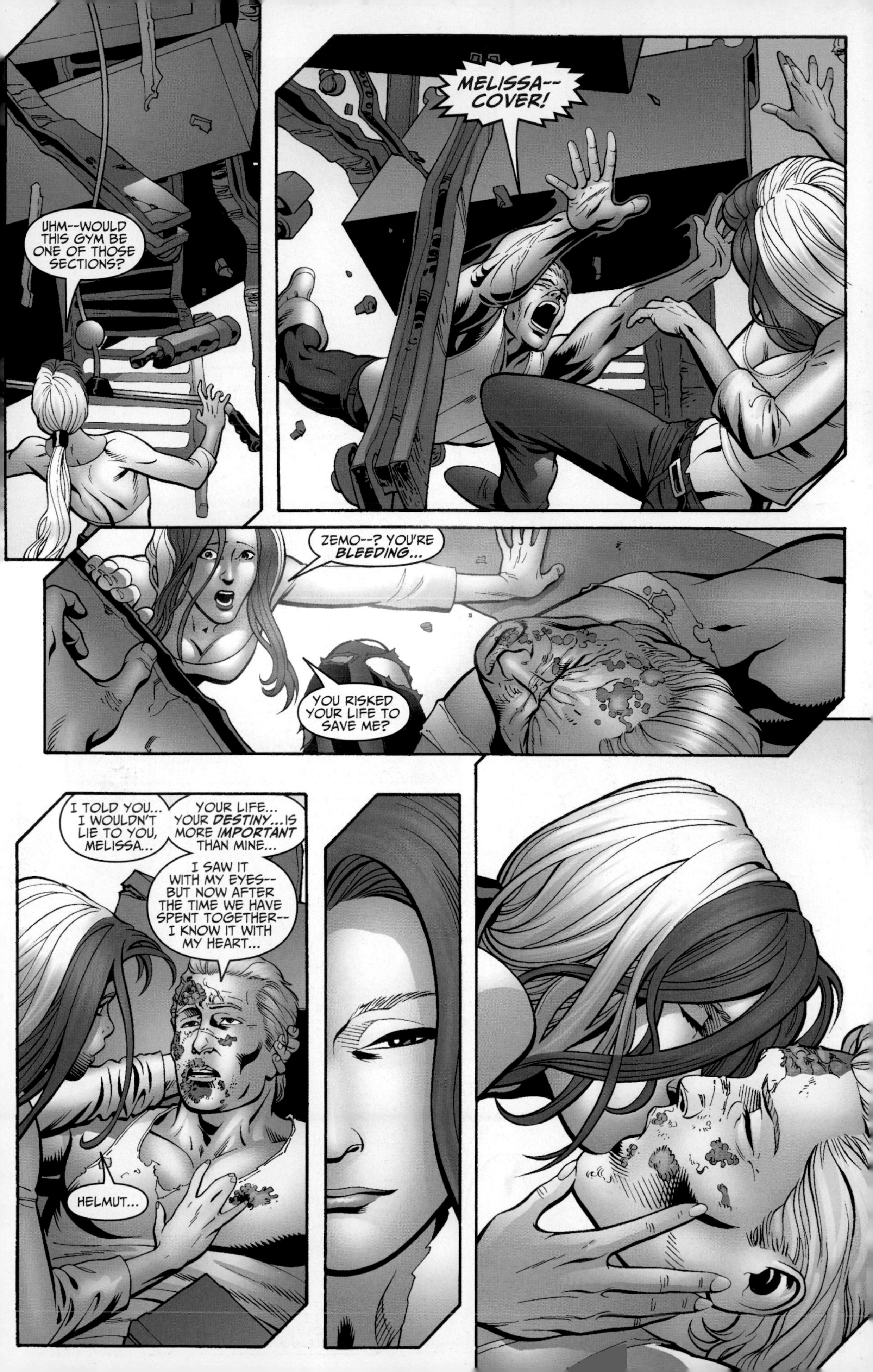
UHM--WOULD THIS GYM BE ONE OF THOSE SECTIONS?
MELISSA-- COVER!
ZEMO--? YOU'RE *BLEEDING*...
YOU RISKED YOUR LIFE TO SAVE ME?
I TOLD YOU... I WOULDN'T LIE TO YOU, MELISSA...
YOUR LIFE... YOUR *DESTINY*... IS MORE *IMPORTANT* THAN MINE...
I SAW IT WITH MY EYES-- BUT NOW AFTER THE TIME WE HAVE SPENT TOGETHER-- I KNOW IT WITH MY HEART...
HELMUT...

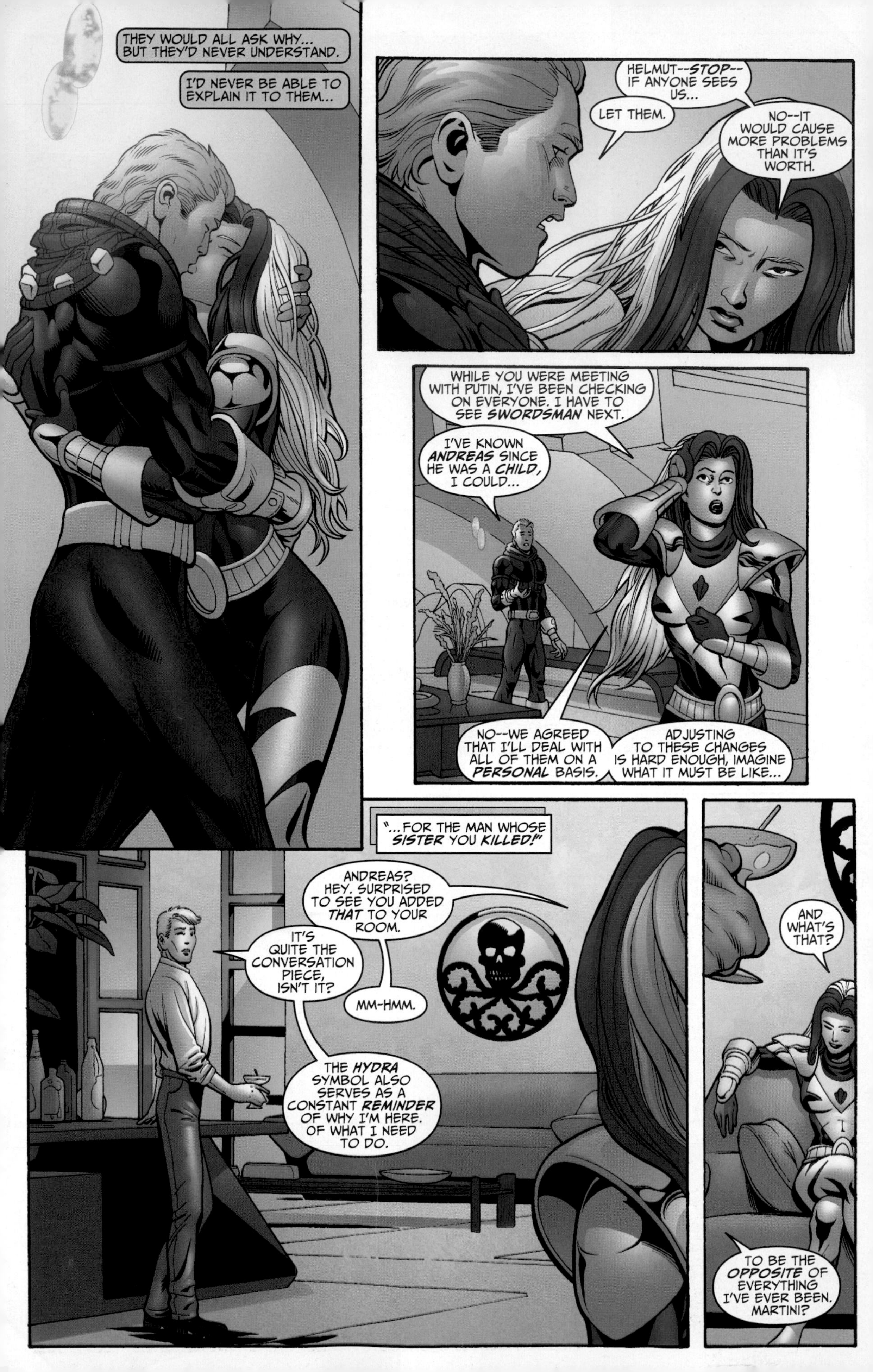
THEY WOULD ALL ASK WHY... BUT THEY'D NEVER UNDERSTAND.
I'D NEVER BE ABLE TO EXPLAIN IT TO THEM...
HELMUT--STOP--IF ANYONE SEES US...
LET THEM.
NO--IT WOULD CAUSE MORE PROBLEMS THAN IT'S WORTH.
WHILE YOU WERE MEETING WITH PUTIN, I'VE BEEN CHECKING ON EVERYONE. I HAVE TO SEE SWORDSMAN NEXT.
I'VE KNOWN ANDREAS SINCE HE WAS A CHILD, I COULD...
NO--WE AGREED THAT I'LL DEAL WITH ALL OF THEM ON A PERSONAL BASIS.
ADJUSTING TO THESE CHANGES IS HARD ENOUGH, IMAGINE WHAT IT MUST BE LIKE...
"...FOR THE MAN WHOSE SISTER YOU KILLED!"
ANDREAS? HEY. SURPRISED TO SEE YOU ADDED THAT TO YOUR ROOM.
IT'S QUITE THE CONVERSATION PIECE, ISN'T IT?
MM-HMM.
THE HYDRA SYMBOL ALSO SERVES AS A CONSTANT REMINDER OF WHY I'M HERE. OF WHAT I NEED TO DO.
AND WHAT'S THAT?
TO BE THE OPPOSITE OF EVERYTHING I'VE EVER BEEN. MARTINI?

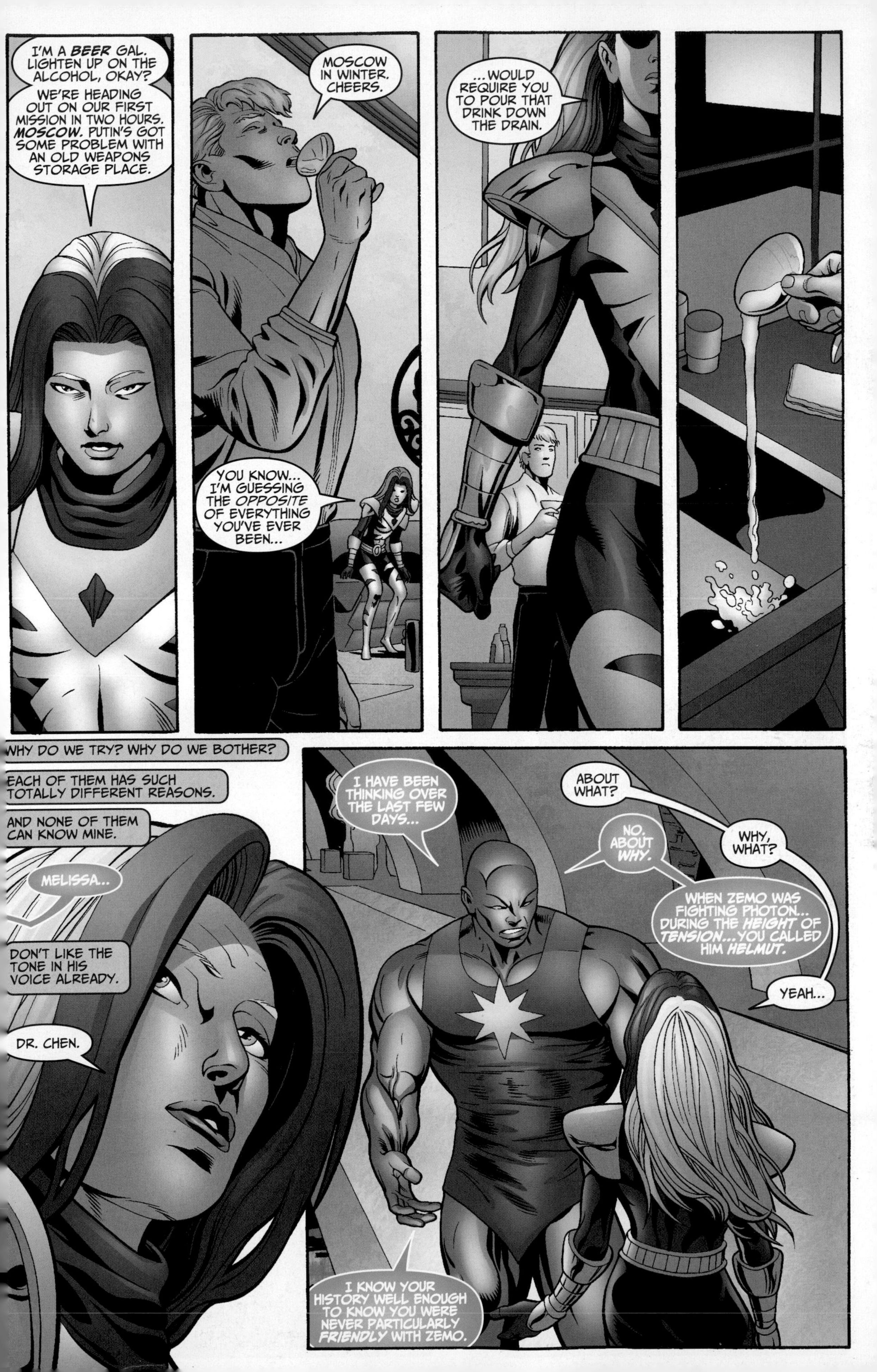
I'M A BEER GAL. LIGHTEN UP ON THE ALCOHOL, OKAY?
WE'RE HEADING OUT ON OUR FIRST MISSION IN TWO HOURS. MOSCOW. PUTIN'S GOT SOME PROBLEM WITH AN OLD WEAPONS STORAGE PLACE.
MOSCOW IN WINTER. CHEERS.
YOU KNOW... I'M GUESSING THE OPPOSITE OF EVERYTHING YOU'VE EVER BEEN...
...WOULD REQUIRE YOU TO POUR THAT DRINK DOWN THE DRAIN.
WHY DO WE TRY? WHY DO WE BOTHER?
EACH OF THEM HAS SUCH TOTALLY DIFFERENT REASONS.
AND NONE OF THEM CAN KNOW MINE.
MELISSA...
DON'T LIKE THE TONE IN HIS VOICE ALREADY.
DR. CHEN.
I HAVE BEEN THINKING OVER THE LAST FEW DAYS...
ABOUT WHAT?
NO. ABOUT WHY.
WHY, WHAT?
WHEN ZEMO WAS FIGHTING PHOTON... DURING THE HEIGHT OF TENSION...YOU CALLED HIM HELMUT.
YEAH...
I KNOW YOUR HISTORY WELL ENOUGH TO KNOW YOU WERE NEVER PARTICULARLY FRIENDLY WITH ZEMO.

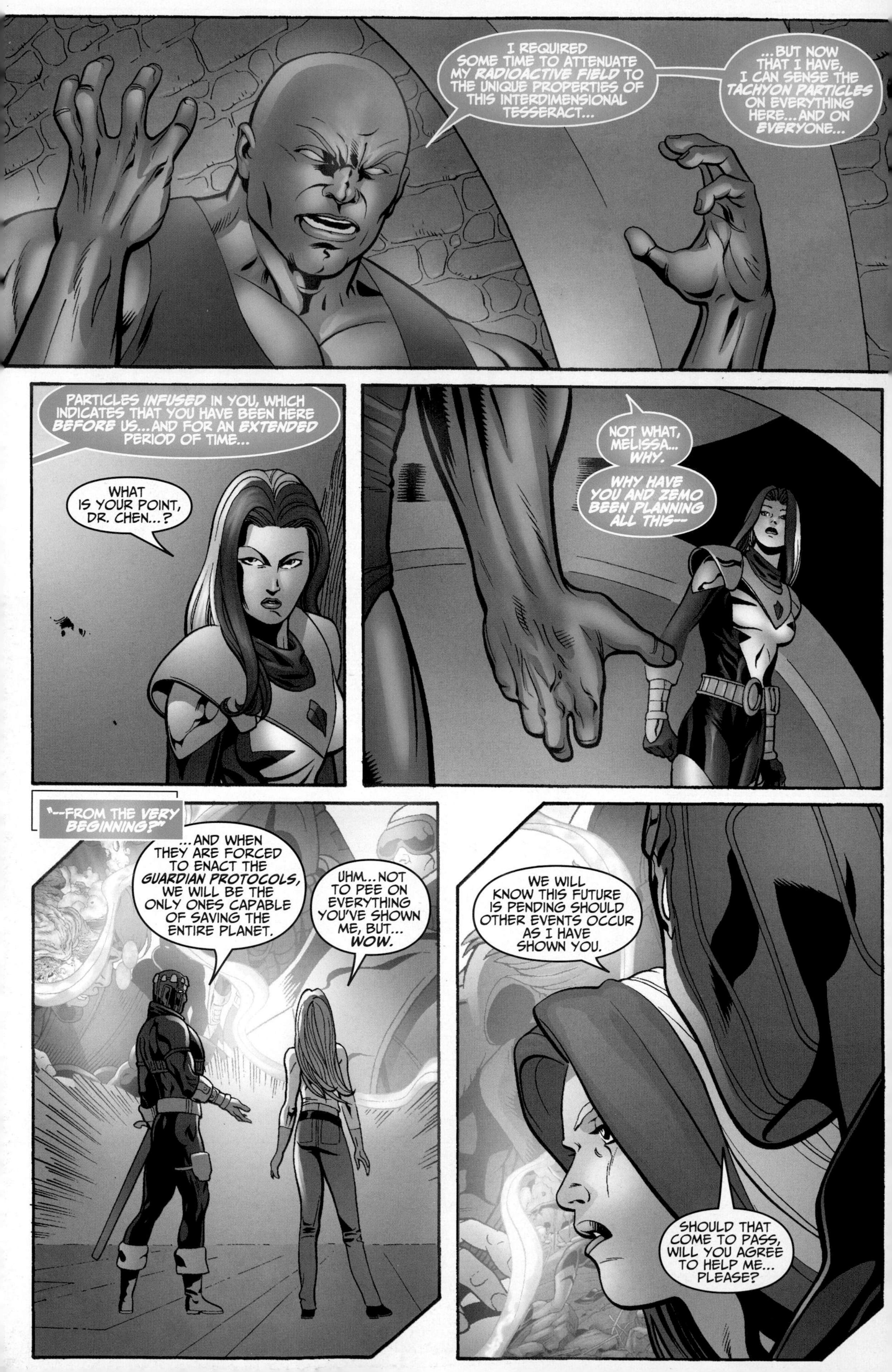

I REQUIRED SOME TIME TO ATTENUATE MY RADIOACTIVE FIELD TO THE UNIQUE PROPERTIES OF THIS INTERDIMENSIONAL TESSERACT...
...BUT NOW THAT I HAVE, I CAN SENSE THE TACHYON PARTICLES ON EVERYTHING HERE...AND ON EVERYONE...
PARTICLES INFUSED IN YOU, WHICH INDICATES THAT YOU HAVE BEEN HERE BEFORE US...AND FOR AN EXTENDED PERIOD OF TIME...
WHAT IS YOUR POINT, DR. CHEN...?
NOT WHAT, MELISSA... WHY.
WHY HAVE YOU AND ZEMO BEEN PLANNING ALL THIS--
"--FROM THE VERY BEGINNING?"
...AND WHEN THEY ARE FORCED TO ENACT THE GUARDIAN PROTOCOLS, WE WILL BE THE ONLY ONES CAPABLE OF SAVING THE ENTIRE PLANET.
UHM...NOT TO PEE ON EVERYTHING YOU'VE SHOWN ME, BUT... WOW.
WE WILL KNOW THIS FUTURE IS PENDING SHOULD OTHER EVENTS OCCUR AS I HAVE SHOWN YOU.
SHOULD THAT COME TO PASS, WILL YOU AGREE TO HELP ME... PLEASE?

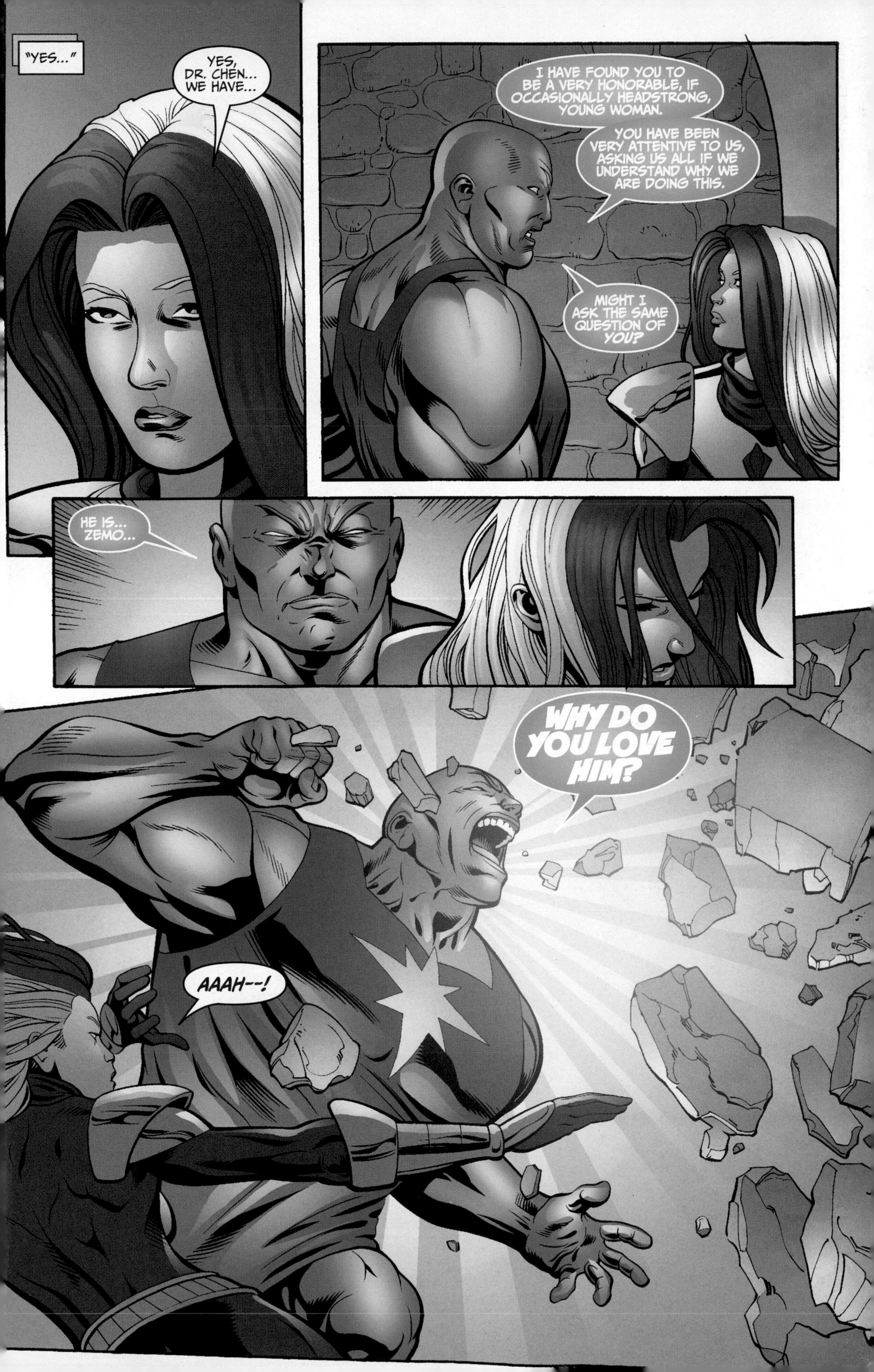
"YES..."
YES, DR. CHEN... WE HAVE...
I HAVE FOUND YOU TO BE A VERY HONORABLE, IF OCCASIONALLY HEADSTRONG, YOUNG WOMAN.
YOU HAVE BEEN VERY ATTENTIVE TO US, ASKING US ALL IF WE UNDERSTAND WHY WE ARE DOING THIS.
MIGHT I ASK THE SAME QUESTION OF YOU?
HE IS... ZEMO...
WHY DO YOU LOVE HIM?
AAAH--!

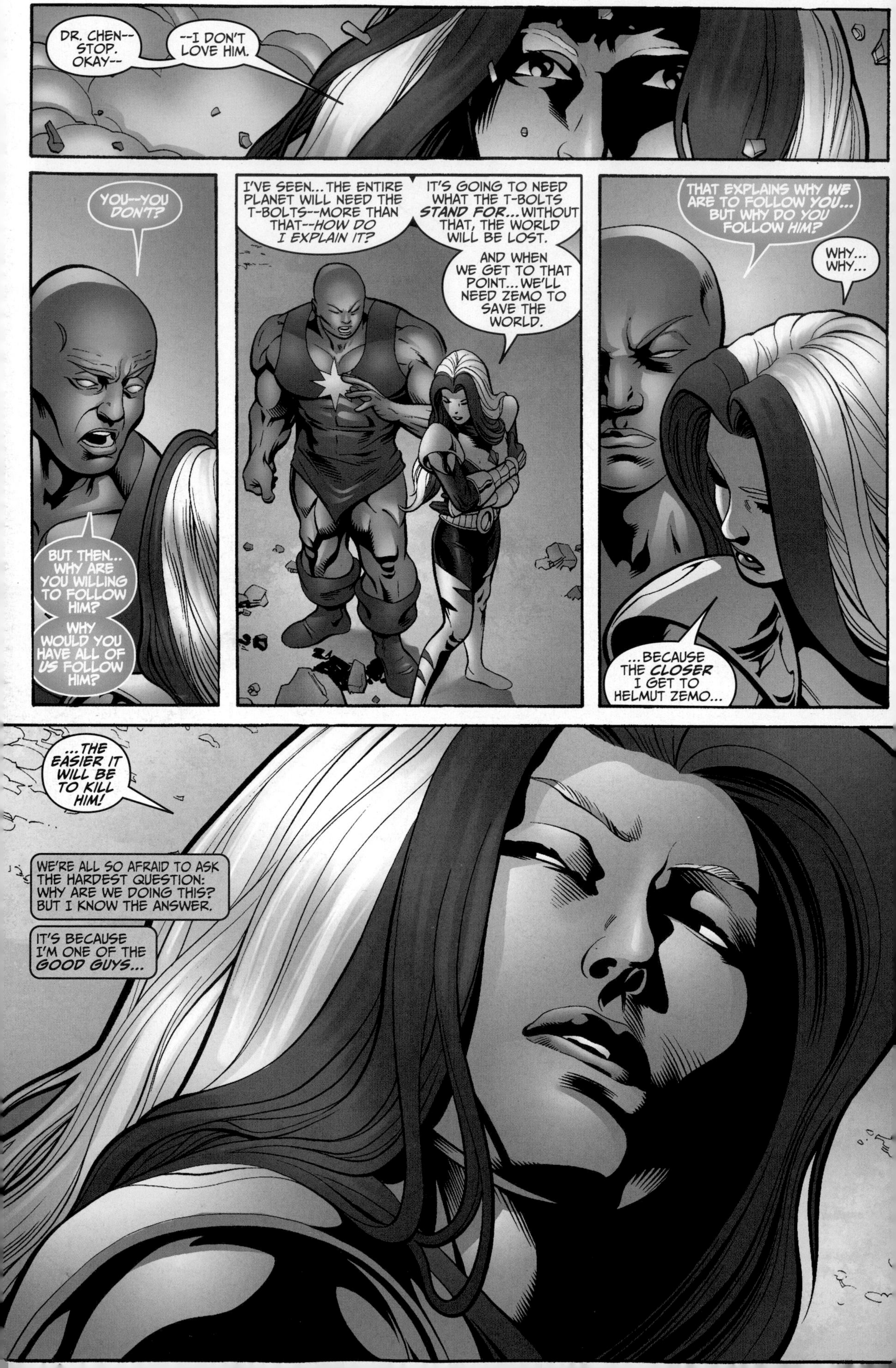
DR. CHEN--STOP. OKAY--
--I DON'T LOVE HIM.
YOU--YOU DON'T?
BUT THEN... WHY ARE YOU WILLING TO FOLLOW HIM?
WHY WOULD YOU HAVE ALL OF US FOLLOW HIM?
I'VE SEEN... THE ENTIRE PLANET WILL NEED THE T-BOLTS--MORE THAN THAT--HOW DO I EXPLAIN IT?
IT'S GOING TO NEED WHAT THE T-BOLTS STAND FOR... WITHOUT THAT, THE WORLD WILL BE LOST.
AND WHEN WE GET TO THAT POINT... WE'LL NEED ZEMO TO SAVE THE WORLD.
THAT EXPLAINS WHY WE ARE TO FOLLOW YOU... BUT WHY DO YOU FOLLOW HIM?
WHY... WHY...
...BECAUSE THE CLOSER I GET TO HELMUT ZEMO...
...THE EASIER IT WILL BE TO KILL HIM!
WE'RE ALL SO AFRAID TO ASK THE HARDEST QUESTION: WHY ARE WE DOING THIS? BUT I KNOW THE ANSWER.
IT'S BECAUSE I'M ONE OF THE GOOD GUYS...

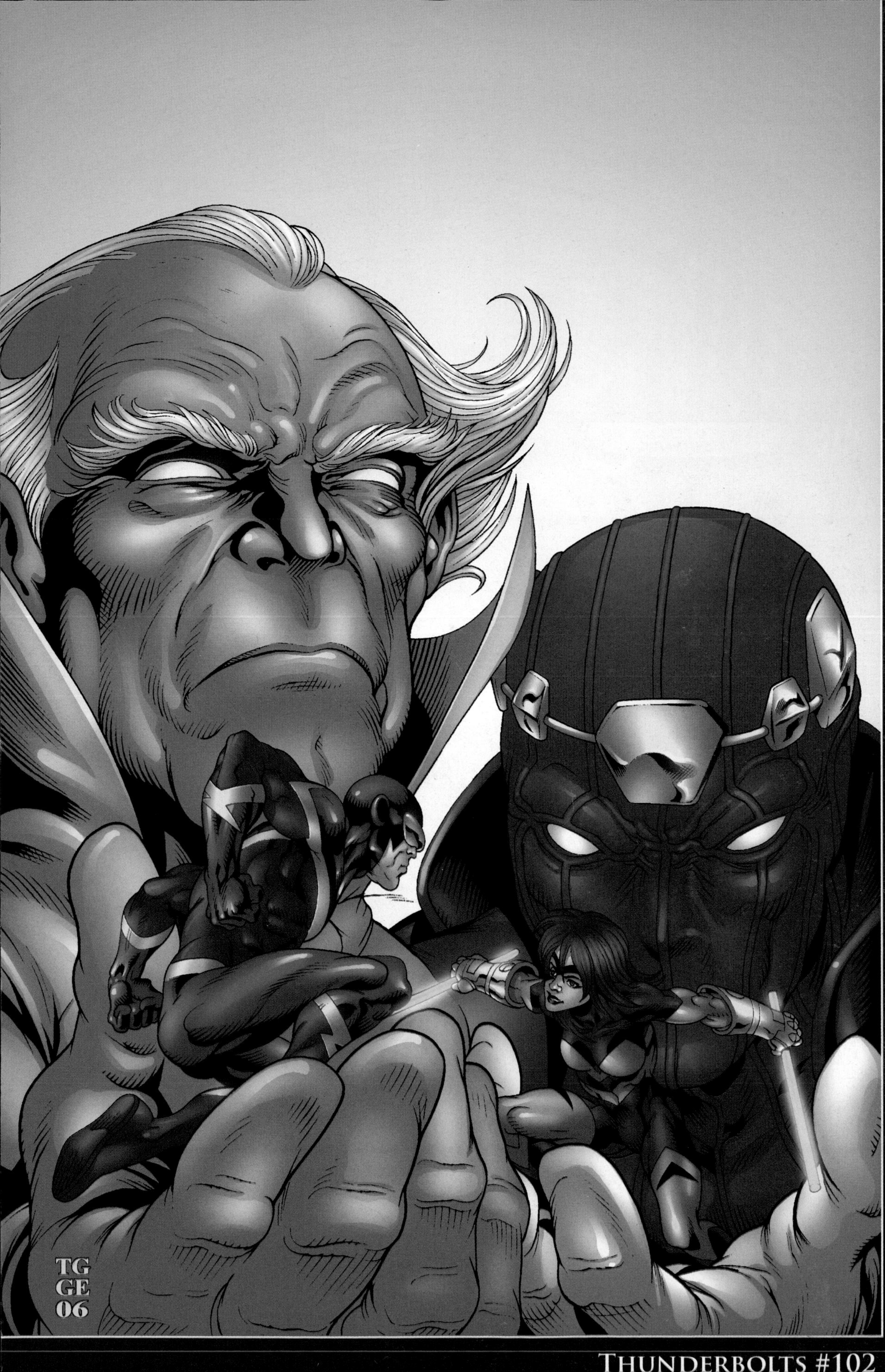
TG
GE
06

THUNDERBOLTS #102

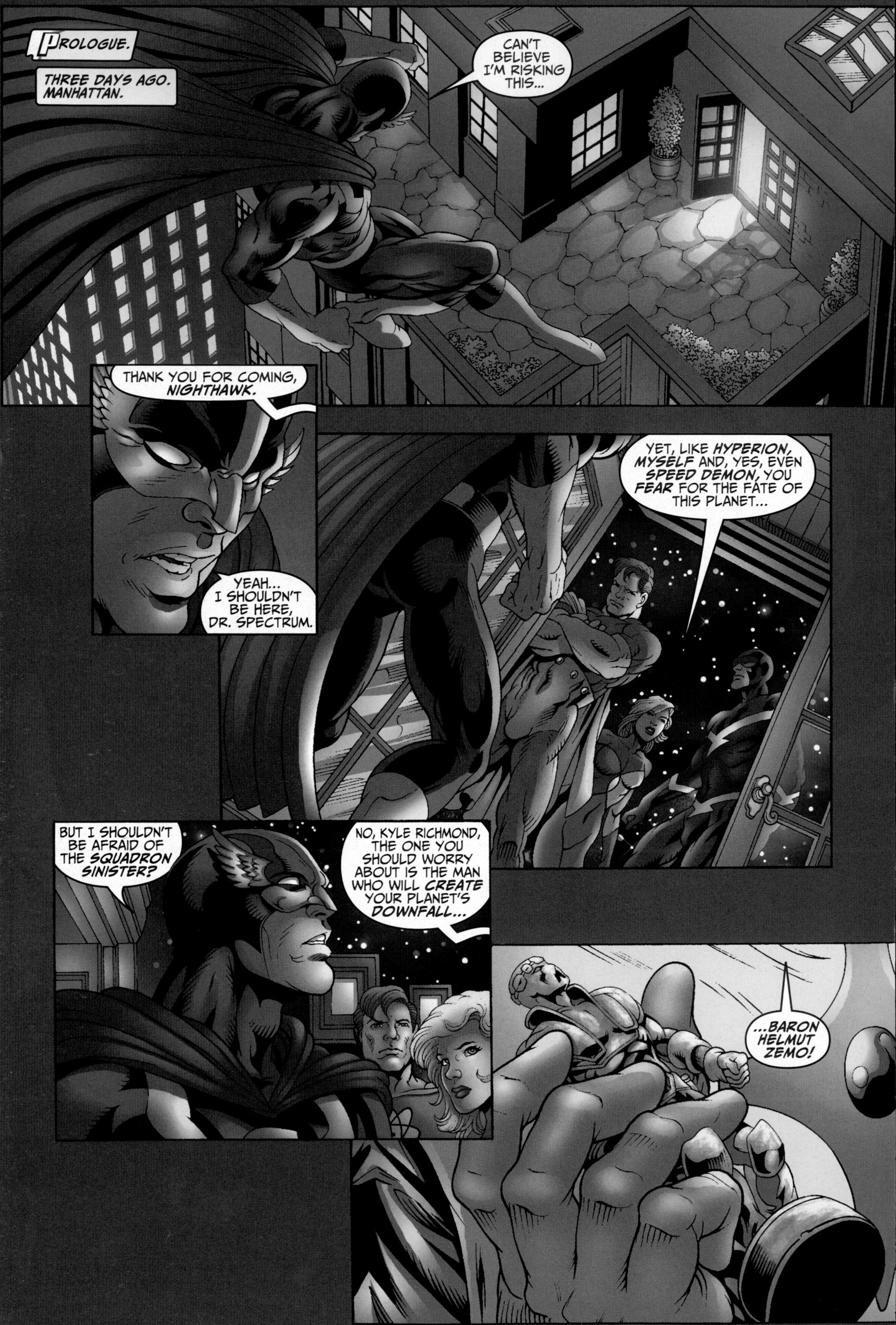
PROLOGUE.
THREE DAYS AGO. MANHATTAN.
CAN'T BELIEVE I'M RISKING THIS...
THANK YOU FOR COMING, NIGHTHAWK.
YEAH... I SHOULDN'T BE HERE, DR. SPECTRUM.
YET, LIKE HYPERION, MYSELF AND, YES, EVEN SPEED DEMON, YOU FEAR FOR THE FATE OF THIS PLANET...
BUT I SHOULDN'T BE AFRAID OF THE SQUADRON SINISTER?
NO, KYLE RICHMOND, THE ONE YOU SHOULD WORRY ABOUT IS THE MAN WHO WILL CREATE YOUR PLANET'S DOWNFALL...
...BARON HELMUT ZEMO!

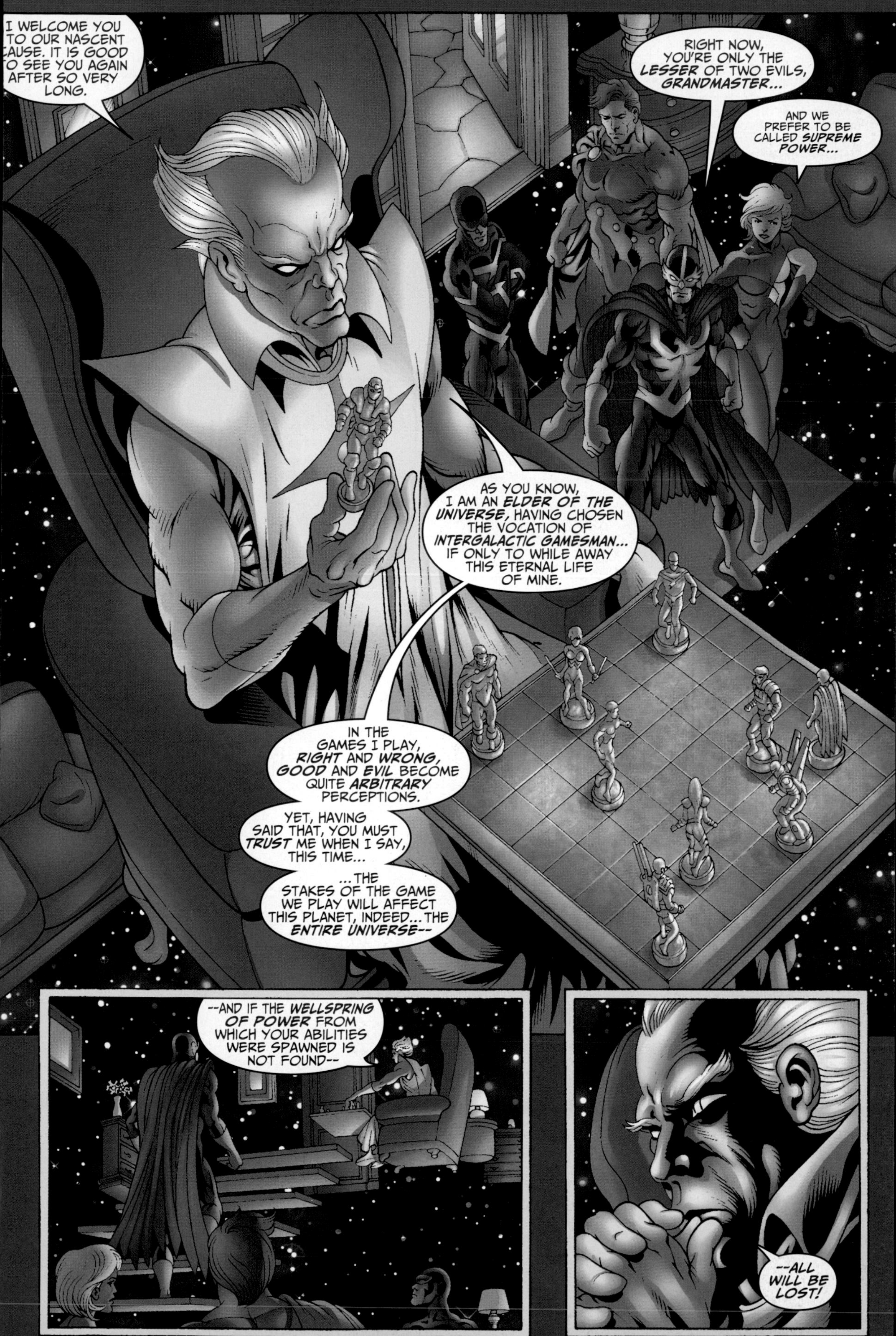
I WELCOME YOU TO OUR NASCENT CAUSE. IT IS GOOD TO SEE YOU AGAIN AFTER SO VERY LONG.
RIGHT NOW, YOU'RE ONLY THE LESSER OF TWO EVILS, GRANDMASTER...
AND WE PREFER TO BE CALLED SUPREME POWER...
AS YOU KNOW, I AM AN ELDER OF THE UNIVERSE, HAVING CHOSEN THE VOCATION OF INTERGALACTIC GAMESMAN... IF ONLY TO WHILE AWAY THIS ETERNAL LIFE OF MINE.
IN THE GAMES I PLAY, RIGHT AND WRONG, GOOD AND EVIL BECOME QUITE ARBITRARY PERCEPTIONS.
YET, HAVING SAID THAT, YOU MUST TRUST ME WHEN I SAY, THIS TIME...
...THE STAKES OF THE GAME WE PLAY WILL AFFECT THIS PLANET, INDEED... THE ENTIRE UNIVERSE--
--AND IF THE WELLSPRING OF POWER FROM WHICH YOUR ABILITIES WERE SPAWNED IS NOT FOUND--
--ALL WILL BE LOST!

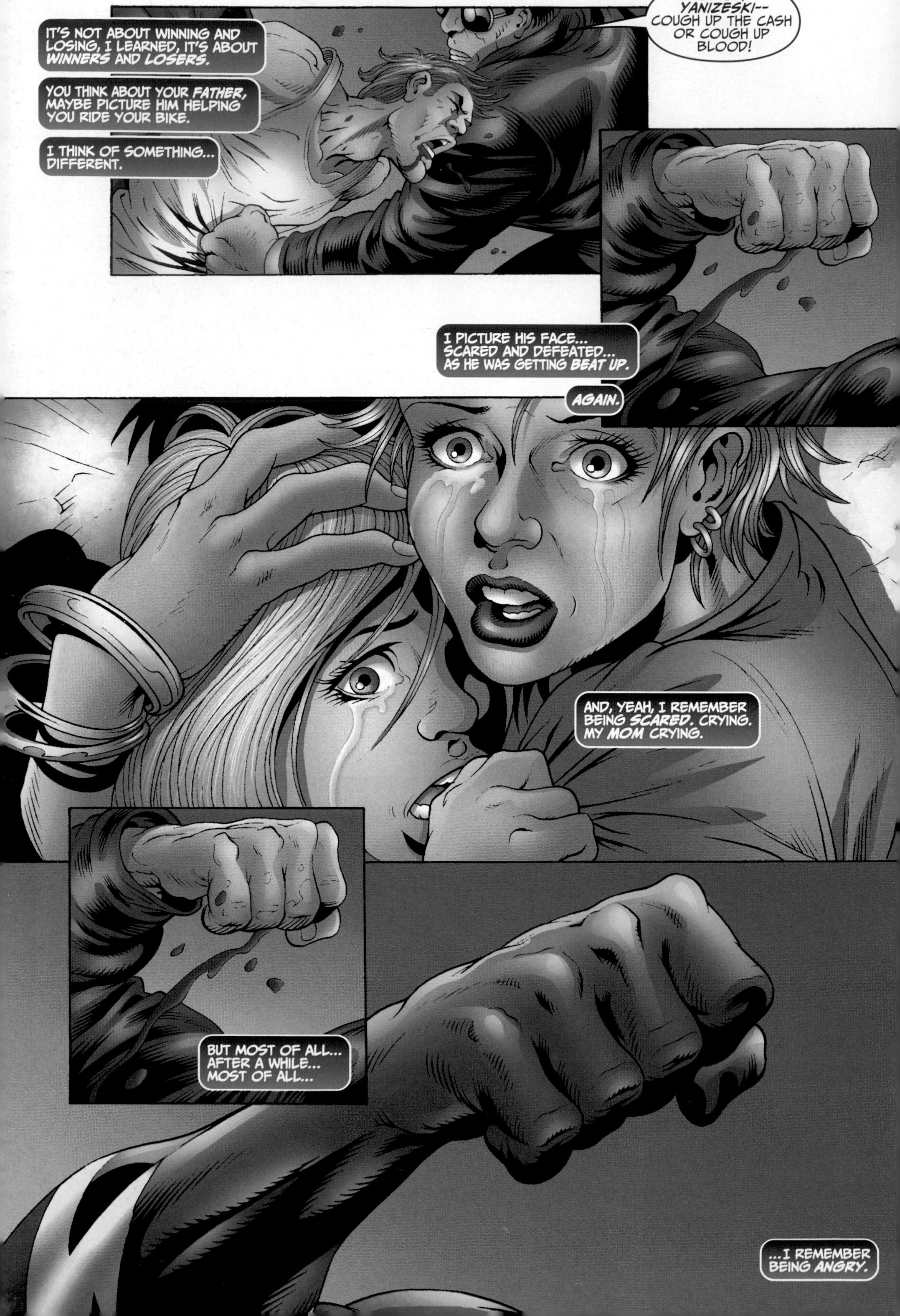
IT'S NOT ABOUT WINNING AND LOSING, I LEARNED, IT'S ABOUT *WINNERS* AND *LOSERS*.
C'MON, *YANIZESKI*-- COUGH UP THE CASH OR COUGH UP BLOOD!
YOU THINK ABOUT YOUR *FATHER*, MAYBE PICTURE HIM HELPING YOU RIDE YOUR BIKE.
I THINK OF SOMETHING... DIFFERENT.
I PICTURE HIS FACE... SCARED AND DEFEATED... AS HE WAS GETTING *BEAT UP*.
*AGAIN*.
AND, YEAH, I REMEMBER BEING *SCARED*. CRYING. MY *MOM* CRYING.
BUT MOST OF ALL... AFTER A WHILE... MOST OF ALL...
...I REMEMBER BEING *ANGRY*.

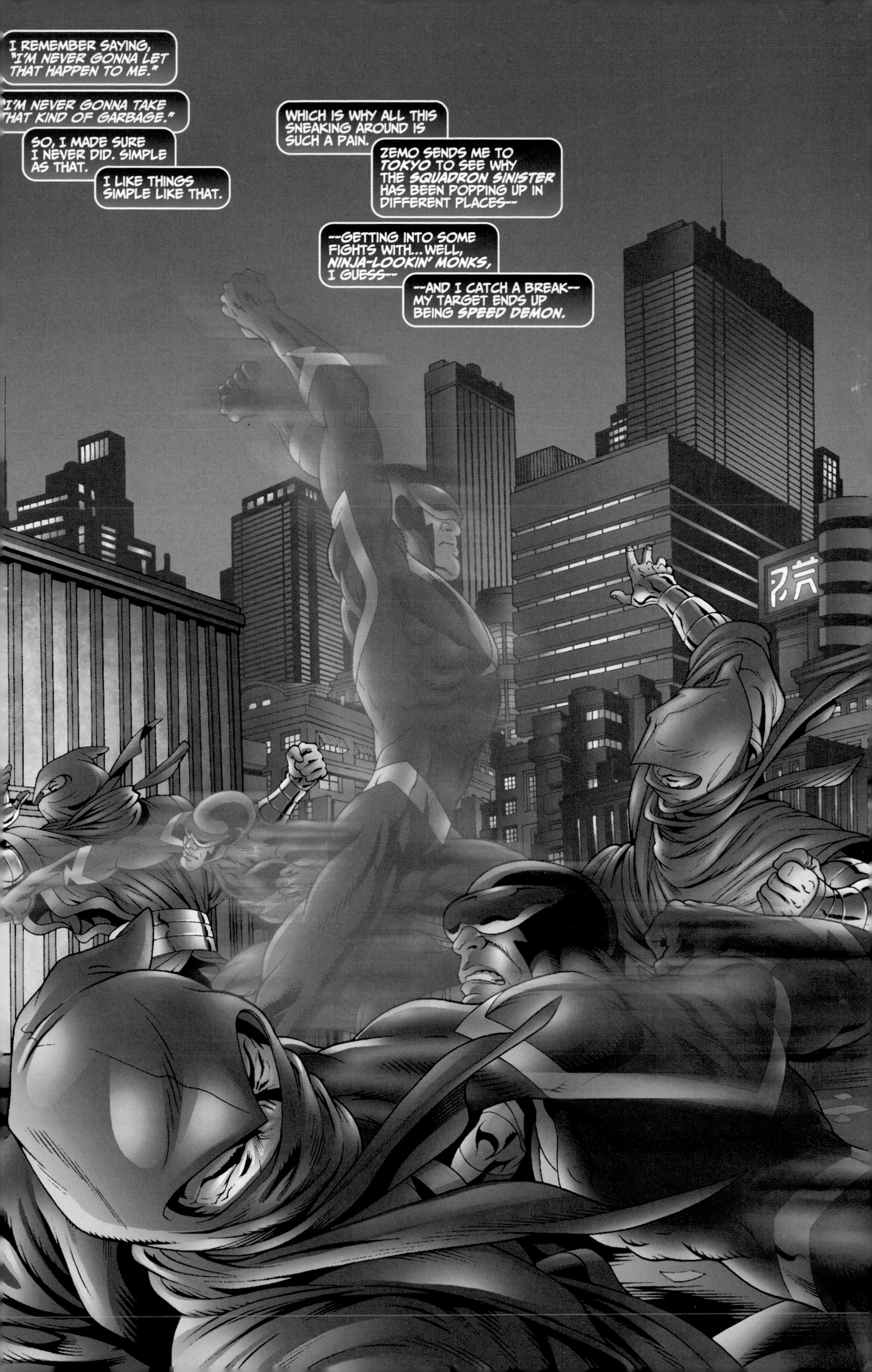
I REMEMBER SAYING, "I'M NEVER GONNA LET THAT HAPPEN TO ME."
"I'M NEVER GONNA TAKE THAT KIND OF GARBAGE."
SO, I MADE SURE I NEVER DID. SIMPLE AS THAT.
I LIKE THINGS SIMPLE LIKE THAT.
WHICH IS WHY ALL THIS SNEAKING AROUND IS SUCH A PAIN.
ZEMO SENDS ME TO TOKYO TO SEE WHY THE SQUADRON SINISTER HAS BEEN POPPING UP IN DIFFERENT PLACES--
--GETTING INTO SOME FIGHTS WITH...WELL, NINJA-LOOKIN' MONKS, I GUESS--
--AND I CATCH A BREAK-- MY TARGET ENDS UP BEING SPEED DEMON.

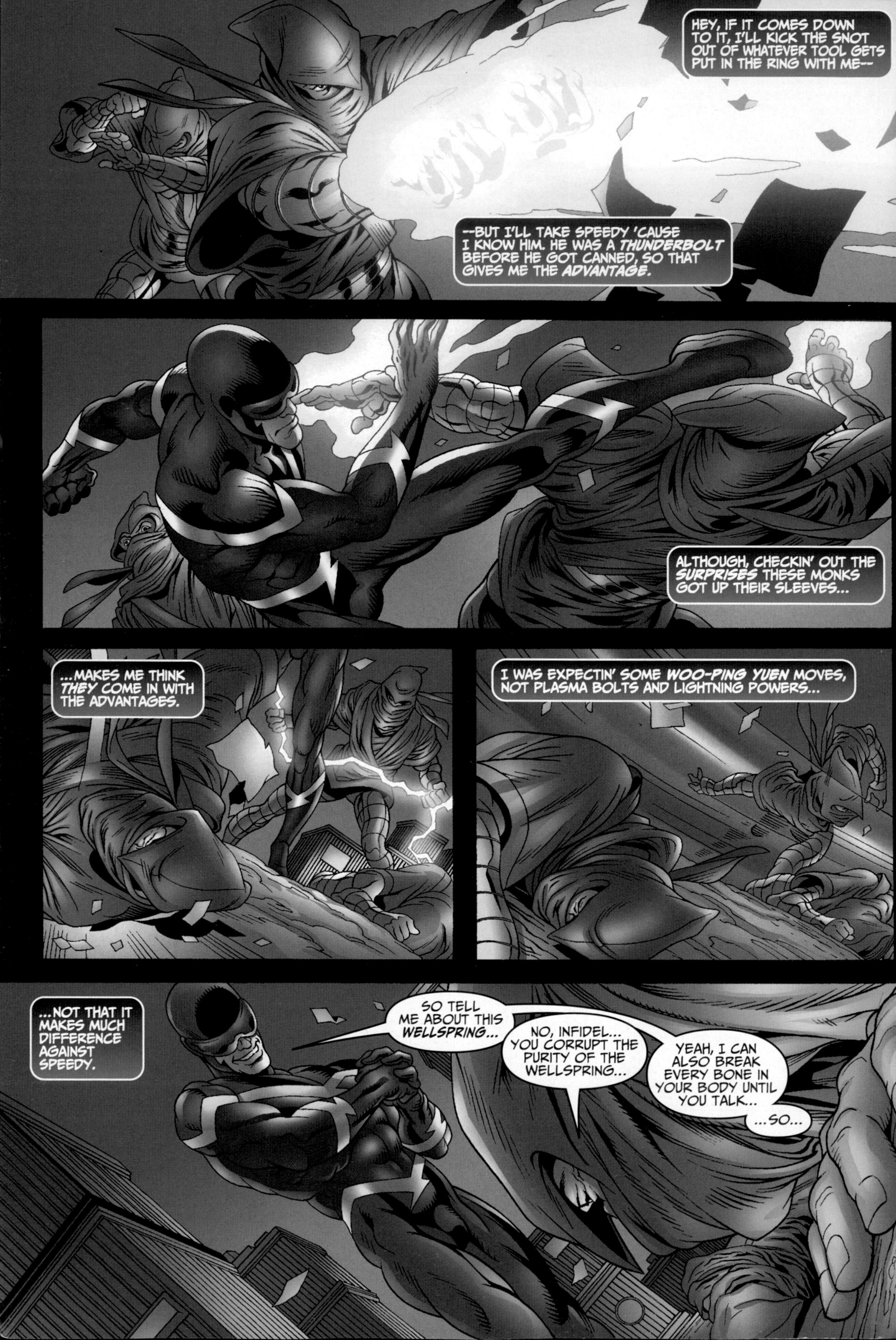
HEY, IF IT COMES DOWN TO IT, I'LL KICK THE SNOT OUT OF WHATEVER TOOL GETS PUT IN THE RING WITH ME--
--BUT I'LL TAKE SPEEDY 'CAUSE I KNOW HIM. HE WAS A *THUNDERBOLT* BEFORE HE GOT CANNED, SO THAT GIVES ME THE *ADVANTAGE*.
ALTHOUGH, CHECKIN' OUT THE *SURPRISES* THESE MONKS GOT UP THEIR SLEEVES...
...MAKES ME THINK *THEY* COME IN WITH THE ADVANTAGES.
I WAS EXPECTIN' SOME *WOO-PING YUEN* MOVES, NOT PLASMA BOLTS AND LIGHTNING POWERS...
...NOT THAT IT MAKES MUCH DIFFERENCE AGAINST SPEEDY.
SO TELL ME ABOUT THIS *WELLSPRING*...
NO, INFIDEL... YOU CORRUPT THE PURITY OF THE WELLSPRING...
YEAH, I CAN ALSO BREAK EVERY BONE IN YOUR BODY UNTIL YOU TALK...
...SO...

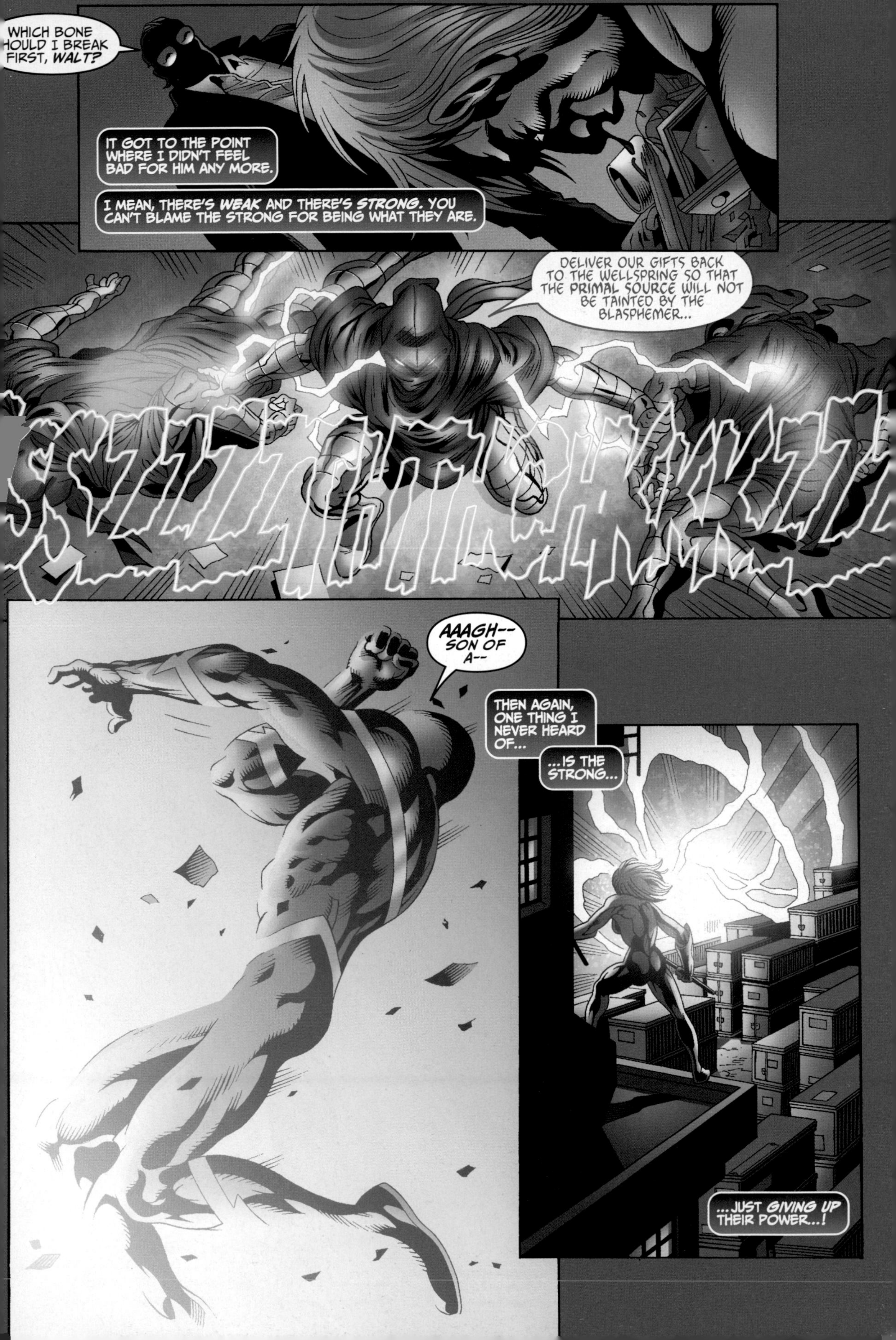
WHICH BONE HOULD I BREAK FIRST, WALT?
IT GOT TO THE POINT WHERE I DIDN'T FEEL BAD FOR HIM ANY MORE.
I MEAN, THERE'S WEAK AND THERE'S STRONG. YOU CAN'T BLAME THE STRONG FOR BEING WHAT THEY ARE.
DELIVER OUR GIFTS BACK TO THE WELLSPRING SO THAT THE PRIMAL SOURCE WILL NOT BE TAINTED BY THE BLASPHEMER...
AAAGH-- SON OF A--
THEN AGAIN, ONE THING I NEVER HEARD OF...
...IS THE STRONG...
...JUST GIVING UP THEIR POWER...!

EVEN TWO BLOCKS AWAY, THE AIR SMELLS LIKE BURNT HAIR.

SPEEDY LOOKS OKAY...

YEAH... YOU CAN *SHUNT* THE ENERGY AROUND... THANKS FOR *CONFIRMING* OUR *SUSPICIONS*...

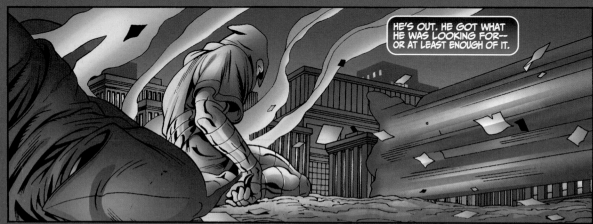

HE'S OUT. HE GOT WHAT HE WAS LOOKING FOR— OR AT LEAST ENOUGH OF IT.

BUT I HAVEN'T...

ONE BROKEN BONE AT A TIME, HE SAID...

...THAT'S PRACTICALLY A PECK ON THE CHEEK COMPARED TO WHAT *I* HAVE PLANNED...

AAH—

KRAK

WHY TAKE A MAN *OUT* WHEN HE'S ALREADY *DOWN*?

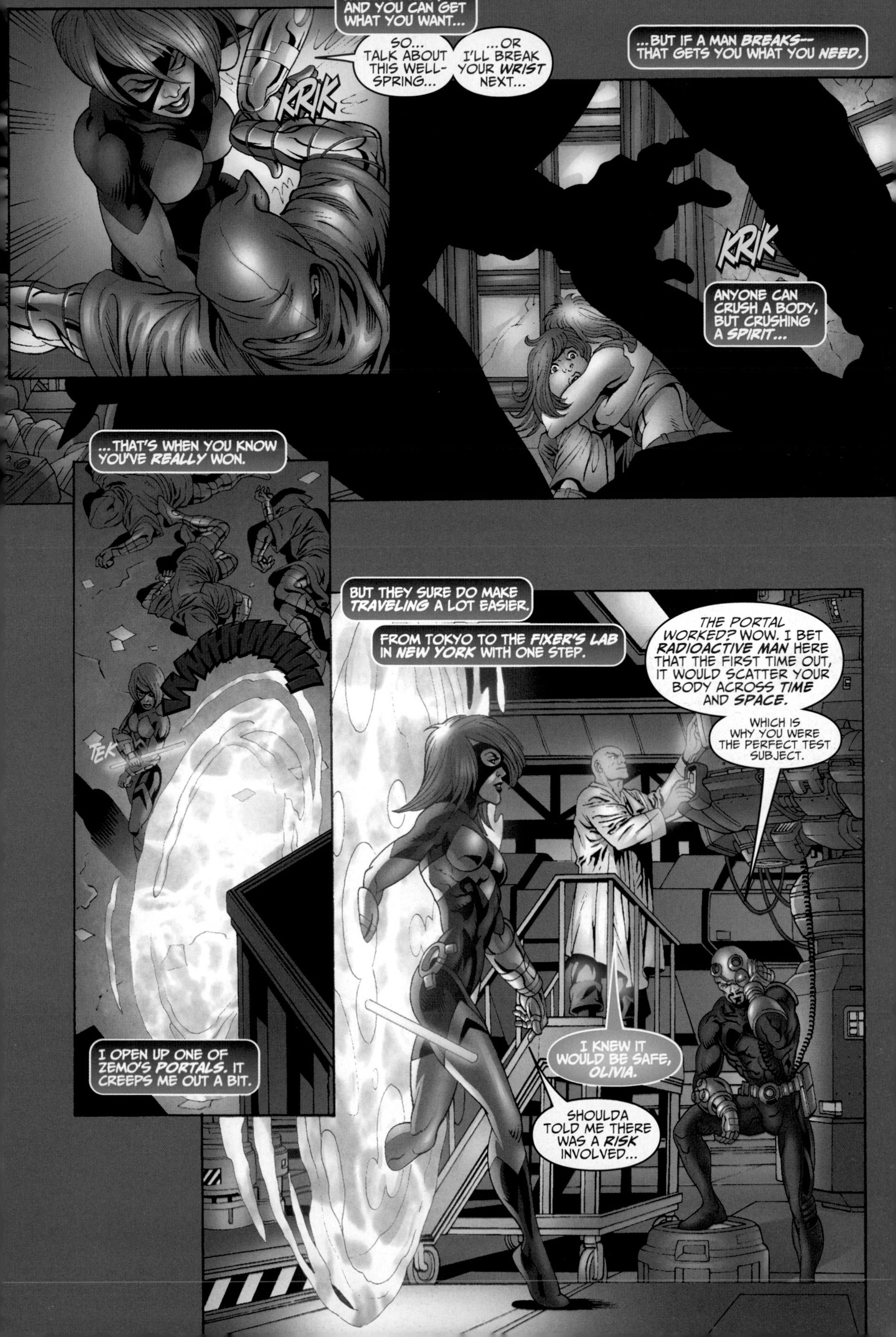

A MAN BENDS, AND YOU CAN GET WHAT YOU WANT...
SO... TALK ABOUT THIS WELL-SPRING...
...OR I'LL BREAK YOUR WRIST NEXT...
KRIK
...BUT IF A MAN BREAKS-- THAT GETS YOU WHAT YOU NEED.
KRIK
ANYONE CAN CRUSH A BODY, BUT CRUSHING A SPIRIT...
...THAT'S WHEN YOU KNOW YOU'VE REALLY WON.
TEK
I OPEN UP ONE OF ZEMO'S PORTALS. IT CREEPS ME OUT A BIT.
BUT THEY SURE DO MAKE TRAVELING A LOT EASIER.
FROM TOKYO TO THE FIXER'S LAB IN NEW YORK WITH ONE STEP.
THE PORTAL WORKED? WOW. I BET RADIOACTIVE MAN HERE THAT THE FIRST TIME OUT, IT WOULD SCATTER YOUR BODY ACROSS TIME AND SPACE.
WHICH IS WHY YOU WERE THE PERFECT TEST SUBJECT.
I KNEW IT WOULD BE SAFE, OLIVIA.
SHOULDA TOLD ME THERE WAS A RISK INVOLVED...

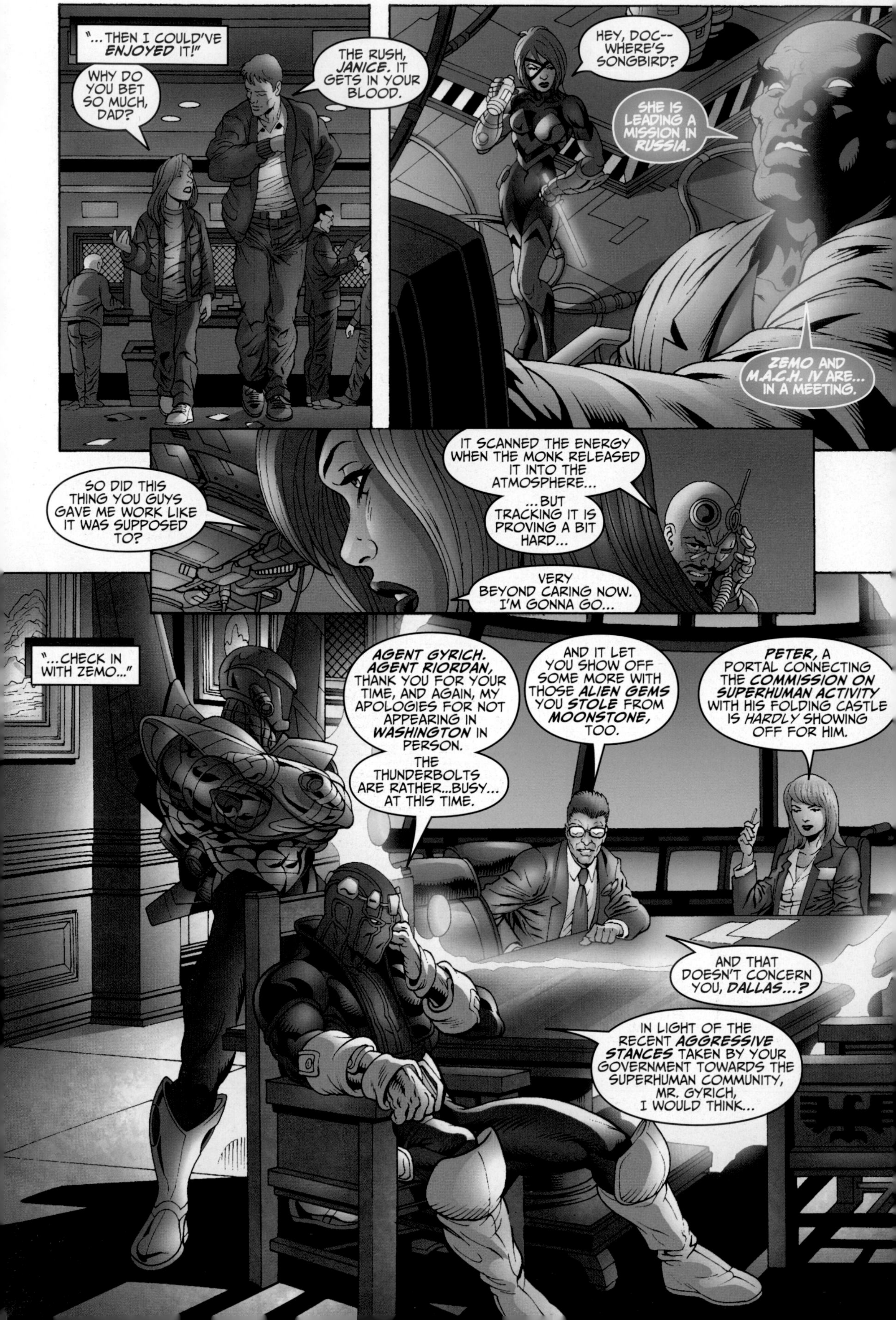
"...THEN I COULD'VE ENJOYED IT!"
WHY DO YOU BET SO MUCH, DAD?
THE RUSH, JANICE. IT GETS IN YOUR BLOOD.
HEY, DOC-- WHERE'S SONGBIRD?
SHE IS LEADING A MISSION IN RUSSIA.
ZEMO AND M.A.C.H. IV ARE... IN A MEETING.
SO DID THIS THING YOU GUYS GAVE ME WORK LIKE IT WAS SUPPOSED TO?
IT SCANNED THE ENERGY WHEN THE MONK RELEASED IT INTO THE ATMOSPHERE...
...BUT TRACKING IT IS PROVING A BIT HARD...
VERY BEYOND CARING NOW. I'M GONNA GO...
"...CHECK IN WITH ZEMO..."
AGENT GYRICH. AGENT RIORDAN, THANK YOU FOR YOUR TIME, AND AGAIN, MY APOLOGIES FOR NOT APPEARING IN WASHINGTON IN PERSON.
THE THUNDERBOLTS ARE RATHER...BUSY... AT THIS TIME.
AND IT LET YOU SHOW OFF SOME MORE WITH THOSE ALIEN GEMS YOU STOLE FROM MOONSTONE, TOO.
PETER, A PORTAL CONNECTING THE COMMISSION ON SUPERHUMAN ACTIVITY WITH HIS FOLDING CASTLE IS HARDLY SHOWING OFF FOR HIM.
AND THAT DOESN'T CONCERN YOU, DALLAS...?
IN LIGHT OF THE RECENT AGGRESSIVE STANCES TAKEN BY YOUR GOVERNMENT TOWARDS THE SUPERHUMAN COMMUNITY, MR. GYRICH, I WOULD THINK...

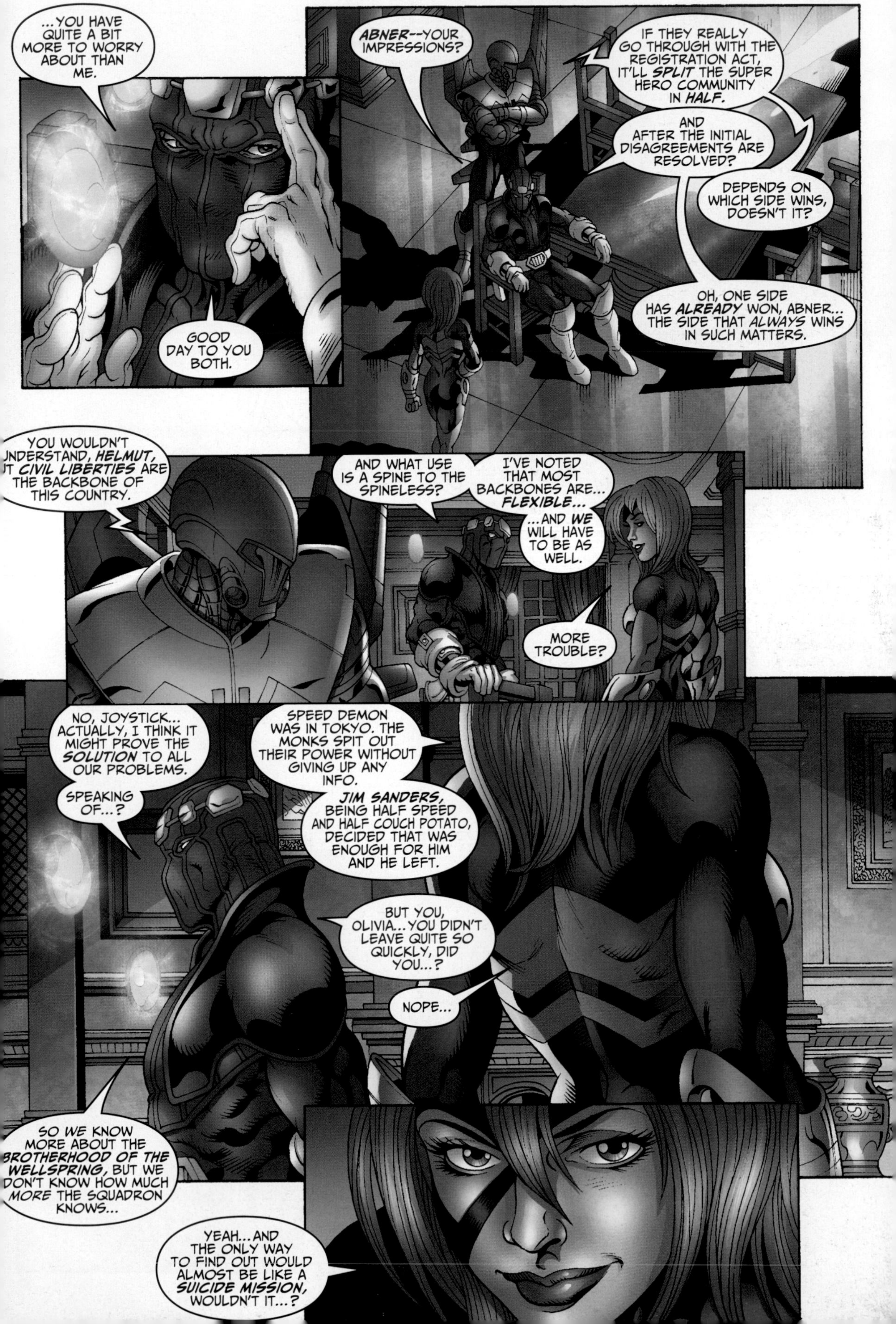
...YOU HAVE QUITE A BIT MORE TO WORRY ABOUT THAN ME.
GOOD DAY TO YOU BOTH.
ABNER--YOUR IMPRESSIONS?
IF THEY REALLY GO THROUGH WITH THE REGISTRATION ACT, IT'LL SPLIT THE SUPER HERO COMMUNITY IN HALF.
AND AFTER THE INITIAL DISAGREEMENTS ARE RESOLVED?
DEPENDS ON WHICH SIDE WINS, DOESN'T IT?
OH, ONE SIDE HAS ALREADY WON, ABNER... THE SIDE THAT ALWAYS WINS IN SUCH MATTERS.
YOU WOULDN'T UNDERSTAND, HELMUT, BUT CIVIL LIBERTIES ARE THE BACKBONE OF THIS COUNTRY.
AND WHAT USE IS A SPINE TO THE SPINELESS?
I'VE NOTED THAT MOST BACKBONES ARE... FLEXIBLE...
...AND WE WILL HAVE TO BE AS WELL.
MORE TROUBLE?
NO, JOYSTICK... ACTUALLY, I THINK IT MIGHT PROVE THE SOLUTION TO ALL OUR PROBLEMS.
SPEAKING OF...?
SPEED DEMON WAS IN TOKYO. THE MONKS SPIT OUT THEIR POWER WITHOUT GIVING UP ANY INFO.
JIM SANDERS, BEING HALF SPEED AND HALF COUCH POTATO, DECIDED THAT WAS ENOUGH FOR HIM AND HE LEFT.
BUT YOU, OLIVIA... YOU DIDN'T LEAVE QUITE SO QUICKLY, DID YOU...?
NOPE...
SO WE KNOW MORE ABOUT THE BROTHERHOOD OF THE WELLSPRING, BUT WE DON'T KNOW HOW MUCH MORE THE SQUADRON KNOWS...
YEAH... AND THE ONLY WAY TO FIND OUT WOULD ALMOST BE LIKE A SUICIDE MISSION, WOULDN'T IT...?

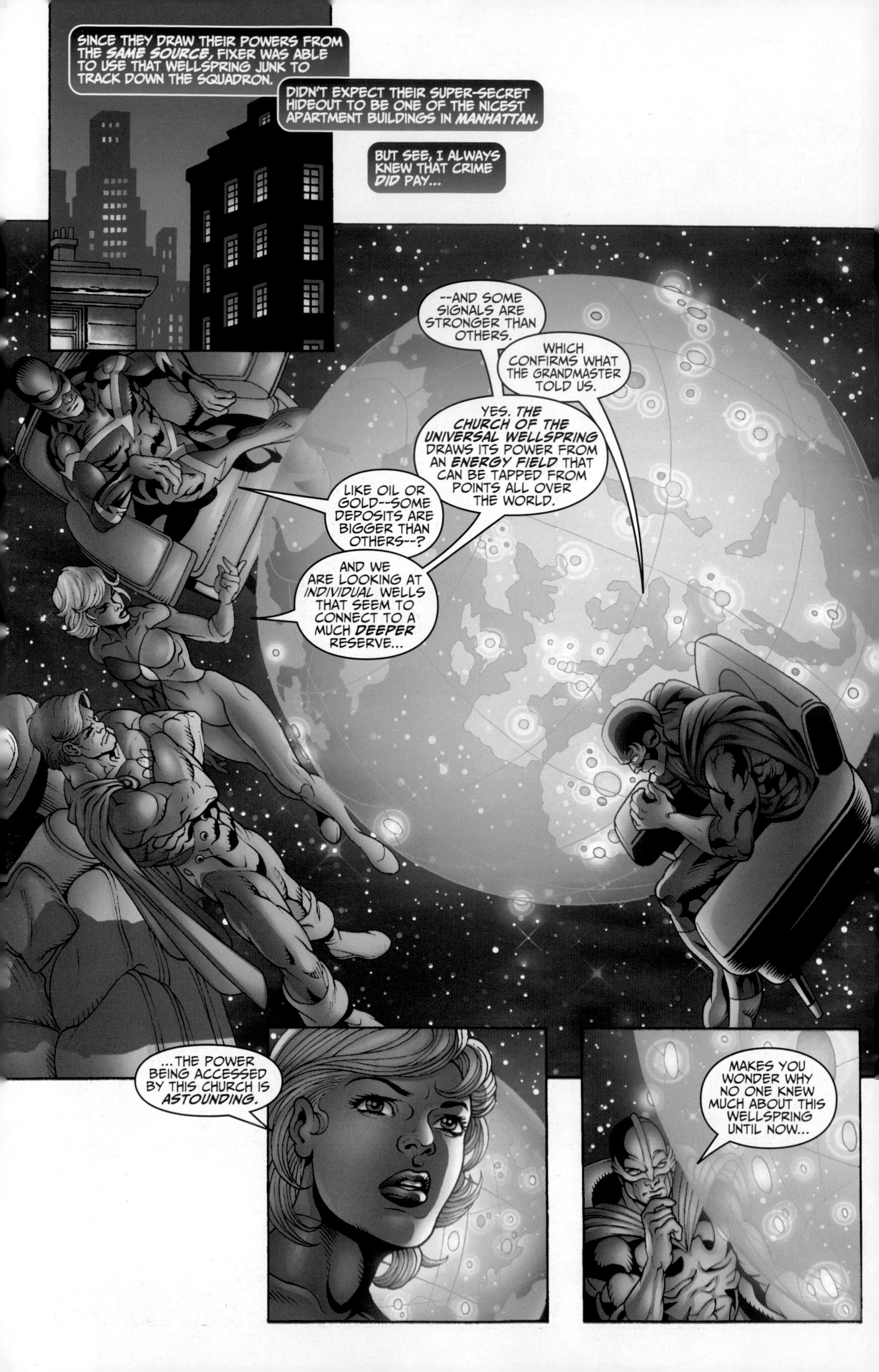
SINCE THEY DRAW THEIR POWERS FROM THE SAME SOURCE, FIXER WAS ABLE TO USE THAT WELLSPRING JUNK TO TRACK DOWN THE SQUADRON.
DIDN'T EXPECT THEIR SUPER-SECRET HIDEOUT TO BE ONE OF THE NICEST APARTMENT BUILDINGS IN MANHATTAN.
BUT SEE, I ALWAYS KNEW THAT CRIME DID PAY...
--AND SOME SIGNALS ARE STRONGER THAN OTHERS.
WHICH CONFIRMS WHAT THE GRANDMASTER TOLD US.
YES. THE CHURCH OF THE UNIVERSAL WELLSPRING DRAWS ITS POWER FROM AN ENERGY FIELD THAT CAN BE TAPPED FROM POINTS ALL OVER THE WORLD.
LIKE OIL OR GOLD--SOME DEPOSITS ARE BIGGER THAN OTHERS--?
AND WE ARE LOOKING AT INDIVIDUAL WELLS THAT SEEM TO CONNECT TO A MUCH DEEPER RESERVE...
...THE POWER BEING ACCESSED BY THIS CHURCH IS ASTOUNDING.
MAKES YOU WONDER WHY NO ONE KNEW MUCH ABOUT THIS WELLSPRING UNTIL NOW...

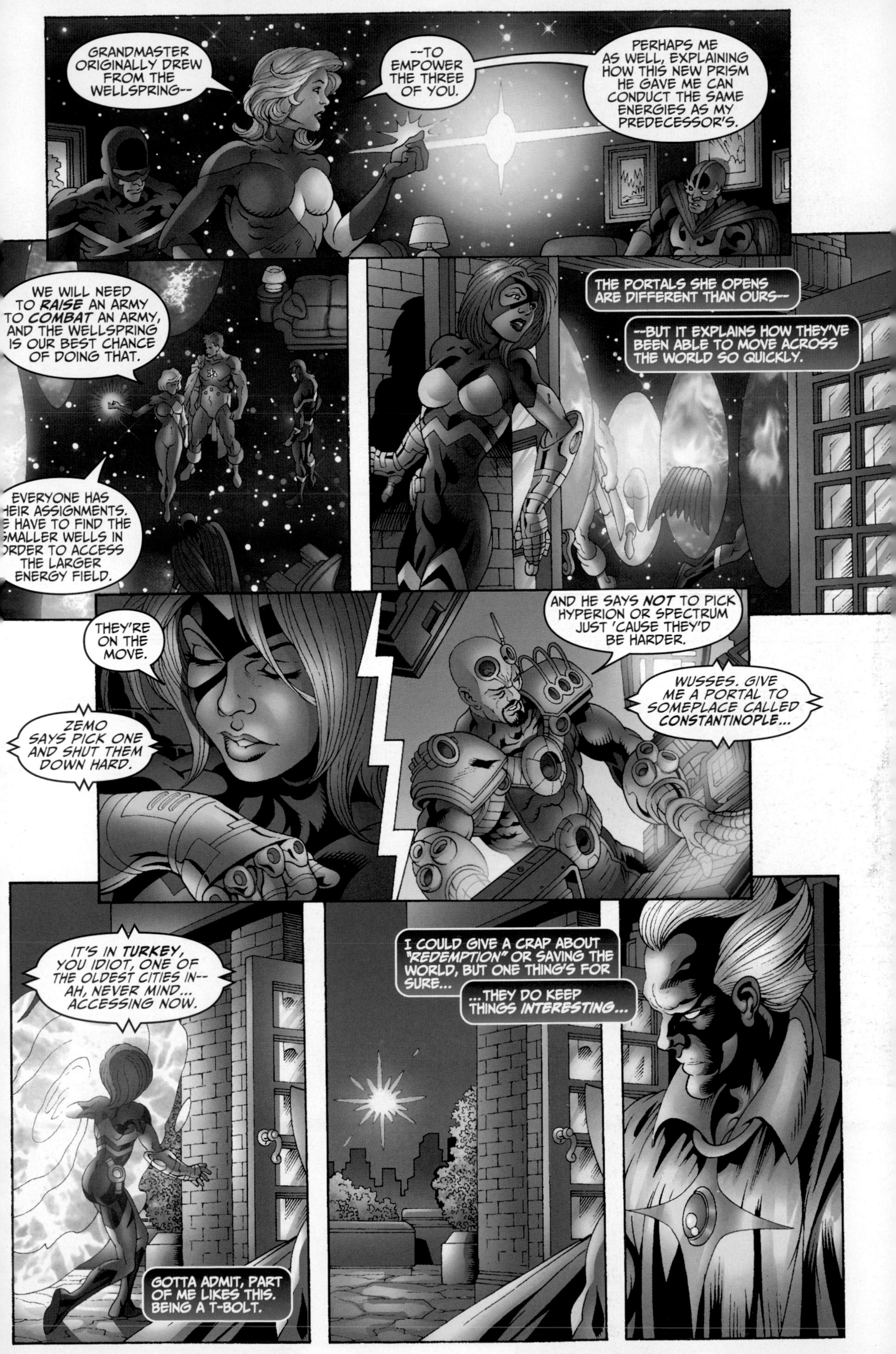
GRANDMASTER ORIGINALLY DREW FROM THE WELLSPRING--
--TO EMPOWER THE THREE OF YOU.
PERHAPS ME AS WELL, EXPLAINING HOW THIS NEW PRISM HE GAVE ME CAN CONDUCT THE SAME ENERGIES AS MY PREDECESSOR'S.
WE WILL NEED TO RAISE AN ARMY TO COMBAT AN ARMY, AND THE WELLSPRING IS OUR BEST CHANCE OF DOING THAT.
EVERYONE HAS THEIR ASSIGNMENTS. WE HAVE TO FIND THE SMALLER WELLS IN ORDER TO ACCESS THE LARGER ENERGY FIELD.
THE PORTALS SHE OPENS ARE DIFFERENT THAN OURS--
--BUT IT EXPLAINS HOW THEY'VE BEEN ABLE TO MOVE ACROSS THE WORLD SO QUICKLY.
THEY'RE ON THE MOVE.
ZEMO SAYS PICK ONE AND SHUT THEM DOWN HARD.
AND HE SAYS NOT TO PICK HYPERION OR SPECTRUM JUST 'CAUSE THEY'D BE HARDER.
WUSSES. GIVE ME A PORTAL TO SOMEPLACE CALLED CONSTANTINOPLE...
IT'S IN TURKEY, YOU IDIOT, ONE OF THE OLDEST CITIES IN-- AH, NEVER MIND... ACCESSING NOW.
GOTTA ADMIT, PART OF ME LIKES THIS. BEING A T-BOLT.
I COULD GIVE A CRAP ABOUT "REDEMPTION" OR SAVING THE WORLD, BUT ONE THING'S FOR SURE...
...THEY DO KEEP THINGS INTERESTING...

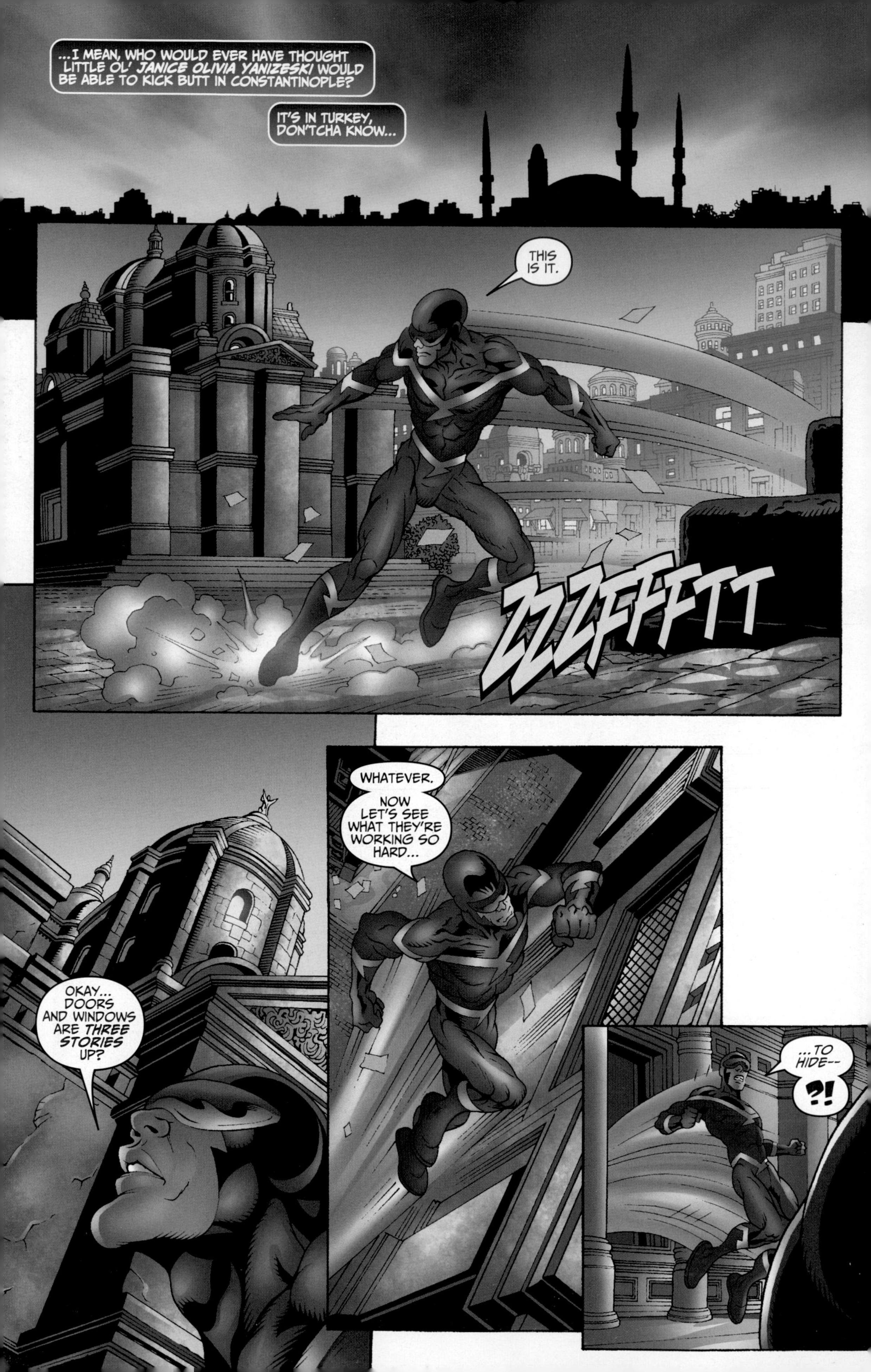
...I MEAN, WHO WOULD EVER HAVE THOUGHT LITTLE OL' JANICE OLIVIA YANIZESKI WOULD BE ABLE TO KICK BUTT IN CONSTANTINOPLE?
IT'S IN TURKEY, DON'TCHA KNOW...
THIS IS IT.
ZZZFFFTT
OKAY... DOORS AND WINDOWS ARE THREE STORIES UP?
WHATEVER.
NOW LET'S SEE WHAT THEY'RE WORKING SO HARD...
...TO HIDE--
?!

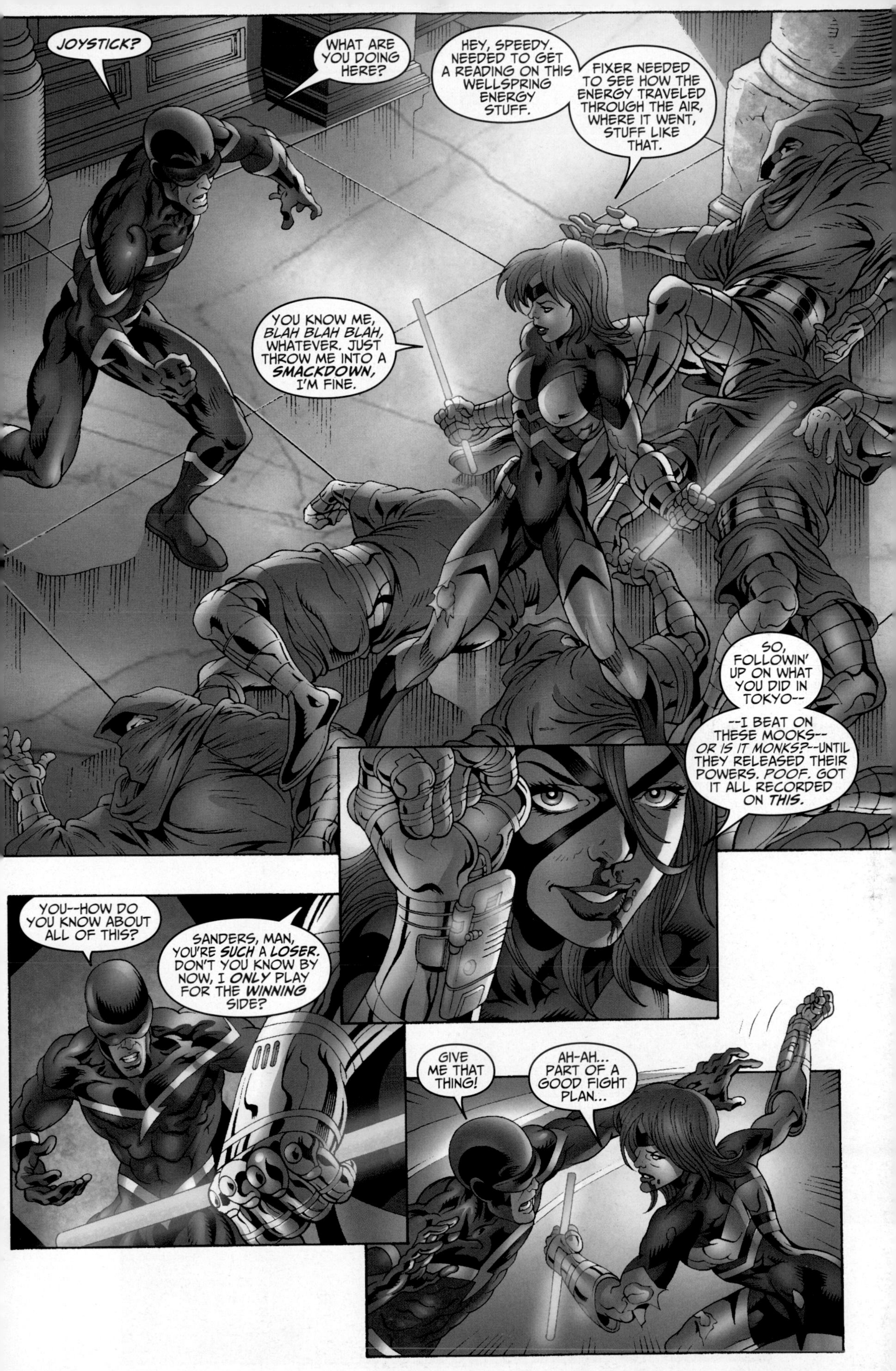
JOYSTICK?
WHAT ARE YOU DOING HERE?
HEY, SPEEDY. NEEDED TO GET A READING ON THIS WELLSPRING ENERGY STUFF.
FIXER NEEDED TO SEE HOW THE ENERGY TRAVELED THROUGH THE AIR, WHERE IT WENT, STUFF LIKE THAT.
YOU KNOW ME, BLAH BLAH BLAH, WHATEVER. JUST THROW ME INTO A SMACKDOWN, I'M FINE.
SO, FOLLOWIN' UP ON WHAT YOU DID IN TOKYO--
--I BEAT ON THESE MOOKS-- OR IS IT MONKS?--UNTIL THEY RELEASED THEIR POWERS. POOF. GOT IT ALL RECORDED ON THIS.
YOU--HOW DO YOU KNOW ABOUT ALL OF THIS?
SANDERS, MAN, YOU'RE SUCH A LOSER. DON'T YOU KNOW BY NOW, I ONLY PLAY FOR THE WINNING SIDE?
GIVE ME THAT THING!
AH-AH... PART OF A GOOD FIGHT PLAN...

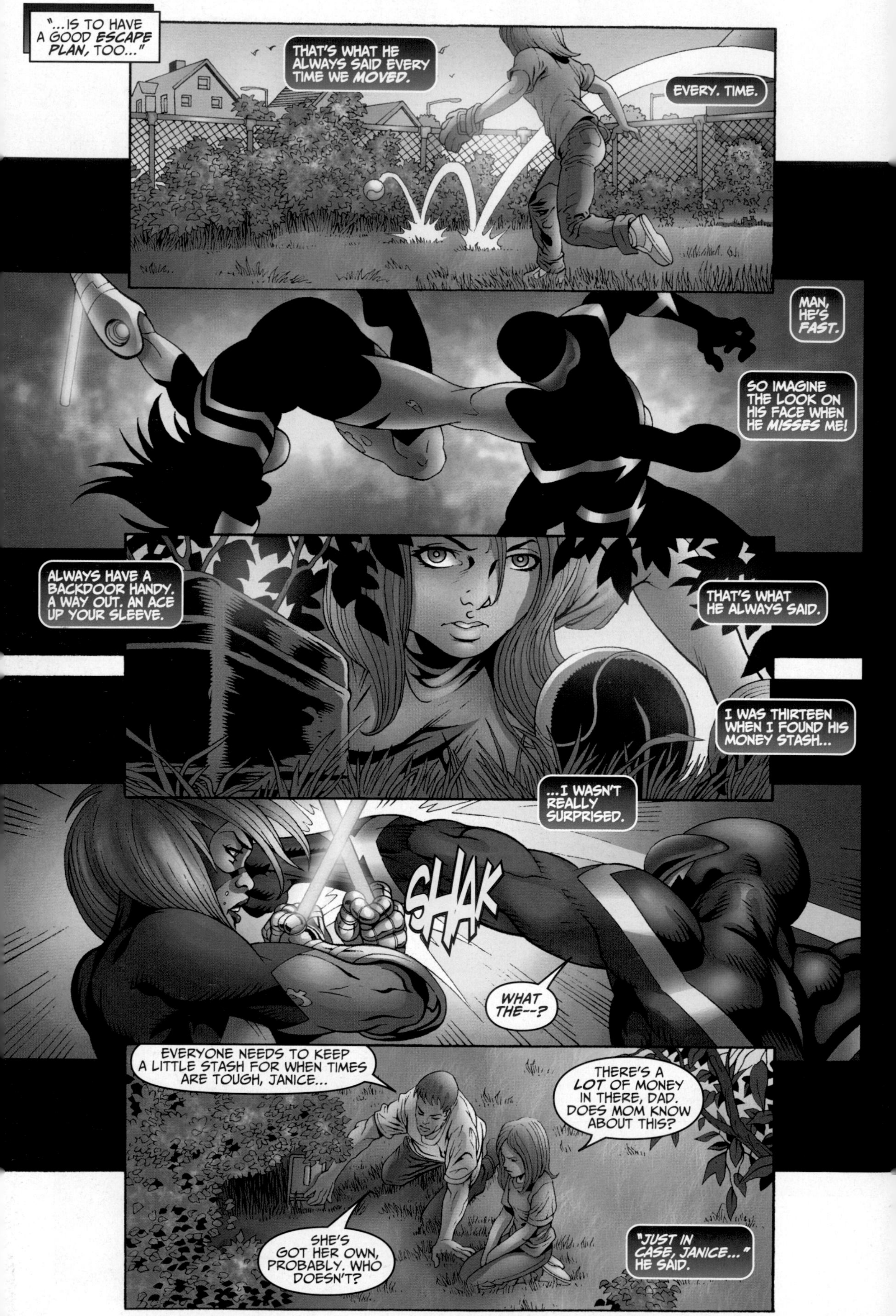
"...IS TO HAVE A GOOD ESCAPE PLAN, TOO..."
THAT'S WHAT HE ALWAYS SAID EVERY TIME WE MOVED.
EVERY. TIME.
MAN, HE'S FAST.
SO IMAGINE THE LOOK ON HIS FACE WHEN HE MISSES ME!
ALWAYS HAVE A BACKDOOR HANDY. A WAY OUT. AN ACE UP YOUR SLEEVE.
THAT'S WHAT HE ALWAYS SAID.
I WAS THIRTEEN WHEN I FOUND HIS MONEY STASH...
...I WASN'T REALLY SURPRISED.
SHAK
WHAT THE--?
EVERYONE NEEDS TO KEEP A LITTLE STASH FOR WHEN TIMES ARE TOUGH, JANICE...
THERE'S A LOT OF MONEY IN THERE, DAD. DOES MOM KNOW ABOUT THIS?
SHE'S GOT HER OWN, PROBABLY. WHO DOESN'T?
"JUST IN CASE, JANICE..." HE SAID.

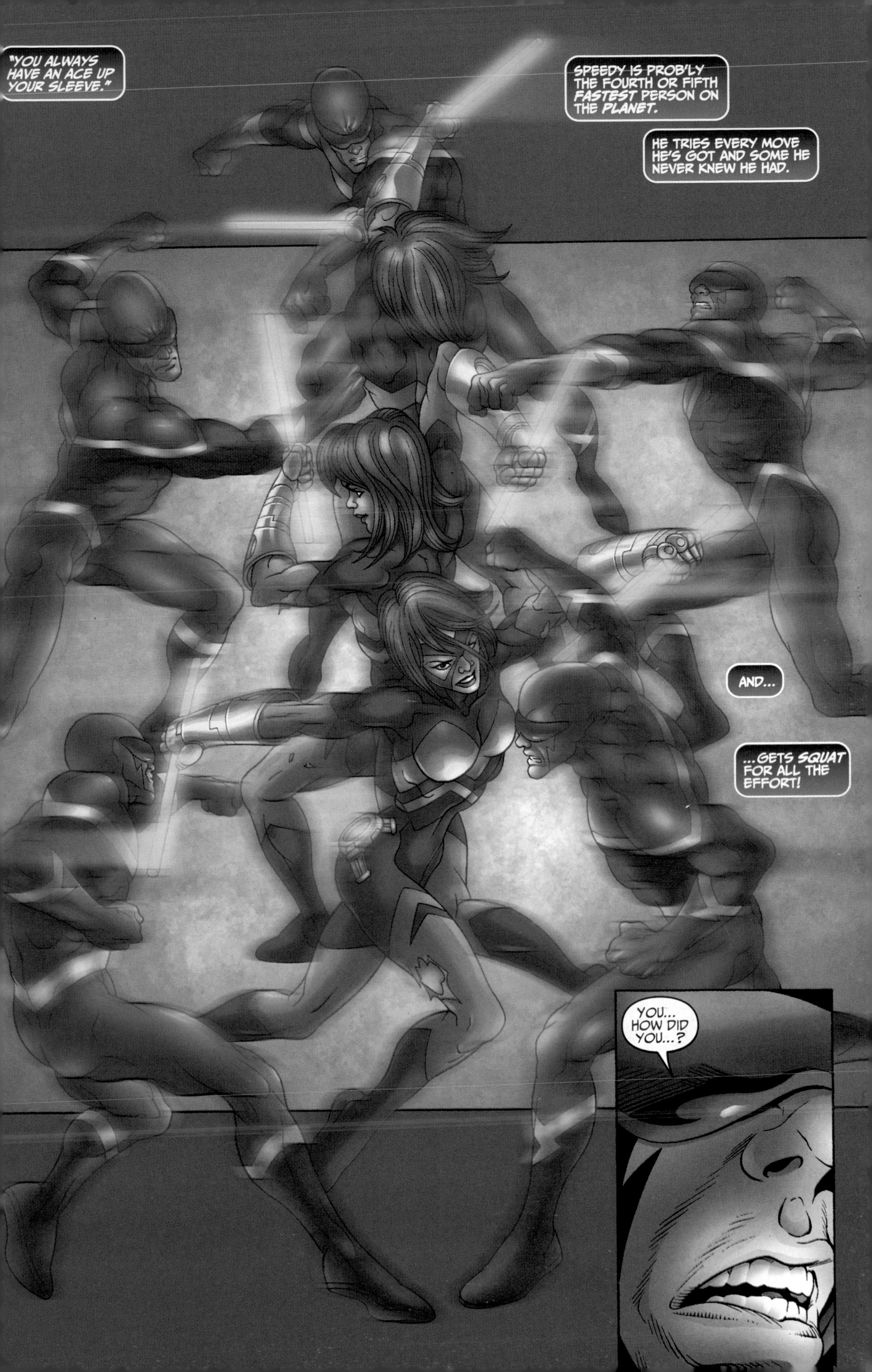
"YOU ALWAYS HAVE AN ACE UP YOUR SLEEVE."
SPEEDY IS PROB'LY THE FOURTH OR FIFTH FASTEST PERSON ON THE PLANET.
HE TRIES EVERY MOVE HE'S GOT AND SOME HE NEVER KNEW HE HAD.
AND...
...GETS SQUAT FOR ALL THE EFFORT!
YOU... HOW DID YOU...?

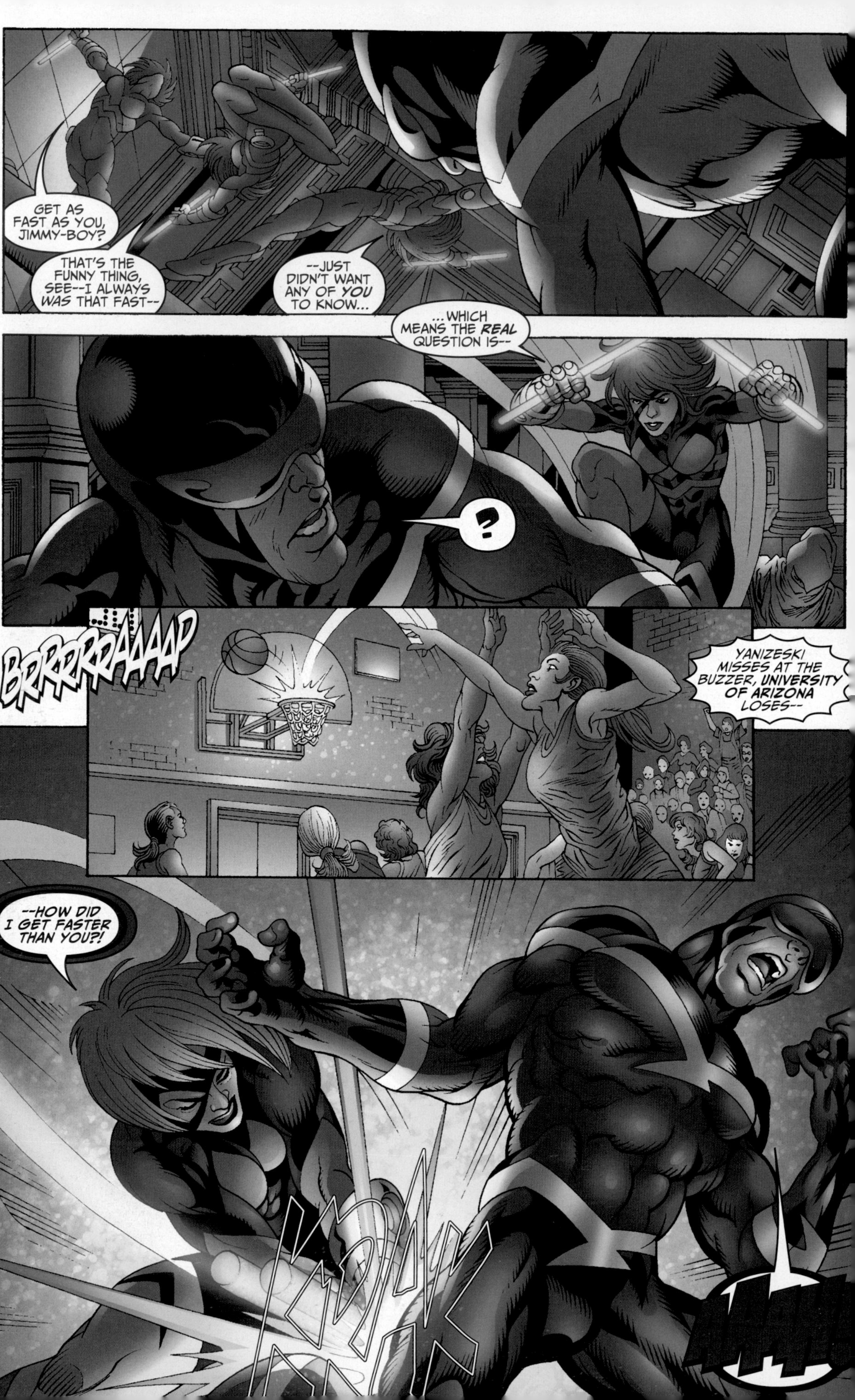
GET AS FAST AS YOU, JIMMY-BOY?
THAT'S THE FUNNY THING, SEE--I ALWAYS WAS THAT FAST--
--JUST DIDN'T WANT ANY OF YOU TO KNOW...
...WHICH MEANS THE REAL QUESTION IS--
?
BRRRRRAAAAP
YANIZESKI MISSES AT THE BUZZER, UNIVERSITY OF ARIZONA LOSES--
--HOW DID I GET FASTER THAN YOU?!

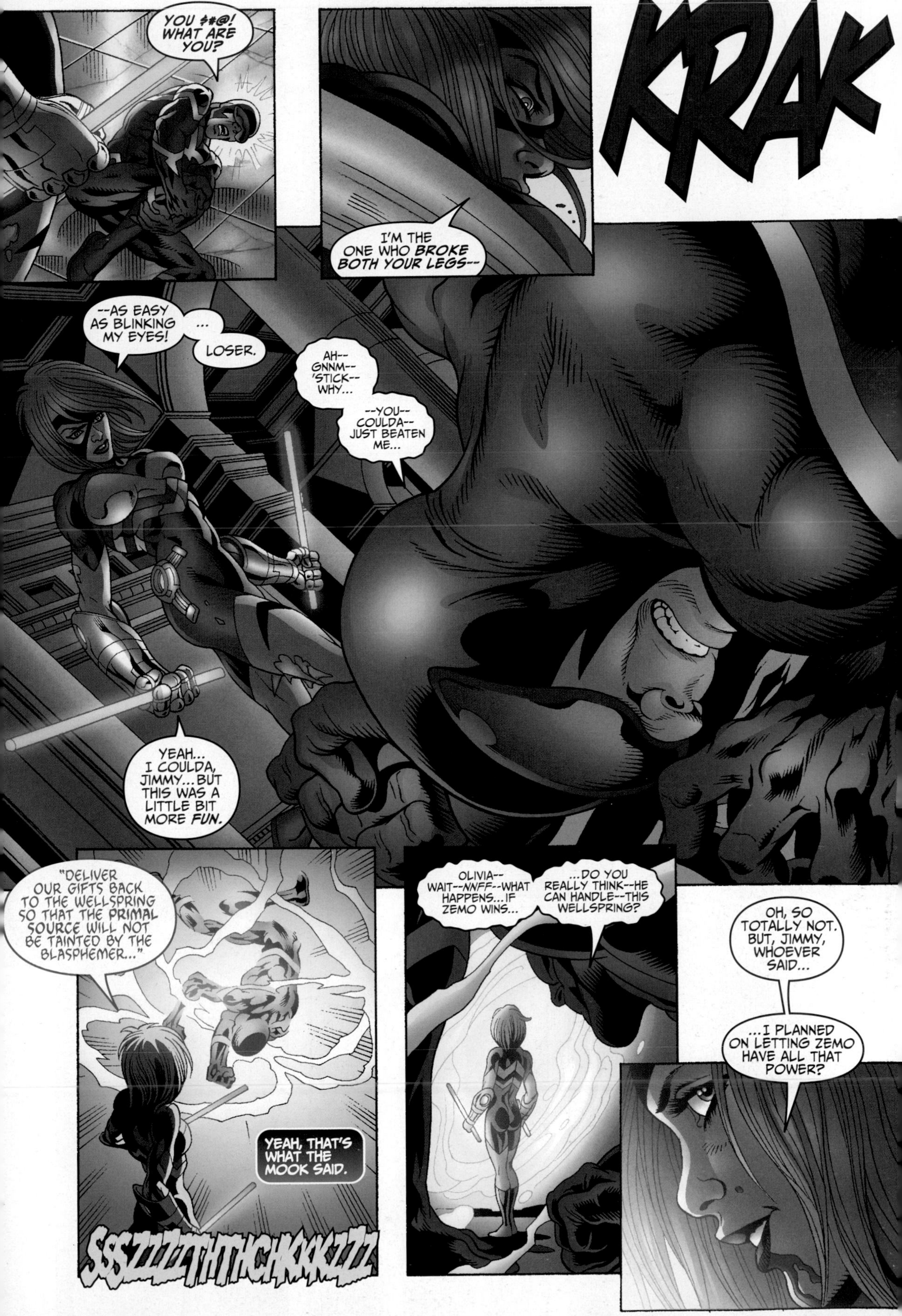

YOU $#@! WHAT ARE YOU?
I'M THE ONE WHO BROKE BOTH YOUR LEGS--
KRAK
--AS EASY AS BLINKING MY EYES!
...
LOSER.
AH-- GNNM-- 'STICK-- WHY...
--YOU-- COULDA-- JUST BEATEN ME...
YEAH... I COULDA, JIMMY... BUT THIS WAS A LITTLE BIT MORE FUN.
"DELIVER OUR GIFTS BACK TO THE WELLSPRING SO THAT THE PRIMAL SOURCE WILL NOT BE TAINTED BY THE BLASPHEMER..."
YEAH, THAT'S WHAT THE MOOK SAID.
SSSZZZZZTHTHCHKKKZZZ
OLIVIA-- WAIT--NNFF--WHAT HAPPENS...IF ZEMO WINS...
...DO YOU REALLY THINK--HE CAN HANDLE--THIS WELLSPRING?
OH, SO TOTALLY NOT. BUT, JIMMY, WHOEVER SAID...
...I PLANNED ON LETTING ZEMO HAVE ALL THAT POWER?

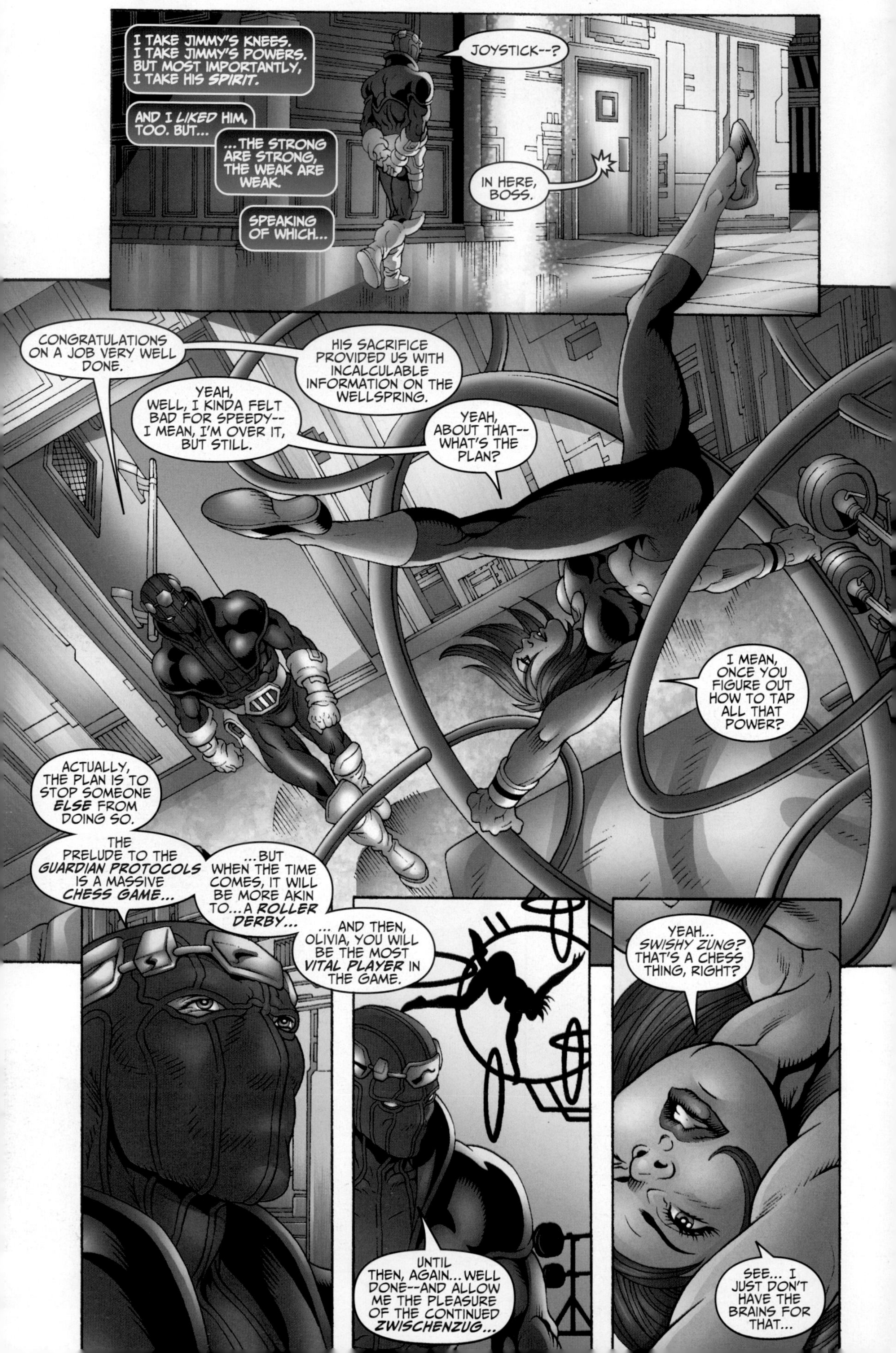
I TAKE JIMMY'S KNEES. I TAKE JIMMY'S POWERS. BUT MOST IMPORTANTLY, I TAKE HIS *SPIRIT*.
AND I *LIKED* HIM, TOO. BUT...
...THE STRONG ARE STRONG, THE WEAK ARE WEAK.
SPEAKING OF WHICH...
JOYSTICK--?
IN HERE, BOSS.
CONGRATULATIONS ON A JOB VERY WELL DONE.
HIS SACRIFICE PROVIDED US WITH INCALCULABLE INFORMATION ON THE WELLSPRING.
YEAH, WELL, I KINDA FELT BAD FOR SPEEDY--I MEAN, I'M OVER IT, BUT STILL.
YEAH, ABOUT THAT--WHAT'S THE PLAN?
I MEAN, ONCE YOU FIGURE OUT HOW TO TAP ALL THAT POWER?
ACTUALLY, THE PLAN IS TO STOP SOMEONE *ELSE* FROM DOING SO.
THE PRELUDE TO THE *GUARDIAN PROTOCOLS* IS A MASSIVE *CHESS GAME*...
...BUT WHEN THE TIME COMES, IT WILL BE MORE AKIN TO...A *ROLLER DERBY*...
... AND THEN, OLIVIA, YOU WILL BE THE MOST *VITAL PLAYER* IN THE GAME.
UNTIL THEN, AGAIN...WELL DONE--AND ALLOW ME THE PLEASURE OF THE CONTINUED *ZWISCHENZUG*...
YEAH... *SWISHY ZUNG*? THAT'S A CHESS THING, RIGHT?
SEE... I JUST DON'T HAVE THE BRAINS FOR THAT...

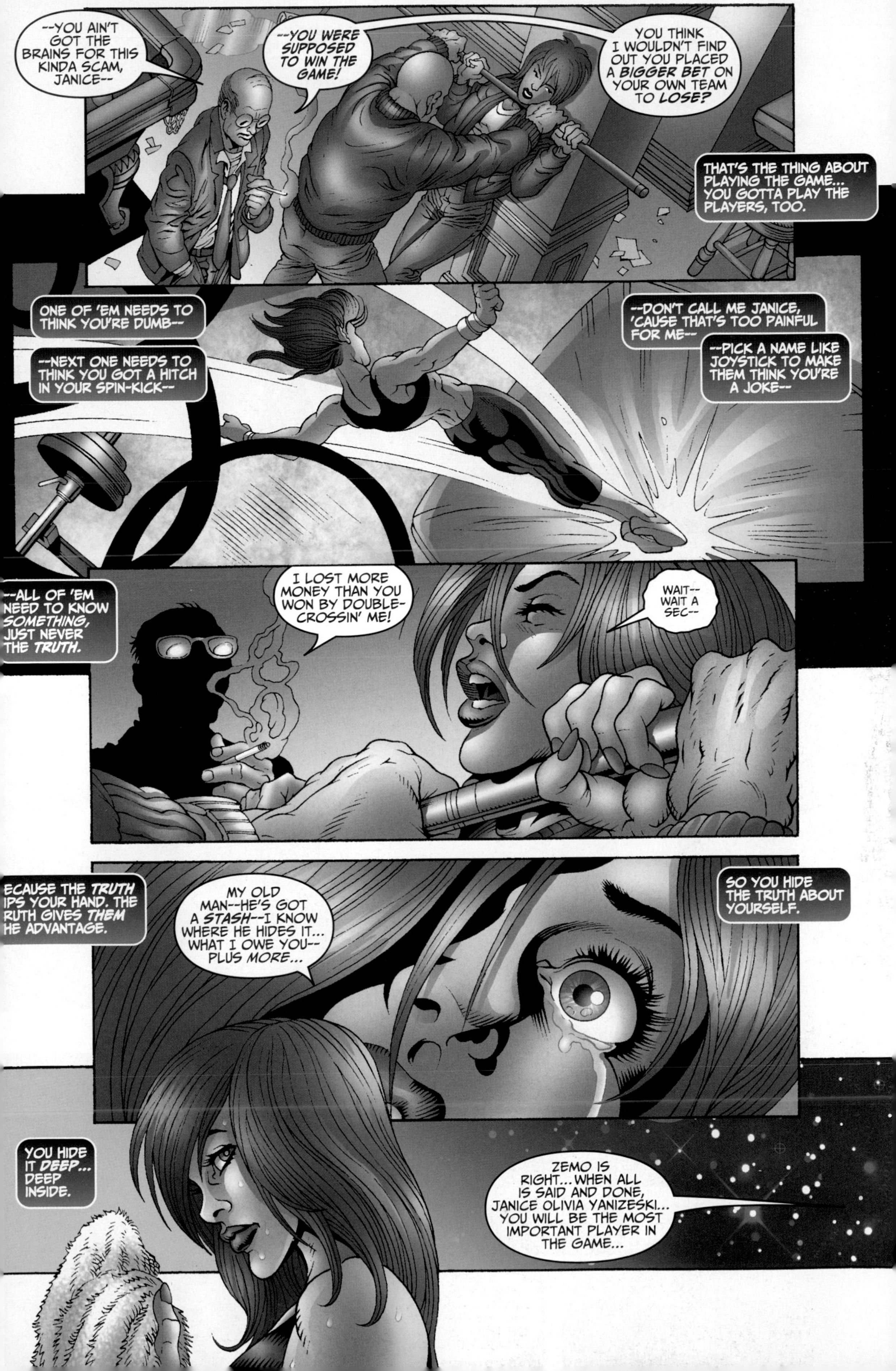
--YOU AIN'T GOT THE BRAINS FOR THIS KINDA SCAM, JANICE--
--YOU WERE SUPPOSED TO WIN THE GAME!
YOU THINK I WOULDN'T FIND OUT YOU PLACED A BIGGER BET ON YOUR OWN TEAM TO LOSE?
THAT'S THE THING ABOUT PLAYING THE GAME... YOU GOTTA PLAY THE PLAYERS, TOO.
ONE OF 'EM NEEDS TO THINK YOU'RE DUMB--
--NEXT ONE NEEDS TO THINK YOU GOT A HITCH IN YOUR SPIN-KICK--
--DON'T CALL ME JANICE, 'CAUSE THAT'S TOO PAINFUL FOR ME--
--PICK A NAME LIKE JOYSTICK TO MAKE THEM THINK YOU'RE A JOKE--
--ALL OF 'EM NEED TO KNOW SOMETHING, JUST NEVER THE TRUTH.
I LOST MORE MONEY THAN YOU WON BY DOUBLE-CROSSIN' ME!
WAIT--WAIT A SEC--
ECAUSE THE TRUTH IPS YOUR HAND. THE RUTH GIVES THEM HE ADVANTAGE.
MY OLD MAN--HE'S GOT A STASH--I KNOW WHERE HE HIDES IT... WHAT I OWE YOU--PLUS MORE...
SO YOU HIDE THE TRUTH ABOUT YOURSELF.
YOU HIDE IT DEEP... DEEP INSIDE.
ZEMO IS RIGHT... WHEN ALL IS SAID AND DONE, JANICE OLIVIA YANIZESKI... YOU WILL BE THE MOST IMPORTANT PLAYER IN THE GAME...

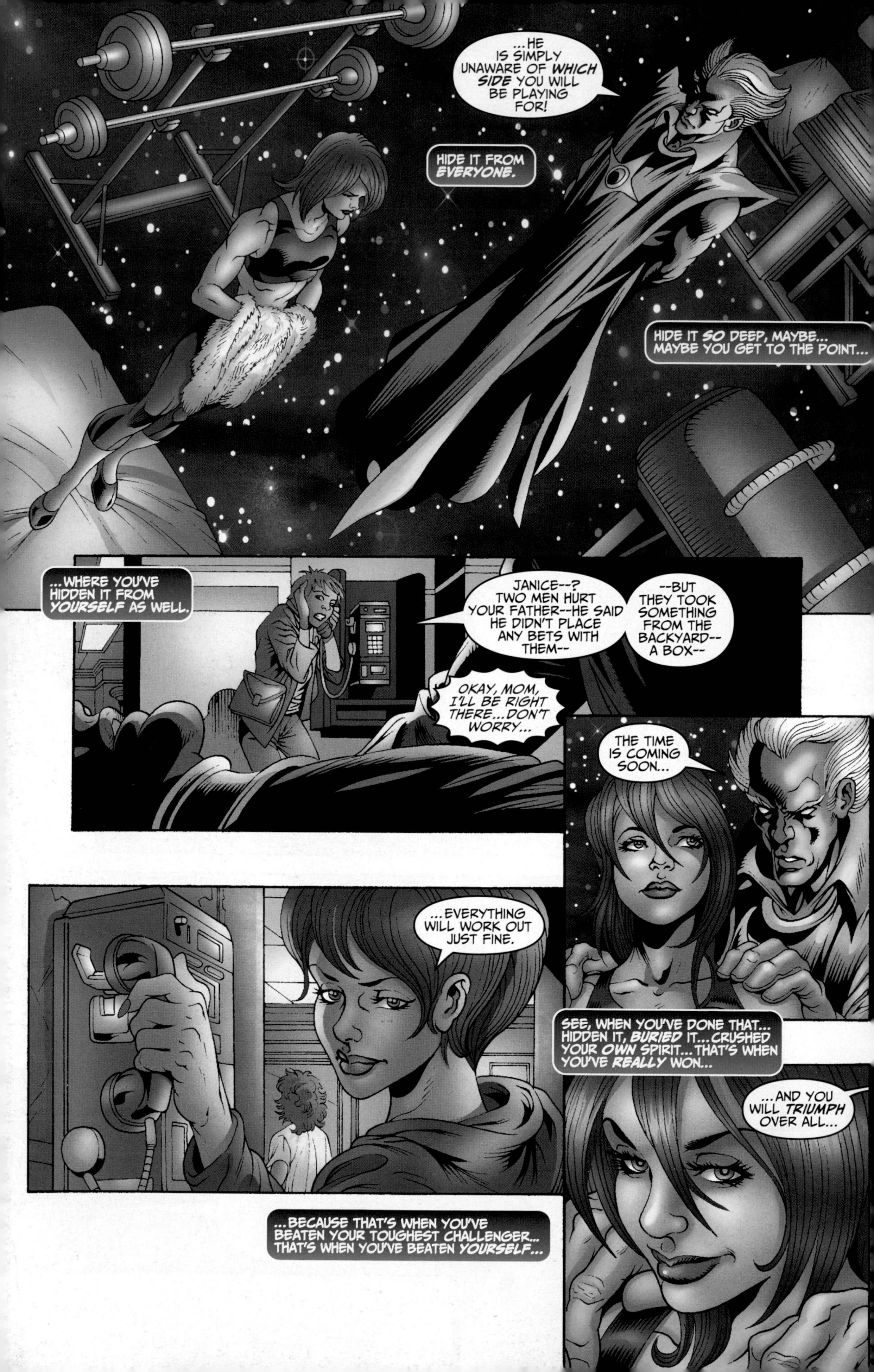
...HE IS SIMPLY UNAWARE OF WHICH SIDE YOU WILL BE PLAYING FOR!
HIDE IT FROM EVERYONE.
HIDE IT SO DEEP, MAYBE... MAYBE YOU GET TO THE POINT...
...WHERE YOU'VE HIDDEN IT FROM YOURSELF AS WELL.
JANICE--? TWO MEN HURT YOUR FATHER--HE SAID HE DIDN'T PLACE ANY BETS WITH THEM--
--BUT THEY TOOK SOMETHING FROM THE BACKYARD--A BOX--
OKAY, MOM, I'LL BE RIGHT THERE...DON'T WORRY...
THE TIME IS COMING SOON...
...EVERYTHING WILL WORK OUT JUST FINE.
SEE, WHEN YOU'VE DONE THAT... HIDDEN IT, BURIED IT...CRUSHED YOUR OWN SPIRIT...THAT'S WHEN YOU'VE REALLY WON...
...AND YOU WILL TRIUMPH OVER ALL...
...BECAUSE THAT'S WHEN YOU'VE BEATEN YOUR TOUGHEST CHALLENGER... THAT'S WHEN YOU'VE BEATEN YOURSELF...

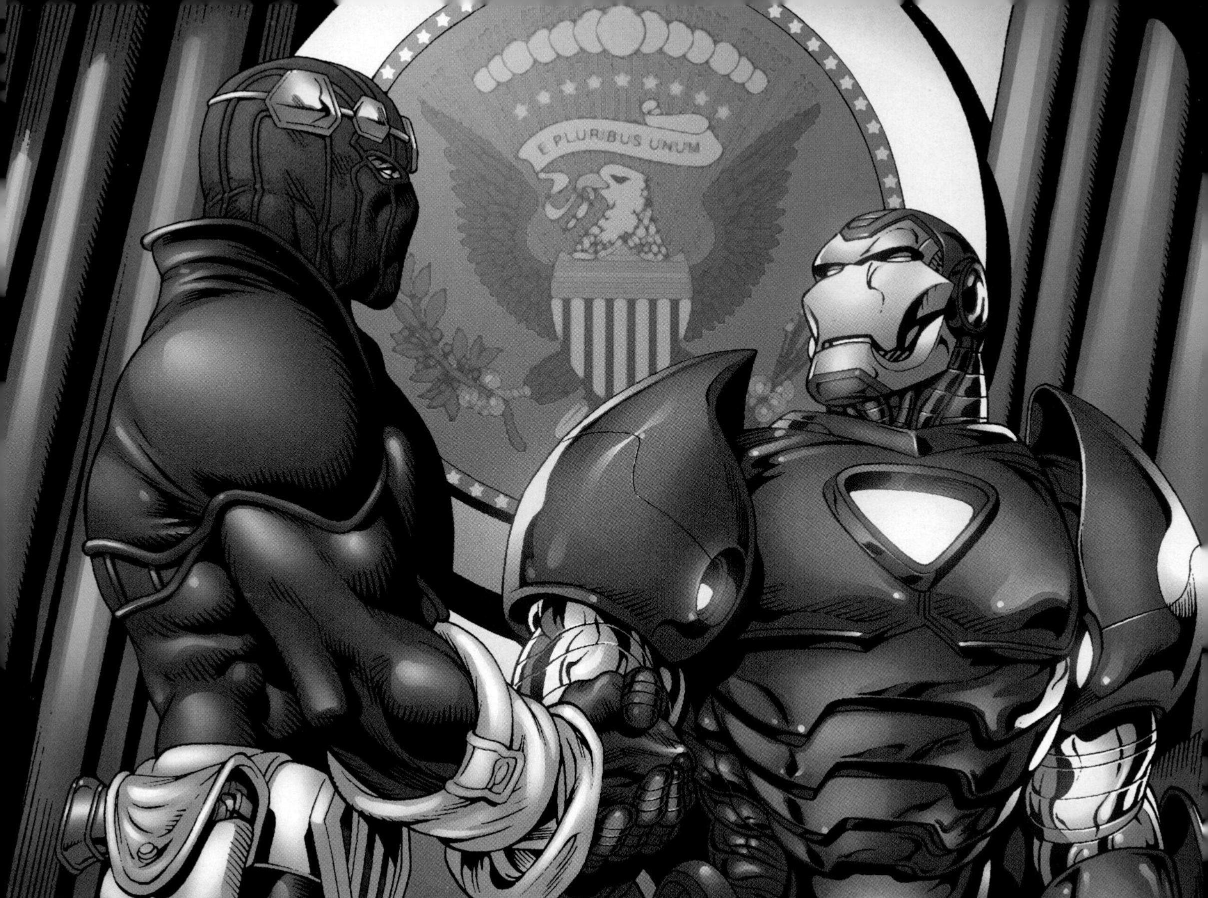
E PLURIBUS UNUM

# THUNDERBOLTS

A MARVEL COMICS EVENT

# CIVIL WAR

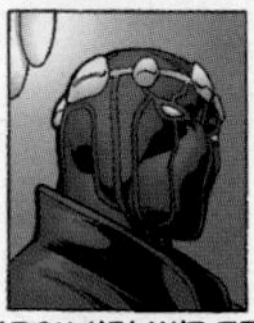

BARON HELMUT ZEMO

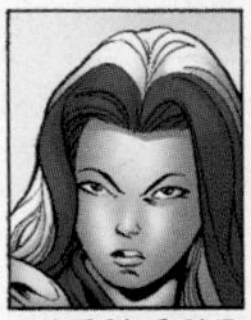

MELISSA GOLD
SONGBIRD

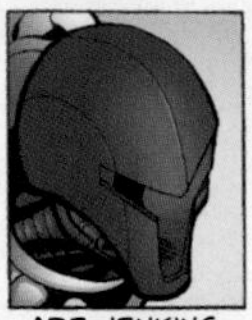

ABE JENKINS
M.A.C.H. IV

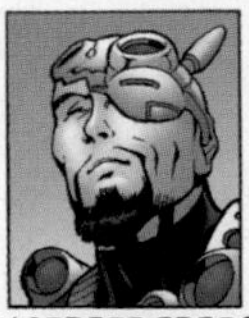

P. NORBERT EBERSOL
FIXER

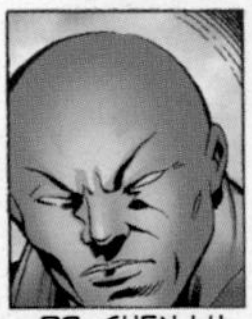

DR. CHEN LU
THE RADIOACTIVE MAN

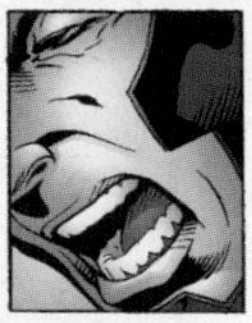

ERIK JOSTEN
ATLAS

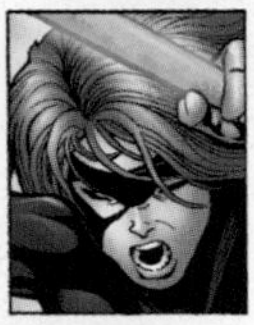

JANICE OLIVIA YANIZESKI
JOYSTICK

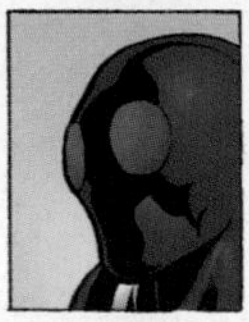

CONRAD JOSTEN
SMUGGLER

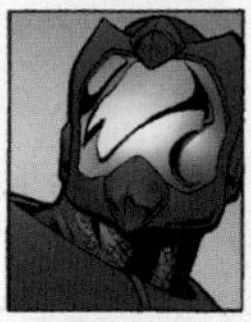

ANDREAS STRUCKER
SWORDSMAN

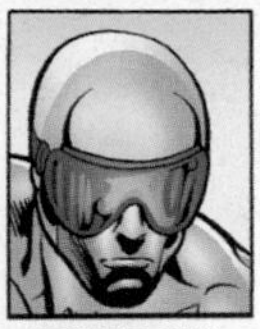

DONNIE GILL
BLIZZARD

The Avengers foiled a plan by Baron Zemo and the Thunderbolts that could have saved the world. They could not trust Zemo, who repaid their doubt by almost sacrificing his life to save Captain America. After those events, the T-Bolts disbanded. A new team was started by M.A.C.H. IV, who didn't know that Zemo and Songbird had worked behind the scenes to prepare his team for an impending and mysterious global threat.

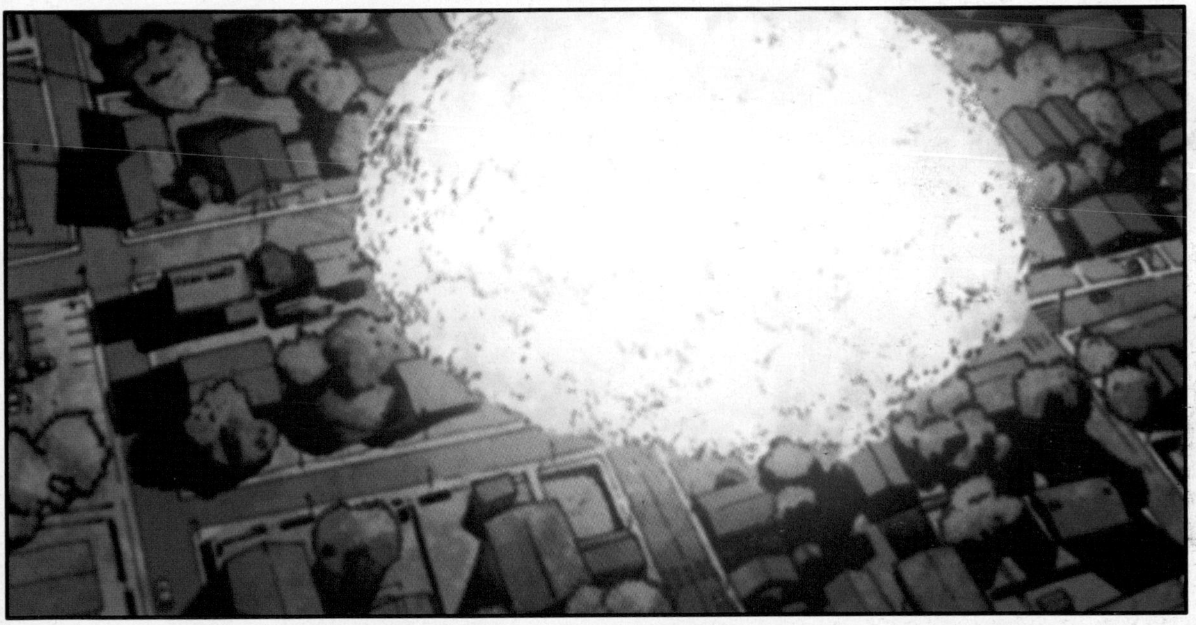

Two Weeks Ago, a horrific explosion at a crowded schoolyard in Stamford, Connecticut killed hundreds of civilians, many of them children. Superhuman irresponsibility was to blame, and the public outcry forced legislators to pass the Superhuman Registration Act. By law, superhumans must now register their identities with the government.

This Act has created a schism in the super hero community. Many have refused to register, including Captain America, who leads a group of renegade heroes against the status quo. Those in favor of using registration to create a nationwide "superhuman police force," have encouraged a startling public unmasking from a hero who has closely guarded his identity...

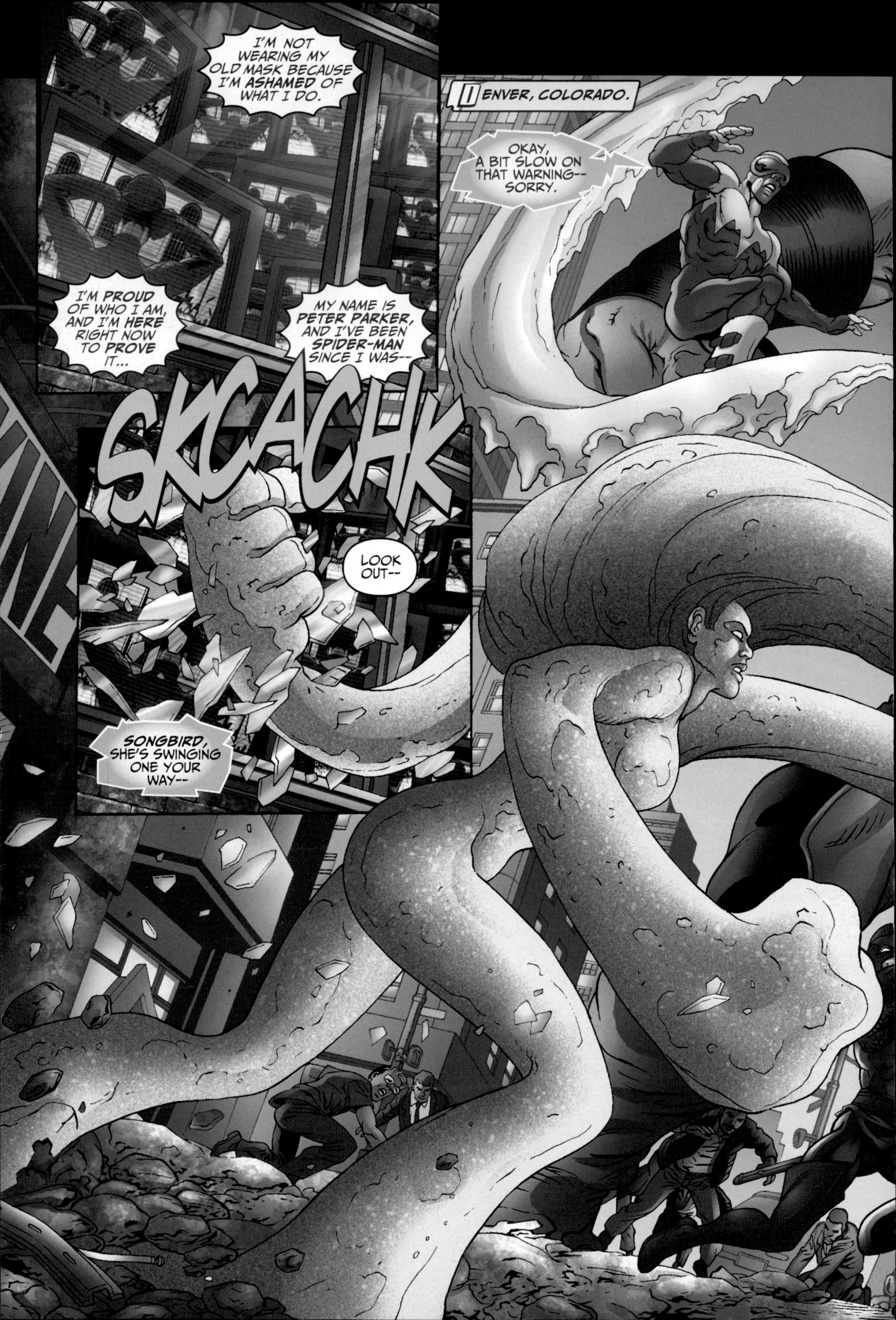
I'M NOT WEARING MY OLD MASK BECAUSE I'M ASHAMED OF WHAT I DO.
I'M PROUD OF WHO I AM, AND I'M HERE RIGHT NOW TO PROVE IT...
MY NAME IS PETER PARKER, AND I'VE BEEN SPIDER-MAN SINCE I WAS--
SKCACHK
LOOK OUT--
SONGBIRD, SHE'S SWINGING ONE YOUR WAY--
DENVER, COLORADO.
OKAY, A BIT SLOW ON THAT WARNING-- SORRY.

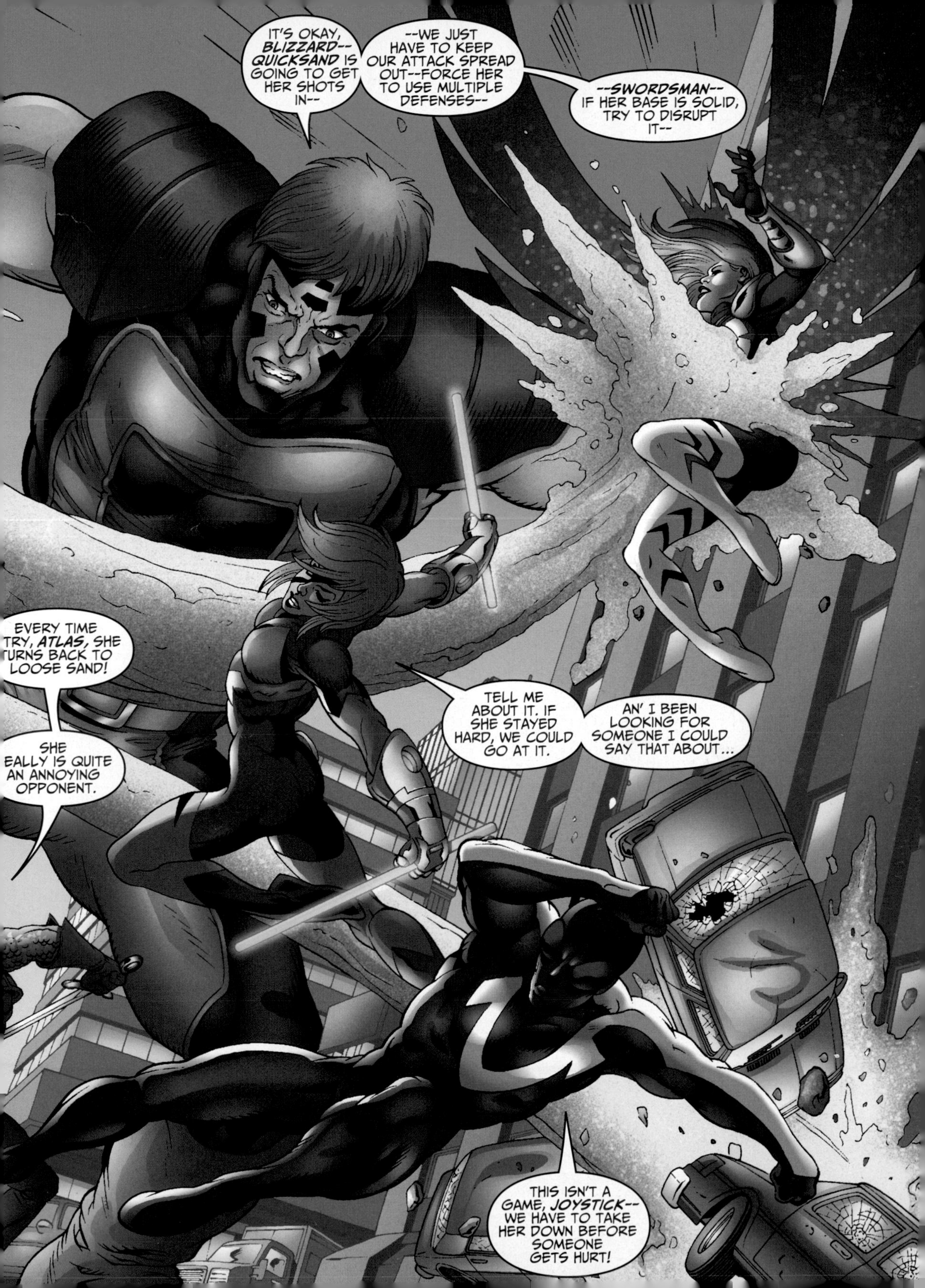
IT'S OKAY, BLIZZARD-- QUICKSAND IS GOING TO GET HER SHOTS IN--
--WE JUST HAVE TO KEEP OUR ATTACK SPREAD OUT--FORCE HER TO USE MULTIPLE DEFENSES--
--SWORDSMAN-- IF HER BASE IS SOLID, TRY TO DISRUPT IT--
EVERY TIME TRY, ATLAS, SHE TURNS BACK TO LOOSE SAND!
SHE EALLY IS QUITE AN ANNOYING OPPONENT.
TELL ME ABOUT IT. IF SHE STAYED HARD, WE COULD GO AT IT.
AN' I BEEN LOOKING FOR SOMEONE I COULD SAY THAT ABOUT...
THIS ISN'T A GAME, JOYSTICK-- WE HAVE TO TAKE HER DOWN BEFORE SOMEONE GETS HURT!

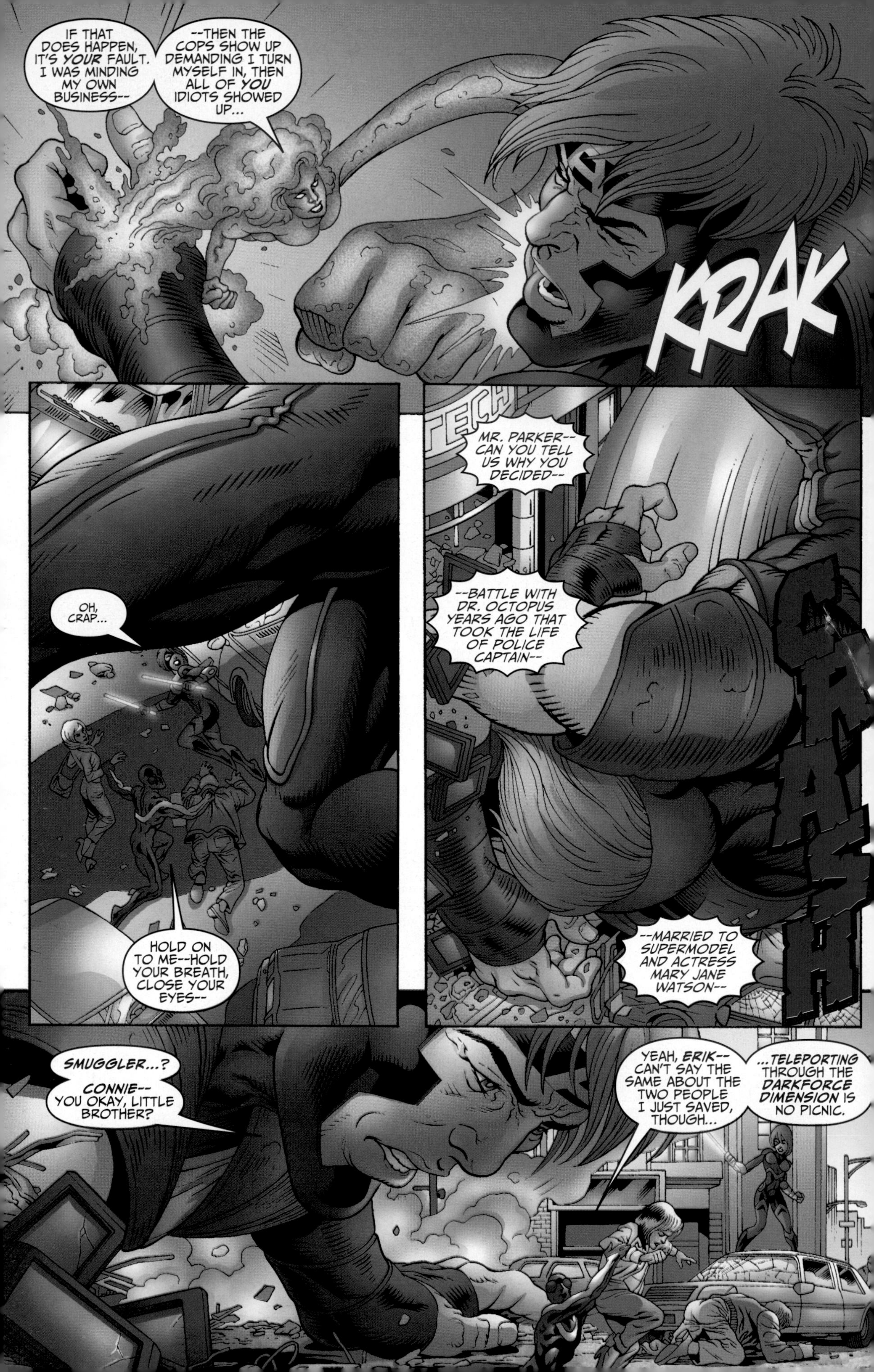
IF THAT DOES HAPPEN, IT'S YOUR FAULT. I WAS MINDING MY OWN BUSINESS--
--THEN THE COPS SHOW UP DEMANDING I TURN MYSELF IN, THEN ALL OF YOU IDIOTS SHOWED UP...
KRAK
OH, CRAP...
HOLD ON TO ME--HOLD YOUR BREATH, CLOSE YOUR EYES--
MR. PARKER-- CAN YOU TELL US WHY YOU DECIDED--
--BATTLE WITH DR. OCTOPUS YEARS AGO THAT TOOK THE LIFE OF POLICE CAPTAIN--
--MARRIED TO SUPERMODEL AND ACTRESS MARY JANE WATSON--
SMUGGLER...?
CONNIE-- YOU OKAY, LITTLE BROTHER?
YEAH, ERIK-- CAN'T SAY THE SAME ABOUT THE TWO PEOPLE I JUST SAVED, THOUGH...
...TELEPORTING THROUGH THE DARKFORCE DIMENSION IS NO PICNIC.

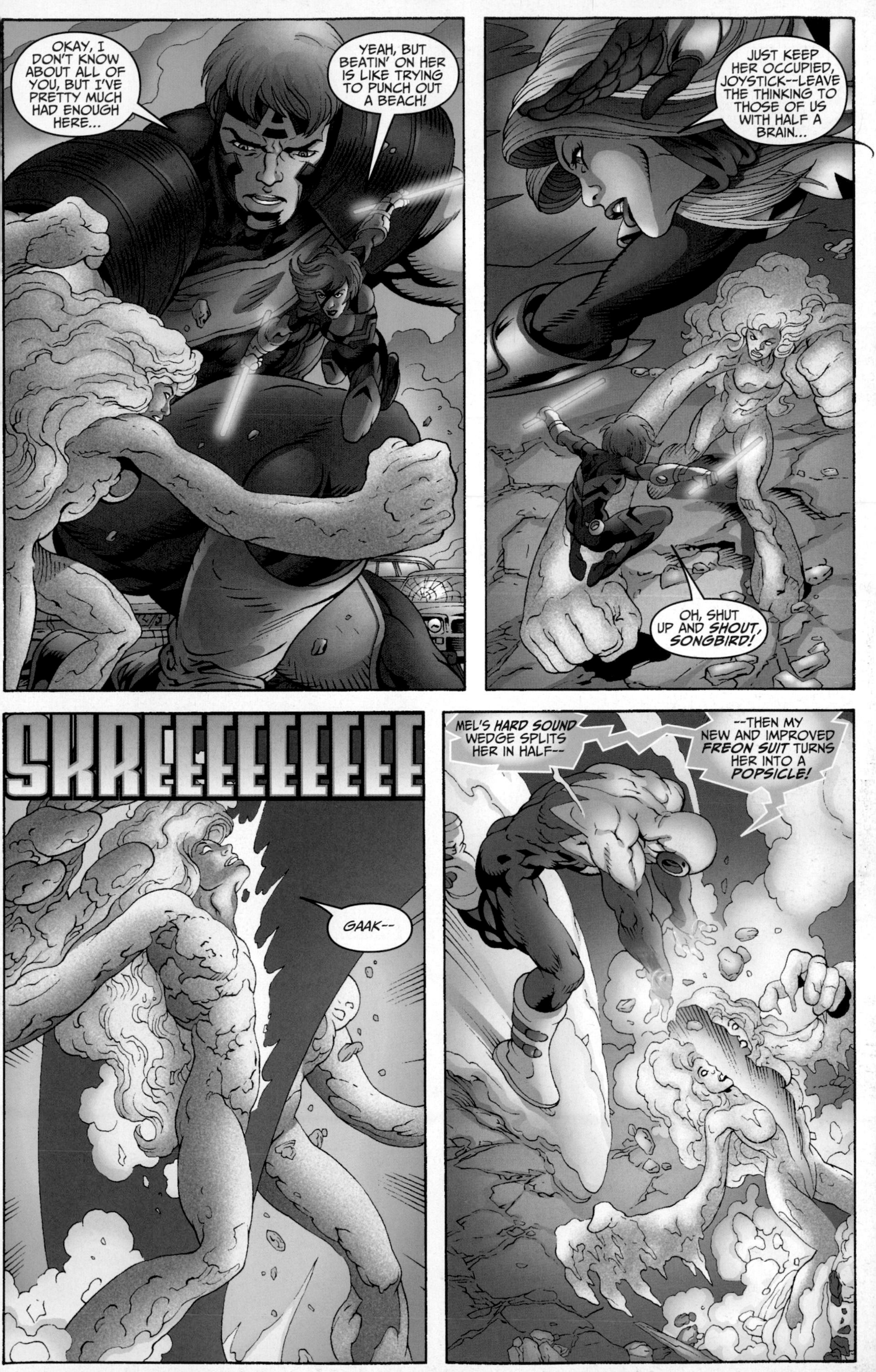
OKAY, I DON'T KNOW ABOUT ALL OF YOU, BUT I'VE PRETTY MUCH HAD ENOUGH HERE...
YEAH, BUT BEATIN' ON HER IS LIKE TRYING TO PUNCH OUT A BEACH!
JUST KEEP HER OCCUPIED, JOYSTICK--LEAVE THE THINKING TO THOSE OF US WITH HALF A BRAIN...
OH, SHUT UP AND SHOUT, SONGBIRD!
SKREEEEEEEEEE
GAAK--
MEL'S HARD SOUND WEDGE SPLITS HER IN HALF--
--THEN MY NEW AND IMPROVED FREON SUIT TURNS HER INTO A POPSICLE!

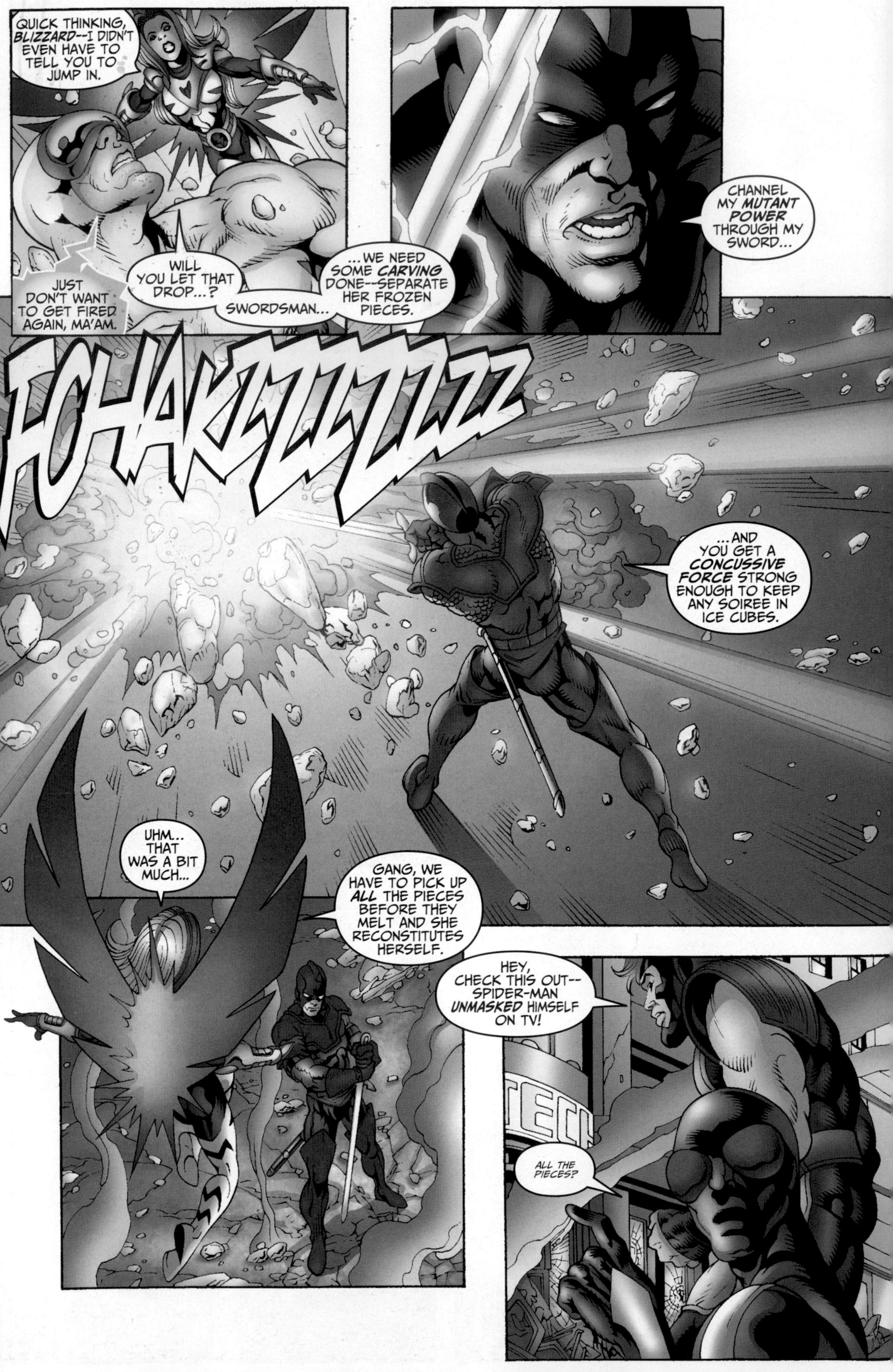
QUICK THINKING, BLIZZARD--I DIDN'T EVEN HAVE TO TELL YOU TO JUMP IN.
JUST DON'T WANT TO GET FIRED AGAIN, MA'AM.
WILL YOU LET THAT DROP...?
SWORDSMAN...
...WE NEED SOME CARVING DONE--SEPARATE HER FROZEN PIECES.
CHANNEL MY MUTANT POWER THROUGH MY SWORD...
FCHAKZZZZZZZZZ
...AND YOU GET A CONCUSSIVE FORCE STRONG ENOUGH TO KEEP ANY SOIREE IN ICE CUBES.
UHM... THAT WAS A BIT MUCH...
GANG, WE HAVE TO PICK UP ALL THE PIECES BEFORE THEY MELT AND SHE RECONSTITUTES HERSELF.
HEY, CHECK THIS OUT--SPIDER-MAN UNMASKED HIMSELF ON TV!
ALL THE PIECES?

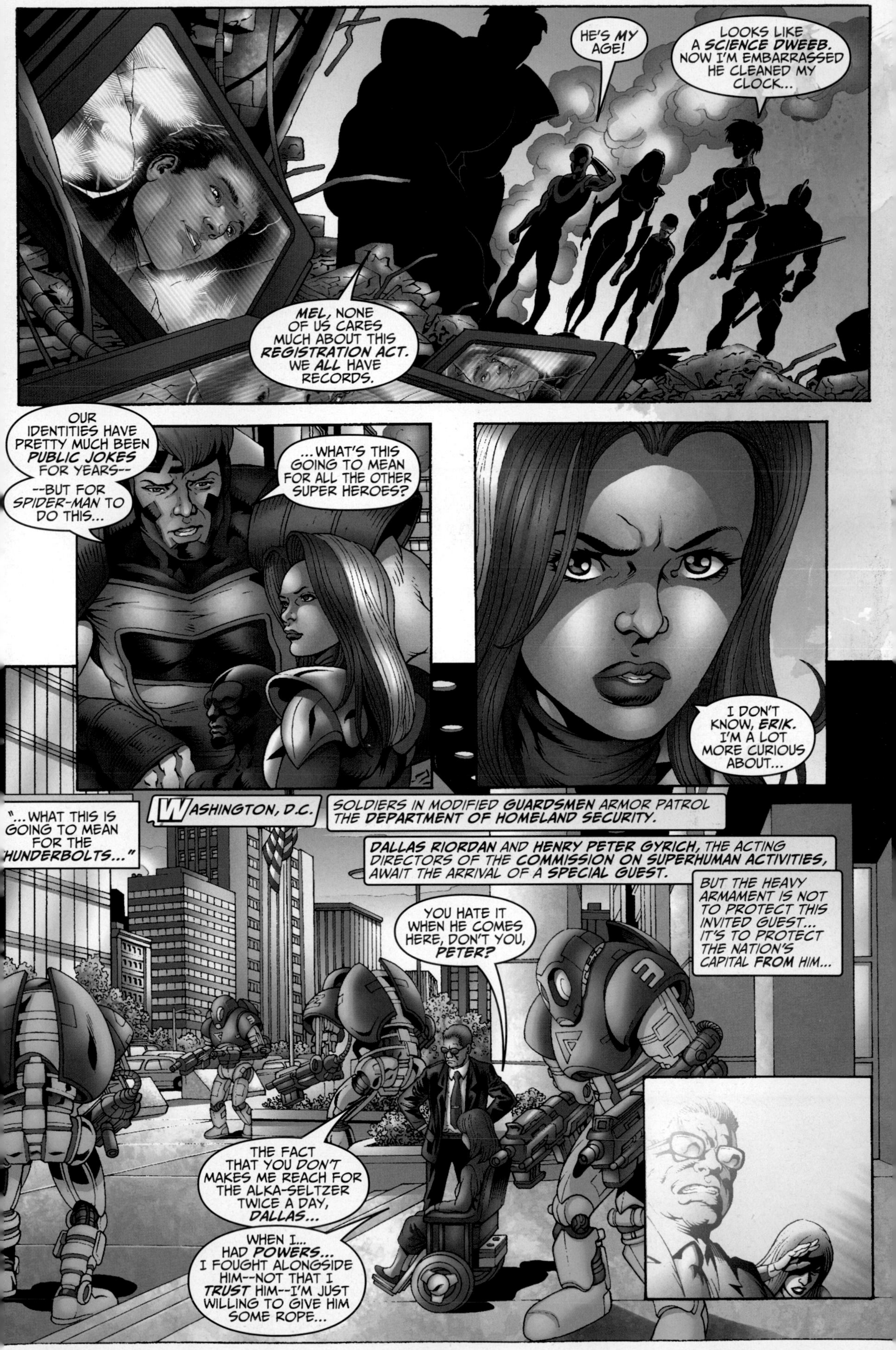
HE'S MY AGE!
LOOKS LIKE A SCIENCE DWEEB. NOW I'M EMBARRASSED HE CLEANED MY CLOCK...
MEL, NONE OF US CARES MUCH ABOUT THIS REGISTRATION ACT. WE ALL HAVE RECORDS.
OUR IDENTITIES HAVE PRETTY MUCH BEEN PUBLIC JOKES FOR YEARS--
--BUT FOR SPIDER-MAN TO DO THIS...
...WHAT'S THIS GOING TO MEAN FOR ALL THE OTHER SUPER HEROES?
I DON'T KNOW, ERIK. I'M A LOT MORE CURIOUS ABOUT...
"...WHAT THIS IS GOING TO MEAN FOR THE HUNDERBOLTS..."
WASHINGTON, D.C.
SOLDIERS IN MODIFIED GUARDSMEN ARMOR PATROL THE DEPARTMENT OF HOMELAND SECURITY.
DALLAS RIORDAN AND HENRY PETER GYRICH, THE ACTING DIRECTORS OF THE COMMISSION ON SUPERHUMAN ACTIVITIES, AWAIT THE ARRIVAL OF A SPECIAL GUEST.
BUT THE HEAVY ARMAMENT IS NOT TO PROTECT THIS INVITED GUEST... IT'S TO PROTECT THE NATION'S CAPITAL FROM HIM...
YOU HATE IT WHEN HE COMES HERE, DON'T YOU, PETER?
THE FACT THAT YOU DON'T MAKES ME REACH FOR THE ALKA-SELTZER TWICE A DAY, DALLAS...
WHEN I... HAD POWERS... I FOUGHT ALONGSIDE HIM--NOT THAT I TRUST HIM--I'M JUST WILLING TO GIVE HIM SOME ROPE...

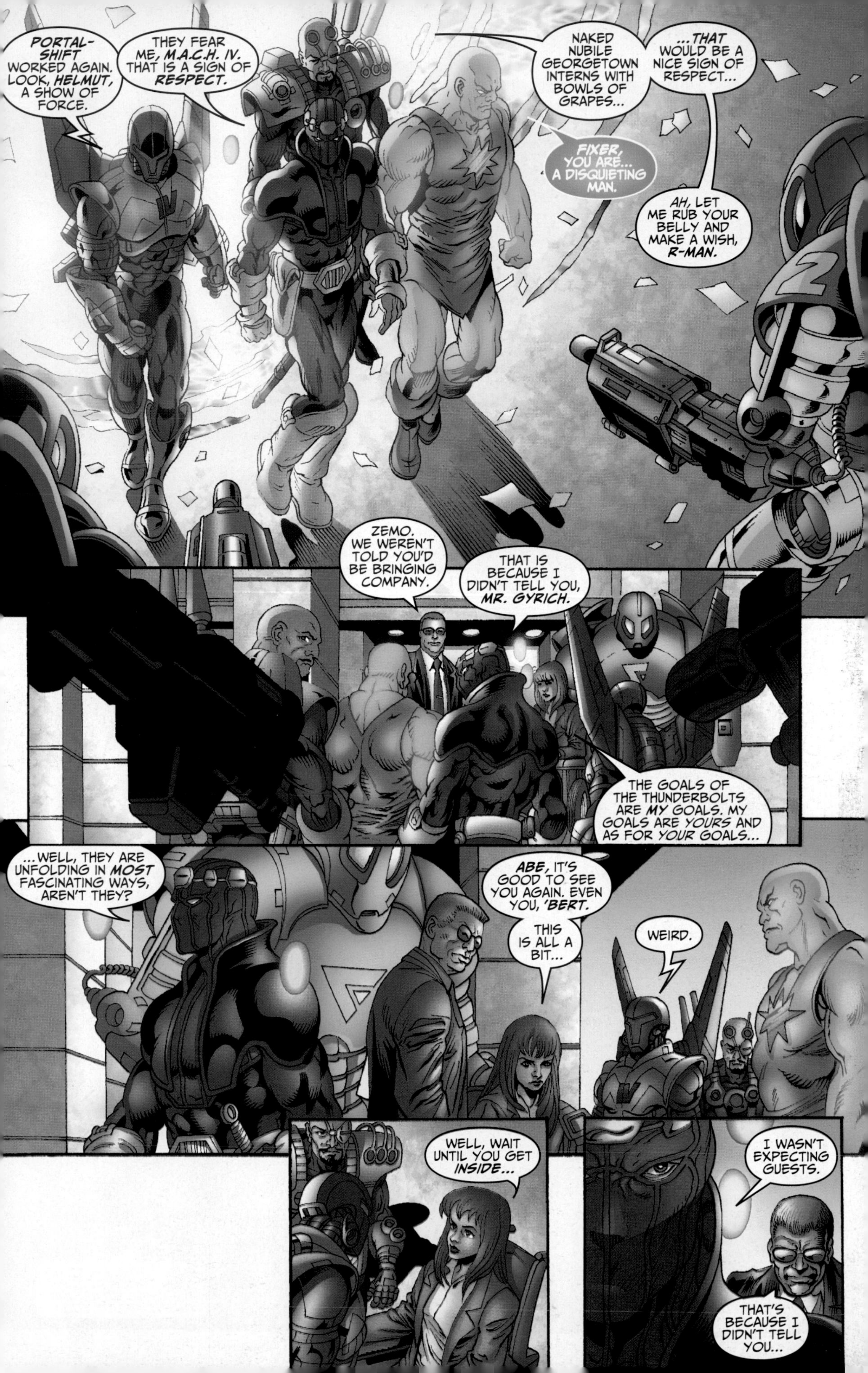
PORTAL-SHIFT WORKED AGAIN. LOOK, HELMUT, A SHOW OF FORCE.
THEY FEAR ME, M.A.C.H. IV. THAT IS A SIGN OF RESPECT.
NAKED NUBILE GEORGETOWN INTERNS WITH BOWLS OF GRAPES...
...THAT WOULD BE A NICE SIGN OF RESPECT...
FIXER, YOU ARE... A DISQUIETING MAN.
AH, LET ME RUB YOUR BELLY AND MAKE A WISH, R-MAN.
ZEMO. WE WEREN'T TOLD YOU'D BE BRINGING COMPANY.
THAT IS BECAUSE I DIDN'T TELL YOU, MR. GYRICH.
THE GOALS OF THE THUNDERBOLTS ARE MY GOALS. MY GOALS ARE YOURS AND AS FOR YOUR GOALS...
...WELL, THEY ARE UNFOLDING IN MOST FASCINATING WAYS, AREN'T THEY?
ABE, IT'S GOOD TO SEE YOU AGAIN. EVEN YOU, 'BERT.
THIS IS ALL A BIT...
WEIRD.
WELL, WAIT UNTIL YOU GET INSIDE...
I WASN'T EXPECTING GUESTS.
THAT'S BECAUSE I DIDN'T TELL YOU...

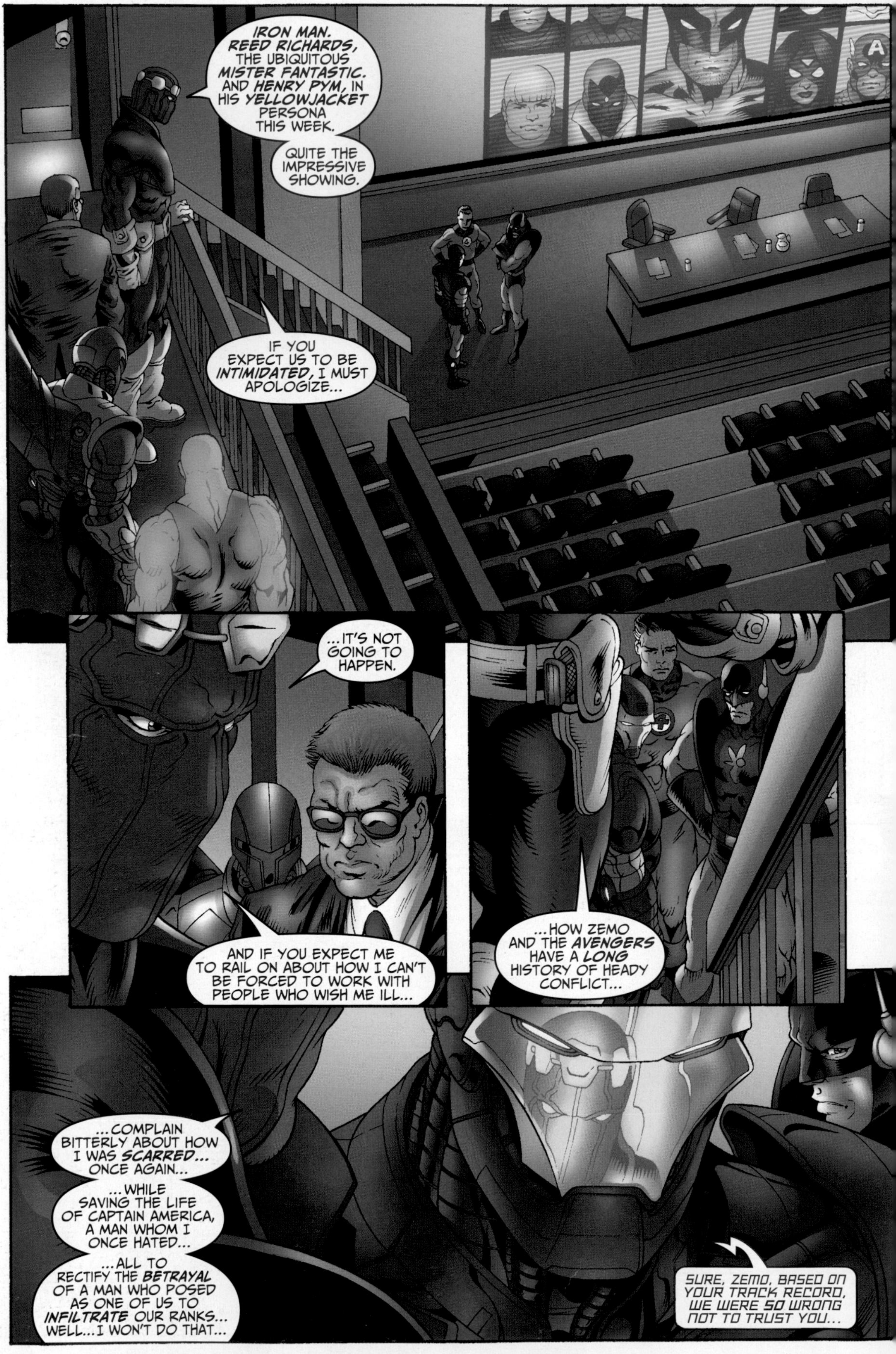
IRON MAN. REED RICHARDS, THE UBIQUITOUS MISTER FANTASTIC. AND HENRY PYM, IN HIS YELLOWJACKET PERSONA THIS WEEK.
QUITE THE IMPRESSIVE SHOWING.
IF YOU EXPECT US TO BE INTIMIDATED, I MUST APOLOGIZE...
...IT'S NOT GOING TO HAPPEN.
AND IF YOU EXPECT ME TO RAIL ON ABOUT HOW I CAN'T BE FORCED TO WORK WITH PEOPLE WHO WISH ME ILL...
...HOW ZEMO AND THE AVENGERS HAVE A LONG HISTORY OF HEADY CONFLICT...
...COMPLAIN BITTERLY ABOUT HOW I WAS SCARRED... ONCE AGAIN...
...WHILE SAVING THE LIFE OF CAPTAIN AMERICA, A MAN WHOM I ONCE HATED...
...ALL TO RECTIFY THE BETRAYAL OF A MAN WHO POSED AS ONE OF US TO INFILTRATE OUR RANKS... WELL...I WON'T DO THAT...
SURE, ZEMO, BASED ON YOUR TRACK RECORD, WE WERE SO WRONG NOT TO TRUST YOU...

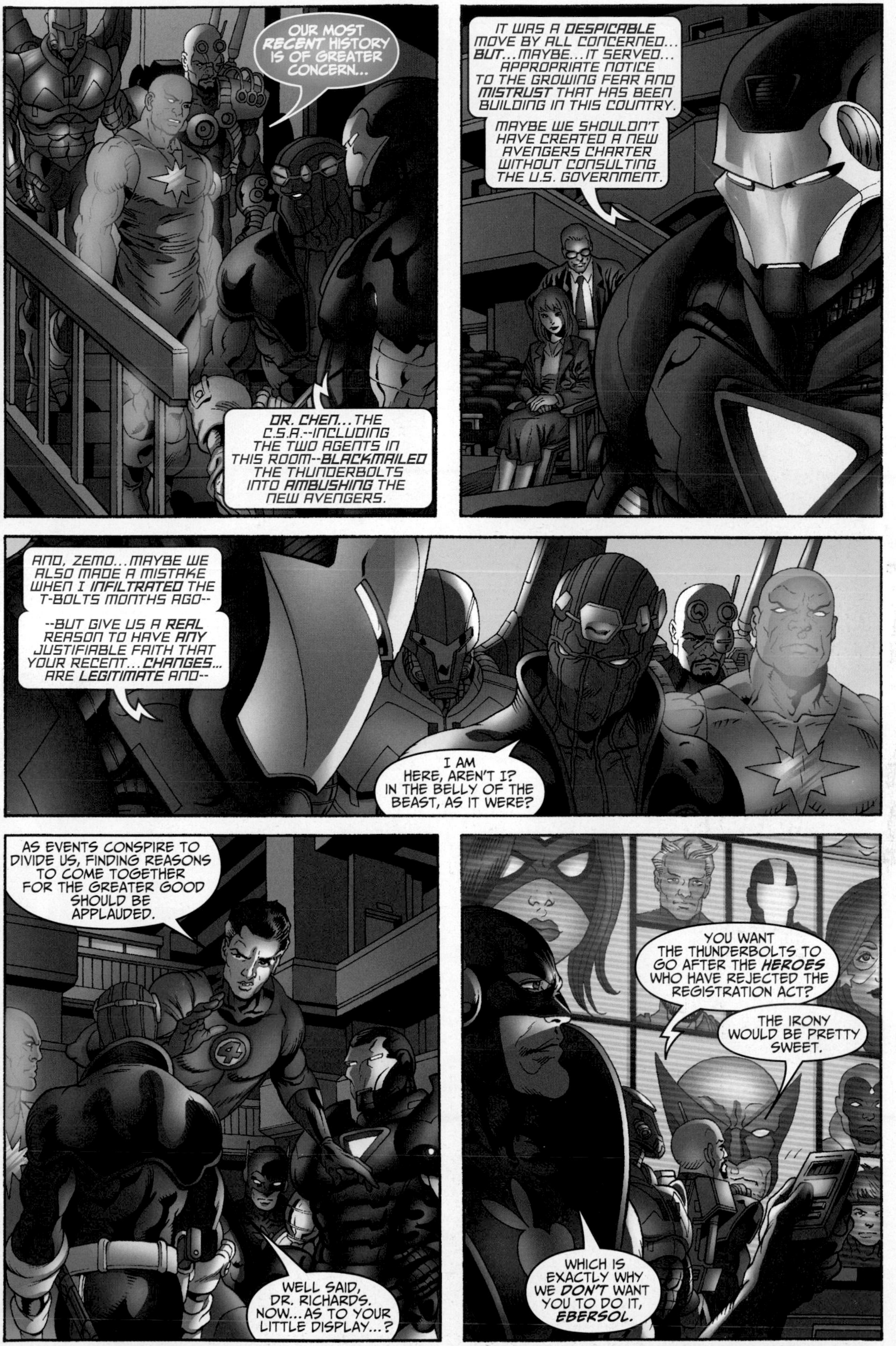
OUR MOST RECENT HISTORY IS OF GREATER CONCERN...
DR. CHEN... THE C.S.A.--INCLUDING THE TWO AGENTS IN THIS ROOM--BLACKMAILED THE THUNDERBOLTS INTO AMBUSHING THE NEW AVENGERS.
IT WAS A DESPICABLE MOVE BY ALL CONCERNED... BUT... MAYBE... IT SERVED... APPROPRIATE NOTICE TO THE GROWING FEAR AND MISTRUST THAT HAS BEEN BUILDING IN THIS COUNTRY.
MAYBE WE SHOULDN'T HAVE CREATED A NEW AVENGERS CHARTER WITHOUT CONSULTING THE U.S. GOVERNMENT.
AND, ZEMO... MAYBE WE ALSO MADE A MISTAKE WHEN I INFILTRATED THE T-BOLTS MONTHS AGO--
--BUT GIVE US A REAL REASON TO HAVE ANY JUSTIFIABLE FAITH THAT YOUR RECENT... CHANGES... ARE LEGITIMATE AND--
I AM HERE, AREN'T I? IN THE BELLY OF THE BEAST, AS IT WERE?
AS EVENTS CONSPIRE TO DIVIDE US, FINDING REASONS TO COME TOGETHER FOR THE GREATER GOOD SHOULD BE APPLAUDED.
WELL SAID, DR. RICHARDS. NOW... AS TO YOUR LITTLE DISPLAY...?
YOU WANT THE THUNDERBOLTS TO GO AFTER THE HEROES WHO HAVE REJECTED THE REGISTRATION ACT?
THE IRONY WOULD BE PRETTY SWEET.
WHICH IS EXACTLY WHY WE DON'T WANT YOU TO DO IT, EBERSOL.

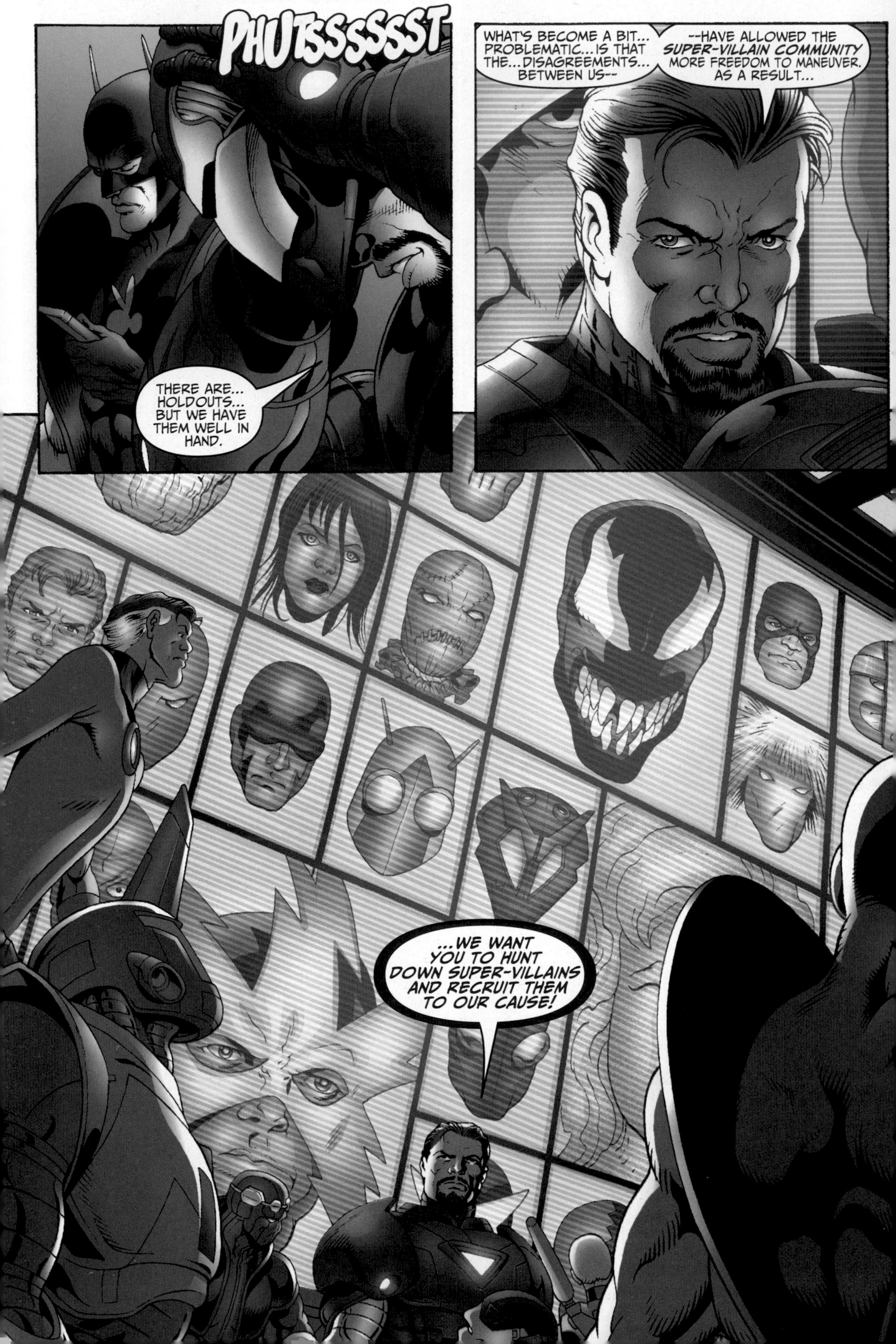
PHUTSSSSSST
THERE ARE... HOLDOUTS... BUT WE HAVE THEM WELL IN HAND.
WHAT'S BECOME A BIT... PROBLEMATIC...IS THAT THE...DISAGREEMENTS... BETWEEN US--
--HAVE ALLOWED THE SUPER-VILLAIN COMMUNITY MORE FREEDOM TO MANEUVER. AS A RESULT...
...WE WANT YOU TO HUNT DOWN SUPER-VILLAINS AND RECRUIT THEM TO OUR CAUSE!

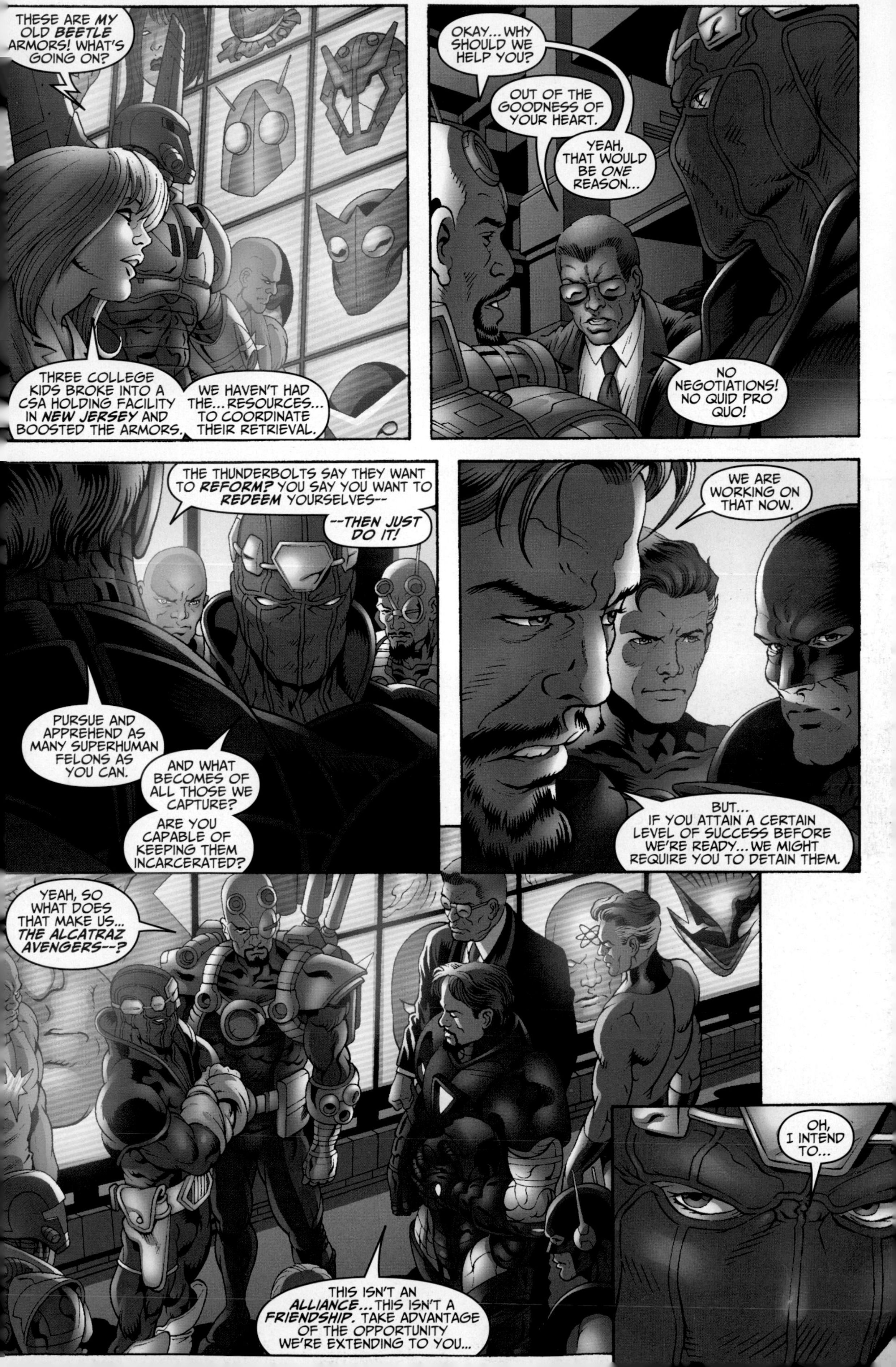
THESE ARE MY OLD BEETLE ARMORS! WHAT'S GOING ON?
THREE COLLEGE KIDS BROKE INTO A CSA HOLDING FACILITY IN NEW JERSEY AND BOOSTED THE ARMORS.
WE HAVEN'T HAD THE... RESOURCES... TO COORDINATE THEIR RETRIEVAL.
OKAY... WHY SHOULD WE HELP YOU?
OUT OF THE GOODNESS OF YOUR HEART.
YEAH, THAT WOULD BE ONE REASON...
NO NEGOTIATIONS! NO QUID PRO QUO!
THE THUNDERBOLTS SAY THEY WANT TO REFORM? YOU SAY YOU WANT TO REDEEM YOURSELVES--
--THEN JUST DO IT!
PURSUE AND APPREHEND AS MANY SUPERHUMAN FELONS AS YOU CAN.
AND WHAT BECOMES OF ALL THOSE WE CAPTURE?
ARE YOU CAPABLE OF KEEPING THEM INCARCERATED?
WE ARE WORKING ON THAT NOW.
BUT... IF YOU ATTAIN A CERTAIN LEVEL OF SUCCESS BEFORE WE'RE READY... WE MIGHT REQUIRE YOU TO DETAIN THEM.
YEAH, SO WHAT DOES THAT MAKE US... THE ALCATRAZ AVENGERS--?
THIS ISN'T AN ALLIANCE... THIS ISN'T A FRIENDSHIP. TAKE ADVANTAGE OF THE OPPORTUNITY WE'RE EXTENDING TO YOU...
OH, I INTEND TO...

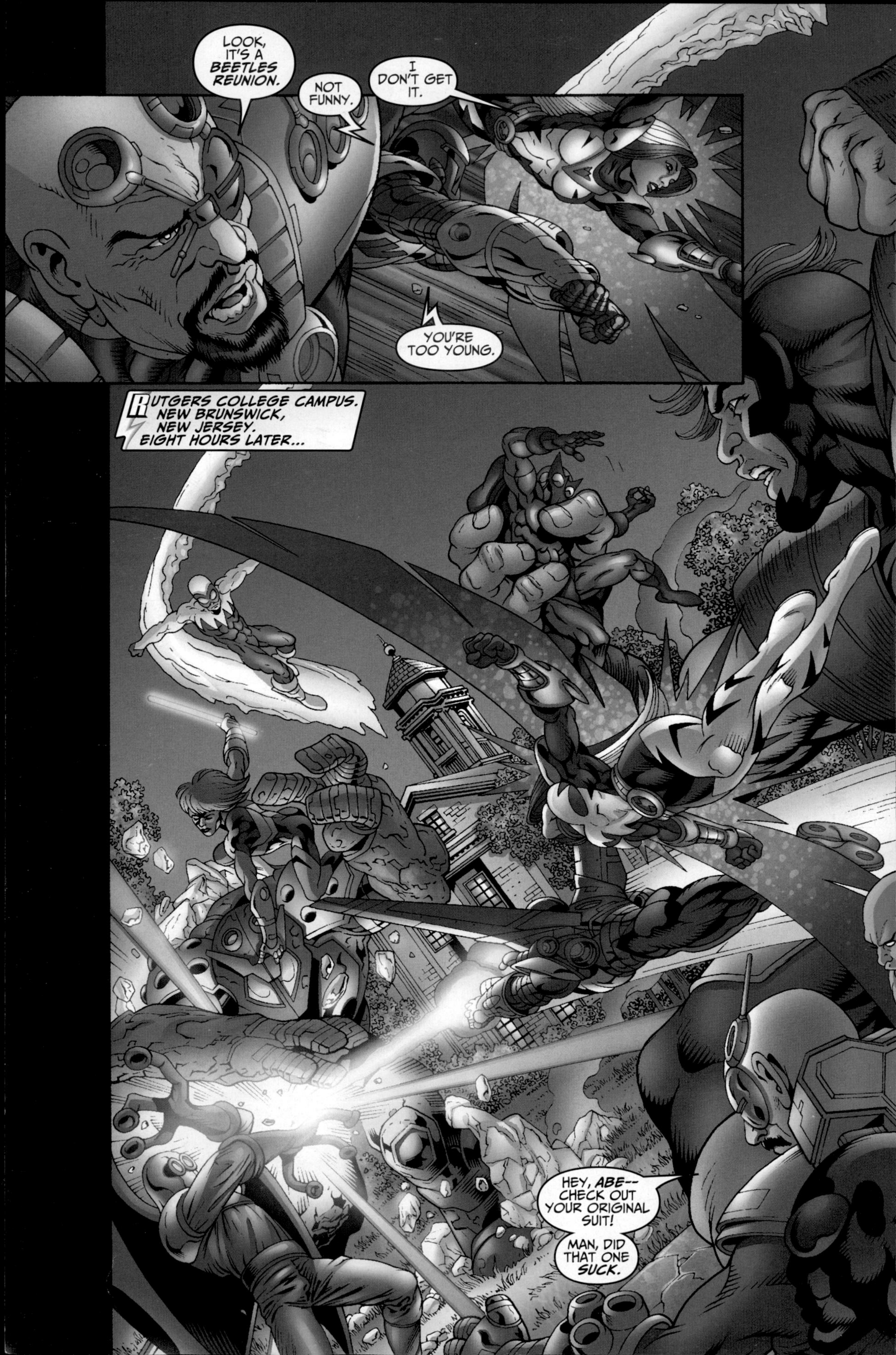
LOOK, IT'S A BEETLES REUNION.
NOT FUNNY.
I DON'T GET IT.
YOU'RE TOO YOUNG.
RUTGERS COLLEGE CAMPUS. NEW BRUNSWICK, NEW JERSEY. EIGHT HOURS LATER...
HEY, ABE-- CHECK OUT YOUR ORIGINAL SUIT!
MAN, DID THAT ONE SUCK.

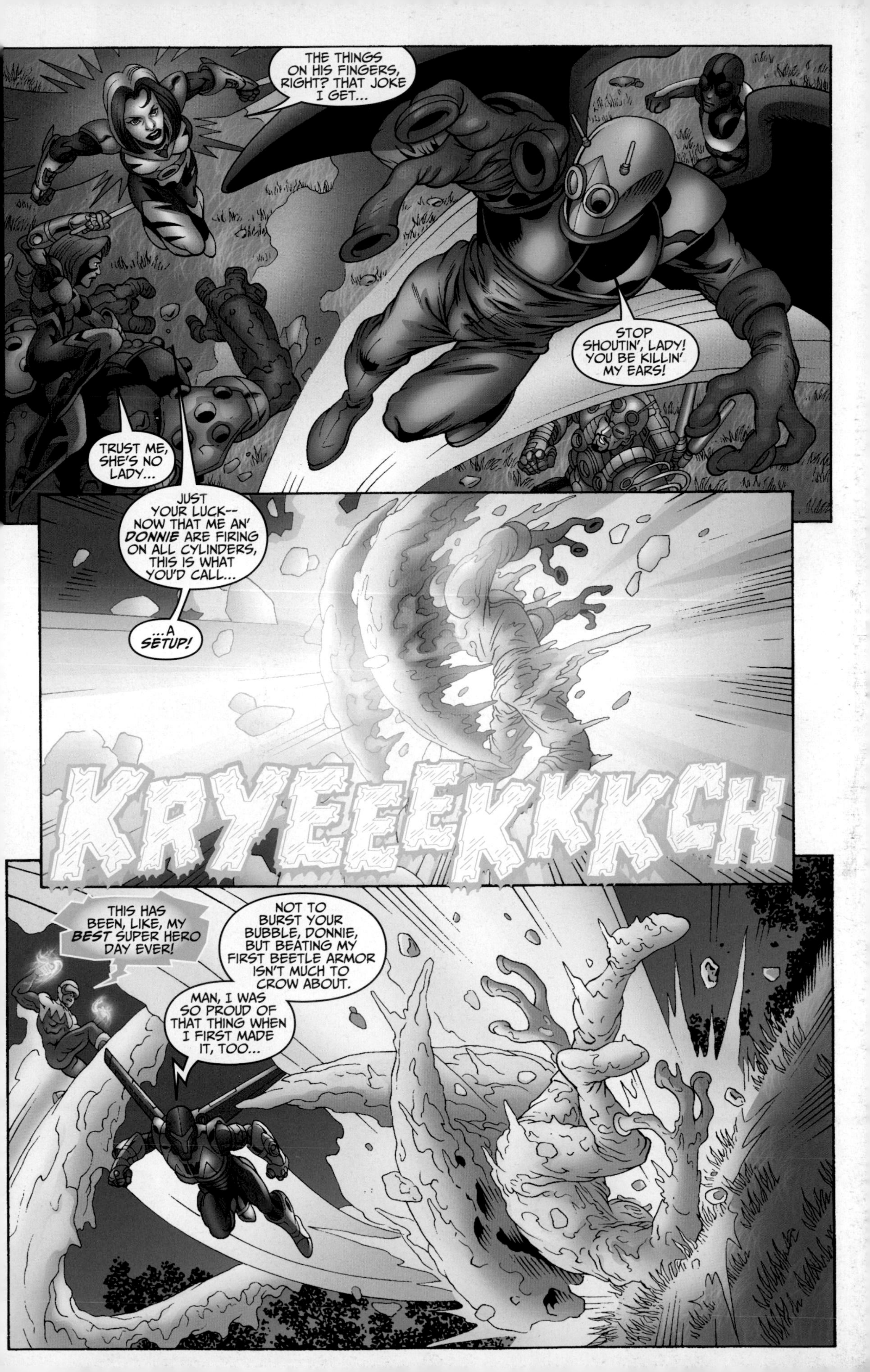
THE THINGS ON HIS FINGERS, RIGHT? THAT JOKE I GET...
STOP SHOUTIN', LADY! YOU BE KILLIN' MY EARS!
TRUST ME, SHE'S NO LADY...
JUST YOUR LUCK-- NOW THAT ME AN' DONNIE ARE FIRING ON ALL CYLINDERS, THIS IS WHAT YOU'D CALL...
...A SETUP!
KRYEEEKKKCH
THIS HAS BEEN, LIKE, MY BEST SUPER HERO DAY EVER!
NOT TO BURST YOUR BUBBLE, DONNIE, BUT BEATING MY FIRST BEETLE ARMOR ISN'T MUCH TO CROW ABOUT.
MAN, I WAS SO PROUD OF THAT THING WHEN I FIRST MADE IT, TOO...

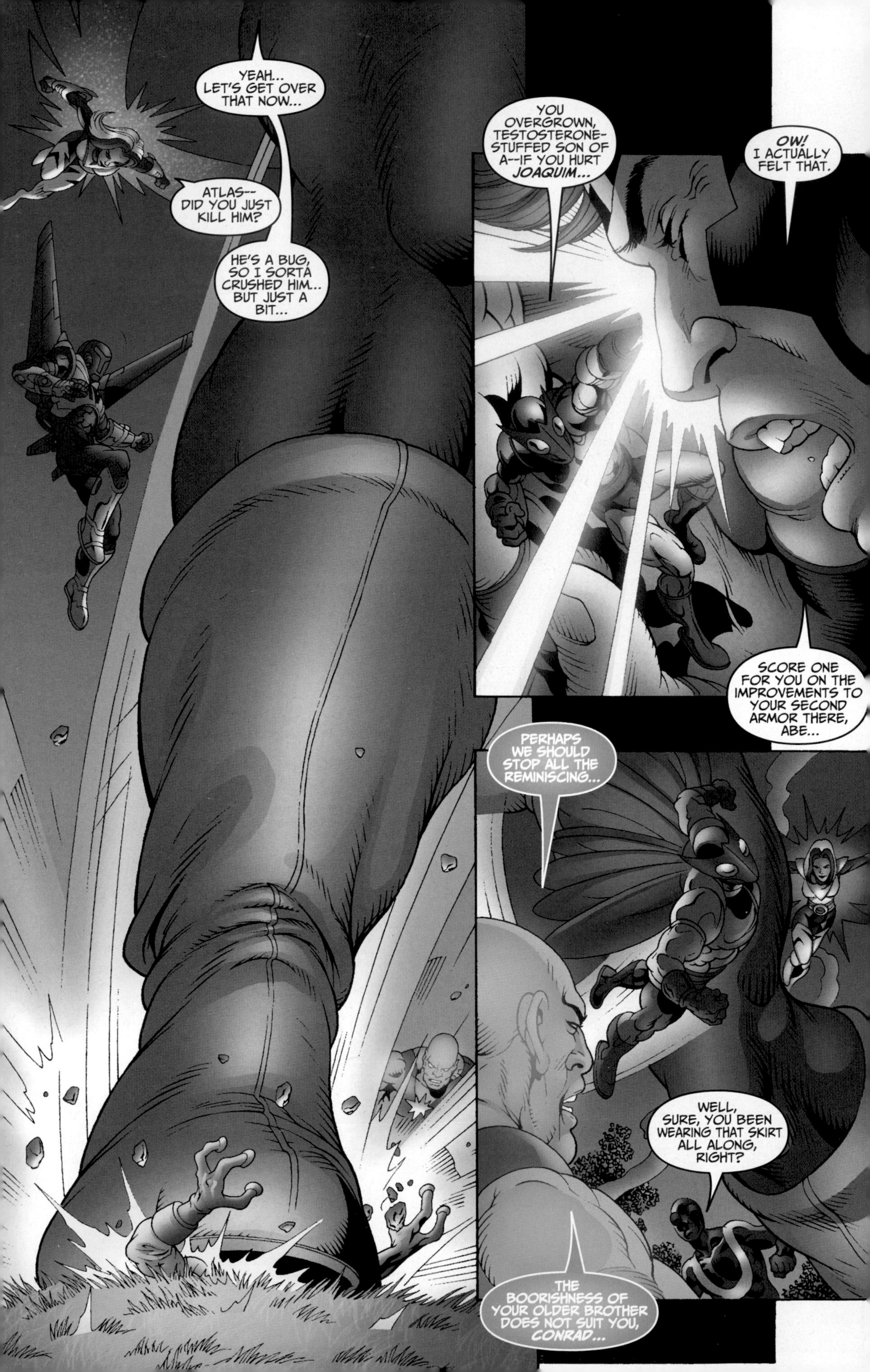
YEAH... LET'S GET OVER THAT NOW...
ATLAS-- DID YOU JUST KILL HIM?
HE'S A BUG, SO I SORTA CRUSHED HIM... BUT JUST A BIT...
YOU OVERGROWN, TESTOSTERONE-STUFFED SON OF A--IF YOU HURT JOAQUIM...
OW! I ACTUALLY FELT THAT.
SCORE ONE FOR YOU ON THE IMPROVEMENTS TO YOUR SECOND ARMOR THERE, ABE...
PERHAPS WE SHOULD STOP ALL THE REMINISCING...
WELL, SURE, YOU BEEN WEARING THAT SKIRT ALL ALONG, RIGHT?
THE BOORISHNESS OF YOUR OLDER BROTHER DOES NOT SUIT YOU, CONRAD...

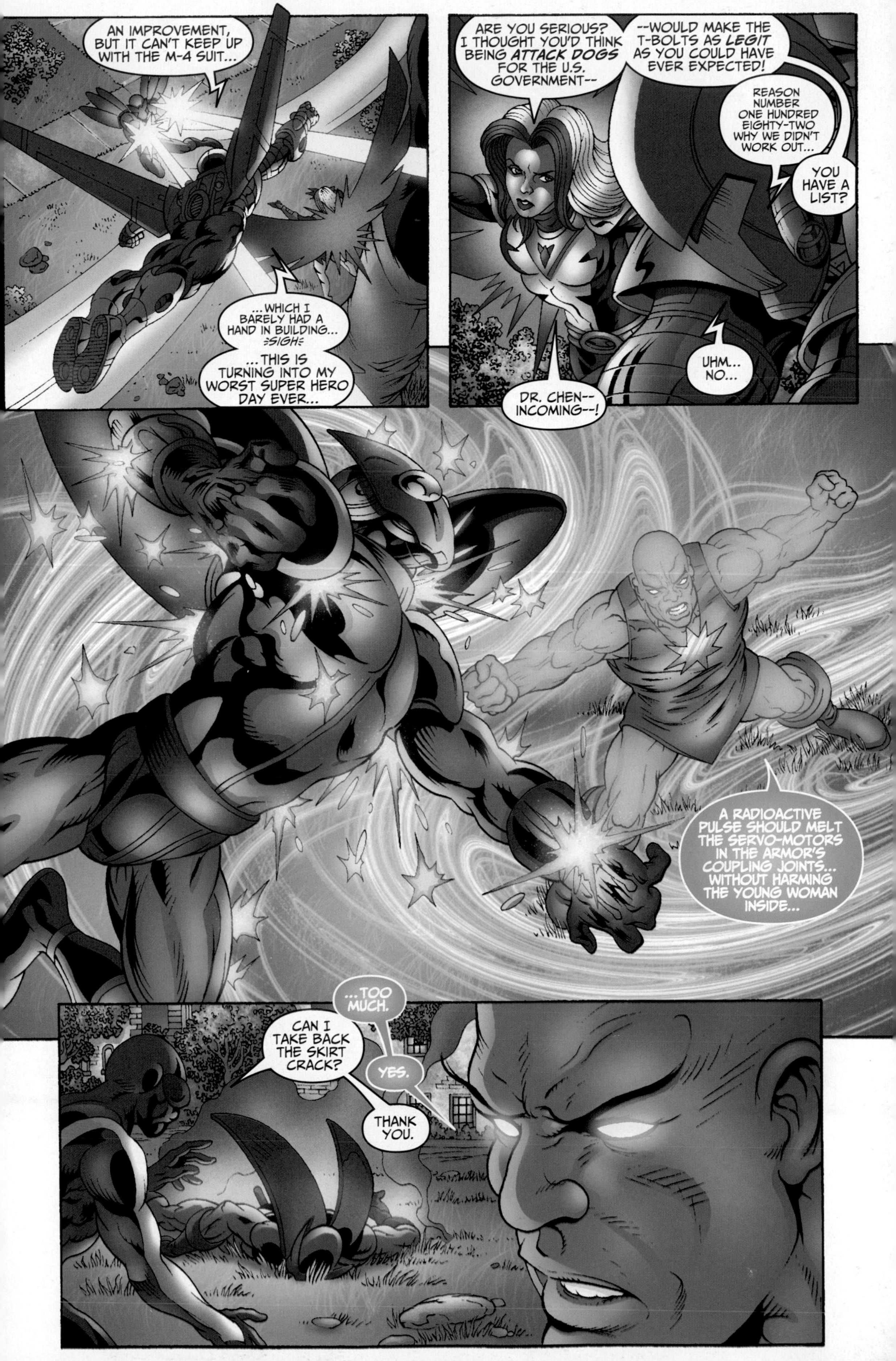

AN IMPROVEMENT, BUT IT CAN'T KEEP UP WITH THE M-4 SUIT...
...WHICH I BARELY HAD A HAND IN BUILDING... SIGH
...THIS IS TURNING INTO MY WORST SUPER HERO DAY EVER...
ARE YOU SERIOUS? I THOUGHT YOU'D THINK BEING ATTACK DOGS FOR THE U.S. GOVERNMENT--
--WOULD MAKE THE T-BOLTS AS LEGIT AS YOU COULD HAVE EVER EXPECTED!
REASON NUMBER ONE HUNDRED EIGHTY-TWO WHY WE DIDN'T WORK OUT...
YOU HAVE A LIST?
UHM... NO...
DR. CHEN-- INCOMING--!
A RADIOACTIVE PULSE SHOULD MELT THE SERVO-MOTORS IN THE ARMOR'S COUPLING JOINTS... WITHOUT HARMING THE YOUNG WOMAN INSIDE...
...TOO MUCH.
CAN I TAKE BACK THE SKIRT CRACK?
YES.
THANK YOU.

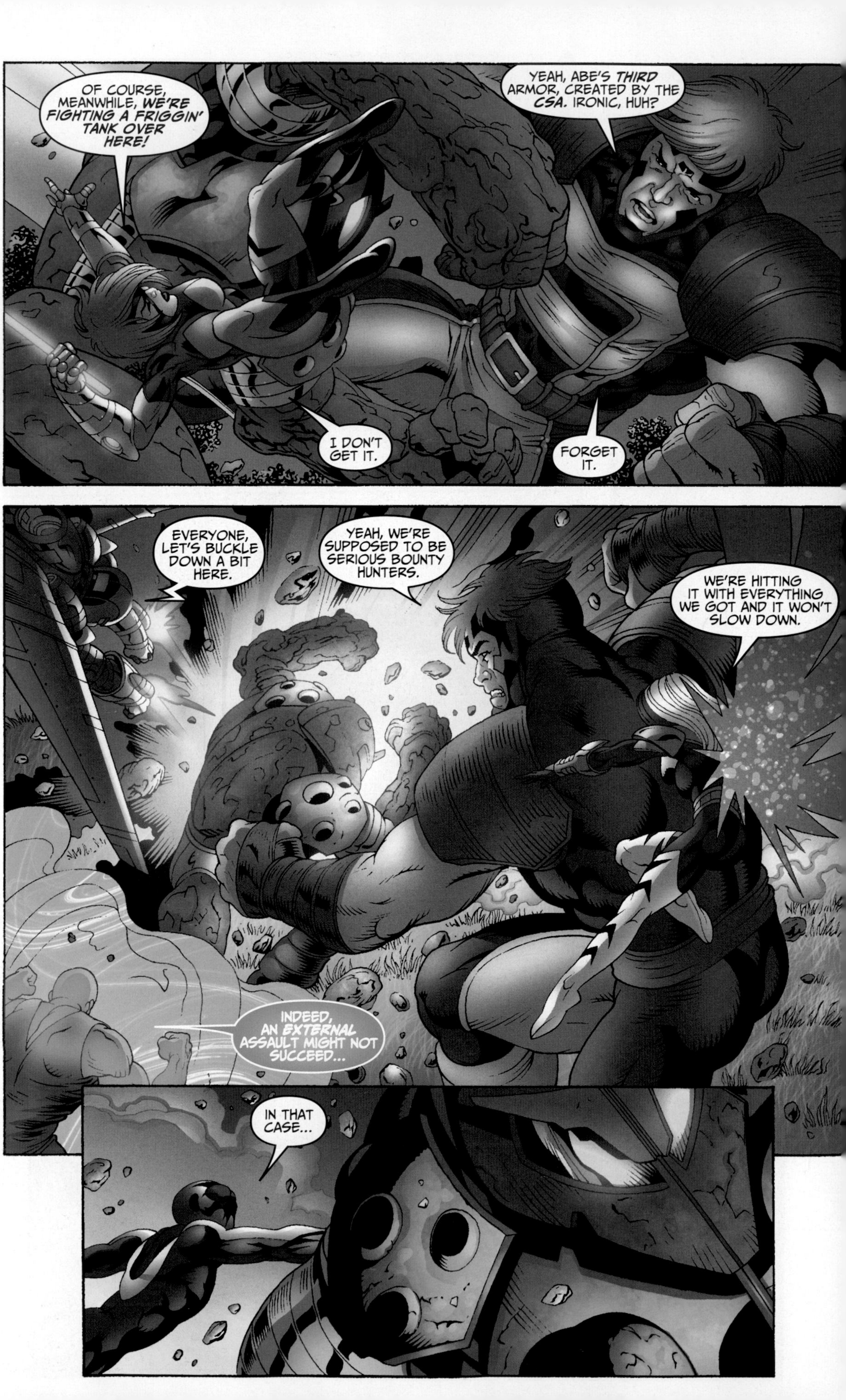

OF COURSE, MEANWHILE, WE'RE FIGHTING A FRIGGIN' TANK OVER HERE!
YEAH, ABE'S THIRD ARMOR, CREATED BY THE CSA. IRONIC, HUH?
I DON'T GET IT.
FORGET IT.
EVERYONE, LET'S BUCKLE DOWN A BIT HERE.
YEAH, WE'RE SUPPOSED TO BE SERIOUS BOUNTY HUNTERS.
WE'RE HITTING IT WITH EVERYTHING WE GOT AND IT WON'T SLOW DOWN.
INDEED, AN EXTERNAL ASSAULT MIGHT NOT SUCCEED...
IN THAT CASE...

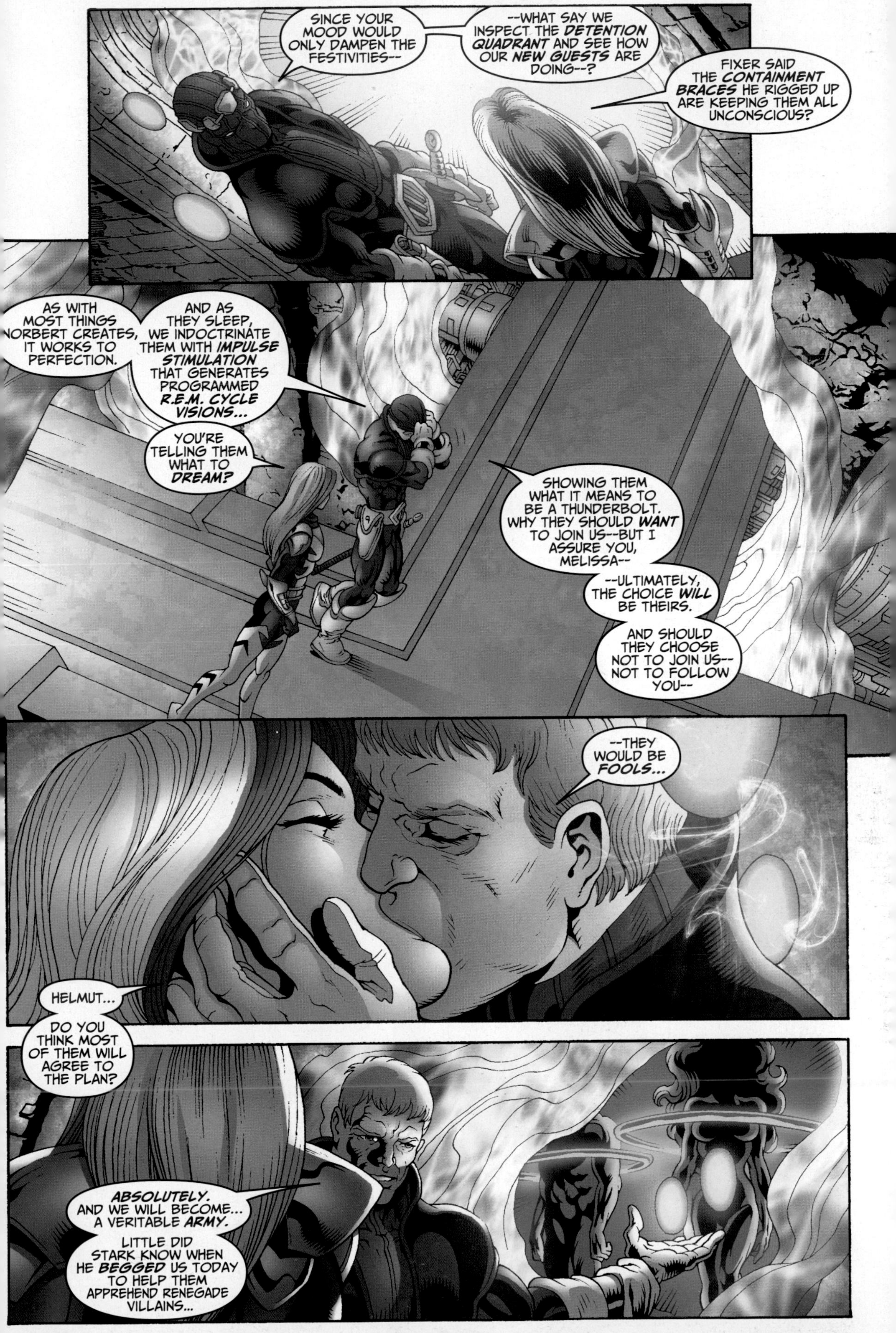
SINCE YOUR MOOD WOULD ONLY DAMPEN THE FESTIVITIES--
--WHAT SAY WE INSPECT THE DETENTION QUADRANT AND SEE HOW OUR NEW GUESTS ARE DOING--?
FIXER SAID THE CONTAINMENT BRACES HE RIGGED UP ARE KEEPING THEM ALL UNCONSCIOUS?
AS WITH MOST THINGS NORBERT CREATES, IT WORKS TO PERFECTION.
AND AS THEY SLEEP, WE INDOCTRINATE THEM WITH IMPULSE STIMULATION THAT GENERATES PROGRAMMED R.E.M. CYCLE VISIONS...
YOU'RE TELLING THEM WHAT TO DREAM?
SHOWING THEM WHAT IT MEANS TO BE A THUNDERBOLT. WHY THEY SHOULD WANT TO JOIN US--BUT I ASSURE YOU, MELISSA--
--ULTIMATELY, THE CHOICE WILL BE THEIRS.
AND SHOULD THEY CHOOSE NOT TO JOIN US-- NOT TO FOLLOW YOU--
--THEY WOULD BE FOOLS...
HELMUT...
DO YOU THINK MOST OF THEM WILL AGREE TO THE PLAN?
ABSOLUTELY. AND WE WILL BECOME... A VERITABLE ARMY.
LITTLE DID STARK KNOW WHEN HE BEGGED US TODAY TO HELP THEM APPREHEND RENEGADE VILLAINS...

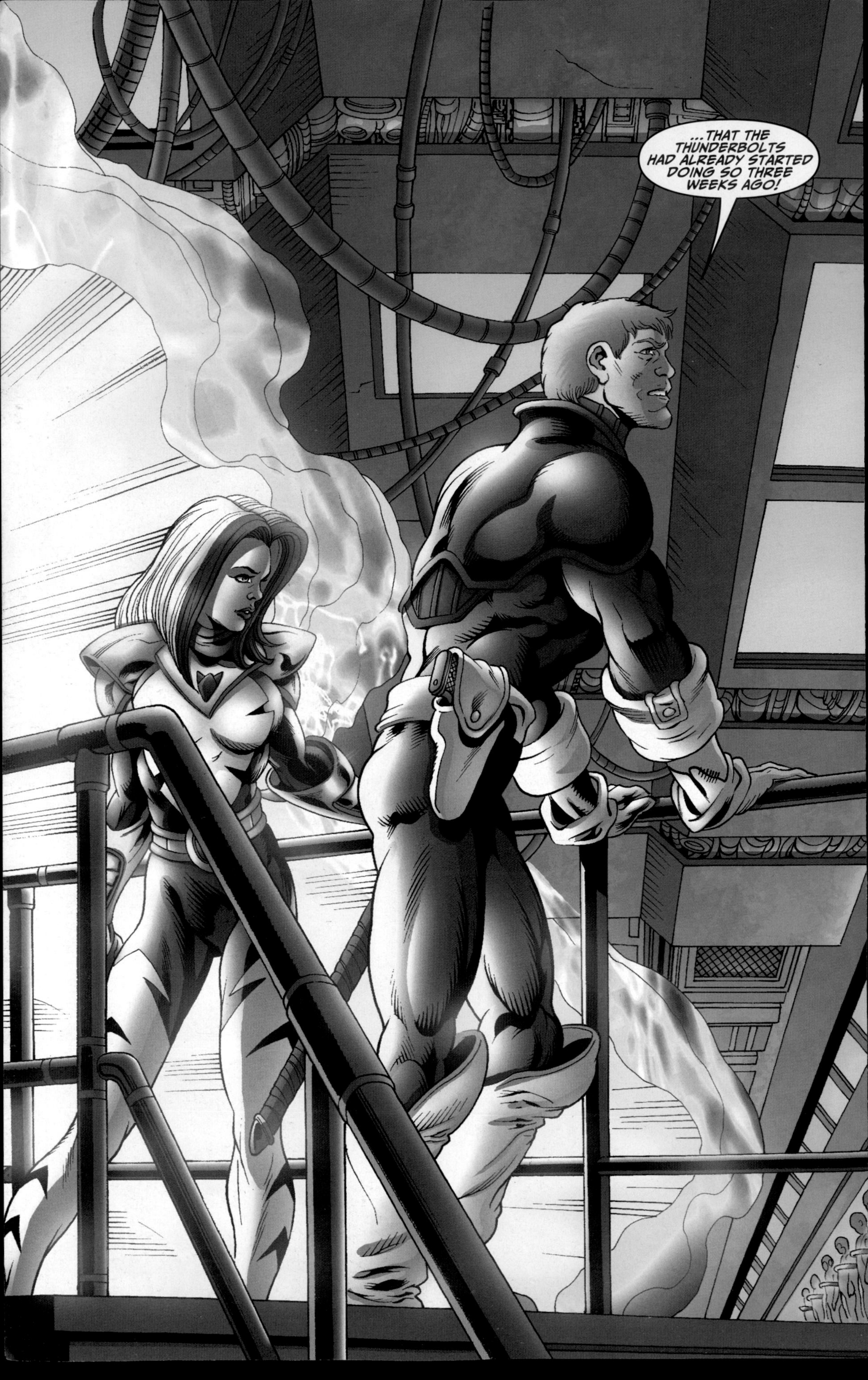
...THAT THE THUNDERBOLTS HAD ALREADY STARTED DOING SO THREE WEEKS AGO!

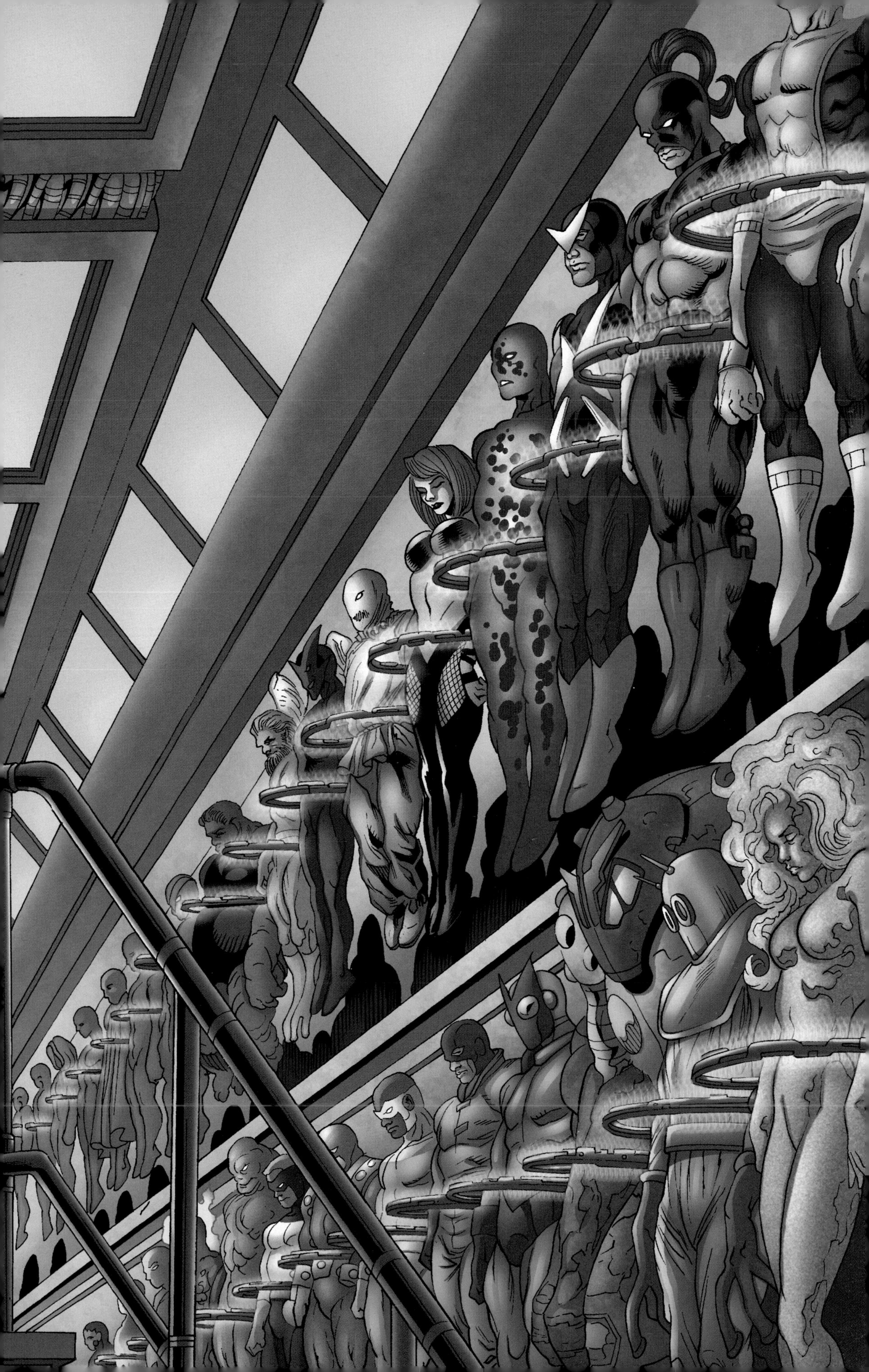

# THUNDERBOLTS
## A MARVEL COMICS EVENT

# CIVIL
WAR

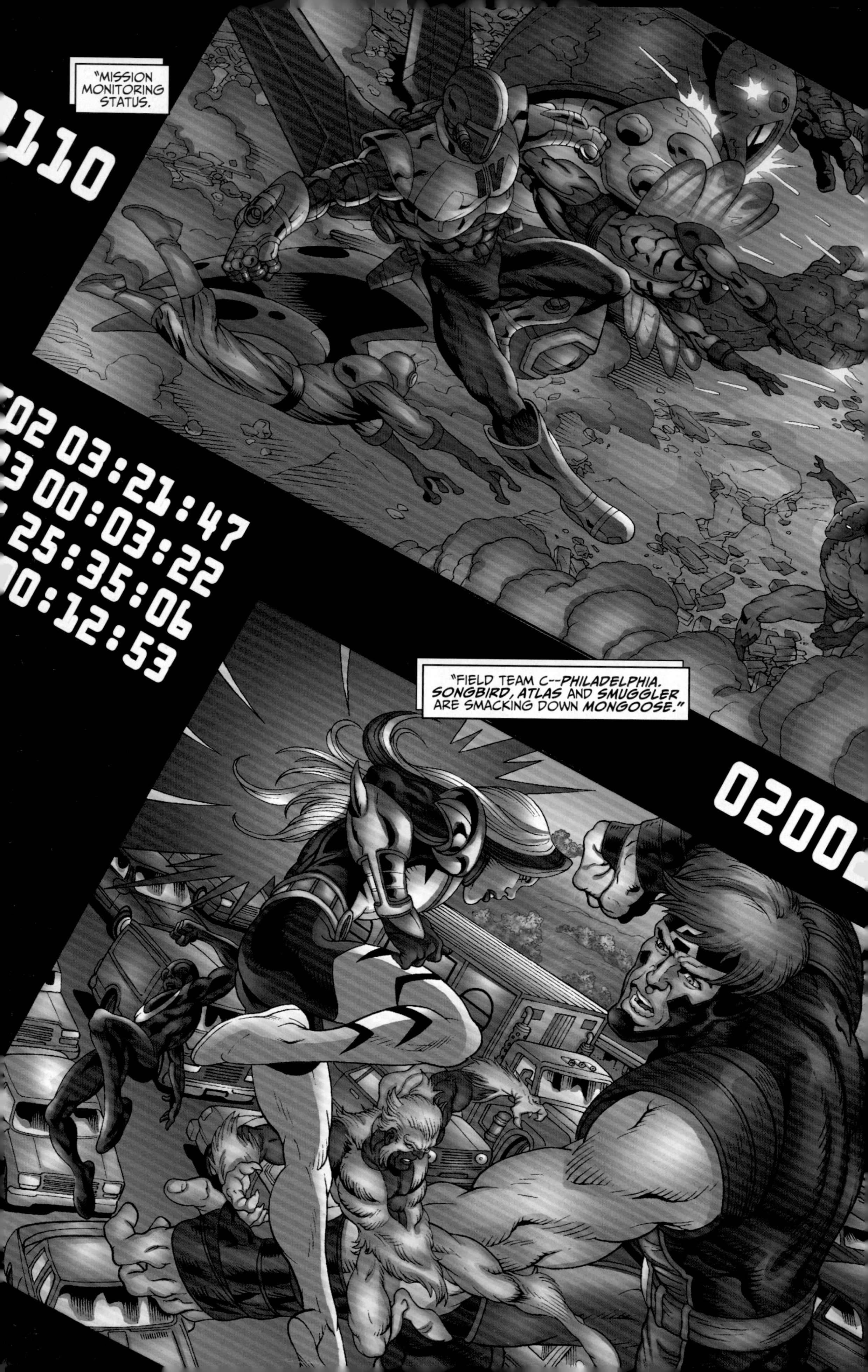
"MISSION MONITORING STATUS.
110
03:21:47
00:03:22
25:35:06
12:53
"FIELD TEAM C--PHILADELPHIA. SONGBIRD, ATLAS AND SMUGGLER ARE SMACKING DOWN MONGOOSE."
0200

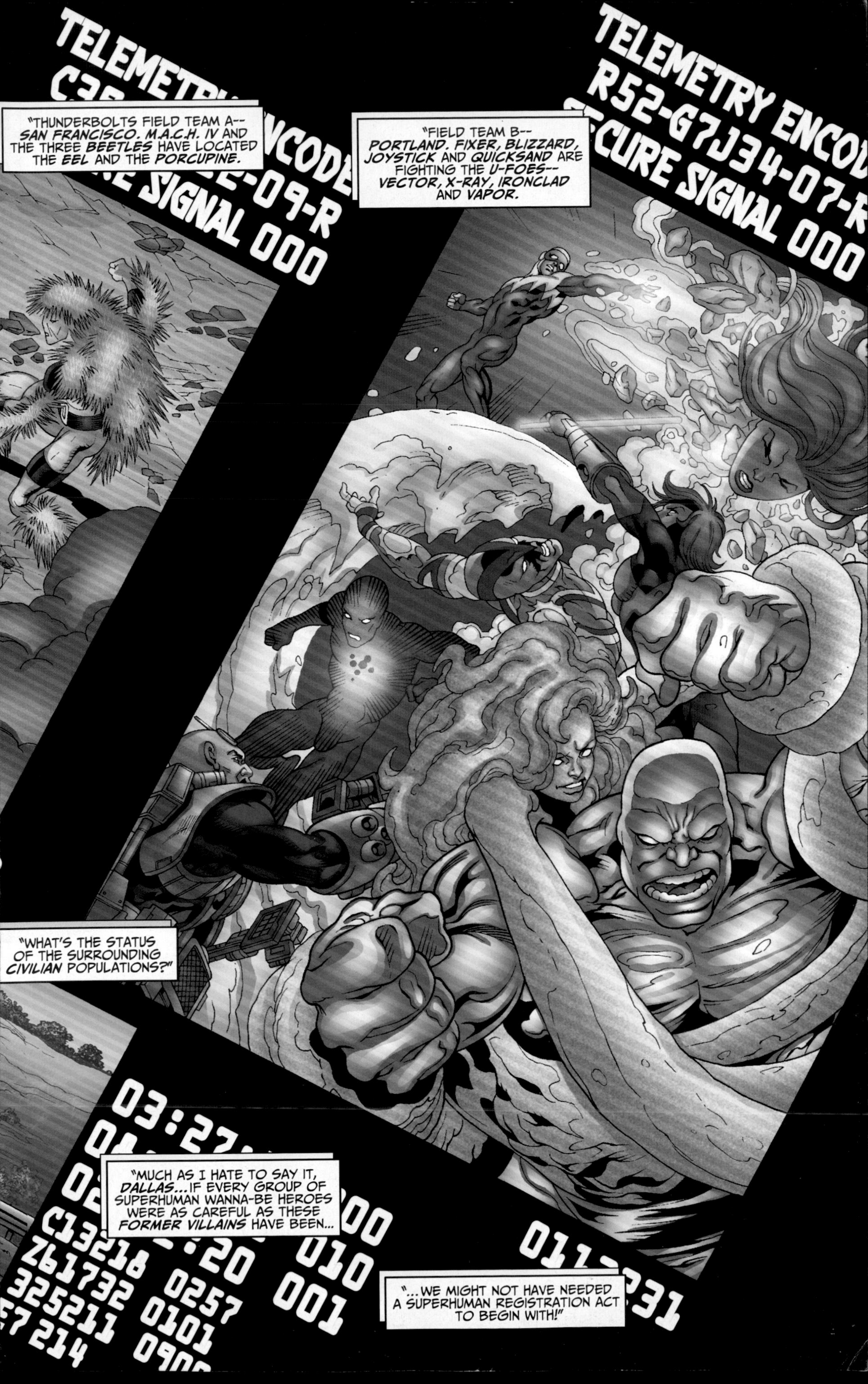
"THUNDERBOLTS FIELD TEAM A--SAN FRANCISCO. M.A.C.H. IV AND THE THREE BEETLES HAVE LOCATED THE EEL AND THE PORCUPINE.
"FIELD TEAM B--PORTLAND. FIXER, BLIZZARD, JOYSTICK AND QUICKSAND ARE FIGHTING THE U-FOES--VECTOR, X-RAY, IRONCLAD AND VAPOR.
"WHAT'S THE STATUS OF THE SURROUNDING CIVILIAN POPULATIONS?"
"MUCH AS I HATE TO SAY IT, DALLAS...IF EVERY GROUP OF SUPERHUMAN WANNA-BE HEROES WERE AS CAREFUL AS THESE FORMER VILLAINS HAVE BEEN...
"...WE MIGHT NOT HAVE NEEDED A SUPERHUMAN REGISTRATION ACT TO BEGIN WITH!"

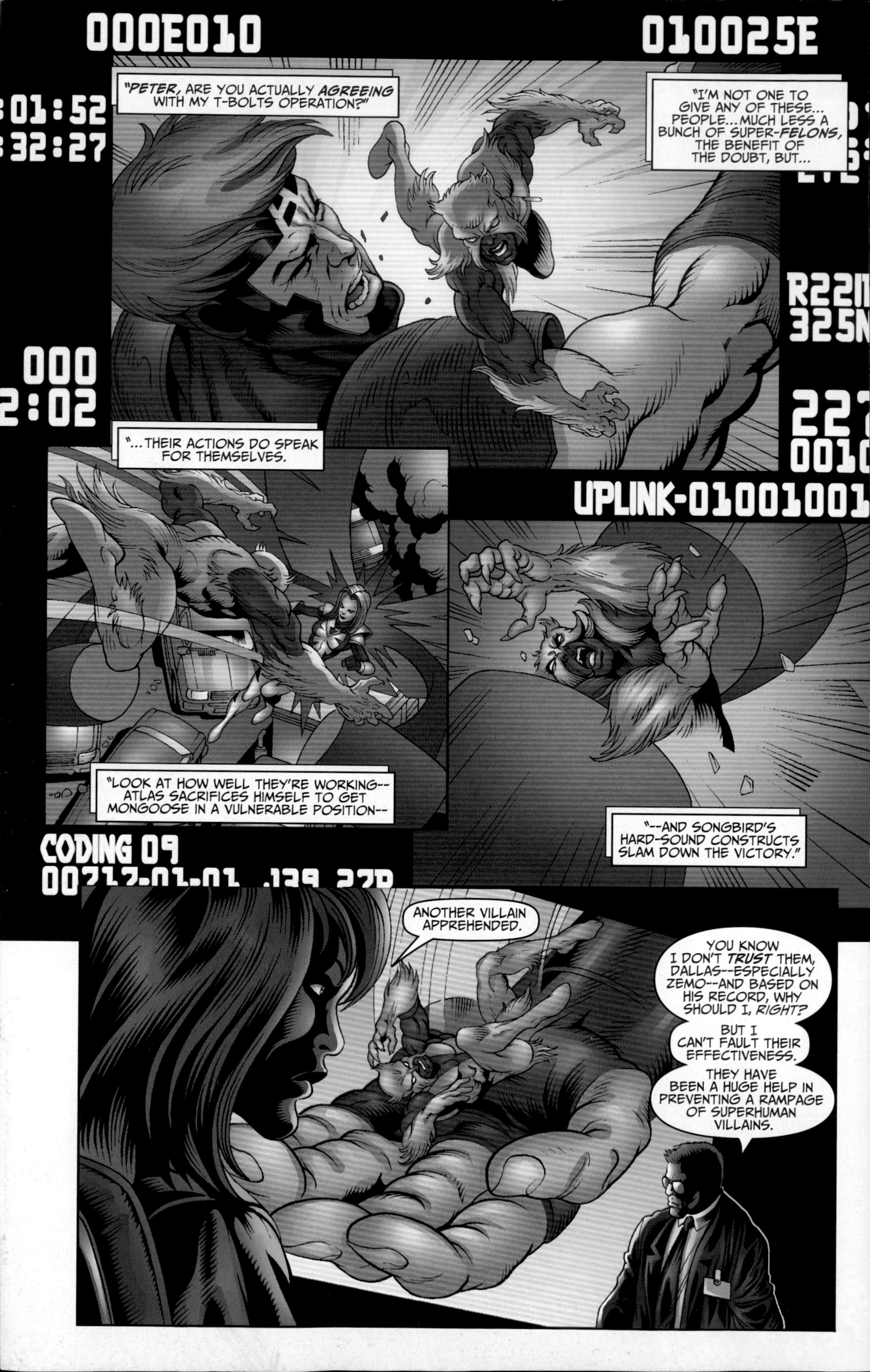
000E010
010025E
"PETER, ARE YOU ACTUALLY AGREEING WITH MY T-BOLTS OPERATION?"
"I'M NOT ONE TO GIVE ANY OF THESE... PEOPLE...MUCH LESS A BUNCH OF SUPER-FELONS, THE BENEFIT OF THE DOUBT, BUT...
"...THEIR ACTIONS DO SPEAK FOR THEMSELVES.
UPLINK-01001001
"LOOK AT HOW WELL THEY'RE WORKING-- ATLAS SACRIFICES HIMSELF TO GET MONGOOSE IN A VULNERABLE POSITION--
"--AND SONGBIRD'S HARD-SOUND CONSTRUCTS SLAM DOWN THE VICTORY."
CODING 09
ANOTHER VILLAIN APPREHENDED.
YOU KNOW I DON'T TRUST THEM, DALLAS--ESPECIALLY ZEMO--AND BASED ON HIS RECORD, WHY SHOULD I, RIGHT?
BUT I CAN'T FAULT THEIR EFFECTIVENESS.
THEY HAVE BEEN A HUGE HELP IN PREVENTING A RAMPAGE OF SUPERHUMAN VILLAINS.

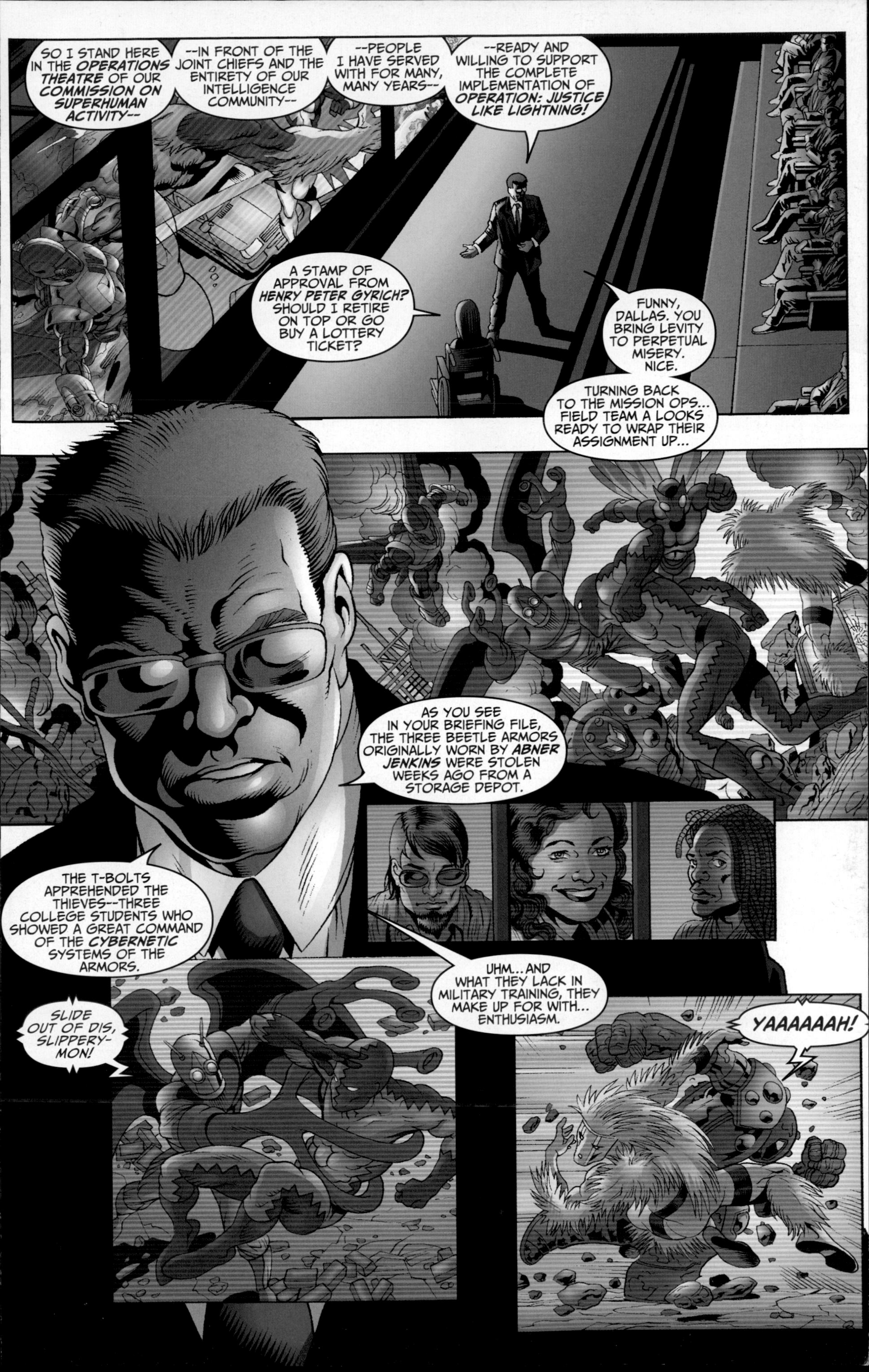
SO I STAND HERE IN THE OPERATIONS THEATRE OF OUR COMMISSION ON SUPERHUMAN ACTIVITY--
--IN FRONT OF THE JOINT CHIEFS AND THE ENTIRETY OF OUR INTELLIGENCE COMMUNITY--
--PEOPLE I HAVE SERVED WITH FOR MANY, MANY YEARS--
--READY AND WILLING TO SUPPORT THE COMPLETE IMPLEMENTATION OF OPERATION: JUSTICE LIKE LIGHTNING!
A STAMP OF APPROVAL FROM HENRY PETER GYRICH? SHOULD I RETIRE ON TOP OR GO BUY A LOTTERY TICKET?
FUNNY, DALLAS. YOU BRING LEVITY TO PERPETUAL MISERY. NICE.
TURNING BACK TO THE MISSION OPS... FIELD TEAM A LOOKS READY TO WRAP THEIR ASSIGNMENT UP...
AS YOU SEE IN YOUR BRIEFING FILE, THE THREE BEETLE ARMORS ORIGINALLY WORN BY ABNER JENKINS WERE STOLEN WEEKS AGO FROM A STORAGE DEPOT.
THE T-BOLTS APPREHENDED THE THIEVES--THREE COLLEGE STUDENTS WHO SHOWED A GREAT COMMAND OF THE CYBERNETIC SYSTEMS OF THE ARMORS.
UHM...AND WHAT THEY LACK IN MILITARY TRAINING, THEY MAKE UP FOR WITH... ENTHUSIASM.
SLIDE OUT OF DIS, SLIPPERY-MON!
YAAAAAAH!

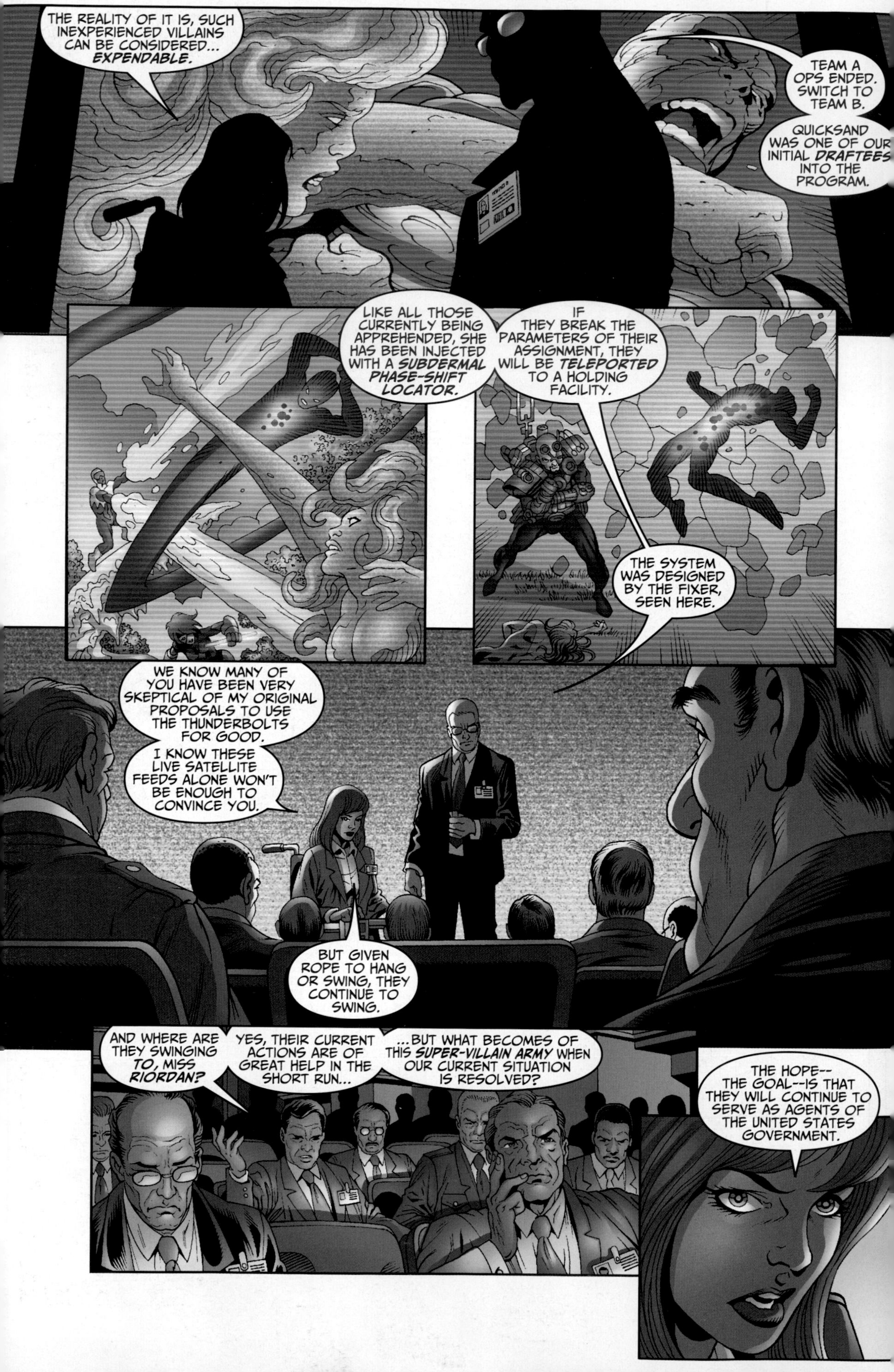
THE REALITY OF IT IS, SUCH INEXPERIENCED VILLAINS CAN BE CONSIDERED... EXPENDABLE.
TEAM A OPS ENDED. SWITCH TO TEAM B.
QUICKSAND WAS ONE OF OUR INITIAL DRAFTEES INTO THE PROGRAM.
LIKE ALL THOSE CURRENTLY BEING APPREHENDED, SHE HAS BEEN INJECTED WITH A SUBDERMAL PHASE-SHIFT LOCATOR.
IF THEY BREAK THE PARAMETERS OF THEIR ASSIGNMENT, THEY WILL BE TELEPORTED TO A HOLDING FACILITY.
THE SYSTEM WAS DESIGNED BY THE FIXER, SEEN HERE.
WE KNOW MANY OF YOU HAVE BEEN VERY SKEPTICAL OF MY ORIGINAL PROPOSALS TO USE THE THUNDERBOLTS FOR GOOD.
I KNOW THESE LIVE SATELLITE FEEDS ALONE WON'T BE ENOUGH TO CONVINCE YOU.
BUT GIVEN ROPE TO HANG OR SWING, THEY CONTINUE TO SWING.
AND WHERE ARE THEY SWINGING TO, MISS RIORDAN?
YES, THEIR CURRENT ACTIONS ARE OF GREAT HELP IN THE SHORT RUN...
...BUT WHAT BECOMES OF THIS SUPER-VILLAIN ARMY WHEN OUR CURRENT SITUATION IS RESOLVED?
THE HOPE-- THE GOAL--IS THAT THEY WILL CONTINUE TO SERVE AS AGENTS OF THE UNITED STATES GOVERNMENT.

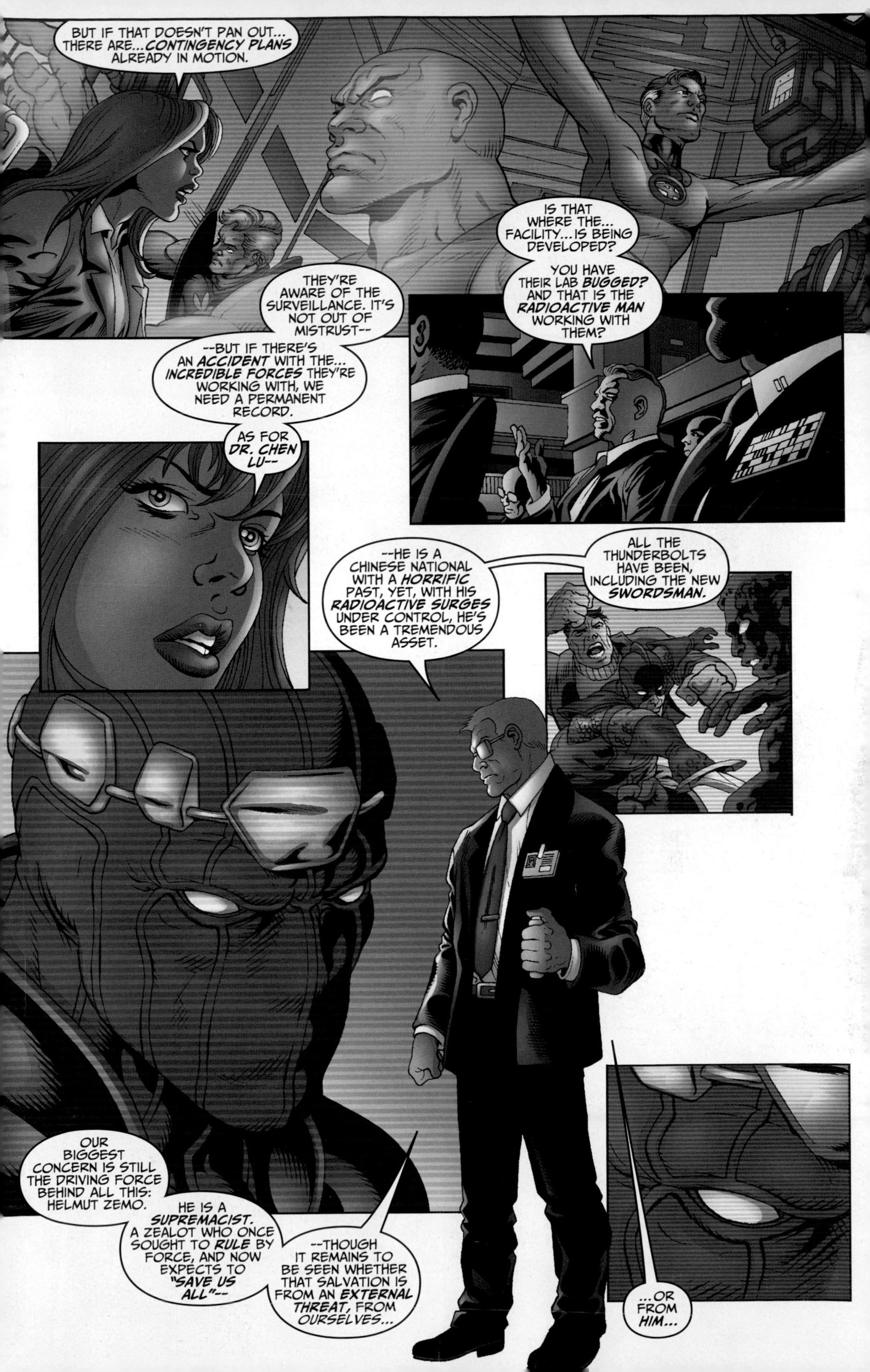
BUT IF THAT DOESN'T PAN OUT... THERE ARE... CONTINGENCY PLANS ALREADY IN MOTION.
IS THAT WHERE THE... FACILITY... IS BEING DEVELOPED?
YOU HAVE THEIR LAB BUGGED? AND THAT IS THE RADIOACTIVE MAN WORKING WITH THEM?
THEY'RE AWARE OF THE SURVEILLANCE. IT'S NOT OUT OF MISTRUST--
--BUT IF THERE'S AN ACCIDENT WITH THE... INCREDIBLE FORCES THEY'RE WORKING WITH, WE NEED A PERMANENT RECORD.
AS FOR DR. CHEN LU--
--HE IS A CHINESE NATIONAL WITH A HORRIFIC PAST, YET, WITH HIS RADIOACTIVE SURGES UNDER CONTROL, HE'S BEEN A TREMENDOUS ASSET.
ALL THE THUNDERBOLTS HAVE BEEN, INCLUDING THE NEW SWORDSMAN.
OUR BIGGEST CONCERN IS STILL THE DRIVING FORCE BEHIND ALL THIS: HELMUT ZEMO.
HE IS A SUPREMACIST. A ZEALOT WHO ONCE SOUGHT TO RULE BY FORCE, AND NOW EXPECTS TO "SAVE US ALL"--
--THOUGH IT REMAINS TO BE SEEN WHETHER THAT SALVATION IS FROM AN EXTERNAL THREAT, FROM OURSELVES...
...OR FROM HIM...

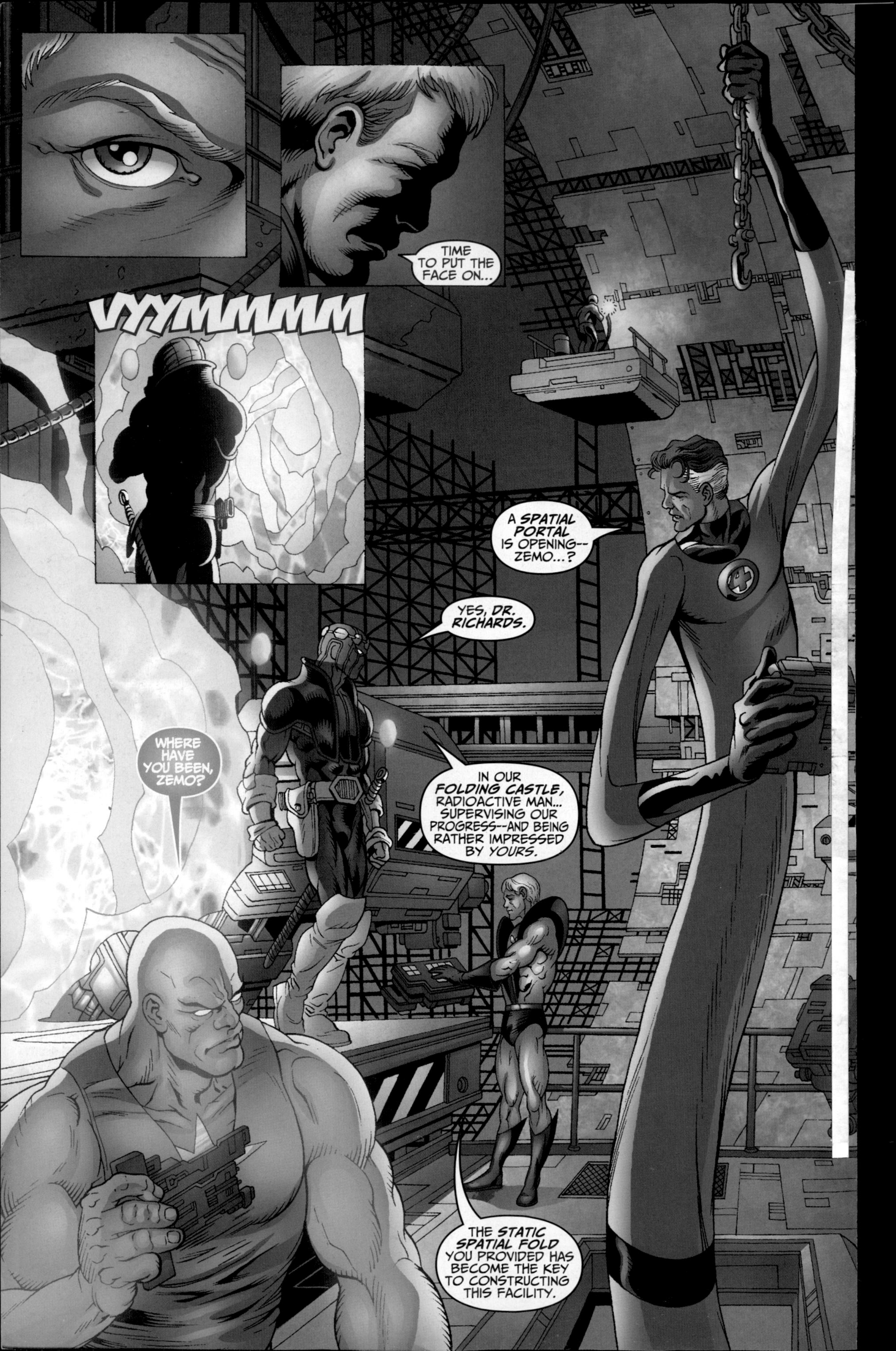
TIME TO PUT THE FACE ON...
VYYMMMMM
A SPATIAL PORTAL IS OPENING-- ZEMO...?
YES, DR. RICHARDS.
WHERE HAVE YOU BEEN, ZEMO?
IN OUR FOLDING CASTLE, RADIOACTIVE MAN... SUPERVISING OUR PROGRESS--AND BEING RATHER IMPRESSED BY YOURS.
THE STATIC SPATIAL FOLD YOU PROVIDED HAS BECOME THE KEY TO CONSTRUCTING THIS FACILITY.

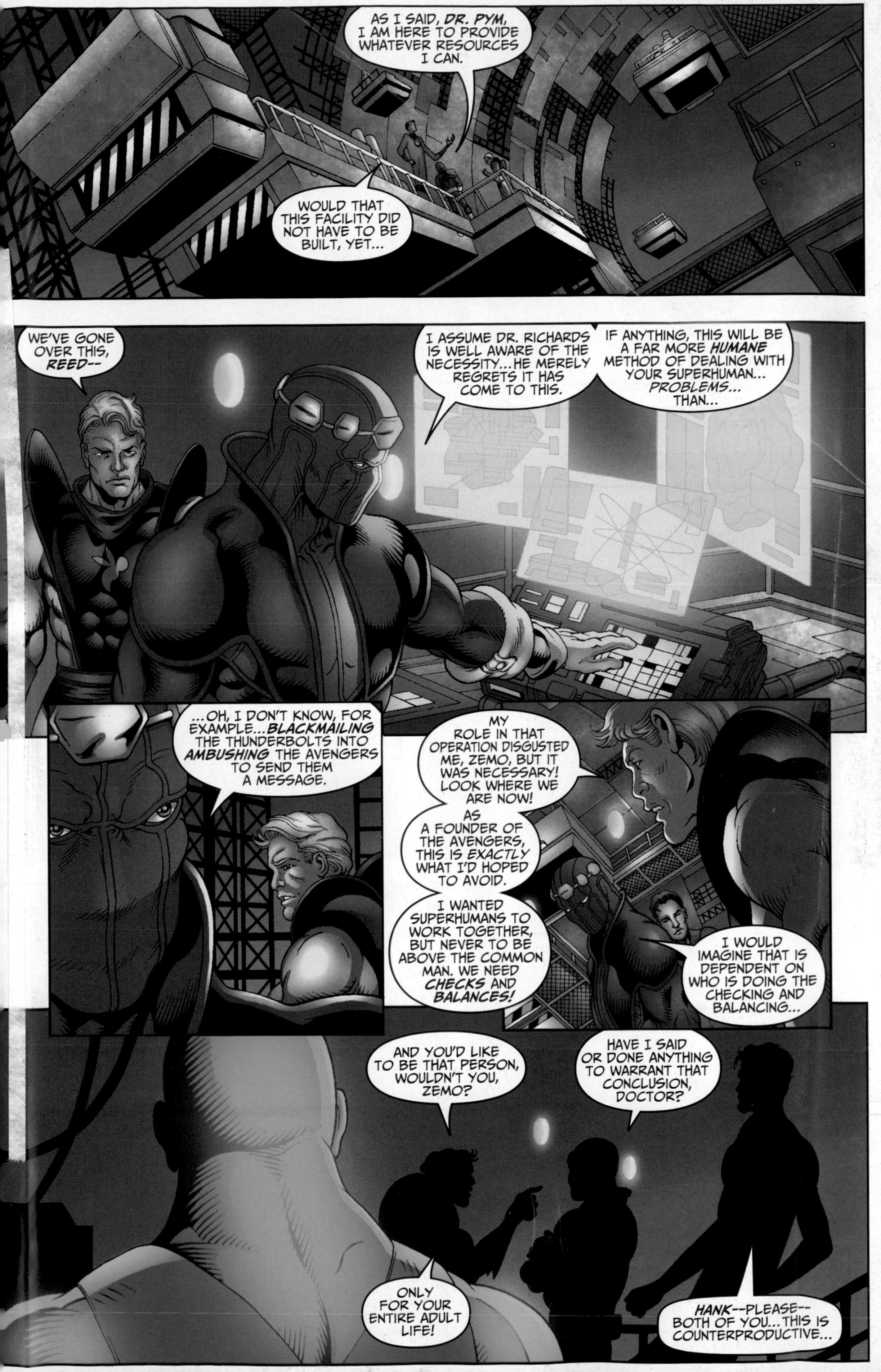
AS I SAID, DR. PYM, I AM HERE TO PROVIDE WHATEVER RESOURCES I CAN.
WOULD THAT THIS FACILITY DID NOT HAVE TO BE BUILT, YET...
WE'VE GONE OVER THIS, REED--
I ASSUME DR. RICHARDS IS WELL AWARE OF THE NECESSITY...HE MERELY REGRETS IT HAS COME TO THIS.
IF ANYTHING, THIS WILL BE A FAR MORE HUMANE METHOD OF DEALING WITH YOUR SUPERHUMAN... PROBLEMS... THAN...
...OH, I DON'T KNOW, FOR EXAMPLE...BLACKMAILING THE THUNDERBOLTS INTO AMBUSHING THE AVENGERS TO SEND THEM A MESSAGE.
MY ROLE IN THAT OPERATION DISGUSTED ME, ZEMO, BUT IT WAS NECESSARY! LOOK WHERE WE ARE NOW!
AS A FOUNDER OF THE AVENGERS, THIS IS EXACTLY WHAT I'D HOPED TO AVOID.
I WANTED SUPERHUMANS TO WORK TOGETHER, BUT NEVER TO BE ABOVE THE COMMON MAN. WE NEED CHECKS AND BALANCES!
I WOULD IMAGINE THAT IS DEPENDENT ON WHO IS DOING THE CHECKING AND BALANCING...
AND YOU'D LIKE TO BE THAT PERSON, WOULDN'T YOU, ZEMO?
HAVE I SAID OR DONE ANYTHING TO WARRANT THAT CONCLUSION, DOCTOR?
ONLY FOR YOUR ENTIRE ADULT LIFE!
HANK--PLEASE--BOTH OF YOU...THIS IS COUNTERPRODUCTIVE...

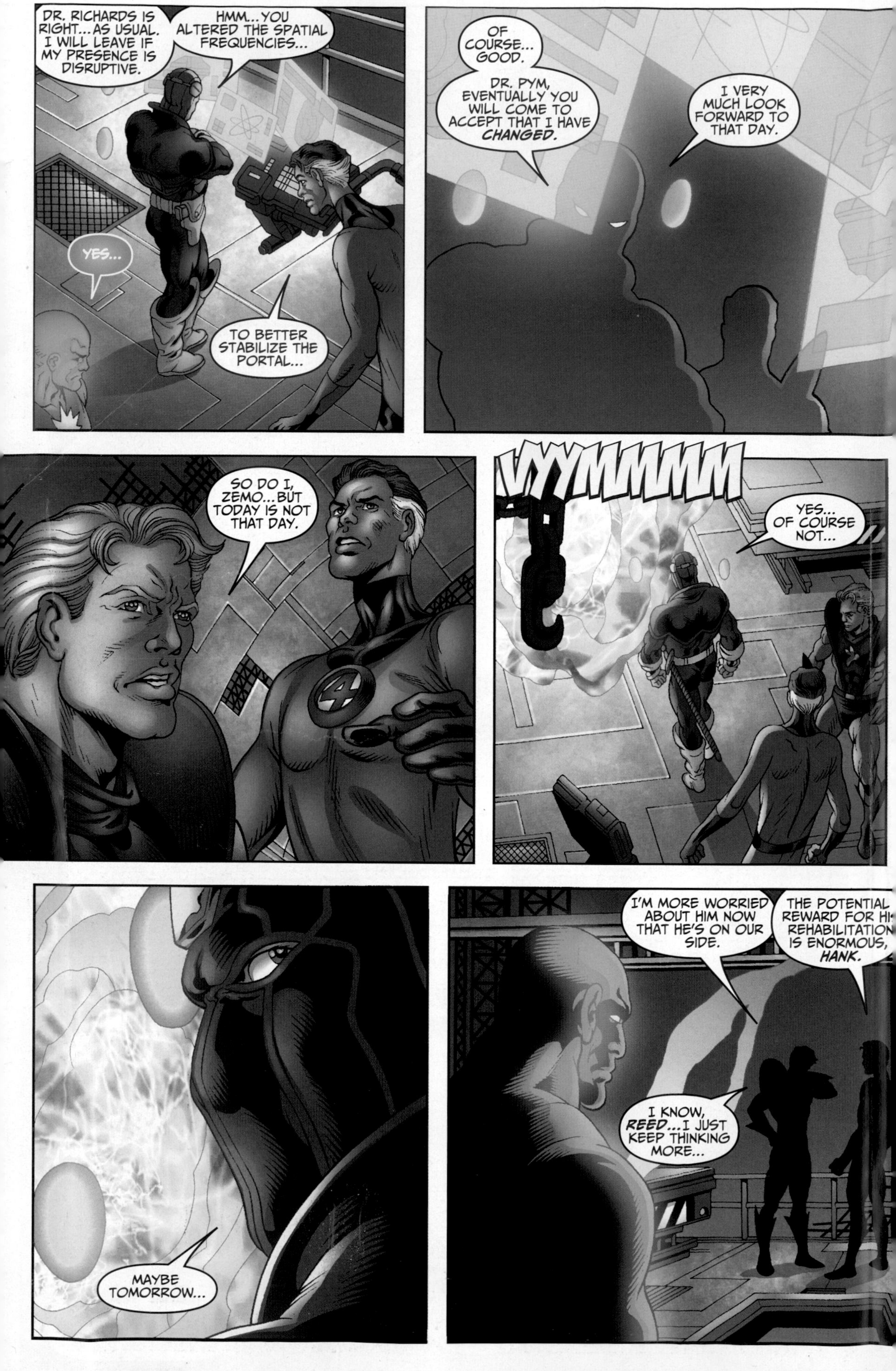
DR. RICHARDS IS RIGHT...AS USUAL. I WILL LEAVE IF MY PRESENCE IS DISRUPTIVE.
HMM...YOU ALTERED THE SPATIAL FREQUENCIES...
YES...
TO BETTER STABILIZE THE PORTAL...
OF COURSE... GOOD.
DR. PYM, EVENTUALLY YOU WILL COME TO ACCEPT THAT I HAVE CHANGED.
I VERY MUCH LOOK FORWARD TO THAT DAY.
SO DO I, ZEMO...BUT TODAY IS NOT THAT DAY.
VYYMMMMM
YES... OF COURSE NOT...
MAYBE TOMORROW...
I'M MORE WORRIED ABOUT HIM NOW THAT HE'S ON OUR SIDE.
THE POTENTIAL REWARD FOR HIS REHABILITATION IS ENORMOUS, HANK.
I KNOW, REED...I JUST KEEP THINKING MORE...

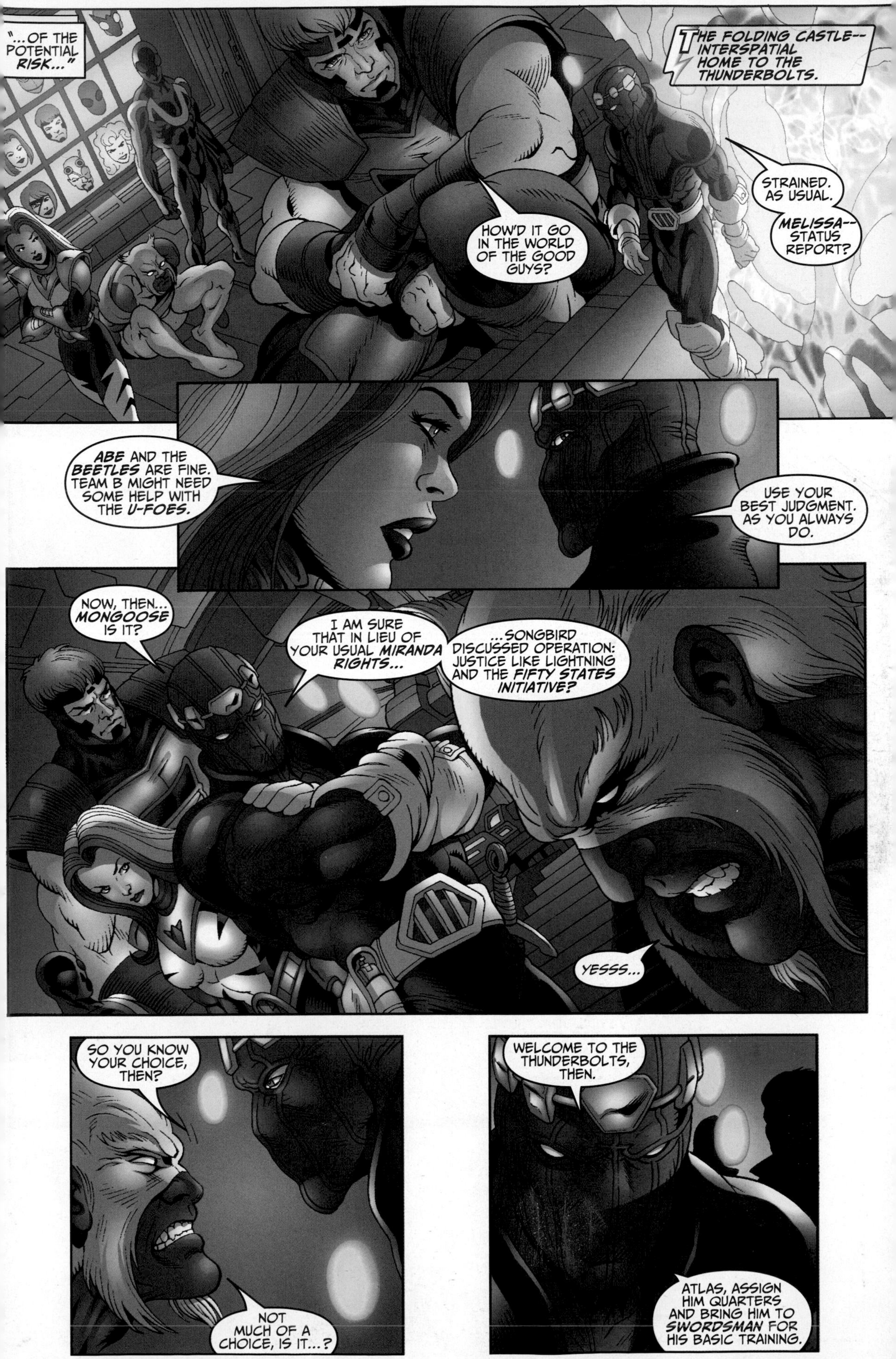
"...OF THE POTENTIAL RISK..."
THE FOLDING CASTLE--INTERSPATIAL HOME TO THE THUNDERBOLTS.
HOW'D IT GO IN THE WORLD OF THE GOOD GUYS?
STRAINED. AS USUAL.
MELISSA--STATUS REPORT?
ABE AND THE BEETLES ARE FINE. TEAM B MIGHT NEED SOME HELP WITH THE U-FOES.
USE YOUR BEST JUDGMENT. AS YOU ALWAYS DO.
NOW, THEN... MONGOOSE IS IT?
I AM SURE THAT IN LIEU OF YOUR USUAL MIRANDA RIGHTS...
...SONGBIRD DISCUSSED OPERATION: JUSTICE LIKE LIGHTNING AND THE FIFTY STATES INITIATIVE?
YESSS...
SO YOU KNOW YOUR CHOICE, THEN?
NOT MUCH OF A CHOICE, IS IT...?
WELCOME TO THE THUNDERBOLTS, THEN.
ATLAS, ASSIGN HIM QUARTERS AND BRING HIM TO SWORDSMAN FOR HIS BASIC TRAINING.

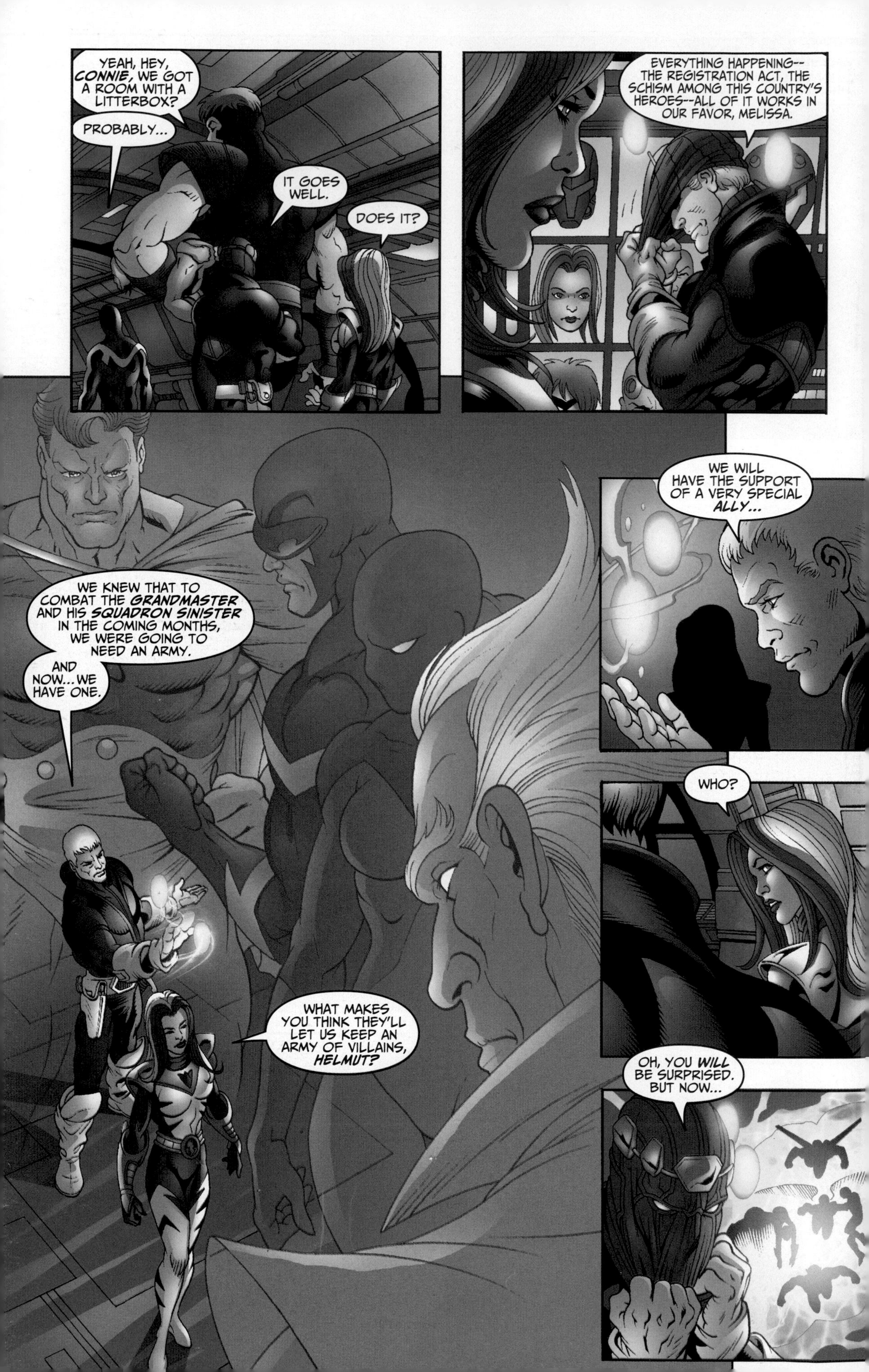
YEAH, HEY, CONNIE, WE GOT A ROOM WITH A LITTERBOX?
PROBABLY...
IT GOES WELL.
DOES IT?
EVERYTHING HAPPENING-- THE REGISTRATION ACT, THE SCHISM AMONG THIS COUNTRY'S HEROES--ALL OF IT WORKS IN OUR FAVOR, MELISSA.
WE KNEW THAT TO COMBAT THE GRANDMASTER AND HIS SQUADRON SINISTER IN THE COMING MONTHS, WE WERE GOING TO NEED AN ARMY.
AND NOW... WE HAVE ONE.
WHAT MAKES YOU THINK THEY'LL LET US KEEP AN ARMY OF VILLAINS, HELMUT?
WE WILL HAVE THE SUPPORT OF A VERY SPECIAL ALLY...
WHO?
OH, YOU WILL BE SURPRISED. BUT NOW...

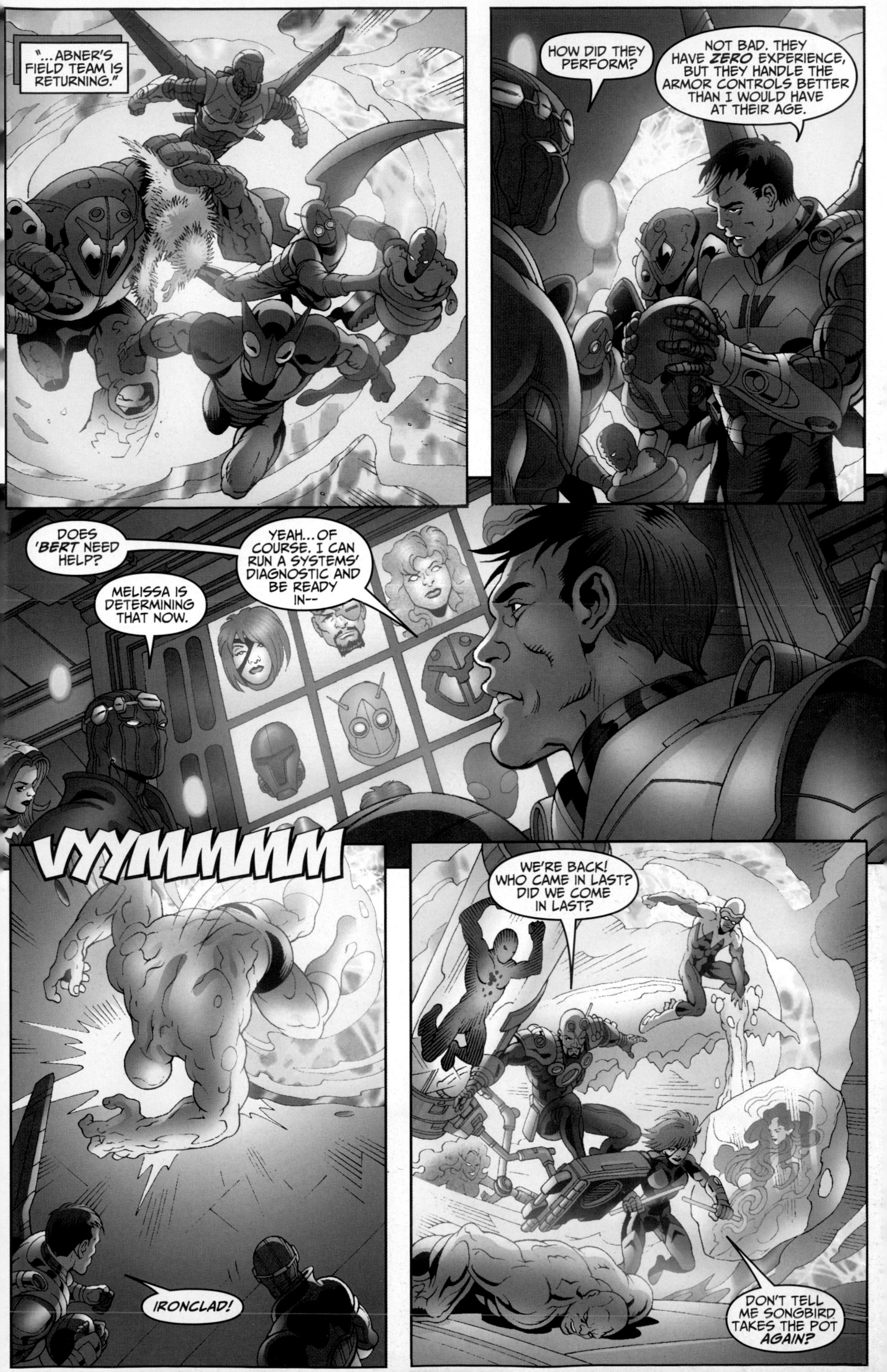
"...ABNER'S FIELD TEAM IS RETURNING."
HOW DID THEY PERFORM?
NOT BAD. THEY HAVE ZERO EXPERIENCE, BUT THEY HANDLE THE ARMOR CONTROLS BETTER THAN I WOULD HAVE AT THEIR AGE.
DOES 'BERT NEED HELP?
YEAH...OF COURSE. I CAN RUN A SYSTEMS' DIAGNOSTIC AND BE READY IN--
MELISSA IS DETERMINING THAT NOW.
VYYMMMMM
IRONCLAD!
WE'RE BACK! WHO CAME IN LAST? DID WE COME IN LAST?
DON'T TELL ME SONGBIRD TAKES THE POT AGAIN?

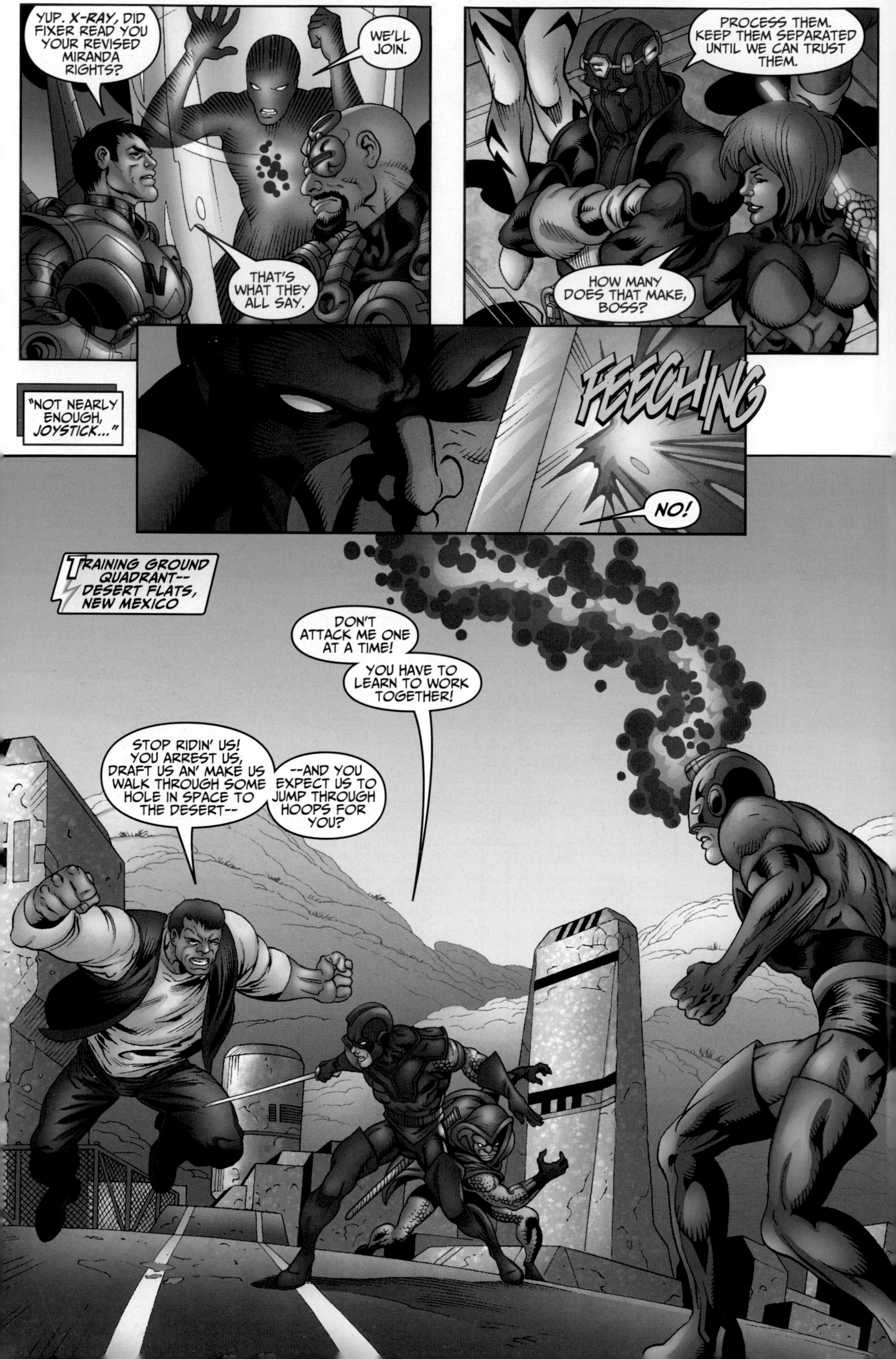
YUP. X-RAY, DID FIXER READ YOU YOUR REVISED MIRANDA RIGHTS?
WE'LL JOIN.
THAT'S WHAT THEY ALL SAY.
PROCESS THEM. KEEP THEM SEPARATED UNTIL WE CAN TRUST THEM.
HOW MANY DOES THAT MAKE, BOSS?
"NOT NEARLY ENOUGH, JOYSTICK..."
FEECHING
NO!
TRAINING GROUND QUADRANT-- DESERT FLATS, NEW MEXICO
DON'T ATTACK ME ONE AT A TIME!
YOU HAVE TO LEARN TO WORK TOGETHER!
STOP RIDIN' US! YOU ARREST US, DRAFT US AN' MAKE US WALK THROUGH SOME HOLE IN SPACE TO THE DESERT--
--AND YOU EXPECT US TO JUMP THROUGH HOOPS FOR YOU?

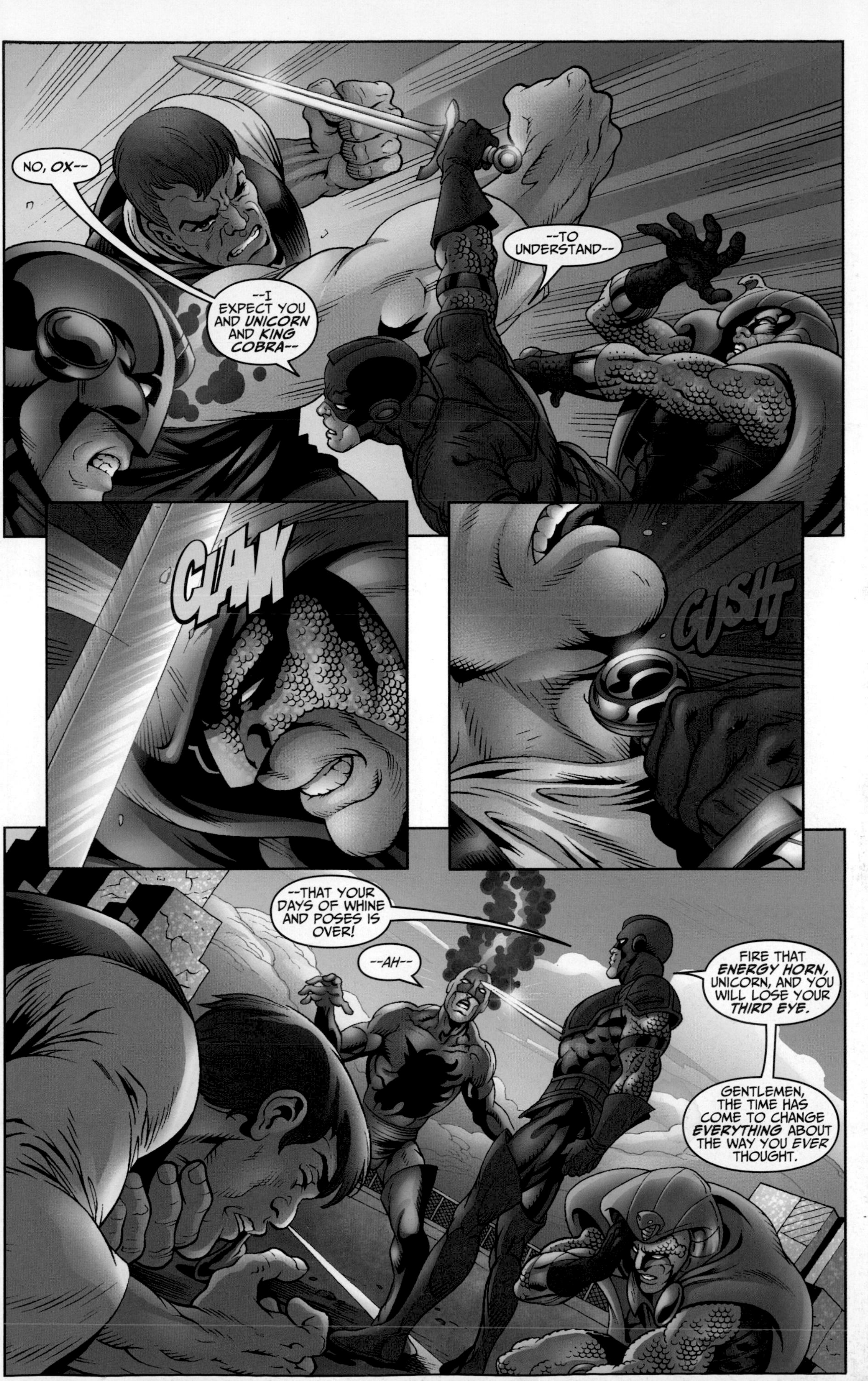
NO, OX--
--I EXPECT YOU AND UNICORN AND KING COBRA--
--TO UNDERSTAND--
CLANK
GUSH
--THAT YOUR DAYS OF WHINE AND POSES IS OVER!
--AH--
FIRE THAT ENERGY HORN, UNICORN, AND YOU WILL LOSE YOUR THIRD EYE.
GENTLEMEN, THE TIME HAS COME TO CHANGE EVERYTHING ABOUT THE WAY YOU EVER THOUGHT.

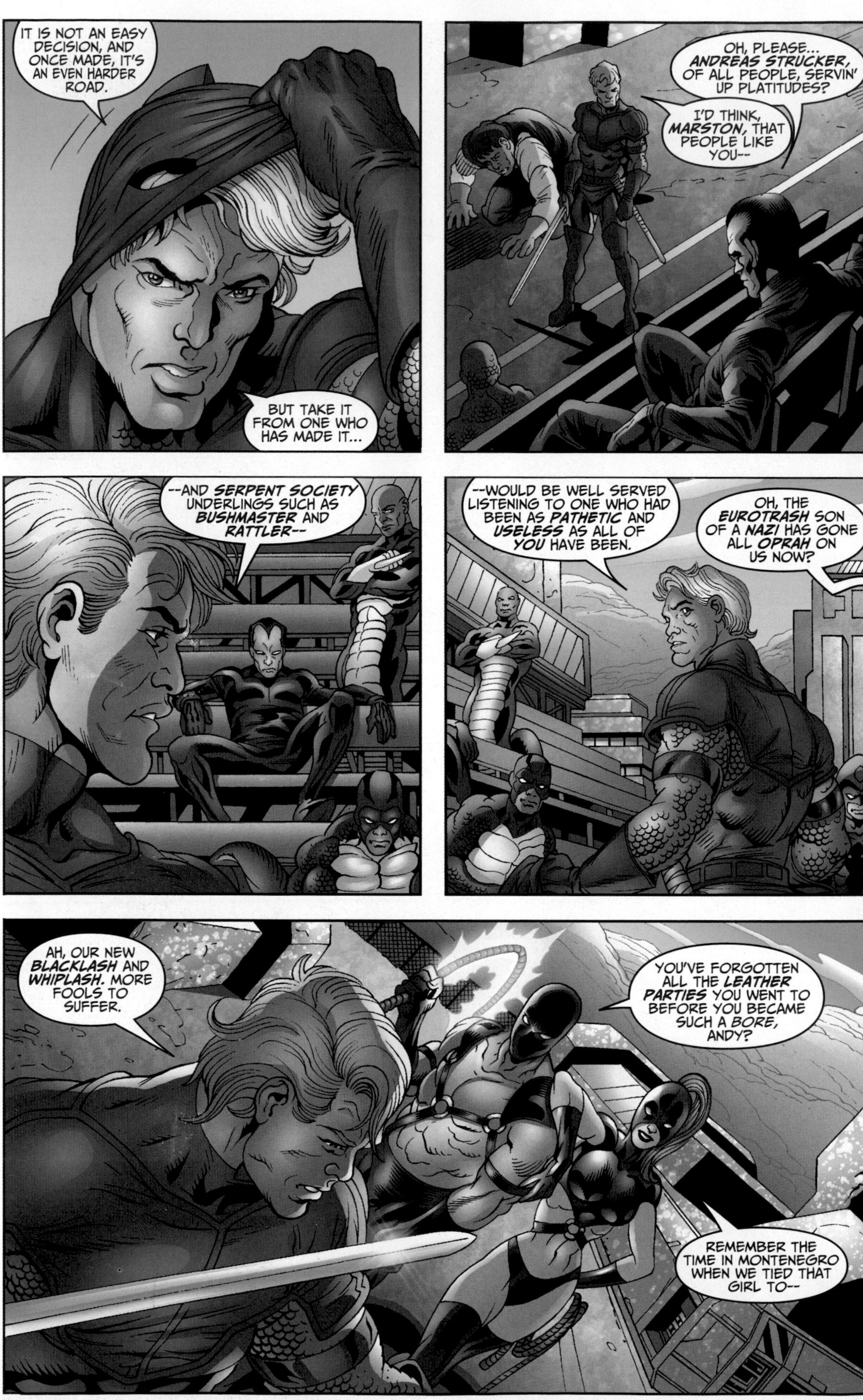
IT IS NOT AN EASY DECISION, AND ONCE MADE, IT'S AN EVEN HARDER ROAD.
BUT TAKE IT FROM ONE WHO HAS MADE IT...
OH, PLEASE... ANDREAS STRUCKER, OF ALL PEOPLE, SERVIN' UP PLATITUDES?
I'D THINK, MARSTON, THAT PEOPLE LIKE YOU--
--AND SERPENT SOCIETY UNDERLINGS SUCH AS BUSHMASTER AND RATTLER--
--WOULD BE WELL SERVED LISTENING TO ONE WHO HAD BEEN AS PATHETIC AND USELESS AS ALL OF YOU HAVE BEEN.
OH, THE EUROTRASH SON OF A NAZI HAS GONE ALL OPRAH ON US NOW?
AH, OUR NEW BLACKLASH AND WHIPLASH. MORE FOOLS TO SUFFER.
YOU'VE FORGOTTEN ALL THE LEATHER PARTIES YOU WENT TO BEFORE YOU BECAME SUCH A BORE, ANDY?
REMEMBER THE TIME IN MONTENEGRO WHEN WE TIED THAT GIRL TO--

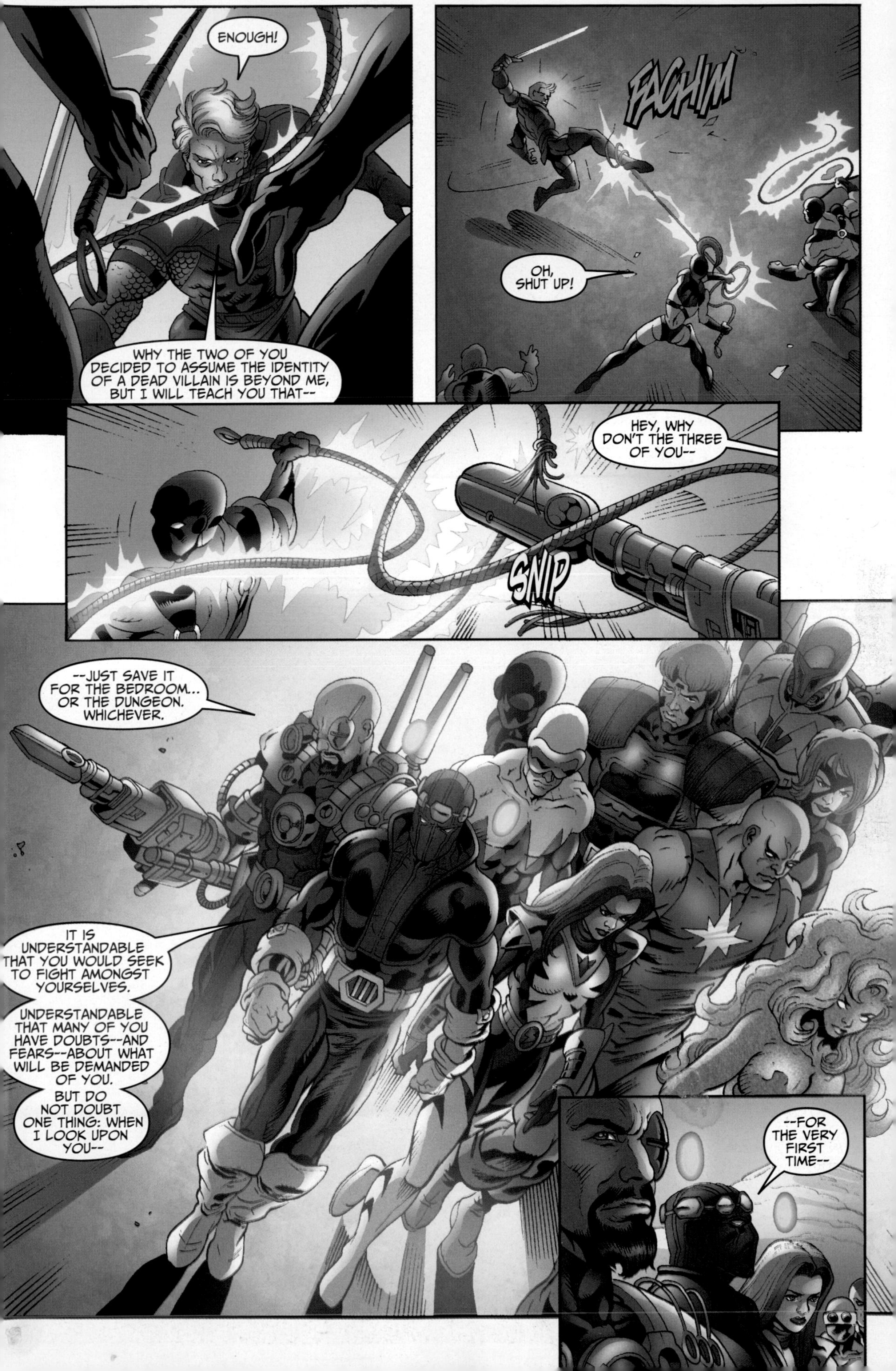
ENOUGH!
WHY THE TWO OF YOU DECIDED TO ASSUME THE IDENTITY OF A DEAD VILLAIN IS BEYOND ME, BUT I WILL TEACH YOU THAT--
FACHIM
OH, SHUT UP!
HEY, WHY DON'T THE THREE OF YOU--
SNIP
--JUST SAVE IT FOR THE BEDROOM... OR THE DUNGEON. WHICHEVER.
IT IS UNDERSTANDABLE THAT YOU WOULD SEEK TO FIGHT AMONGST YOURSELVES.
UNDERSTANDABLE THAT MANY OF YOU HAVE DOUBTS--AND FEARS--ABOUT WHAT WILL BE DEMANDED OF YOU.
BUT DO NOT DOUBT ONE THING: WHEN I LOOK UPON YOU--
--FOR THE VERY FIRST TIME--

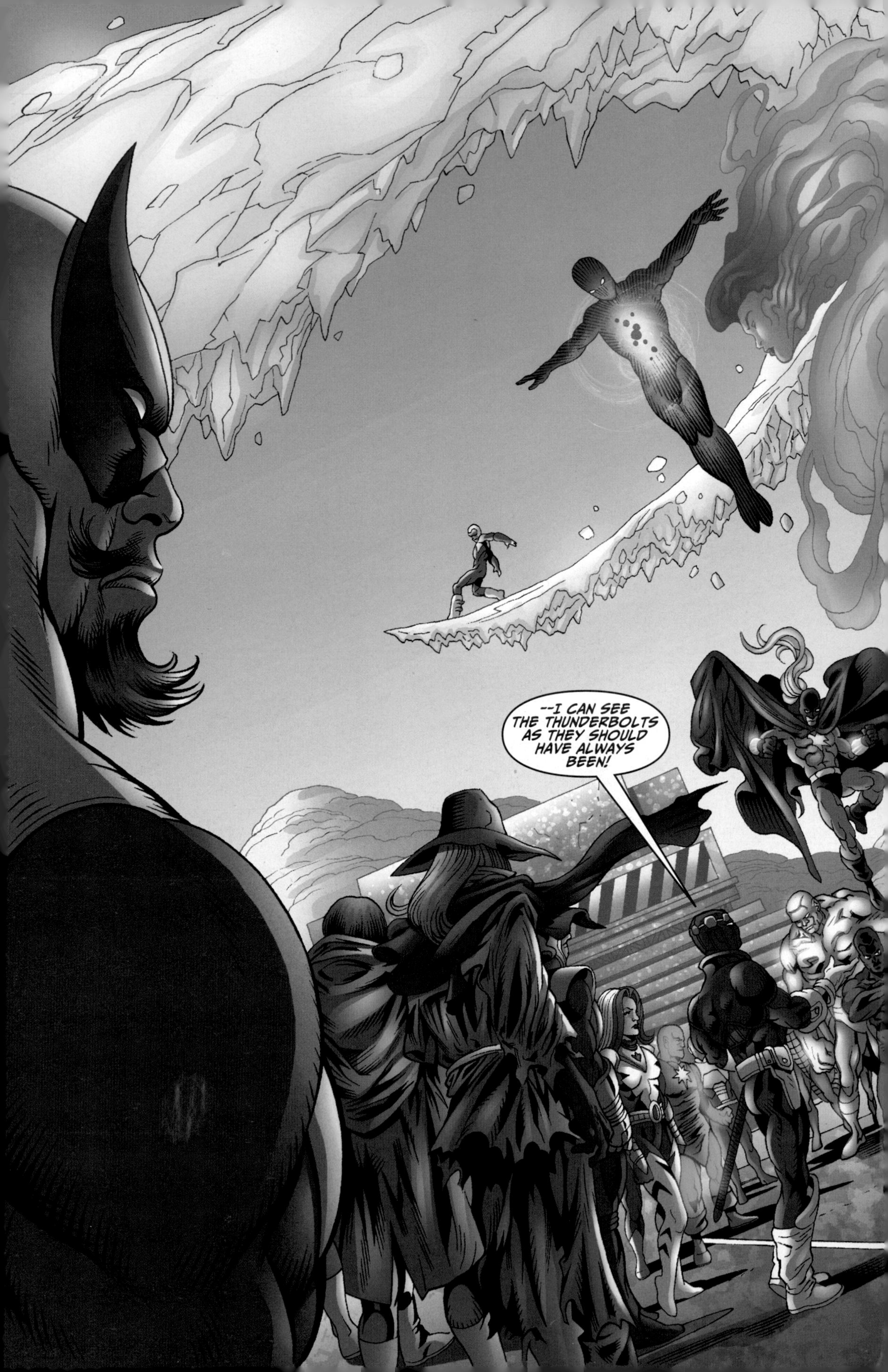
--I CAN SEE THE THUNDERBOLTS AS THEY SHOULD HAVE ALWAYS BEEN!

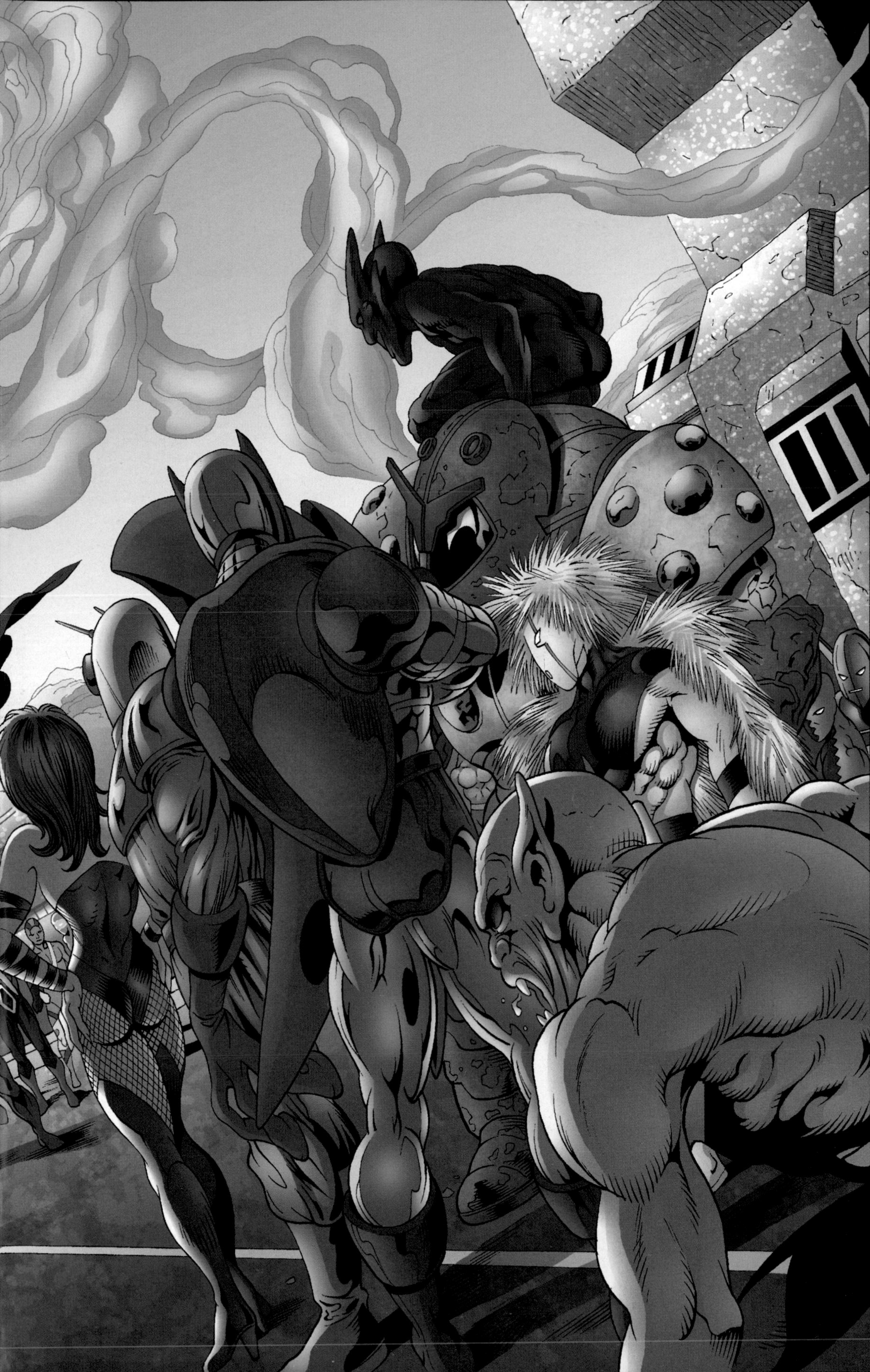

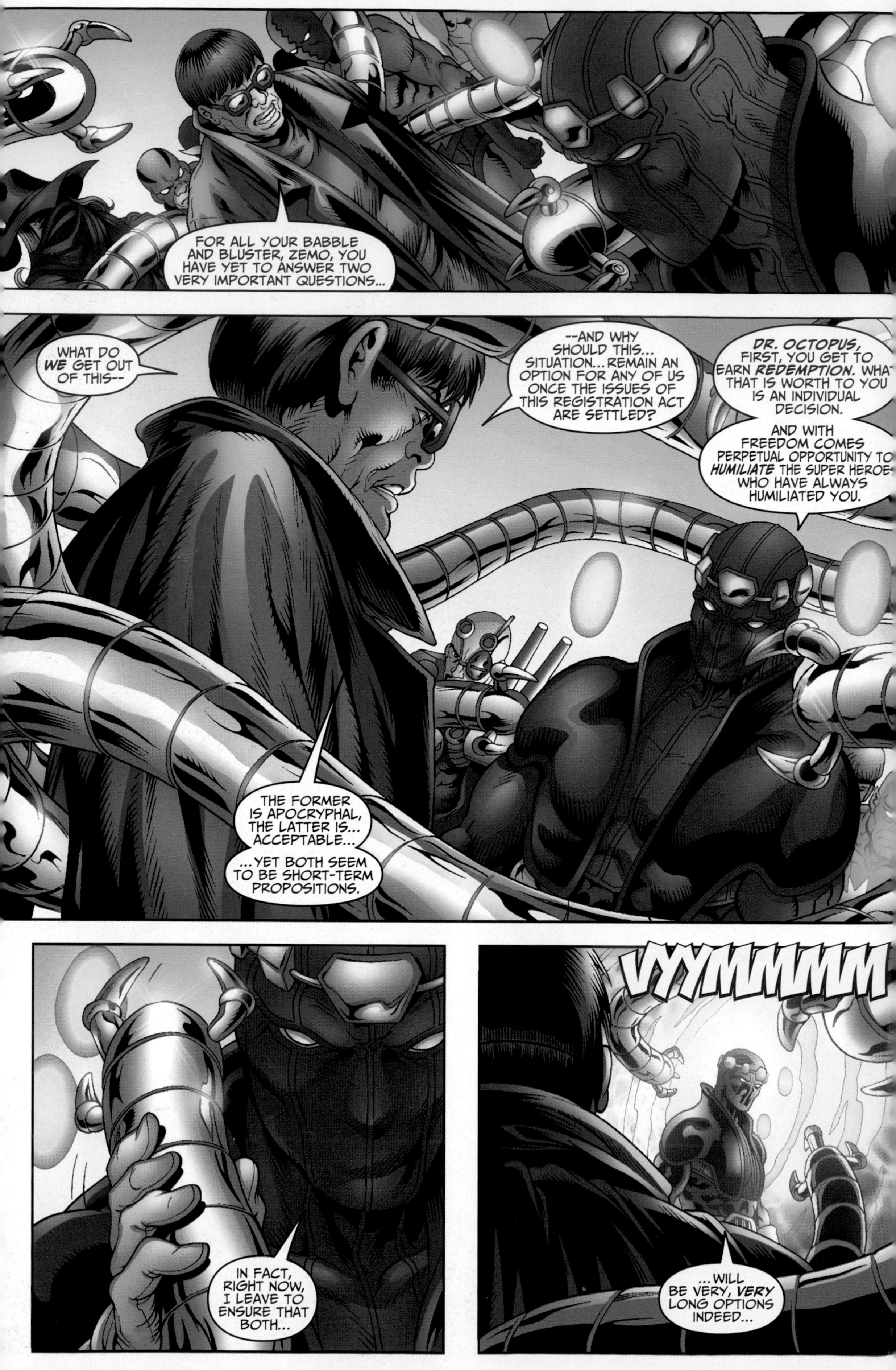

FOR ALL YOUR BABBLE AND BLUSTER, ZEMO, YOU HAVE YET TO ANSWER TWO VERY IMPORTANT QUESTIONS...
WHAT DO *WE* GET OUT OF THIS--
--AND WHY SHOULD THIS... SITUATION... REMAIN AN OPTION FOR ANY OF US ONCE THE ISSUES OF THIS REGISTRATION ACT ARE SETTLED?
*DR. OCTOPUS,* FIRST, YOU GET TO EARN *REDEMPTION.* WHAT THAT IS WORTH TO YOU IS AN INDIVIDUAL DECISION.
AND WITH FREEDOM COMES PERPETUAL OPPORTUNITY TO *HUMILIATE* THE SUPER HEROES WHO HAVE ALWAYS HUMILIATED YOU.
THE FORMER IS APOCRYPHAL, THE LATTER IS... ACCEPTABLE...
...YET BOTH SEEM TO BE SHORT-TERM PROPOSITIONS.
IN FACT, RIGHT NOW, I LEAVE TO ENSURE THAT BOTH...
VYYMMMMM
...WILL BE VERY, *VERY* LONG OPTIONS INDEED...

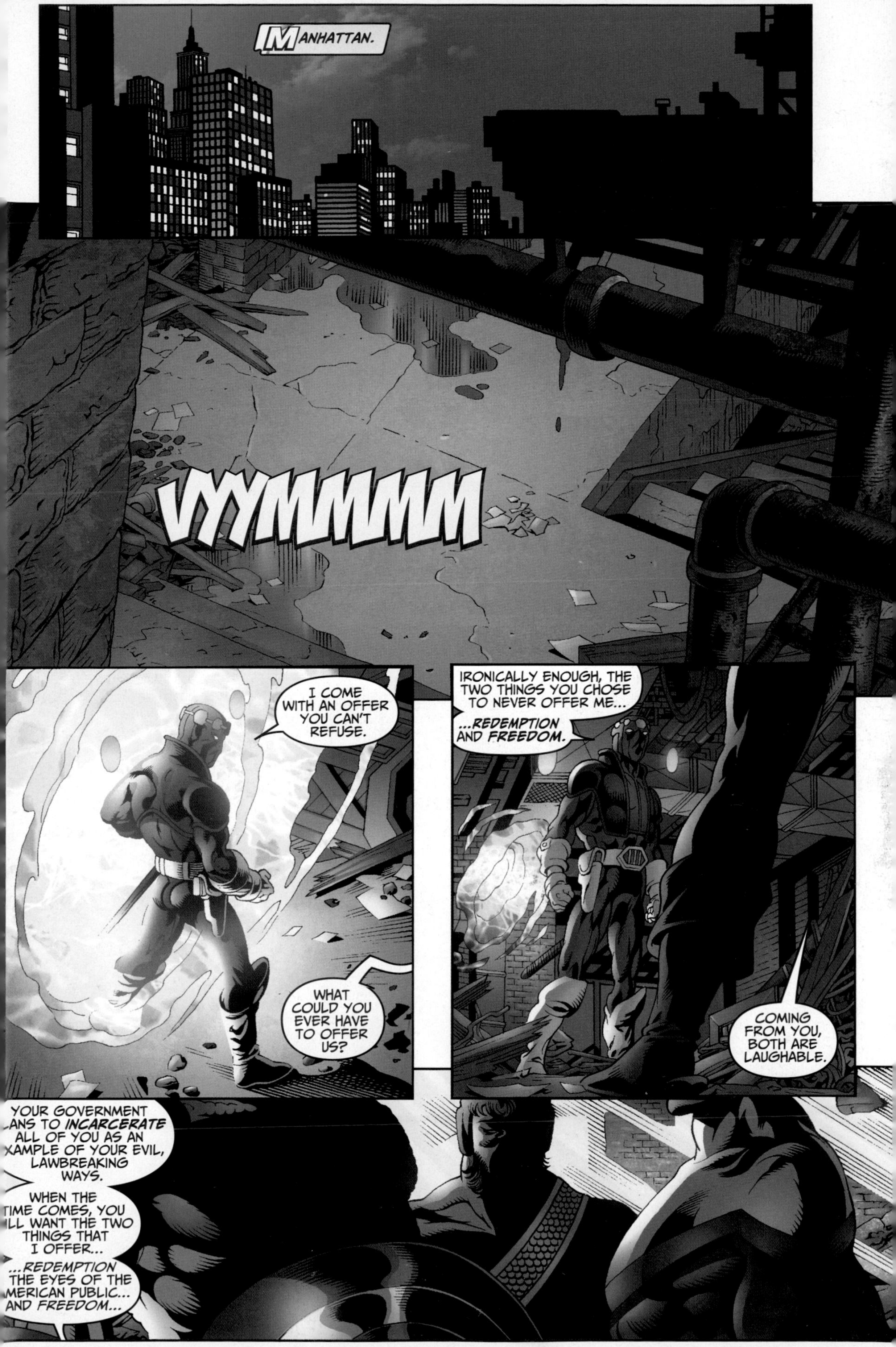
MANHATTAN.
VYYMMMMM
I COME WITH AN OFFER YOU CAN'T REFUSE.
WHAT COULD YOU EVER HAVE TO OFFER US?
IRONICALLY ENOUGH, THE TWO THINGS YOU CHOSE TO NEVER OFFER ME...
...REDEMPTION AND FREEDOM.
COMING FROM YOU, BOTH ARE LAUGHABLE.
YOUR GOVERNMENT LANS TO INCARCERATE ALL OF YOU AS AN XAMPLE OF YOUR EVIL, LAWBREAKING WAYS.
WHEN THE TIME COMES, YOU ILL WANT THE TWO THINGS THAT I OFFER...
...REDEMPTION THE EYES OF THE MERICAN PUBLIC... AND FREEDOM...

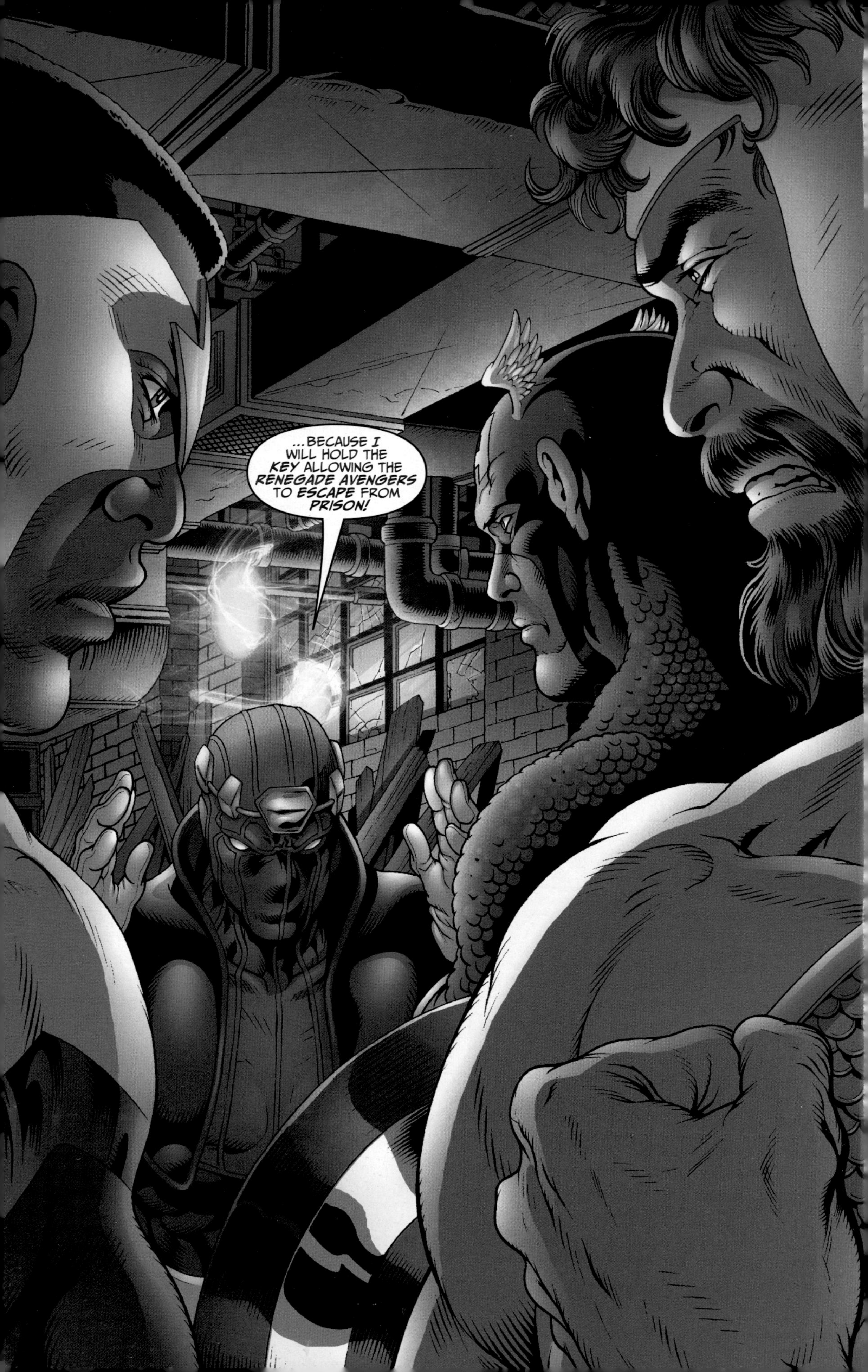
...BECAUSE I WILL HOLD THE KEY ALLOWING THE RENEGADE AVENGERS TO ESCAPE FROM PRISON!

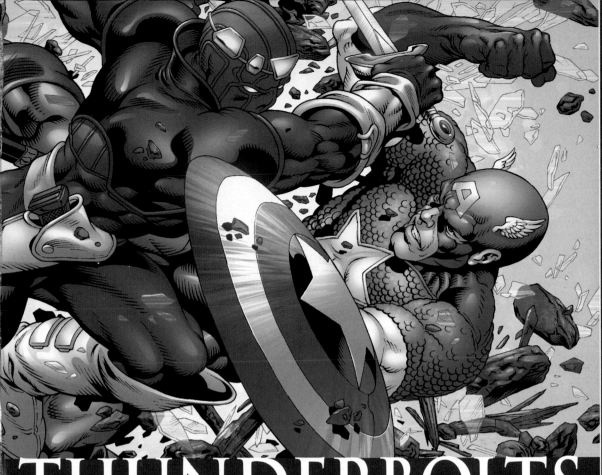

# THUNDERBOLTS

A MARVEL COMICS EVENT

# CIVIL
WAR

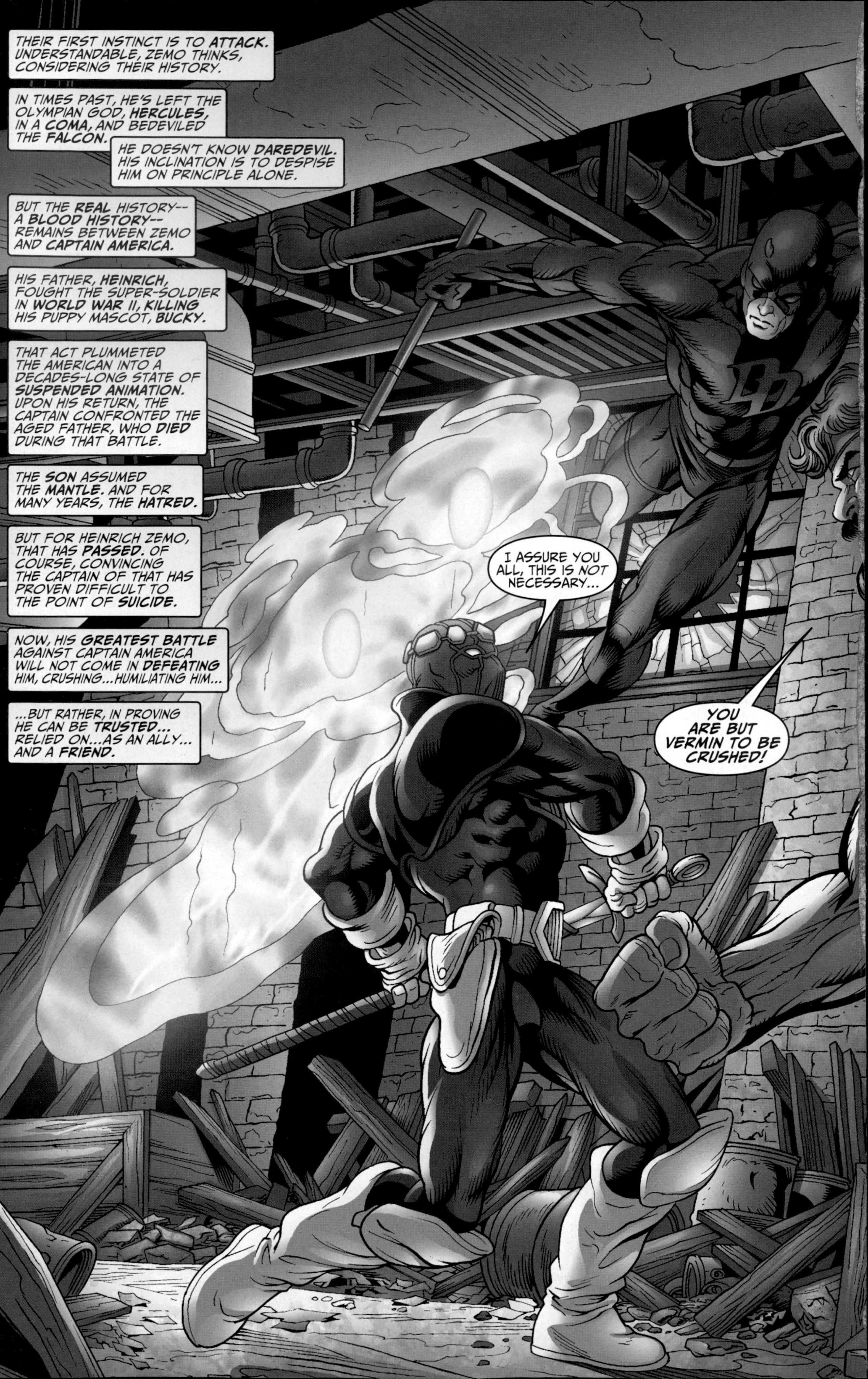
THEIR FIRST INSTINCT IS TO ATTACK. UNDERSTANDABLE, ZEMO THINKS, CONSIDERING THEIR HISTORY.
IN TIMES PAST, HE'S LEFT THE OLYMPIAN GOD, HERCULES, IN A COMA, AND BEDEVILED THE FALCON.
HE DOESN'T KNOW DAREDEVIL. HIS INCLINATION IS TO DESPISE HIM ON PRINCIPLE ALONE.
BUT THE REAL HISTORY-- A BLOOD HISTORY-- REMAINS BETWEEN ZEMO AND CAPTAIN AMERICA.
HIS FATHER, HEINRICH, FOUGHT THE SUPER-SOLDIER IN WORLD WAR II, KILLING HIS PUPPY MASCOT, BUCKY.
THAT ACT PLUMMETED THE AMERICAN INTO A DECADES-LONG STATE OF SUSPENDED ANIMATION. UPON HIS RETURN, THE CAPTAIN CONFRONTED THE AGED FATHER, WHO DIED DURING THAT BATTLE.
THE SON ASSUMED THE MANTLE. AND FOR MANY YEARS, THE HATRED.
BUT FOR HEINRICH ZEMO, THAT HAS PASSED. OF COURSE, CONVINCING THE CAPTAIN OF THAT HAS PROVEN DIFFICULT TO THE POINT OF SUICIDE.
NOW, HIS GREATEST BATTLE AGAINST CAPTAIN AMERICA WILL NOT COME IN DEFEATING HIM, CRUSHING...HUMILIATING HIM...
...BUT RATHER, IN PROVING HE CAN BE TRUSTED... RELIED ON...AS AN ALLY... AND A FRIEND.
I ASSURE YOU ALL, THIS IS NOT NECESSARY...
YOU ARE BUT VERMIN TO BE CRUSHED!

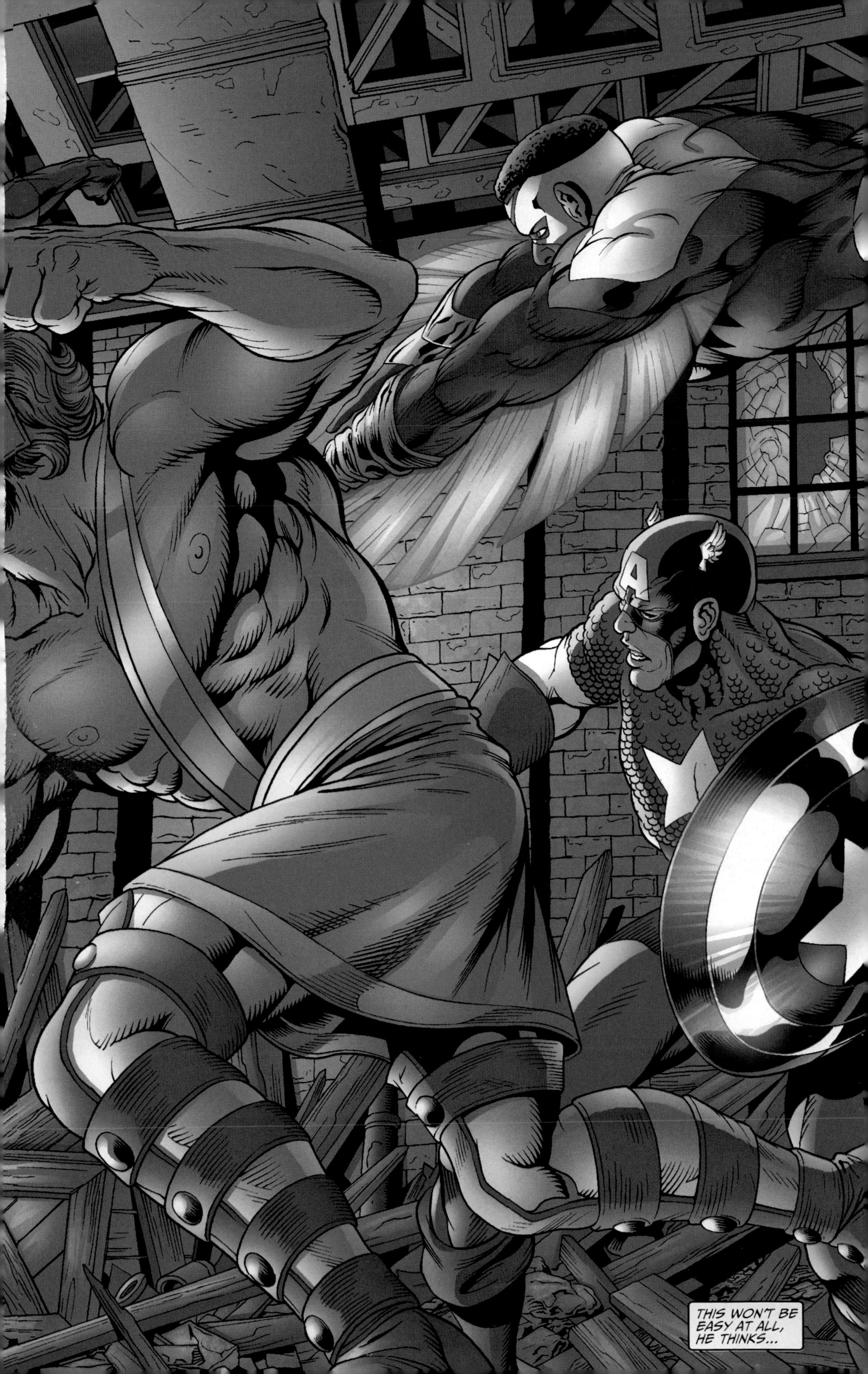
THIS WON'T BE EASY AT ALL, HE THINKS...

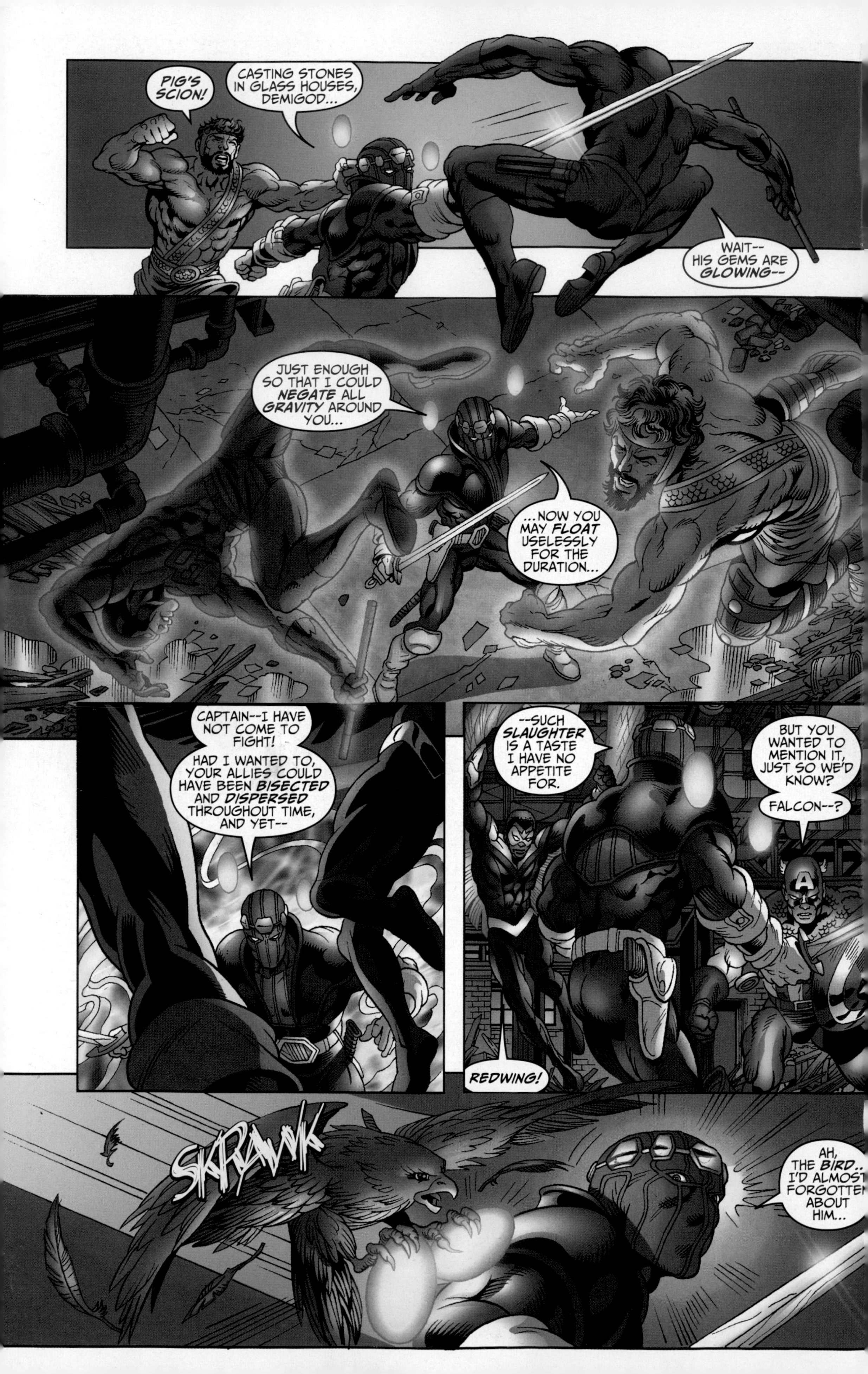
PIG'S SCION!
CASTING STONES IN GLASS HOUSES, DEMIGOD...
WAIT-- HIS GEMS ARE GLOWING--
JUST ENOUGH SO THAT I COULD NEGATE ALL GRAVITY AROUND YOU...
...NOW YOU MAY FLOAT USELESSLY FOR THE DURATION...
CAPTAIN--I HAVE NOT COME TO FIGHT!
HAD I WANTED TO, YOUR ALLIES COULD HAVE BEEN BISECTED AND DISPERSED THROUGHOUT TIME, AND YET--
--SUCH SLAUGHTER IS A TASTE I HAVE NO APPETITE FOR.
BUT YOU WANTED TO MENTION IT, JUST SO WE'D KNOW?
FALCON--?
REDWING!
SKRAWK
AH, THE BIRD.. I'D ALMOST FORGOTTEN ABOUT HIM...

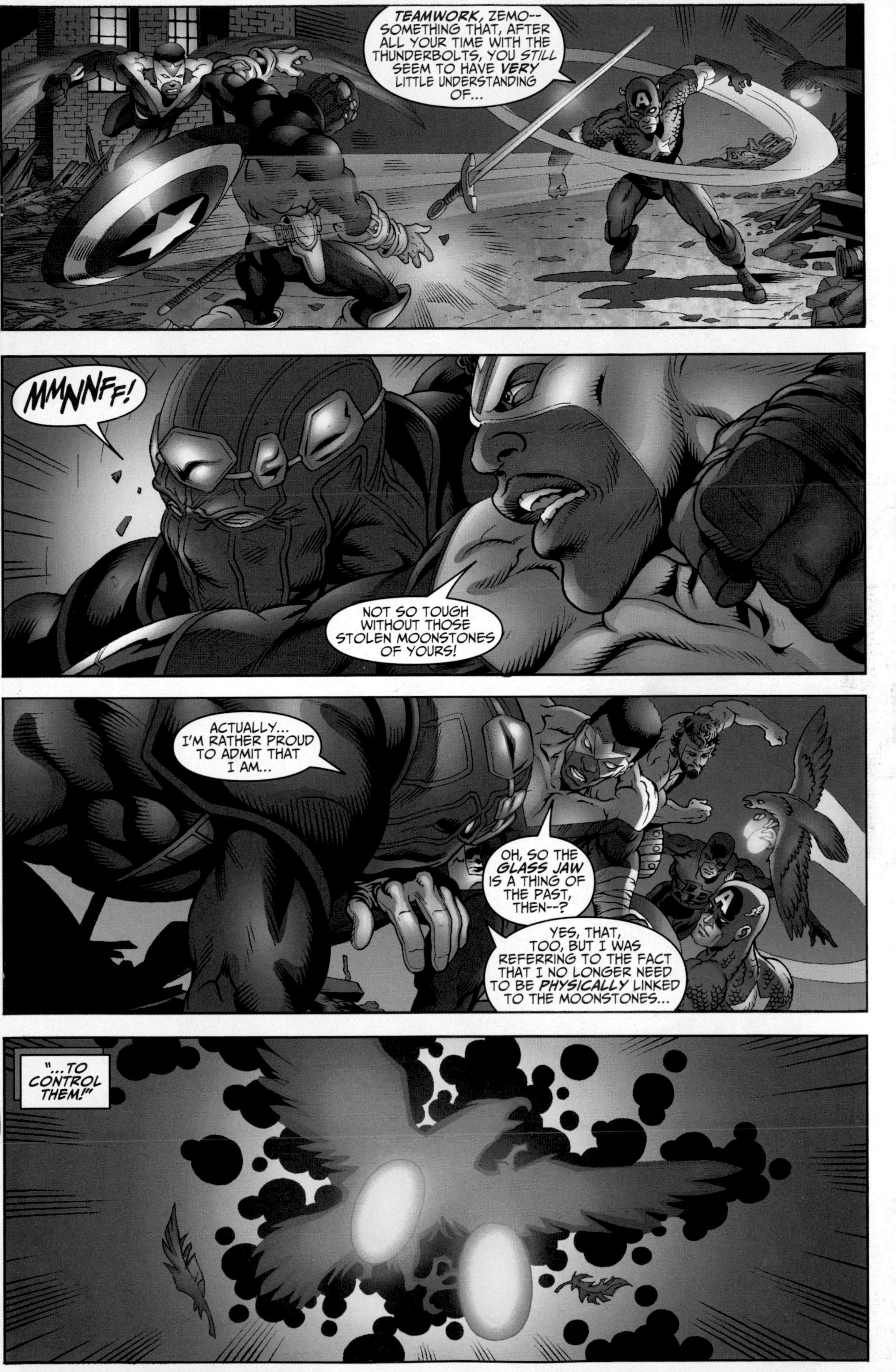

TEAMWORK, ZEMO-- SOMETHING THAT, AFTER ALL YOUR TIME WITH THE THUNDERBOLTS, YOU STILL SEEM TO HAVE VERY LITTLE UNDERSTANDING OF...
MMNNFF!
NOT SO TOUGH WITHOUT THOSE STOLEN MOONSTONES OF YOURS!
ACTUALLY... I'M RATHER PROUD TO ADMIT THAT I AM...
OH, SO THE GLASS JAW IS A THING OF THE PAST, THEN--?
YES, THAT, TOO, BUT I WAS REFERRING TO THE FACT THAT I NO LONGER NEED TO BE PHYSICALLY LINKED TO THE MOONSTONES...
"...TO CONTROL THEM!"

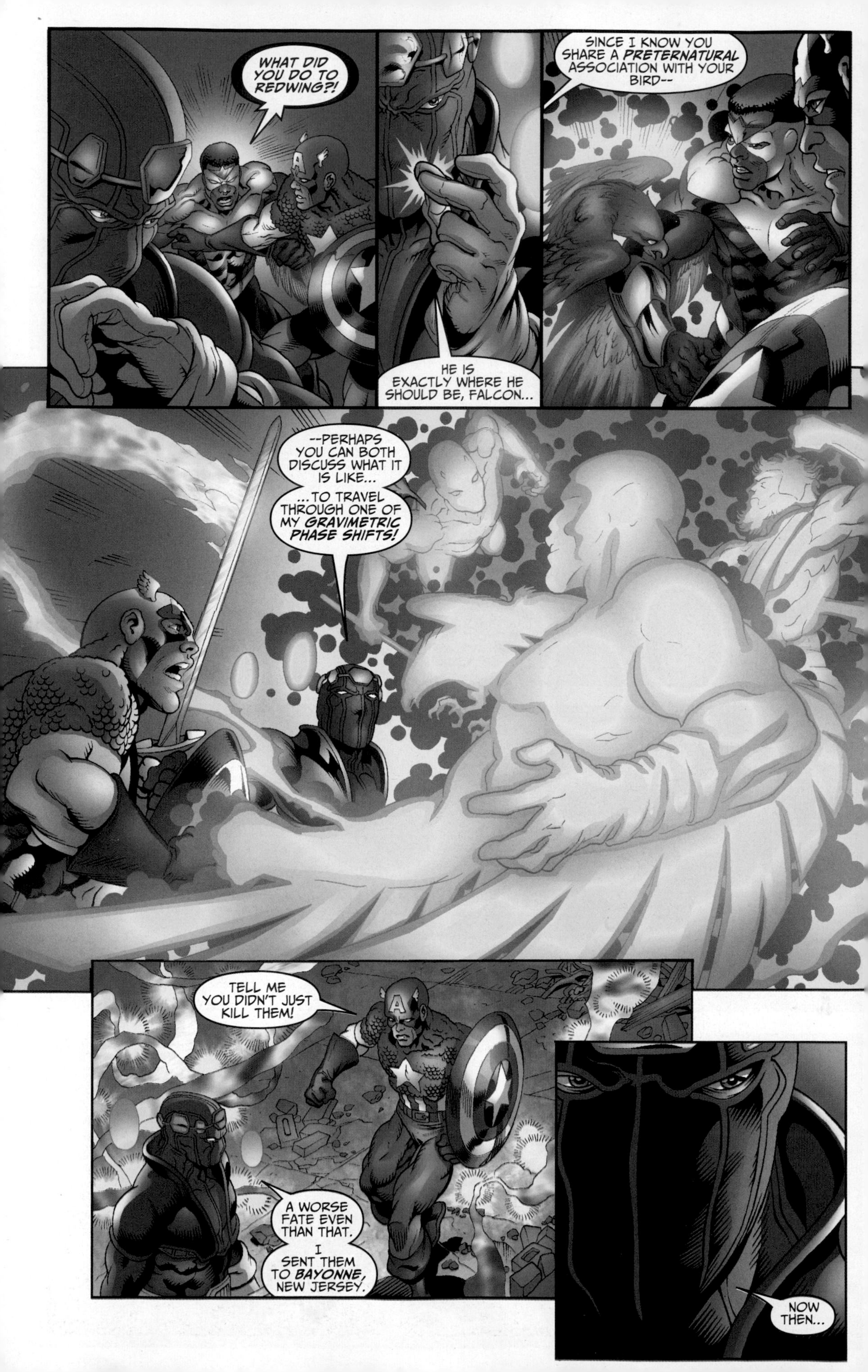
WHAT DID YOU DO TO REDWING?!
HE IS EXACTLY WHERE HE SHOULD BE, FALCON...
SINCE I KNOW YOU SHARE A PRETERNATURAL ASSOCIATION WITH YOUR BIRD--
--PERHAPS YOU CAN BOTH DISCUSS WHAT IT IS LIKE...
...TO TRAVEL THROUGH ONE OF MY GRAVIMETRIC PHASE SHIFTS!
TELL ME YOU DIDN'T JUST KILL THEM!
A WORSE FATE EVEN THAN THAT.
I SENT THEM TO BAYONNE, NEW JERSEY.
NOW THEN...

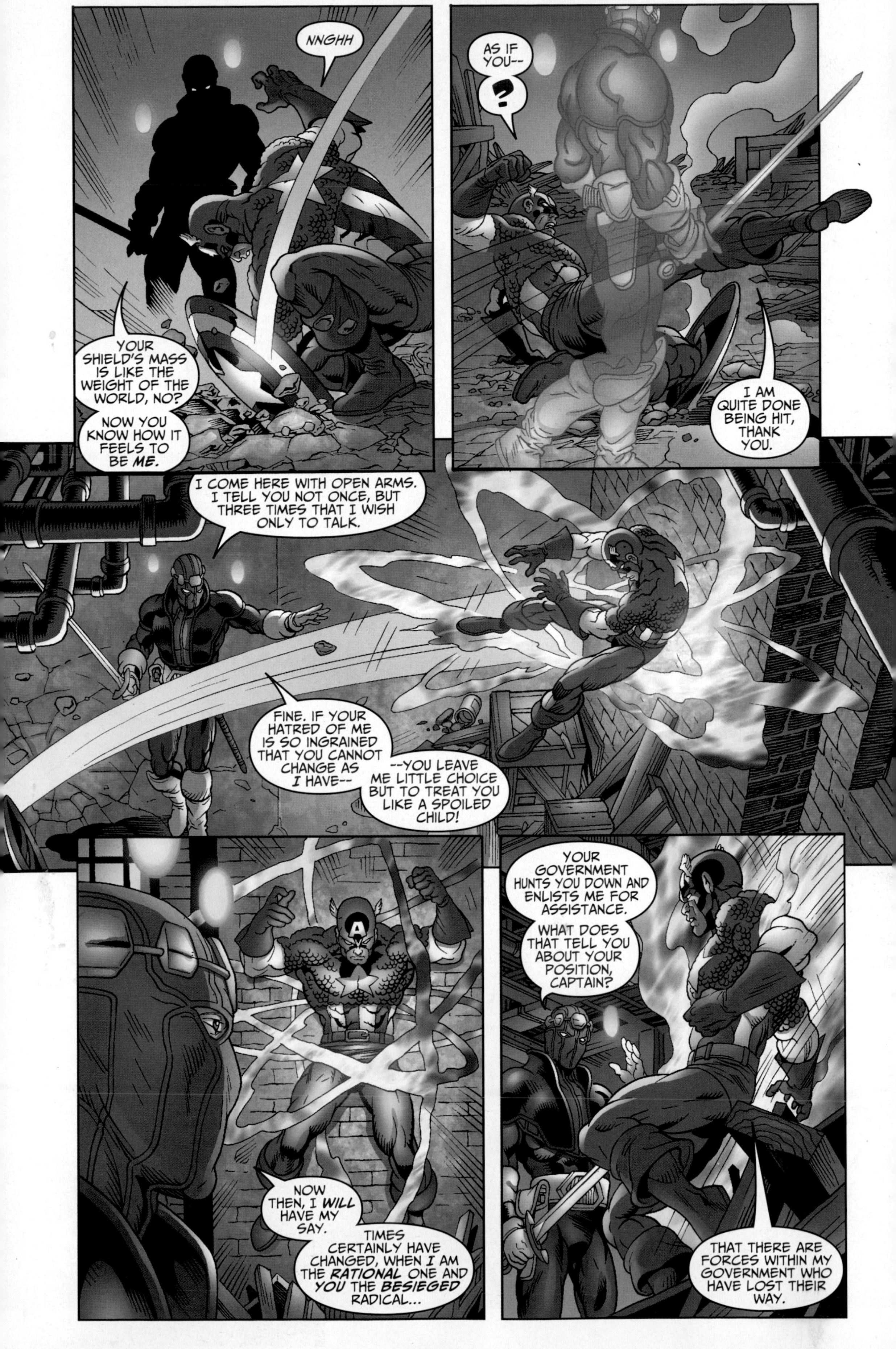
NNGHH
YOUR SHIELD'S MASS IS LIKE THE WEIGHT OF THE WORLD, NO?
NOW YOU KNOW HOW IT FEELS TO BE **ME.**
AS IF YOU--
?
I AM QUITE DONE BEING HIT, THANK YOU.
I COME HERE WITH OPEN ARMS. I TELL YOU NOT ONCE, BUT THREE TIMES THAT I WISH ONLY TO TALK.
FINE. IF YOUR HATRED OF ME IS SO INGRAINED THAT YOU CANNOT CHANGE AS *I HAVE--*
--YOU LEAVE ME LITTLE CHOICE BUT TO TREAT YOU LIKE A SPOILED CHILD!
NOW THEN, I ***WILL*** HAVE MY SAY.
TIMES CERTAINLY HAVE CHANGED, WHEN ***I*** AM THE ***RATIONAL*** ONE AND ***YOU*** THE ***BESIEGED*** RADICAL...
YOUR GOVERNMENT HUNTS YOU DOWN AND ENLISTS ME FOR ASSISTANCE.
WHAT DOES THAT TELL YOU ABOUT YOUR POSITION, CAPTAIN?
THAT THERE ARE FORCES WITHIN MY GOVERNMENT WHO HAVE LOST THEIR WAY.

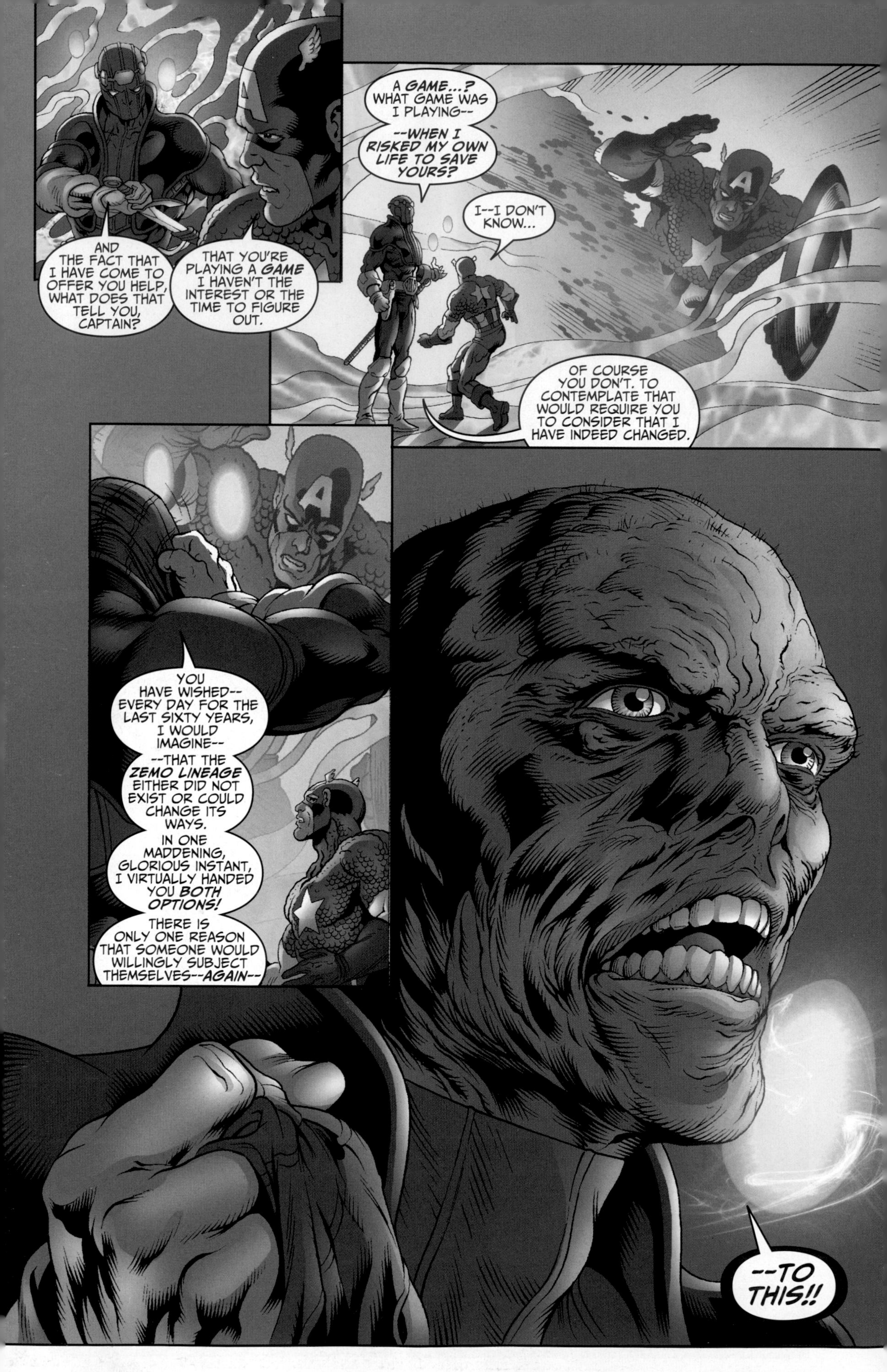
AND THE FACT THAT I HAVE COME TO OFFER YOU HELP, WHAT DOES THAT TELL YOU, CAPTAIN?
THAT YOU'RE PLAYING A GAME I HAVEN'T THE INTEREST OR THE TIME TO FIGURE OUT.
A GAME...? WHAT GAME WAS I PLAYING--
--WHEN I RISKED MY OWN LIFE TO SAVE YOURS?
I--I DON'T KNOW...
OF COURSE YOU DON'T. TO CONTEMPLATE THAT WOULD REQUIRE YOU TO CONSIDER THAT I HAVE INDEED CHANGED.
YOU HAVE WISHED-- EVERY DAY FOR THE LAST SIXTY YEARS, I WOULD IMAGINE--
--THAT THE ZEMO LINEAGE EITHER DID NOT EXIST OR COULD CHANGE ITS WAYS.
IN ONE MADDENING, GLORIOUS INSTANT, I VIRTUALLY HANDED YOU BOTH OPTIONS!
THERE IS ONLY ONE REASON THAT SOMEONE WOULD WILLINGLY SUBJECT THEMSELVES--AGAIN--
--TO THIS!!

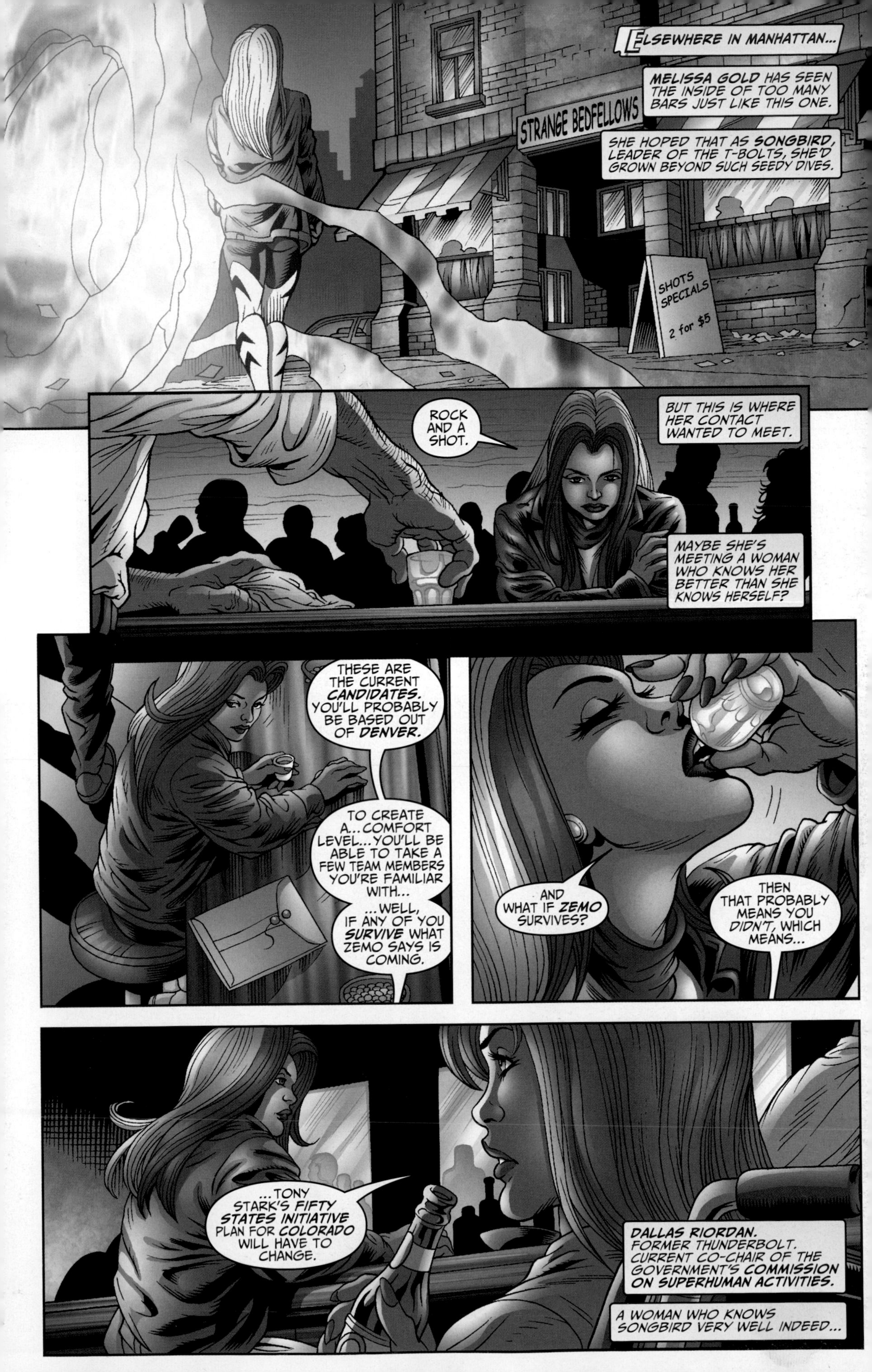
ELSEWHERE IN MANHATTAN...
MELISSA GOLD HAS SEEN THE INSIDE OF TOO MANY BARS JUST LIKE THIS ONE.
STRANGE BEDFELLOWS
SHE HOPED THAT AS SONGBIRD, LEADER OF THE T-BOLTS, SHE'D GROWN BEYOND SUCH SEEDY DIVES.
SHOTS SPECIALS 2 for $5
ROCK AND A SHOT.
BUT THIS IS WHERE HER CONTACT WANTED TO MEET.
MAYBE SHE'S MEETING A WOMAN WHO KNOWS HER BETTER THAN SHE KNOWS HERSELF?
THESE ARE THE CURRENT CANDIDATES. YOU'LL PROBABLY BE BASED OUT OF DENVER.
TO CREATE A...COMFORT LEVEL...YOU'LL BE ABLE TO TAKE A FEW TEAM MEMBERS YOU'RE FAMILIAR WITH...
...WELL, IF ANY OF YOU SURVIVE WHAT ZEMO SAYS IS COMING.
AND WHAT IF ZEMO SURVIVES?
THEN THAT PROBABLY MEANS YOU DIDN'T, WHICH MEANS...
...TONY STARK'S FIFTY STATES INITIATIVE PLAN FOR COLORADO WILL HAVE TO CHANGE.
DALLAS RIORDAN. FORMER THUNDERBOLT. CURRENT CO-CHAIR OF THE GOVERNMENT'S COMMISSION ON SUPERHUMAN ACTIVITIES.
A WOMAN WHO KNOWS SONGBIRD VERY WELL INDEED...

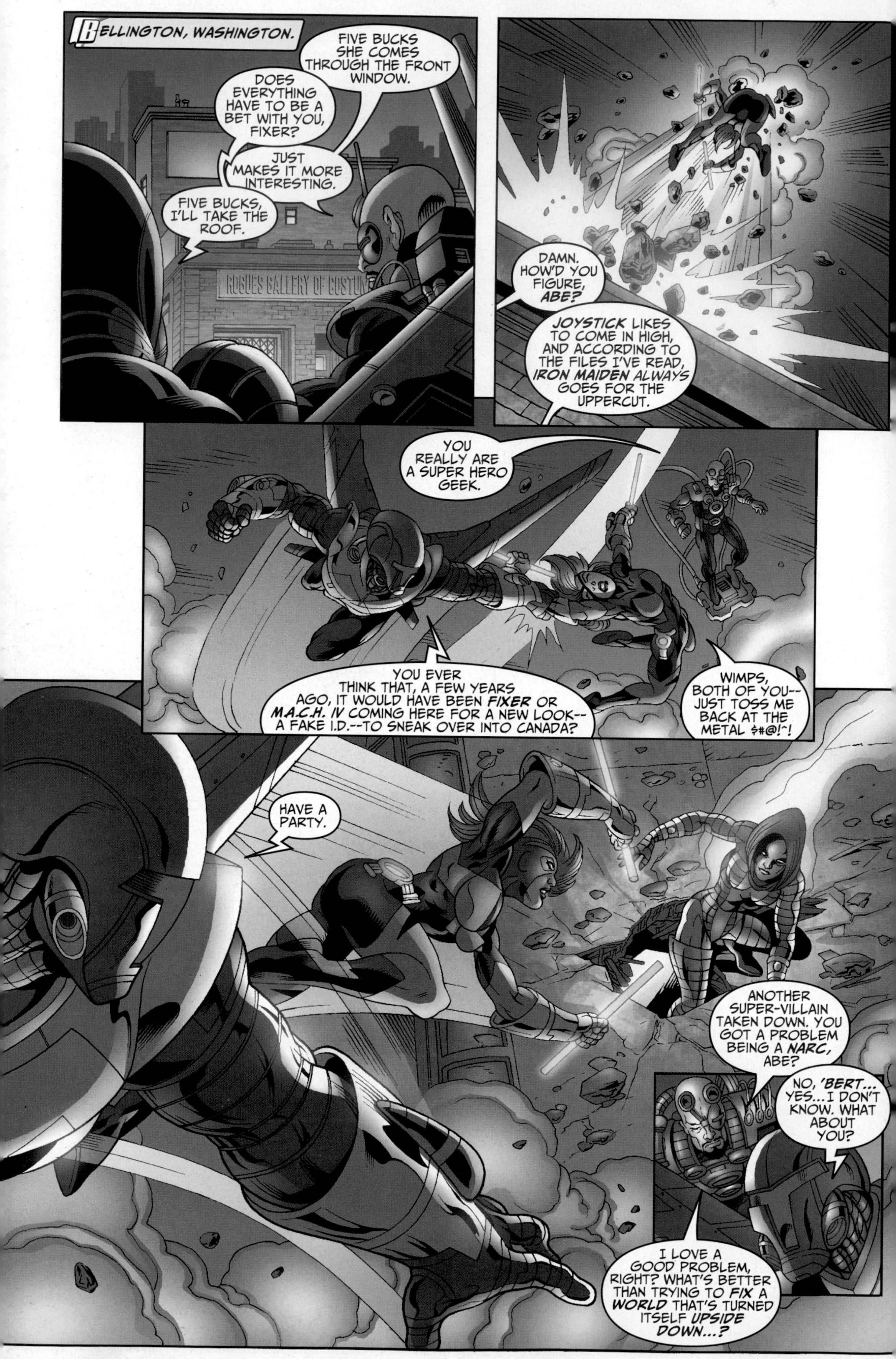
BELLINGTON, WASHINGTON.
FIVE BUCKS SHE COMES THROUGH THE FRONT WINDOW.
DOES EVERYTHING HAVE TO BE A BET WITH YOU, FIXER?
JUST MAKES IT MORE INTERESTING.
FIVE BUCKS, I'LL TAKE THE ROOF.
ROGUES GALLERY OF COSTU
DAMN. HOW'D YOU FIGURE, ABE?
JOYSTICK LIKES TO COME IN HIGH, AND ACCORDING TO THE FILES I'VE READ, IRON MAIDEN ALWAYS GOES FOR THE UPPERCUT.
YOU REALLY ARE A SUPER HERO GEEK.
YOU EVER THINK THAT, A FEW YEARS AGO, IT WOULD HAVE BEEN FIXER OR M.A.C.H. IV COMING HERE FOR A NEW LOOK-- A FAKE I.D.--TO SNEAK OVER INTO CANADA?
WIMPS, BOTH OF YOU-- JUST TOSS ME BACK AT THE METAL $#@!~!
HAVE A PARTY.
ANOTHER SUPER-VILLAIN TAKEN DOWN. YOU GOT A PROBLEM BEING A NARC, ABE?
NO, 'BERT... YES...I DON'T KNOW. WHAT ABOUT YOU?
I LOVE A GOOD PROBLEM, RIGHT? WHAT'S BETTER THAN TRYING TO FIX A WORLD THAT'S TURNED ITSELF UPSIDE DOWN...?

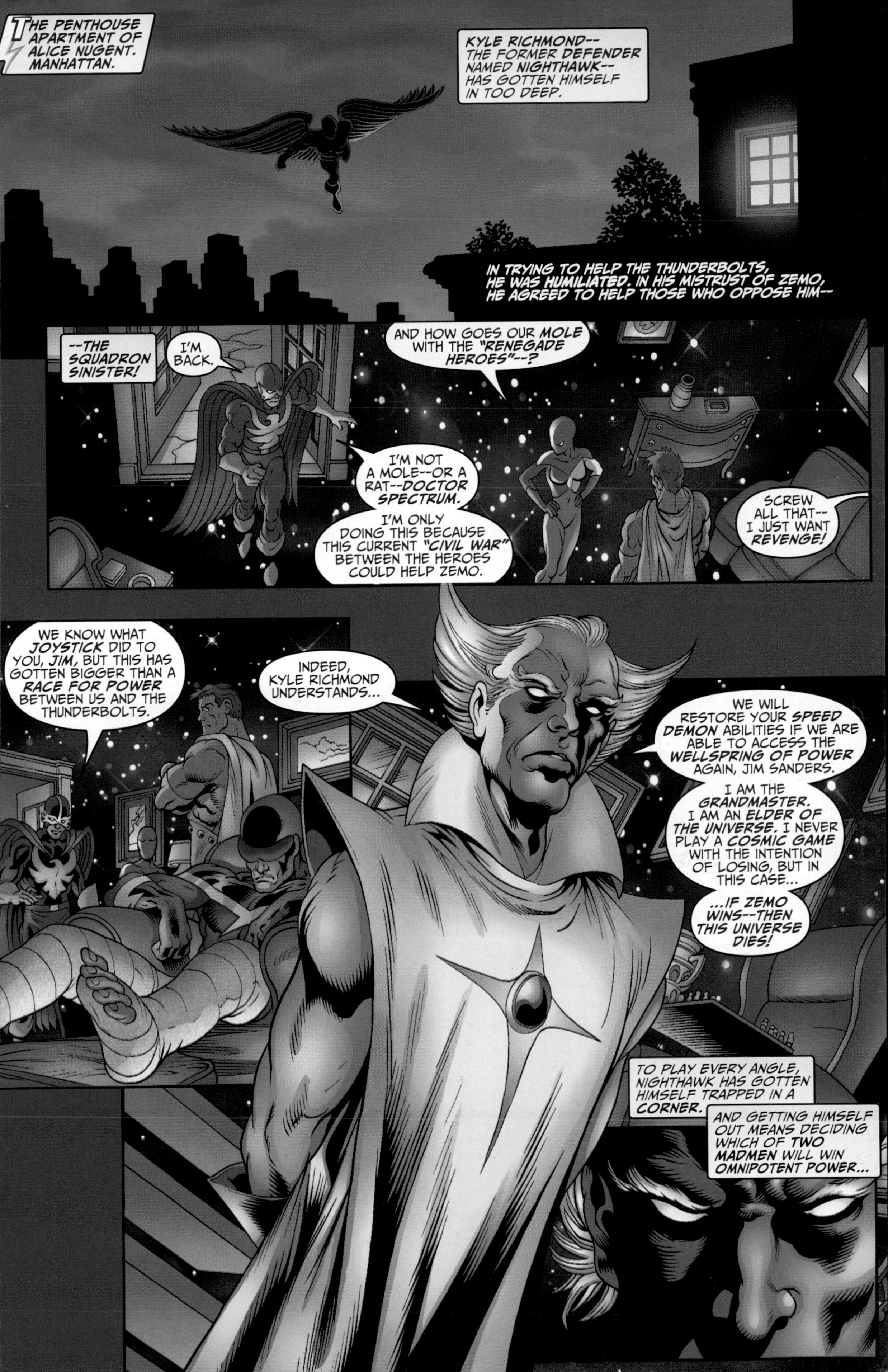
THE PENTHOUSE APARTMENT OF ALICE NUGENT. MANHATTAN.
KYLE RICHMOND-- THE FORMER DEFENDER NAMED NIGHTHAWK-- HAS GOTTEN HIMSELF IN TOO DEEP.
IN TRYING TO HELP THE THUNDERBOLTS, HE WAS HUMILIATED. IN HIS MISTRUST OF ZEMO, HE AGREED TO HELP THOSE WHO OPPOSE HIM--
--THE SQUADRON SINISTER!
I'M BACK.
AND HOW GOES OUR MOLE WITH THE "RENEGADE HEROES"--?
I'M NOT A MOLE--OR A RAT--DOCTOR SPECTRUM.
I'M ONLY DOING THIS BECAUSE THIS CURRENT "CIVIL WAR" BETWEEN THE HEROES COULD HELP ZEMO.
SCREW ALL THAT-- I JUST WANT REVENGE!
WE KNOW WHAT JOYSTICK DID TO YOU, JIM, BUT THIS HAS GOTTEN BIGGER THAN A RACE FOR POWER BETWEEN US AND THE THUNDERBOLTS.
INDEED, KYLE RICHMOND UNDERSTANDS...
WE WILL RESTORE YOUR SPEED DEMON ABILITIES IF WE ARE ABLE TO ACCESS THE WELLSPRING OF POWER AGAIN, JIM SANDERS.
I AM THE GRANDMASTER. I AM AN ELDER OF THE UNIVERSE. I NEVER PLAY A COSMIC GAME WITH THE INTENTION OF LOSING, BUT IN THIS CASE...
...IF ZEMO WINS--THEN THIS UNIVERSE DIES!
TO PLAY EVERY ANGLE, NIGHTHAWK HAS GOTTEN HIMSELF TRAPPED IN A CORNER.
AND GETTING HIMSELF OUT MEANS DECIDING WHICH OF TWO MADMEN WILL WIN OMNIPOTENT POWER...

THE BAXTER BUILDING, HEADQUARTERS OF THE FANTASTIC FOUR.

THE SEEPAGE OF AMBIENT ENERGY CONTINUES TO REGISTER AT UNACCEPTABLE LEVELS.

RADIOACTIVE MAN IS RIGHT. WE STILL HAVEN'T FOUND THE WAY TO COMPLETELY SEAL THE *PORTAL.*

WE ARE PHASING THE FACILITY BETWEEN DISTINCT SPATIAL PLANES, *HANK.* CAN WE EXPECT TO SCREEN OUT ALL AMBIENT ENERGIES?

THE MAIN QUESTION, *REED,* IS, WOULD THAT ENDANGER ANY OF THE *"GUESTS"* WHO WILL BE IN *"RESIDENCE"--?*

DR. CHEN LU, THE RADIOACTIVE MAN, LISTENS TO *HANK PYM* AND *REED RICHARDS,* THE HEROES NAMED *YELLOWJACKET* AND *MR. FANTASTIC.*

LISTENS TO THEIR EUPHEMISMS, THEIR CLINICAL DETACHMENT TO THEIR SITUATION.

LISTENS...UNTIL HE'S HAD ENOUGH...

AS A *CHINESE NATIONAL* WITH A LONG HISTORY OF OPPOSING THIS COUNTRY'S GOVERNMENT--

--I FIND IT RATHER IRONIC THAT THE *BRIGHTEST MINDS* OF THE UNITED STATES...THEIR *ELECTED LEADERS...*

...ARE CREATING A SOCIAL CLIMATE SO *SIMILAR* TO THE ONES YOU HAVE SO LONG RAILED *AGAINST.*

THAT'S A BIT OF AN EXAGGERATION, DR. CHEN--

CAPTAIN AMERICA.

EXCUSE ME?

YOU INTEND TO *APPREHEND* AND *INCARCERATE* CAPTAIN AMERICA.

SAY *THOSE* WORDS ALOUD... CONSIDER THEIR *TRUE* IMPLICATION...

...AND THEN CLAIM *MY* WORDS HAVE NO MERIT...

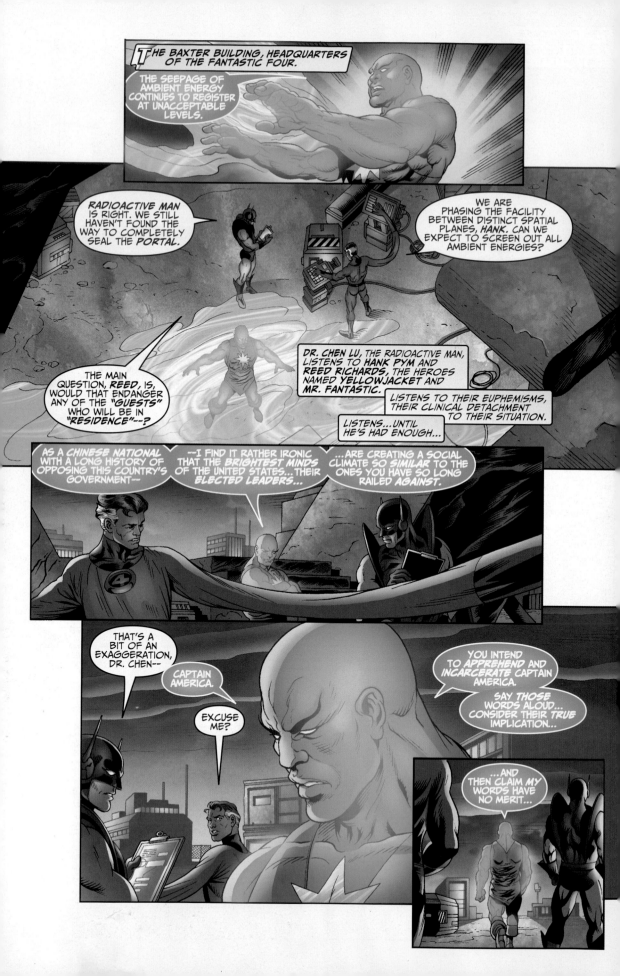

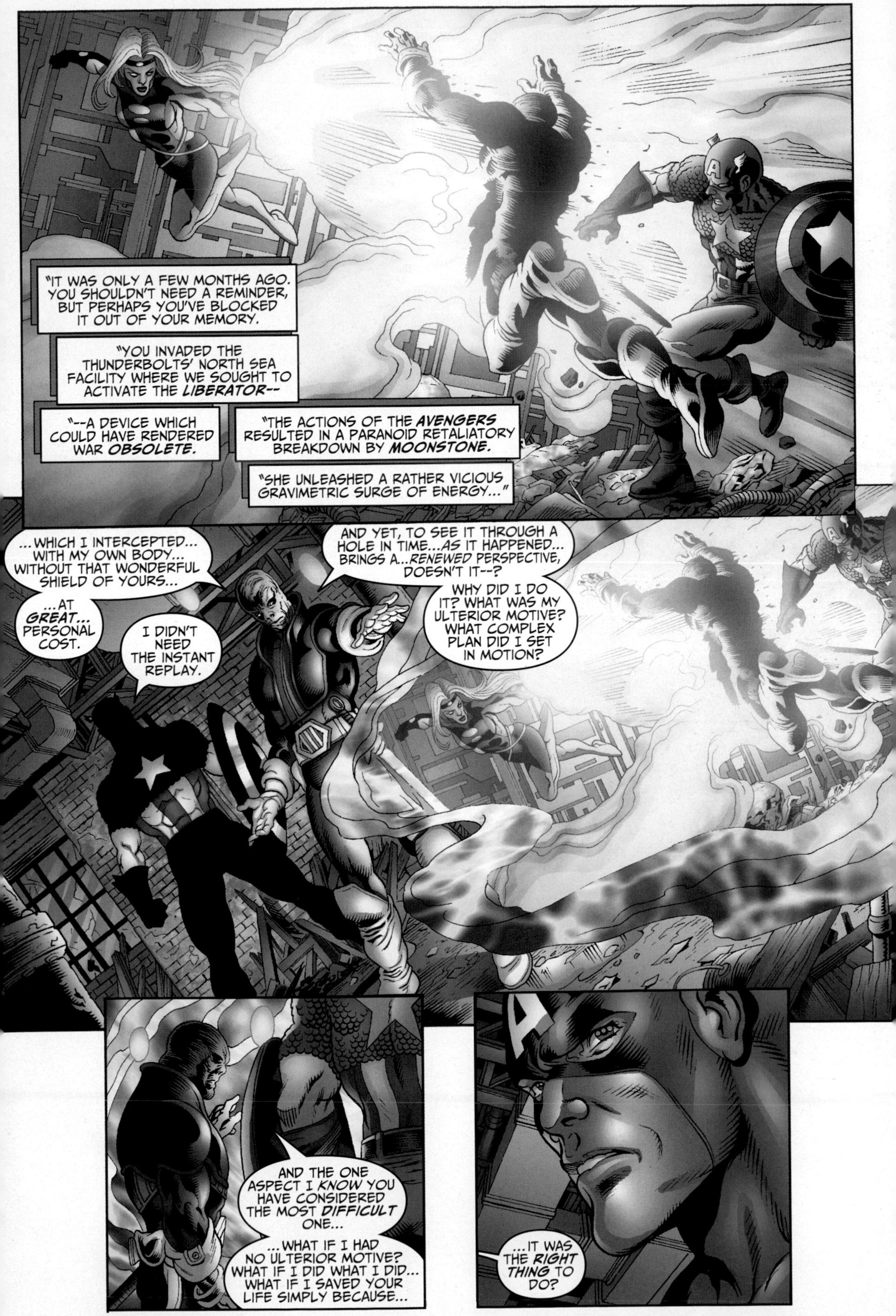
"IT WAS ONLY A FEW MONTHS AGO. YOU SHOULDN'T NEED A REMINDER, BUT PERHAPS YOU'VE BLOCKED IT OUT OF YOUR MEMORY.
"YOU INVADED THE THUNDERBOLTS' NORTH SEA FACILITY WHERE WE SOUGHT TO ACTIVATE THE LIBERATOR--
"--A DEVICE WHICH COULD HAVE RENDERED WAR OBSOLETE.
"THE ACTIONS OF THE AVENGERS RESULTED IN A PARANOID RETALIATORY BREAKDOWN BY MOONSTONE.
"SHE UNLEASHED A RATHER VICIOUS GRAVIMETRIC SURGE OF ENERGY..."
...WHICH I INTERCEPTED... WITH MY OWN BODY... WITHOUT THAT WONDERFUL SHIELD OF YOURS...
...AT GREAT... PERSONAL COST.
I DIDN'T NEED THE INSTANT REPLAY.
AND YET, TO SEE IT THROUGH A HOLE IN TIME...AS IT HAPPENED... BRINGS A...RENEWED PERSPECTIVE, DOESN'T IT--?
WHY DID I DO IT? WHAT WAS MY ULTERIOR MOTIVE? WHAT COMPLEX PLAN DID I SET IN MOTION?
AND THE ONE ASPECT I KNOW YOU HAVE CONSIDERED THE MOST DIFFICULT ONE...
...WHAT IF I HAD NO ULTERIOR MOTIVE? WHAT IF I DID WHAT I DID... WHAT IF I SAVED YOUR LIFE SIMPLY BECAUSE...
...IT WAS THE RIGHT THING TO DO?

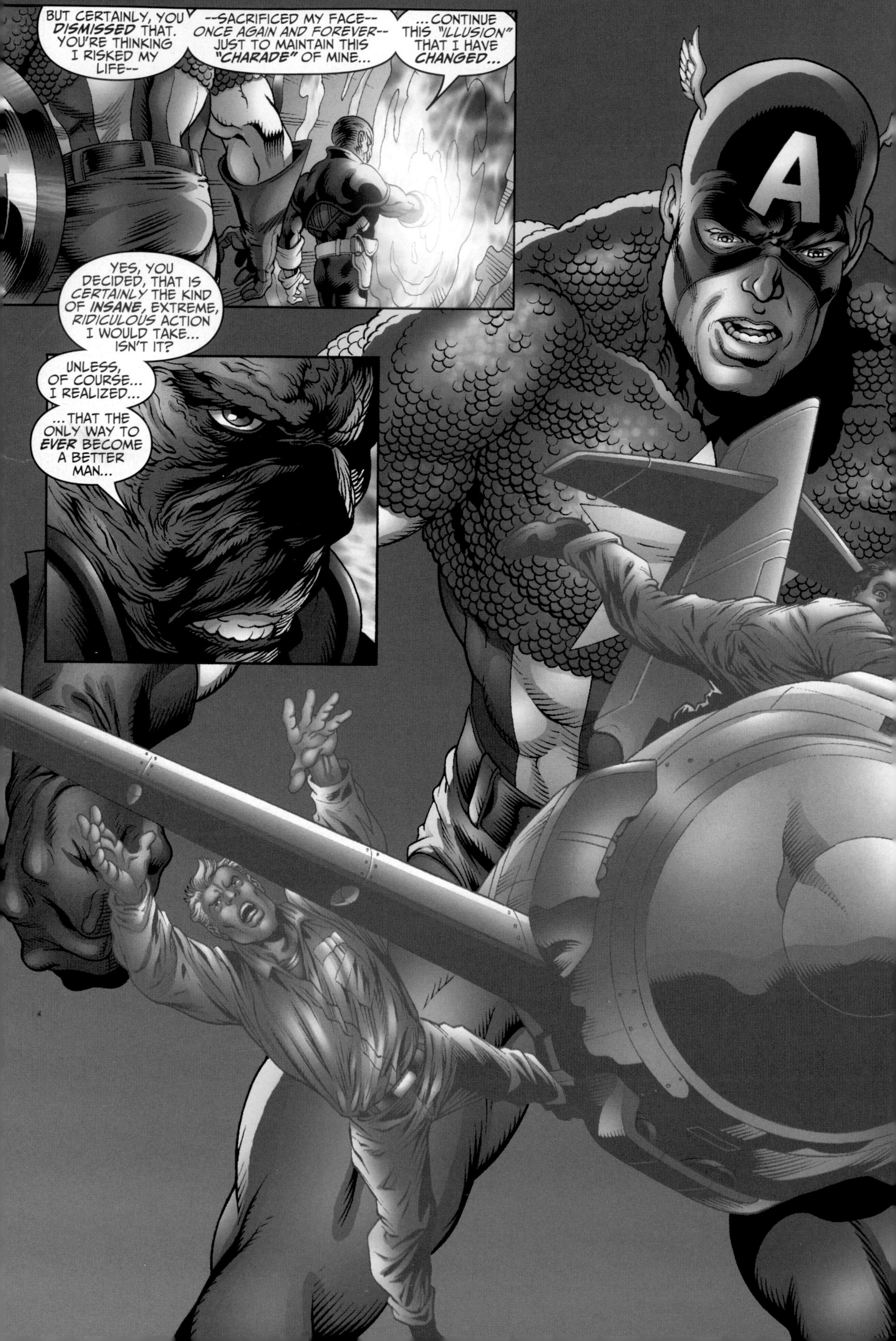
BUT CERTAINLY, YOU DISMISSED THAT. YOU'RE THINKING I RISKED MY LIFE--
--SACRIFICED MY FACE-- ONCE AGAIN AND FOREVER-- JUST TO MAINTAIN THIS "CHARADE" OF MINE...
...CONTINUE THIS "ILLUSION" THAT I HAVE CHANGED...
YES, YOU DECIDED, THAT IS CERTAINLY THE KIND OF INSANE, EXTREME, RIDICULOUS ACTION I WOULD TAKE... ISN'T IT?
UNLESS, OF COURSE... I REALIZED...
...THAT THE ONLY WAY TO EVER BECOME A BETTER MAN...

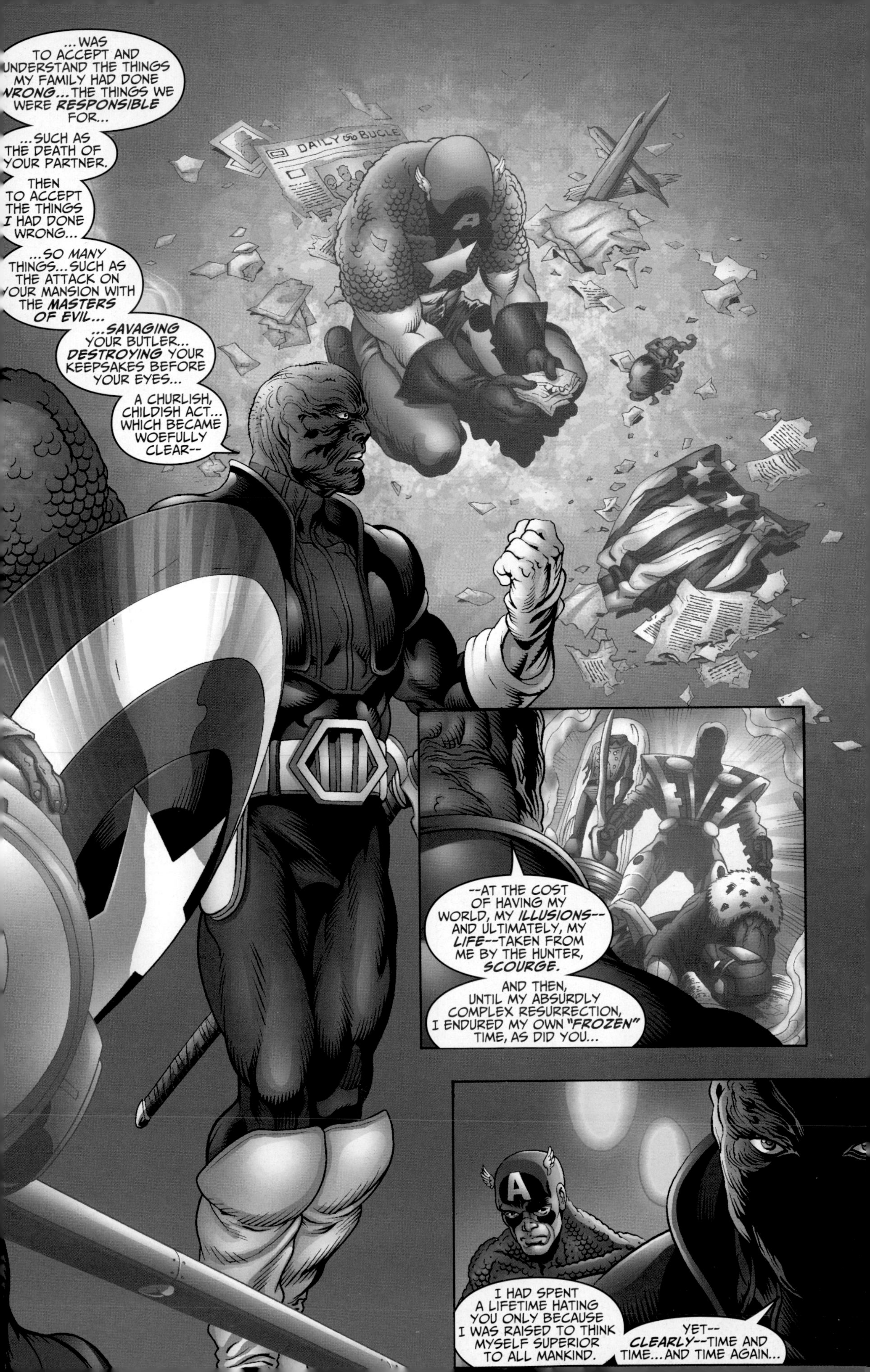
...WAS TO ACCEPT AND UNDERSTAND THE THINGS MY FAMILY HAD DONE WRONG... THE THINGS WE WERE RESPONSIBLE FOR...
...SUCH AS THE DEATH OF YOUR PARTNER.
THEN TO ACCEPT THE THINGS I HAD DONE WRONG...
...SO MANY THINGS... SUCH AS THE ATTACK ON YOUR MANSION WITH THE MASTERS OF EVIL...
...SAVAGING YOUR BUTLER... DESTROYING YOUR KEEPSAKES BEFORE YOUR EYES...
A CHURLISH, CHILDISH ACT... WHICH BECAME WOEFULLY CLEAR--
DAILY BUGLE
--AT THE COST OF HAVING MY WORLD, MY ILLUSIONS-- AND ULTIMATELY, MY LIFE--TAKEN FROM ME BY THE HUNTER, SCOURGE.
AND THEN, UNTIL MY ABSURDLY COMPLEX RESURRECTION, I ENDURED MY OWN "FROZEN" TIME, AS DID YOU...
I HAD SPENT A LIFETIME HATING YOU ONLY BECAUSE I WAS RAISED TO THINK MYSELF SUPERIOR TO ALL MANKIND.
YET-- CLEARLY--TIME AND TIME... AND TIME AGAIN...

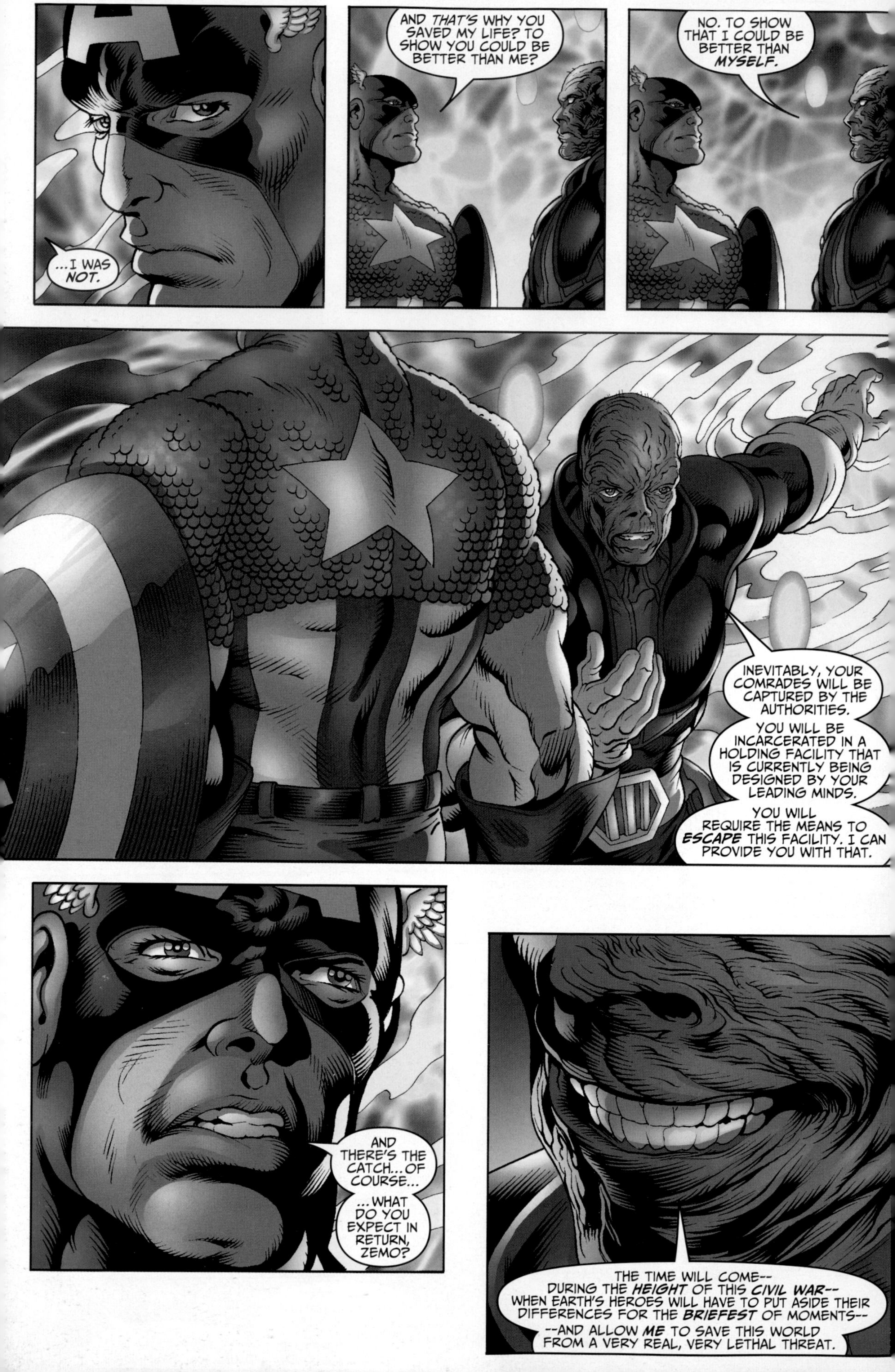
...I WAS *NOT.*
AND *THAT'S* WHY YOU SAVED MY LIFE? TO SHOW YOU COULD BE BETTER THAN ME?
NO. TO SHOW THAT I COULD BE BETTER THAN *MYSELF.*
INEVITABLY, YOUR COMRADES WILL BE CAPTURED BY THE AUTHORITIES.
YOU WILL BE INCARCERATED IN A HOLDING FACILITY THAT IS CURRENTLY BEING DESIGNED BY YOUR LEADING MINDS.
YOU WILL REQUIRE THE MEANS TO *ESCAPE* THIS FACILITY. I CAN PROVIDE YOU WITH THAT.
AND THERE'S THE CATCH... OF COURSE...
...WHAT DO YOU EXPECT IN RETURN, ZEMO?
THE TIME WILL COME-- DURING THE *HEIGHT* OF THIS *CIVIL WAR*-- WHEN EARTH'S HEROES WILL HAVE TO PUT ASIDE THEIR DIFFERENCES FOR THE *BRIEFEST* OF MOMENTS--
--AND ALLOW *ME* TO SAVE THIS WORLD FROM A VERY REAL, VERY LETHAL THREAT.

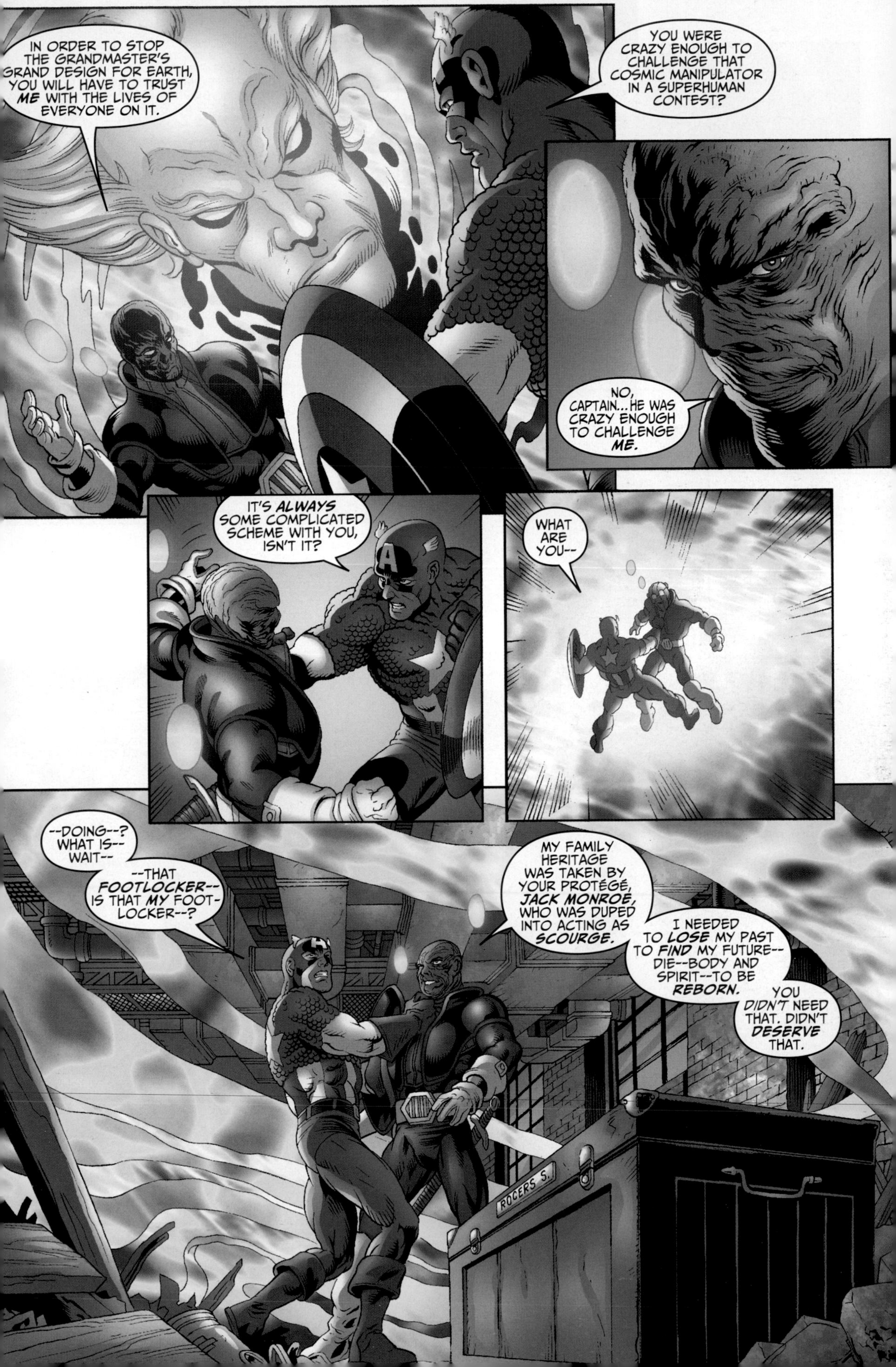

IN ORDER TO STOP THE GRANDMASTER'S GRAND DESIGN FOR EARTH, YOU WILL HAVE TO TRUST *ME* WITH THE LIVES OF EVERYONE ON IT.
YOU WERE CRAZY ENOUGH TO CHALLENGE THAT COSMIC MANIPULATOR IN A SUPERHUMAN CONTEST?
NO, CAPTAIN... HE WAS CRAZY ENOUGH TO CHALLENGE *ME.*
IT'S *ALWAYS* SOME COMPLICATED SCHEME WITH YOU, ISN'T IT?
WHAT ARE YOU--
--DOING--? WHAT IS-- WAIT--
--THAT *FOOTLOCKER*-- IS THAT *MY* FOOT-LOCKER--?
MY FAMILY HERITAGE WAS TAKEN BY YOUR PROTÉGÉ, *JACK MONROE*, WHO WAS DUPED INTO ACTING AS *SCOURGE.*
I NEEDED TO *LOSE* MY PAST TO *FIND* MY FUTURE-- DIE--BODY AND SPIRIT--TO BE *REBORN.*
YOU *DIDN'T* NEED THAT. DIDN'T *DESERVE* THAT.
ROGERS S.

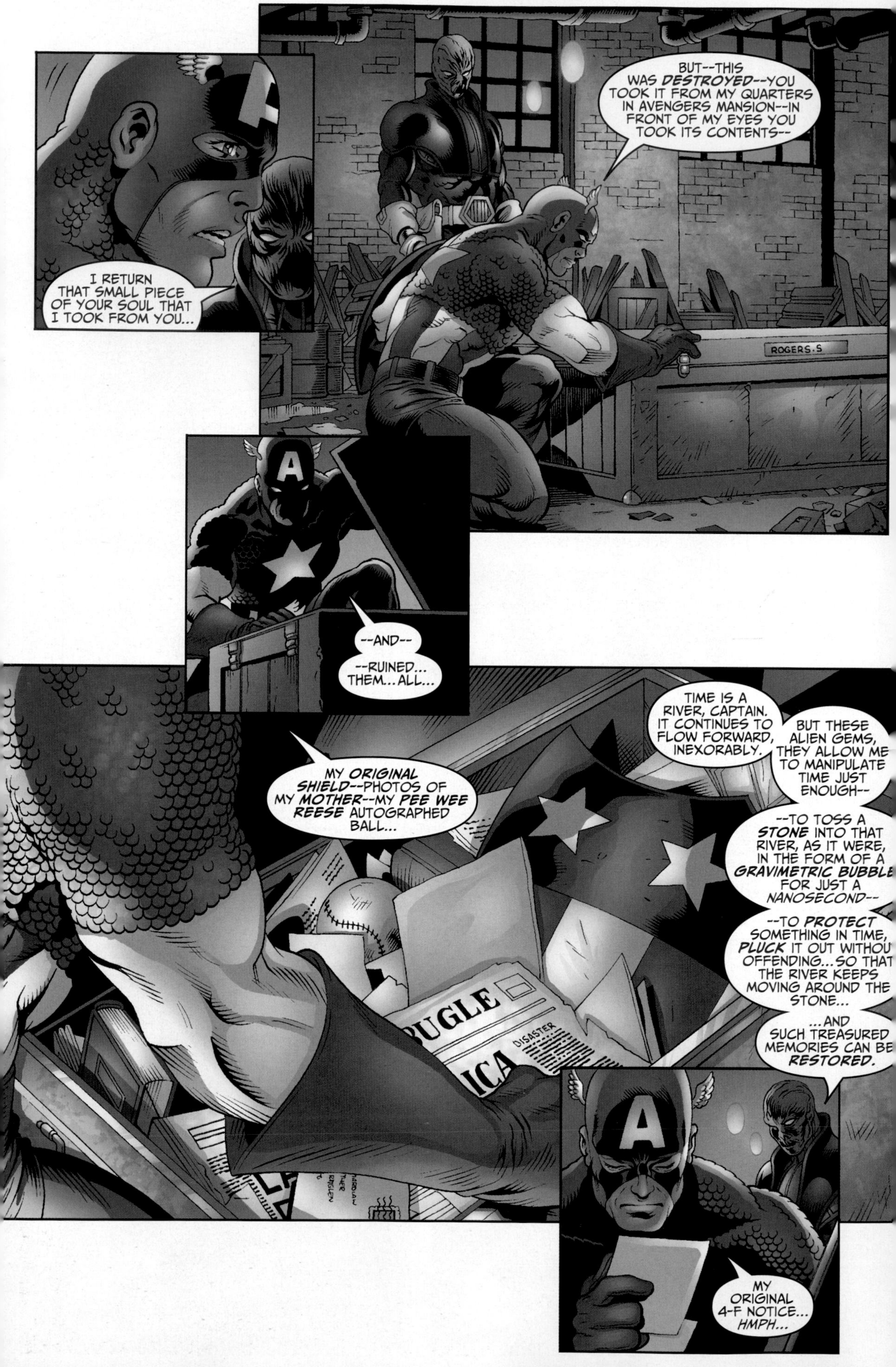
I RETURN THAT SMALL PIECE OF YOUR SOUL THAT I TOOK FROM YOU...
BUT--THIS WAS **DESTROYED**--YOU TOOK IT FROM MY QUARTERS IN AVENGERS MANSION--IN FRONT OF MY EYES YOU TOOK ITS CONTENTS--
ROGERS.S
--AND--
--RUINED... THEM...ALL...
MY **ORIGINAL SHIELD**--PHOTOS OF MY **MOTHER**--MY **PEE WEE REESE** AUTOGRAPHED BALL...
BUGLE
DISASTER
TIME IS A RIVER, CAPTAIN. IT CONTINUES TO FLOW FORWARD, INEXORABLY.
BUT THESE ALIEN GEMS, THEY ALLOW ME TO MANIPULATE TIME JUST ENOUGH--
--TO TOSS A **STONE** INTO THAT RIVER, AS IT WERE, IN THE FORM OF A **GRAVIMETRIC BUBBL** FOR JUST A *NANOSECOND*--
--TO **PROTECT** SOMETHING IN TIME, **PLUCK** IT OUT WITHOU OFFENDING...SO THAT THE RIVER KEEPS MOVING AROUND THE STONE...
...AND SUCH TREASURED MEMORIES CAN BE **RESTORED**.
MY ORIGINAL 4-F NOTICE... **HMPH...**

WITH THESE GEMSTONES, CAPTAIN, I COULD *RULE THE WORLD.*

IT IS AN ELECTRONIC SPATIAL INTERFACE THAT WILL ENABLE YOU TO *ESCAPE* THE *CAGE* THAT AWAITS YOU.

HOW CAN YOU BE SO *CERTAIN* I'LL BE CAUGHT?

TO PROVE YOUR CAUSE JUST, YOU WOULD *WANT* TO BE CAUGHT ANYWAY, *RIGHT...?*

I CHOOSE *NOT* TO.

I AM *NOT* YOUR ENEMY ANYMORE.

THIS *KEY*-- FIGURATIVELY AND LITERALLY-- PROVES THAT.

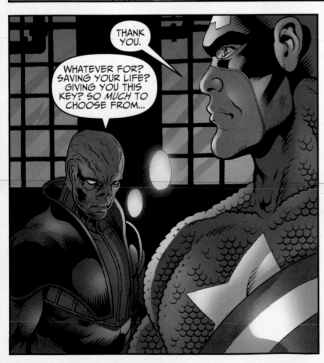

THANK YOU.

WHATEVER FOR? SAVING YOUR LIFE? GIVING YOU THIS KEY? SO *MUCH* TO CHOOSE FROM...

THANK YOU FOR GIVING ME *HOPE...*

...THAT THE *STRUGGLE* IS WORTH THE *COST...*

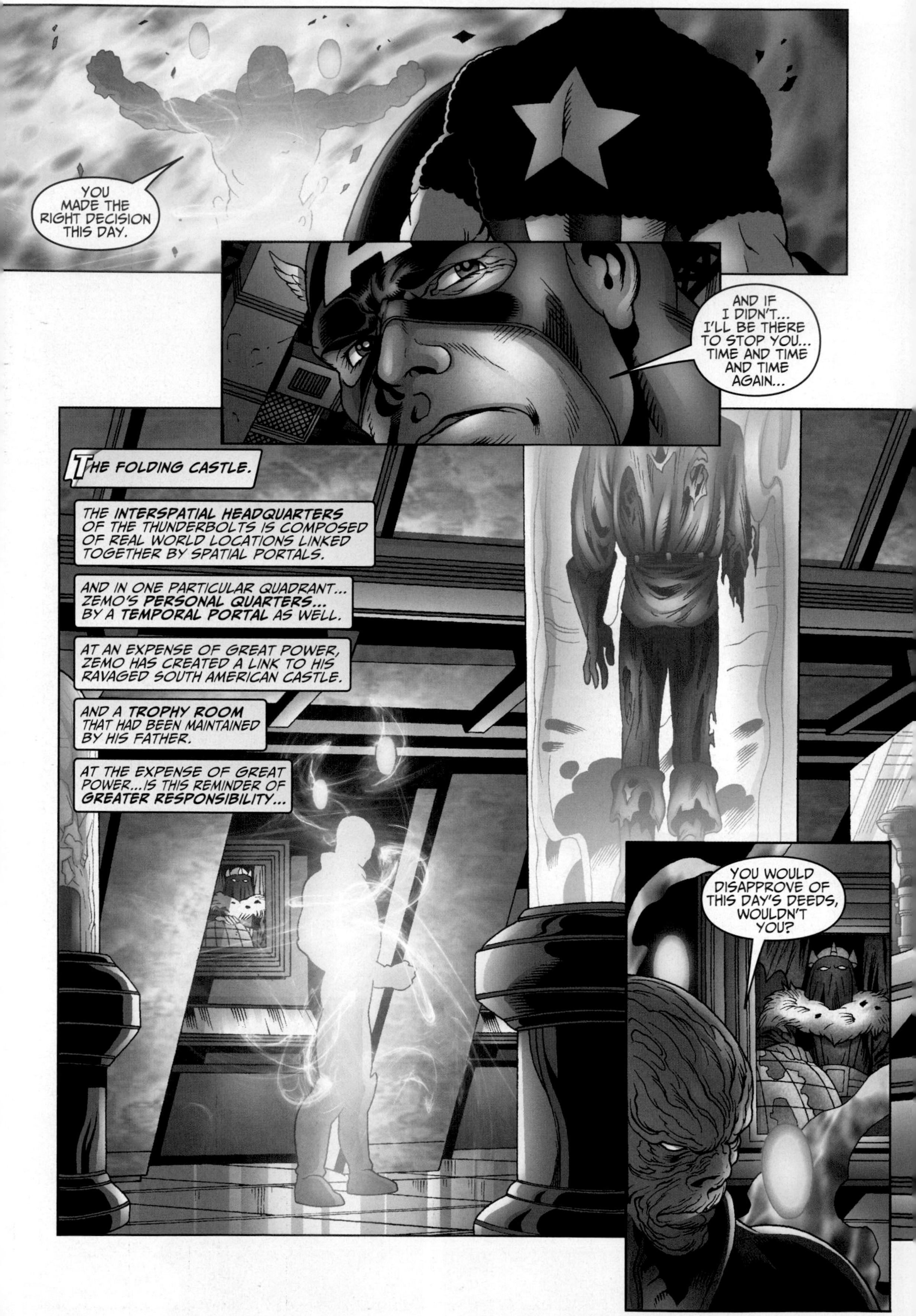

YOU MADE THE RIGHT DECISION THIS DAY.
AND IF I DIDN'T... I'LL BE THERE TO STOP YOU... TIME AND TIME AND TIME AGAIN...
THE FOLDING CASTLE.
THE INTERSPATIAL HEADQUARTERS OF THE THUNDERBOLTS IS COMPOSED OF REAL WORLD LOCATIONS LINKED TOGETHER BY SPATIAL PORTALS.
AND IN ONE PARTICULAR QUADRANT... ZEMO'S PERSONAL QUARTERS... BY A TEMPORAL PORTAL AS WELL.
AT AN EXPENSE OF GREAT POWER, ZEMO HAS CREATED A LINK TO HIS RAVAGED SOUTH AMERICAN CASTLE.
AND A TROPHY ROOM THAT HAD BEEN MAINTAINED BY HIS FATHER.
AT THE EXPENSE OF GREAT POWER...IS THIS REMINDER OF GREATER RESPONSIBILITY...
YOU WOULD DISAPPROVE OF THIS DAY'S DEEDS, WOULDN'T YOU?

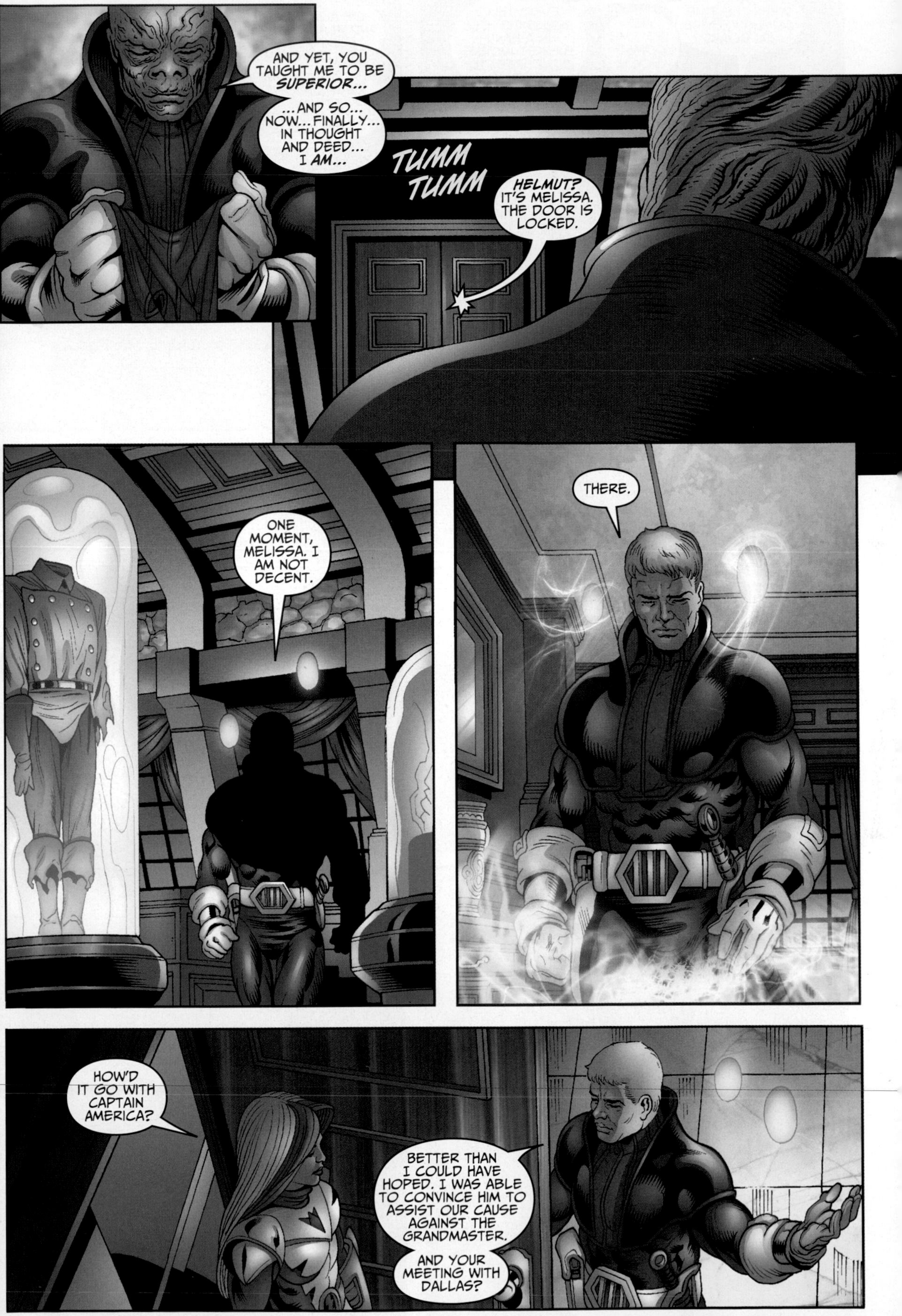
AND YET, YOU TAUGHT ME TO BE *SUPERIOR...*
...AND SO... NOW...FINALLY... IN THOUGHT AND DEED... I *AM...*
TUMM TUMM
*HELMUT?* IT'S MELISSA. THE DOOR IS LOCKED.
ONE MOMENT, MELISSA. I AM NOT DECENT.
THERE.
HOW'D IT GO WITH CAPTAIN AMERICA?
BETTER THAN I COULD HAVE HOPED. I WAS ABLE TO CONVINCE HIM TO ASSIST OUR CAUSE AGAINST THE GRANDMASTER.
AND YOUR MEETING WITH DALLAS?

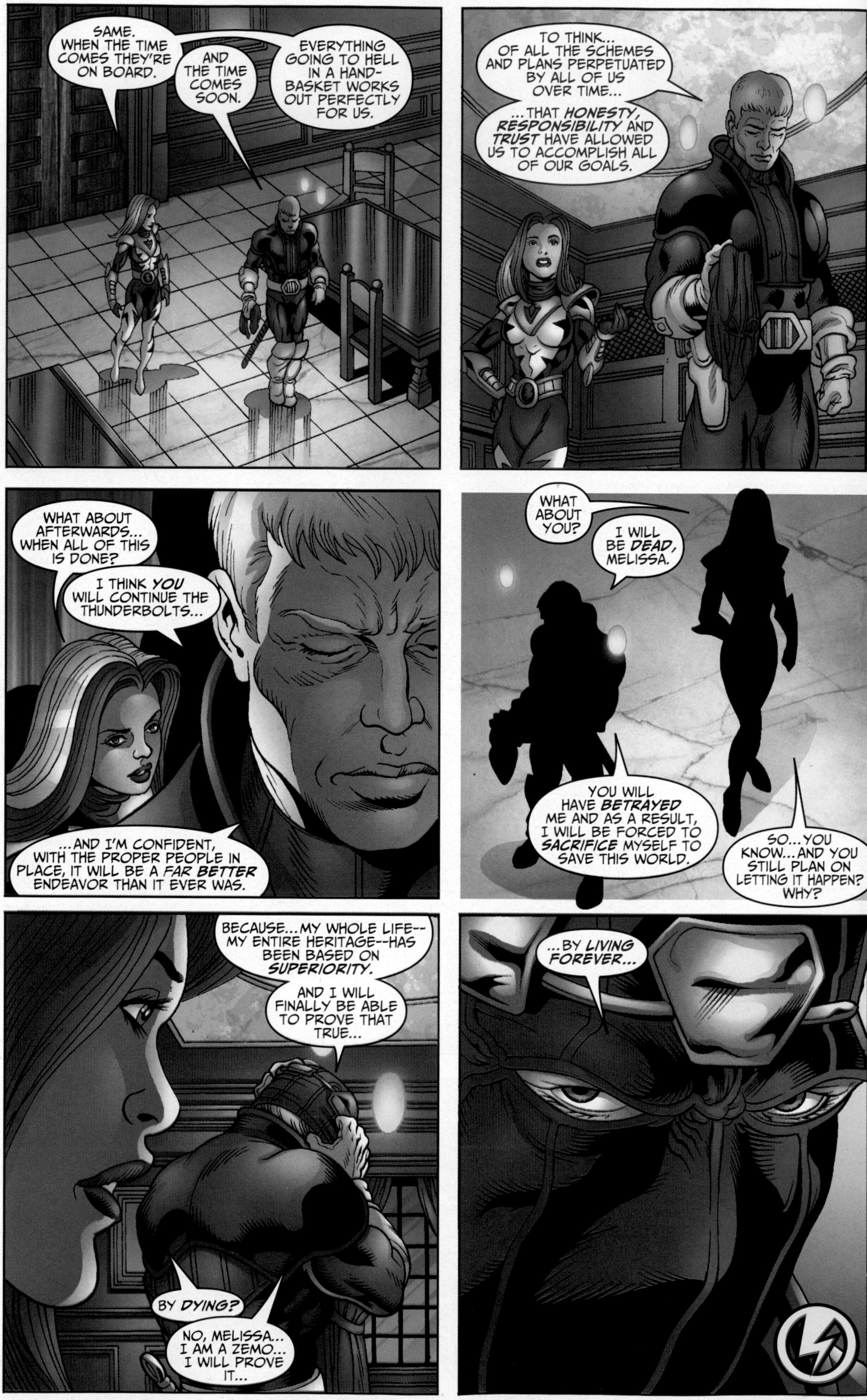
SAME. WHEN THE TIME COMES THEY'RE ON BOARD.
AND THE TIME COMES SOON.
EVERYTHING GOING TO HELL IN A HAND-BASKET WORKS OUT PERFECTLY FOR US.
TO THINK... OF ALL THE SCHEMES AND PLANS PERPETUATED BY ALL OF US OVER TIME...
...THAT HONESTY, RESPONSIBILITY AND TRUST HAVE ALLOWED US TO ACCOMPLISH ALL OF OUR GOALS.
WHAT ABOUT AFTERWARDS... WHEN ALL OF THIS IS DONE?
I THINK YOU WILL CONTINUE THE THUNDERBOLTS...
...AND I'M CONFIDENT, WITH THE PROPER PEOPLE IN PLACE, IT WILL BE A FAR BETTER ENDEAVOR THAN IT EVER WAS.
WHAT ABOUT YOU?
I WILL BE DEAD, MELISSA.
YOU WILL HAVE BETRAYED ME AND AS A RESULT, I WILL BE FORCED TO SACRIFICE MYSELF TO SAVE THIS WORLD.
SO...YOU KNOW...AND YOU STILL PLAN ON LETTING IT HAPPEN? WHY?
BECAUSE...MY WHOLE LIFE--MY ENTIRE HERITAGE--HAS BEEN BASED ON SUPERIORITY.
AND I WILL FINALLY BE ABLE TO PROVE THAT TRUE...
BY DYING?
NO, MELISSA... I AM A ZEMO... I WILL PROVE IT...
...BY LIVING FOREVER...

# HEROES
## FOR HIRE
### A MARVEL COMICS EVENT

## CIVIL
## WAR

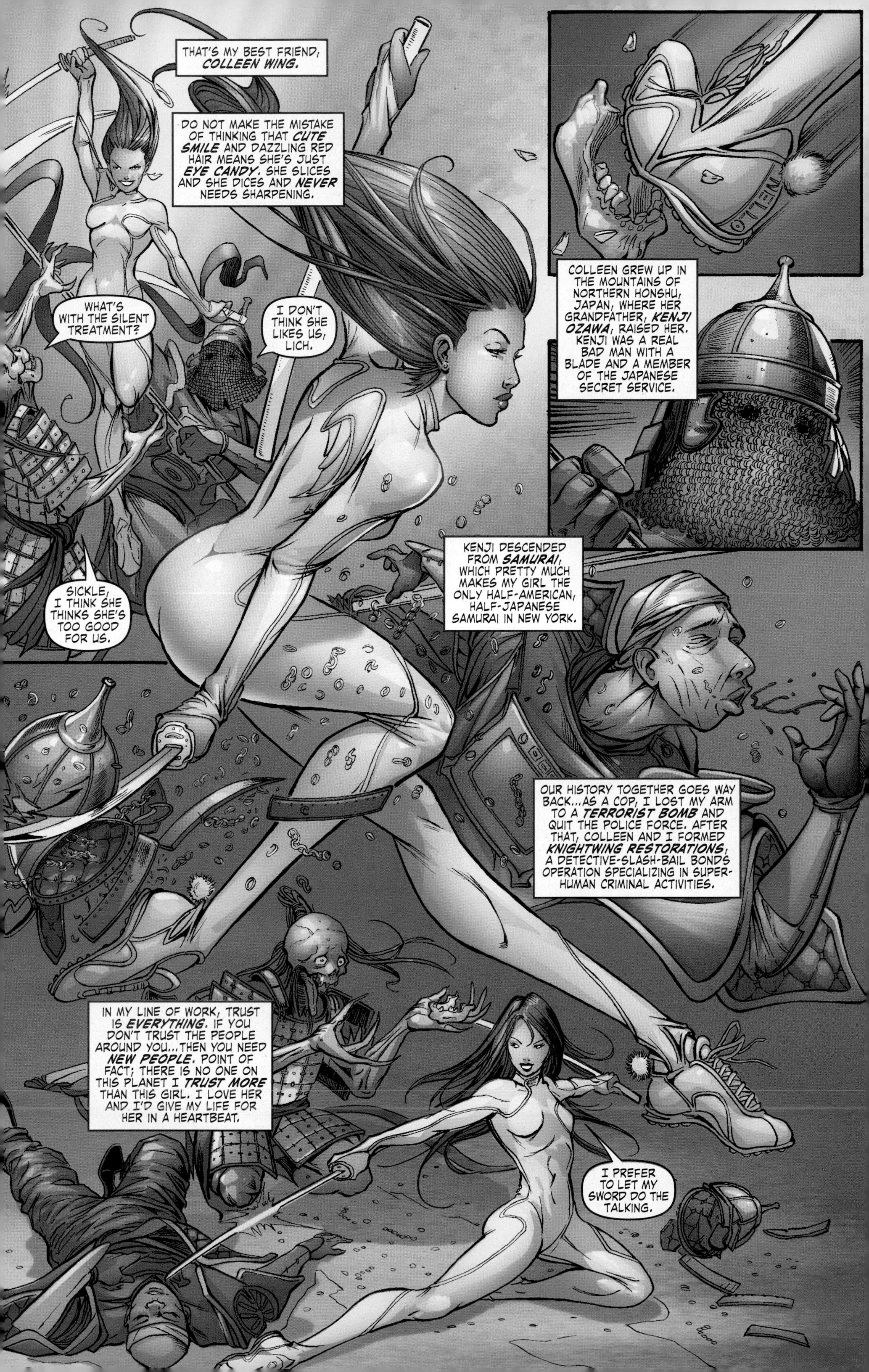

THAT'S MY BEST FRIEND, COLLEEN WING.
DO NOT MAKE THE MISTAKE OF THINKING THAT CUTE SMILE AND DAZZLING RED HAIR MEANS SHE'S JUST EYE CANDY. SHE SLICES AND SHE DICES AND NEVER NEEDS SHARPENING.
COLLEEN GREW UP IN THE MOUNTAINS OF NORTHERN HONSHU, JAPAN, WHERE HER GRANDFATHER, KENJI OZAWA, RAISED HER. KENJI WAS A REAL BAD MAN WITH A BLADE AND A MEMBER OF THE JAPANESE SECRET SERVICE.
WHAT'S WITH THE SILENT TREATMENT?
I DON'T THINK SHE LIKES US, LICH.
KENJI DESCENDED FROM SAMURAI, WHICH PRETTY MUCH MAKES MY GIRL THE ONLY HALF-AMERICAN, HALF-JAPANESE SAMURAI IN NEW YORK.
SICKLE, I THINK SHE THINKS SHE'S TOO GOOD FOR US.
OUR HISTORY TOGETHER GOES WAY BACK...AS A COP, I LOST MY ARM TO A TERRORIST BOMB AND QUIT THE POLICE FORCE. AFTER THAT, COLLEEN AND I FORMED KNIGHTWING RESTORATIONS, A DETECTIVE-SLASH-BAIL BONDS OPERATION SPECIALIZING IN SUPER-HUMAN CRIMINAL ACTIVITIES.
IN MY LINE OF WORK, TRUST IS EVERYTHING. IF YOU DON'T TRUST THE PEOPLE AROUND YOU...THEN YOU NEED NEW PEOPLE. POINT OF FACT; THERE IS NO ONE ON THIS PLANET I TRUST MORE THAN THIS GIRL. I LOVE HER AND I'D GIVE MY LIFE FOR HER IN A HEARTBEAT.
I PREFER TO LET MY SWORD DO THE TALKING.

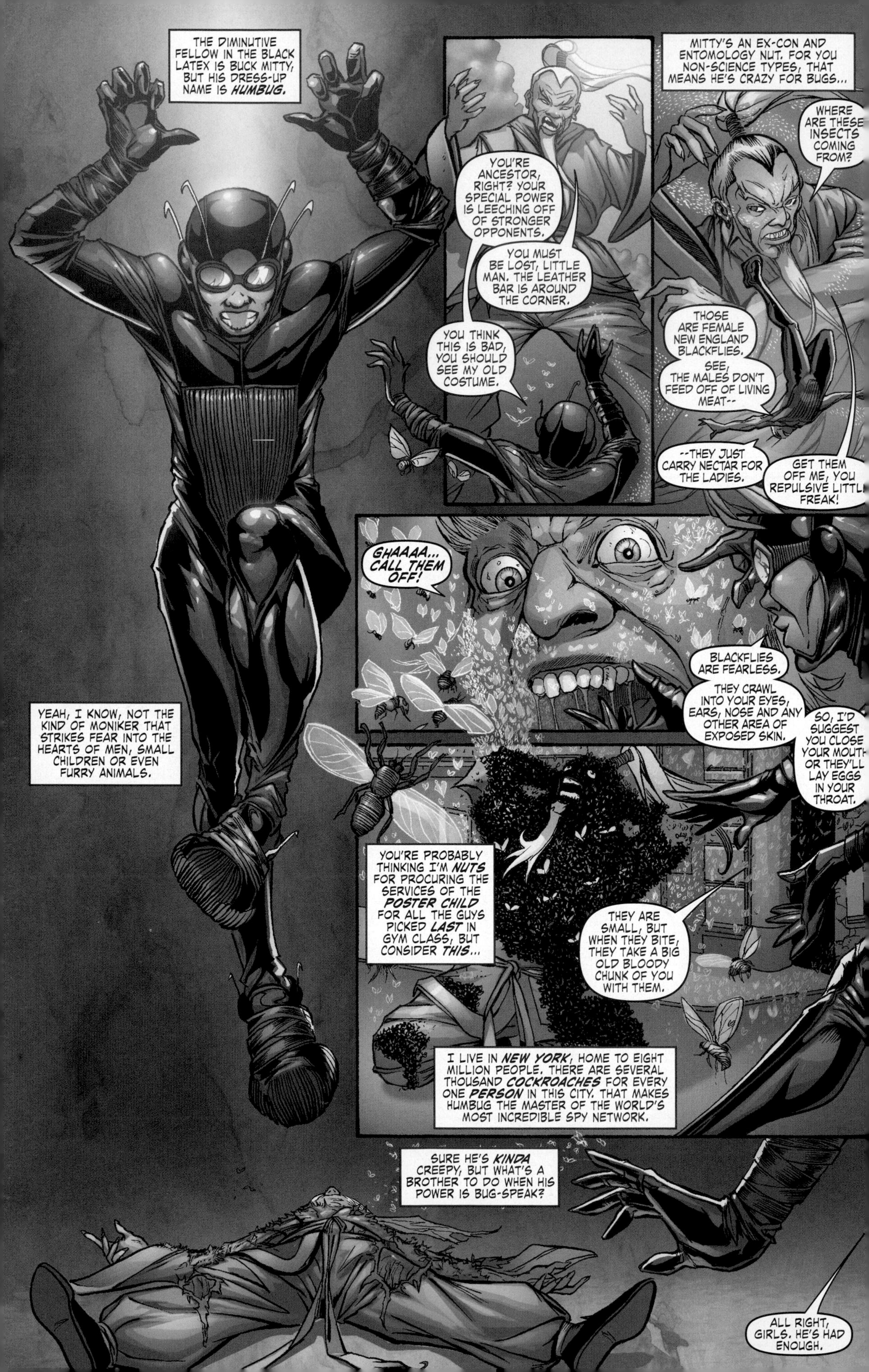
THE DIMINUTIVE FELLOW IN THE BLACK LATEX IS BUCK MITTY, BUT HIS DRESS-UP NAME IS HUMBUG.
YEAH, I KNOW, NOT THE KIND OF MONIKER THAT STRIKES FEAR INTO THE HEARTS OF MEN, SMALL CHILDREN OR EVEN FURRY ANIMALS.
YOU'RE ANCESTOR, RIGHT? YOUR SPECIAL POWER IS LEECHING OFF OF STRONGER OPPONENTS.
YOU MUST BE LOST, LITTLE MAN. THE LEATHER BAR IS AROUND THE CORNER.
YOU THINK THIS IS BAD, YOU SHOULD SEE MY OLD COSTUME.
MITTY'S AN EX-CON AND ENTOMOLOGY NUT. FOR YOU NON-SCIENCE TYPES, THAT MEANS HE'S CRAZY FOR BUGS...
WHERE ARE THESE INSECTS COMING FROM?
THOSE ARE FEMALE NEW ENGLAND BLACKFLIES.
SEE, THE MALES DON'T FEED OFF OF LIVING MEAT--
--THEY JUST CARRY NECTAR FOR THE LADIES.
GET THEM OFF ME, YOU REPULSIVE LITTLE FREAK!
GHAAAA... CALL THEM OFF!
BLACKFLIES ARE FEARLESS.
THEY CRAWL INTO YOUR EYES, EARS, NOSE AND ANY OTHER AREA OF EXPOSED SKIN.
SO, I'D SUGGEST YOU CLOSE YOUR MOUTH OR THEY'LL LAY EGGS IN YOUR THROAT.
YOU'RE PROBABLY THINKING I'M NUTS FOR PROCURING THE SERVICES OF THE POSTER CHILD FOR ALL THE GUYS PICKED LAST IN GYM CLASS, BUT CONSIDER THIS...
THEY ARE SMALL, BUT WHEN THEY BITE, THEY TAKE A BIG OLD BLOODY CHUNK OF YOU WITH THEM.
I LIVE IN NEW YORK, HOME TO EIGHT MILLION PEOPLE. THERE ARE SEVERAL THOUSAND COCKROACHES FOR EVERY ONE PERSON IN THIS CITY. THAT MAKES HUMBUG THE MASTER OF THE WORLD'S MOST INCREDIBLE SPY NETWORK.
SURE HE'S KINDA CREEPY, BUT WHAT'S A BROTHER TO DO WHEN HIS POWER IS BUG-SPEAK?
ALL RIGHT, GIRLS. HE'S HAD ENOUGH.

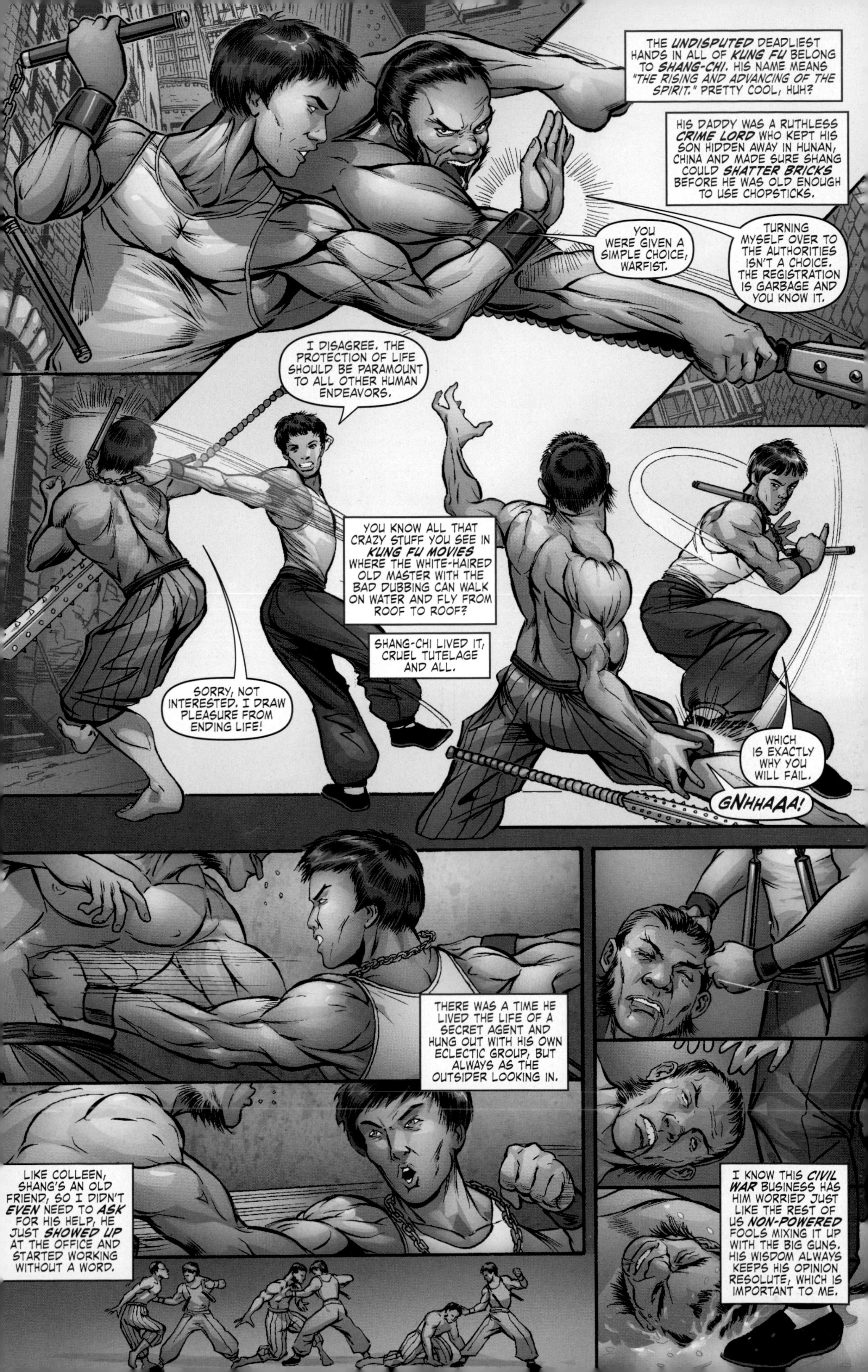

THE UNDISPUTED DEADLIEST HANDS IN ALL OF KUNG FU BELONG TO SHANG-CHI. HIS NAME MEANS "THE RISING AND ADVANCING OF THE SPIRIT." PRETTY COOL, HUH?
HIS DADDY WAS A RUTHLESS CRIME LORD WHO KEPT HIS SON HIDDEN AWAY IN HUNAN, CHINA AND MADE SURE SHANG COULD SHATTER BRICKS BEFORE HE WAS OLD ENOUGH TO USE CHOPSTICKS.
YOU WERE GIVEN A SIMPLE CHOICE, WARFIST.
TURNING MYSELF OVER TO THE AUTHORITIES ISN'T A CHOICE. THE REGISTRATION IS GARBAGE AND YOU KNOW IT.
I DISAGREE. THE PROTECTION OF LIFE SHOULD BE PARAMOUNT TO ALL OTHER HUMAN ENDEAVORS.
YOU KNOW ALL THAT CRAZY STUFF YOU SEE IN KUNG FU MOVIES WHERE THE WHITE-HAIRED OLD MASTER WITH THE BAD DUBBING CAN WALK ON WATER AND FLY FROM ROOF TO ROOF?
SHANG-CHI LIVED IT, CRUEL TUTELAGE AND ALL.
SORRY, NOT INTERESTED. I DRAW PLEASURE FROM ENDING LIFE!
WHICH IS EXACTLY WHY YOU WILL FAIL.
GNHHAAA!
THERE WAS A TIME HE LIVED THE LIFE OF A SECRET AGENT AND HUNG OUT WITH HIS OWN ECLECTIC GROUP, BUT ALWAYS AS THE OUTSIDER LOOKING IN.
LIKE COLLEEN, SHANG'S AN OLD FRIEND, SO I DIDN'T EVEN NEED TO ASK FOR HIS HELP, HE JUST SHOWED UP AT THE OFFICE AND STARTED WORKING WITHOUT A WORD.
I KNOW THIS CIVIL WAR BUSINESS HAS HIM WORRIED JUST LIKE THE REST OF US NON-POWERED FOOLS MIXING IT UP WITH THE BIG GUNS. HIS WISDOM ALWAYS KEEPS HIS OPINION RESOLUTE, WHICH IS IMPORTANT TO ME.

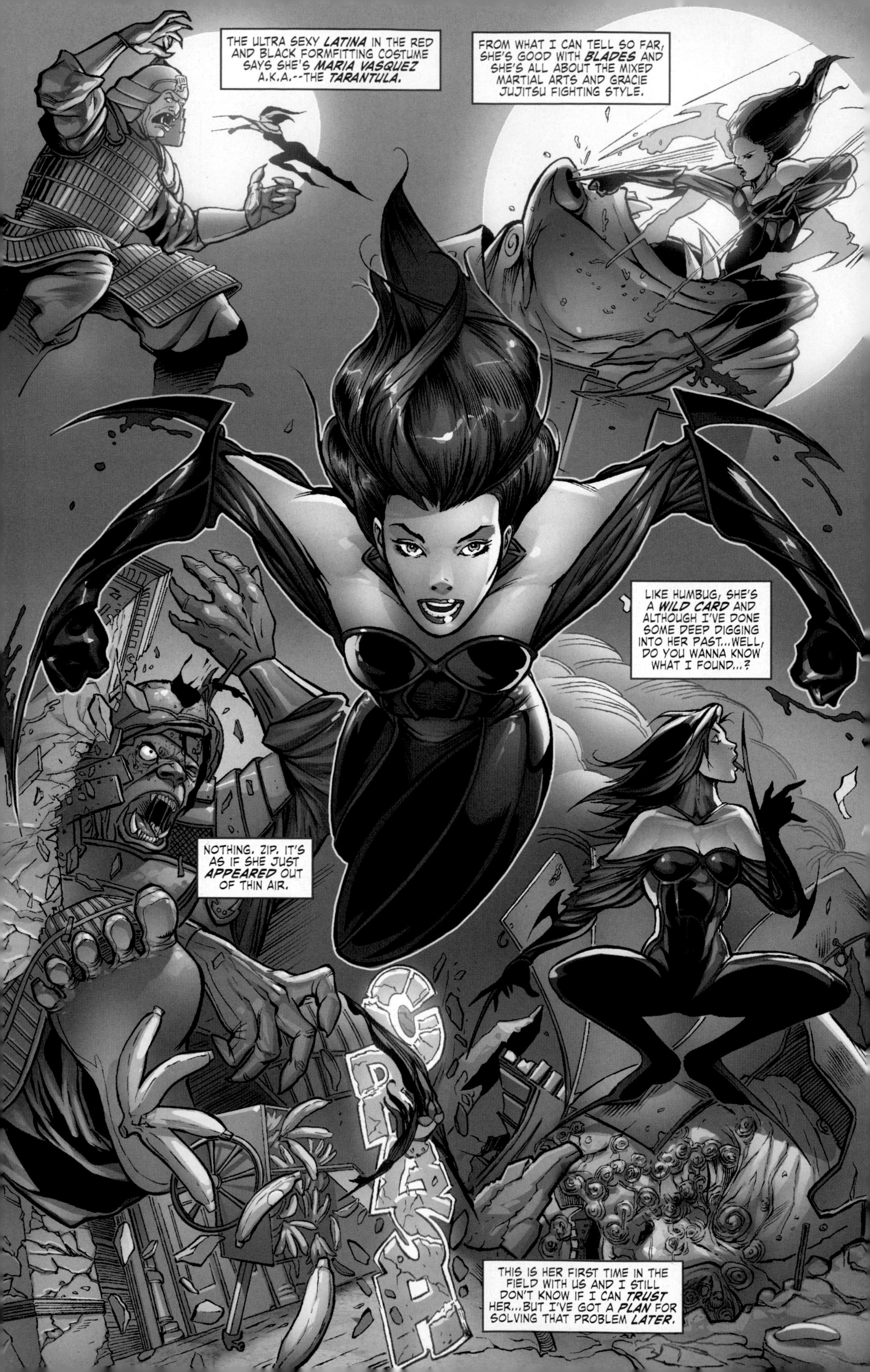
THE ULTRA SEXY LATINA IN THE RED AND BLACK FORMFITTING COSTUME SAYS SHE'S MARIA VASQUEZ A.K.A.--THE TARANTULA.
FROM WHAT I CAN TELL SO FAR, SHE'S GOOD WITH BLADES AND SHE'S ALL ABOUT THE MIXED MARTIAL ARTS AND GRACIE JUJITSU FIGHTING STYLE.
LIKE HUMBUG, SHE'S A WILD CARD AND ALTHOUGH I'VE DONE SOME DEEP DIGGING INTO HER PAST...WELL, DO YOU WANNA KNOW WHAT I FOUND...?
NOTHING. ZIP. IT'S AS IF SHE JUST APPEARED OUT OF THIN AIR.
THIS IS HER FIRST TIME IN THE FIELD WITH US AND I STILL DON'T KNOW IF I CAN TRUST HER...BUT I'VE GOT A PLAN FOR SOLVING THAT PROBLEM LATER.

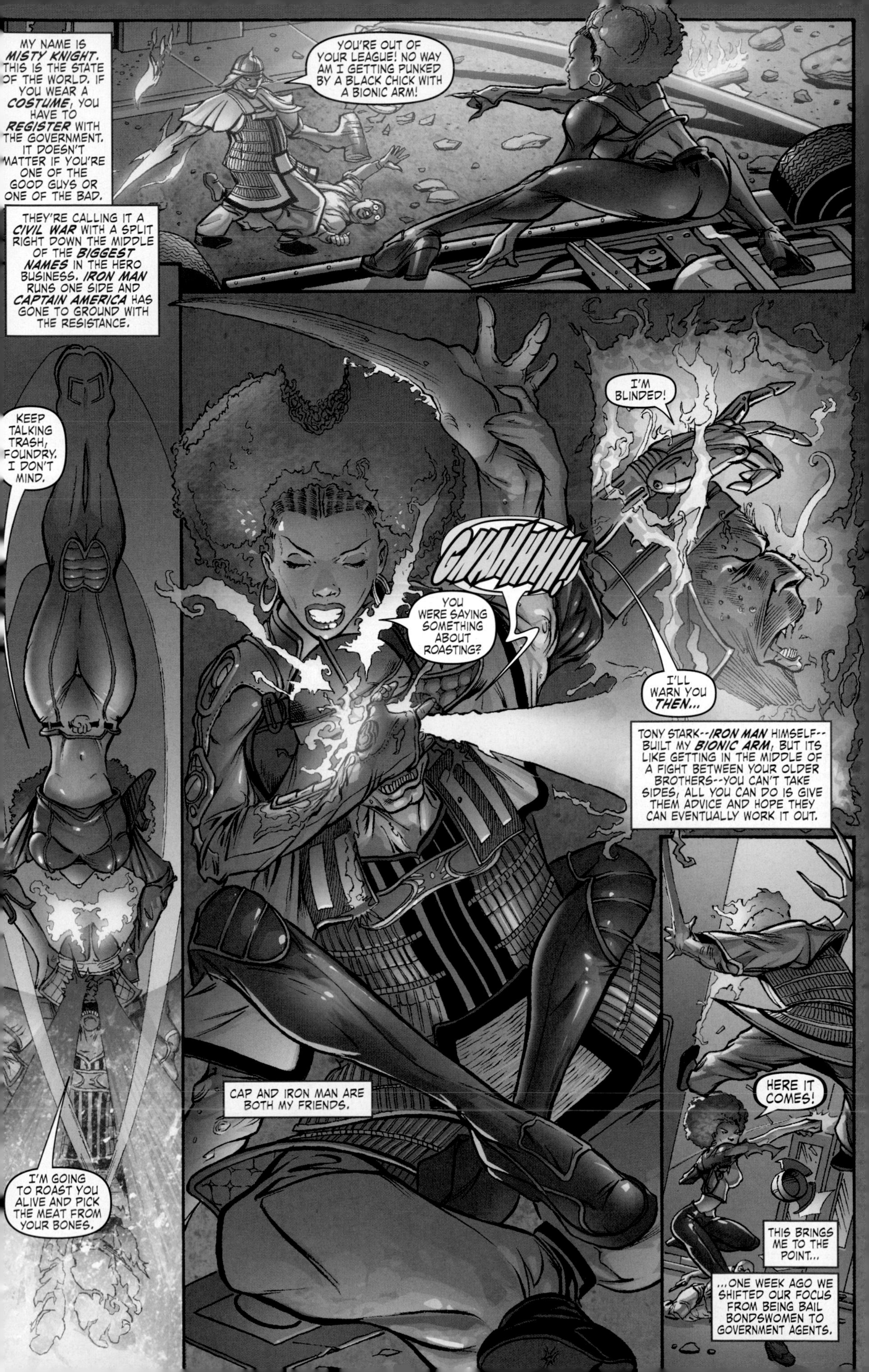
MY NAME IS MISTY KNIGHT. THIS IS THE STATE OF THE WORLD. IF YOU WEAR A COSTUME, YOU HAVE TO REGISTER WITH THE GOVERNMENT. IT DOESN'T MATTER IF YOU'RE ONE OF THE GOOD GUYS OR ONE OF THE BAD.
YOU'RE OUT OF YOUR LEAGUE! NO WAY AM I GETTING PUNKED BY A BLACK CHICK WITH A BIONIC ARM!
THEY'RE CALLING IT A CIVIL WAR WITH A SPLIT RIGHT DOWN THE MIDDLE OF THE BIGGEST NAMES IN THE HERO BUSINESS. IRON MAN RUNS ONE SIDE AND CAPTAIN AMERICA HAS GONE TO GROUND WITH THE RESISTANCE.
KEEP TALKING TRASH, FOUNDRY. I DON'T MIND.
I'M GOING TO ROAST YOU ALIVE AND PICK THE MEAT FROM YOUR BONES.
YOU WERE SAYING SOMETHING ABOUT ROASTING?
GWAHHHH!
I'M BLINDED!
I'LL WARN YOU THEN...
CAP AND IRON MAN ARE BOTH MY FRIENDS.
TONY STARK--IRON MAN HIMSELF--BUILT MY BIONIC ARM, BUT ITS LIKE GETTING IN THE MIDDLE OF A FIGHT BETWEEN YOUR OLDER BROTHERS--YOU CAN'T TAKE SIDES, ALL YOU CAN DO IS GIVE THEM ADVICE AND HOPE THEY CAN EVENTUALLY WORK IT OUT.
HERE IT COMES!
THIS BRINGS ME TO THE POINT...
...ONE WEEK AGO WE SHIFTED OUR FOCUS FROM BEING BAIL BONDSWOMEN TO GOVERNMENT AGENTS.

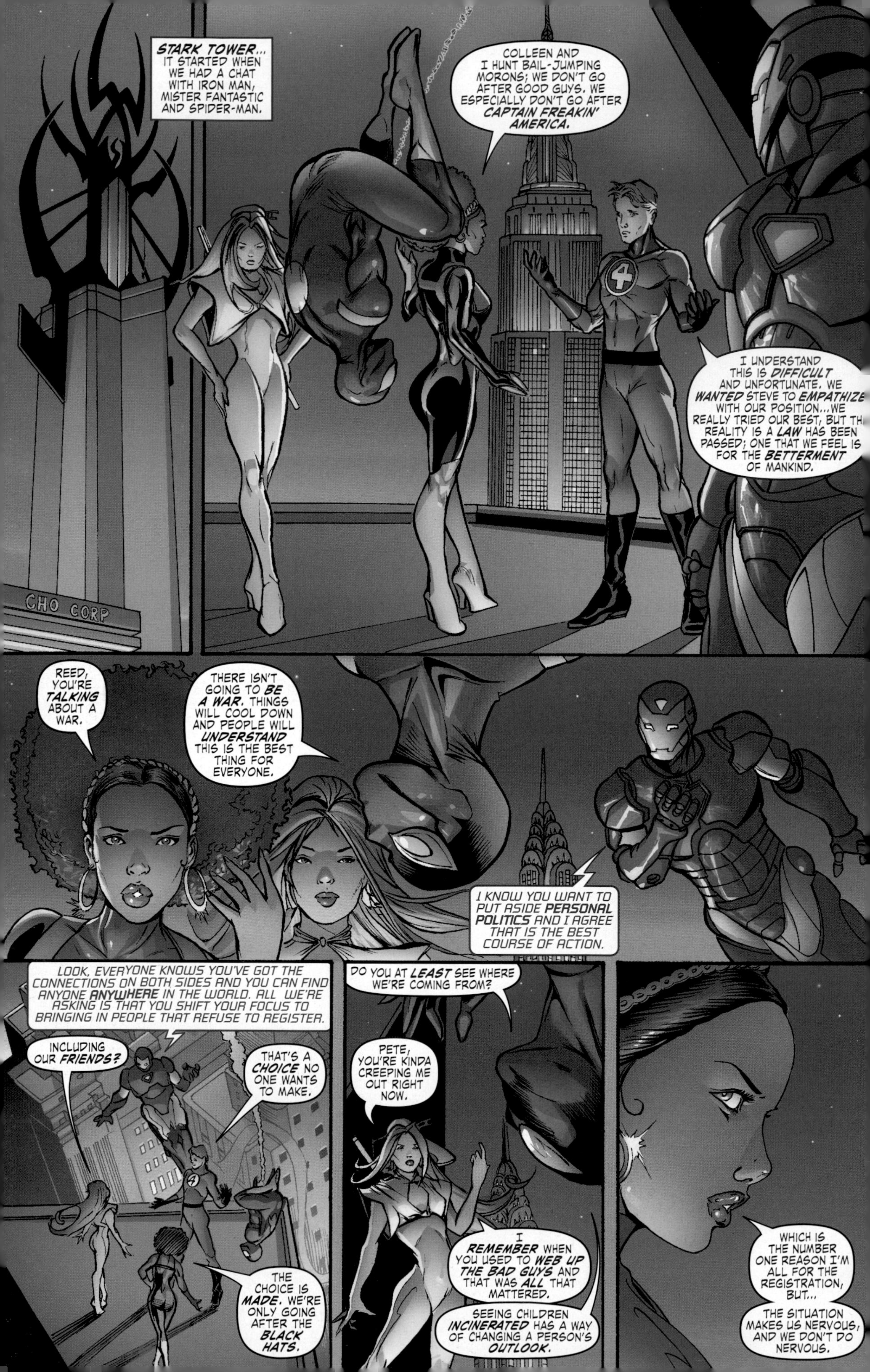
STARK TOWER... IT STARTED WHEN WE HAD A CHAT WITH IRON MAN, MISTER FANTASTIC AND SPIDER-MAN.
COLLEEN AND I HUNT BAIL-JUMPING MORONS; WE DON'T GO AFTER GOOD GUYS. WE ESPECIALLY DON'T GO AFTER CAPTAIN FREAKIN' AMERICA.
I UNDERSTAND THIS IS DIFFICULT AND UNFORTUNATE. WE WANTED STEVE TO EMPATHIZE WITH OUR POSITION... WE REALLY TRIED OUR BEST, BUT THE REALITY IS A LAW HAS BEEN PASSED; ONE THAT WE FEEL IS FOR THE BETTERMENT OF MANKIND.
CHO CORP
REED, YOU'RE TALKING ABOUT A WAR.
THERE ISN'T GOING TO BE A WAR. THINGS WILL COOL DOWN AND PEOPLE WILL UNDERSTAND THIS IS THE BEST THING FOR EVERYONE.
I KNOW YOU WANT TO PUT ASIDE PERSONAL POLITICS AND I AGREE THAT IS THE BEST COURSE OF ACTION.
LOOK, EVERYONE KNOWS YOU'VE GOT THE CONNECTIONS ON BOTH SIDES AND YOU CAN FIND ANYONE ANYWHERE IN THE WORLD. ALL WE'RE ASKING IS THAT YOU SHIFT YOUR FOCUS TO BRINGING IN PEOPLE THAT REFUSE TO REGISTER.
INCLUDING OUR FRIENDS?
THAT'S A CHOICE NO ONE WANTS TO MAKE.
THE CHOICE IS MADE. WE'RE ONLY GOING AFTER THE BLACK HATS.
DO YOU AT LEAST SEE WHERE WE'RE COMING FROM?
PETE, YOU'RE KINDA CREEPING ME OUT RIGHT NOW.
I REMEMBER WHEN YOU USED TO WEB UP THE BAD GUYS AND THAT WAS ALL THAT MATTERED.
SEEING CHILDREN INCINERATED HAS A WAY OF CHANGING A PERSON'S OUTLOOK.
WHICH IS THE NUMBER ONE REASON I'M ALL FOR THE REGISTRATION, BUT...
THE SITUATION MAKES US NERVOUS, AND WE DON'T DO NERVOUS.

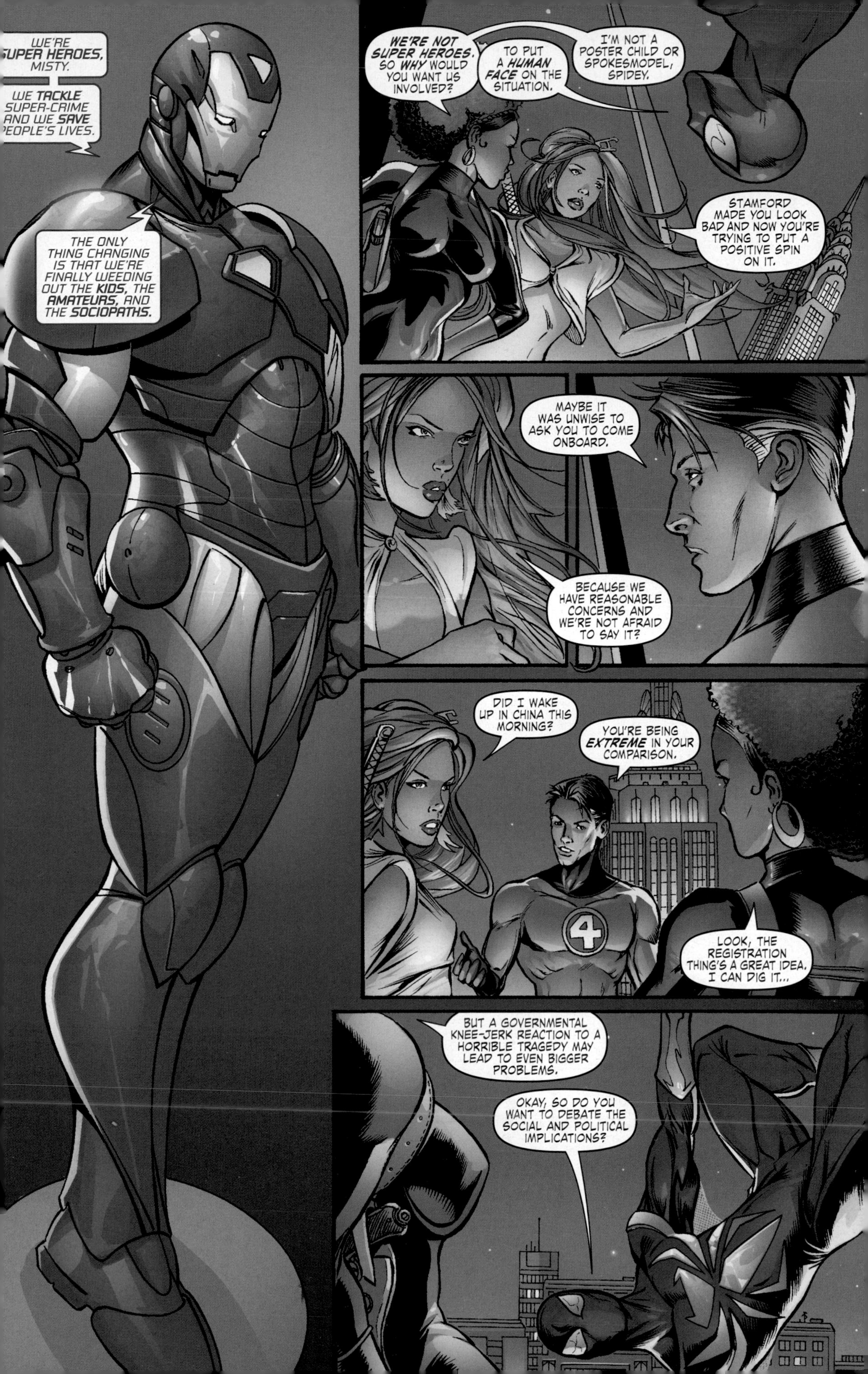
WE'RE SUPER HEROES, MISTY.
WE TACKLE SUPER-CRIME AND WE SAVE PEOPLE'S LIVES.
THE ONLY THING CHANGING IS THAT WE'RE FINALLY WEEDING OUT THE KIDS, THE AMATEURS, AND THE SOCIOPATHS.
WE'RE NOT SUPER HEROES, SO WHY WOULD YOU WANT US INVOLVED?
TO PUT A HUMAN FACE ON THE SITUATION.
I'M NOT A POSTER CHILD OR SPOKESMODEL, SPIDEY.
STAMFORD MADE YOU LOOK BAD AND NOW YOU'RE TRYING TO PUT A POSITIVE SPIN ON IT.
MAYBE IT WAS UNWISE TO ASK YOU TO COME ONBOARD.
BECAUSE WE HAVE REASONABLE CONCERNS AND WE'RE NOT AFRAID TO SAY IT?
DID I WAKE UP IN CHINA THIS MORNING?
YOU'RE BEING EXTREME IN YOUR COMPARISON.
LOOK, THE REGISTRATION THING'S A GREAT IDEA. I CAN DIG IT...
BUT A GOVERNMENTAL KNEE-JERK REACTION TO A HORRIBLE TRAGEDY MAY LEAD TO EVEN BIGGER PROBLEMS.
OKAY, SO DO YOU WANT TO DEBATE THE SOCIAL AND POLITICAL IMPLICATIONS?

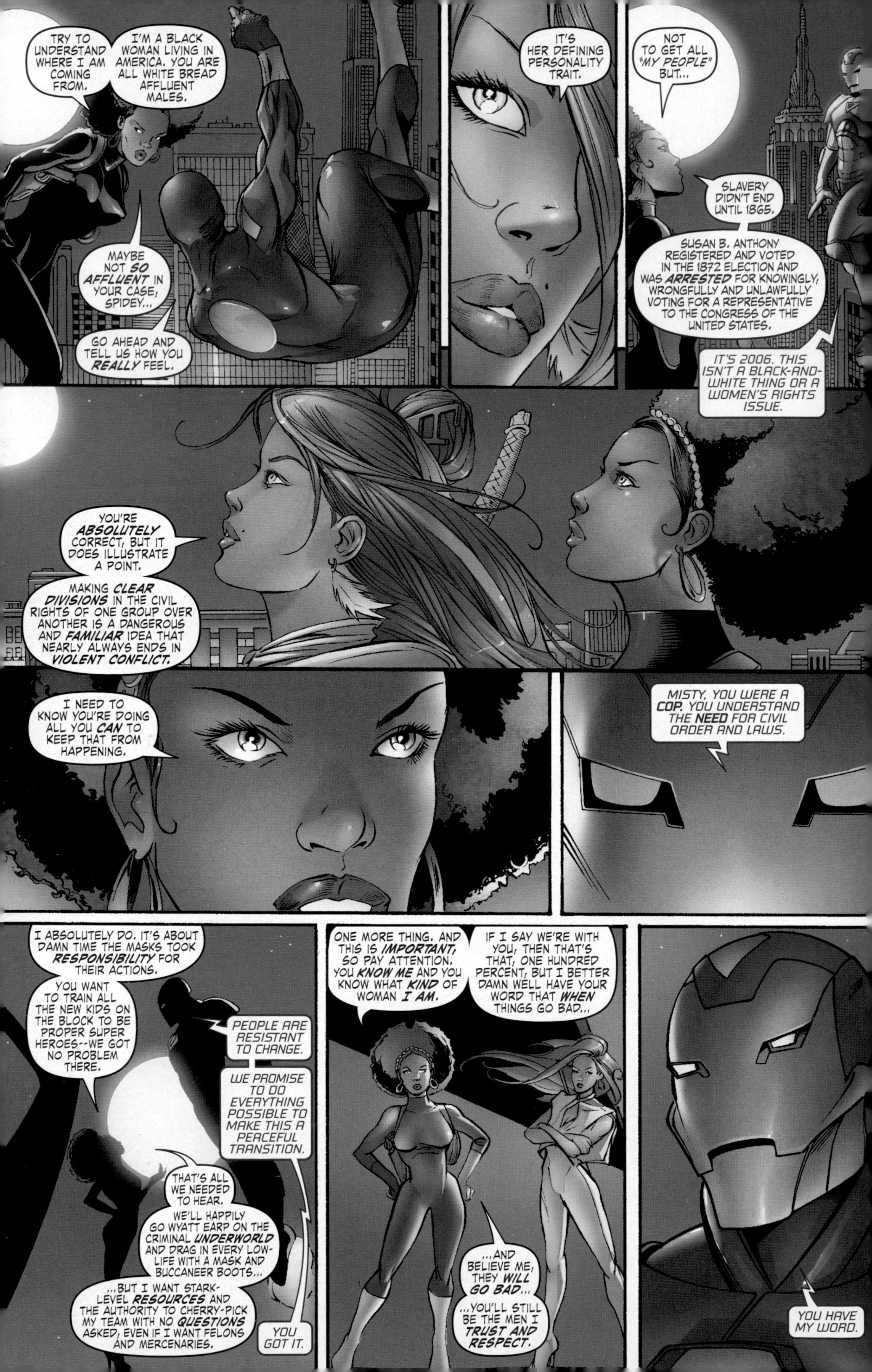
TRY TO UNDERSTAND WHERE I AM COMING FROM.
I'M A BLACK WOMAN LIVING IN AMERICA. YOU ARE ALL WHITE BREAD AFFLUENT MALES.
MAYBE NOT SO AFFLUENT IN YOUR CASE, SPIDEY...
GO AHEAD AND TELL US HOW YOU REALLY FEEL.
IT'S HER DEFINING PERSONALITY TRAIT.
NOT TO GET ALL "MY PEOPLE" BUT...
SLAVERY DIDN'T END UNTIL 1865.
SUSAN B. ANTHONY REGISTERED AND VOTED IN THE 1872 ELECTION AND WAS ARRESTED FOR KNOWINGLY, WRONGFULLY AND UNLAWFULLY VOTING FOR A REPRESENTATIVE TO THE CONGRESS OF THE UNITED STATES.
IT'S 2006. THIS ISN'T A BLACK-AND-WHITE THING OR A WOMEN'S RIGHTS ISSUE.
YOU'RE ABSOLUTELY CORRECT, BUT IT DOES ILLUSTRATE A POINT.
MAKING CLEAR DIVISIONS IN THE CIVIL RIGHTS OF ONE GROUP OVER ANOTHER IS A DANGEROUS AND FAMILIAR IDEA THAT NEARLY ALWAYS ENDS IN VIOLENT CONFLICT.
I NEED TO KNOW YOU'RE DOING ALL YOU CAN TO KEEP THAT FROM HAPPENING.
MISTY, YOU WERE A COP. YOU UNDERSTAND THE NEED FOR CIVIL ORDER AND LAWS.
I ABSOLUTELY DO. IT'S ABOUT DAMN TIME THE MASKS TOOK RESPONSIBILITY FOR THEIR ACTIONS.
YOU WANT TO TRAIN ALL THE NEW KIDS ON THE BLOCK TO BE PROPER SUPER HEROES--WE GOT NO PROBLEM THERE.
PEOPLE ARE RESISTANT TO CHANGE.
WE PROMISE TO DO EVERYTHING POSSIBLE TO MAKE THIS A PEACEFUL TRANSITION.
THAT'S ALL WE NEEDED TO HEAR.
WE'LL HAPPILY GO WYATT EARP ON THE CRIMINAL UNDERWORLD AND DRAG IN EVERY LOW-LIFE WITH A MASK AND BUCCANEER BOOTS...
...BUT I WANT STARK-LEVEL RESOURCES AND THE AUTHORITY TO CHERRY-PICK MY TEAM WITH NO QUESTIONS ASKED, EVEN IF I WANT FELONS AND MERCENARIES.
YOU GOT IT.
ONE MORE THING. AND THIS IS IMPORTANT, SO PAY ATTENTION. YOU KNOW ME AND YOU KNOW WHAT KIND OF WOMAN I AM.
IF I SAY WE'RE WITH YOU, THEN THAT'S THAT, ONE HUNDRED PERCENT, BUT I BETTER DAMN WELL HAVE YOUR WORD THAT WHEN THINGS GO BAD...
...AND BELIEVE ME, THEY WILL GO BAD...
...YOU'LL STILL BE THE MEN I TRUST AND RESPECT.
YOU HAVE MY WORD.

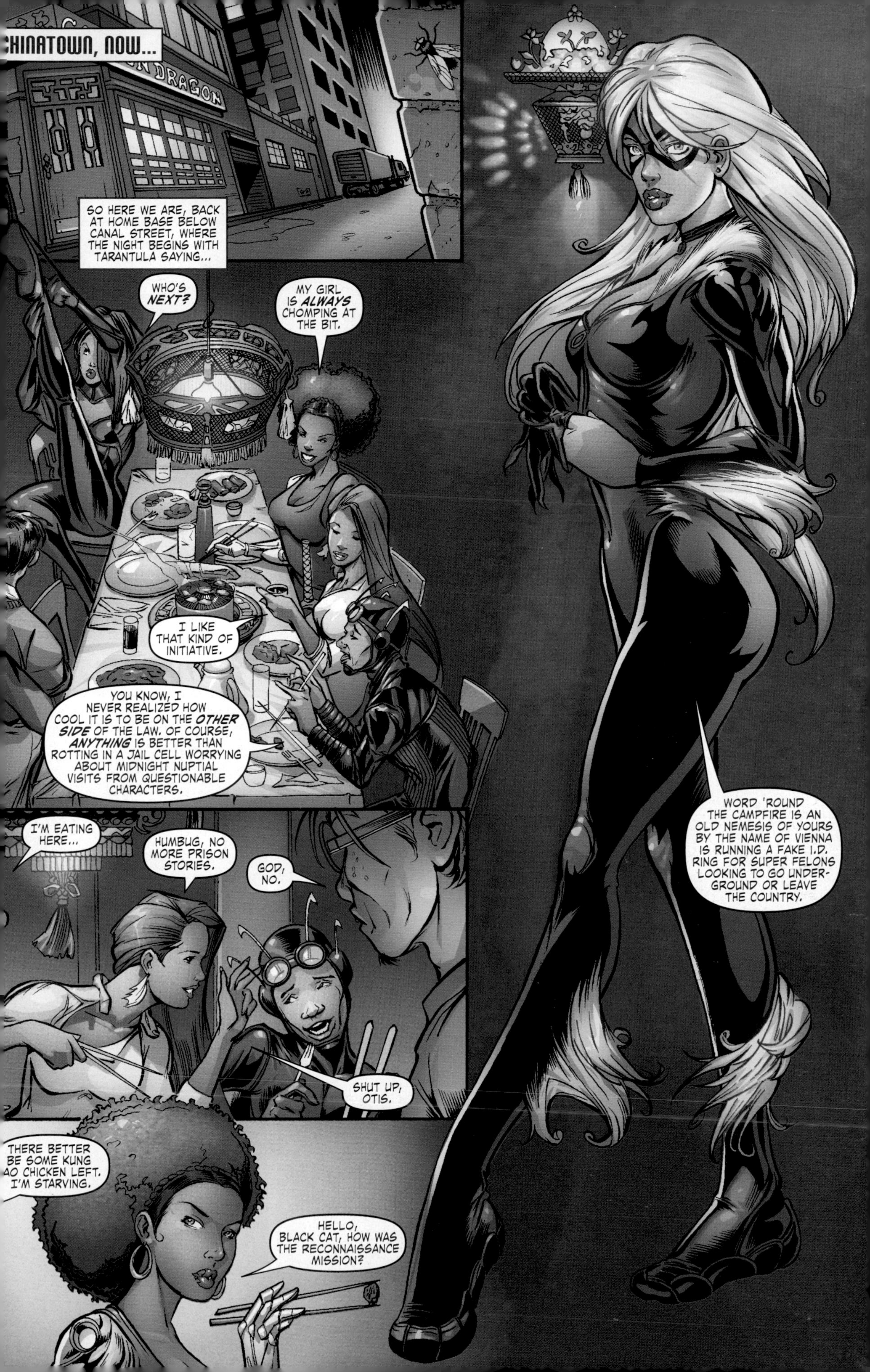
CHINATOWN, NOW...
SO HERE WE ARE, BACK AT HOME BASE BELOW CANAL STREET, WHERE THE NIGHT BEGINS WITH TARANTULA SAYING...
WHO'S NEXT?
MY GIRL IS ALWAYS CHOMPING AT THE BIT.
I LIKE THAT KIND OF INITIATIVE.
YOU KNOW, I NEVER REALIZED HOW COOL IT IS TO BE ON THE OTHER SIDE OF THE LAW. OF COURSE, ANYTHING IS BETTER THAN ROTTING IN A JAIL CELL WORRYING ABOUT MIDNIGHT NUPTIAL VISITS FROM QUESTIONABLE CHARACTERS.
I'M EATING HERE...
HUMBUG, NO MORE PRISON STORIES.
GOD, NO.
SHUT UP, OTIS.
THERE BETTER BE SOME KUNG PAO CHICKEN LEFT. I'M STARVING.
HELLO, BLACK CAT, HOW WAS THE RECONNAISSANCE MISSION?
WORD 'ROUND THE CAMPFIRE IS AN OLD NEMESIS OF YOURS BY THE NAME OF VIENNA IS RUNNING A FAKE I.D. RING FOR SUPER FELONS LOOKING TO GO UNDERGROUND OR LEAVE THE COUNTRY.

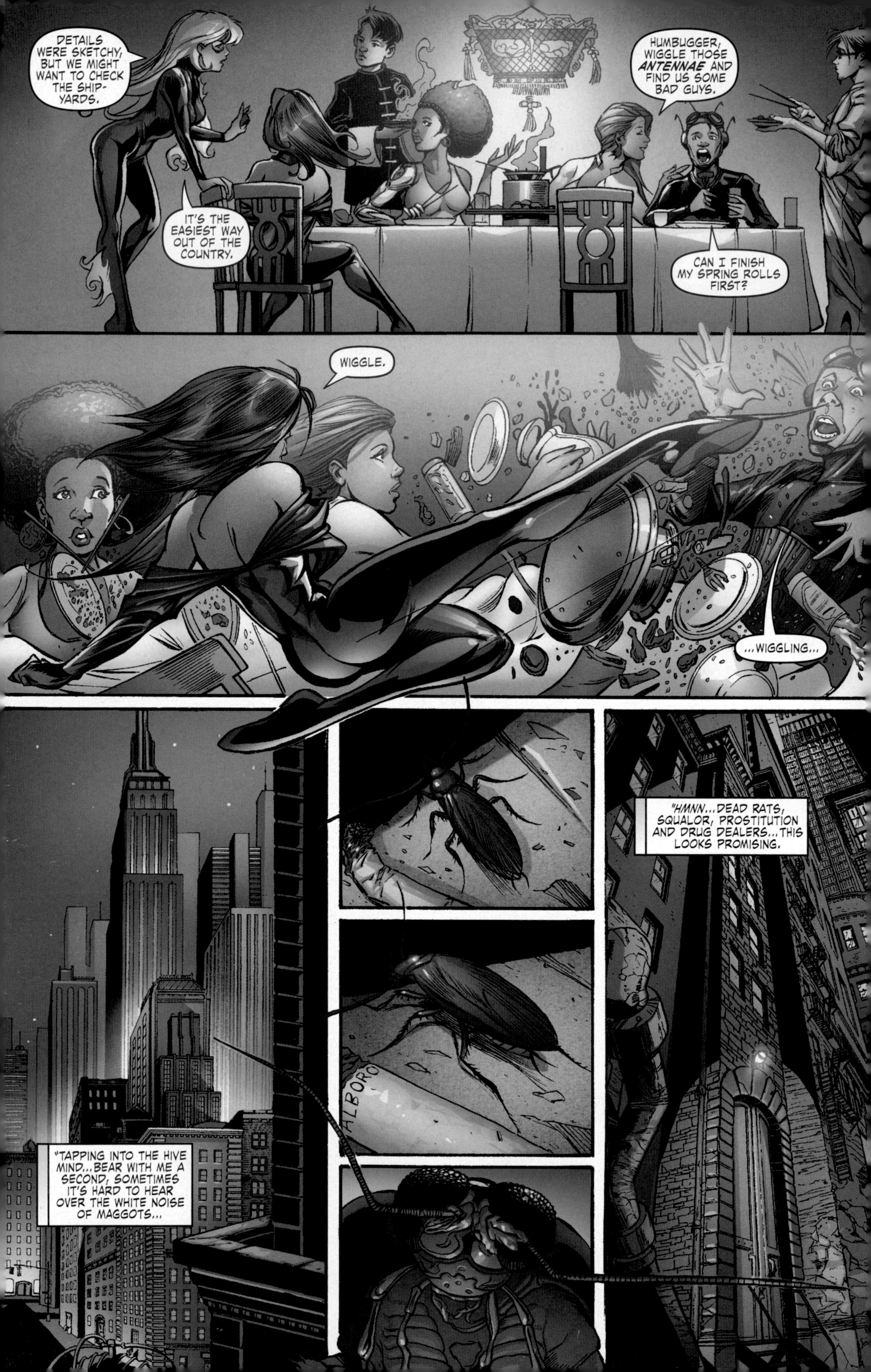

DETAILS WERE SKETCHY, BUT WE MIGHT WANT TO CHECK THE SHIP-YARDS.
IT'S THE EASIEST WAY OUT OF THE COUNTRY.
HUMBUGGER, WIGGLE THOSE *ANTENNAE* AND FIND US SOME BAD GUYS.
CAN I FINISH MY SPRING ROLLS FIRST?
WIGGLE.
...WIGGLING...
"TAPPING INTO THE HIVE MIND...BEAR WITH ME A SECOND, SOMETIMES IT'S HARD TO HEAR OVER THE WHITE NOISE OF MAGGOTS...
"HMNN...DEAD RATS, SQUALOR, PROSTITUTION AND DRUG DEALERS...THIS LOOKS PROMISING.

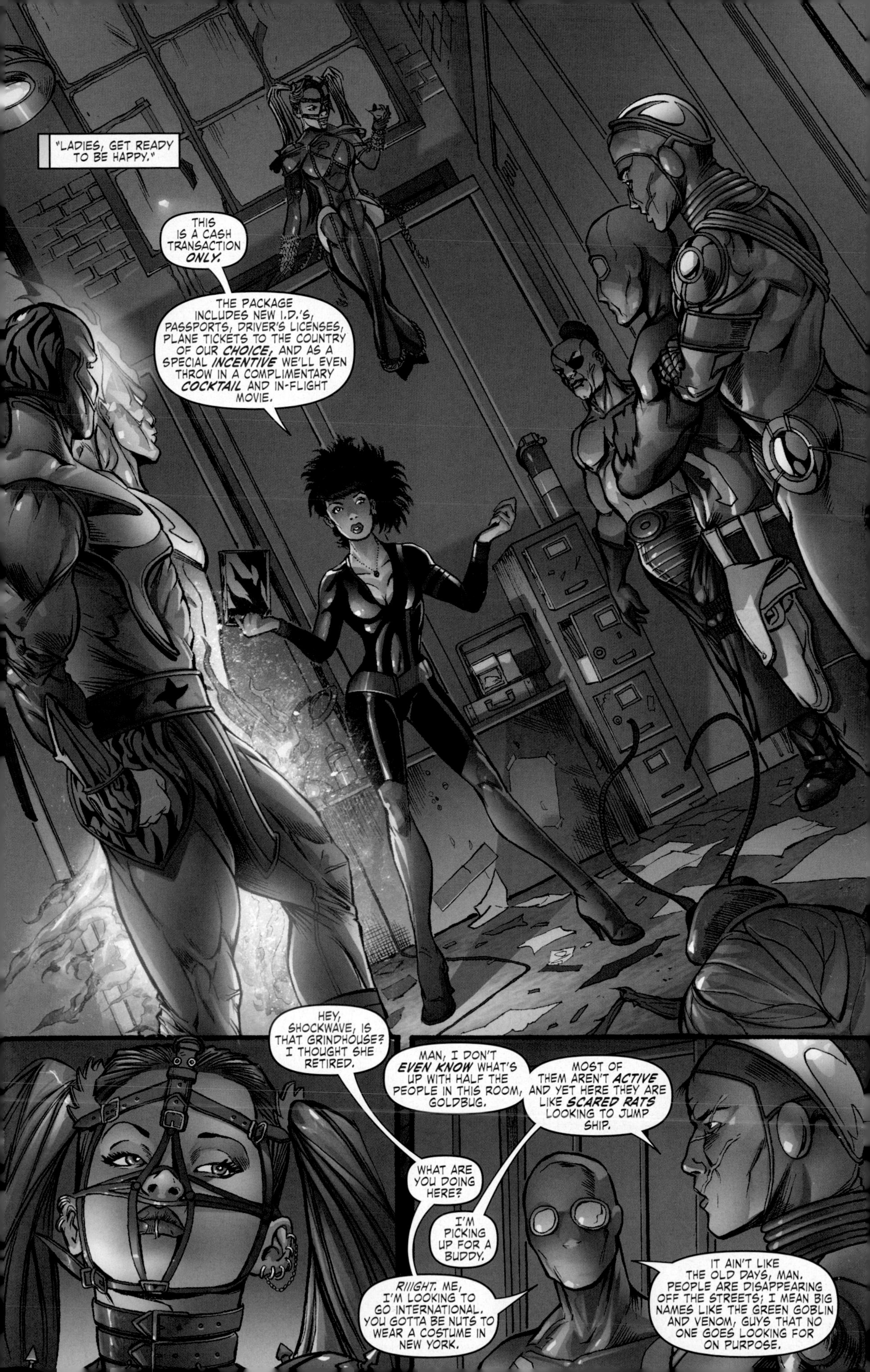
"LADIES, GET READY TO BE HAPPY."
THIS IS A CASH TRANSACTION *ONLY.*
THE PACKAGE INCLUDES NEW I.D.'S, PASSPORTS, DRIVER'S LICENSES, PLANE TICKETS TO THE COUNTRY OF OUR *CHOICE,* AND AS A SPECIAL *INCENTIVE* WE'LL EVEN THROW IN A COMPLIMENTARY *COCKTAIL* AND IN-FLIGHT MOVIE.
HEY, SHOCKWAVE, IS THAT GRINDHOUSE? I THOUGHT SHE RETIRED.
MAN, I DON'T *EVEN KNOW* WHAT'S UP WITH HALF THE PEOPLE IN THIS ROOM, GOLDBUG.
MOST OF THEM AREN'T *ACTIVE* AND YET HERE THEY ARE LIKE *SCARED RATS* LOOKING TO JUMP SHIP.
WHAT ARE YOU DOING HERE?
I'M PICKING UP FOR A BUDDY.
*RIIIGHT.* ME, I'M LOOKING TO GO INTERNATIONAL. YOU GOTTA BE NUTS TO WEAR A COSTUME IN NEW YORK.
IT AIN'T LIKE THE OLD DAYS, MAN. PEOPLE ARE DISAPPEARING OFF THE STREETS; I MEAN BIG NAMES LIKE THE GREEN GOBLIN AND VENOM, GUYS THAT NO ONE GOES LOOKING FOR ON PURPOSE.

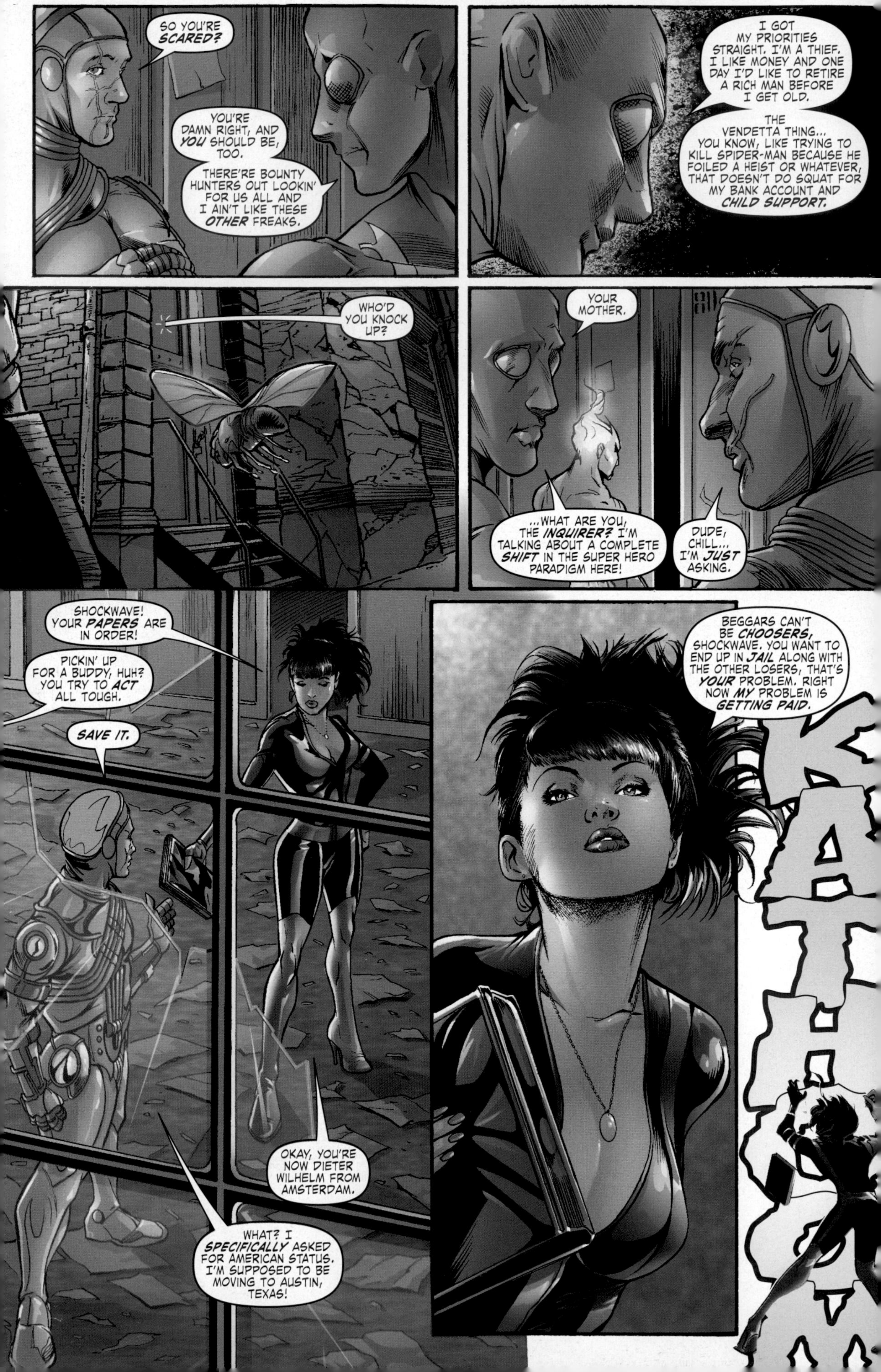

SO YOU'RE *SCARED?*
YOU'RE DAMN RIGHT, AND *YOU* SHOULD BE, TOO.
THERE'RE BOUNTY HUNTERS OUT LOOKIN' FOR US ALL AND I AIN'T LIKE THESE *OTHER* FREAKS.
I GOT MY PRIORITIES STRAIGHT. I'M A THIEF. I LIKE MONEY AND ONE DAY I'D LIKE TO RETIRE A RICH MAN BEFORE I GET OLD.
THE VENDETTA THING... YOU KNOW, LIKE TRYING TO KILL SPIDER-MAN BECAUSE HE FOILED A HEIST OR WHATEVER, THAT DOESN'T DO SQUAT FOR MY BANK ACCOUNT AND *CHILD SUPPORT.*
WHO'D YOU KNOCK UP?
YOUR MOTHER.
...WHAT ARE YOU, THE *INQUIRER?* I'M TALKING ABOUT A COMPLETE *SHIFT* IN THE SUPER HERO PARADIGM HERE!
DUDE, CHILL... I'M *JUST* ASKING.
SHOCKWAVE! YOUR *PAPERS* ARE IN ORDER!
PICKIN' UP FOR A BUDDY, HUH? YOU TRY TO *ACT* ALL TOUGH.
*SAVE IT.*
OKAY, YOU'RE NOW DIETER WILHELM FROM AMSTERDAM.
WHAT? I *SPECIFICALLY* ASKED FOR AMERICAN STATUS. I'M SUPPOSED TO BE MOVING TO AUSTIN, TEXAS!
BEGGARS CAN'T BE *CHOOSERS,* SHOCKWAVE. YOU WANT TO END UP IN *JAIL* ALONG WITH THE OTHER LOSERS, THAT'S *YOUR* PROBLEM. RIGHT NOW *MY* PROBLEM IS *GETTING PAID.*

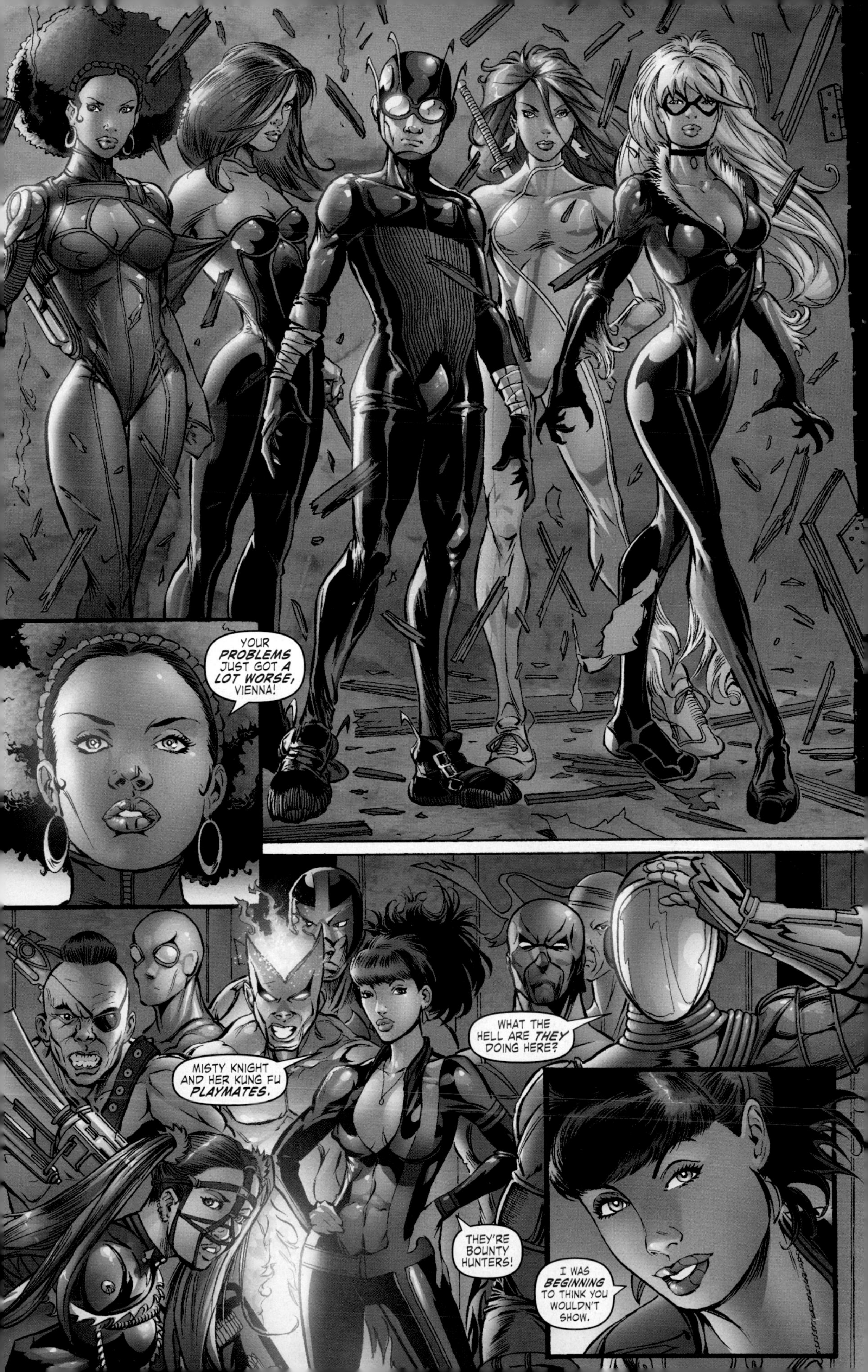
YOUR PROBLEMS JUST GOT A LOT WORSE, VIENNA!
WHAT THE HELL ARE THEY DOING HERE?
MISTY KNIGHT AND HER KUNG FU PLAYMATES.
THEY'RE BOUNTY HUNTERS!
I WAS BEGINNING TO THINK YOU WOULDN'T SHOW.

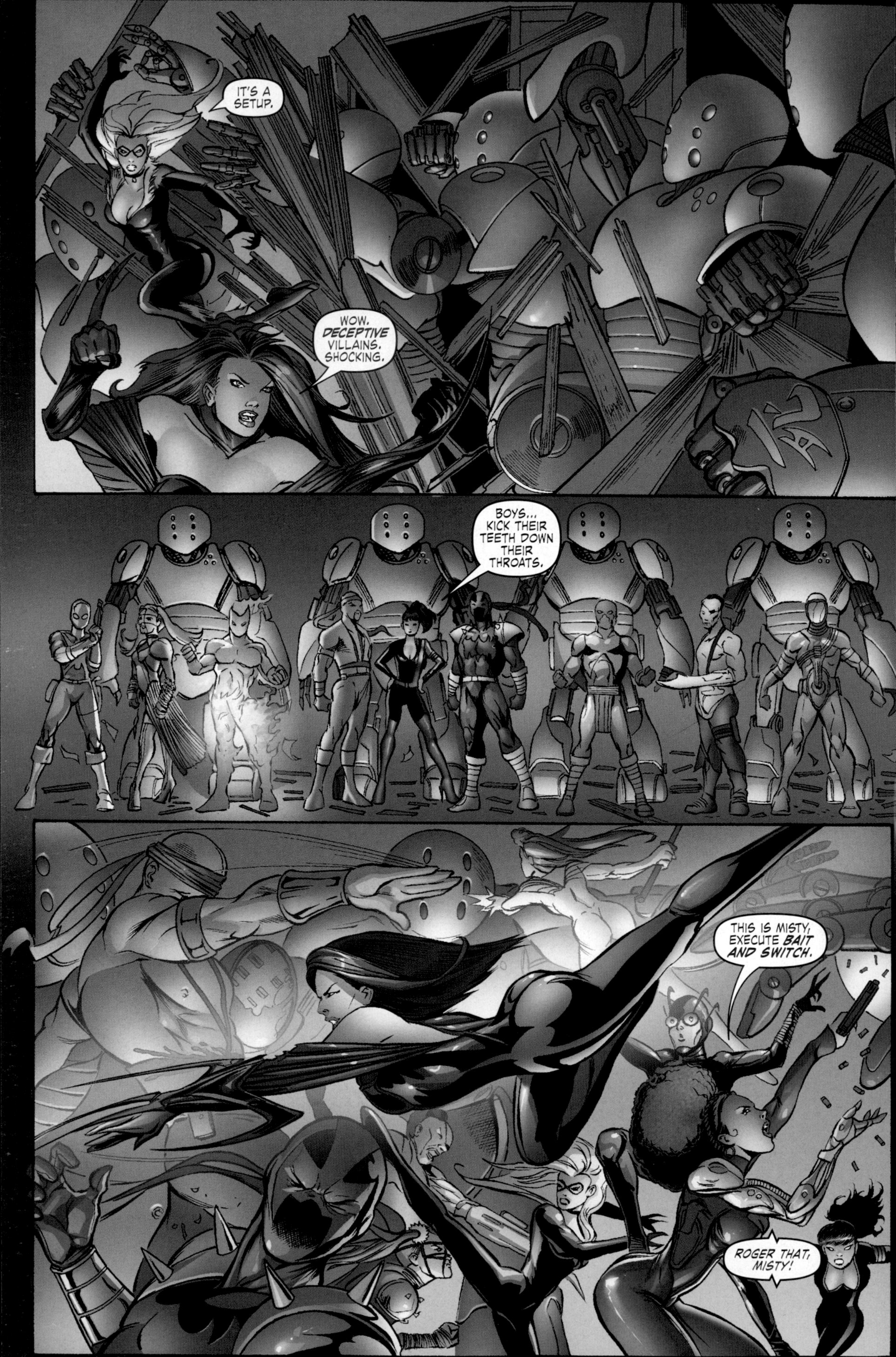
IT'S A SETUP.
WOW. DECEPTIVE VILLAINS. SHOCKING.
BOYS... KICK THEIR TEETH DOWN THEIR THROATS.
THIS IS MISTY, EXECUTE BAIT AND SWITCH.
ROGER THAT, MISTY!

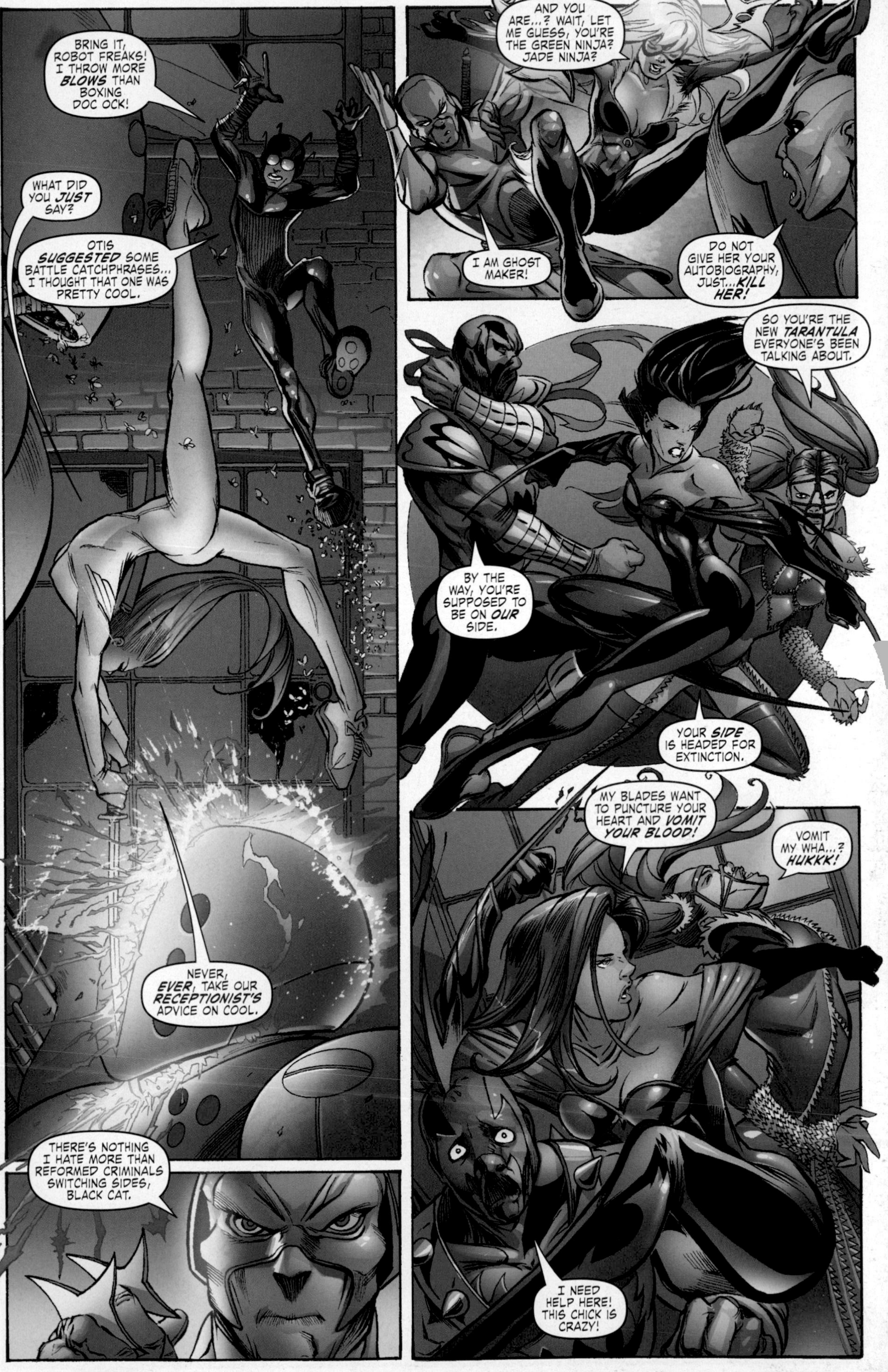

BRING IT, ROBOT FREAKS! I THROW MORE BLOWS THAN BOXING DOC OCK!
WHAT DID YOU JUST SAY?
OTIS SUGGESTED SOME BATTLE CATCHPHRASES... I THOUGHT THAT ONE WAS PRETTY COOL.
NEVER, EVER, TAKE OUR RECEPTIONIST'S ADVICE ON COOL.
AND YOU ARE...? WAIT, LET ME GUESS, YOU'RE THE GREEN NINJA? JADE NINJA?
I AM GHOST MAKER!
DO NOT GIVE HER YOUR AUTOBIOGRAPHY, JUST...KILL HER!
SO YOU'RE THE NEW TARANTULA EVERYONE'S BEEN TALKING ABOUT.
BY THE WAY, YOU'RE SUPPOSED TO BE ON OUR SIDE.
YOUR SIDE IS HEADED FOR EXTINCTION.
THERE'S NOTHING I HATE MORE THAN REFORMED CRIMINALS SWITCHING SIDES, BLACK CAT.
MY BLADES WANT TO PUNCTURE YOUR HEART AND VOMIT YOUR BLOOD!
VOMIT MY WHA...? HUKKK!
I NEED HELP HERE! THIS CHICK IS CRAZY!

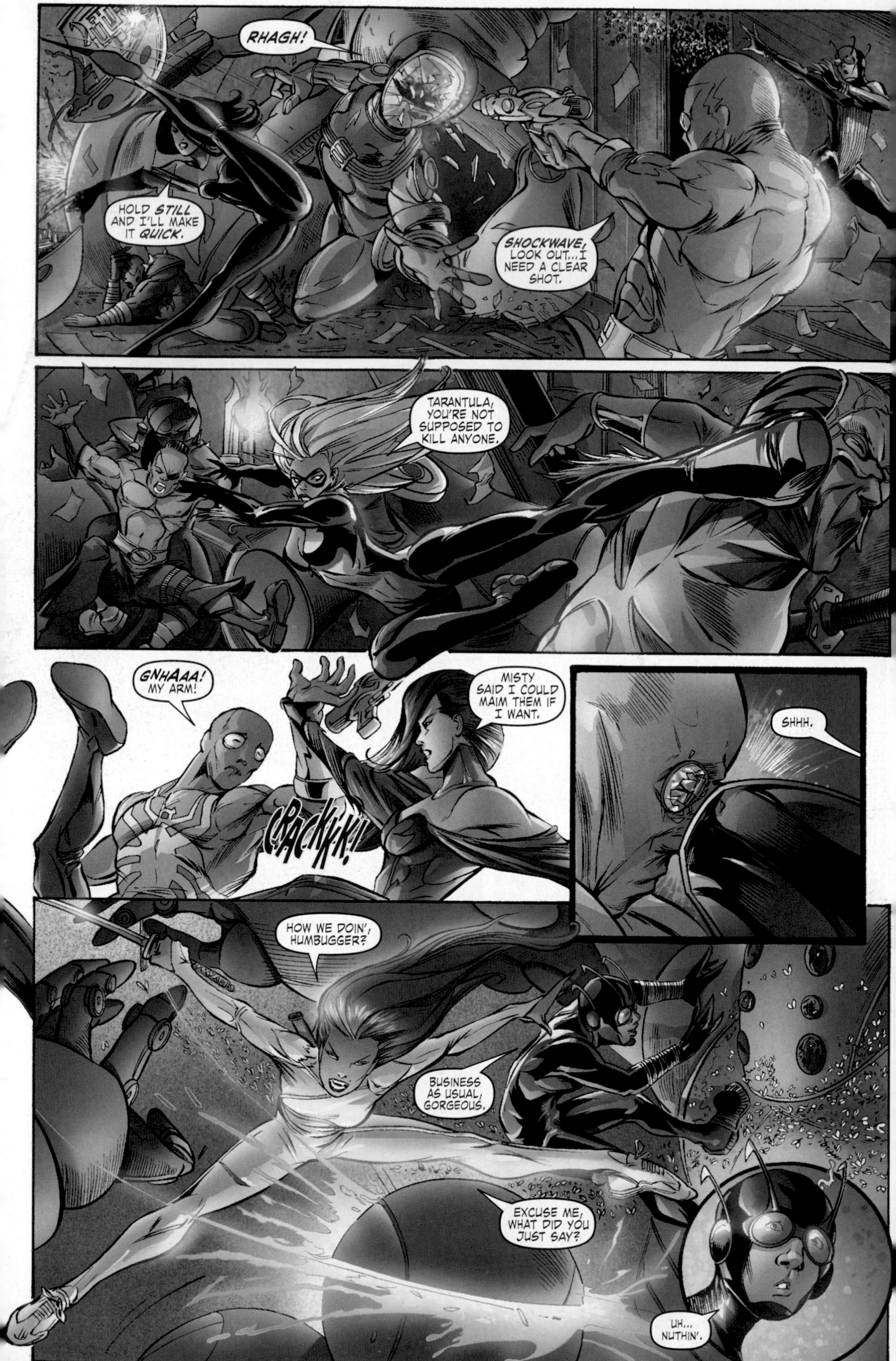
RHAGH!
HOLD STILL AND I'LL MAKE IT QUICK.
SHOCKWAVE, LOOK OUT...I NEED A CLEAR SHOT.
TARANTULA, YOU'RE NOT SUPPOSED TO KILL ANYONE.
GNHAAA! MY ARM!
CRACKK-K!
MISTY SAID I COULD MAIM THEM IF I WANT.
SHHH.
HOW WE DOIN', HUMBUGGER?
BUSINESS AS USUAL, GORGEOUS.
EXCUSE ME, WHAT DID YOU JUST SAY?
UH... NUTHIN'.

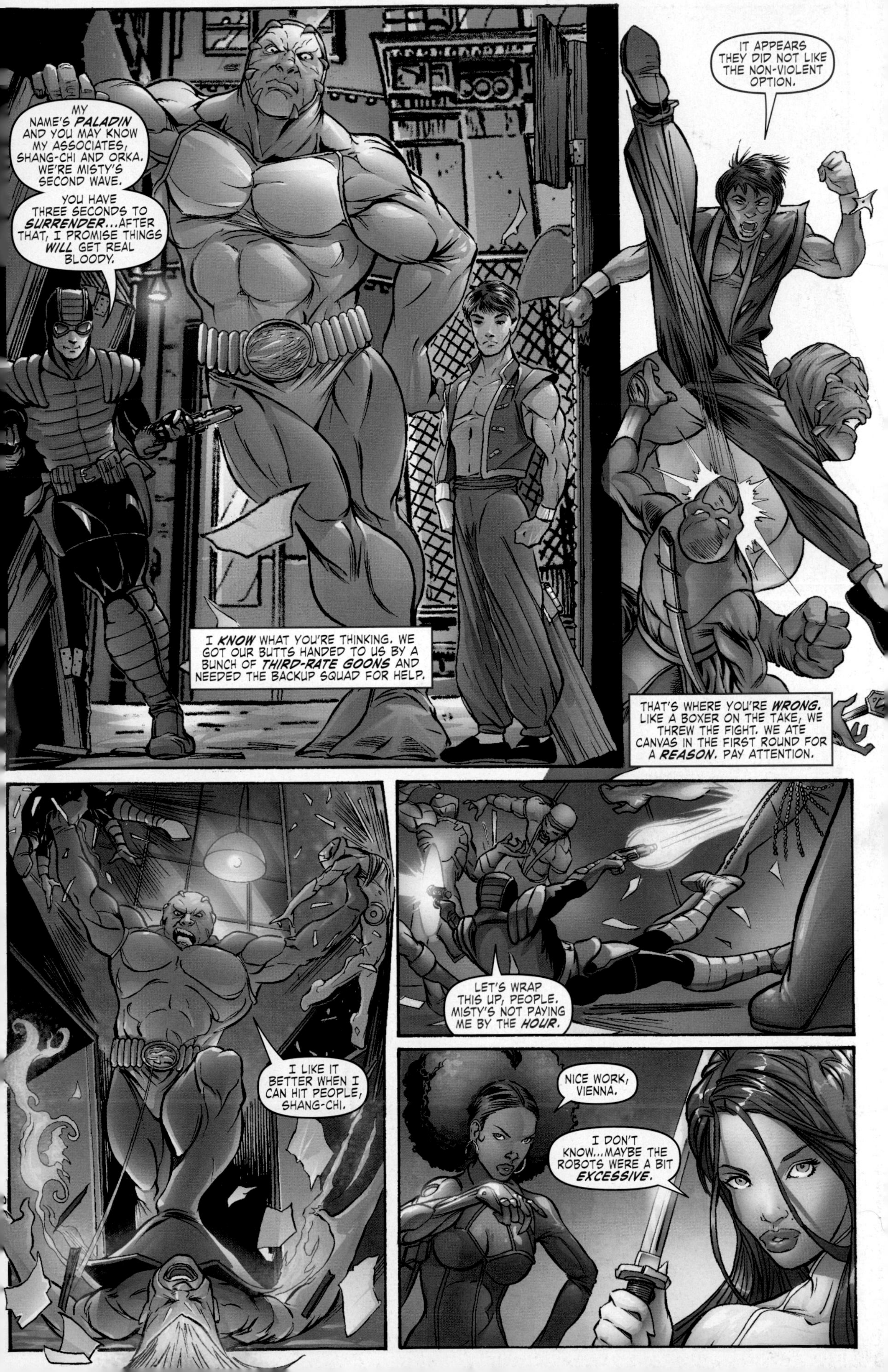

MY NAME'S PALADIN AND YOU MAY KNOW MY ASSOCIATES, SHANG-CHI AND ORKA. WE'RE MISTY'S SECOND WAVE.
YOU HAVE THREE SECONDS TO SURRENDER...AFTER THAT, I PROMISE THINGS WILL GET REAL BLOODY.
I KNOW WHAT YOU'RE THINKING. WE GOT OUR BUTTS HANDED TO US BY A BUNCH OF THIRD-RATE GOONS AND NEEDED THE BACKUP SQUAD FOR HELP.
IT APPEARS THEY DID NOT LIKE THE NON-VIOLENT OPTION.
THAT'S WHERE YOU'RE WRONG. LIKE A BOXER ON THE TAKE, WE THREW THE FIGHT. WE ATE CANVAS IN THE FIRST ROUND FOR A REASON. PAY ATTENTION.
I LIKE IT BETTER WHEN I CAN HIT PEOPLE, SHANG-CHI.
LET'S WRAP THIS UP, PEOPLE. MISTY'S NOT PAYING ME BY THE HOUR.
NICE WORK, VIENNA.
I DON'T KNOW...MAYBE THE ROBOTS WERE A BIT EXCESSIVE.

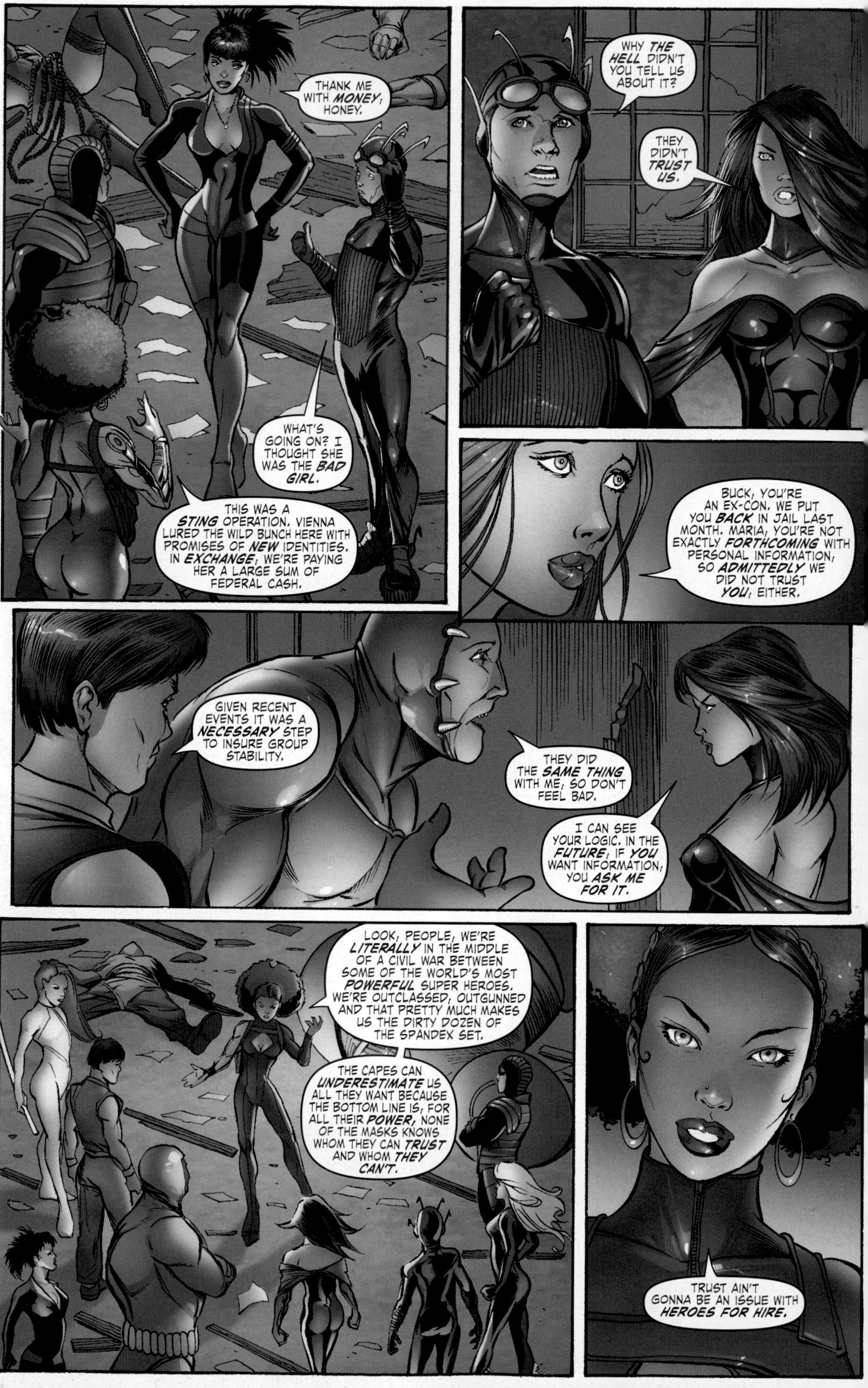

THANK ME WITH MONEY, HONEY.
WHAT'S GOING ON? I THOUGHT SHE WAS THE BAD GIRL.
THIS WAS A STING OPERATION. VIENNA LURED THE WILD BUNCH HERE WITH PROMISES OF NEW IDENTITIES. IN EXCHANGE, WE'RE PAYING HER A LARGE SUM OF FEDERAL CASH.
WHY THE HELL DIDN'T YOU TELL US ABOUT IT?
THEY DIDN'T TRUST US.
BUCK, YOU'RE AN EX-CON. WE PUT YOU BACK IN JAIL LAST MONTH. MARIA, YOU'RE NOT EXACTLY FORTHCOMING WITH PERSONAL INFORMATION, SO ADMITTEDLY WE DID NOT TRUST YOU, EITHER.
GIVEN RECENT EVENTS IT WAS A NECESSARY STEP TO INSURE GROUP STABILITY.
THEY DID THE SAME THING WITH ME, SO DON'T FEEL BAD.
I CAN SEE YOUR LOGIC. IN THE FUTURE, IF YOU WANT INFORMATION, YOU ASK ME FOR IT.
LOOK, PEOPLE, WE'RE LITERALLY IN THE MIDDLE OF A CIVIL WAR BETWEEN SOME OF THE WORLD'S MOST POWERFUL SUPER HEROES. WE'RE OUTCLASSED, OUTGUNNED AND THAT PRETTY MUCH MAKES US THE DIRTY DOZEN OF THE SPANDEX SET.
THE CAPES CAN UNDERESTIMATE US ALL THEY WANT BECAUSE THE BOTTOM LINE IS, FOR ALL THEIR POWER, NONE OF THE MASKS KNOWS WHOM THEY CAN TRUST AND WHOM THEY CAN'T.
TRUST AIN'T GONNA BE AN ISSUE WITH HEROES FOR HIRE.

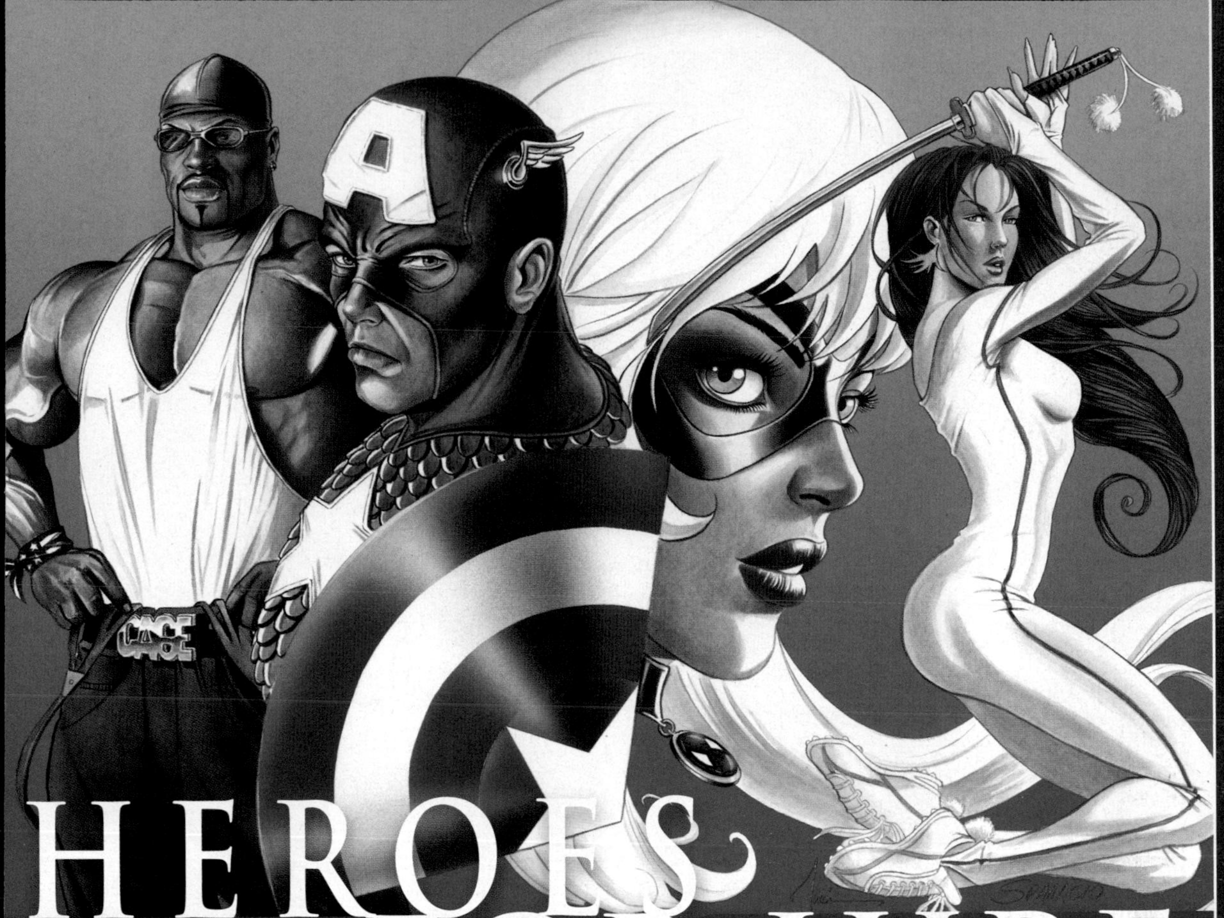
CAGE

# HEROES FOR HIRE

A MARVEL COMICS EVENT

## CIVIL WAR

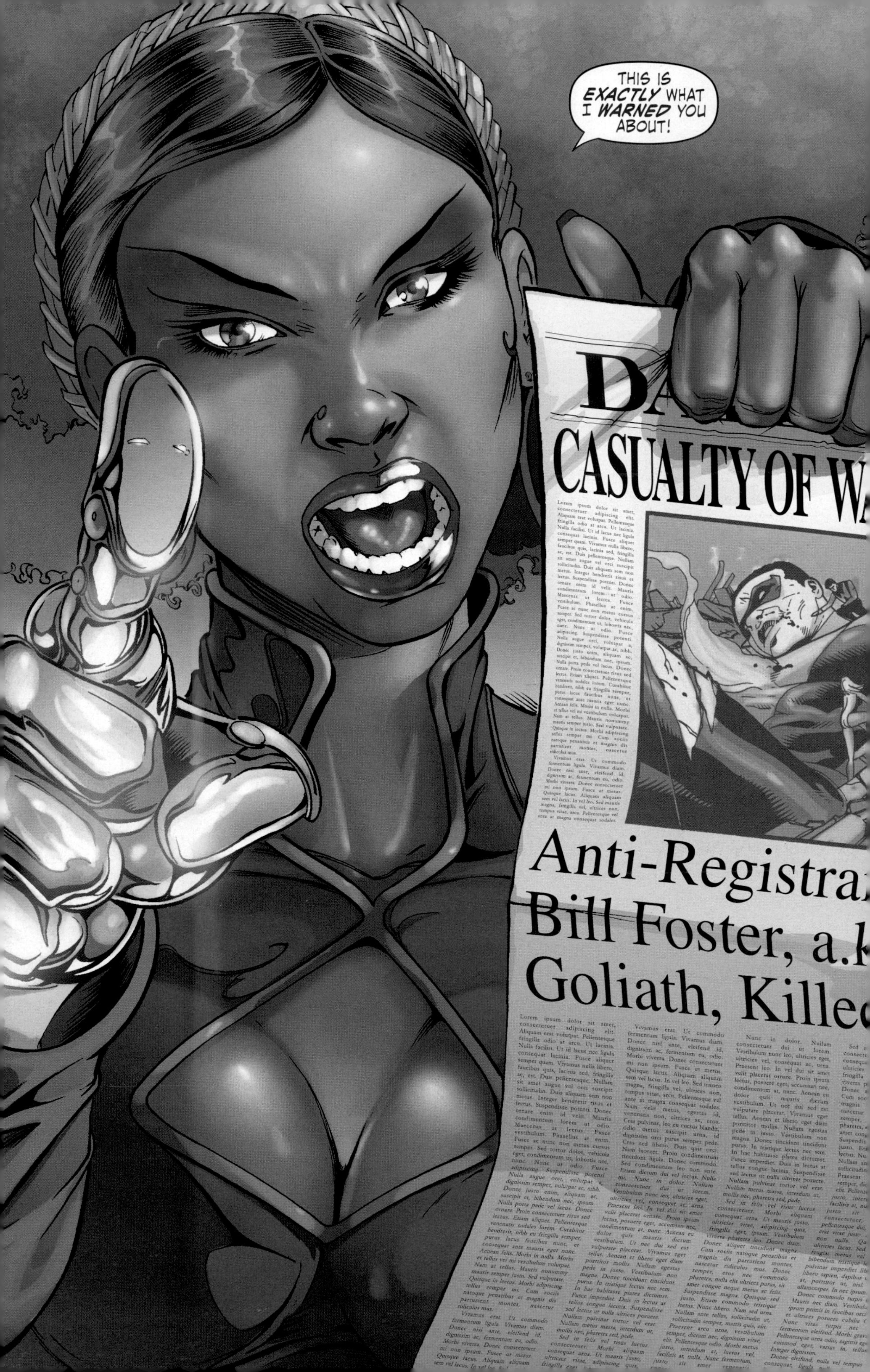
THIS IS EXACTLY WHAT I WARNED YOU ABOUT!
CASUALTY OF WA
Anti-Registra
Bill Foster, a.k
Goliath, Kille

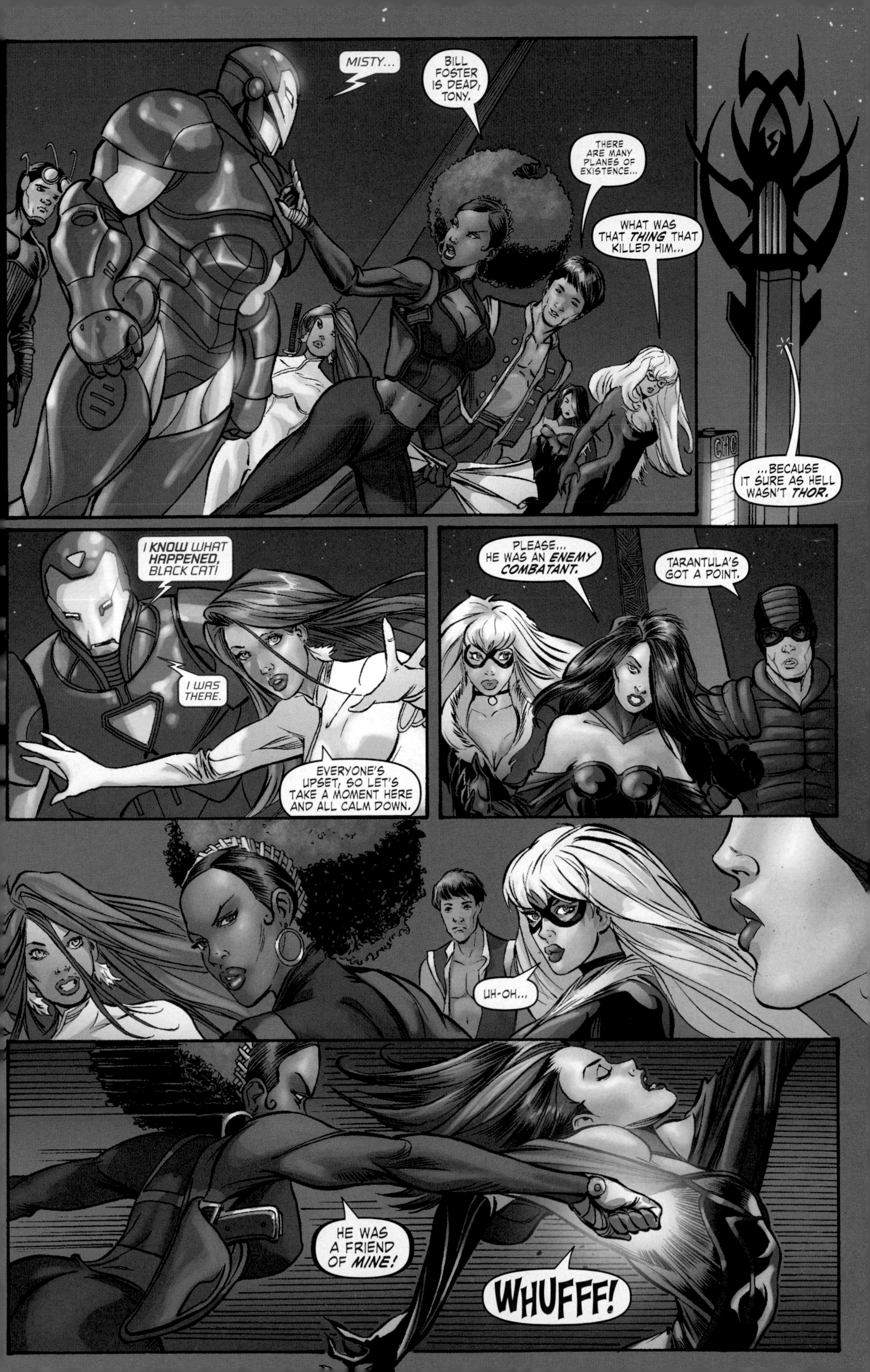
MISTY...
BILL FOSTER IS DEAD, TONY.
THERE ARE MANY PLANES OF EXISTENCE...
WHAT WAS THAT THING THAT KILLED HIM...
...BECAUSE IT SURE AS HELL WASN'T THOR.
I KNOW WHAT HAPPENED, BLACK CAT!
I WAS THERE.
EVERYONE'S UPSET, SO LET'S TAKE A MOMENT HERE AND ALL CALM DOWN.
PLEASE... HE WAS AN ENEMY COMBATANT.
TARANTULA'S GOT A POINT.
UH-OH...
HE WAS A FRIEND OF MINE!
WHUFFF!

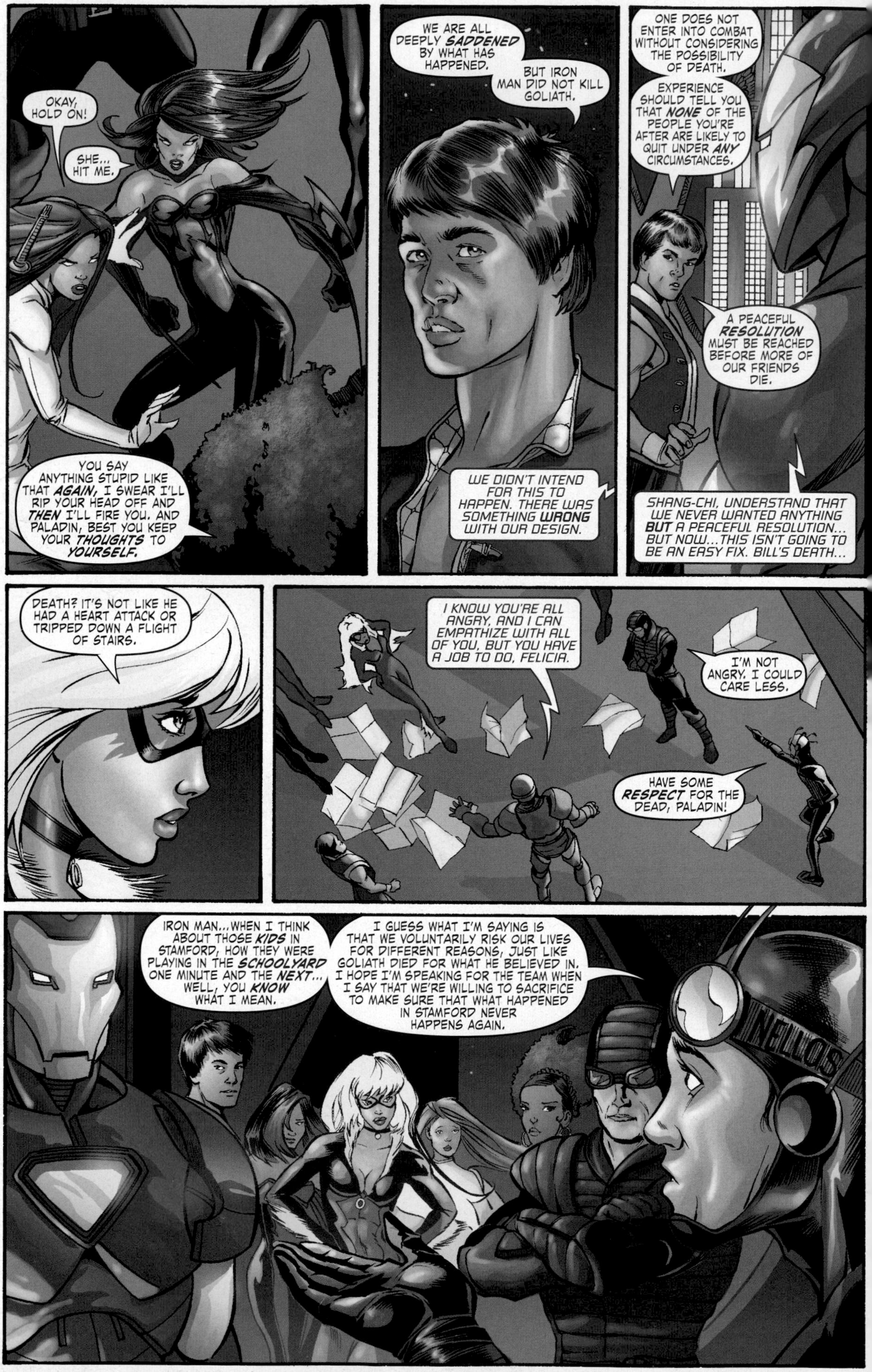
OKAY, HOLD ON!
SHE... HIT ME.
YOU SAY ANYTHING STUPID LIKE THAT AGAIN, I SWEAR I'LL RIP YOUR HEAD OFF AND THEN I'LL FIRE YOU. AND PALADIN, BEST YOU KEEP YOUR THOUGHTS TO YOURSELF.
WE ARE ALL DEEPLY SADDENED BY WHAT HAS HAPPENED.
BUT IRON MAN DID NOT KILL GOLIATH.
WE DIDN'T INTEND FOR THIS TO HAPPEN. THERE WAS SOMETHING WRONG WITH OUR DESIGN.
ONE DOES NOT ENTER INTO COMBAT WITHOUT CONSIDERING THE POSSIBILITY OF DEATH.
EXPERIENCE SHOULD TELL YOU THAT NONE OF THE PEOPLE YOU'RE AFTER ARE LIKELY TO QUIT UNDER ANY CIRCUMSTANCES.
A PEACEFUL RESOLUTION MUST BE REACHED BEFORE MORE OF OUR FRIENDS DIE.
SHANG-CHI, UNDERSTAND THAT WE NEVER WANTED ANYTHING BUT A PEACEFUL RESOLUTION... BUT NOW... THIS ISN'T GOING TO BE AN EASY FIX. BILL'S DEATH...
DEATH? IT'S NOT LIKE HE HAD A HEART ATTACK OR TRIPPED DOWN A FLIGHT OF STAIRS.
I KNOW YOU'RE ALL ANGRY, AND I CAN EMPATHIZE WITH ALL OF YOU, BUT YOU HAVE A JOB TO DO, FELICIA.
I'M NOT ANGRY. I COULD CARE LESS.
HAVE SOME RESPECT FOR THE DEAD, PALADIN!
IRON MAN... WHEN I THINK ABOUT THOSE KIDS IN STAMFORD, HOW THEY WERE PLAYING IN THE SCHOOLYARD ONE MINUTE AND THE NEXT... WELL, YOU KNOW WHAT I MEAN.
I GUESS WHAT I'M SAYING IS THAT WE VOLUNTARILY RISK OUR LIVES FOR DIFFERENT REASONS, JUST LIKE GOLIATH DIED FOR WHAT HE BELIEVED IN. I HOPE I'M SPEAKING FOR THE TEAM WHEN I SAY THAT WE'RE WILLING TO SACRIFICE TO MAKE SURE THAT WHAT HAPPENED IN STAMFORD NEVER HAPPENS AGAIN.

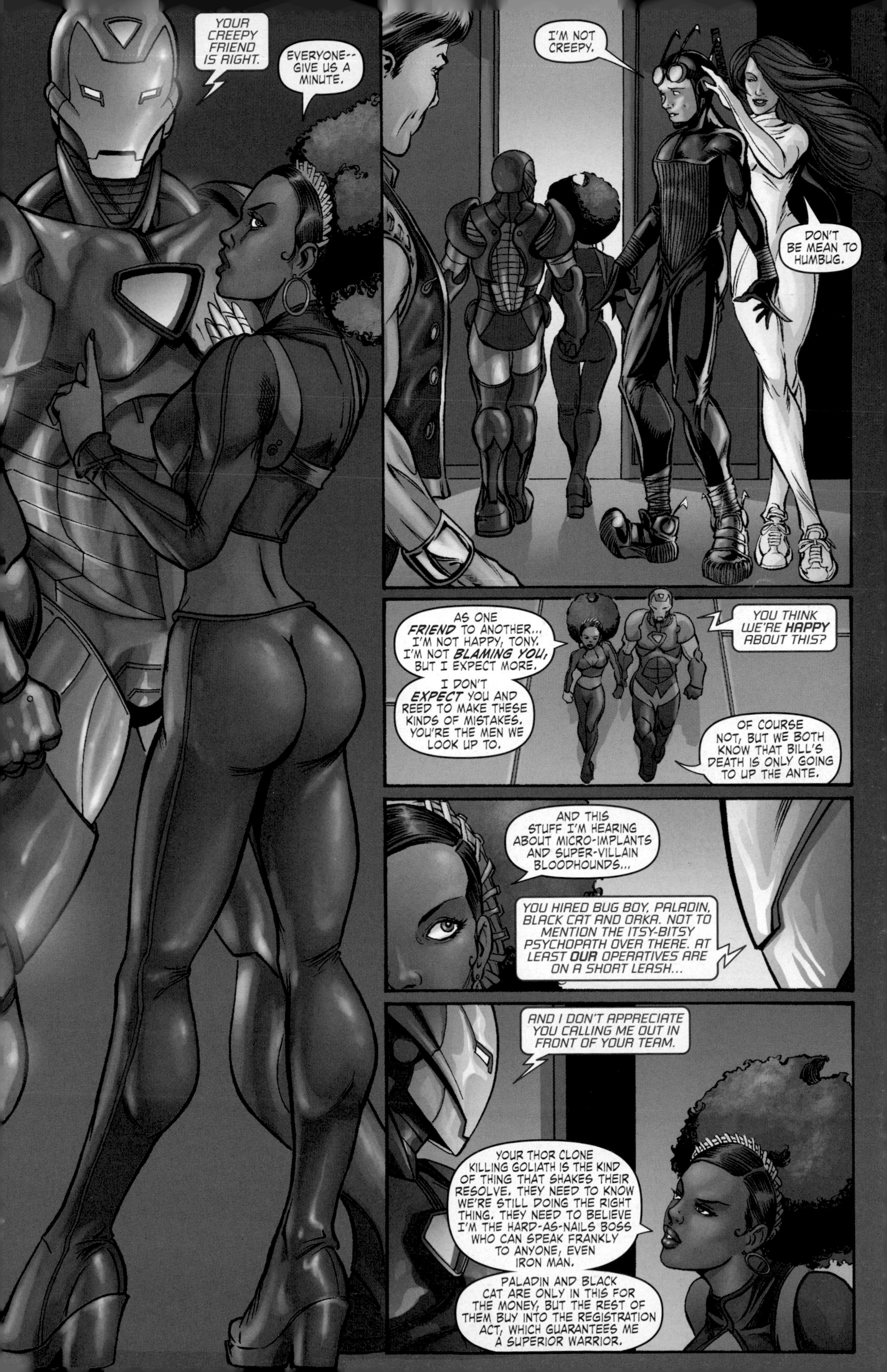
YOUR CREEPY FRIEND IS RIGHT.
EVERYONE-- GIVE US A MINUTE.
I'M NOT CREEPY.
DON'T BE MEAN TO HUMBUG.
AS ONE FRIEND TO ANOTHER... I'M NOT HAPPY, TONY. I'M NOT BLAMING YOU, BUT I EXPECT MORE.
I DON'T EXPECT YOU AND REED TO MAKE THESE KINDS OF MISTAKES. YOU'RE THE MEN WE LOOK UP TO.
YOU THINK WE'RE HAPPY ABOUT THIS?
OF COURSE NOT, BUT WE BOTH KNOW THAT BILL'S DEATH IS ONLY GOING TO UP THE ANTE.
AND THIS STUFF I'M HEARING ABOUT MICRO-IMPLANTS AND SUPER-VILLAIN BLOODHOUNDS...
YOU HIRED BUG BOY, PALADIN, BLACK CAT AND ORKA. NOT TO MENTION THE ITSY-BITSY PSYCHOPATH OVER THERE. AT LEAST OUR OPERATIVES ARE ON A SHORT LEASH...
AND I DON'T APPRECIATE YOU CALLING ME OUT IN FRONT OF YOUR TEAM.
YOUR THOR CLONE KILLING GOLIATH IS THE KIND OF THING THAT SHAKES THEIR RESOLVE. THEY NEED TO KNOW WE'RE STILL DOING THE RIGHT THING. THEY NEED TO BELIEVE I'M THE HARD-AS-NAILS BOSS WHO CAN SPEAK FRANKLY TO ANYONE, EVEN IRON MAN.
PALADIN AND BLACK CAT ARE ONLY IN THIS FOR THE MONEY, BUT THE REST OF THEM BUY INTO THE REGISTRATION ACT, WHICH GUARANTEES ME A SUPERIOR WARRIOR.

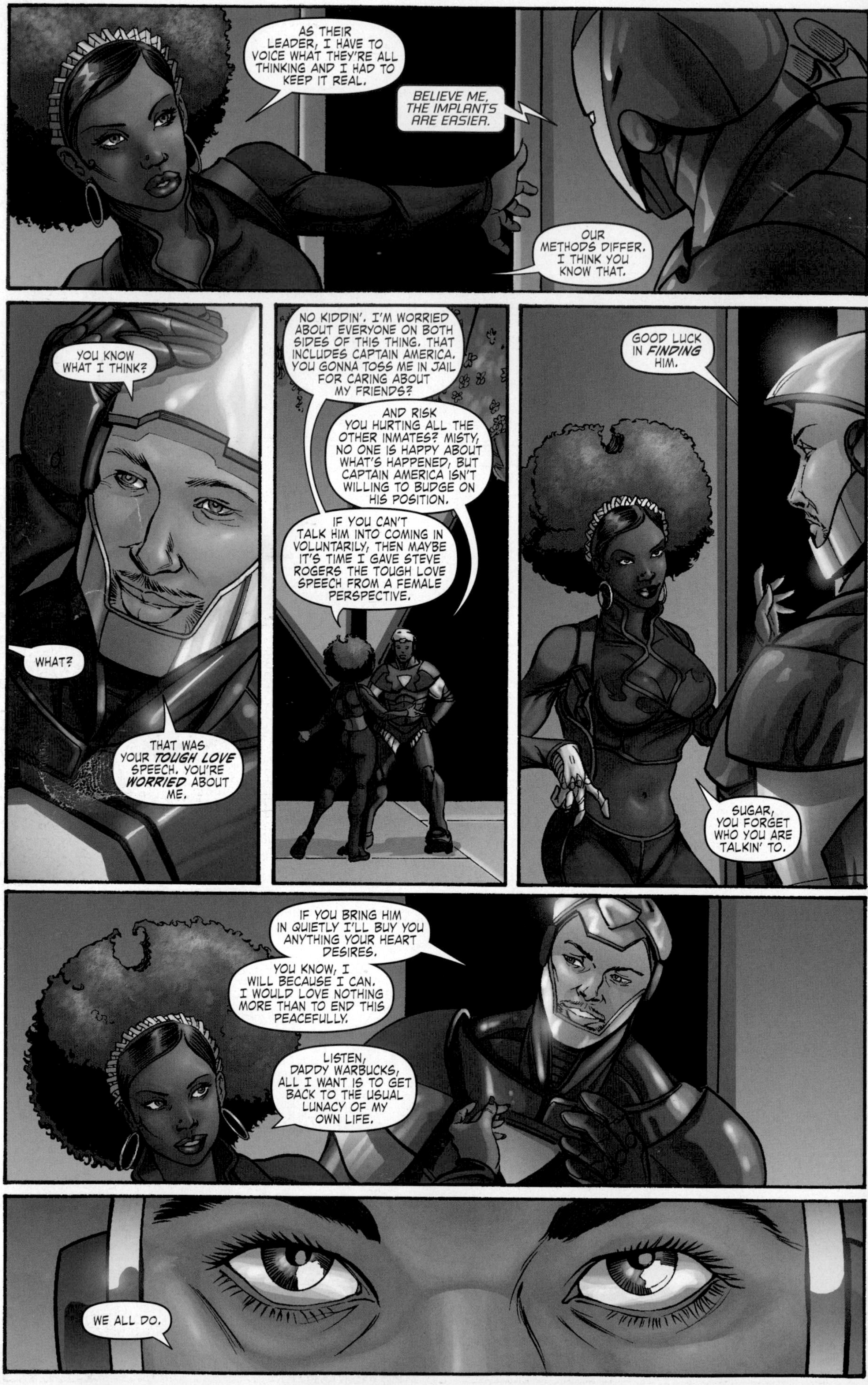
AS THEIR LEADER, I HAVE TO VOICE WHAT THEY'RE ALL THINKING AND I HAD TO KEEP IT REAL.
BELIEVE ME, THE IMPLANTS ARE EASIER.
OUR METHODS DIFFER. I THINK YOU KNOW THAT.
YOU KNOW WHAT I THINK?
WHAT?
THAT WAS YOUR TOUGH LOVE SPEECH. YOU'RE WORRIED ABOUT ME.
NO KIDDIN'. I'M WORRIED ABOUT EVERYONE ON BOTH SIDES OF THIS THING. THAT INCLUDES CAPTAIN AMERICA. YOU GONNA TOSS ME IN JAIL FOR CARING ABOUT MY FRIENDS?
AND RISK YOU HURTING ALL THE OTHER INMATES? MISTY, NO ONE IS HAPPY ABOUT WHAT'S HAPPENED, BUT CAPTAIN AMERICA ISN'T WILLING TO BUDGE ON HIS POSITION.
IF YOU CAN'T TALK HIM INTO COMING IN VOLUNTARILY, THEN MAYBE IT'S TIME I GAVE STEVE ROGERS THE TOUGH LOVE SPEECH FROM A FEMALE PERSPECTIVE.
GOOD LUCK IN FINDING HIM.
SUGAR, YOU FORGET WHO YOU ARE TALKIN' TO.
IF YOU BRING HIM IN QUIETLY I'LL BUY YOU ANYTHING YOUR HEART DESIRES.
YOU KNOW, I WILL BECAUSE I CAN. I WOULD LOVE NOTHING MORE THAN TO END THIS PEACEFULLY.
LISTEN, DADDY WARBUCKS, ALL I WANT IS TO GET BACK TO THE USUAL LUNACY OF MY OWN LIFE.
WE ALL DO.

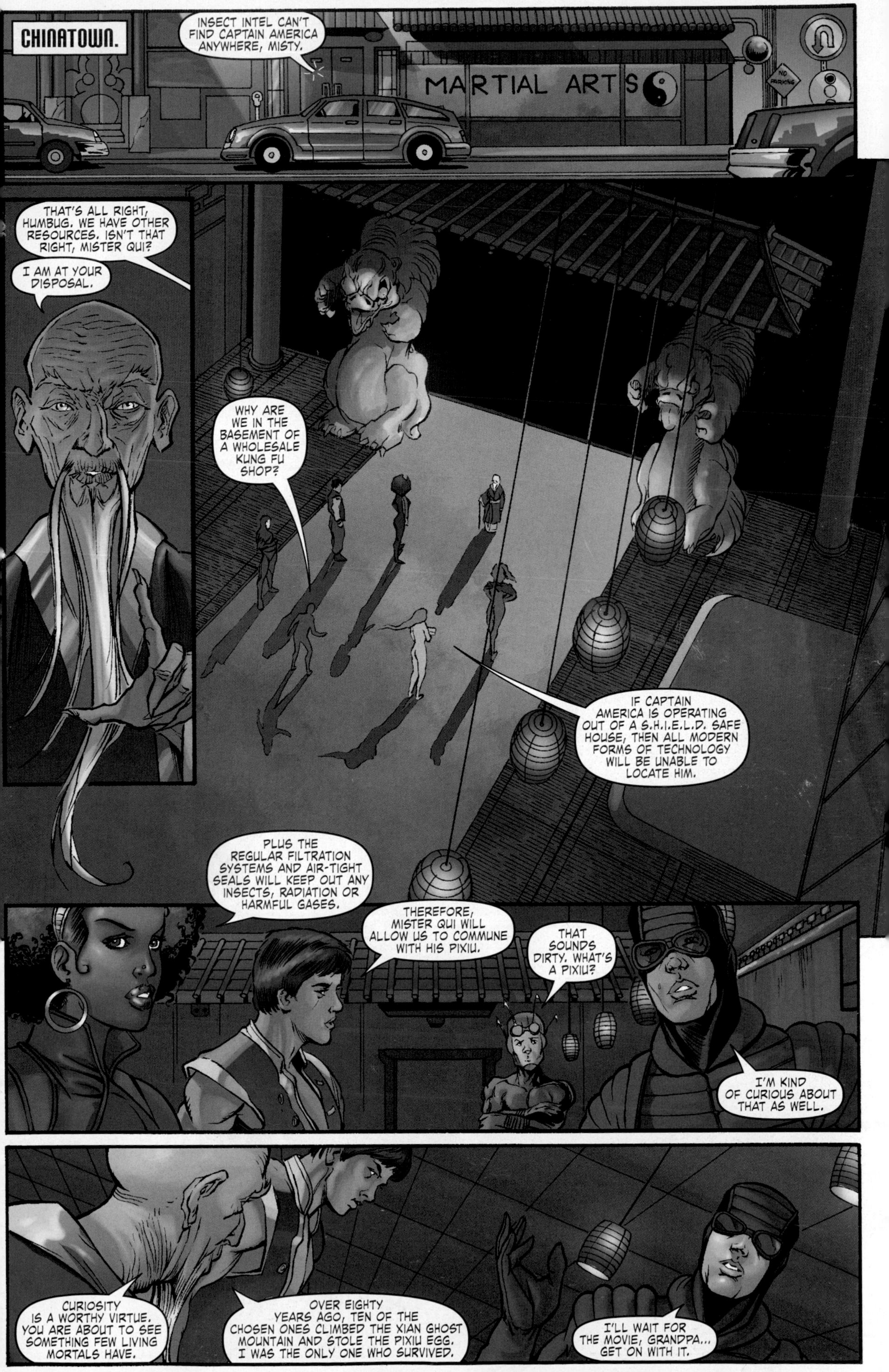
CHINATOWN.
INSECT INTEL CAN'T FIND CAPTAIN AMERICA ANYWHERE, MISTY.
MARTIAL ARTS
NO PARKING
THAT'S ALL RIGHT, HUMBUG. WE HAVE OTHER RESOURCES. ISN'T THAT RIGHT, MISTER QUI?
I AM AT YOUR DISPOSAL.
WHY ARE WE IN THE BASEMENT OF A WHOLESALE KUNG FU SHOP?
IF CAPTAIN AMERICA IS OPERATING OUT OF A S.H.I.E.L.D. SAFE HOUSE, THEN ALL MODERN FORMS OF TECHNOLOGY WILL BE UNABLE TO LOCATE HIM.
PLUS THE REGULAR FILTRATION SYSTEMS AND AIR-TIGHT SEALS WILL KEEP OUT ANY INSECTS, RADIATION OR HARMFUL GASES.
THEREFORE, MISTER QUI WILL ALLOW US TO COMMUNE WITH HIS PIXIU.
THAT SOUNDS DIRTY. WHAT'S A PIXIU?
I'M KIND OF CURIOUS ABOUT THAT AS WELL.
CURIOSITY IS A WORTHY VIRTUE. YOU ARE ABOUT TO SEE SOMETHING FEW LIVING MORTALS HAVE.
OVER EIGHTY YEARS AGO, TEN OF THE CHOSEN ONES CLIMBED THE XIAN GHOST MOUNTAIN AND STOLE THE PIXIU EGG. I WAS THE ONLY ONE WHO SURVIVED.
I'LL WAIT FOR THE MOVIE, GRANDPA... GET ON WITH IT.

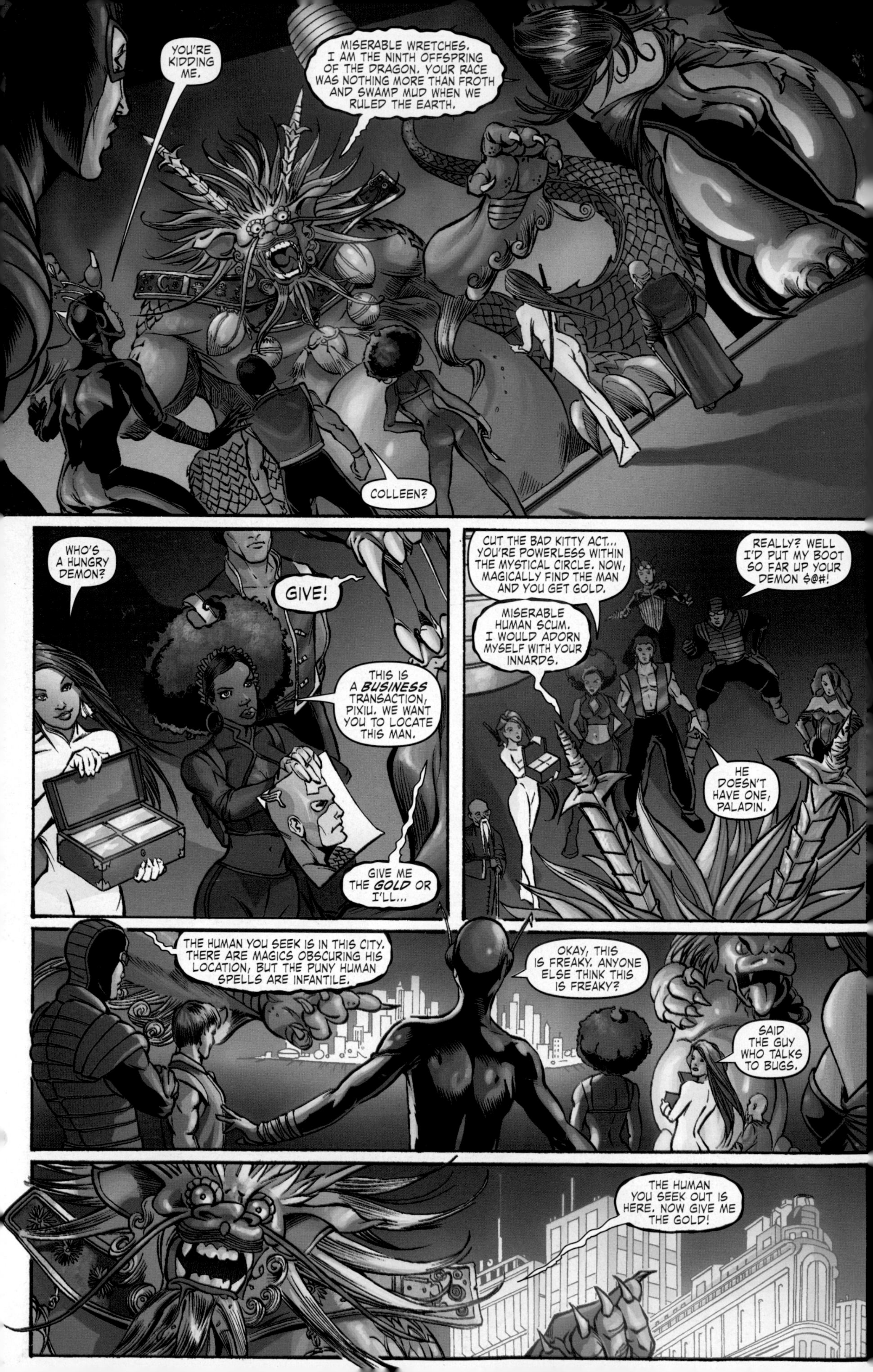
YOU'RE KIDDING ME.
MISERABLE WRETCHES. I AM THE NINTH OFFSPRING OF THE DRAGON. YOUR RACE WAS NOTHING MORE THAN FROTH AND SWAMP MUD WHEN WE RULED THE EARTH.
COLLEEN?
WHO'S A HUNGRY DEMON?
GIVE!
THIS IS A BUSINESS TRANSACTION, PIXIU. WE WANT YOU TO LOCATE THIS MAN.
GIVE ME THE GOLD OR I'LL...
CUT THE BAD KITTY ACT... YOU'RE POWERLESS WITHIN THE MYSTICAL CIRCLE. NOW, MAGICALLY FIND THE MAN AND YOU GET GOLD.
MISERABLE HUMAN SCUM. I WOULD ADORN MYSELF WITH YOUR INNARDS.
REALLY? WELL I'D PUT MY BOOT SO FAR UP YOUR DEMON $@#!
HE DOESN'T HAVE ONE, PALADIN.
THE HUMAN YOU SEEK IS IN THIS CITY. THERE ARE MAGICS OBSCURING HIS LOCATION, BUT THE PUNY HUMAN SPELLS ARE INFANTILE.
OKAY, THIS IS FREAKY. ANYONE ELSE THINK THIS IS FREAKY?
SAID THE GUY WHO TALKS TO BUGS.
THE HUMAN YOU SEEK OUT IS HERE. NOW GIVE ME THE GOLD!

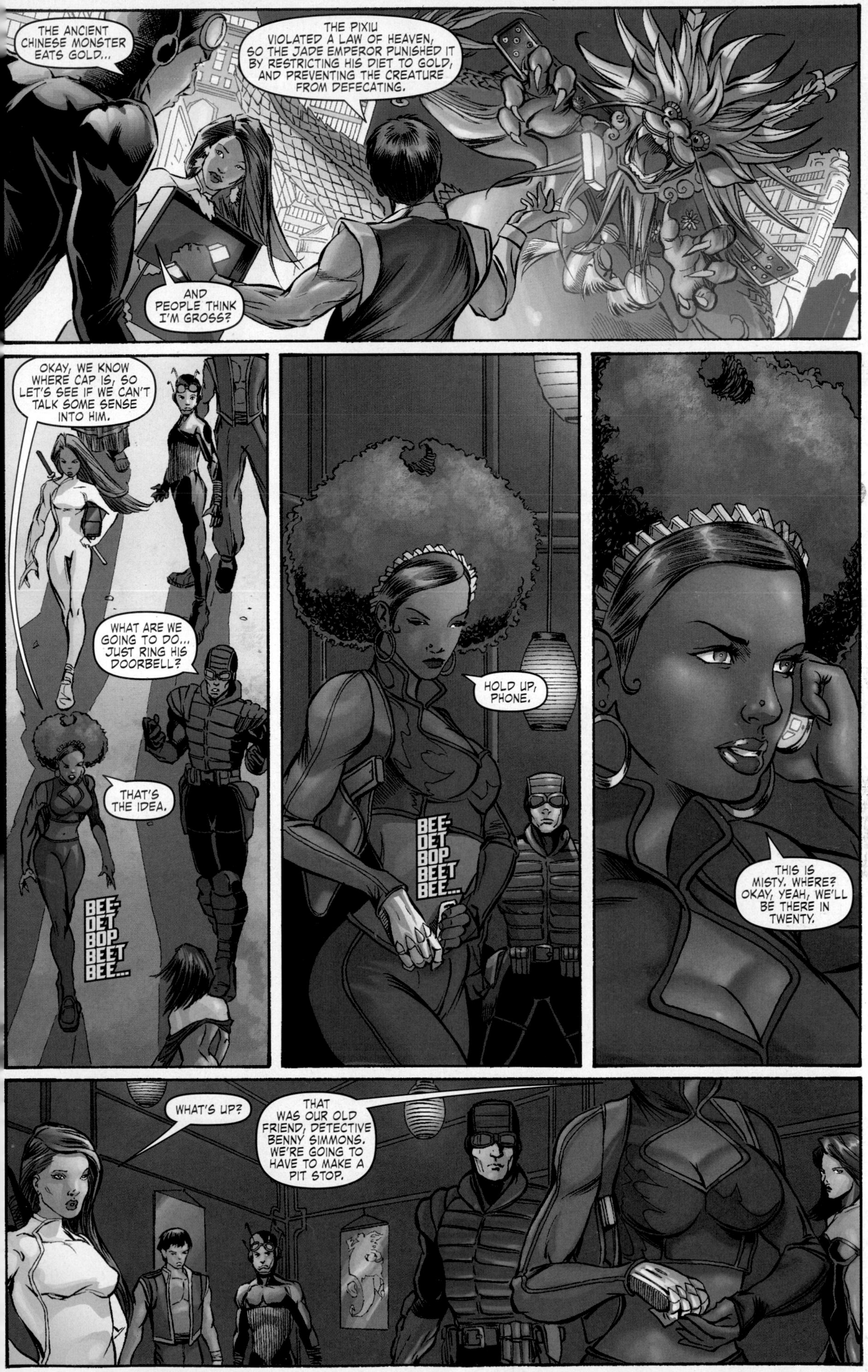
THE ANCIENT CHINESE MONSTER EATS GOLD...
THE PIXIU VIOLATED A LAW OF HEAVEN, SO THE JADE EMPEROR PUNISHED IT BY RESTRICTING HIS DIET TO GOLD, AND PREVENTING THE CREATURE FROM DEFECATING.
AND PEOPLE THINK I'M GROSS?
OKAY, WE KNOW WHERE CAP IS, SO LET'S SEE IF WE CAN'T TALK SOME SENSE INTO HIM.
WHAT ARE WE GOING TO DO... JUST RING HIS DOORBELL?
THAT'S THE IDEA.
BEE-DET BOP BEET BEE...
HOLD UP, PHONE.
BEE-DET BOP BEET BEE...
THIS IS MISTY. WHERE? OKAY, YEAH, WE'LL BE THERE IN TWENTY.
WHAT'S UP?
THAT WAS OUR OLD FRIEND, DETECTIVE BENNY SIMMONS. WE'RE GOING TO HAVE TO MAKE A PIT STOP.

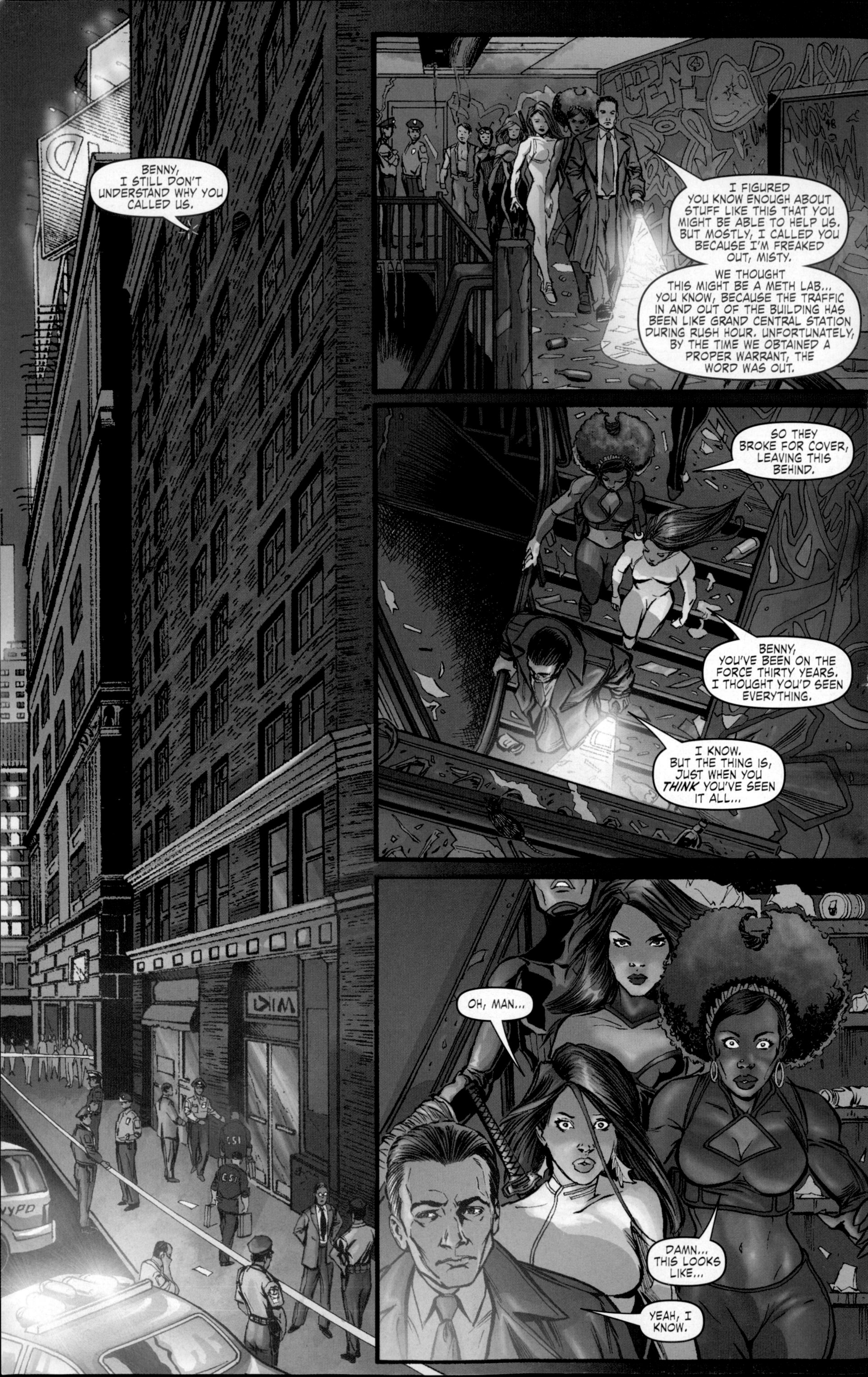
BENNY, I STILL DON'T UNDERSTAND WHY YOU CALLED US.
I FIGURED YOU KNOW ENOUGH ABOUT STUFF LIKE THIS THAT YOU MIGHT BE ABLE TO HELP US. BUT MOSTLY, I CALLED YOU BECAUSE I'M FREAKED OUT, MISTY.
WE THOUGHT THIS MIGHT BE A METH LAB... YOU KNOW, BECAUSE THE TRAFFIC IN AND OUT OF THE BUILDING HAS BEEN LIKE GRAND CENTRAL STATION DURING RUSH HOUR. UNFORTUNATELY, BY THE TIME WE OBTAINED A PROPER WARRANT, THE WORD WAS OUT.
SO THEY BROKE FOR COVER, LEAVING THIS BEHIND.
BENNY, YOU'VE BEEN ON THE FORCE THIRTY YEARS. I THOUGHT YOU'D SEEN EVERYTHING.
I KNOW. BUT THE THING IS, JUST WHEN YOU *THINK* YOU'VE SEEN IT ALL...
OH, MAN...
DAMN... THIS LOOKS LIKE...
YEAH, I KNOW.
NYPD
CSI

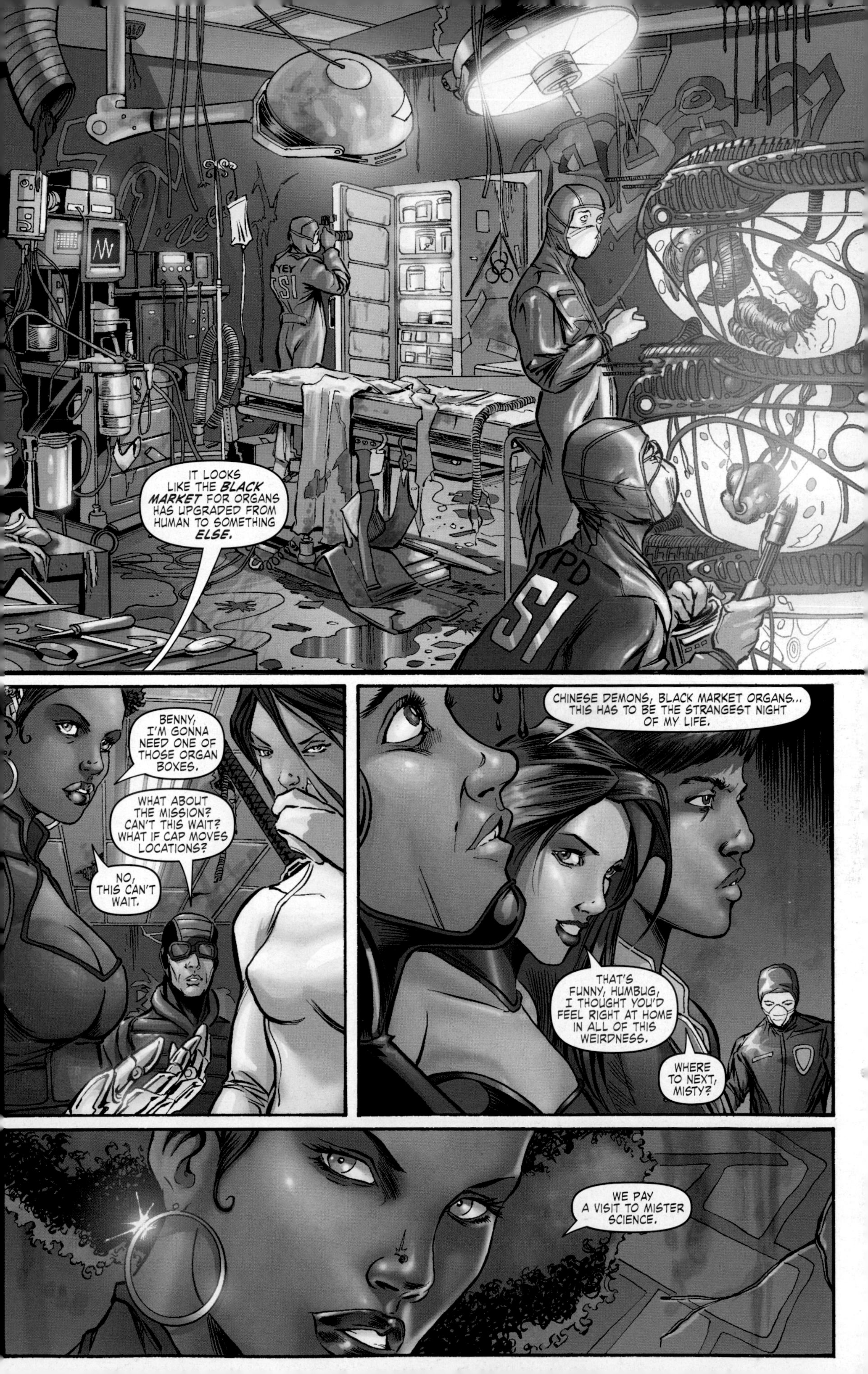
IT LOOKS LIKE THE BLACK MARKET FOR ORGANS HAS UPGRADED FROM HUMAN TO SOMETHING ELSE.
BENNY, I'M GONNA NEED ONE OF THOSE ORGAN BOXES.
WHAT ABOUT THE MISSION? CAN'T THIS WAIT? WHAT IF CAP MOVES LOCATIONS?
NO, THIS CAN'T WAIT.
CHINESE DEMONS, BLACK MARKET ORGANS... THIS HAS TO BE THE STRANGEST NIGHT OF MY LIFE.
THAT'S FUNNY, HUMBUG, I THOUGHT YOU'D FEEL RIGHT AT HOME IN ALL OF THIS WEIRDNESS.
WHERE TO NEXT, MISTY?
WE PAY A VISIT TO MISTER SCIENCE.

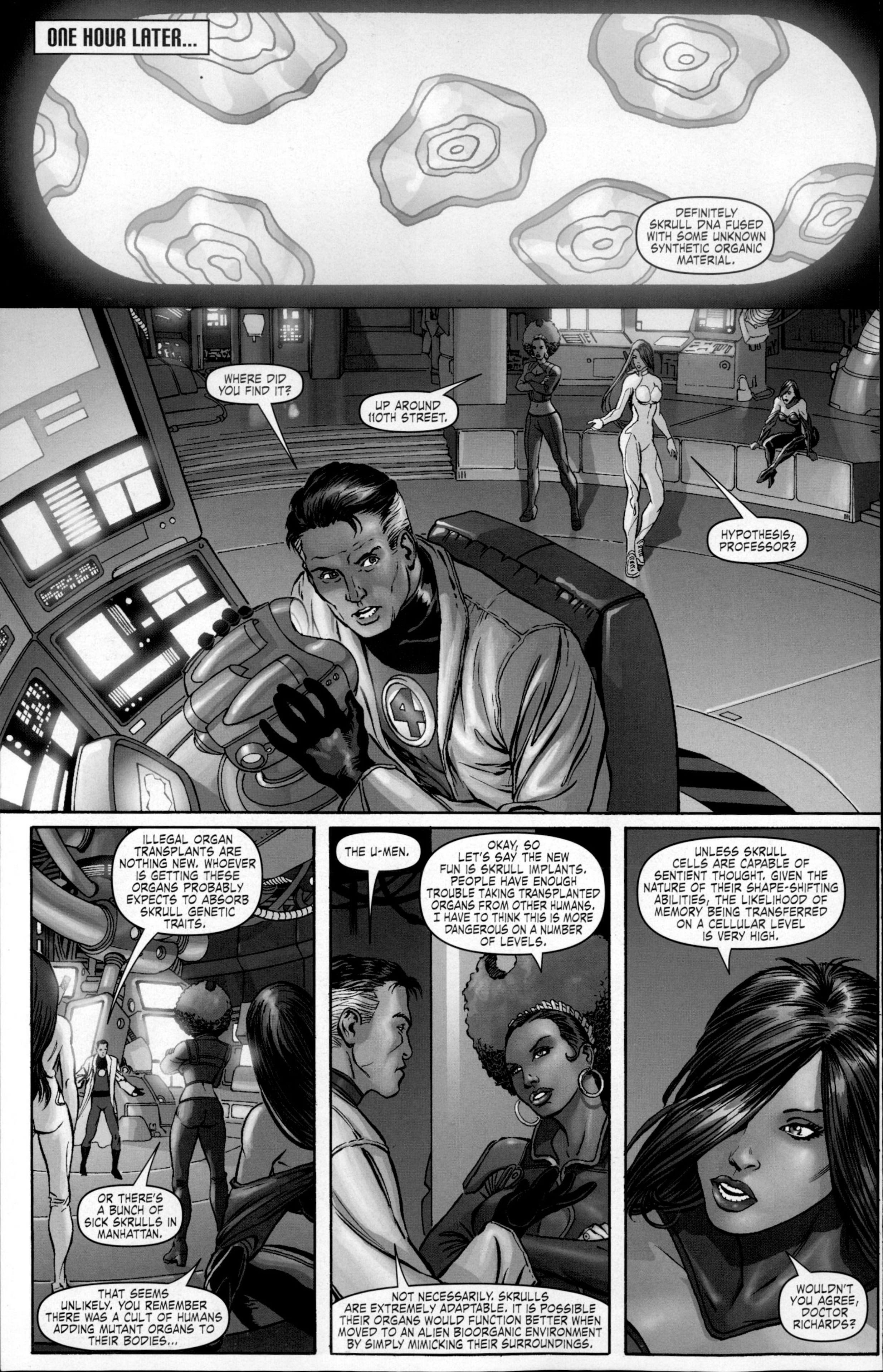
ONE HOUR LATER...
DEFINITELY SKRULL DNA FUSED WITH SOME UNKNOWN SYNTHETIC ORGANIC MATERIAL.
WHERE DID YOU FIND IT?
UP AROUND 110TH STREET.
HYPOTHESIS, PROFESSOR?
ILLEGAL ORGAN TRANSPLANTS ARE NOTHING NEW. WHOEVER IS GETTING THESE ORGANS PROBABLY EXPECTS TO ABSORB SKRULL GENETIC TRAITS.
OR THERE'S A BUNCH OF SICK SKRULLS IN MANHATTAN.
THAT SEEMS UNLIKELY. YOU REMEMBER THERE WAS A CULT OF HUMANS ADDING MUTANT ORGANS TO THEIR BODIES...
THE U-MEN.
OKAY, SO LET'S SAY THE NEW FUN IS SKRULL IMPLANTS. PEOPLE HAVE ENOUGH TROUBLE TAKING TRANSPLANTED ORGANS FROM OTHER HUMANS. I HAVE TO THINK THIS IS MORE DANGEROUS ON A NUMBER OF LEVELS.
NOT NECESSARILY. SKRULLS ARE EXTREMELY ADAPTABLE. IT IS POSSIBLE THEIR ORGANS WOULD FUNCTION BETTER WHEN MOVED TO AN ALIEN BIOORGANIC ENVIRONMENT BY SIMPLY MIMICKING THEIR SURROUNDINGS.
UNLESS SKRULL CELLS ARE CAPABLE OF SENTIENT THOUGHT. GIVEN THE NATURE OF THEIR SHAPE-SHIFTING ABILITIES, THE LIKELIHOOD OF MEMORY BEING TRANSFERRED ON A CELLULAR LEVEL IS VERY HIGH.
WOULDN'T YOU AGREE, DOCTOR RICHARDS?

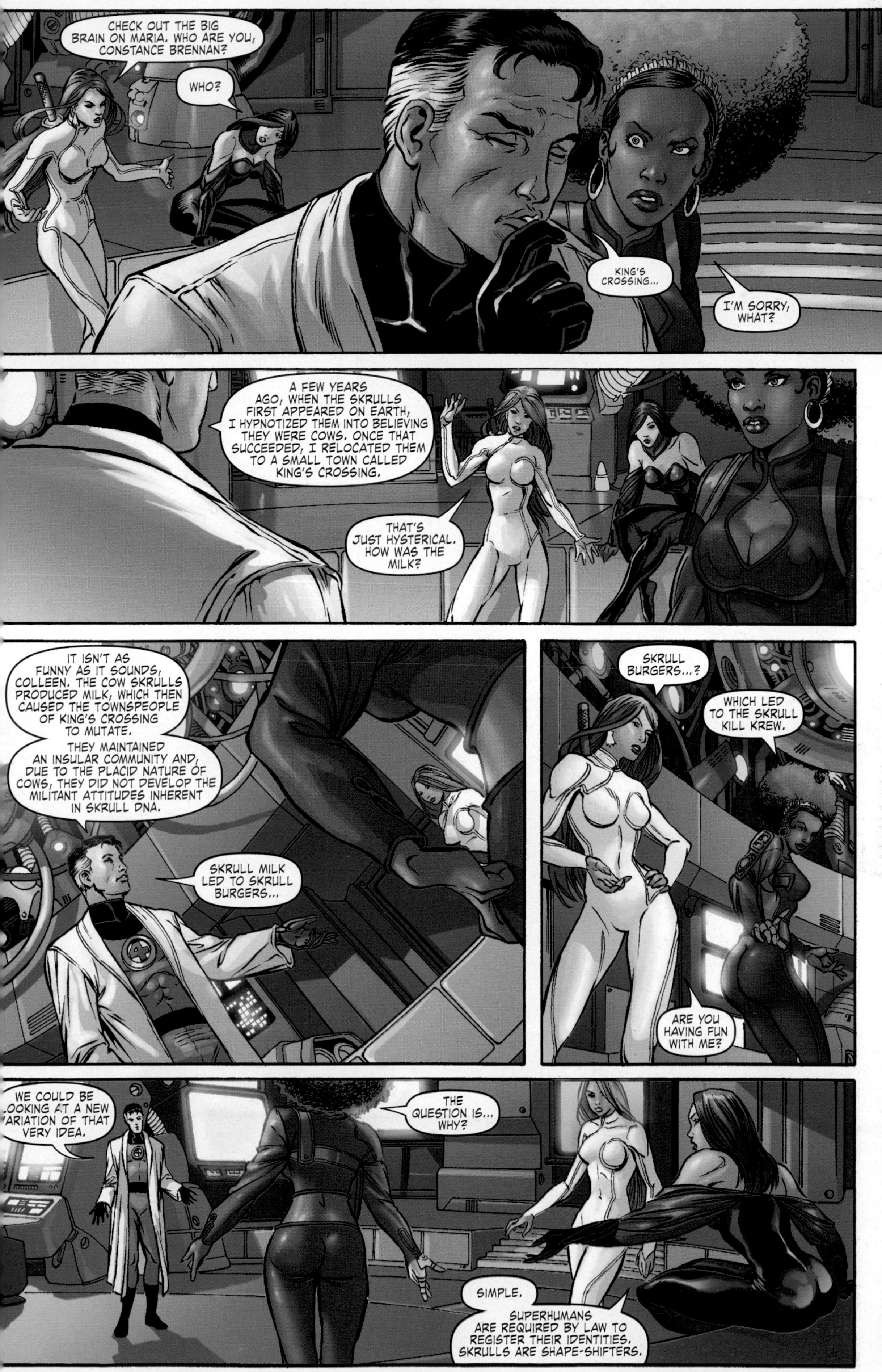
CHECK OUT THE BIG BRAIN ON MARIA. WHO ARE YOU, CONSTANCE BRENNAN?
WHO?
KING'S CROSSING...
I'M SORRY, WHAT?
A FEW YEARS AGO, WHEN THE SKRULLS FIRST APPEARED ON EARTH, I HYPNOTIZED THEM INTO BELIEVING THEY WERE COWS. ONCE THAT SUCCEEDED, I RELOCATED THEM TO A SMALL TOWN CALLED KING'S CROSSING.
THAT'S JUST HYSTERICAL. HOW WAS THE MILK?
IT ISN'T AS FUNNY AS IT SOUNDS, COLLEEN. THE COW SKRULLS PRODUCED MILK, WHICH THEN CAUSED THE TOWNSPEOPLE OF KING'S CROSSING TO MUTATE.
THEY MAINTAINED AN INSULAR COMMUNITY AND, DUE TO THE PLACID NATURE OF COWS, THEY DID NOT DEVELOP THE MILITANT ATTITUDES INHERENT IN SKRULL DNA.
SKRULL MILK LED TO SKRULL BURGERS...
SKRULL BURGERS...?
WHICH LED TO THE SKRULL KILL KREW.
ARE YOU HAVING FUN WITH ME?
WE COULD BE LOOKING AT A NEW VARIATION OF THAT VERY IDEA.
THE QUESTION IS... WHY?
SIMPLE.
SUPERHUMANS ARE REQUIRED BY LAW TO REGISTER THEIR IDENTITIES. SKRULLS ARE SHAPE-SHIFTERS.

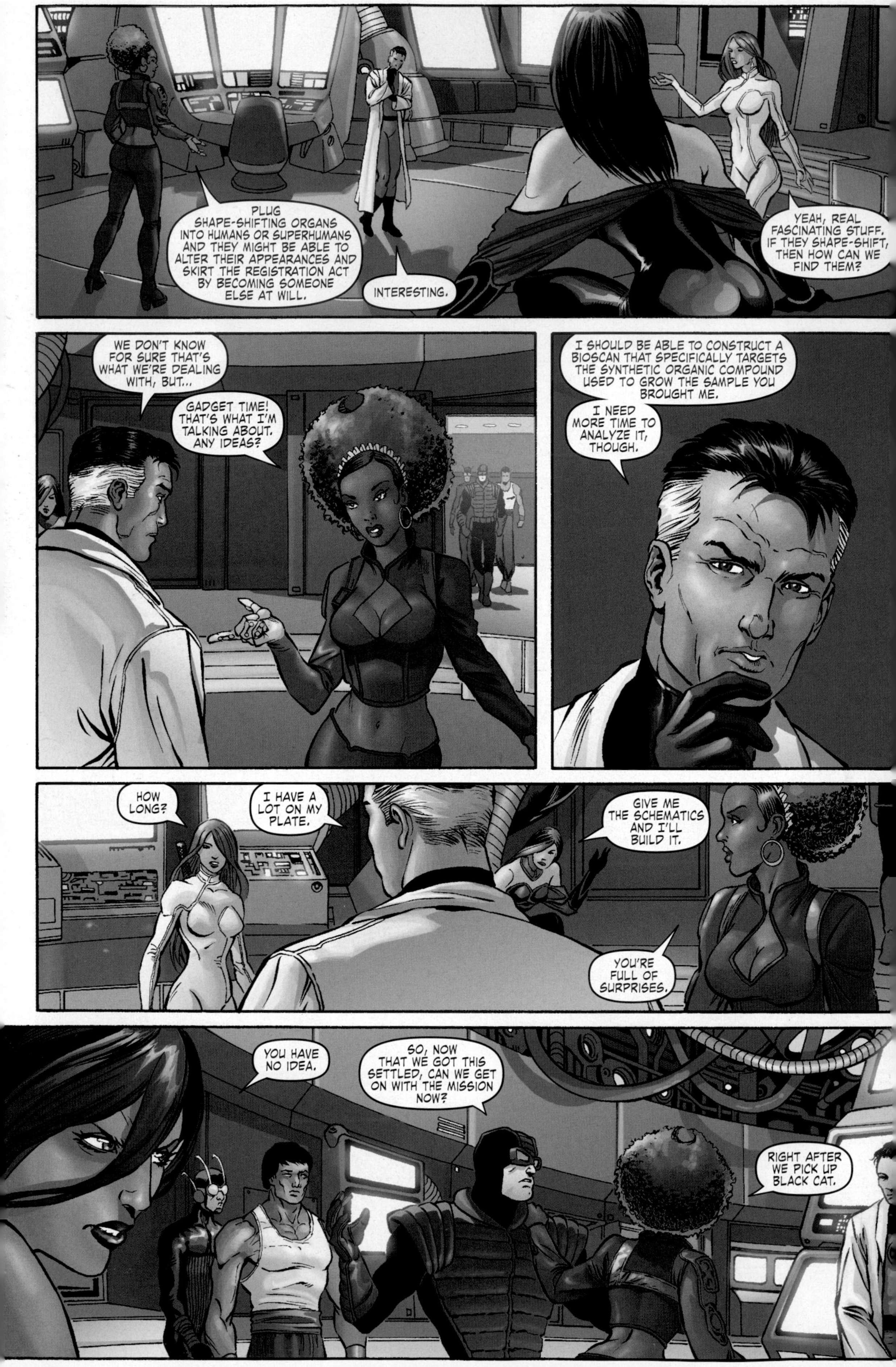
PLUG SHAPE-SHIFTING ORGANS INTO HUMANS OR SUPERHUMANS AND THEY MIGHT BE ABLE TO ALTER THEIR APPEARANCES AND SKIRT THE REGISTRATION ACT BY BECOMING SOMEONE ELSE AT WILL.
INTERESTING.
YEAH, REAL FASCINATING STUFF. IF THEY SHAPE-SHIFT, THEN HOW CAN WE FIND THEM?
WE DON'T KNOW FOR SURE THAT'S WHAT WE'RE DEALING WITH, BUT...
GADGET TIME! THAT'S WHAT I'M TALKING ABOUT. ANY IDEAS?
I SHOULD BE ABLE TO CONSTRUCT A BIOSCAN THAT SPECIFICALLY TARGETS THE SYNTHETIC ORGANIC COMPOUND USED TO GROW THE SAMPLE YOU BROUGHT ME.
I NEED MORE TIME TO ANALYZE IT, THOUGH.
HOW LONG?
I HAVE A LOT ON MY PLATE.
GIVE ME THE SCHEMATICS AND I'LL BUILD IT.
YOU'RE FULL OF SURPRISES.
YOU HAVE NO IDEA.
SO, NOW THAT WE GOT THIS SETTLED, CAN WE GET ON WITH THE MISSION NOW?
RIGHT AFTER WE PICK UP BLACK CAT.

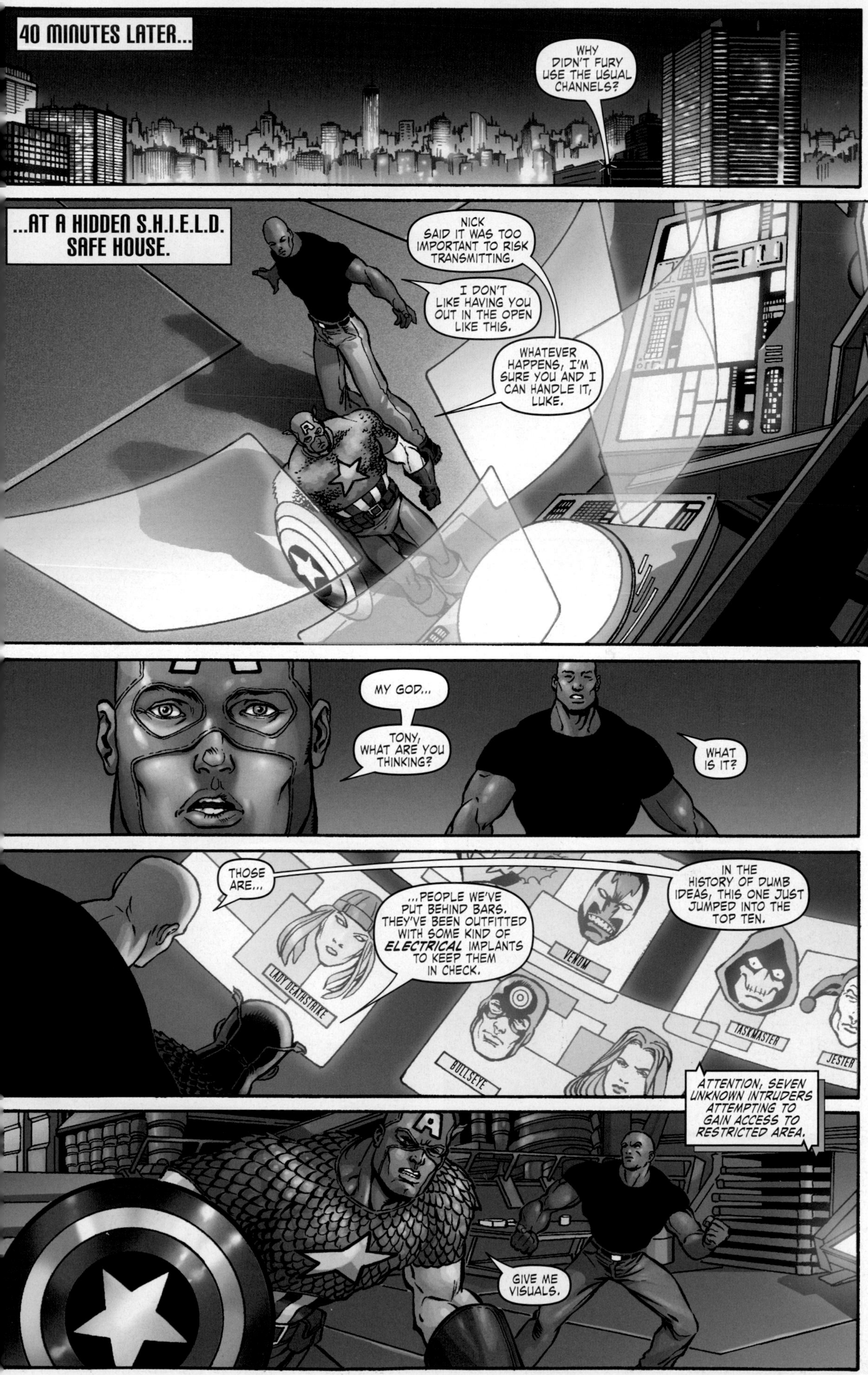
40 MINUTES LATER...
WHY DIDN'T FURY USE THE USUAL CHANNELS?
...AT A HIDDEN S.H.I.E.L.D. SAFE HOUSE.
NICK SAID IT WAS TOO IMPORTANT TO RISK TRANSMITTING.
I DON'T LIKE HAVING YOU OUT IN THE OPEN LIKE THIS.
WHATEVER HAPPENS, I'M SURE YOU AND I CAN HANDLE IT, LUKE.
MY GOD...
TONY, WHAT ARE YOU THINKING?
WHAT IS IT?
THOSE ARE...
...PEOPLE WE'VE PUT BEHIND BARS. THEY'VE BEEN OUTFITTED WITH SOME KIND OF ELECTRICAL IMPLANTS TO KEEP THEM IN CHECK.
IN THE HISTORY OF DUMB IDEAS, THIS ONE JUST JUMPED INTO THE TOP TEN.
LADY DEATHSTRIKE
VENOM
BULLSEYE
TASKMASTER
JESTER
ATTENTION, SEVEN UNKNOWN INTRUDERS ATTEMPTING TO GAIN ACCESS TO RESTRICTED AREA.
GIVE ME VISUALS.

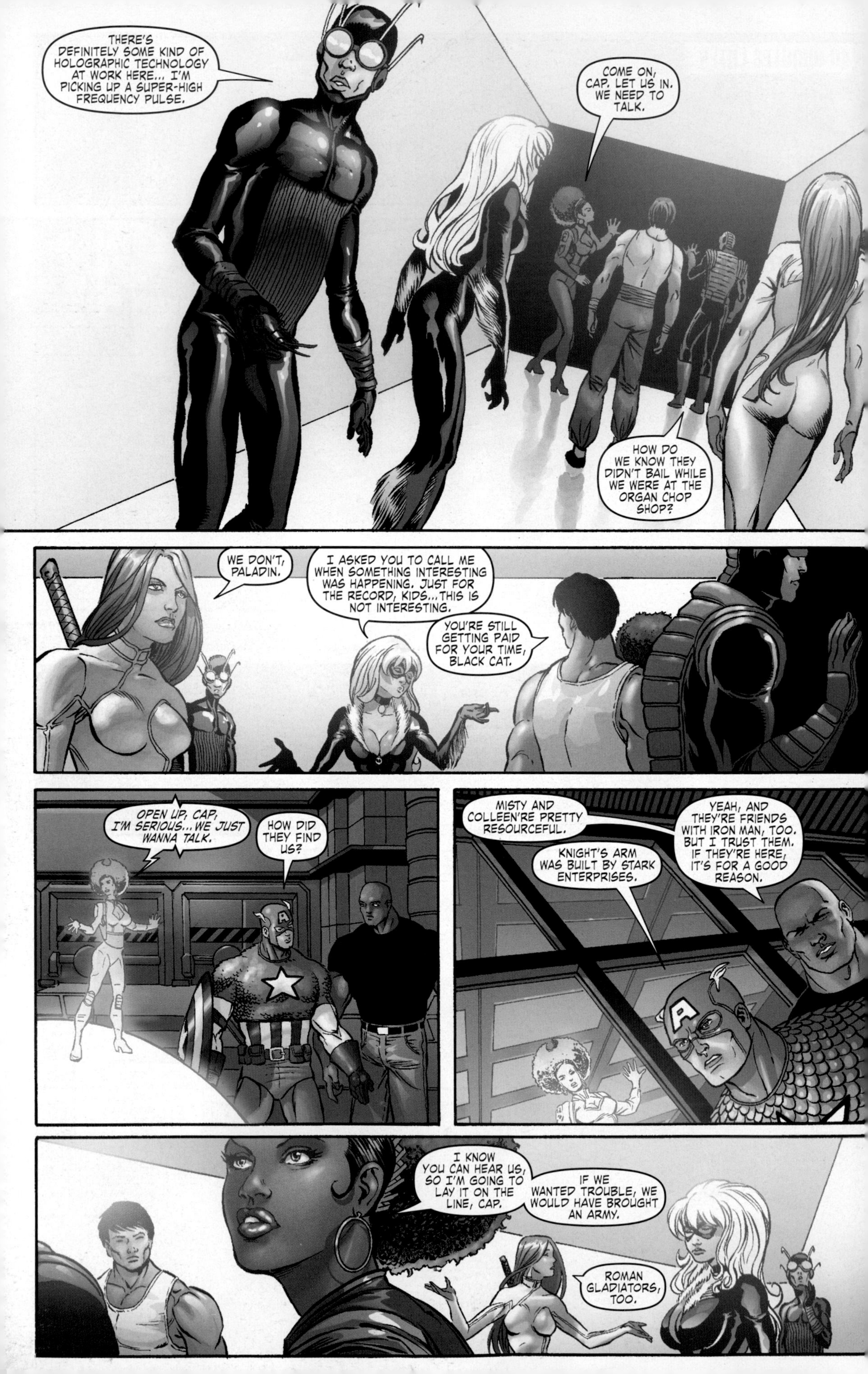
THERE'S DEFINITELY SOME KIND OF HOLOGRAPHIC TECHNOLOGY AT WORK HERE... I'M PICKING UP A SUPER-HIGH FREQUENCY PULSE.
COME ON, CAP. LET US IN. WE NEED TO TALK.
HOW DO WE KNOW THEY DIDN'T BAIL WHILE WE WERE AT THE ORGAN CHOP SHOP?
WE DON'T, PALADIN.
I ASKED YOU TO CALL ME WHEN SOMETHING INTERESTING WAS HAPPENING. JUST FOR THE RECORD, KIDS... THIS IS NOT INTERESTING.
YOU'RE STILL GETTING PAID FOR YOUR TIME, BLACK CAT.
OPEN UP, CAP, I'M SERIOUS... WE JUST WANNA TALK.
HOW DID THEY FIND US?
MISTY AND COLLEEN'RE PRETTY RESOURCEFUL.
KNIGHT'S ARM WAS BUILT BY STARK ENTERPRISES.
YEAH, AND THEY'RE FRIENDS WITH IRON MAN, TOO. BUT I TRUST THEM. IF THEY'RE HERE, IT'S FOR A GOOD REASON.
I KNOW YOU CAN HEAR US, SO I'M GOING TO LAY IT ON THE LINE, CAP.
IF WE WANTED TROUBLE, WE WOULD HAVE BROUGHT AN ARMY.
ROMAN GLADIATORS, TOO.

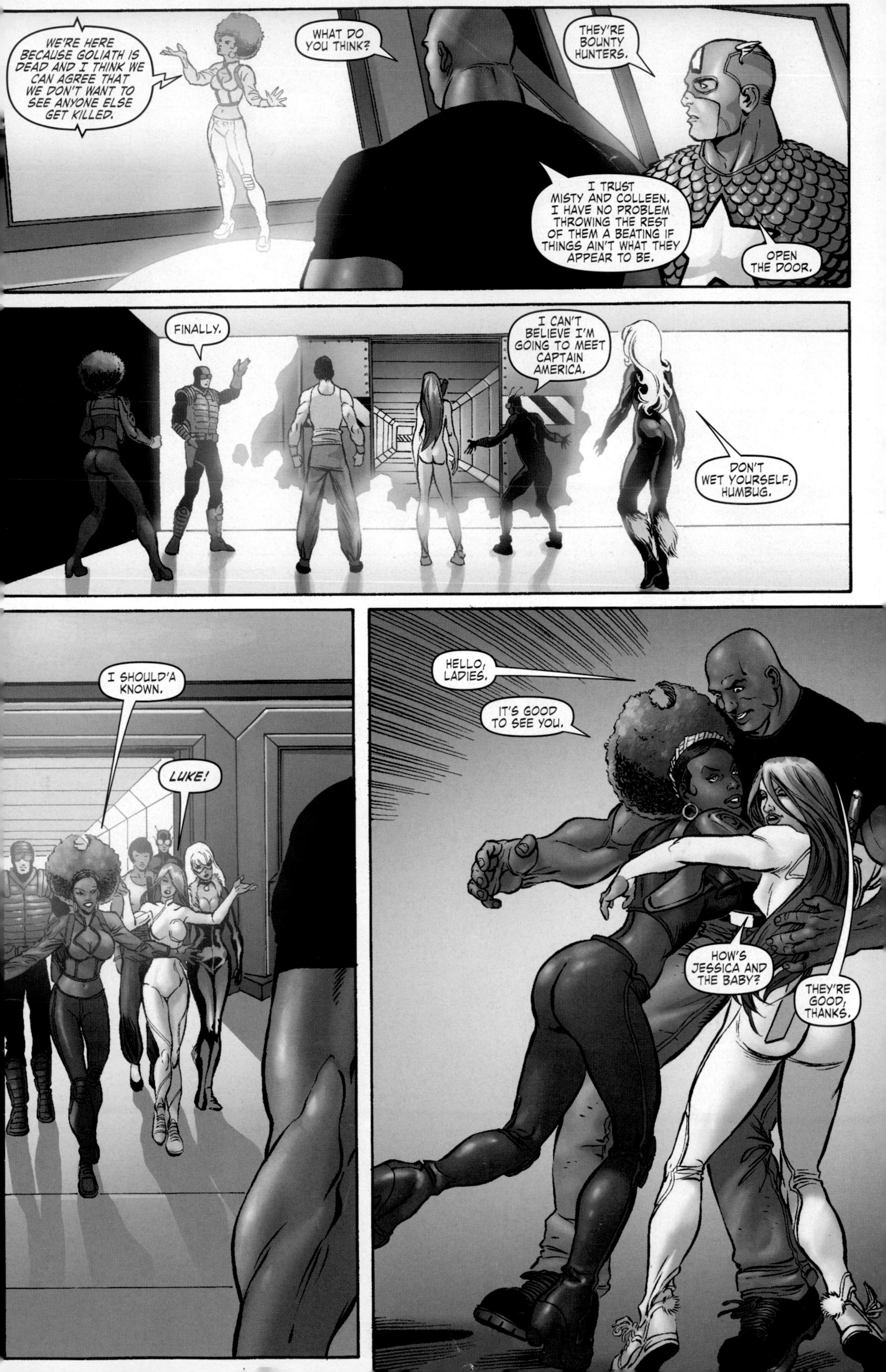
WE'RE HERE BECAUSE GOLIATH IS DEAD AND I THINK WE CAN AGREE THAT WE DON'T WANT TO SEE ANYONE ELSE GET KILLED.
WHAT DO YOU THINK?
THEY'RE BOUNTY HUNTERS.
I TRUST MISTY AND COLLEEN. I HAVE NO PROBLEM THROWING THE REST OF THEM A BEATING IF THINGS AIN'T WHAT THEY APPEAR TO BE.
OPEN THE DOOR.
FINALLY.
I CAN'T BELIEVE I'M GOING TO MEET CAPTAIN AMERICA.
DON'T WET YOURSELF, HUMBUG.
I SHOULD'A KNOWN.
LUKE!
HELLO, LADIES.
IT'S GOOD TO SEE YOU.
HOW'S JESSICA AND THE BABY?
THEY'RE GOOD, THANKS.

YOU WANTED TO TALK, MISTY. START TALKING.

IT'S...SIR... IT'S A HUGE HONOR...

SETTLE DOWN, HUMMER... AND LOSE THE SALUTE.

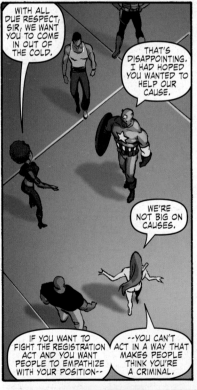

WITH ALL DUE RESPECT, SIR, WE WANT YOU TO COME IN OUT OF THE COLD.

THAT'S DISAPPOINTING. I HAD HOPED YOU WANTED TO HELP OUR CAUSE.

WE'RE NOT BIG ON CAUSES.

IF YOU WANT TO FIGHT THE REGISTRATION ACT AND YOU WANT PEOPLE TO EMPATHIZE WITH YOUR POSITION--

I'M NOT SURRENDERING TO A LAW THAT CONTRADICTS EVERYTHING THIS COUNTRY STANDS FOR.

CAPTAIN AMERICA, WE'D LIKE TO BRING ABOUT A PEACEFUL RESOLUTION TO THE CONFLICT. THIS IS WITHIN YOUR GRASP.

THE TERMS ARE COMPLETELY UNACCEPTABLE.

--YOU CAN'T ACT IN A WAY THAT MAKES PEOPLE THINK YOU'RE A CRIMINAL.

I DON'T KNOW ABOUT YOU, BUT I DON'T WANT TO LIVE IN A WORLD WHERE THERE'S A SUPERHUMAN COP FLOATING OUTSIDE EVERY WINDOW.

NOBODY WANTS THAT.

IRON MAN HAS TURNED SOME OF THE MOST DANGEROUS PEOPLE IN THE WORLD, OUR ENEMIES, INTO HIS PERSONAL BLOODHOUNDS.

I FEEL FUNNY SAYING THIS, YA KNOW, BEING A FORMER THIEF--

--BUT CRIME IS DOWN, AND BY DOWN, I MEAN LOWER THAN I CAN EVER REMEMBER.

THAT'S A GREAT SELLING TOOL TO THE PUBLIC AS THEY WATCH THEIR CIVIL LIBERTIES ERODE.

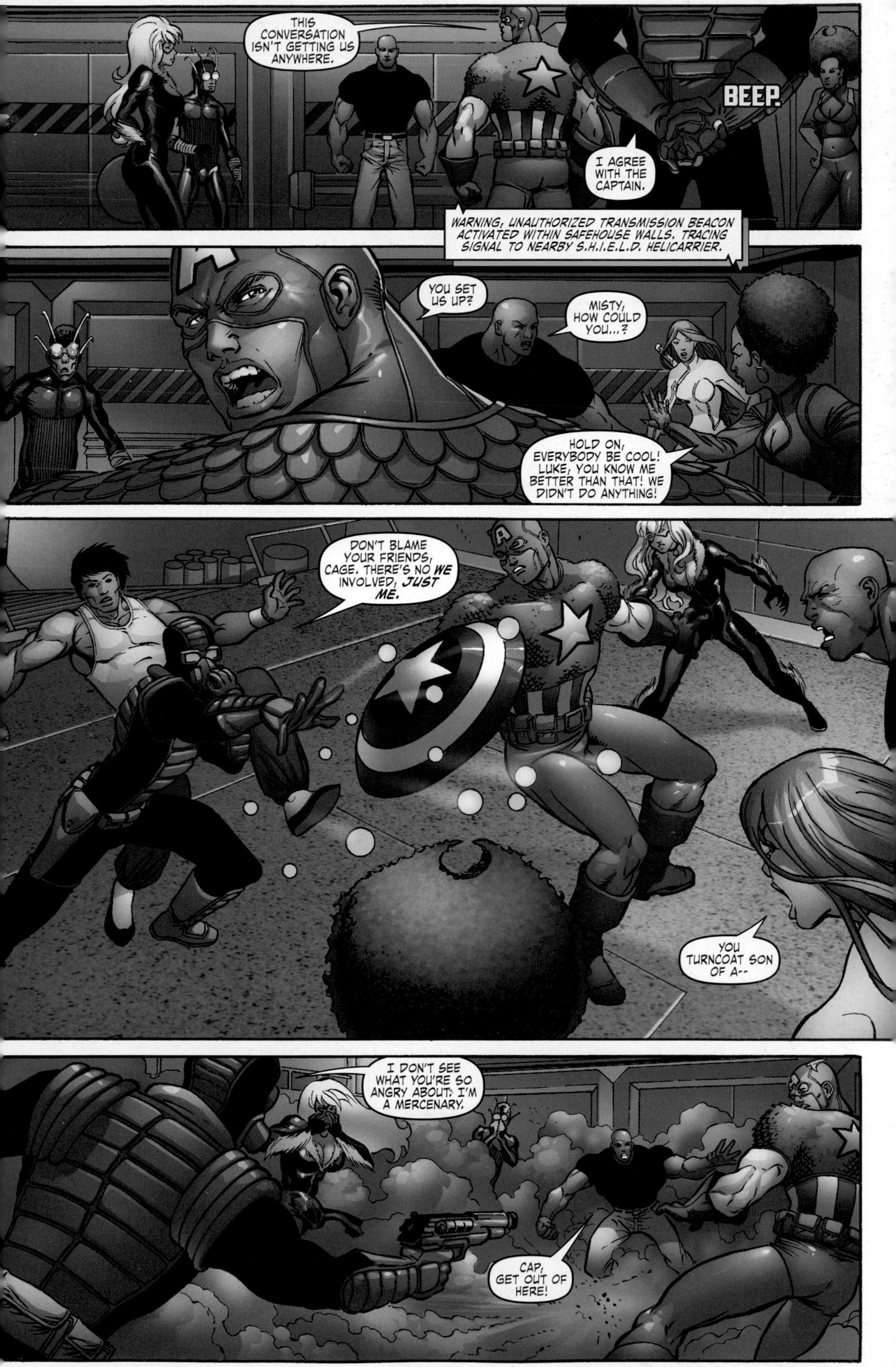
THIS CONVERSATION ISN'T GETTING US ANYWHERE.
BEEP.
I AGREE WITH THE CAPTAIN.
WARNING, UNAUTHORIZED TRANSMISSION BEACON ACTIVATED WITHIN SAFEHOUSE WALLS. TRACING SIGNAL TO NEARBY S.H.I.E.L.D. HELICARRIER.
YOU SET US UP?
MISTY, HOW COULD YOU...?
HOLD ON, EVERYBODY BE COOL! LUKE, YOU KNOW ME BETTER THAN THAT! WE DIDN'T DO ANYTHING!
DON'T BLAME YOUR FRIENDS, CAGE. THERE'S NO *WE* INVOLVED, ***JUST ME.***
YOU TURNCOAT SON OF A--
I DON'T SEE WHAT YOU'RE SO ANGRY ABOUT; I'M A MERCENARY.
CAP, GET OUT OF HERE!

I'M NOT RUNNING!

YOU'VE ONLY GOT TEN SECONDS BEFORE THE GAS SHUTS YOU DOWN. MAKE THIS GOOD.

SORRY, CAT, I'VE GOT A SUPER-SMART ELECTROMAGNETIC FIELD GENERATOR...

...CAP'S SHIELD CAN'T TOUCH ME.

DO YOU TRUST ME?

I'M NOT LEAVING LUKE BEHIND.

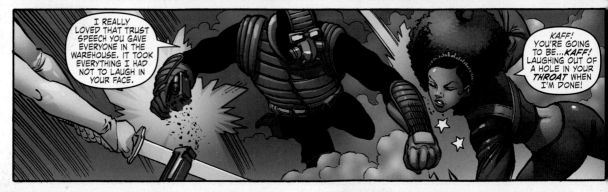

I REALLY LOVED THAT TRUST SPEECH YOU GAVE EVERYONE IN THE WAREHOUSE. IT TOOK EVERYTHING I HAD NOT TO LAUGH IN YOUR FACE.

KAFF! YOU'RE GOING TO BE...KAFF! LAUGHING OUT OF A HOLE IN YOUR THROAT WHEN I'M DONE!

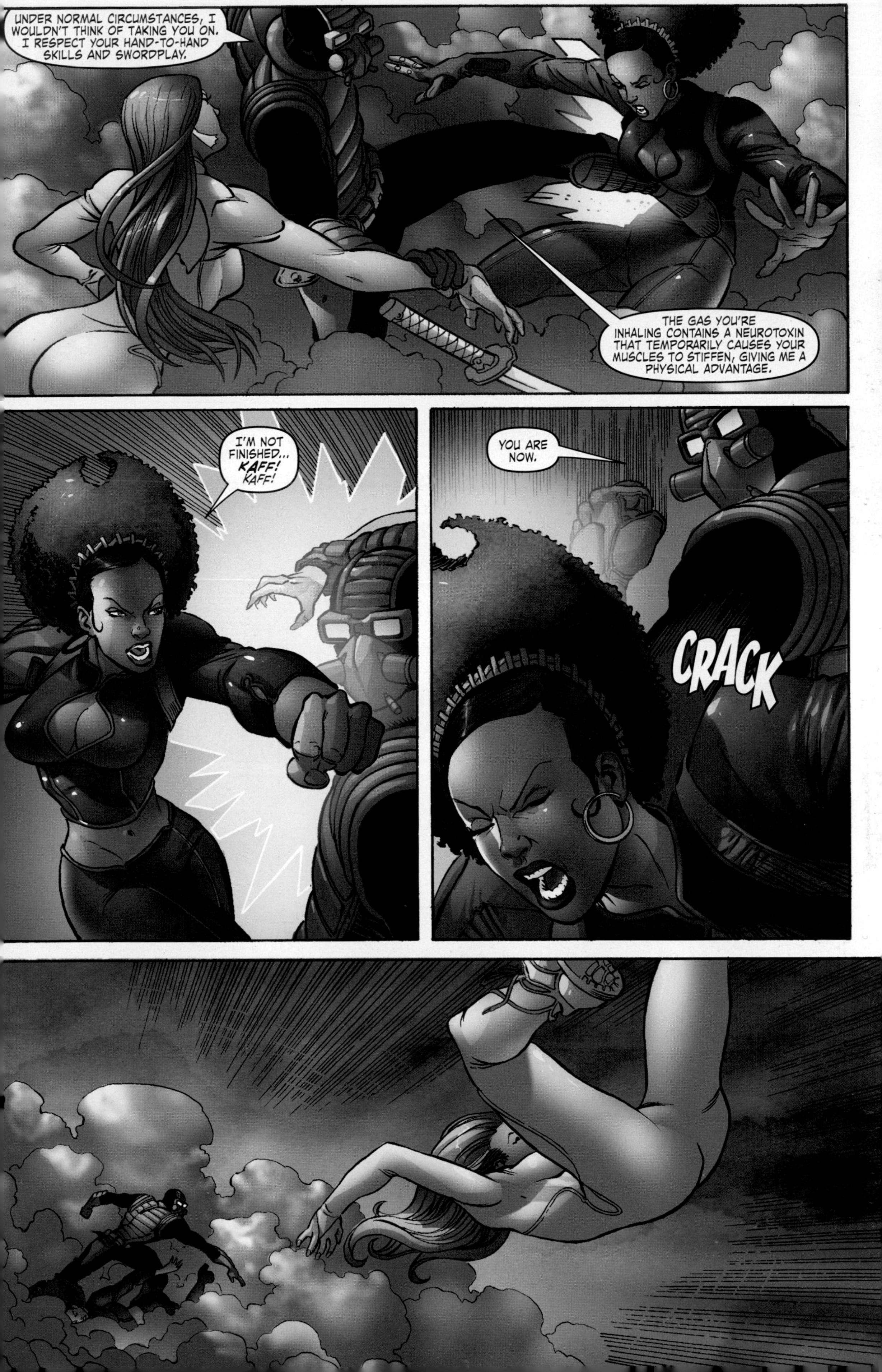
UNDER NORMAL CIRCUMSTANCES, I WOULDN'T THINK OF TAKING YOU ON. I RESPECT YOUR HAND-TO-HAND SKILLS AND SWORDPLAY.
THE GAS YOU'RE INHALING CONTAINS A NEUROTOXIN THAT TEMPORARILY CAUSES YOUR MUSCLES TO STIFFEN, GIVING ME A PHYSICAL ADVANTAGE.
I'M NOT FINISHED... KAFF! KAFF!
YOU ARE NOW.
CRACK

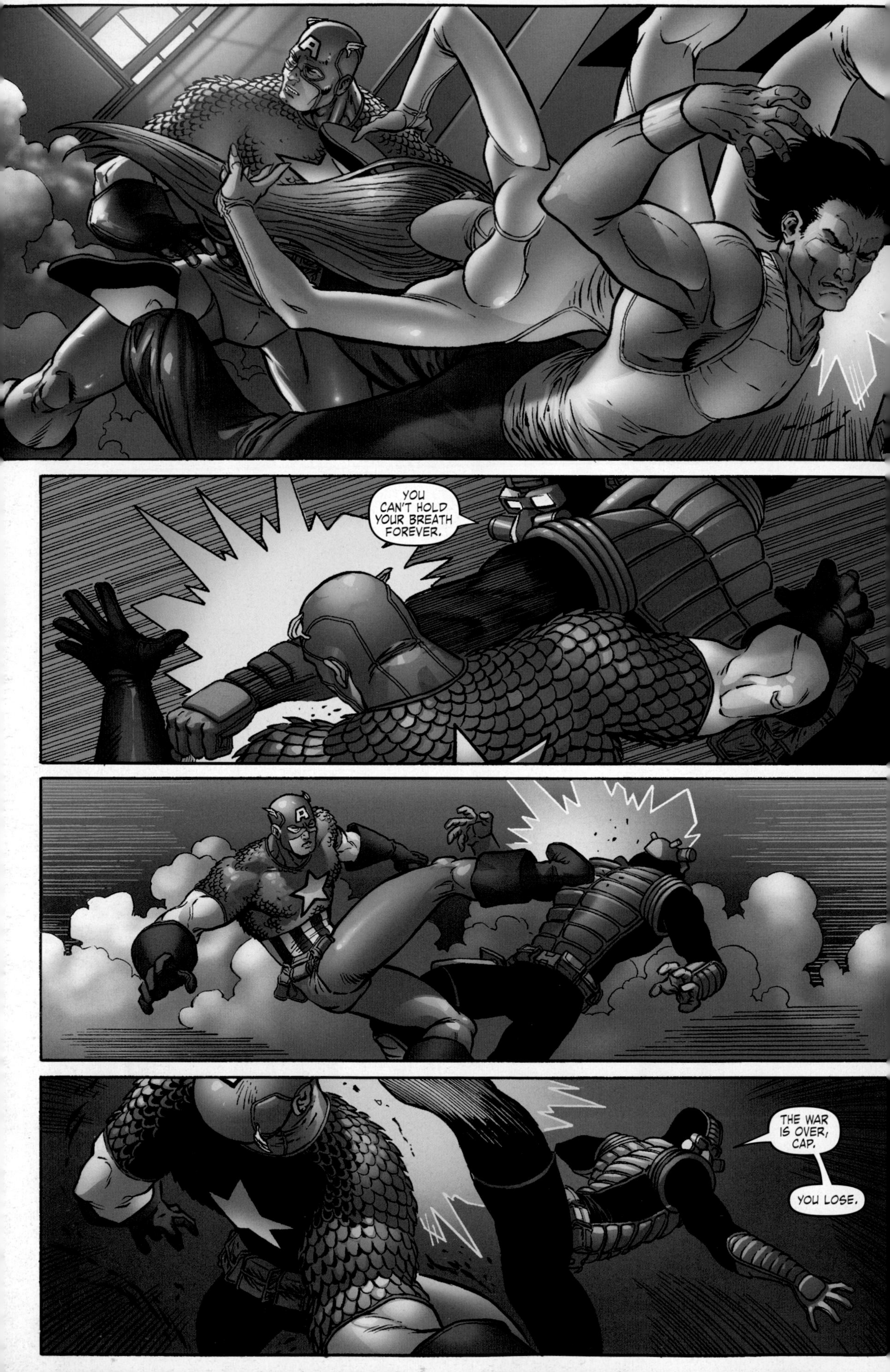
YOU CAN'T HOLD YOUR BREATH FOREVER.
THE WAR IS OVER, CAP.
YOU LOSE.

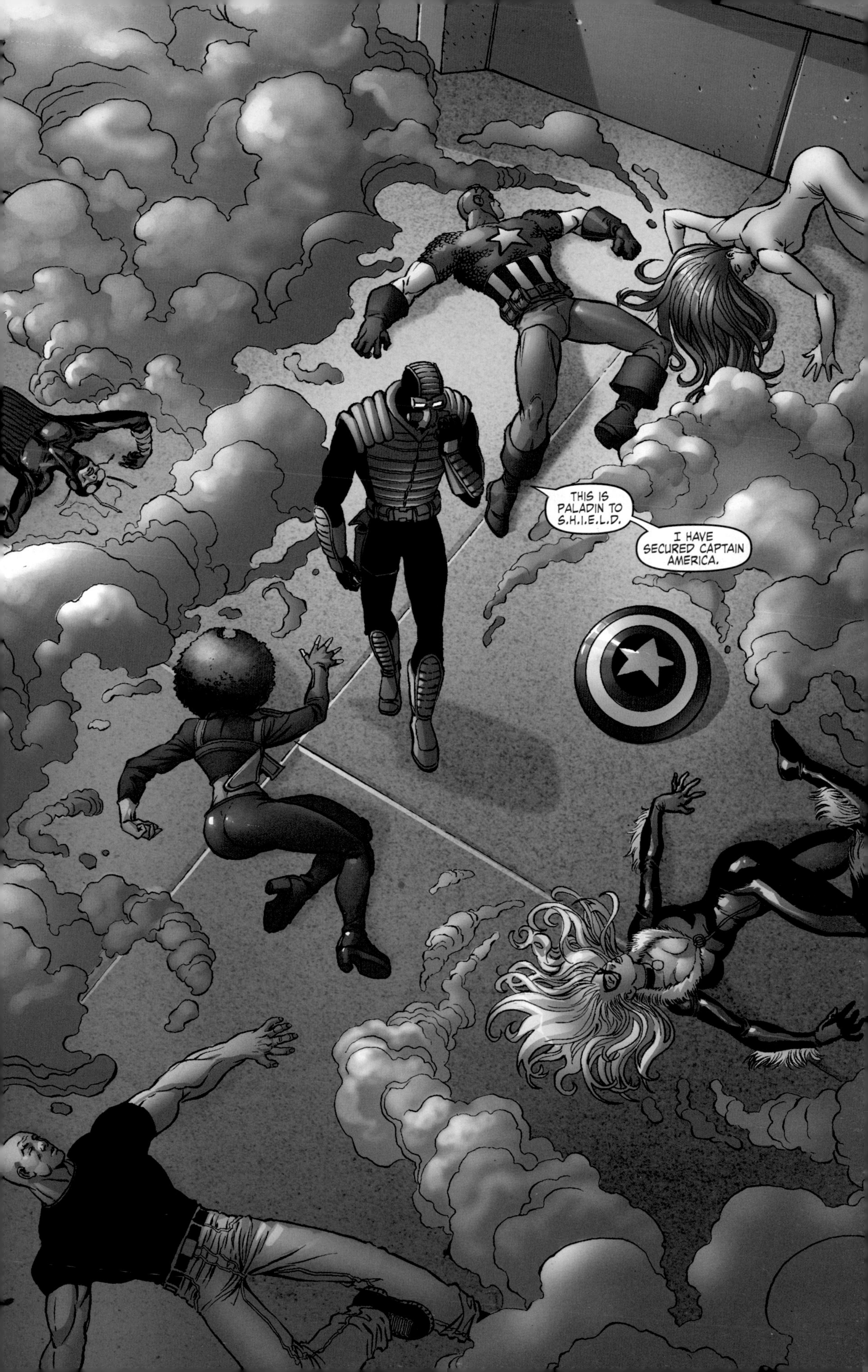
THIS IS PALADIN TO S.H.I.E.L.D.
I HAVE SECURED CAPTAIN AMERICA.

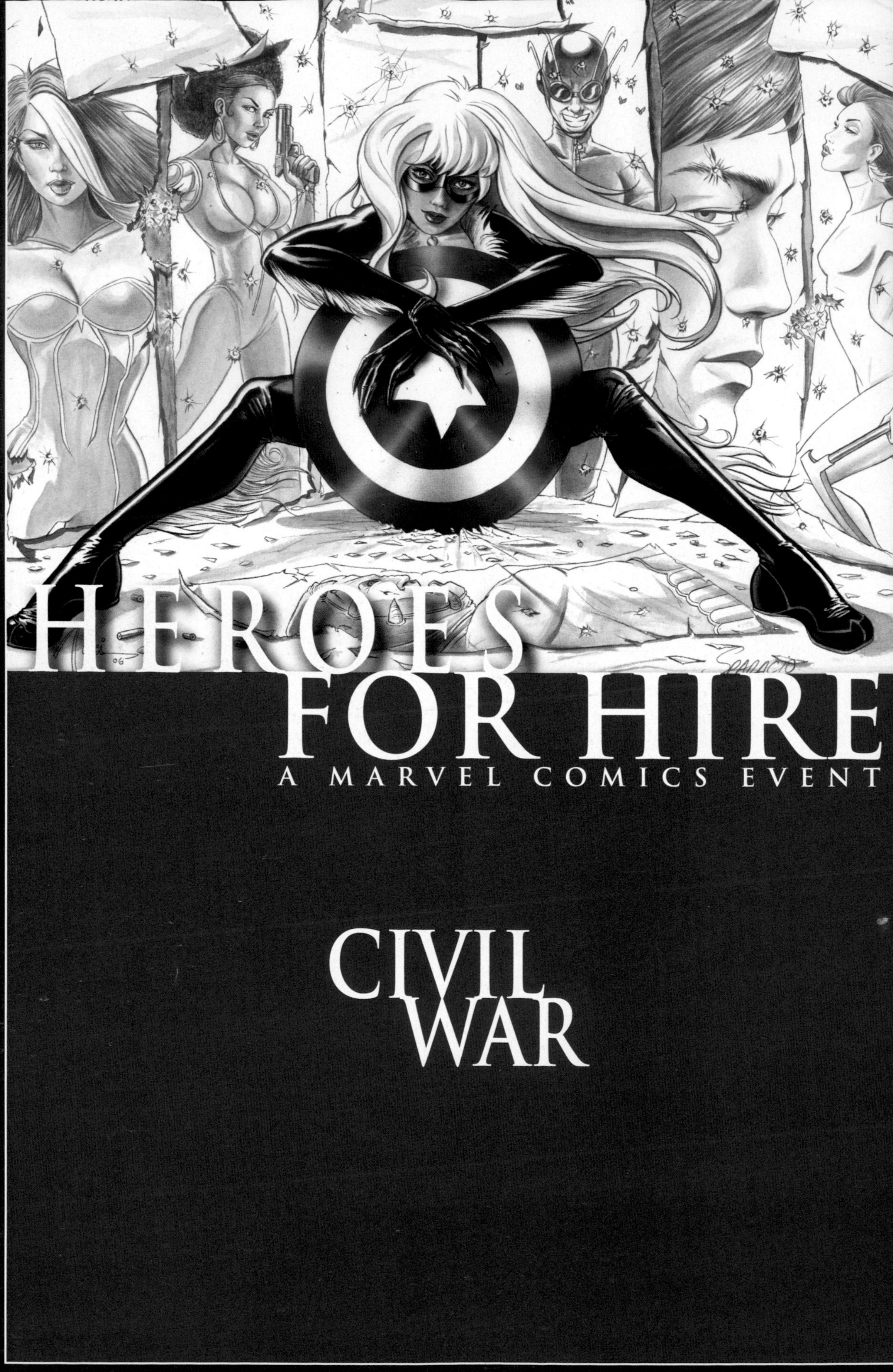
HEROES
FOR HIRE
A MARVEL COMICS EVENT
CIVIL
WAR

HEROES FOR HIRE #3

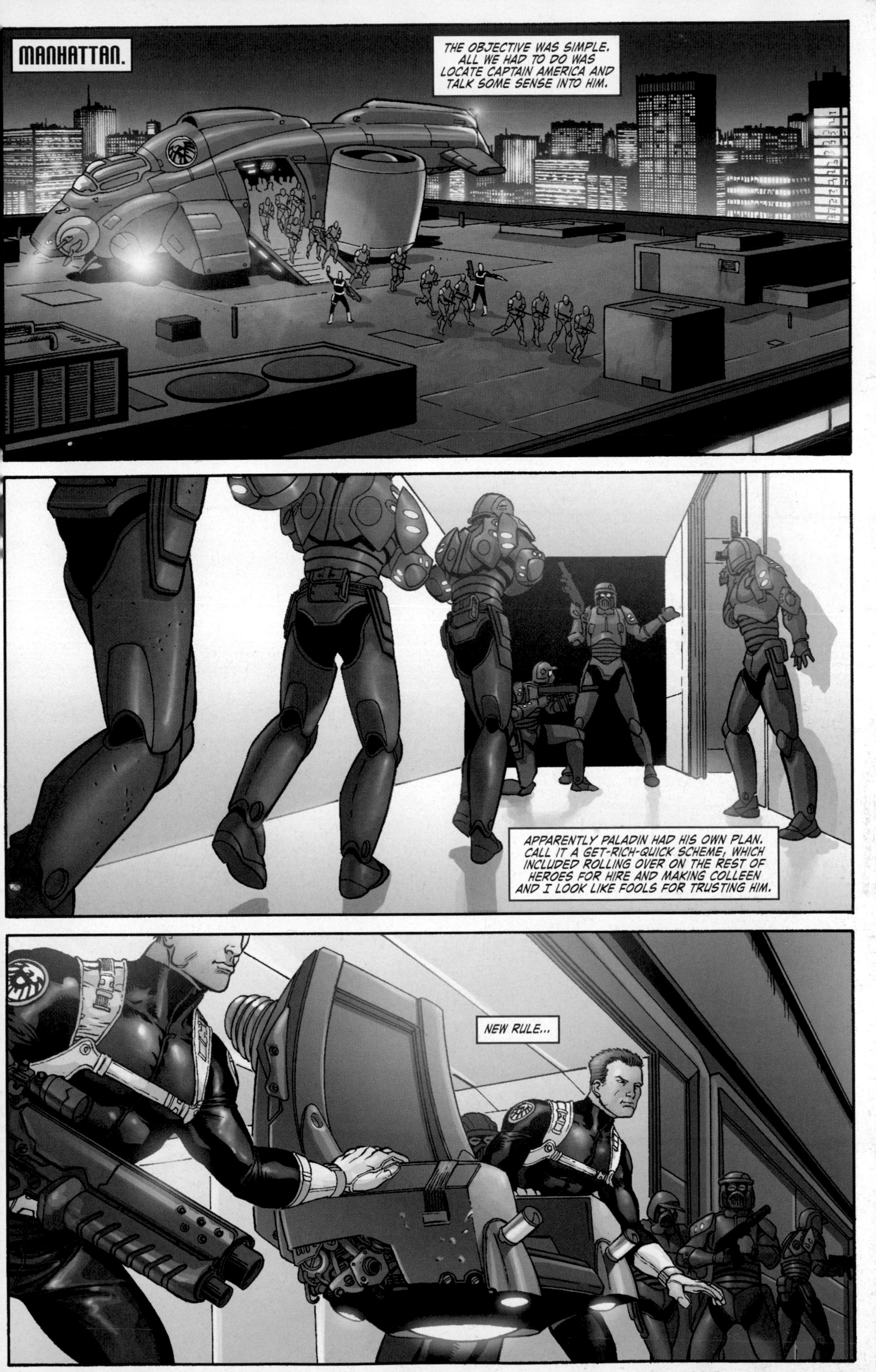
MANHATTAN.
THE OBJECTIVE WAS SIMPLE. ALL WE HAD TO DO WAS LOCATE CAPTAIN AMERICA AND TALK SOME SENSE INTO HIM.
APPARENTLY PALADIN HAD HIS OWN PLAN. CALL IT A GET-RICH-QUICK SCHEME, WHICH INCLUDED ROLLING OVER ON THE REST OF HEROES FOR HIRE AND MAKING COLLEEN AND I LOOK LIKE FOOLS FOR TRUSTING HIM.
NEW RULE...

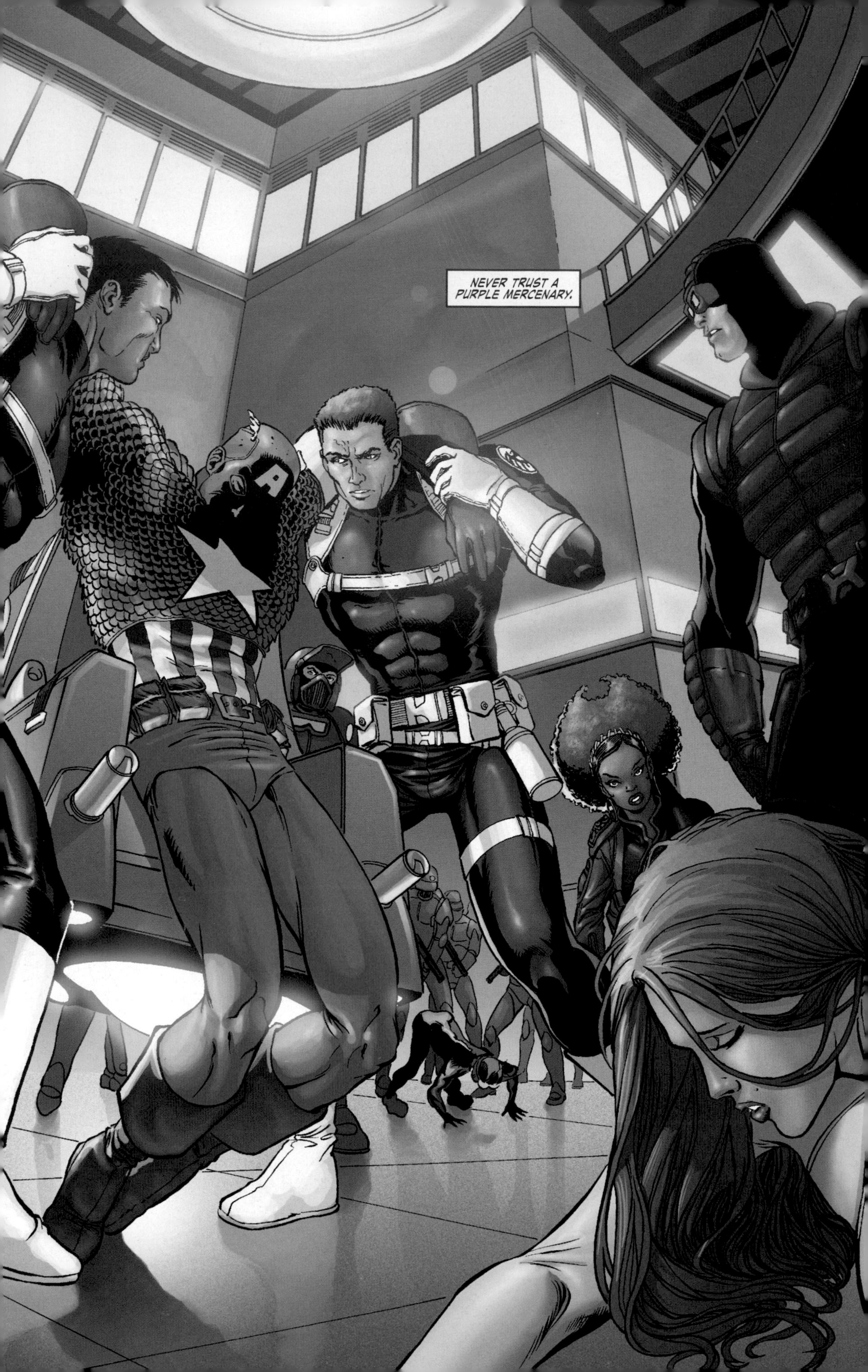
NEVER TRUST A PURPLE MERCENARY.

PALADIN! YOU SONOVA...

YOU KNOW CAPTAIN AMERICA IS A WANTED MAN, MISTY.

NOT BY US HE ISN'T.

LET ME REMIND YOU THIS ARM CAN PRODUCE *THREE THOUSAND POUNDS* OF PRESSURE PER SQUARE INCH. ALL I HAVE TO DO IS *SQUEEZE* AND YOUR HEAD WILL POP CLEAN OFF.

KRK

SHOULD WE BE HELPING HIM--?

WE'VE GOT CAPTAIN AMERICA. HE'S ON HIS *OWN*.

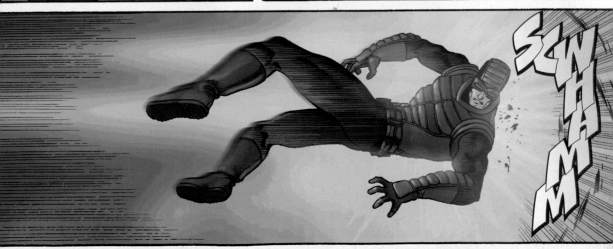

SSWHAMM

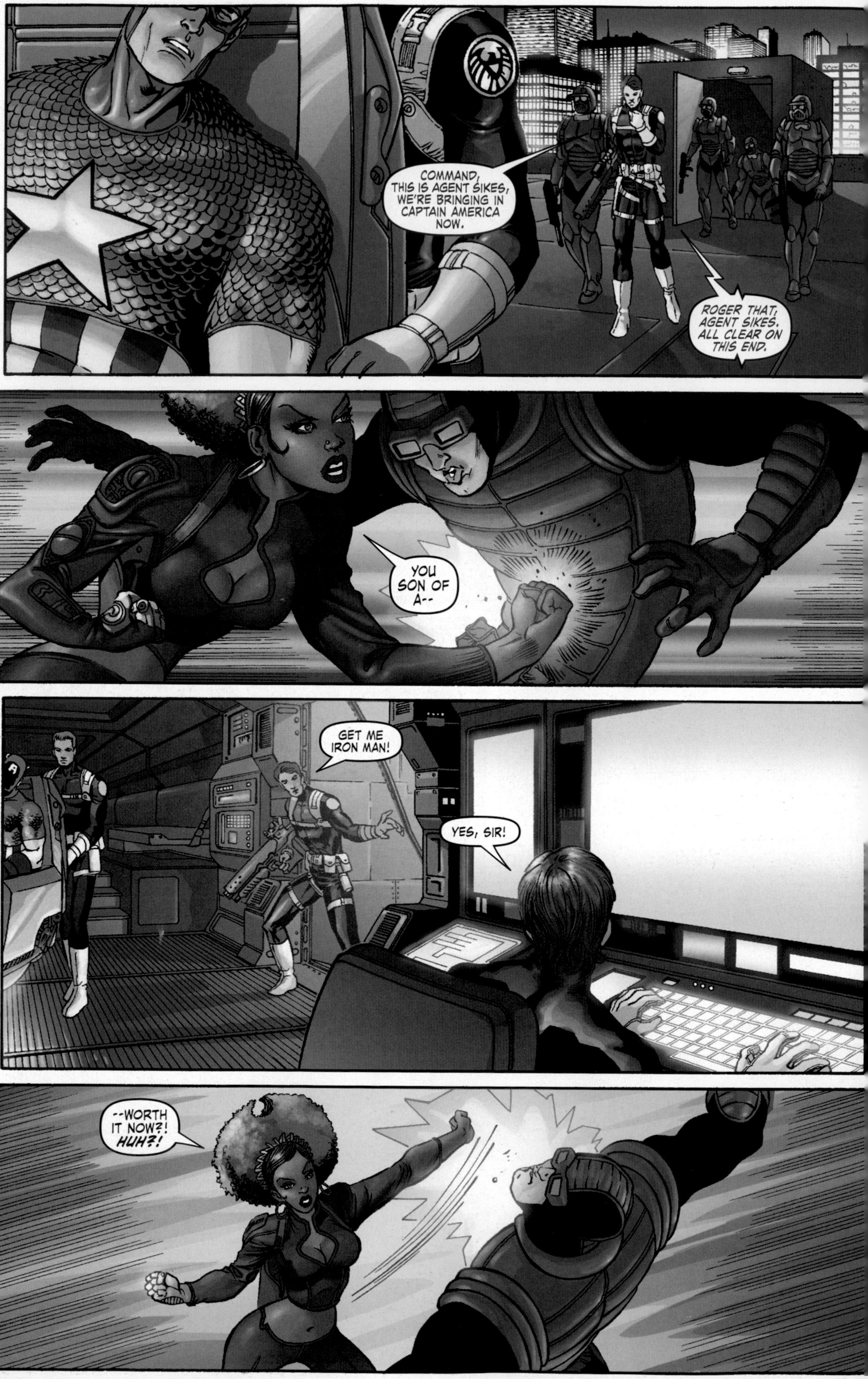
COMMAND, THIS IS AGENT SIKES, WE'RE BRINGING IN CAPTAIN AMERICA NOW.
ROGER THAT, AGENT SIKES. ALL CLEAR ON THIS END.
YOU SON OF A--
GET ME IRON MAN!
YES, SIR!
--WORTH IT NOW?! HUH?!

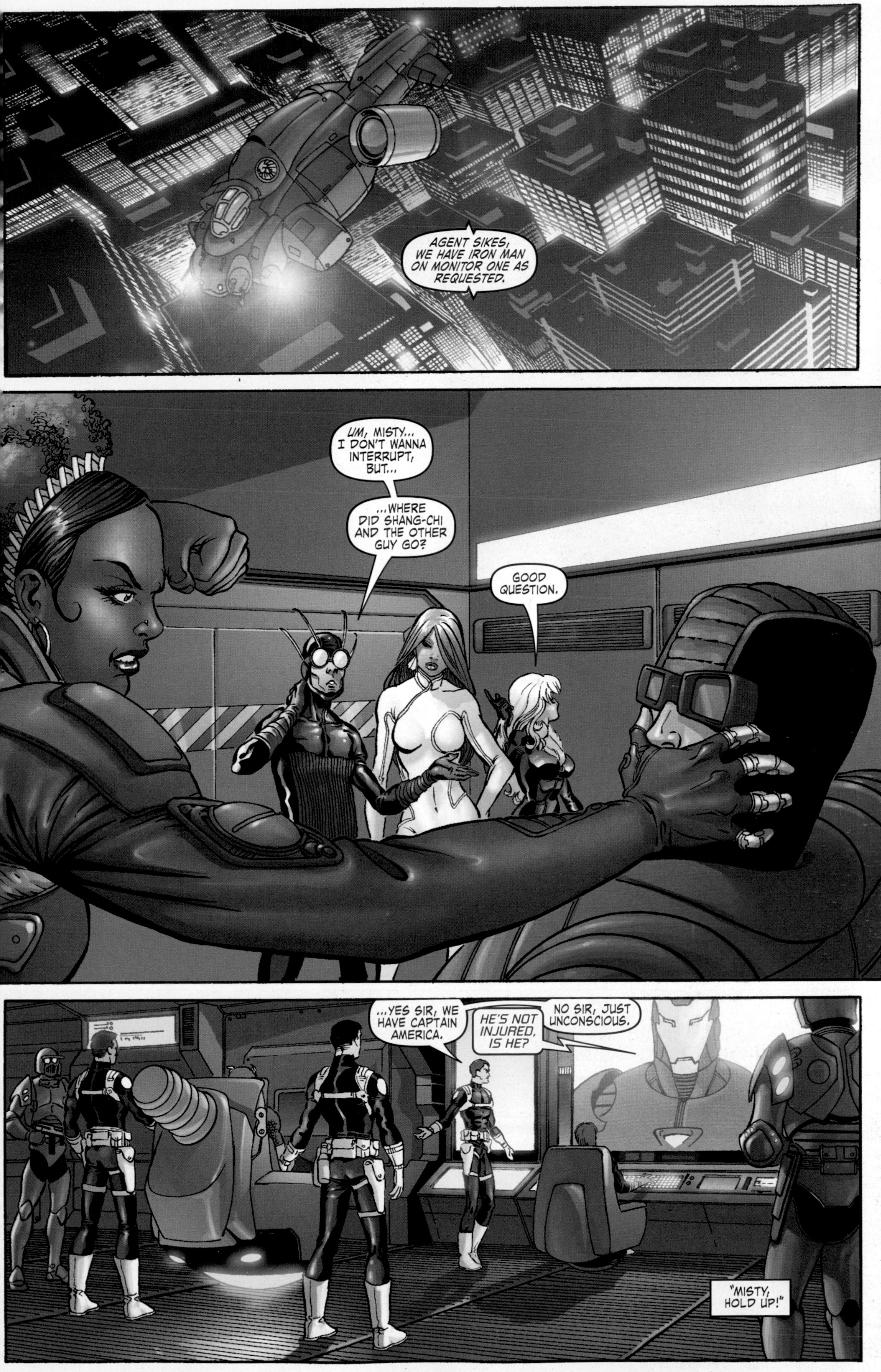
AGENT SIKES, WE HAVE IRON MAN ON MONITOR ONE AS REQUESTED.
UM, MISTY... I DON'T WANNA INTERRUPT, BUT...
...WHERE DID SHANG-CHI AND THE OTHER GUY GO?
GOOD QUESTION.
...YES SIR, WE HAVE CAPTAIN AMERICA.
HE'S NOT INJURED, IS HE?
NO SIR, JUST UNCONSCIOUS.
"MISTY, HOLD UP!"

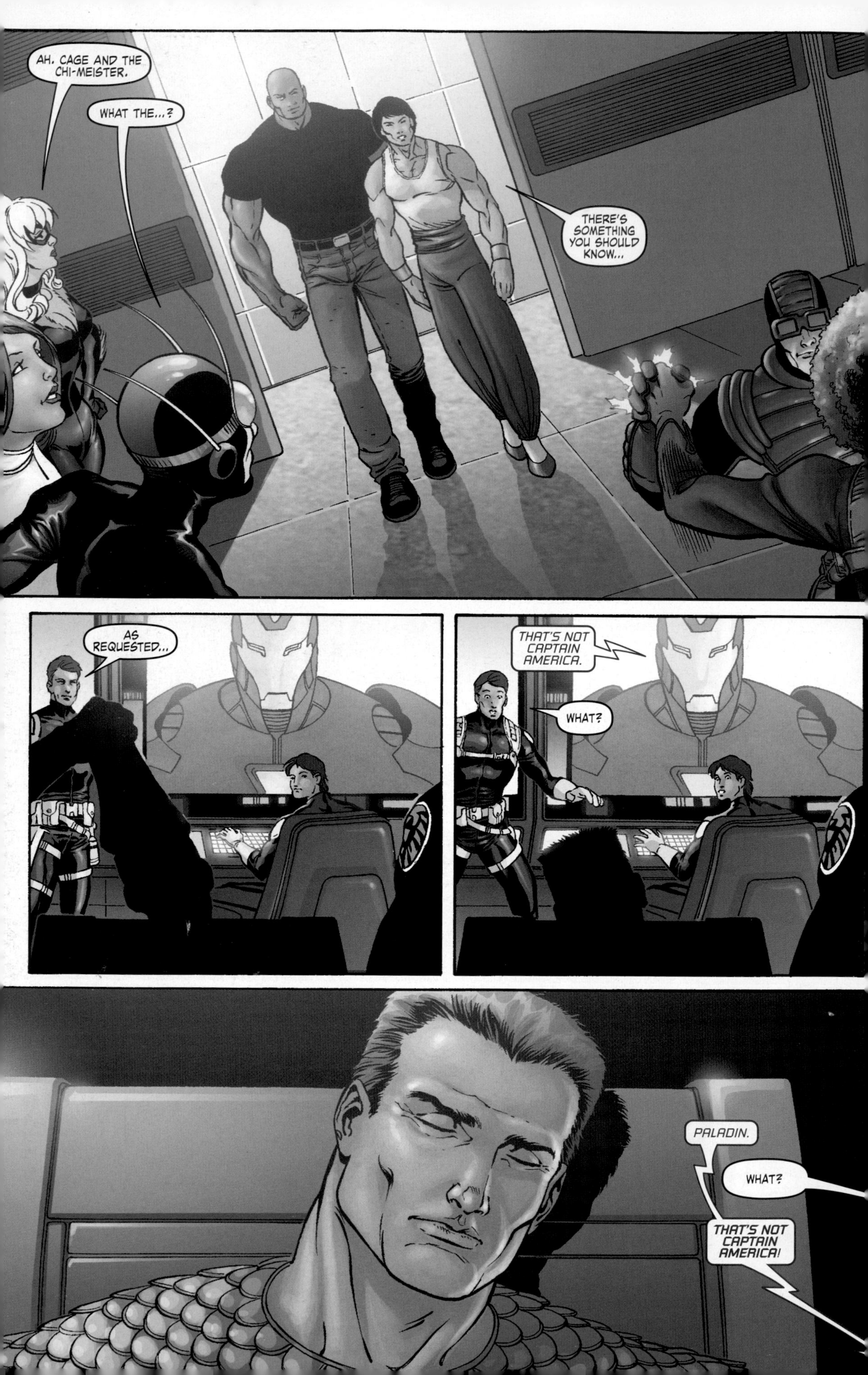
AH. CAGE AND THE CHI-MEISTER.
WHAT THE...?
THERE'S SOMETHING YOU SHOULD KNOW...
AS REQUESTED...
THAT'S NOT CAPTAIN AMERICA.
WHAT?
PALADIN.
WHAT?
THAT'S NOT CAPTAIN AMERICA!

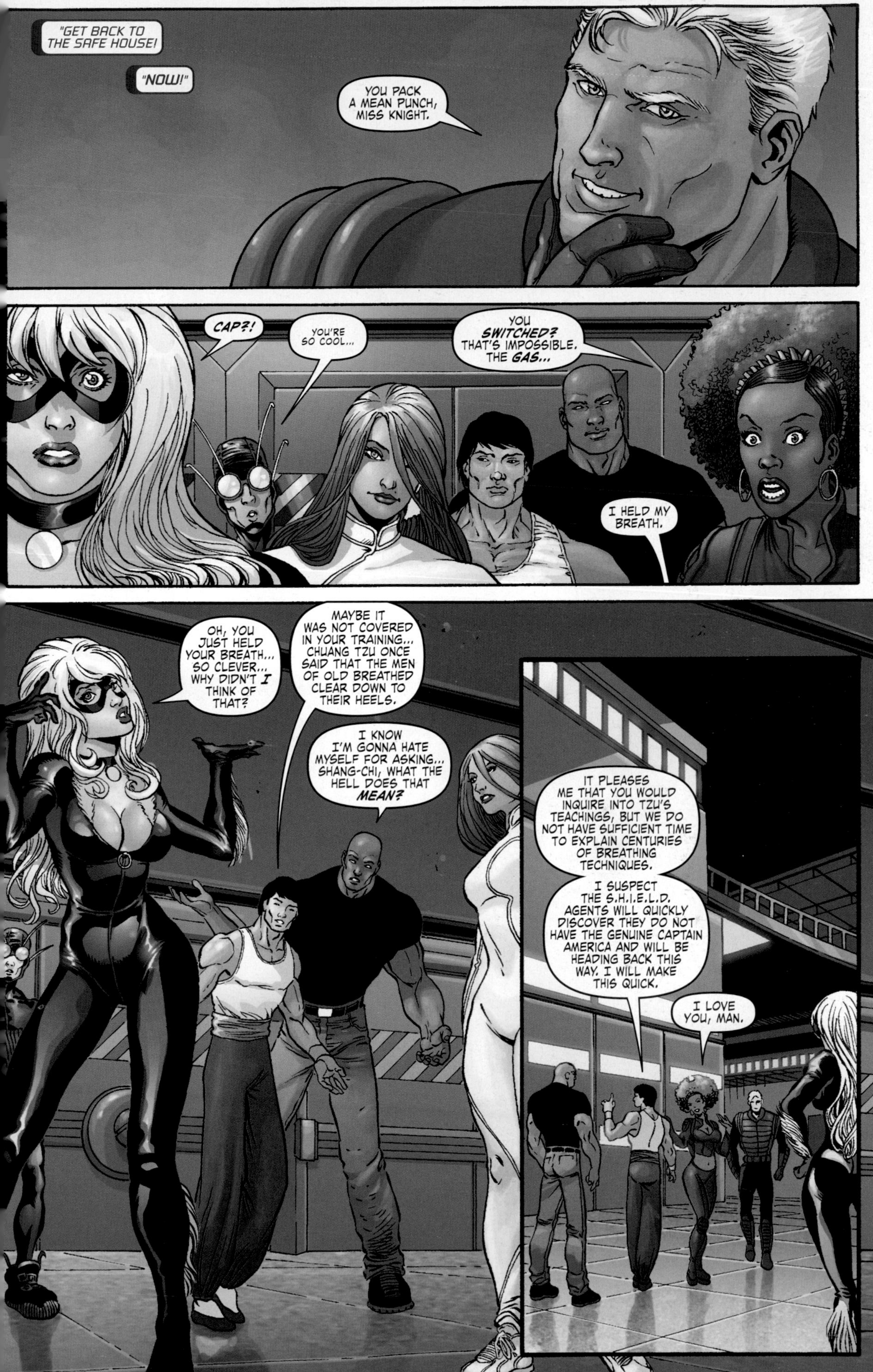
"GET BACK TO THE SAFE HOUSE!
"NOW!"
YOU PACK A MEAN PUNCH, MISS KNIGHT.
CAP?!
YOU'RE SO COOL...
YOU SWITCHED? THAT'S IMPOSSIBLE. THE GAS...
I HELD MY BREATH.
OH, YOU JUST HELD YOUR BREATH... SO CLEVER... WHY DIDN'T I THINK OF THAT?
MAYBE IT WAS NOT COVERED IN YOUR TRAINING... CHUANG TZU ONCE SAID THAT THE MEN OF OLD BREATHED CLEAR DOWN TO THEIR HEELS.
I KNOW I'M GONNA HATE MYSELF FOR ASKING... SHANG-CHI, WHAT THE HELL DOES THAT MEAN?
IT PLEASES ME THAT YOU WOULD INQUIRE INTO TZU'S TEACHINGS, BUT WE DO NOT HAVE SUFFICIENT TIME TO EXPLAIN CENTURIES OF BREATHING TECHNIQUES.
I SUSPECT THE S.H.I.E.L.D. AGENTS WILL QUICKLY DISCOVER THEY DO NOT HAVE THE GENUINE CAPTAIN AMERICA AND WILL BE HEADING BACK THIS WAY. I WILL MAKE THIS QUICK.
I LOVE YOU, MAN.

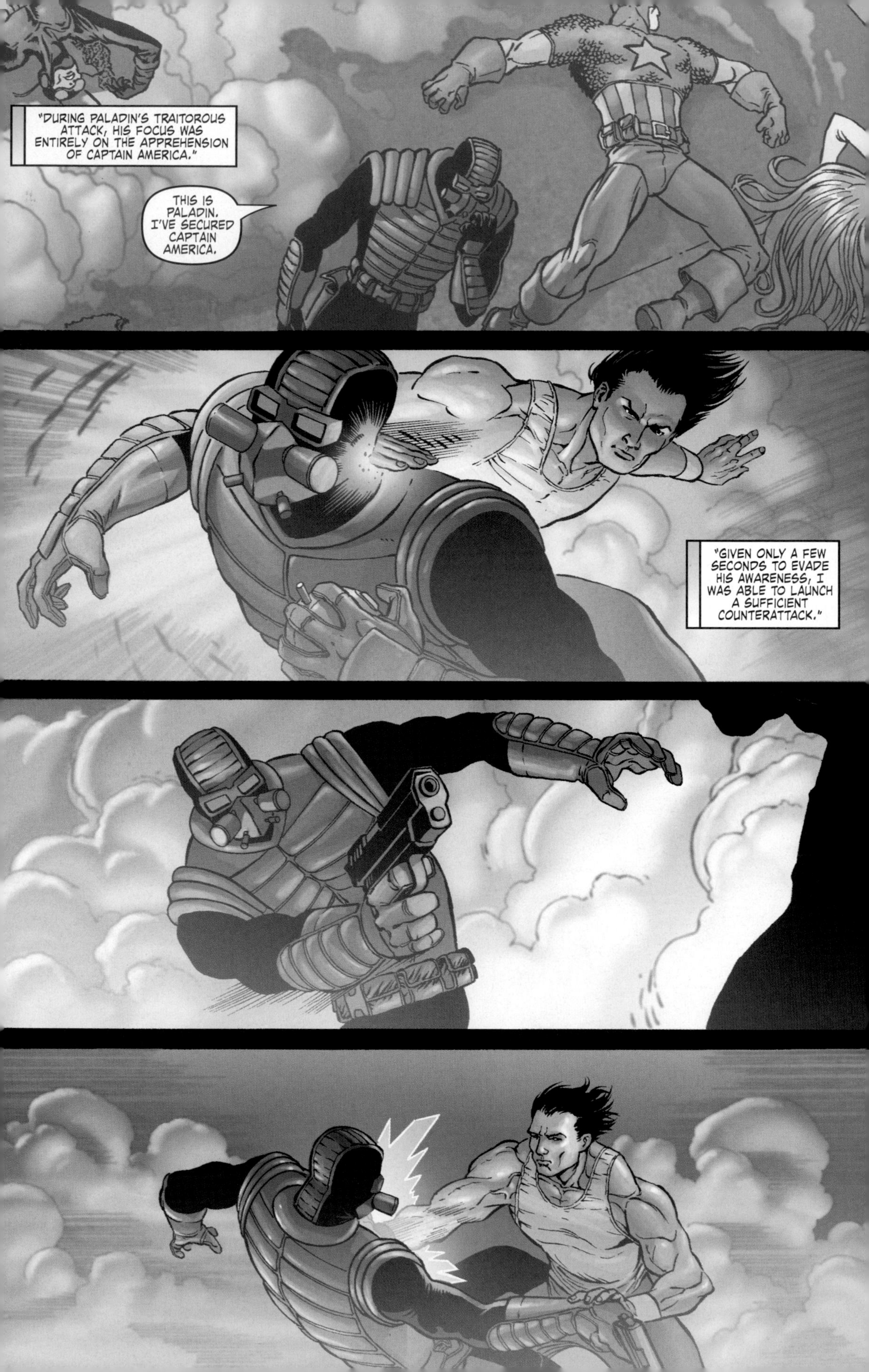
"DURING PALADIN'S TRAITOROUS ATTACK, HIS FOCUS WAS ENTIRELY ON THE APPREHENSION OF CAPTAIN AMERICA."
THIS IS PALADIN. I'VE SECURED CAPTAIN AMERICA.
"GIVEN ONLY A FEW SECONDS TO EVADE HIS AWARENESS, I WAS ABLE TO LAUNCH A SUFFICIENT COUNTERATTACK."

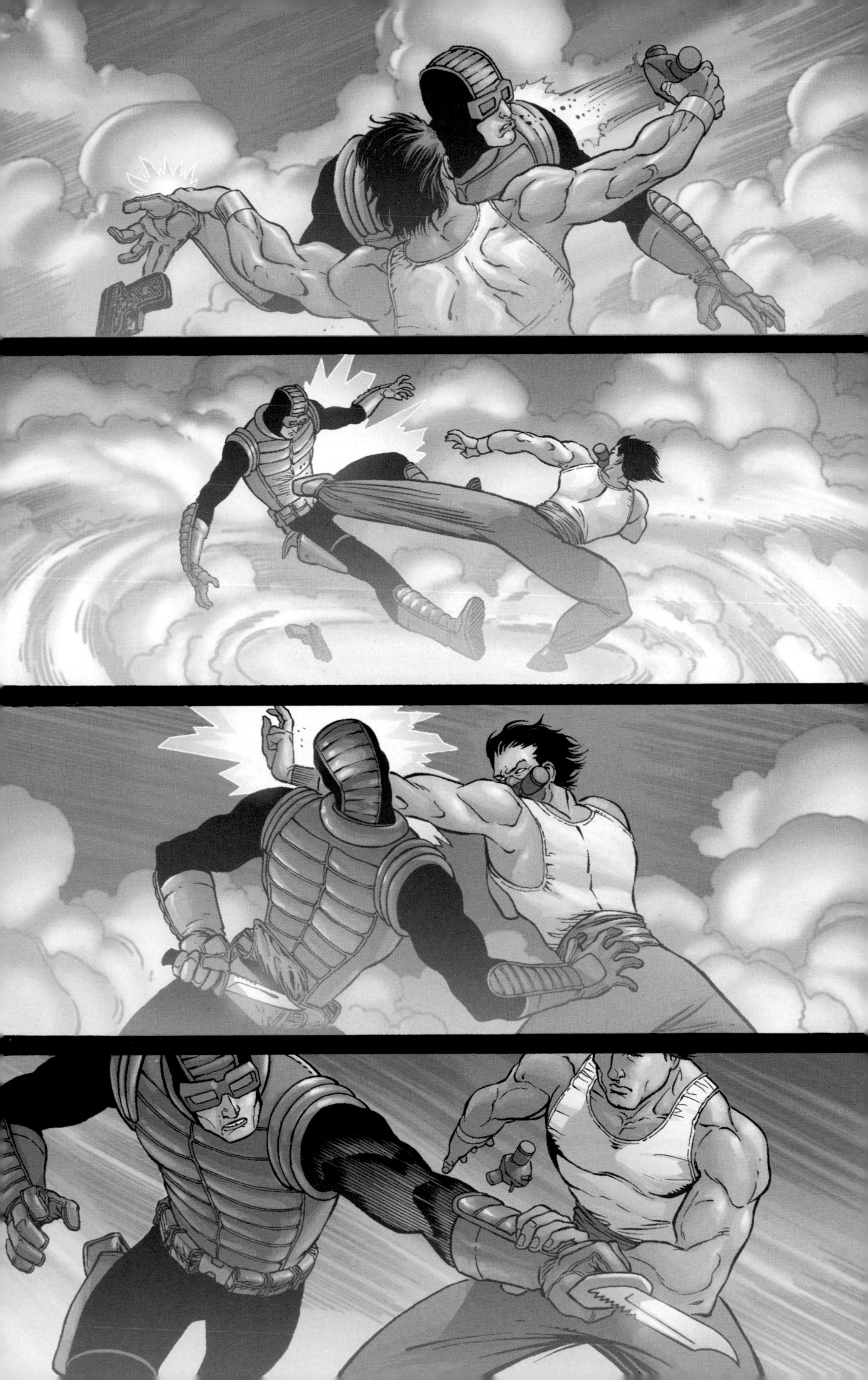

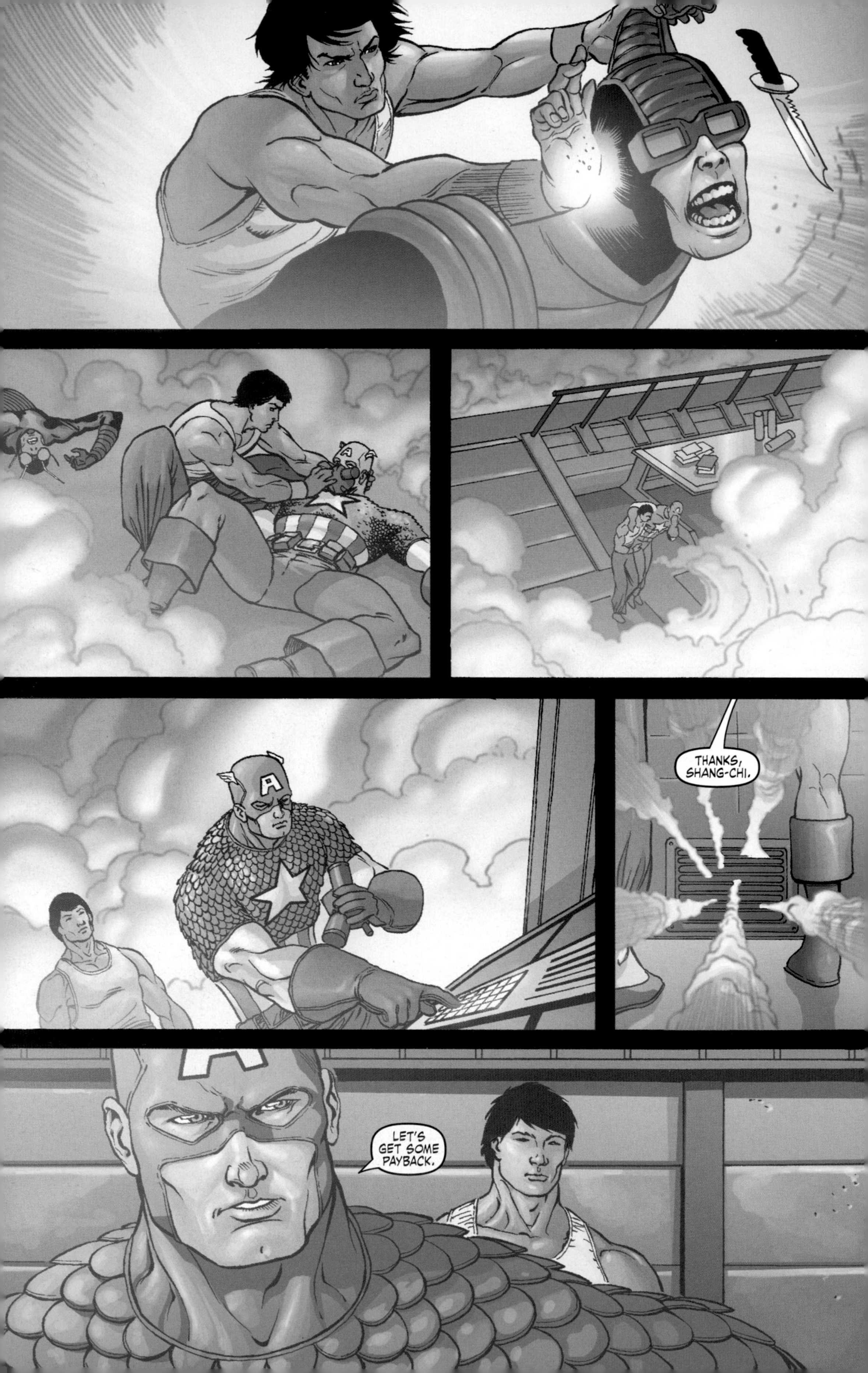
THANKS, SHANG-CHI.
LET'S GET SOME PAYBACK.

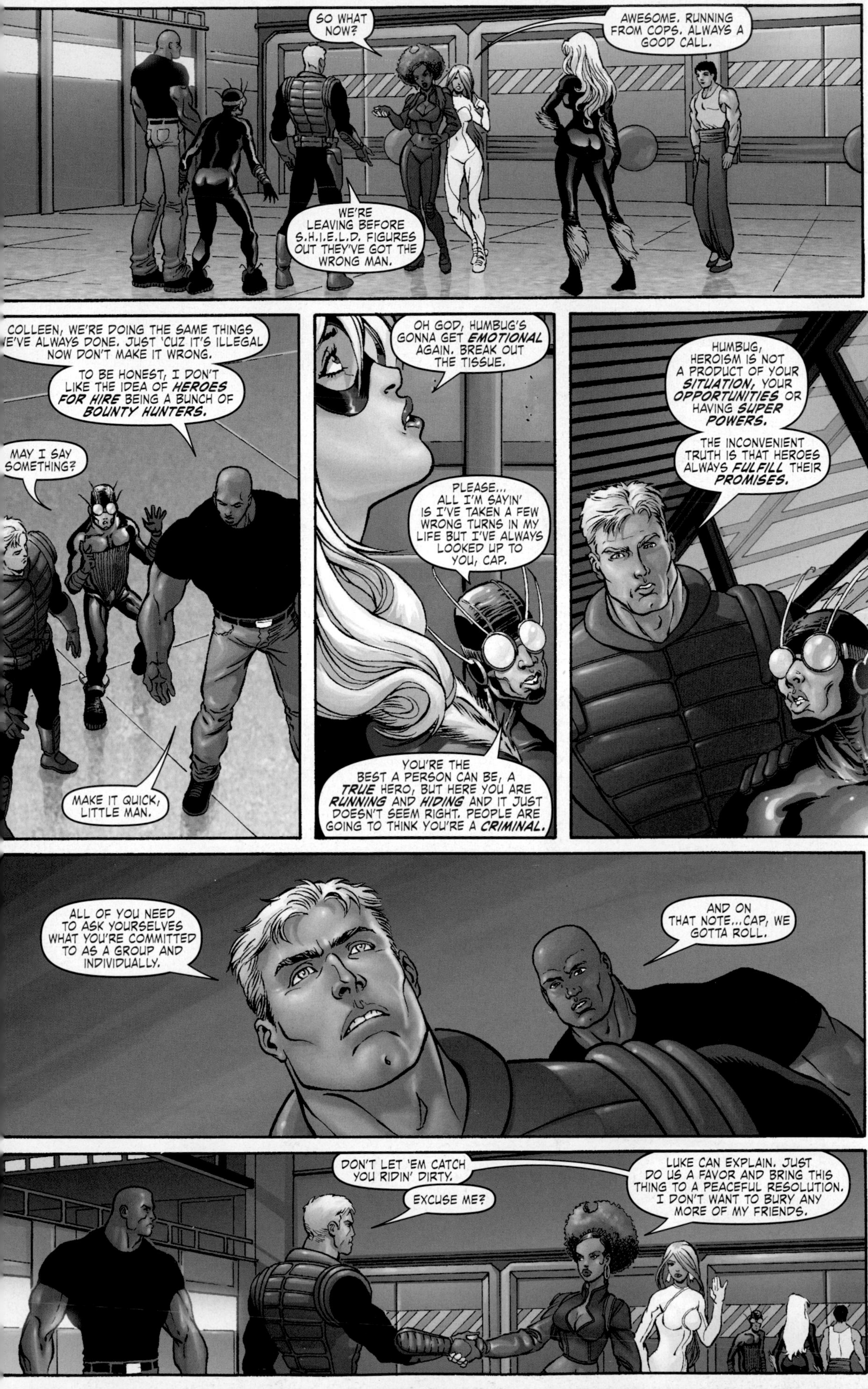
SO WHAT NOW?
AWESOME. RUNNING FROM COPS. ALWAYS A GOOD CALL.
WE'RE LEAVING BEFORE S.H.I.E.L.D. FIGURES OUT THEY'VE GOT THE WRONG MAN.
COLLEEN, WE'RE DOING THE SAME THINGS WE'VE ALWAYS DONE. JUST 'CUZ IT'S ILLEGAL NOW DON'T MAKE IT WRONG.
TO BE HONEST, I DON'T LIKE THE IDEA OF HEROES FOR HIRE BEING A BUNCH OF BOUNTY HUNTERS.
MAY I SAY SOMETHING?
MAKE IT QUICK, LITTLE MAN.
OH GOD, HUMBUG'S GONNA GET EMOTIONAL AGAIN. BREAK OUT THE TISSUE.
PLEASE... ALL I'M SAYIN' IS I'VE TAKEN A FEW WRONG TURNS IN MY LIFE BUT I'VE ALWAYS LOOKED UP TO YOU, CAP.
YOU'RE THE BEST A PERSON CAN BE, A TRUE HERO, BUT HERE YOU ARE RUNNING AND HIDING AND IT JUST DOESN'T SEEM RIGHT. PEOPLE ARE GOING TO THINK YOU'RE A CRIMINAL.
HUMBUG, HEROISM IS NOT A PRODUCT OF YOUR SITUATION, YOUR OPPORTUNITIES OR HAVING SUPER POWERS.
THE INCONVENIENT TRUTH IS THAT HEROES ALWAYS FULFILL THEIR PROMISES.
ALL OF YOU NEED TO ASK YOURSELVES WHAT YOU'RE COMMITTED TO AS A GROUP AND INDIVIDUALLY.
AND ON THAT NOTE...CAP, WE GOTTA ROLL.
DON'T LET 'EM CATCH YOU RIDIN' DIRTY.
EXCUSE ME?
LUKE CAN EXPLAIN. JUST DO US A FAVOR AND BRING THIS THING TO A PEACEFUL RESOLUTION. I DON'T WANT TO BURY ANY MORE OF MY FRIENDS.

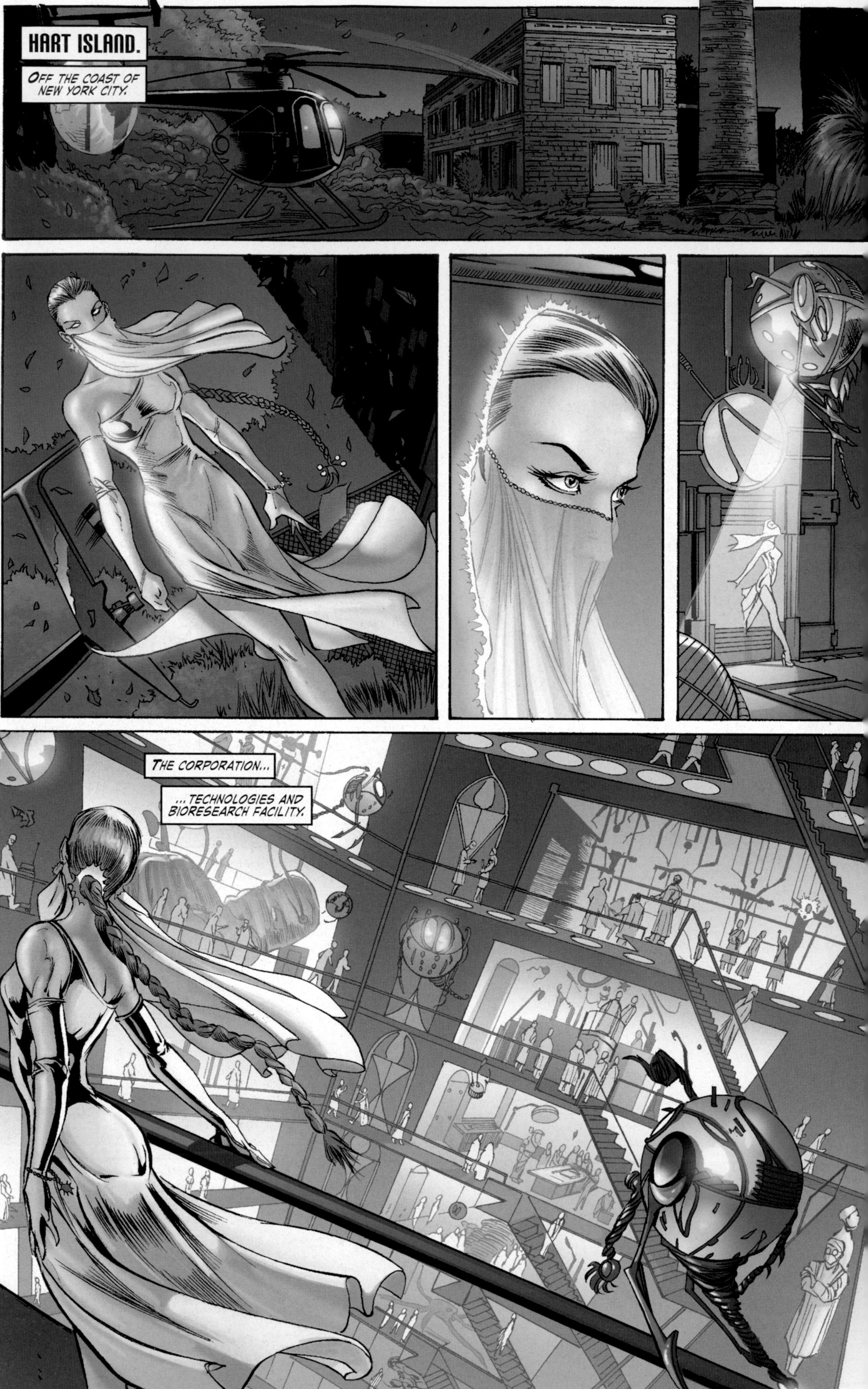
HART ISLAND.
OFF THE COAST OF NEW YORK CITY.
THE CORPORATION...
...TECHNOLOGIES AND BIORESEARCH FACILITY.

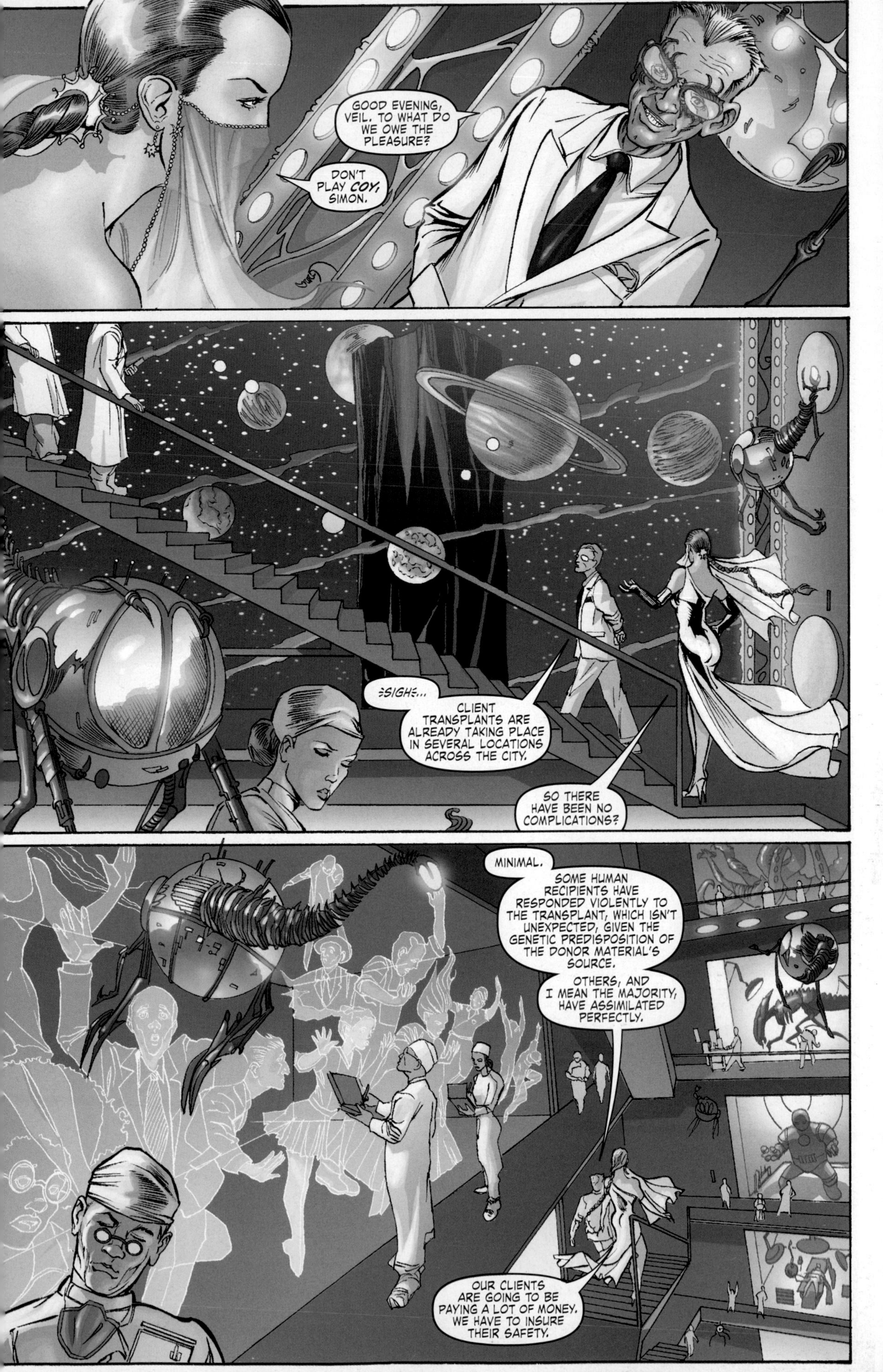
GOOD EVENING, VEIL. TO WHAT DO WE OWE THE PLEASURE?
DON'T PLAY COY, SIMON.
≡SIGH≡...
CLIENT TRANSPLANTS ARE ALREADY TAKING PLACE IN SEVERAL LOCATIONS ACROSS THE CITY.
SO THERE HAVE BEEN NO COMPLICATIONS?
MINIMAL.
SOME HUMAN RECIPIENTS HAVE RESPONDED VIOLENTLY TO THE TRANSPLANT, WHICH ISN'T UNEXPECTED, GIVEN THE GENETIC PREDISPOSITION OF THE DONOR MATERIAL'S SOURCE.
OTHERS, AND I MEAN THE MAJORITY, HAVE ASSIMILATED PERFECTLY.
OUR CLIENTS ARE GOING TO BE PAYING A LOT OF MONEY. WE HAVE TO INSURE THEIR SAFETY.

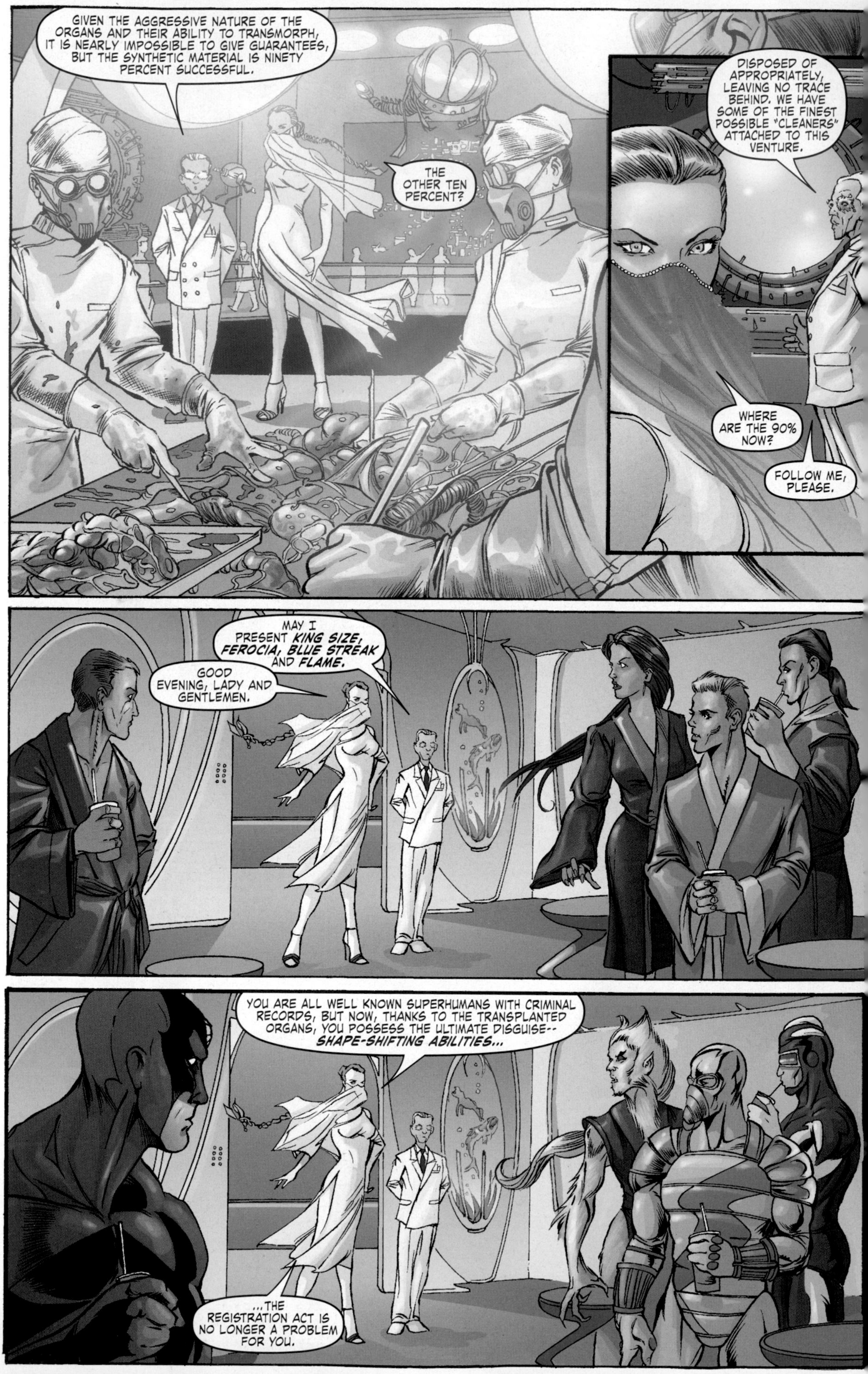
GIVEN THE AGGRESSIVE NATURE OF THE ORGANS AND THEIR ABILITY TO TRANSMORPH, IT IS NEARLY IMPOSSIBLE TO GIVE GUARANTEES, BUT THE SYNTHETIC MATERIAL IS NINETY PERCENT SUCCESSFUL.
THE OTHER TEN PERCENT?
DISPOSED OF APPROPRIATELY, LEAVING NO TRACE BEHIND. WE HAVE SOME OF THE FINEST POSSIBLE "CLEANERS" ATTACHED TO THIS VENTURE.
WHERE ARE THE 90% NOW?
FOLLOW ME, PLEASE.
MAY I PRESENT KING SIZE, FEROCIA, BLUE STREAK AND FLAME.
GOOD EVENING, LADY AND GENTLEMEN.
YOU ARE ALL WELL KNOWN SUPERHUMANS WITH CRIMINAL RECORDS, BUT NOW, THANKS TO THE TRANSPLANTED ORGANS, YOU POSSESS THE ULTIMATE DISGUISE-- SHAPE-SHIFTING ABILITIES...
...THE REGISTRATION ACT IS NO LONGER A PROBLEM FOR YOU.

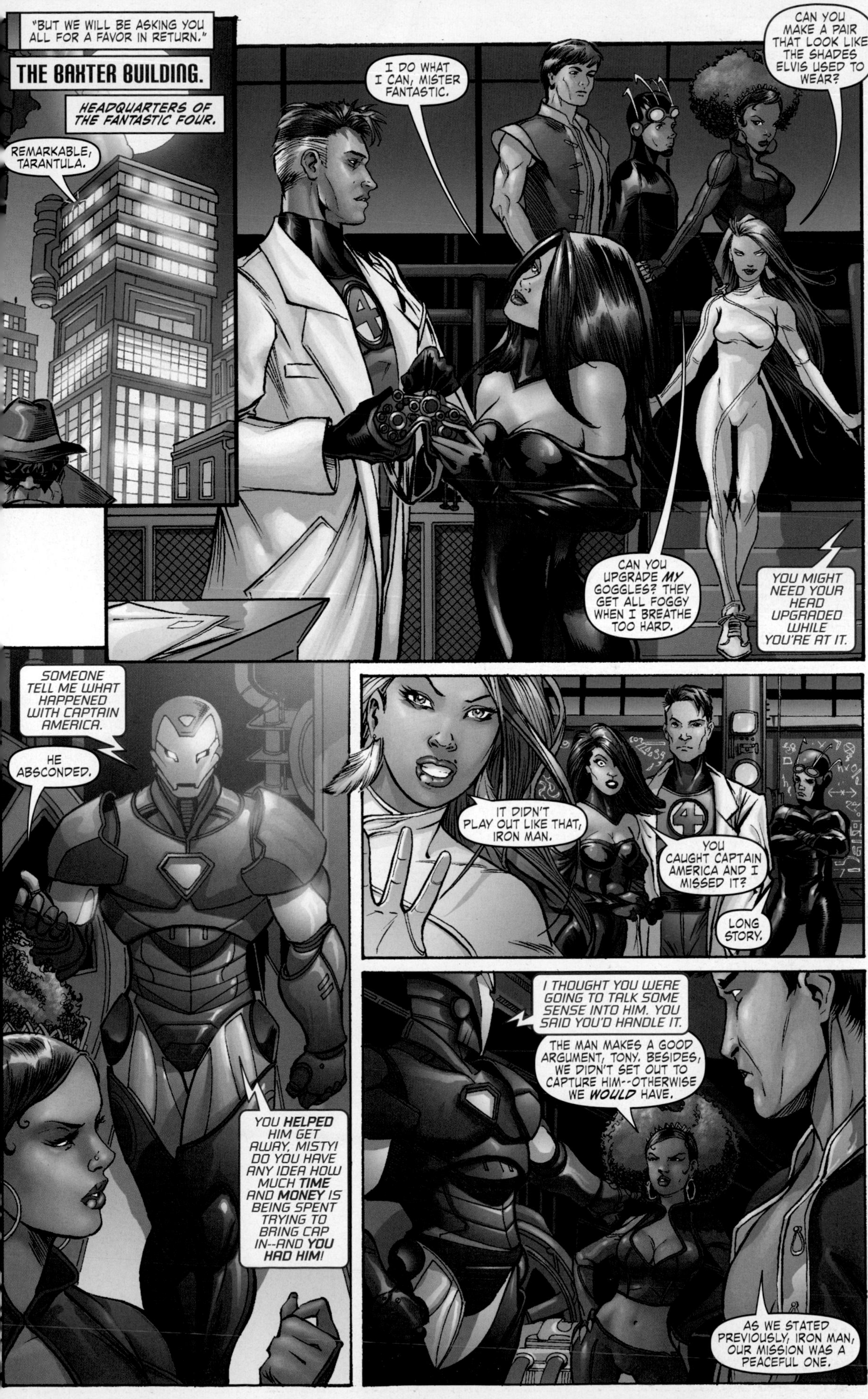
"BUT WE WILL BE ASKING YOU ALL FOR A FAVOR IN RETURN."
THE BAXTER BUILDING.
HEADQUARTERS OF THE FANTASTIC FOUR.
REMARKABLE, TARANTULA.
I DO WHAT I CAN, MISTER FANTASTIC.
CAN YOU MAKE A PAIR THAT LOOK LIKE THE SHADES ELVIS USED TO WEAR?
CAN YOU UPGRADE MY GOGGLES? THEY GET ALL FOGGY WHEN I BREATHE TOO HARD.
YOU MIGHT NEED YOUR HEAD UPGRADED WHILE YOU'RE AT IT.
SOMEONE TELL ME WHAT HAPPENED WITH CAPTAIN AMERICA.
HE ABSCONDED.
YOU HELPED HIM GET AWAY, MISTY! DO YOU HAVE ANY IDEA HOW MUCH TIME AND MONEY IS BEING SPENT TRYING TO BRING CAP IN--AND YOU HAD HIM!
IT DIDN'T PLAY OUT LIKE THAT, IRON MAN.
YOU CAUGHT CAPTAIN AMERICA AND I MISSED IT?
LONG STORY.
I THOUGHT YOU WERE GOING TO TALK SOME SENSE INTO HIM. YOU SAID YOU'D HANDLE IT.
THE MAN MAKES A GOOD ARGUMENT, TONY. BESIDES, WE DIDN'T SET OUT TO CAPTURE HIM--OTHERWISE WE WOULD HAVE.
AS WE STATED PREVIOUSLY, IRON MAN, OUR MISSION WAS A PEACEFUL ONE.

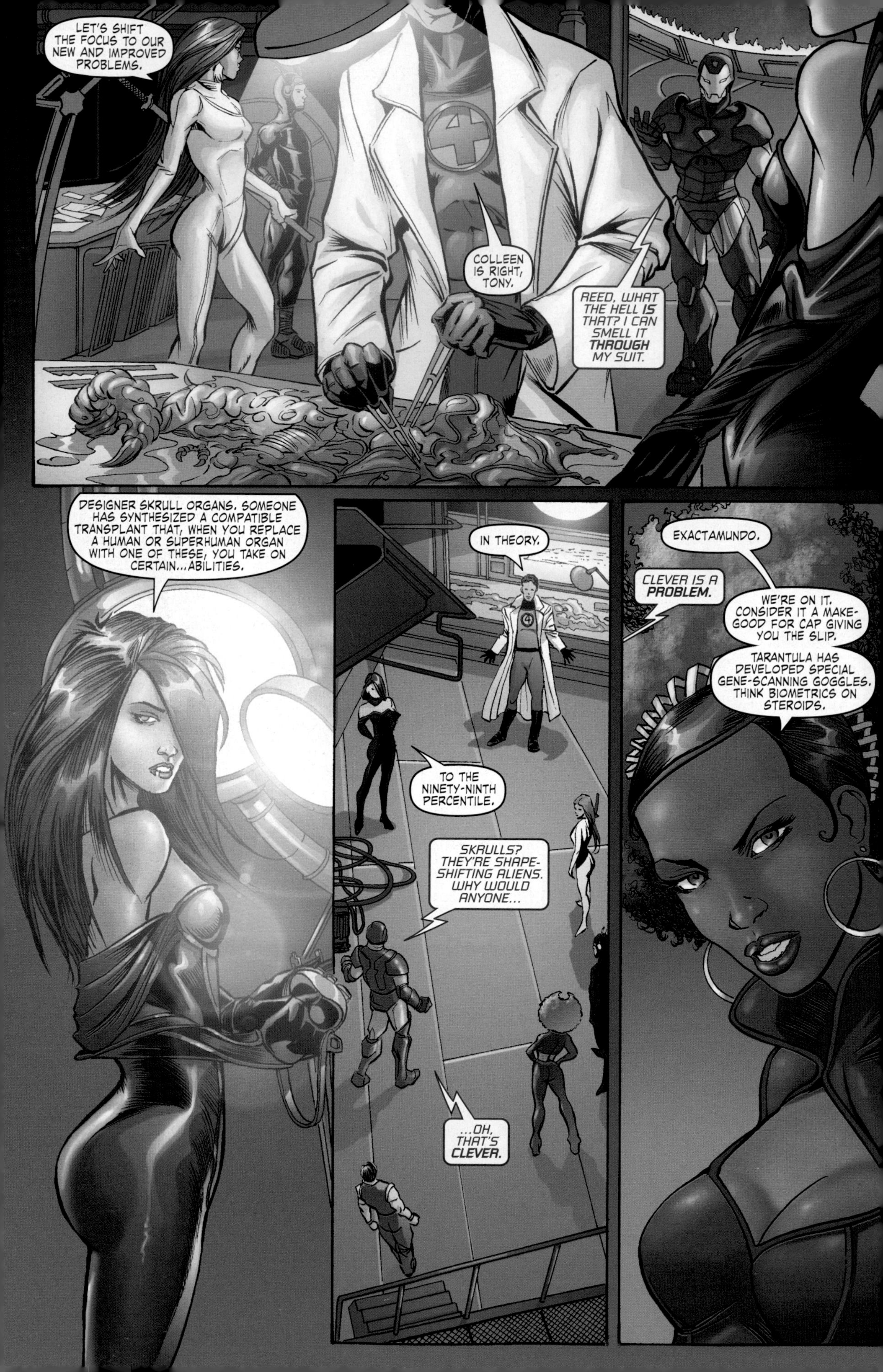
LET'S SHIFT THE FOCUS TO OUR NEW AND IMPROVED PROBLEMS.
COLLEEN IS RIGHT, TONY.
REED, WHAT THE HELL **IS** THAT? I CAN SMELL IT **THROUGH** MY SUIT.
DESIGNER SKRULL ORGANS. SOMEONE HAS SYNTHESIZED A COMPATIBLE TRANSPLANT THAT, WHEN YOU REPLACE A HUMAN OR SUPERHUMAN ORGAN WITH ONE OF THESE, YOU TAKE ON CERTAIN...ABILITIES.
IN THEORY.
TO THE NINETY-NINTH PERCENTILE.
SKRULLS? THEY'RE SHAPE-SHIFTING ALIENS. WHY WOULD ANYONE...
...OH, THAT'S **CLEVER**.
EXACTAMUNDO.
CLEVER IS A **PROBLEM**.
WE'RE ON IT. CONSIDER IT A MAKE-GOOD FOR CAP GIVING YOU THE SLIP.
TARANTULA HAS DEVELOPED SPECIAL GENE-SCANNING GOGGLES. THINK BIOMETRICS ON STEROIDS.

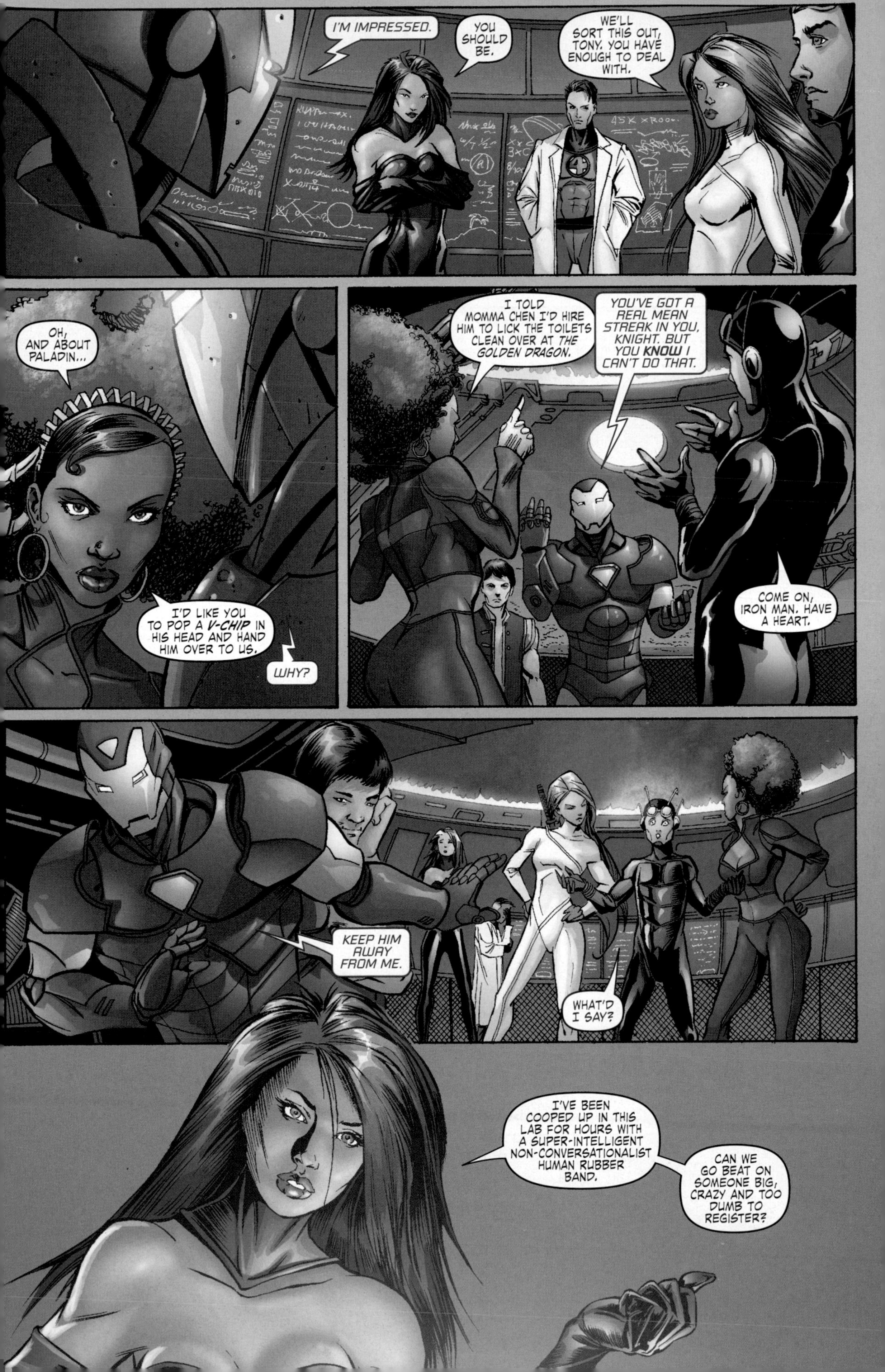
I'M IMPRESSED.
YOU SHOULD BE.
WE'LL SORT THIS OUT, TONY. YOU HAVE ENOUGH TO DEAL WITH.
OH, AND ABOUT PALADIN...
I'D LIKE YOU TO POP A V-CHIP IN HIS HEAD AND HAND HIM OVER TO US.
WHY?
I TOLD MOMMA CHEN I'D HIRE HIM TO LICK THE TOILETS CLEAN OVER AT THE GOLDEN DRAGON.
YOU'VE GOT A REAL MEAN STREAK IN YOU, KNIGHT. BUT YOU KNOW I CAN'T DO THAT.
COME ON, IRON MAN. HAVE A HEART.
KEEP HIM AWAY FROM ME.
WHAT'D I SAY?
I'VE BEEN COOPED UP IN THIS LAB FOR HOURS WITH A SUPER-INTELLIGENT NON-CONVERSATIONALIST HUMAN RUBBER BAND.
CAN WE GO BEAT ON SOMEONE BIG, CRAZY AND TOO DUMB TO REGISTER?

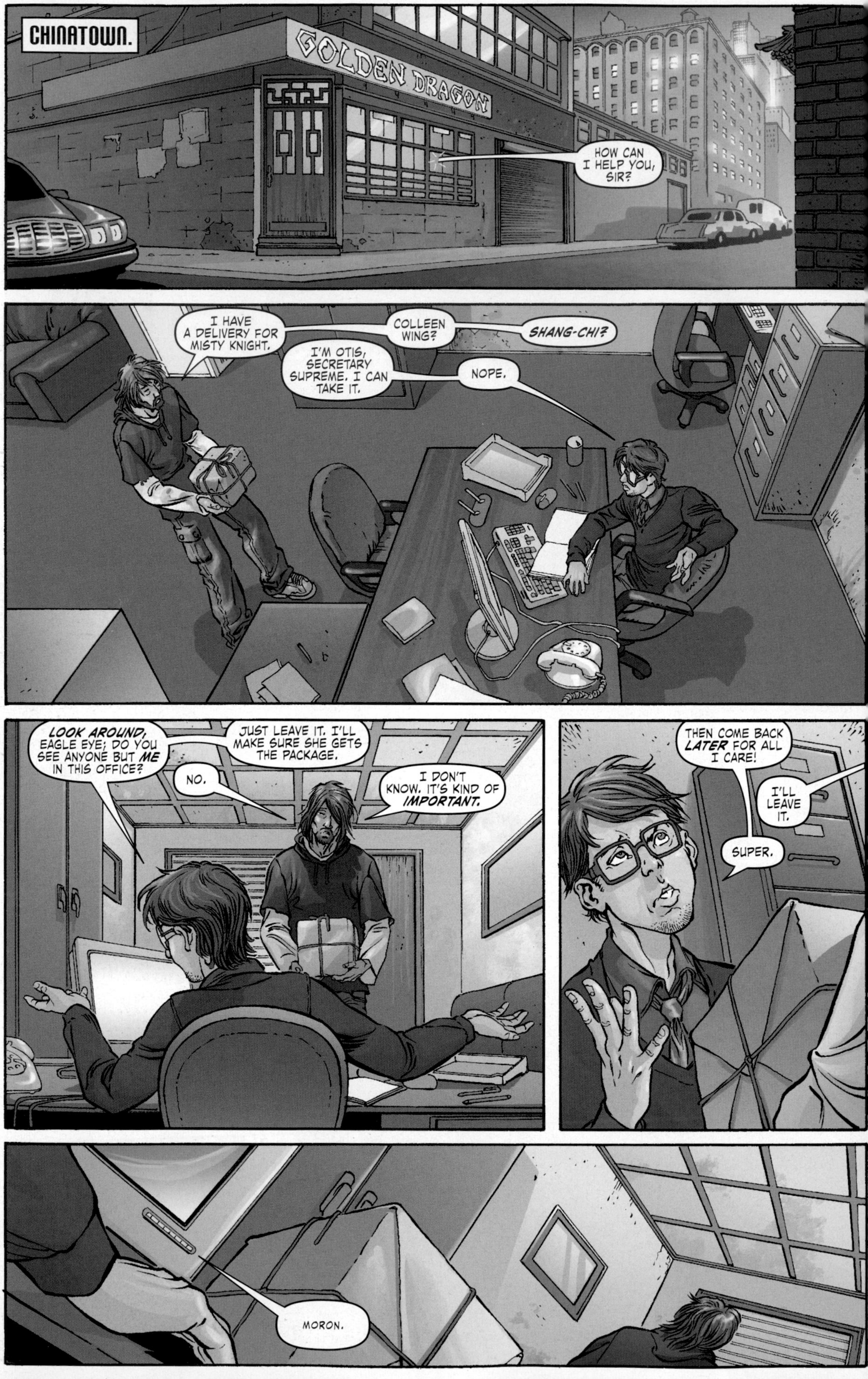
CHINATOWN.
GOLDEN DRAGON
HOW CAN I HELP YOU, SIR?
I HAVE A DELIVERY FOR MISTY KNIGHT.
COLLEEN WING?
SHANG-CHI?
I'M OTIS, SECRETARY SUPREME. I CAN TAKE IT.
NOPE.
LOOK AROUND, EAGLE EYE; DO YOU SEE ANYONE BUT ME IN THIS OFFICE?
NO.
JUST LEAVE IT. I'LL MAKE SURE SHE GETS THE PACKAGE.
I DON'T KNOW. IT'S KIND OF IMPORTANT.
THEN COME BACK LATER FOR ALL I CARE!
I'LL LEAVE IT.
SUPER.
MORON.

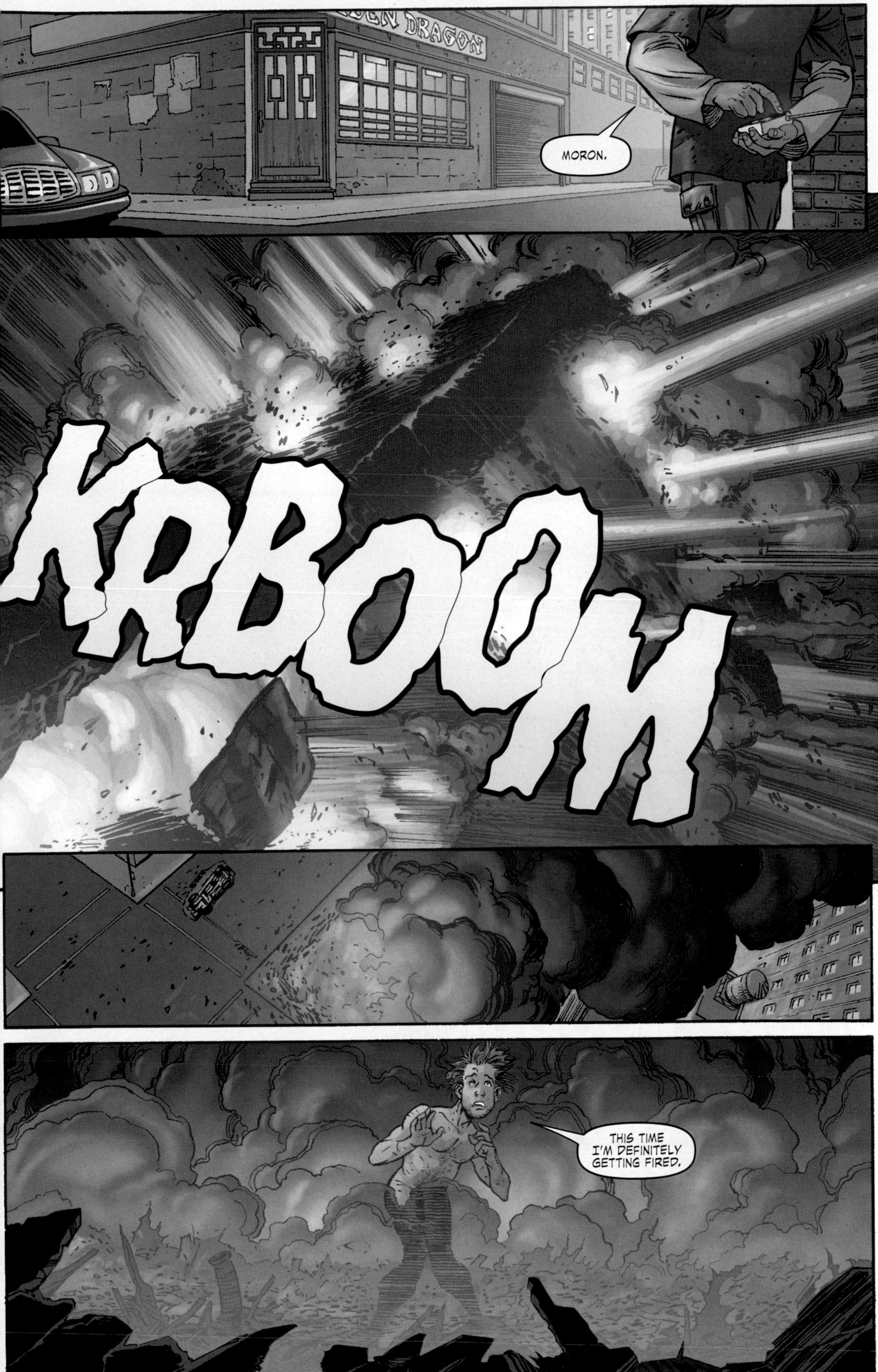
MORON.
KRBOOM
THIS TIME I'M DEFINITELY GETTING FIRED.

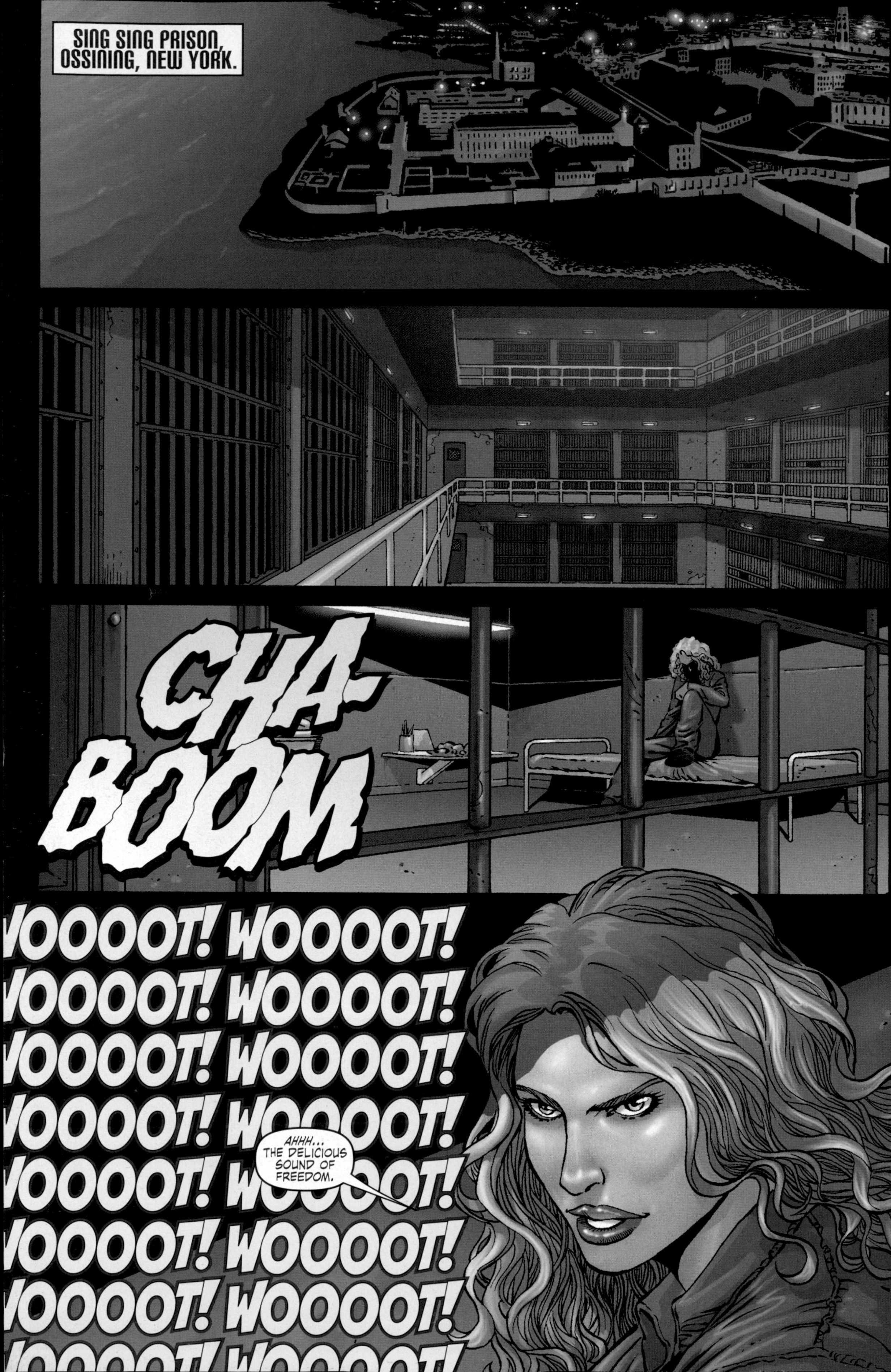
SING SING PRISON, OSSINING, NEW YORK.
CHA-BOOM
WOOOOT! WOOOOT!
WOOOOT! WOOOOT!
WOOOOT! WOOOOT!
WOOOOT! WOOOOT!
WOOOOT! WOOOOT!
WOOOOT! WOOOOT!
WOOOOT! WOOOOT!
AHHH... THE DELICIOUS SOUND OF FREEDOM.

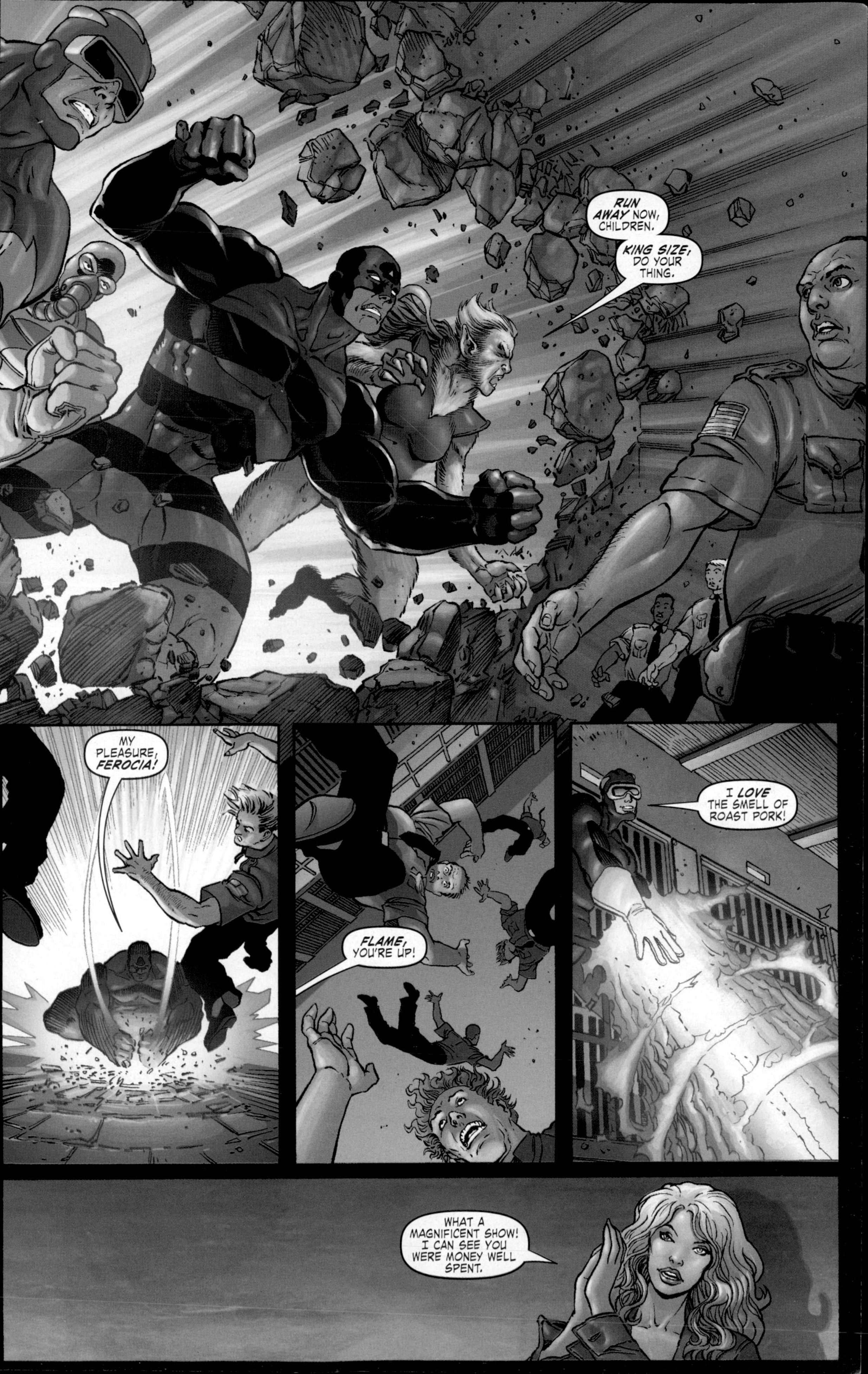
RUN AWAY NOW, CHILDREN.
KING SIZE; DO YOUR THING.
MY PLEASURE, FEROCIA!
FLAME, YOU'RE UP!
I LOVE THE SMELL OF ROAST PORK!
WHAT A MAGNIFICENT SHOW! I CAN SEE YOU WERE MONEY WELL SPENT.

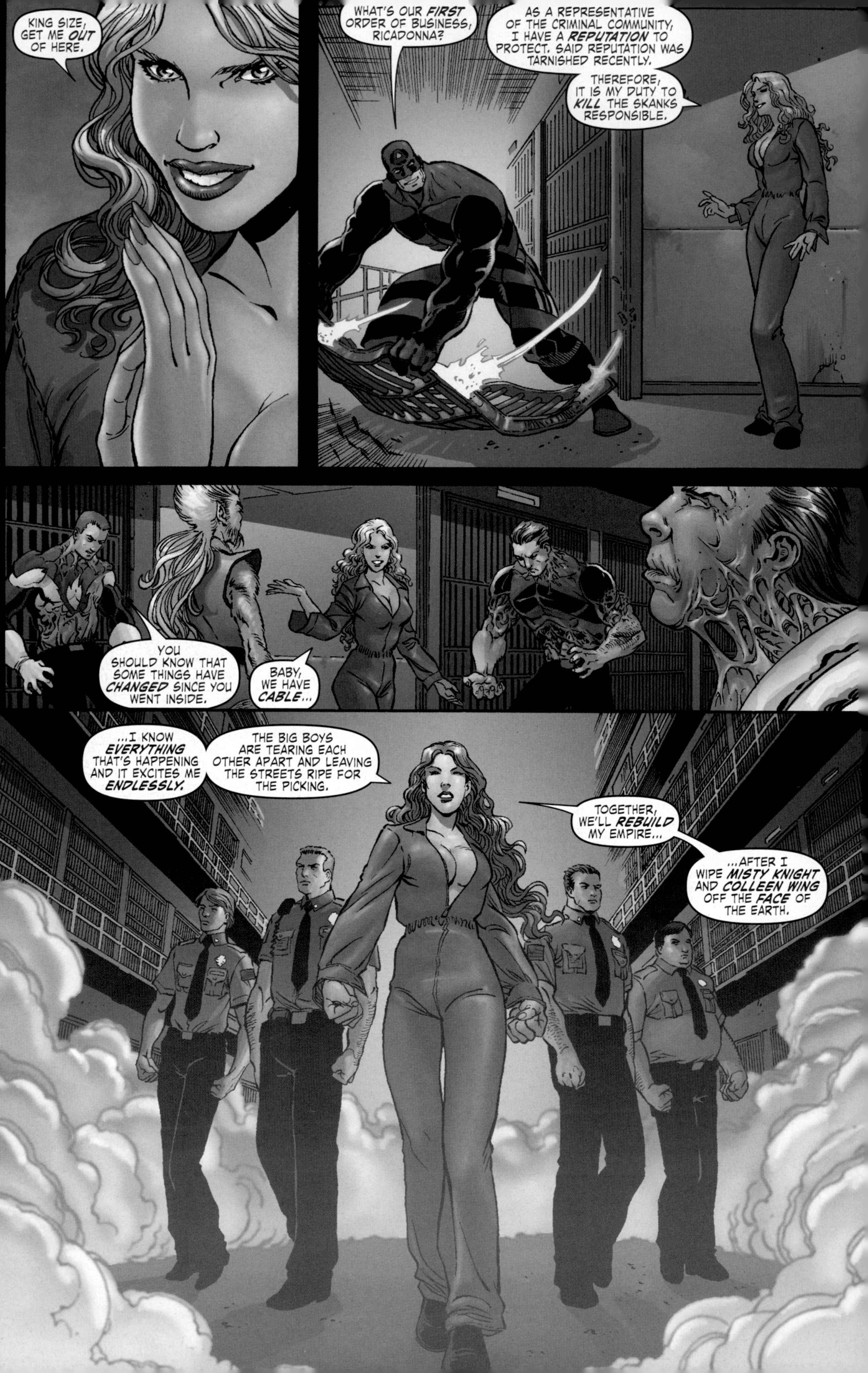
KING SIZE, GET ME OUT OF HERE.
WHAT'S OUR FIRST ORDER OF BUSINESS, RICADONNA?
AS A REPRESENTATIVE OF THE CRIMINAL COMMUNITY, I HAVE A REPUTATION TO PROTECT. SAID REPUTATION WAS TARNISHED RECENTLY.
THEREFORE, IT IS MY DUTY TO KILL THE SKANKS RESPONSIBLE.
YOU SHOULD KNOW THAT SOME THINGS HAVE CHANGED SINCE YOU WENT INSIDE.
BABY, WE HAVE CABLE...
...I KNOW EVERYTHING THAT'S HAPPENING AND IT EXCITES ME ENDLESSLY.
THE BIG BOYS ARE TEARING EACH OTHER APART AND LEAVING THE STREETS RIPE FOR THE PICKING.
TOGETHER, WE'LL REBUILD MY EMPIRE...
...AFTER I WIPE MISTY KNIGHT AND COLLEEN WING OFF THE FACE OF THE EARTH.

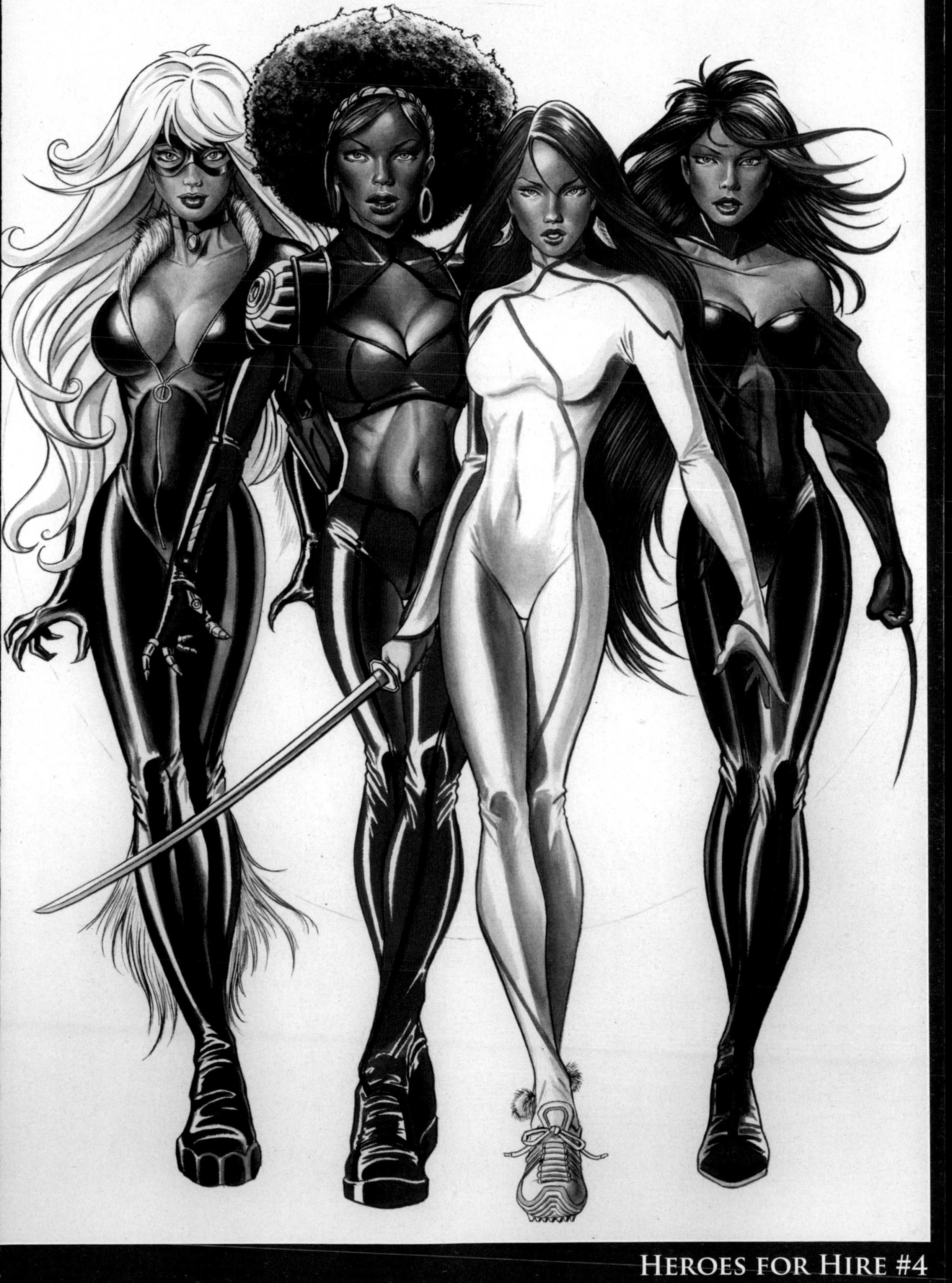

HEROES FOR HIRE #4

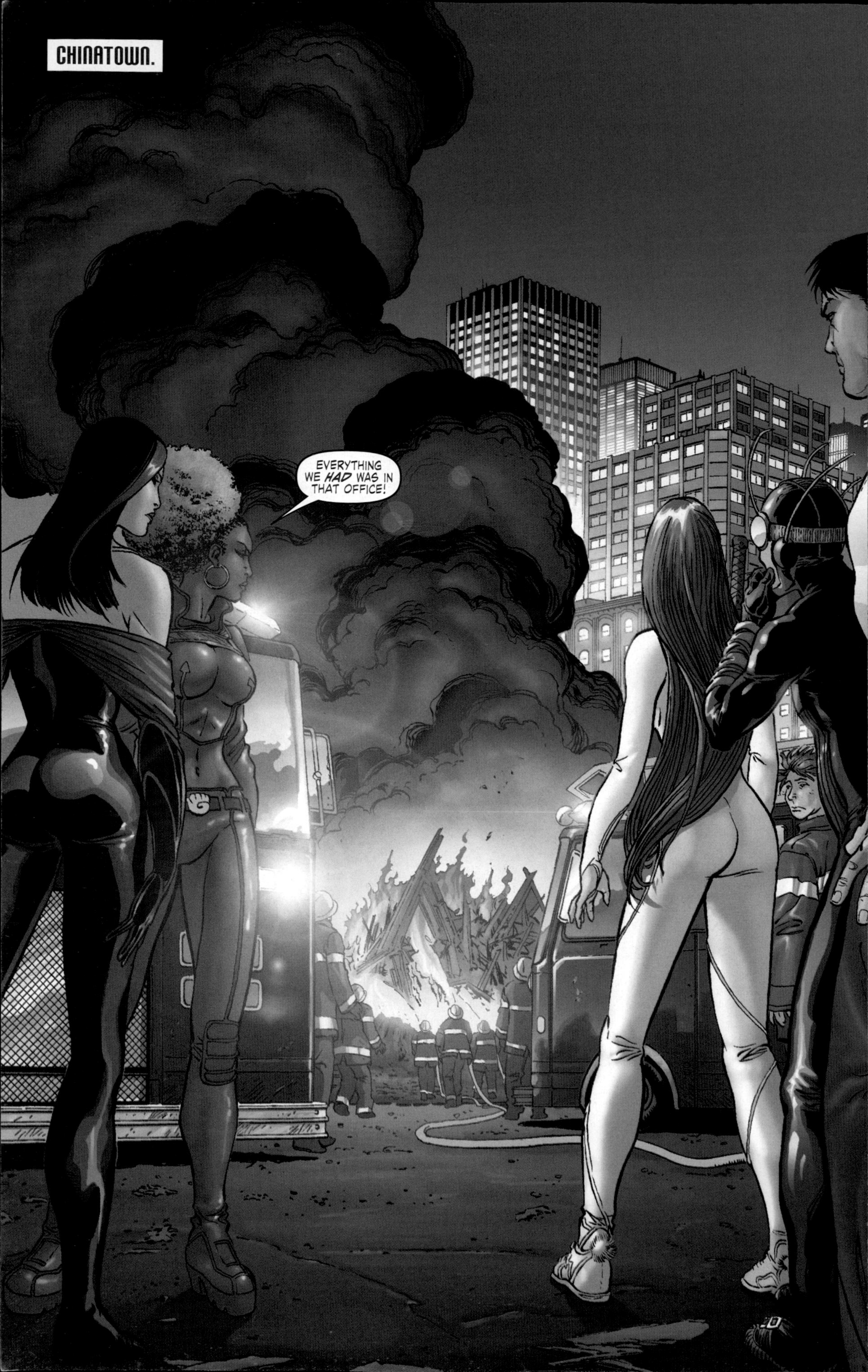
CHINATOWN.
EVERYTHING WE HAD WAS IN THAT OFFICE!

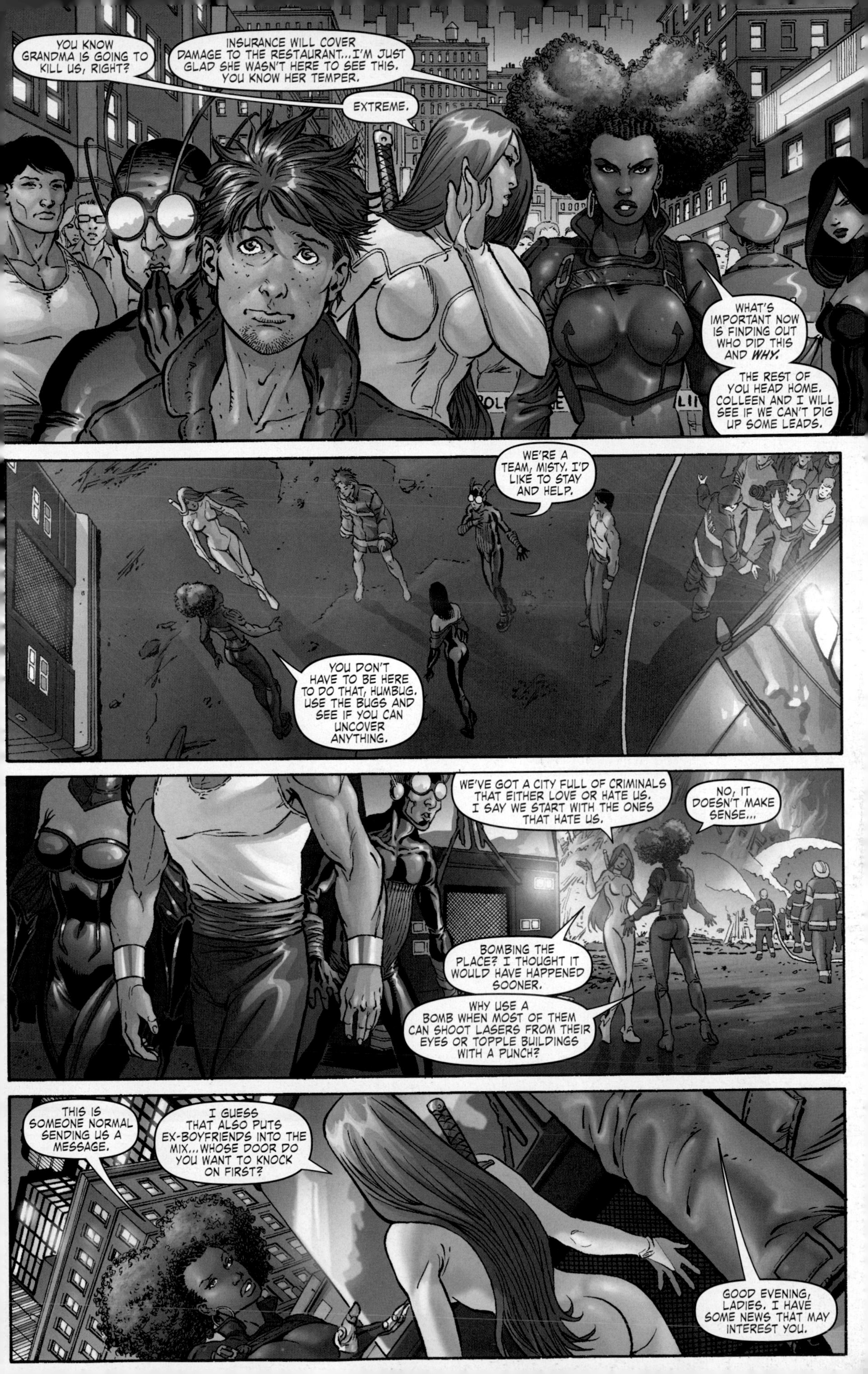
YOU KNOW GRANDMA IS GOING TO KILL US, RIGHT?
INSURANCE WILL COVER DAMAGE TO THE RESTAURANT... I'M JUST GLAD SHE WASN'T HERE TO SEE THIS. YOU KNOW HER TEMPER.
EXTREME.
WHAT'S IMPORTANT NOW IS FINDING OUT WHO DID THIS AND WHY.
THE REST OF YOU HEAD HOME. COLLEEN AND I WILL SEE IF WE CAN'T DIG UP SOME LEADS.
WE'RE A TEAM, MISTY. I'D LIKE TO STAY AND HELP.
YOU DON'T HAVE TO BE HERE TO DO THAT, HUMBUG. USE THE BUGS AND SEE IF YOU CAN UNCOVER ANYTHING.
WE'VE GOT A CITY FULL OF CRIMINALS THAT EITHER LOVE OR HATE US. I SAY WE START WITH THE ONES THAT HATE US.
NO, IT DOESN'T MAKE SENSE...
BOMBING THE PLACE? I THOUGHT IT WOULD HAVE HAPPENED SOONER.
WHY USE A BOMB WHEN MOST OF THEM CAN SHOOT LASERS FROM THEIR EYES OR TOPPLE BUILDINGS WITH A PUNCH?
THIS IS SOMEONE NORMAL SENDING US A MESSAGE.
I GUESS THAT ALSO PUTS EX-BOYFRIENDS INTO THE MIX... WHOSE DOOR DO YOU WANT TO KNOCK ON FIRST?
GOOD EVENING, LADIES. I HAVE SOME NEWS THAT MAY INTEREST YOU.

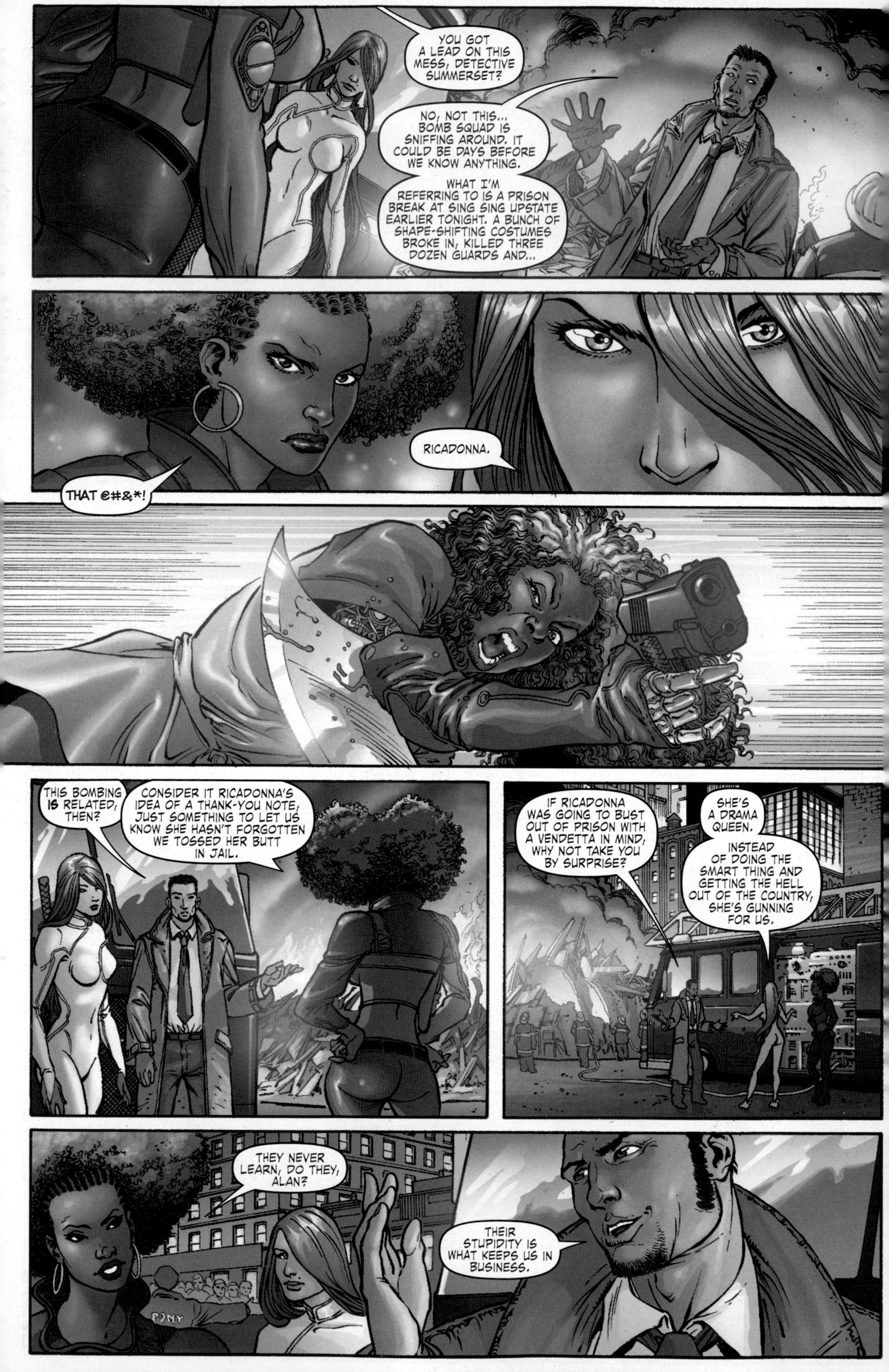
YOU GOT A LEAD ON THIS MESS, DETECTIVE SUMMERSET?
NO, NOT THIS... BOMB SQUAD IS SNIFFING AROUND. IT COULD BE DAYS BEFORE WE KNOW ANYTHING.
WHAT I'M REFERRING TO IS A PRISON BREAK AT SING SING UPSTATE EARLIER TONIGHT. A BUNCH OF SHAPE-SHIFTING COSTUMES BROKE IN, KILLED THREE DOZEN GUARDS AND...
RICADONNA.
THAT @#&*!
THIS BOMBING IS RELATED, THEN?
CONSIDER IT RICADONNA'S IDEA OF A THANK-YOU NOTE, JUST SOMETHING TO LET US KNOW SHE HASN'T FORGOTTEN WE TOSSED HER BUTT IN JAIL.
IF RICADONNA WAS GOING TO BUST OUT OF PRISON WITH A VENDETTA IN MIND, WHY NOT TAKE YOU BY SURPRISE?
SHE'S A DRAMA QUEEN.
INSTEAD OF DOING THE SMART THING AND GETTING THE HELL OUT OF THE COUNTRY, SHE'S GUNNING FOR US.
THEY NEVER LEARN, DO THEY, ALAN?
THEIR STUPIDITY IS WHAT KEEPS US IN BUSINESS.
PDNY

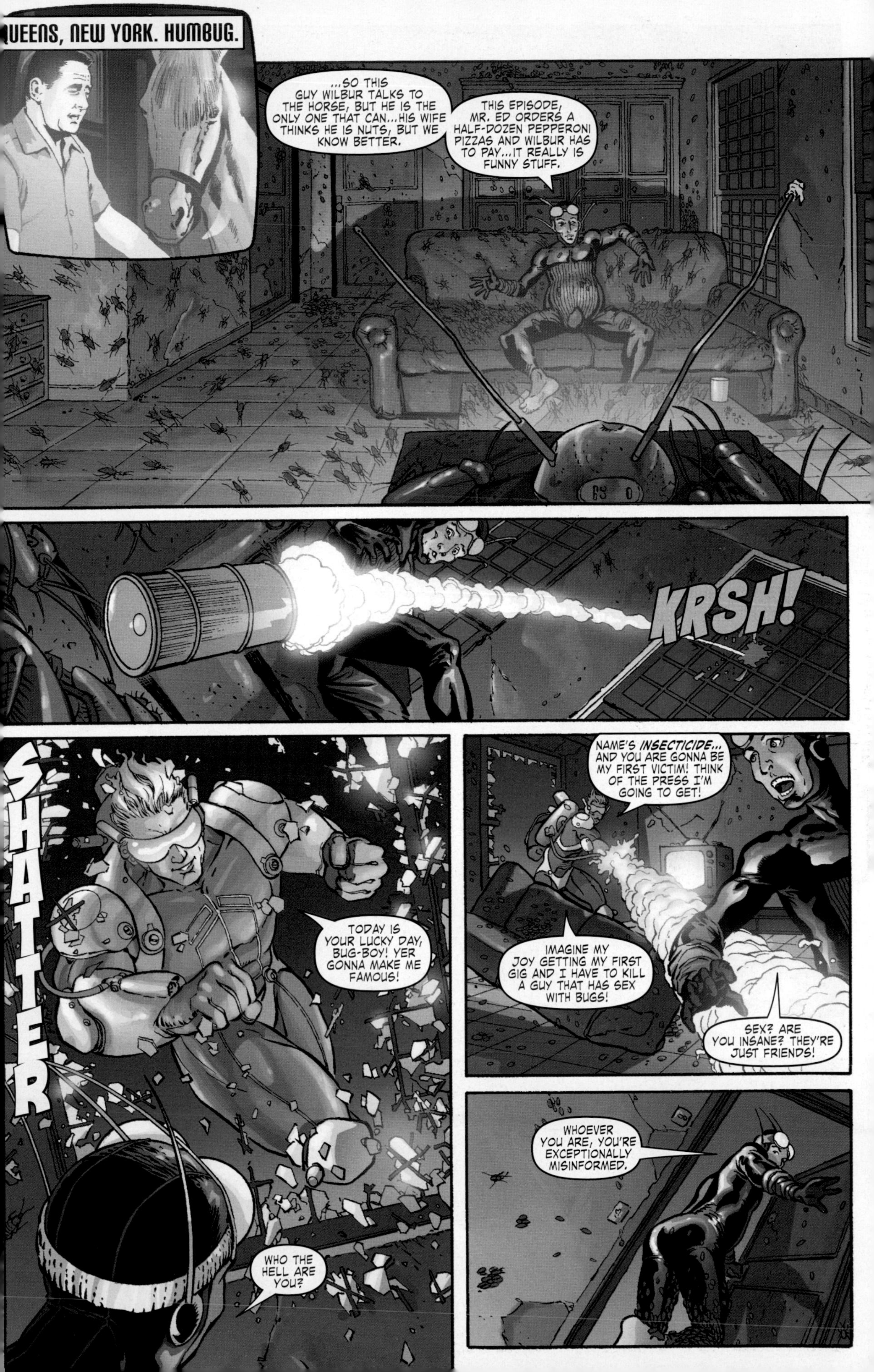
QUEENS, NEW YORK. HUMBUG.
...SO THIS GUY WILBUR TALKS TO THE HORSE, BUT HE IS THE ONLY ONE THAT CAN...HIS WIFE THINKS HE IS NUTS, BUT WE KNOW BETTER.
THIS EPISODE, MR. ED ORDERS A HALF-DOZEN PEPPERONI PIZZAS AND WILBUR HAS TO PAY...IT REALLY IS FUNNY STUFF.
KRSH!
SHATTER
TODAY IS YOUR LUCKY DAY, BUG-BOY! YER GONNA MAKE ME FAMOUS!
WHO THE HELL ARE YOU?
NAME'S INSECTICIDE... AND YOU ARE GONNA BE MY FIRST VICTIM! THINK OF THE PRESS I'M GOING TO GET!
IMAGINE MY JOY GETTING MY FIRST GIG AND I HAVE TO KILL A GUY THAT HAS SEX WITH BUGS!
SEX? ARE YOU INSANE? THEY'RE JUST FRIENDS!
WHOEVER YOU ARE, YOU'RE EXCEPTIONALLY MISINFORMED.

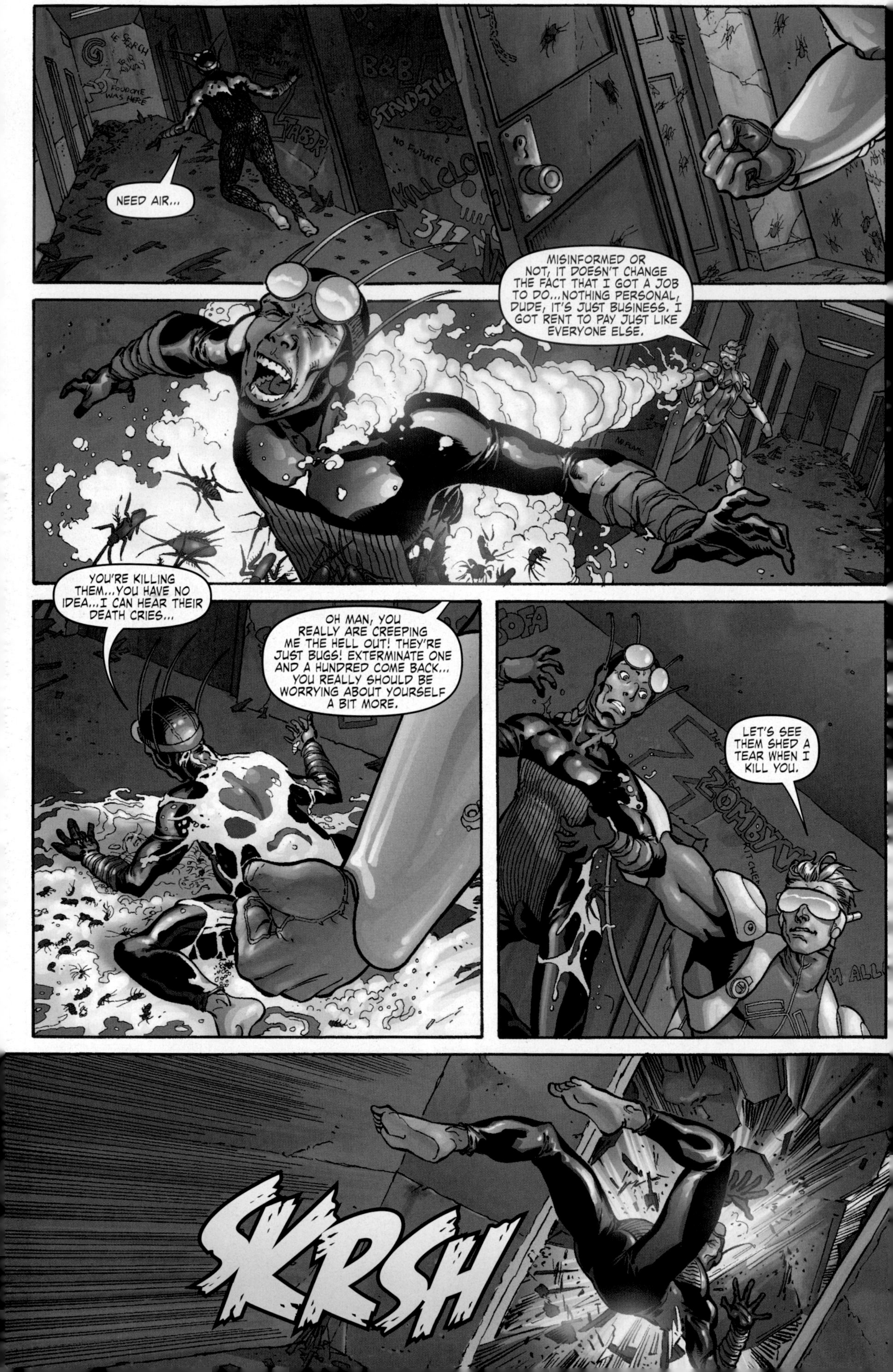
NEED AIR...
MISINFORMED OR NOT, IT DOESN'T CHANGE THE FACT THAT I GOT A JOB TO DO...NOTHING PERSONAL, DUDE, IT'S JUST BUSINESS. I GOT RENT TO PAY JUST LIKE EVERYONE ELSE.
YOU'RE KILLING THEM...YOU HAVE NO IDEA...I CAN HEAR THEIR DEATH CRIES...
OH MAN, YOU REALLY ARE CREEPING ME THE HELL OUT! THEY'RE JUST BUGS! EXTERMINATE ONE AND A HUNDRED COME BACK... YOU REALLY SHOULD BE WORRYING ABOUT YOURSELF A BIT MORE.
LET'S SEE THEM SHED A TEAR WHEN I KILL YOU.
SKRSH

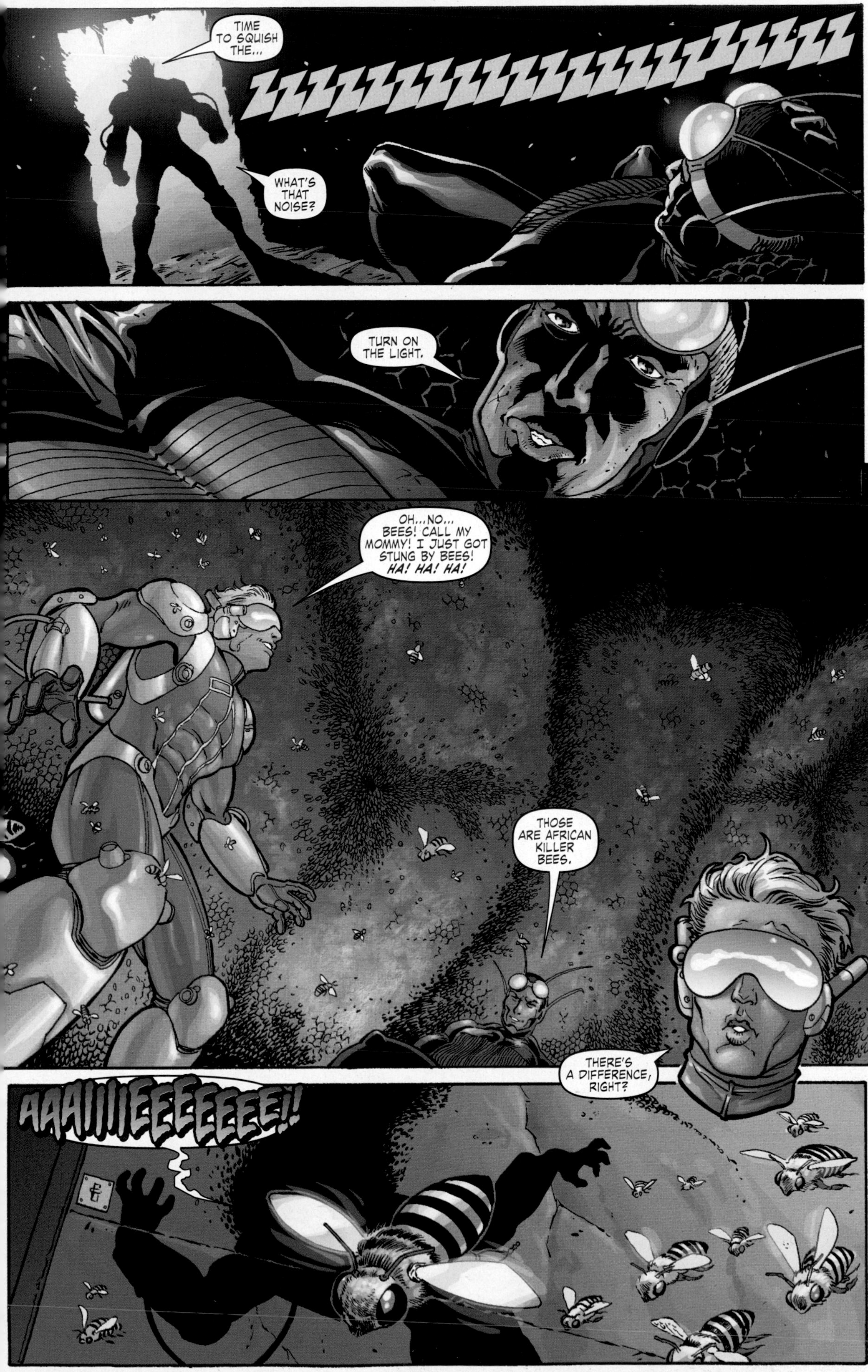
TIME TO SQUISH THE...
ZZZZZZZZZZZZZZZZZZZZZZZZZ
WHAT'S THAT NOISE?
TURN ON THE LIGHT.
OH...NO... BEES! CALL MY MOMMY! I JUST GOT STUNG BY BEES! HA! HA! HA!
THOSE ARE AFRICAN KILLER BEES.
THERE'S A DIFFERENCE, RIGHT?
AAAIIIIIEEEEEEEE!!

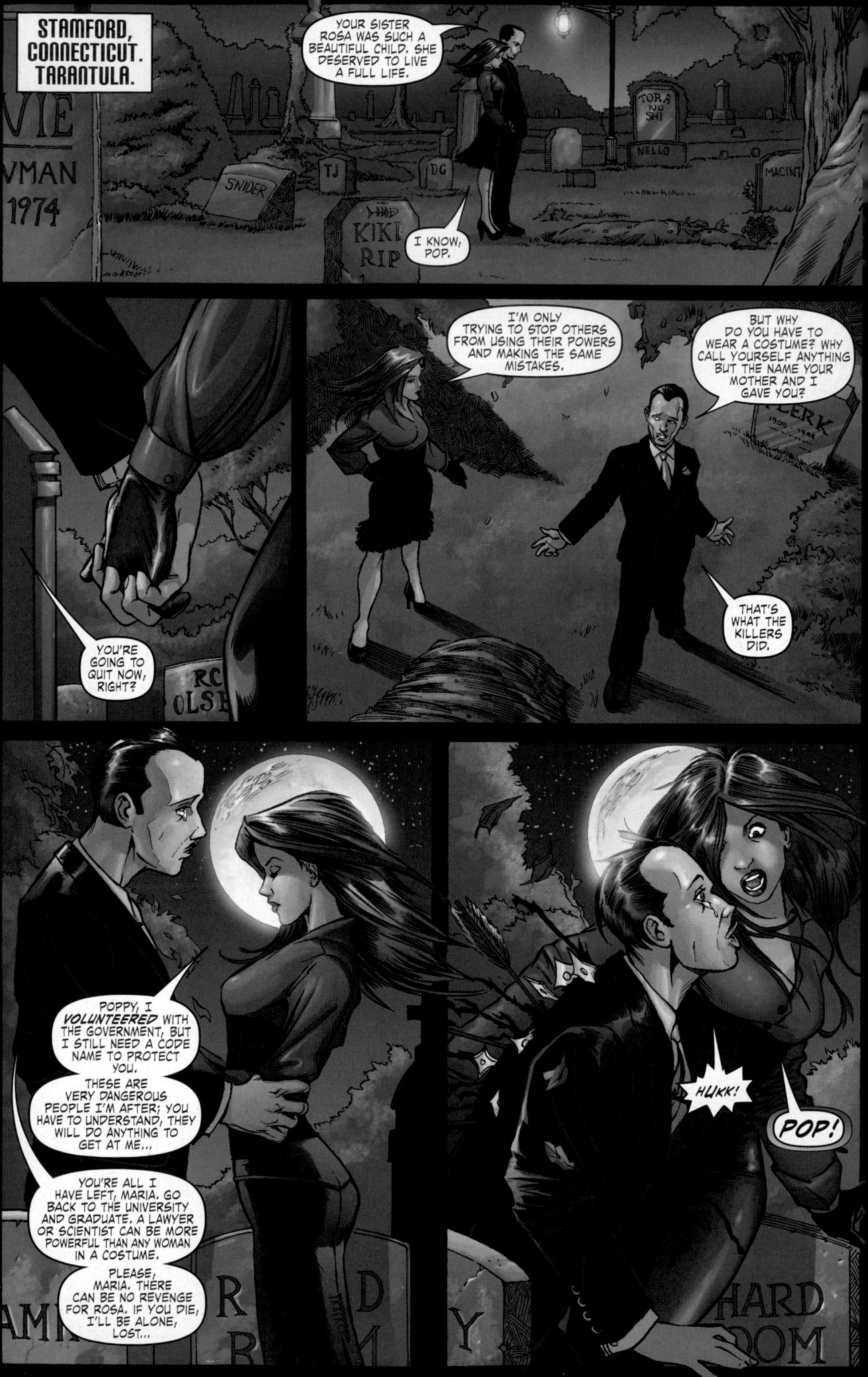

STAMFORD, CONNECTICUT. TARANTULA.
YOUR SISTER ROSA WAS SUCH A BEAUTIFUL CHILD. SHE DESERVED TO LIVE A FULL LIFE.
I KNOW, POP.
YOU'RE GOING TO QUIT NOW, RIGHT?
I'M ONLY TRYING TO STOP OTHERS FROM USING THEIR POWERS AND MAKING THE SAME MISTAKES.
BUT WHY DO YOU HAVE TO WEAR A COSTUME? WHY CALL YOURSELF ANYTHING BUT THE NAME YOUR MOTHER AND I GAVE YOU?
THAT'S WHAT THE KILLERS DID.
POPPY, I VOLUNTEERED WITH THE GOVERNMENT, BUT I STILL NEED A CODE NAME TO PROTECT YOU.
THESE ARE VERY DANGEROUS PEOPLE I'M AFTER; YOU HAVE TO UNDERSTAND, THEY WILL DO ANYTHING TO GET AT ME...
YOU'RE ALL I HAVE LEFT, MARIA. GO BACK TO THE UNIVERSITY AND GRADUATE. A LAWYER OR SCIENTIST CAN BE MORE POWERFUL THAN ANY WOMAN IN A COSTUME.
PLEASE, MARIA. THERE CAN BE NO REVENGE FOR ROSA. IF YOU DIE, I'LL BE ALONE, LOST...
HUKK!
POP!

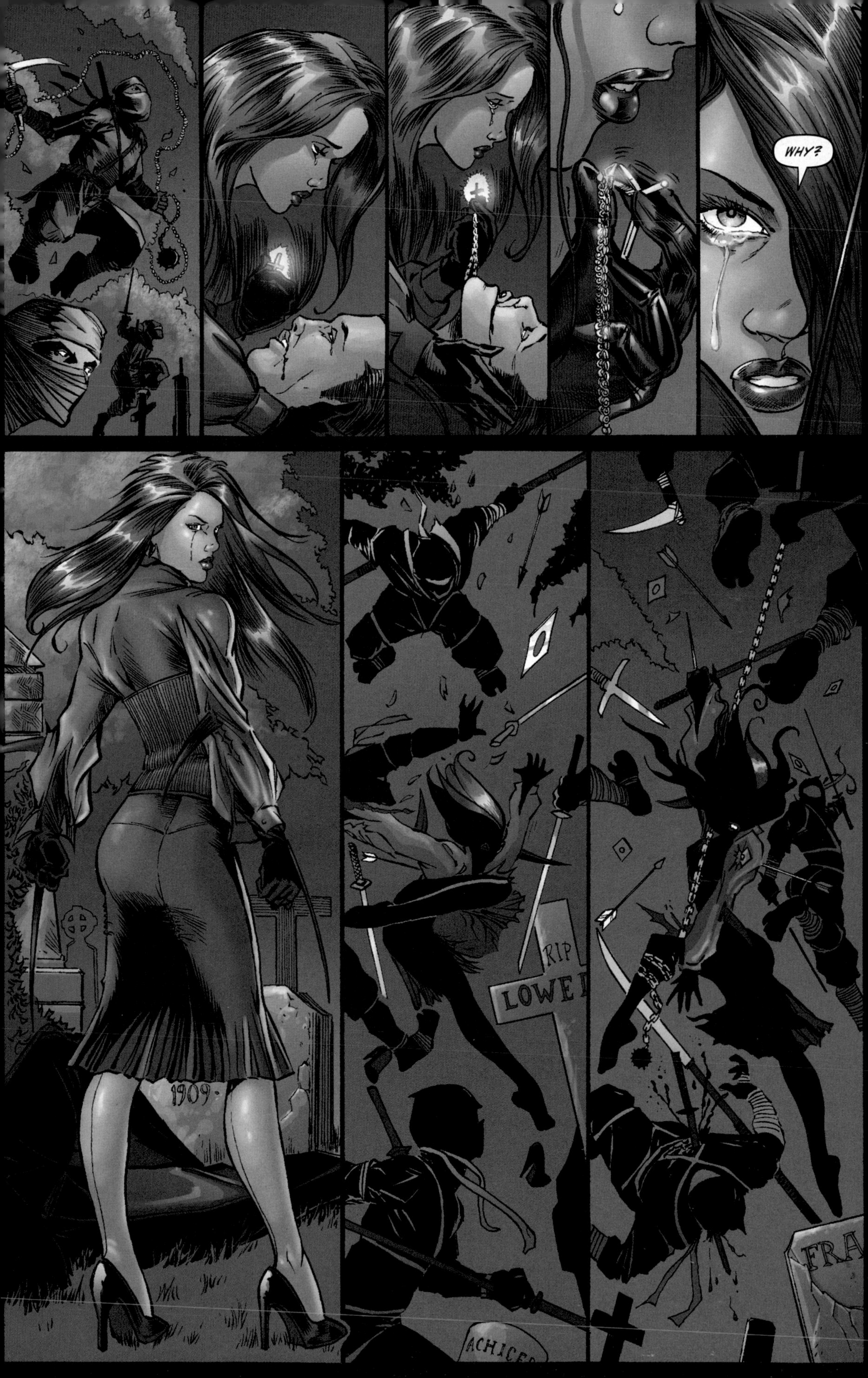
WHY?
RIP
1909

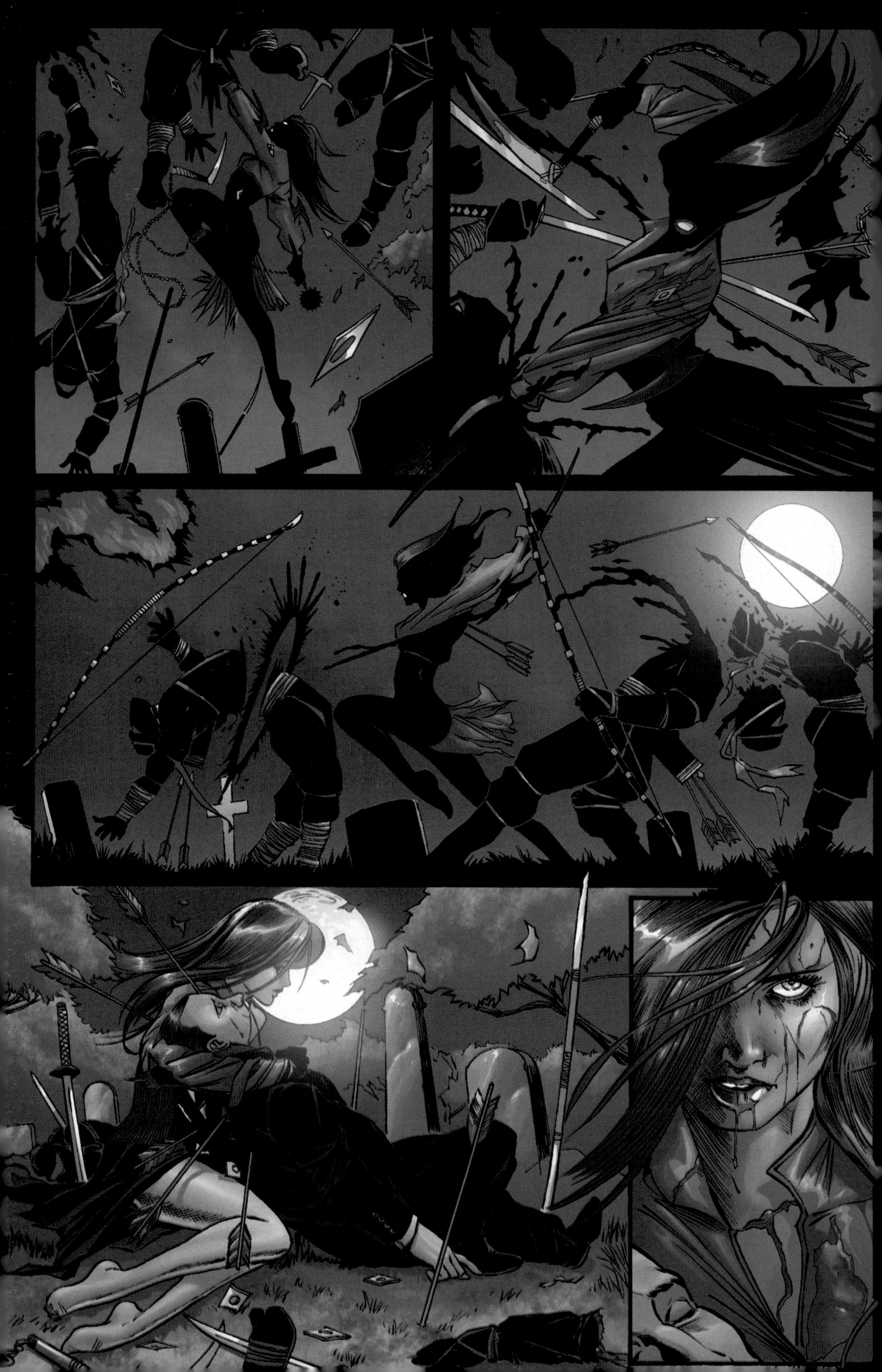

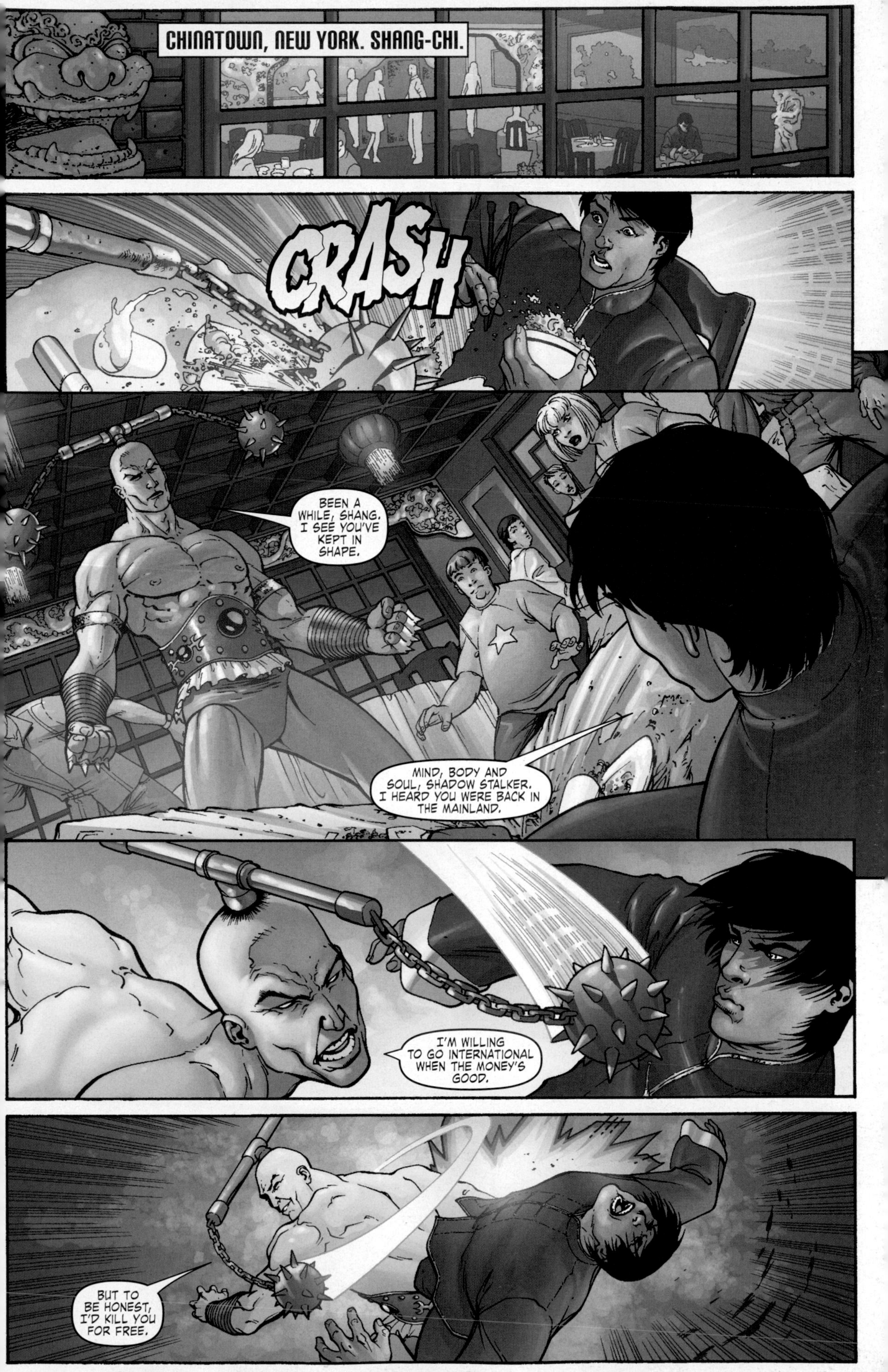
CHINATOWN, NEW YORK. SHANG-CHI.
CRASH
BEEN A WHILE, SHANG. I SEE YOU'VE KEPT IN SHAPE.
MIND, BODY AND SOUL, SHADOW STALKER. I HEARD YOU WERE BACK IN THE MAINLAND.
I'M WILLING TO GO INTERNATIONAL WHEN THE MONEY'S GOOD.
BUT TO BE HONEST, I'D KILL YOU FOR FREE.

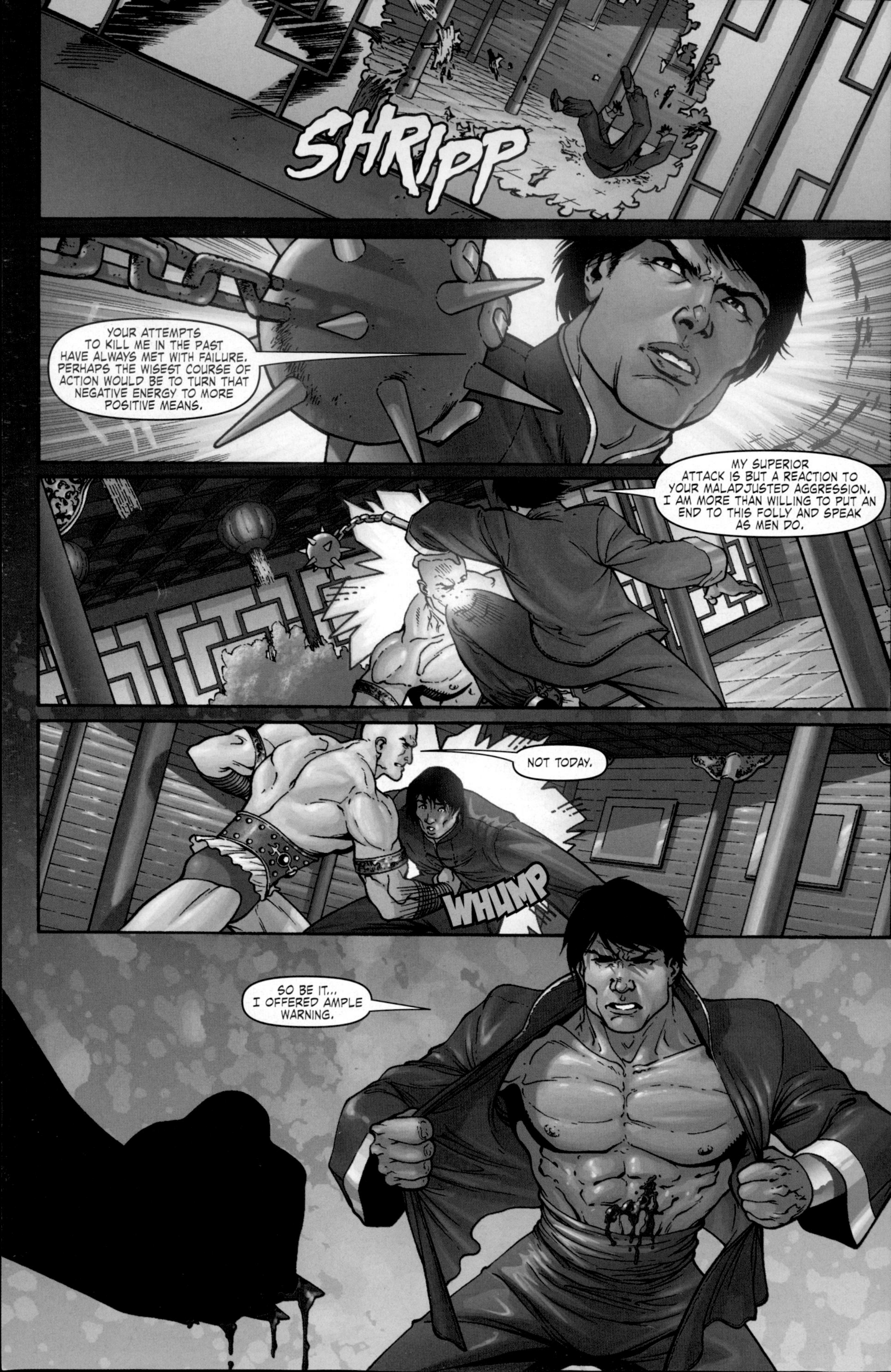
SHRIPP
YOUR ATTEMPTS TO KILL ME IN THE PAST HAVE ALWAYS MET WITH FAILURE. PERHAPS THE WISEST COURSE OF ACTION WOULD BE TO TURN THAT NEGATIVE ENERGY TO MORE POSITIVE MEANS.
MY SUPERIOR ATTACK IS BUT A REACTION TO YOUR MALADJUSTED AGGRESSION. I AM MORE THAN WILLING TO PUT AN END TO THIS FOLLY AND SPEAK AS MEN DO.
NOT TODAY.
WHUMP
SO BE IT... I OFFERED AMPLE WARNING.

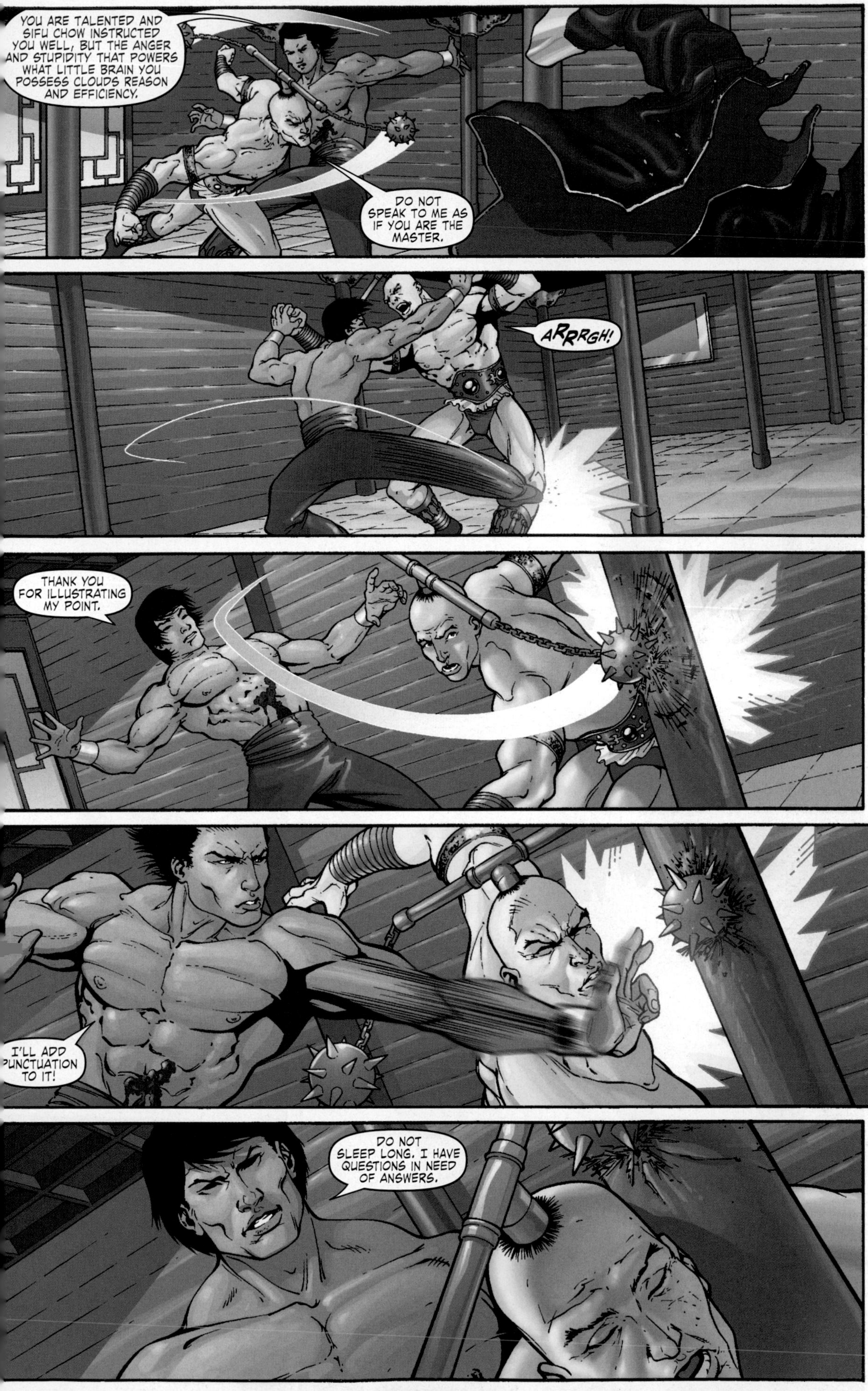
YOU ARE TALENTED AND SIFU CHOW INSTRUCTED YOU WELL, BUT THE ANGER AND STUPIDITY THAT POWERS WHAT LITTLE BRAIN YOU POSSESS CLOUDS REASON AND EFFICIENCY.
DO NOT SPEAK TO ME AS IF YOU ARE THE MASTER.
ARRRGH!
THANK YOU FOR ILLUSTRATING MY POINT.
I'LL ADD PUNCTUATION TO IT!
DO NOT SLEEP LONG. I HAVE QUESTIONS IN NEED OF ANSWERS.

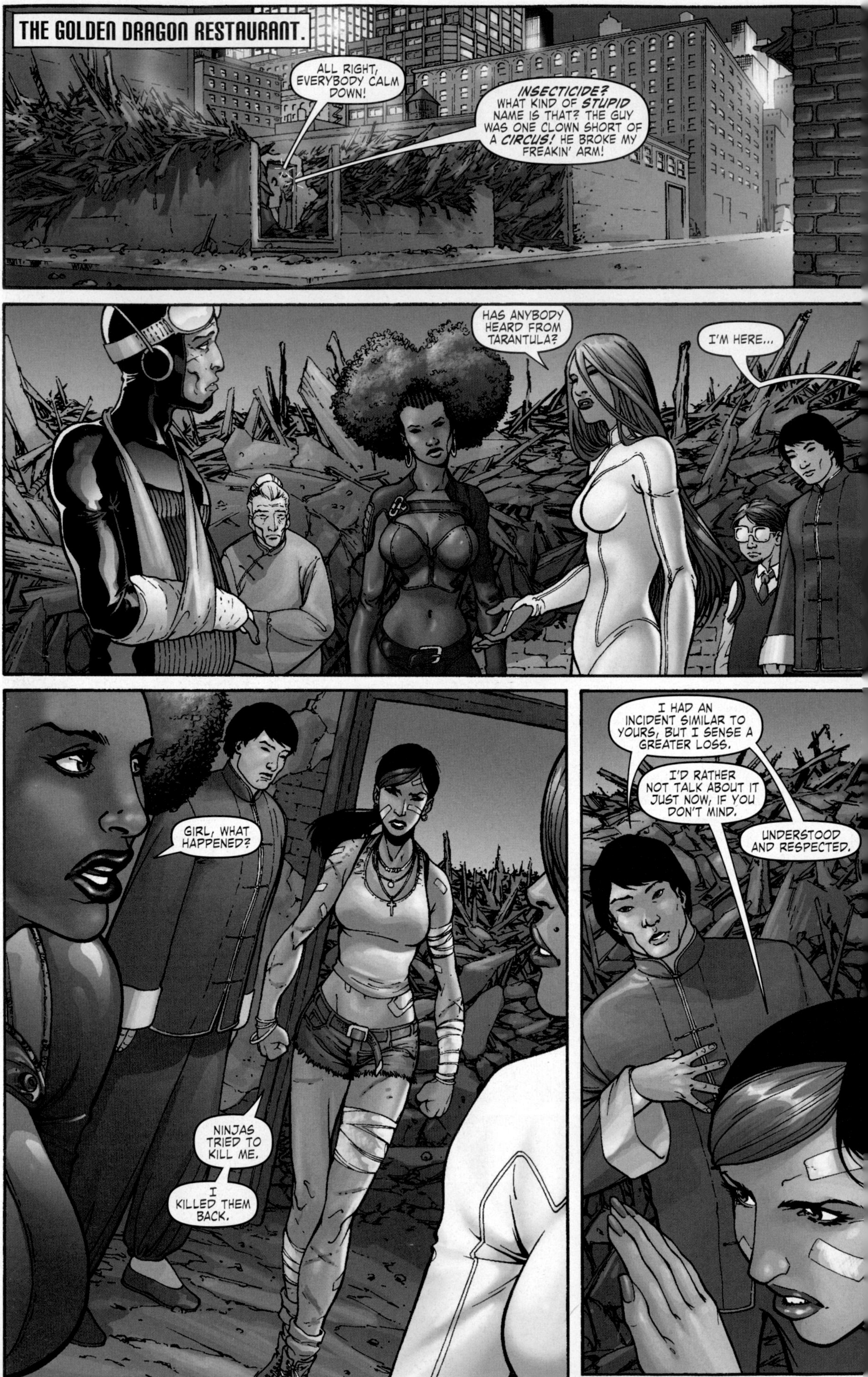
THE GOLDEN DRAGON RESTAURANT.
ALL RIGHT, EVERYBODY CALM DOWN!
INSECTICIDE? WHAT KIND OF STUPID NAME IS THAT? THE GUY WAS ONE CLOWN SHORT OF A CIRCUS! HE BROKE MY FREAKIN' ARM!
HAS ANYBODY HEARD FROM TARANTULA?
I'M HERE...
GIRL, WHAT HAPPENED?
NINJAS TRIED TO KILL ME.
I KILLED THEM BACK.
I HAD AN INCIDENT SIMILAR TO YOURS, BUT I SENSE A GREATER LOSS.
I'D RATHER NOT TALK ABOUT IT JUST NOW, IF YOU DON'T MIND.
UNDERSTOOD AND RESPECTED.

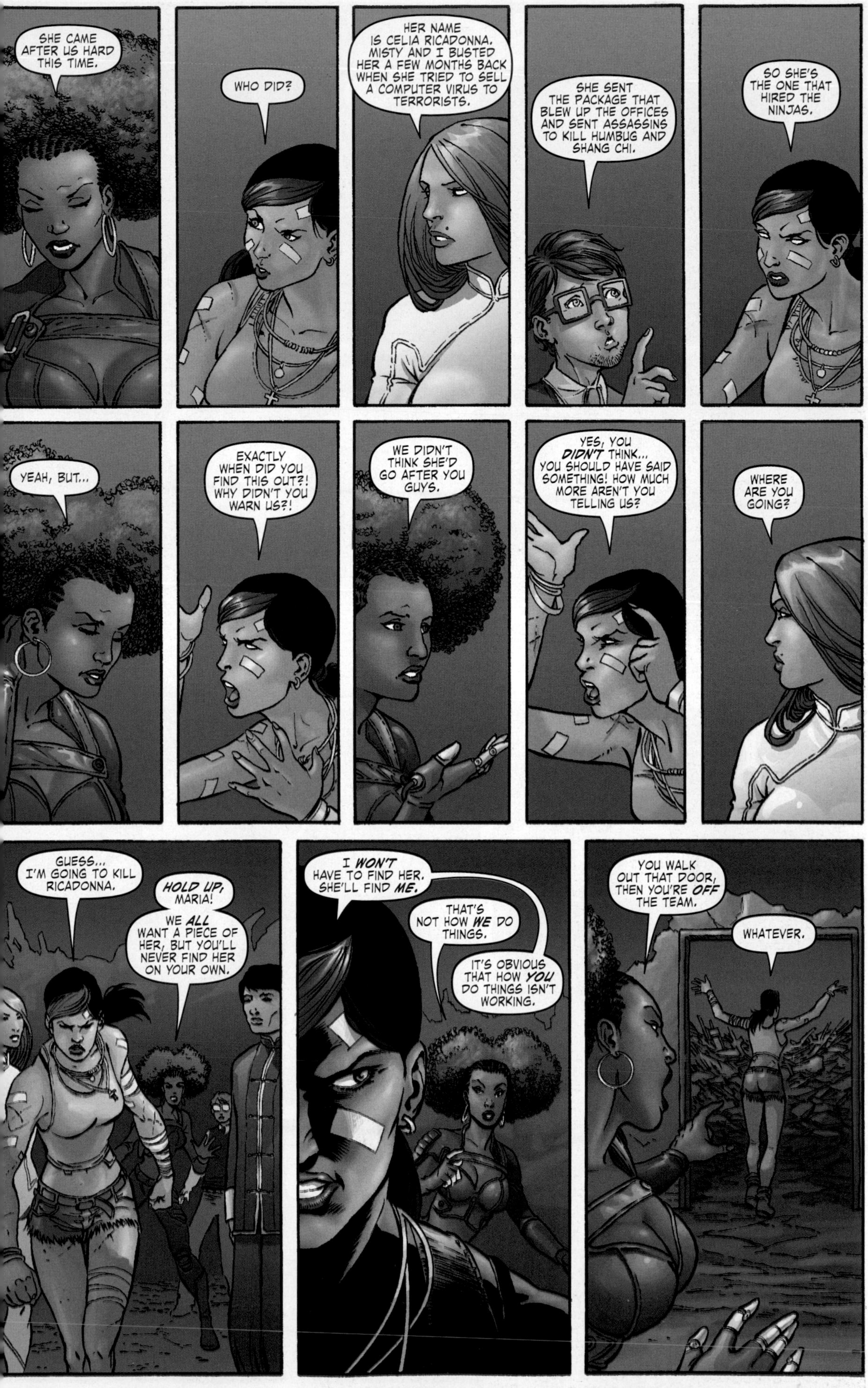
SHE CAME AFTER US HARD THIS TIME.
WHO DID?
HER NAME IS CELIA RICADONNA. MISTY AND I BUSTED HER A FEW MONTHS BACK WHEN SHE TRIED TO SELL A COMPUTER VIRUS TO TERRORISTS.
SHE SENT THE PACKAGE THAT BLEW UP THE OFFICES AND SENT ASSASSINS TO KILL HUMBUG AND SHANG CHI.
SO SHE'S THE ONE THAT HIRED THE NINJAS.
YEAH, BUT...
EXACTLY WHEN DID YOU FIND THIS OUT?! WHY DIDN'T YOU WARN US?!
WE DIDN'T THINK SHE'D GO AFTER YOU GUYS.
YES, YOU *DIDN'T* THINK... YOU SHOULD HAVE SAID SOMETHING! HOW MUCH MORE AREN'T YOU TELLING US?
WHERE ARE YOU GOING?
GUESS... I'M GOING TO KILL RICADONNA.
*HOLD UP,* MARIA!
WE *ALL* WANT A PIECE OF HER, BUT YOU'LL NEVER FIND HER ON YOUR OWN.
I *WON'T* HAVE TO FIND HER. SHE'LL FIND *ME.*
THAT'S NOT HOW *WE* DO THINGS.
IT'S OBVIOUS THAT HOW *YOU* DO THINGS ISN'T WORKING.
YOU WALK OUT THAT DOOR, THEN YOU'RE *OFF* THE TEAM.
WHATEVER.

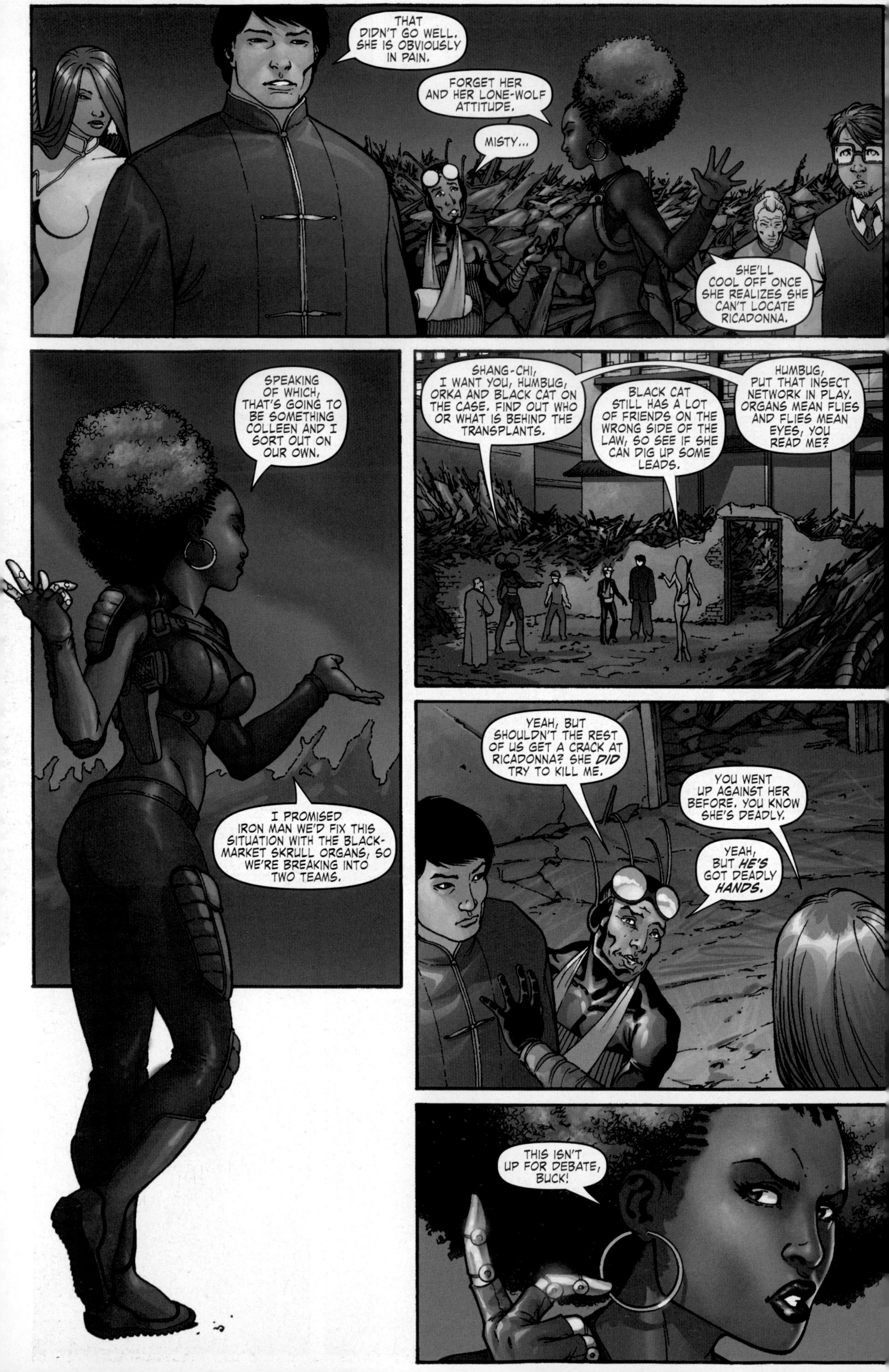
THAT DIDN'T GO WELL. SHE IS OBVIOUSLY IN PAIN.
FORGET HER AND HER LONE-WOLF ATTITUDE.
MISTY...
SHE'LL COOL OFF ONCE SHE REALIZES SHE CAN'T LOCATE RICADONNA.
SPEAKING OF WHICH, THAT'S GOING TO BE SOMETHING COLLEEN AND I SORT OUT ON OUR OWN.
I PROMISED IRON MAN WE'D FIX THIS SITUATION WITH THE BLACK-MARKET SKRULL ORGANS, SO WE'RE BREAKING INTO TWO TEAMS.
SHANG-CHI, I WANT YOU, HUMBUG, ORKA AND BLACK CAT ON THE CASE. FIND OUT WHO OR WHAT IS BEHIND THE TRANSPLANTS.
BLACK CAT STILL HAS A LOT OF FRIENDS ON THE WRONG SIDE OF THE LAW, SO SEE IF SHE CAN DIG UP SOME LEADS.
HUMBUG, PUT THAT INSECT NETWORK IN PLAY. ORGANS MEAN FLIES AND FLIES MEAN EYES, YOU READ ME?
YEAH, BUT SHOULDN'T THE REST OF US GET A CRACK AT RICADONNA? SHE DID TRY TO KILL ME.
YOU WENT UP AGAINST HER BEFORE. YOU KNOW SHE'S DEADLY.
YEAH, BUT HE'S GOT DEADLY HANDS.
THIS ISN'T UP FOR DEBATE, BUCK!

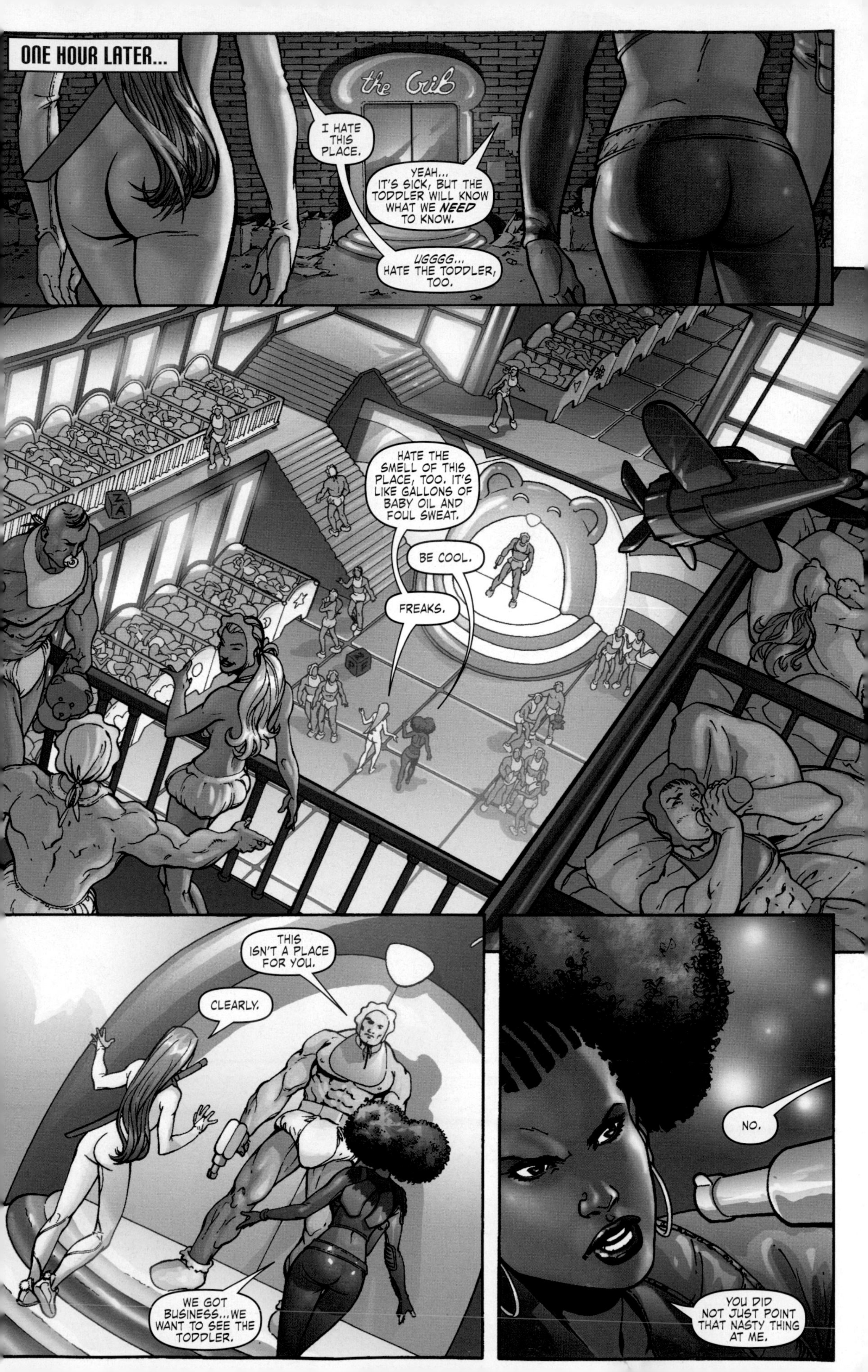
ONE HOUR LATER...
the Crib
I HATE THIS PLACE.
YEAH... IT'S SICK, BUT THE TODDLER WILL KNOW WHAT WE *NEED* TO KNOW.
UGGGG... HATE THE TODDLER, TOO.
HATE THE SMELL OF THIS PLACE, TOO. IT'S LIKE GALLONS OF BABY OIL AND FOUL SWEAT.
BE COOL.
FREAKS.
THIS ISN'T A PLACE FOR YOU.
CLEARLY.
WE GOT BUSINESS... WE WANT TO SEE THE TODDLER.
NO.
YOU DID NOT JUST POINT THAT NASTY THING AT ME.

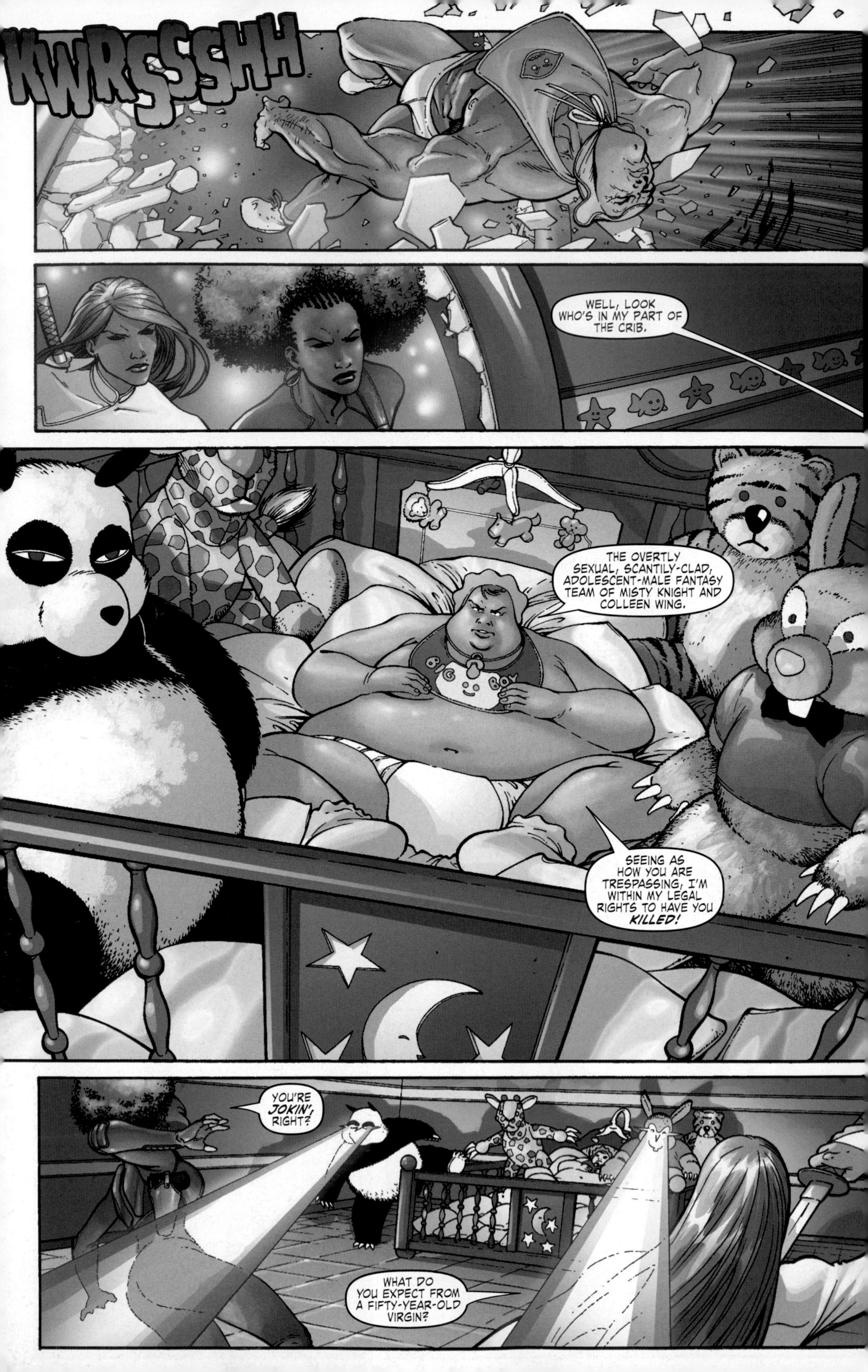
KWRSSSHH
WELL, LOOK WHO'S IN MY PART OF THE CRIB.
THE OVERTLY SEXUAL, SCANTILY-CLAD, ADOLESCENT-MALE FANTASY TEAM OF MISTY KNIGHT AND COLLEEN WING.
SEEING AS HOW YOU ARE TRESPASSING, I'M WITHIN MY LEGAL RIGHTS TO HAVE YOU *KILLED!*
YOU'RE *JOKIN',* RIGHT?
BIG BOY
WHAT DO YOU EXPECT FROM A FIFTY-YEAR-OLD VIRGIN?

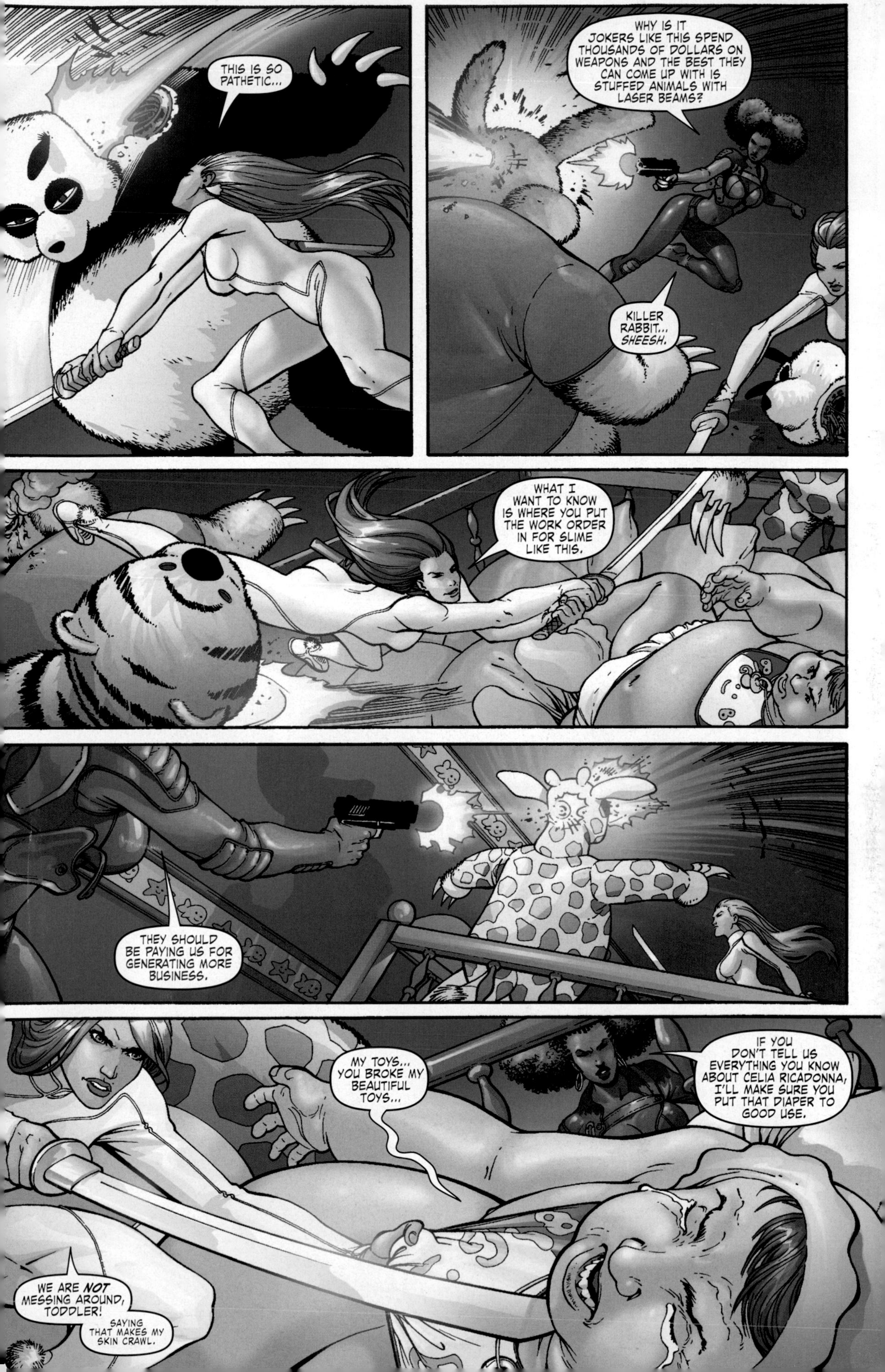
THIS IS SO PATHETIC...
WHY IS IT JOKERS LIKE THIS SPEND THOUSANDS OF DOLLARS ON WEAPONS AND THE BEST THEY CAN COME UP WITH IS STUFFED ANIMALS WITH LASER BEAMS?
KILLER RABBIT... *SHEESH.*
WHAT I WANT TO KNOW IS WHERE YOU PUT THE WORK ORDER IN FOR SLIME LIKE THIS.
THEY SHOULD BE PAYING US FOR GENERATING MORE BUSINESS.
MY TOYS... YOU BROKE MY BEAUTIFUL TOYS...
IF YOU DON'T TELL US EVERYTHING YOU KNOW ABOUT CELIA RICADONNA, I'LL MAKE SURE YOU PUT THAT DIAPER TO GOOD USE.
WE ARE ***NOT*** MESSING AROUND, TODDLER!
SAYING THAT MAKES MY SKIN CRAWL.

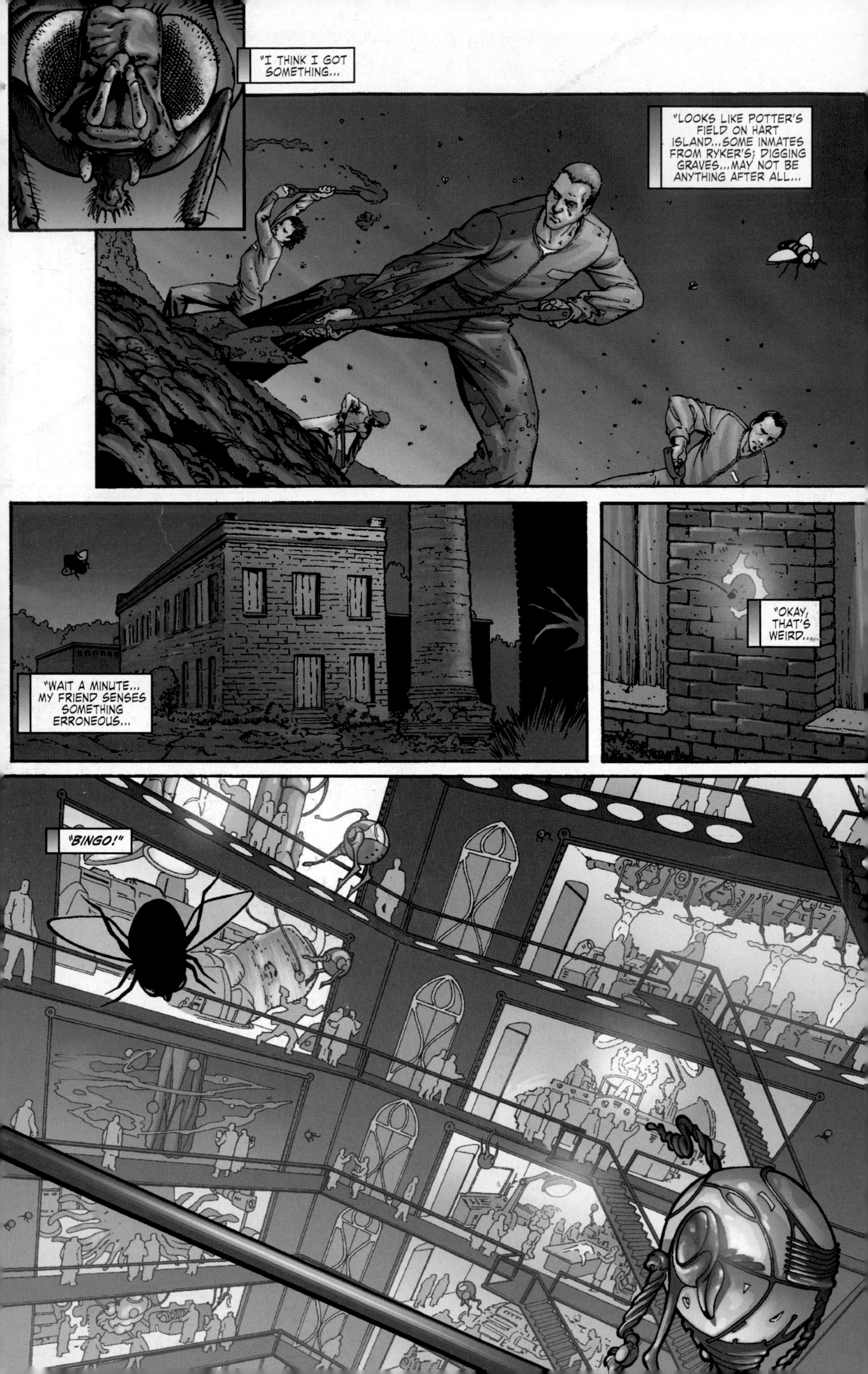
"I THINK I GOT SOMETHING...
"LOOKS LIKE POTTER'S FIELD ON HART ISLAND...SOME INMATES FROM RYKER'S; DIGGING GRAVES...MAY NOT BE ANYTHING AFTER ALL...
"WAIT A MINUTE... MY FRIEND SENSES SOMETHING ERRONEOUS...
"OKAY, THAT'S WEIRD...
"BINGO!"

THIS HAS *GOT* TO BE THE PLACE...

LOOKS LIKE A BUNCH OF SCIENTISTS AT WORK...TABLES FILLED WITH...

"...OH, THAT'S JUST *GROSS.*"

WHAT'S GROSS? DID HE GO INTO THE MEN'S SHOWER?

DON'T DISTRACT HIM, BLACK CAT.

KEEP THE VOICE-OVERS GOING, HUMBUG...WHAT'S HAPPENING? WHAT DOES YOUR BUG FRIEND SEE?

PLEASE...

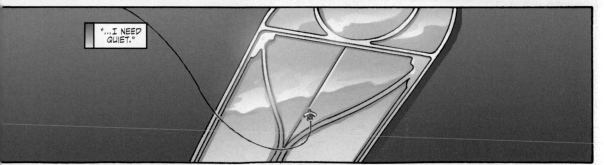

"...I NEED QUIET."

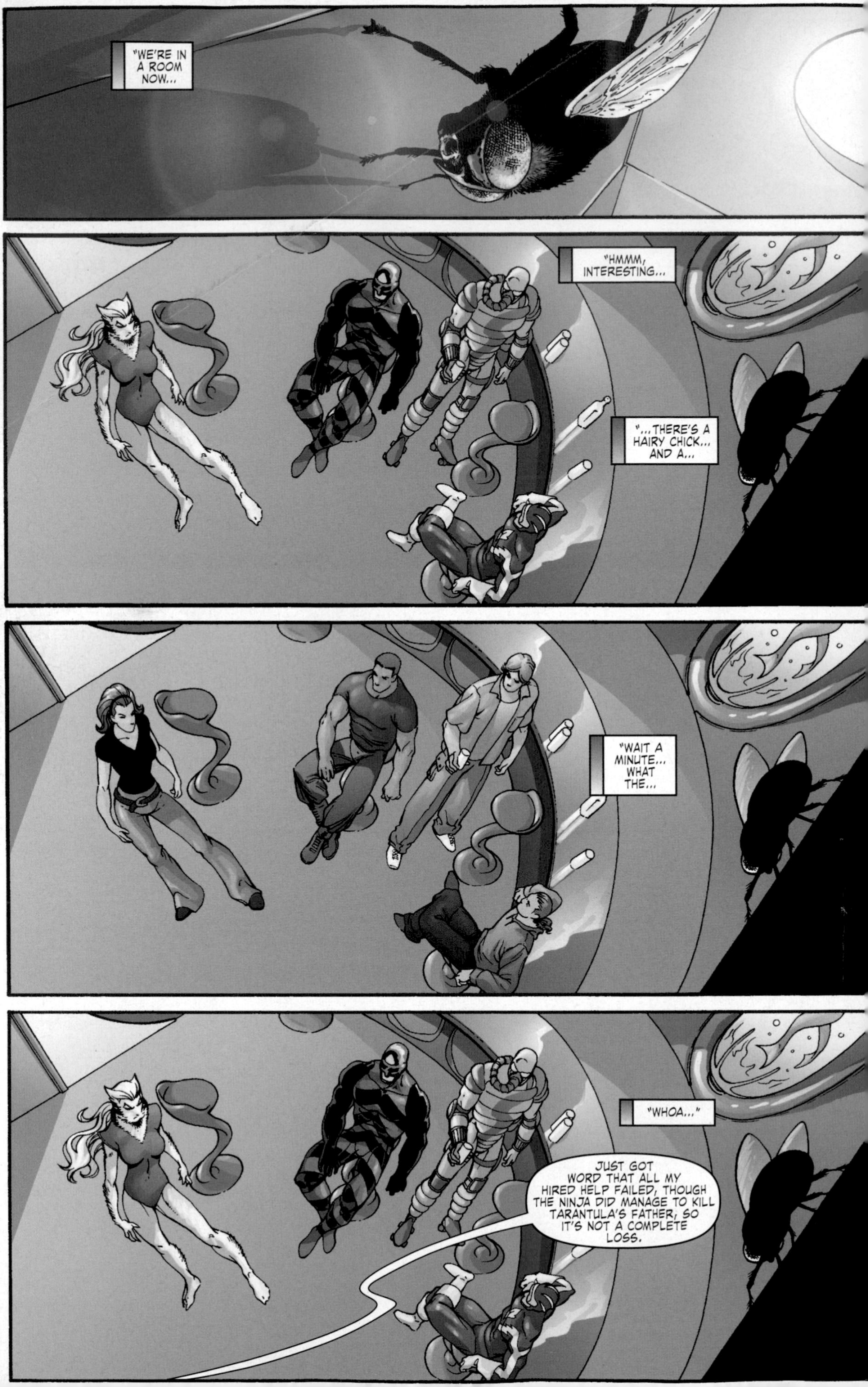
"WE'RE IN A ROOM NOW...
"HMMM, INTERESTING...
"...THERE'S A HAIRY CHICK... AND A...
"WAIT A MINUTE... WHAT THE...
"WHOA..."
JUST GOT WORD THAT ALL MY HIRED HELP FAILED, THOUGH THE NINJA DID MANAGE TO KILL TARANTULA'S FATHER, SO IT'S NOT A COMPLETE LOSS.

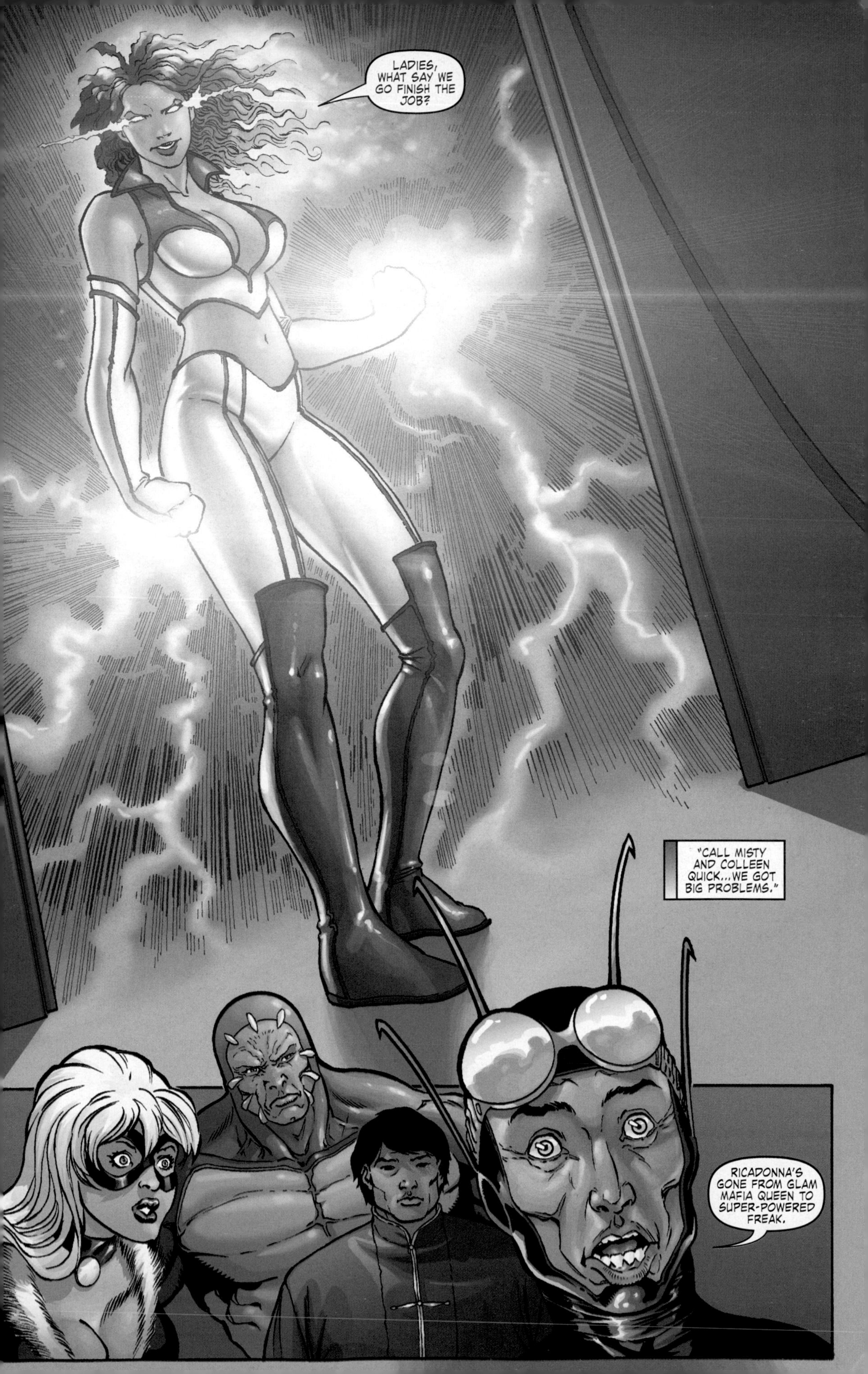
LADIES, WHAT SAY WE GO FINISH THE JOB?
"CALL MISTY AND COLLEEN QUICK...WE GOT BIG PROBLEMS."
RICADONNA'S GONE FROM GLAM MAFIA QUEEN TO SUPER-POWERED FREAK.

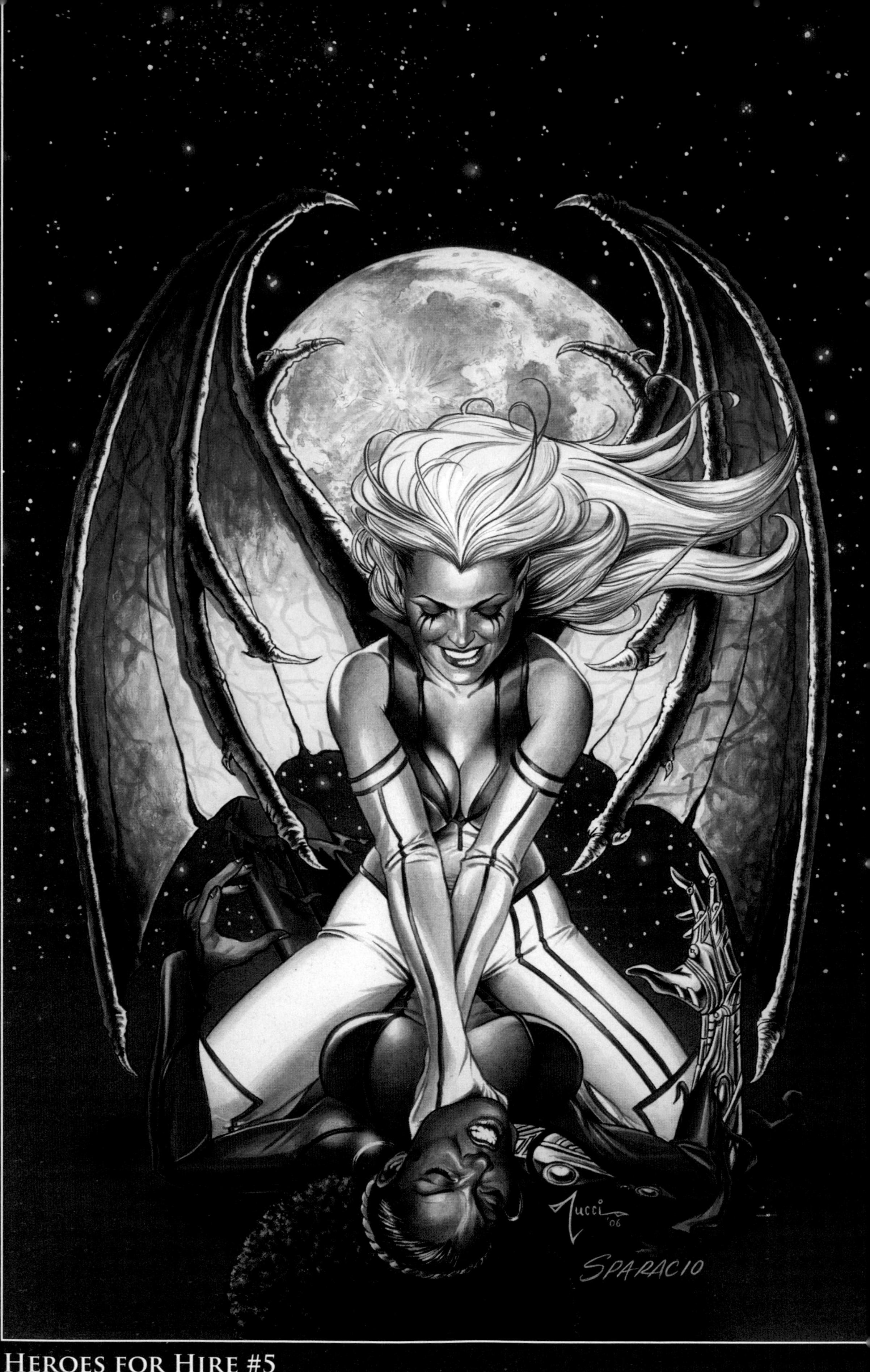
SPARACIO

Heroes for Hire #5

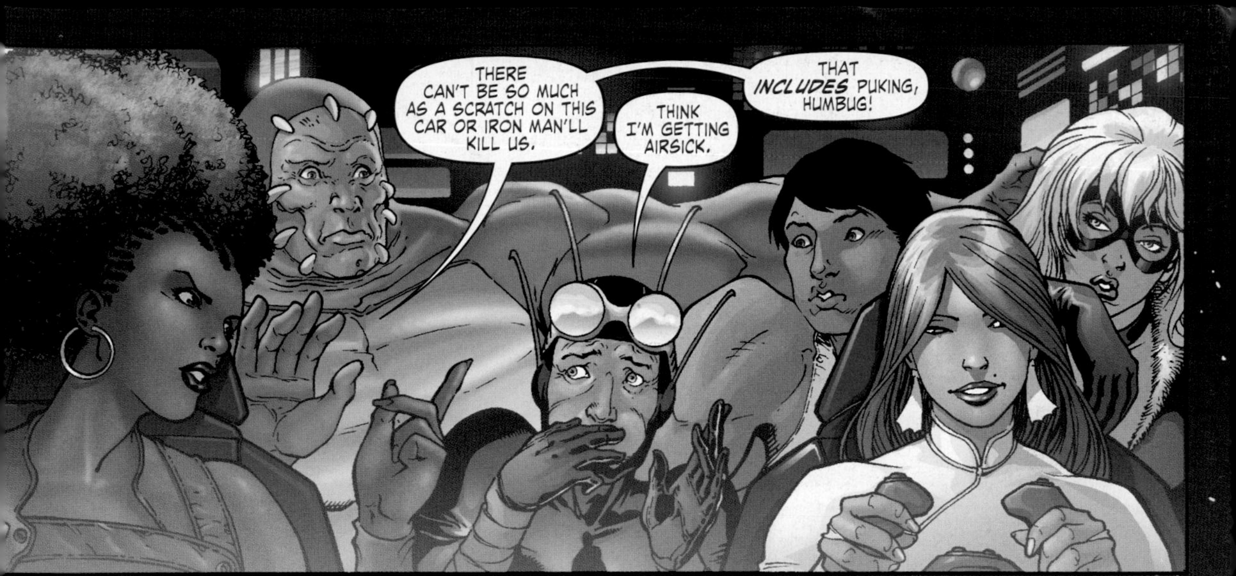
THERE CAN'T BE SO MUCH AS A SCRATCH ON THIS CAR OR IRON MAN'LL KILL US.
THINK I'M GETTING AIRSICK.
THAT *INCLUDES* PUKING, HUMBUG!

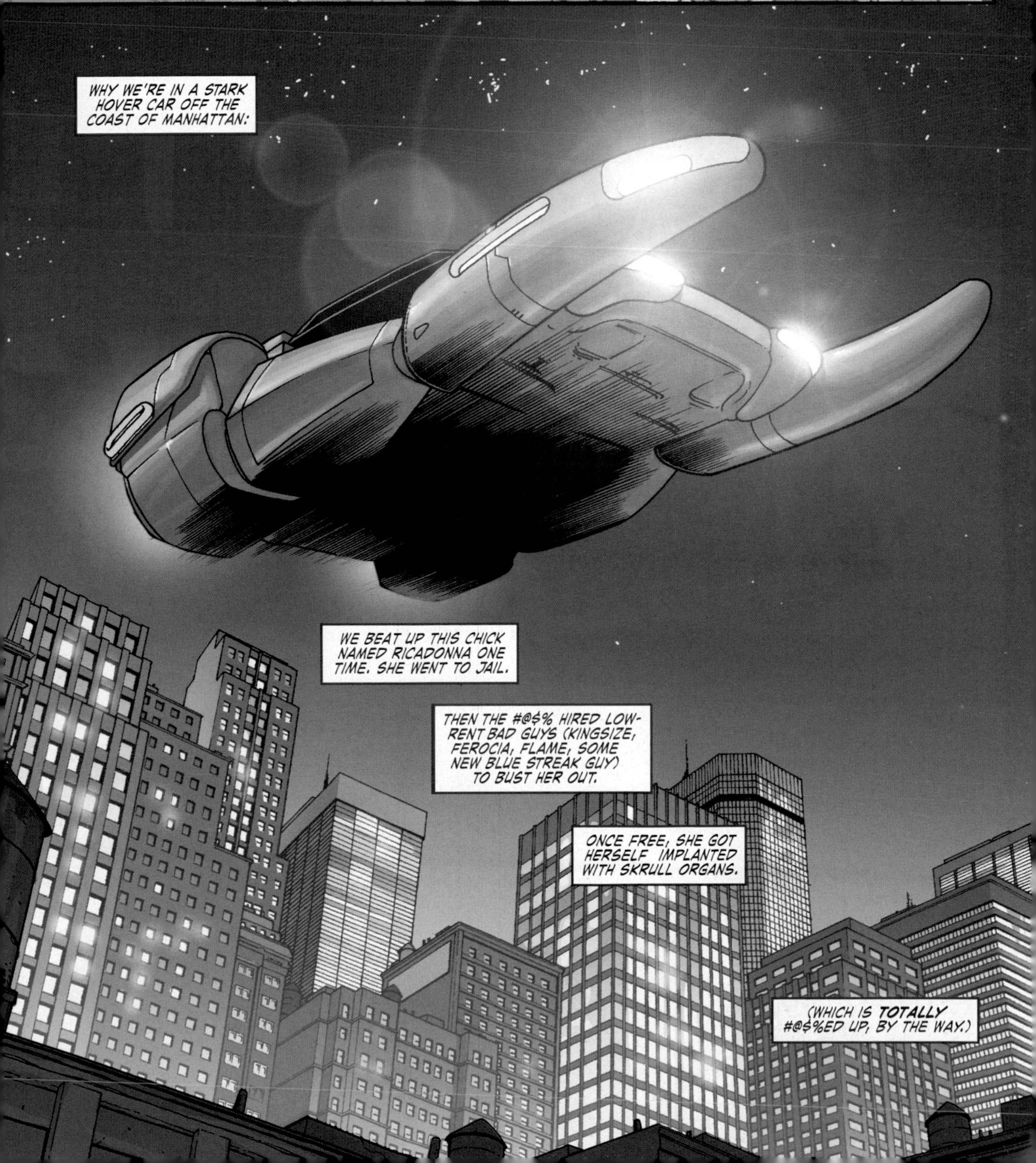
WHY WE'RE IN A STARK HOVER CAR OFF THE COAST OF MANHATTAN:
WE BEAT UP THIS CHICK NAMED RICADONNA ONE TIME. SHE WENT TO JAIL.
THEN THE #@$% HIRED LOW-RENT BAD GUYS (KINGSIZE, FEROCIA, FLAME, SOME NEW BLUE STREAK GUY) TO BUST HER OUT.
ONCE FREE, SHE GOT HERSELF IMPLANTED WITH SKRULL ORGANS.
(WHICH IS *TOTALLY* #@$%ED UP, BY THE WAY.)

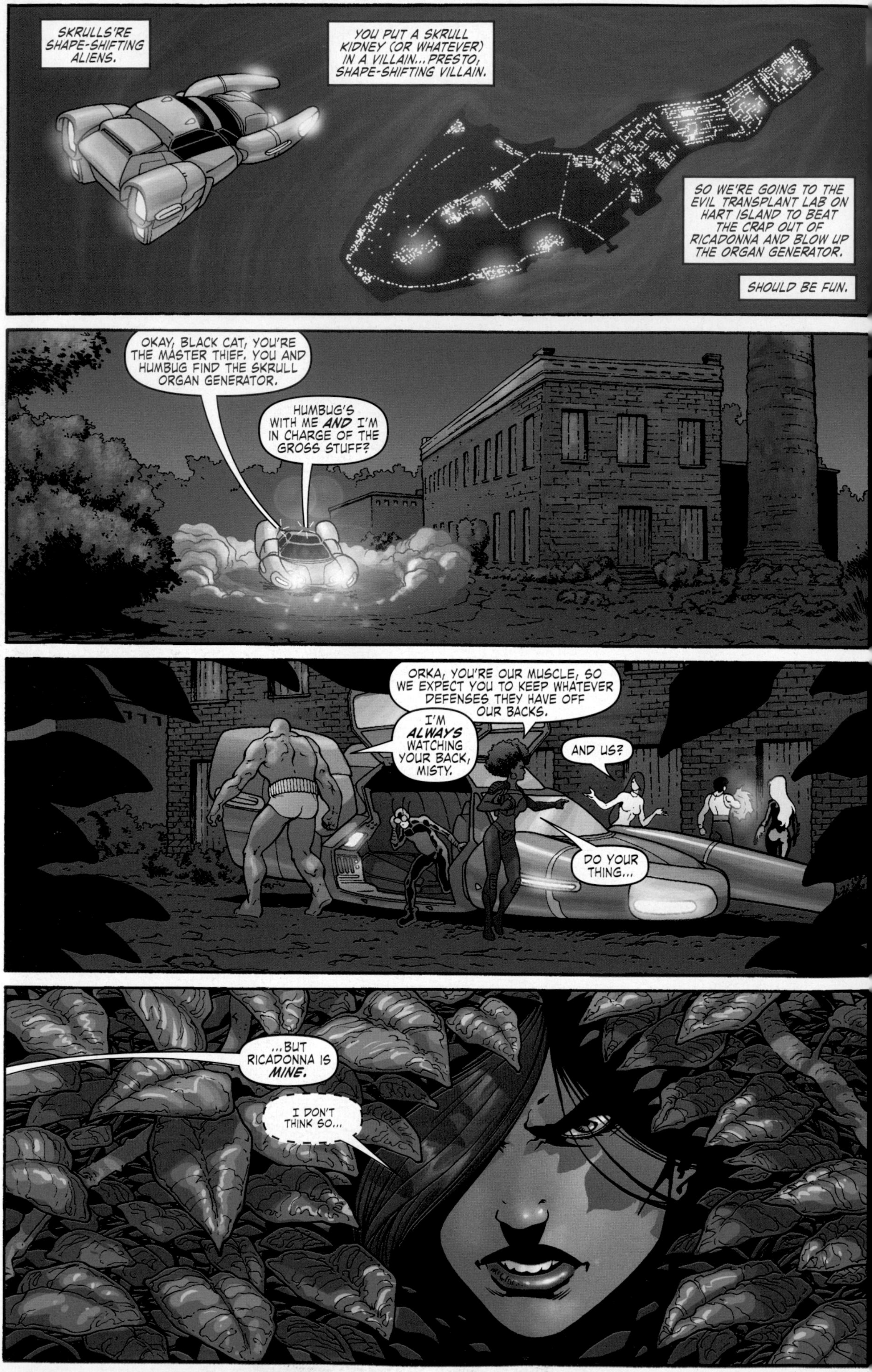
SKRULLS'RE SHAPE-SHIFTING ALIENS.
YOU PUT A SKRULL KIDNEY (OR WHATEVER) IN A VILLAIN... PRESTO, SHAPE-SHIFTING VILLAIN.
SO WE'RE GOING TO THE EVIL TRANSPLANT LAB ON HART ISLAND TO BEAT THE CRAP OUT OF RICADONNA AND BLOW UP THE ORGAN GENERATOR.
SHOULD BE FUN.
OKAY, BLACK CAT, YOU'RE THE MASTER THIEF. YOU AND HUMBUG FIND THE SKRULL ORGAN GENERATOR.
HUMBUG'S WITH ME AND I'M IN CHARGE OF THE GROSS STUFF?
ORKA, YOU'RE OUR MUSCLE, SO WE EXPECT YOU TO KEEP WHATEVER DEFENSES THEY HAVE OFF OUR BACKS.
I'M ALWAYS WATCHING YOUR BACK, MISTY.
AND US?
DO YOUR THING...
...BUT RICADONNA IS MINE.
I DON'T THINK SO...

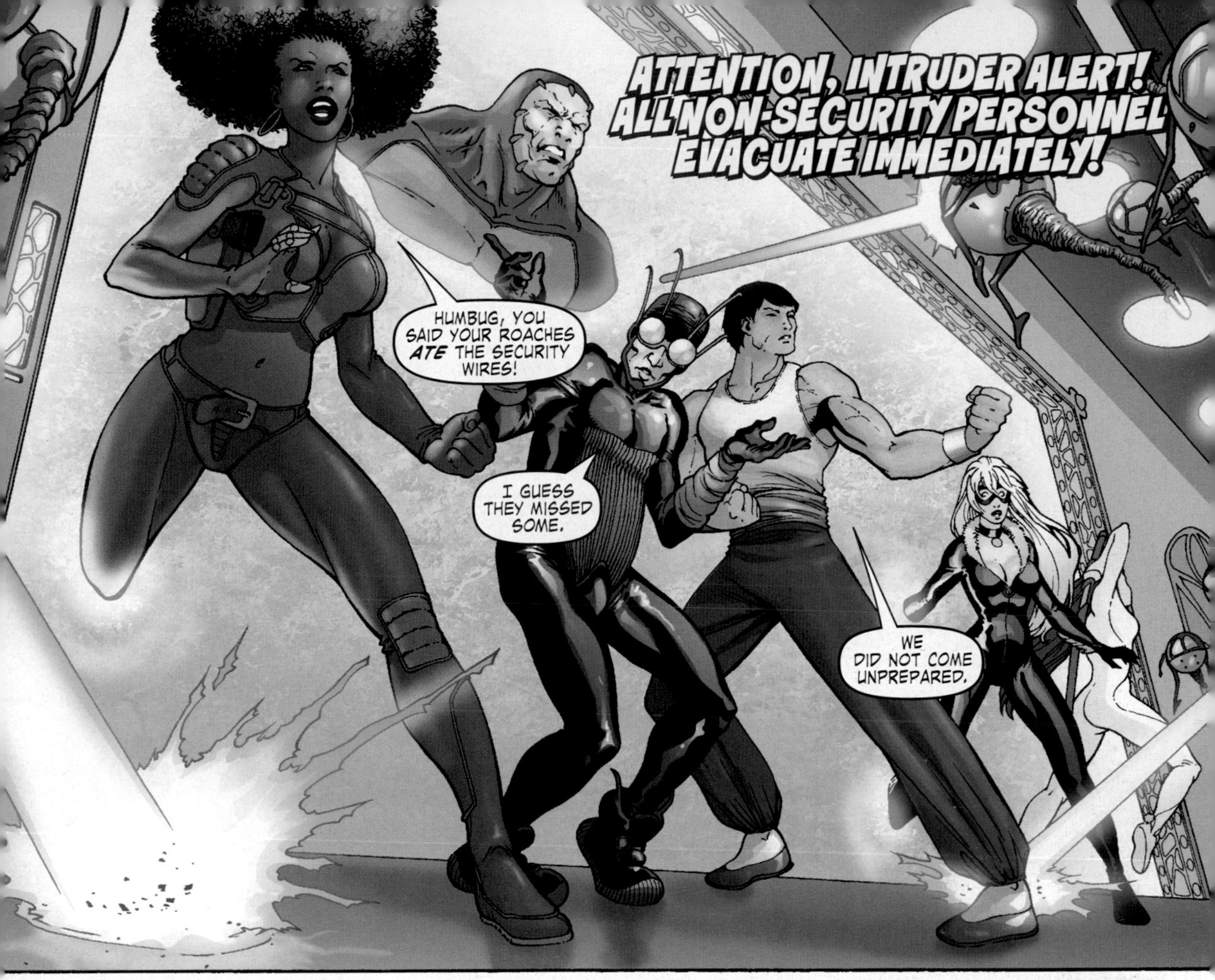
ATTENTION, INTRUDER ALERT! ALL NON-SECURITY PERSONNEL EVACUATE IMMEDIATELY!
HUMBUG, YOU SAID YOUR ROACHES ATE THE SECURITY WIRES!
I GUESS THEY MISSED SOME.
WE DID NOT COME UNPREPARED.

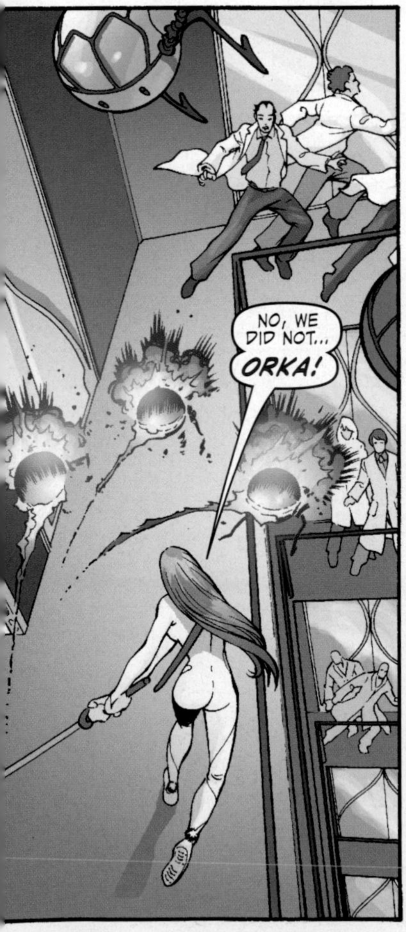
NO, WE DID NOT... ORKA!

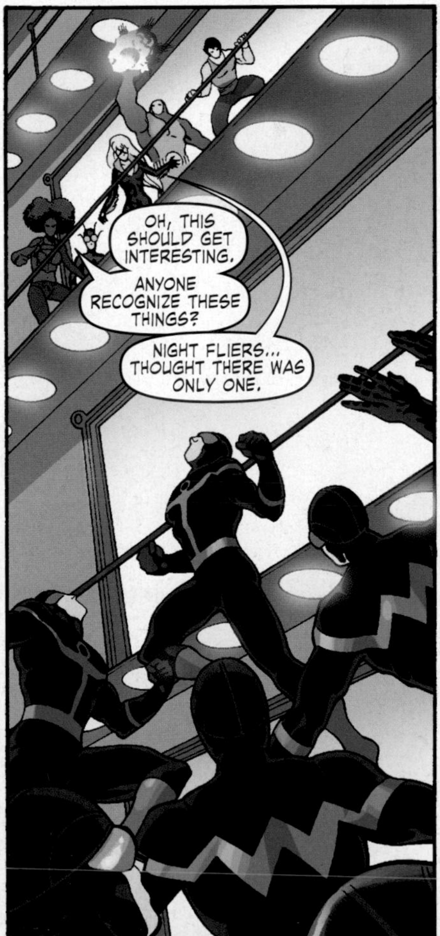
OH, THIS SHOULD GET INTERESTING. ANYONE RECOGNIZE THESE THINGS?
NIGHT FLIERS... THOUGHT THERE WAS ONLY ONE.

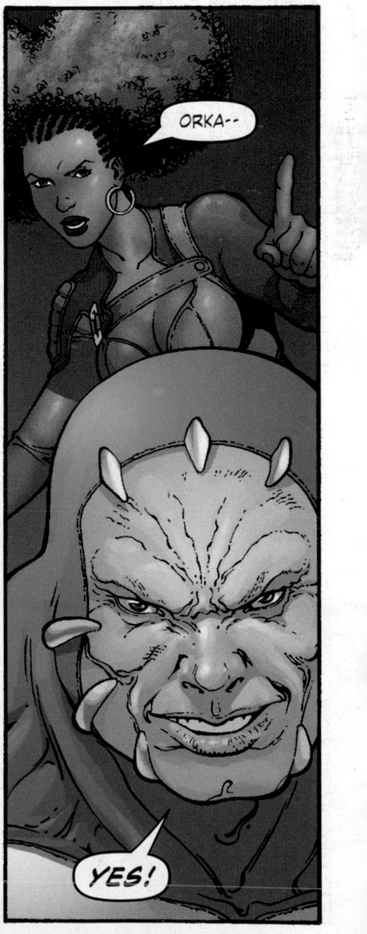
ORKA--
YES!

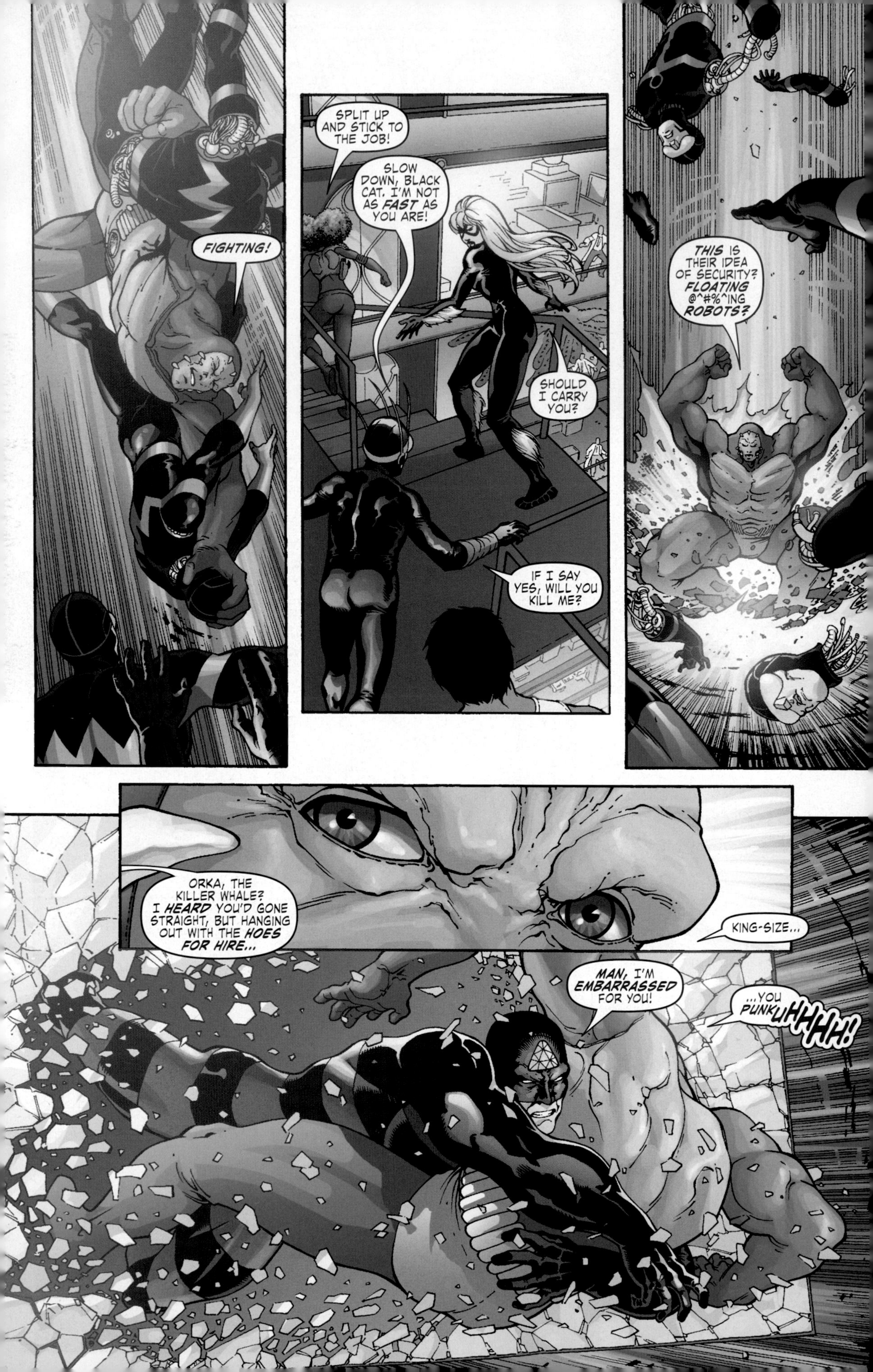

FIGHTING!
SPLIT UP AND STICK TO THE JOB!
SLOW DOWN, BLACK CAT. I'M NOT AS FAST AS YOU ARE!
SHOULD I CARRY YOU?
IF I SAY YES, WILL YOU KILL ME?
THIS IS THEIR IDEA OF SECURITY? FLOATING @^#%^ING ROBOTS?
ORKA, THE KILLER WHALE? I HEARD YOU'D GONE STRAIGHT, BUT HANGING OUT WITH THE HOES FOR HIRE...
KING-SIZE...
MAN, I'M EMBARRASSED FOR YOU!
...YOU PUNKUHHHH!

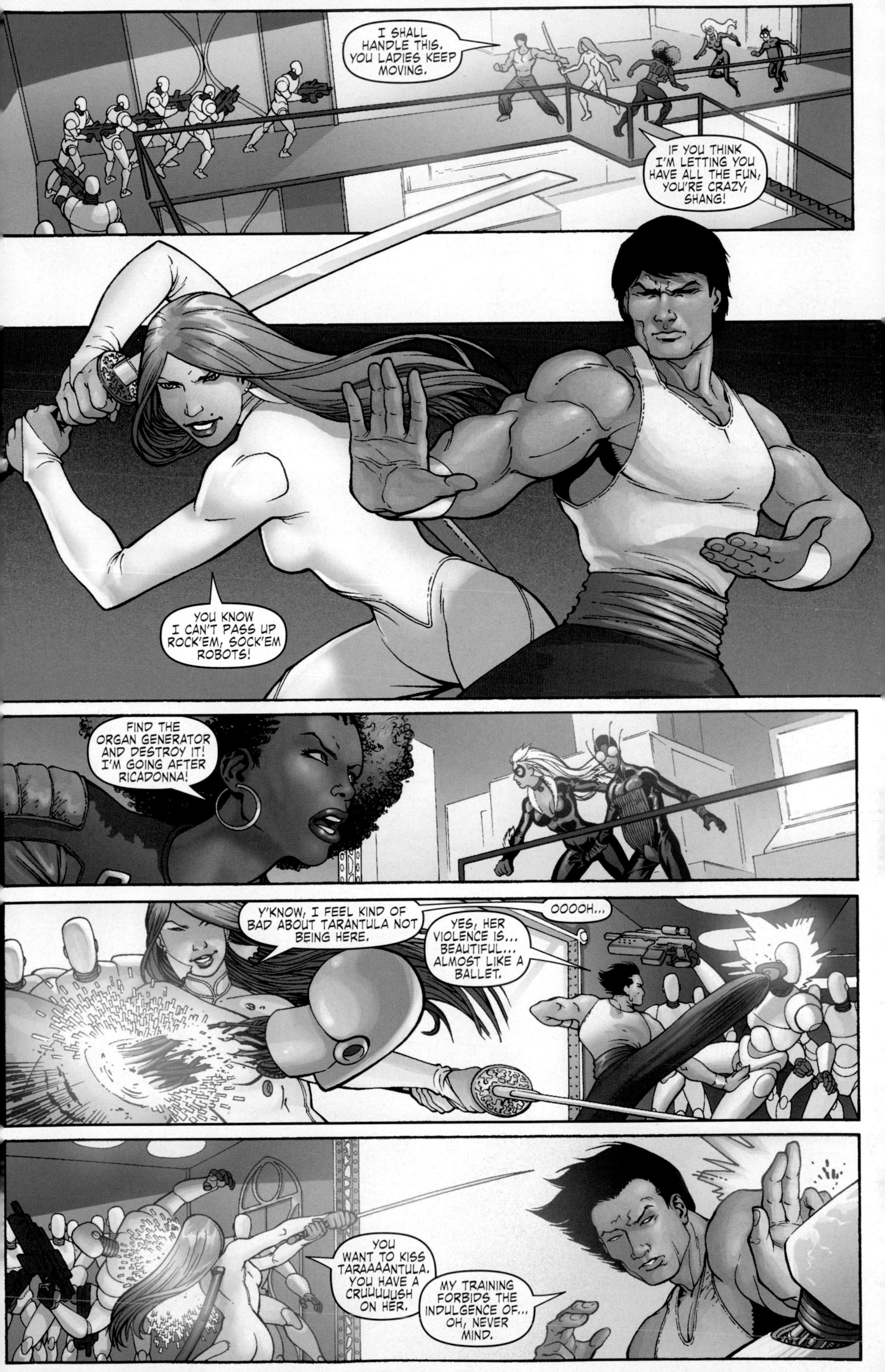
I SHALL HANDLE THIS. YOU LADIES KEEP MOVING.
IF YOU THINK I'M LETTING YOU HAVE ALL THE FUN, YOU'RE CRAZY, SHANG!
YOU KNOW I CAN'T PASS UP ROCK'EM, SOCK'EM ROBOTS!
FIND THE ORGAN GENERATOR AND DESTROY IT! I'M GOING AFTER RICADONNA!
Y'KNOW, I FEEL KIND OF BAD ABOUT TARANTULA NOT BEING HERE.
OOOOH...
YES, HER VIOLENCE IS... BEAUTIFUL... ALMOST LIKE A BALLET.
YOU WANT TO KISS TARAAAANTULA. YOU HAVE A CRUUUUUSH ON HER.
MY TRAINING FORBIDS THE INDULGENCE OF... OH, NEVER MIND.

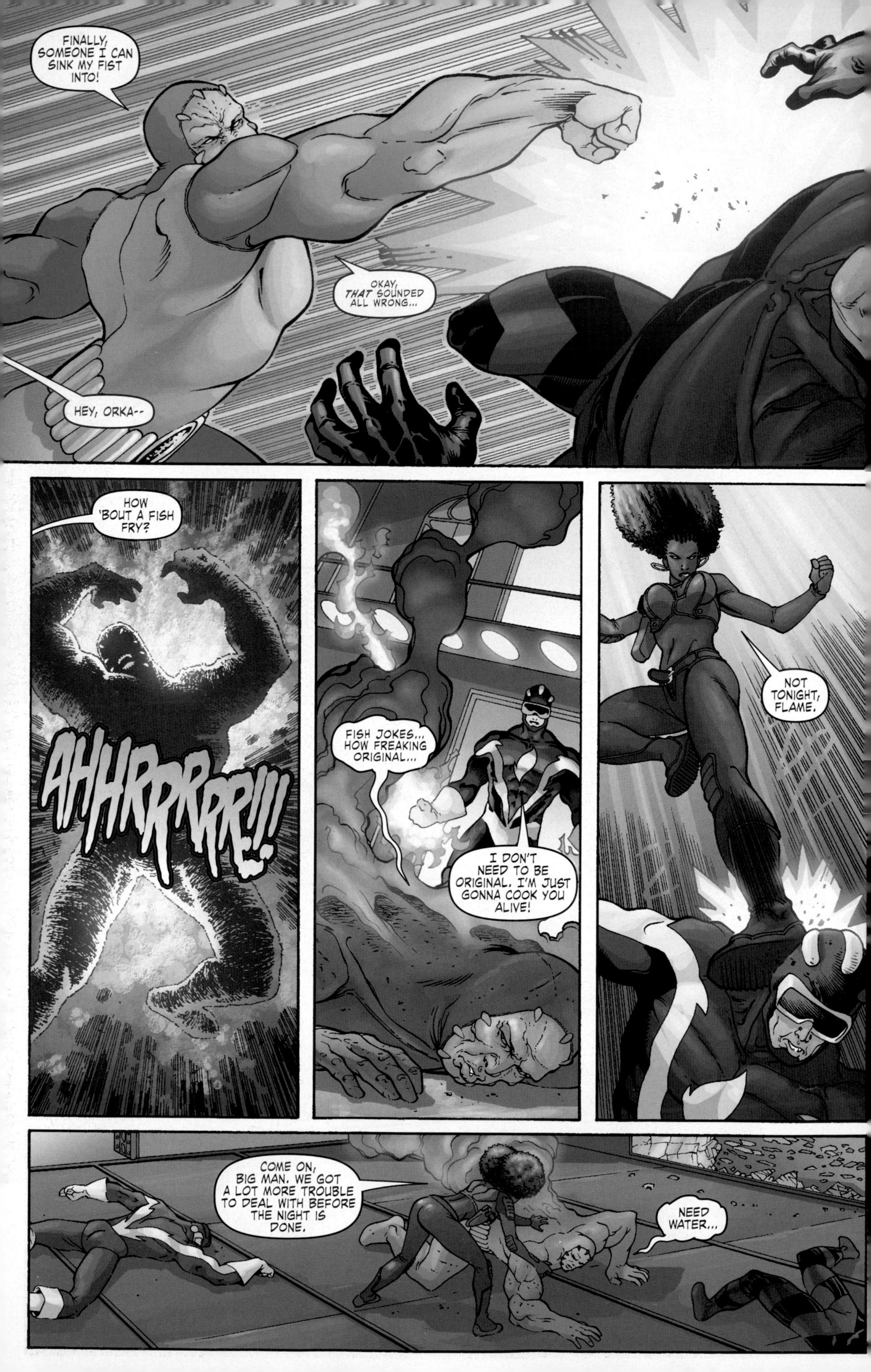
FINALLY, SOMEONE I CAN SINK MY FIST INTO!
OKAY, THAT SOUNDED ALL WRONG...
HEY, ORKA--
HOW 'BOUT A FISH FRY?
AHHRRRRR!!!
FISH JOKES... HOW FREAKING ORIGINAL...
I DON'T NEED TO BE ORIGINAL. I'M JUST GONNA COOK YOU ALIVE!
NOT TONIGHT, FLAME.
COME ON, BIG MAN. WE GOT A LOT MORE TROUBLE TO DEAL WITH BEFORE THE NIGHT IS DONE.
NEED WATER...

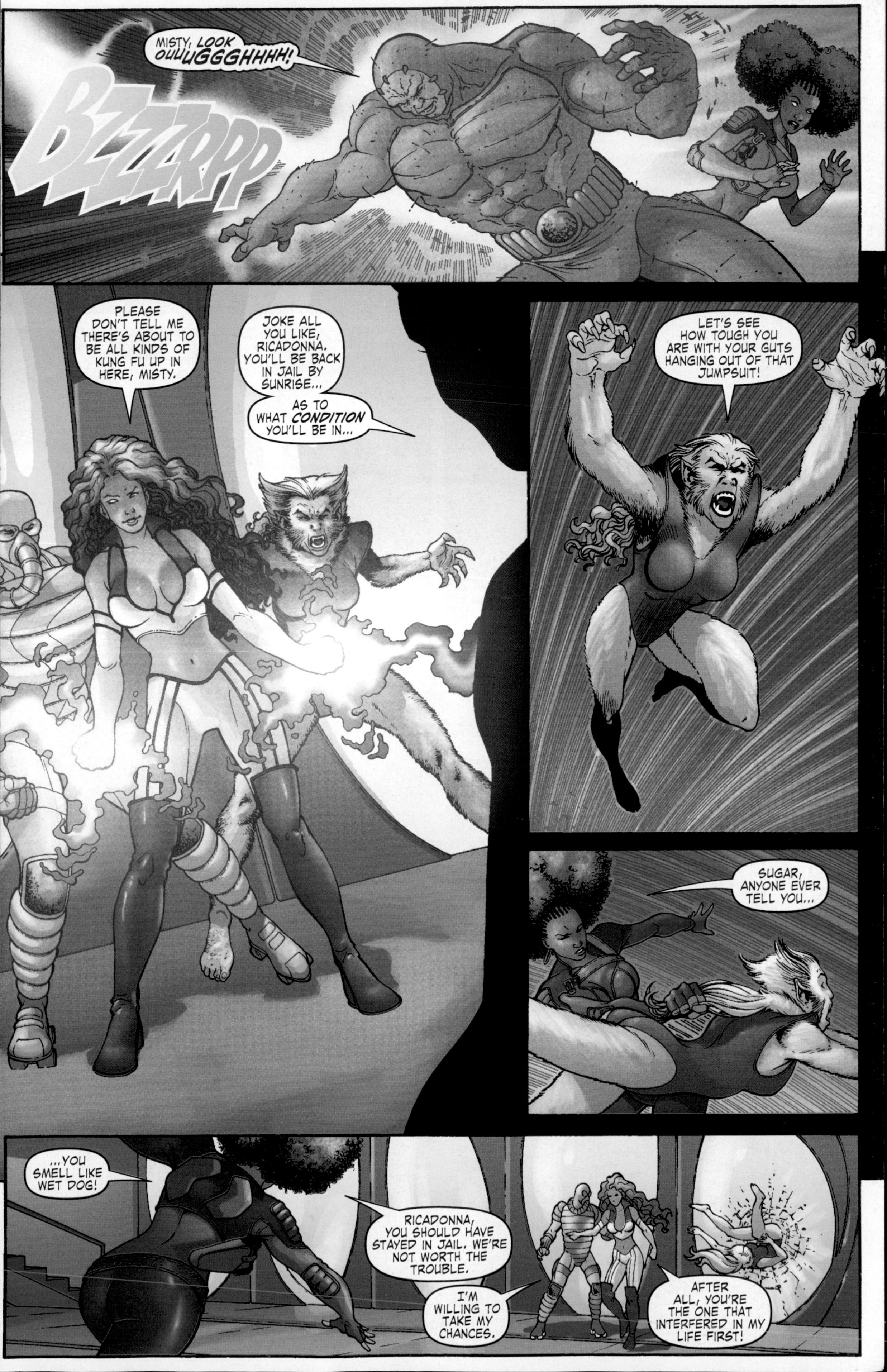
MISTY, LOOK OUUUUGGGHHHH!
BZZZRPP
PLEASE DON'T TELL ME THERE'S ABOUT TO BE ALL KINDS OF KUNG FU UP IN HERE, MISTY.
JOKE ALL YOU LIKE, RICADONNA. YOU'LL BE BACK IN JAIL BY SUNRISE...
AS TO WHAT CONDITION YOU'LL BE IN...
LET'S SEE HOW TOUGH YOU ARE WITH YOUR GUTS HANGING OUT OF THAT JUMPSUIT!
SUGAR, ANYONE EVER TELL YOU...
...YOU SMELL LIKE WET DOG!
RICADONNA, YOU SHOULD HAVE STAYED IN JAIL. WE'RE NOT WORTH THE TROUBLE.
I'M WILLING TO TAKE MY CHANCES.
AFTER ALL, YOU'RE THE ONE THAT INTERFERED IN MY LIFE FIRST!

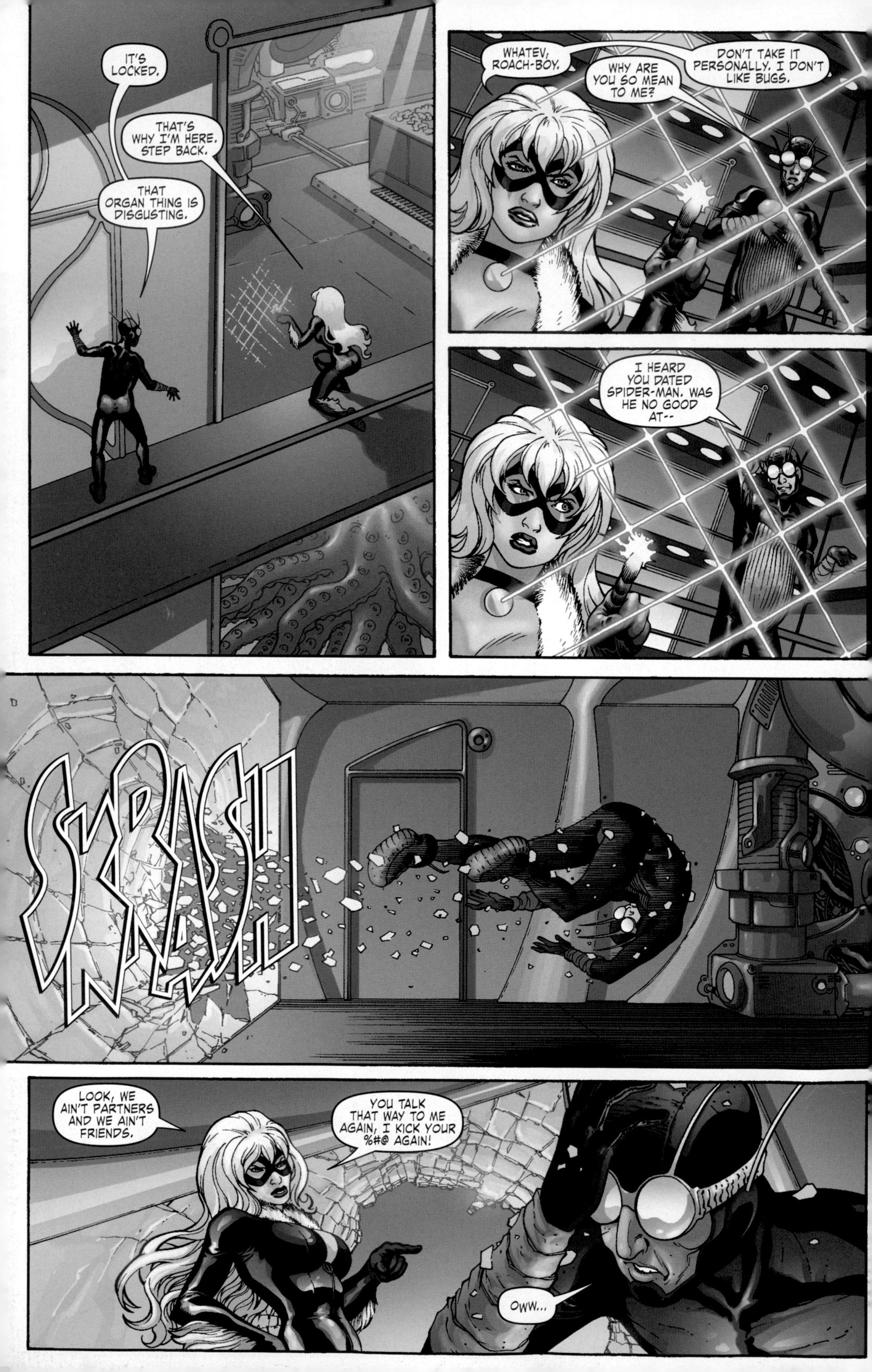
IT'S LOCKED.
THAT'S WHY I'M HERE. STEP BACK.
THAT ORGAN THING IS DISGUSTING.
WHATEV, ROACH-BOY.
WHY ARE YOU SO MEAN TO ME?
DON'T TAKE IT PERSONALLY. I DON'T LIKE BUGS.
I HEARD YOU DATED SPIDER-MAN. WAS HE NO GOOD AT--
SKRASH
LOOK, WE AIN'T PARTNERS AND WE AIN'T FRIENDS.
YOU TALK THAT WAY TO ME AGAIN, I KICK YOUR %#@ AGAIN!
OWW...

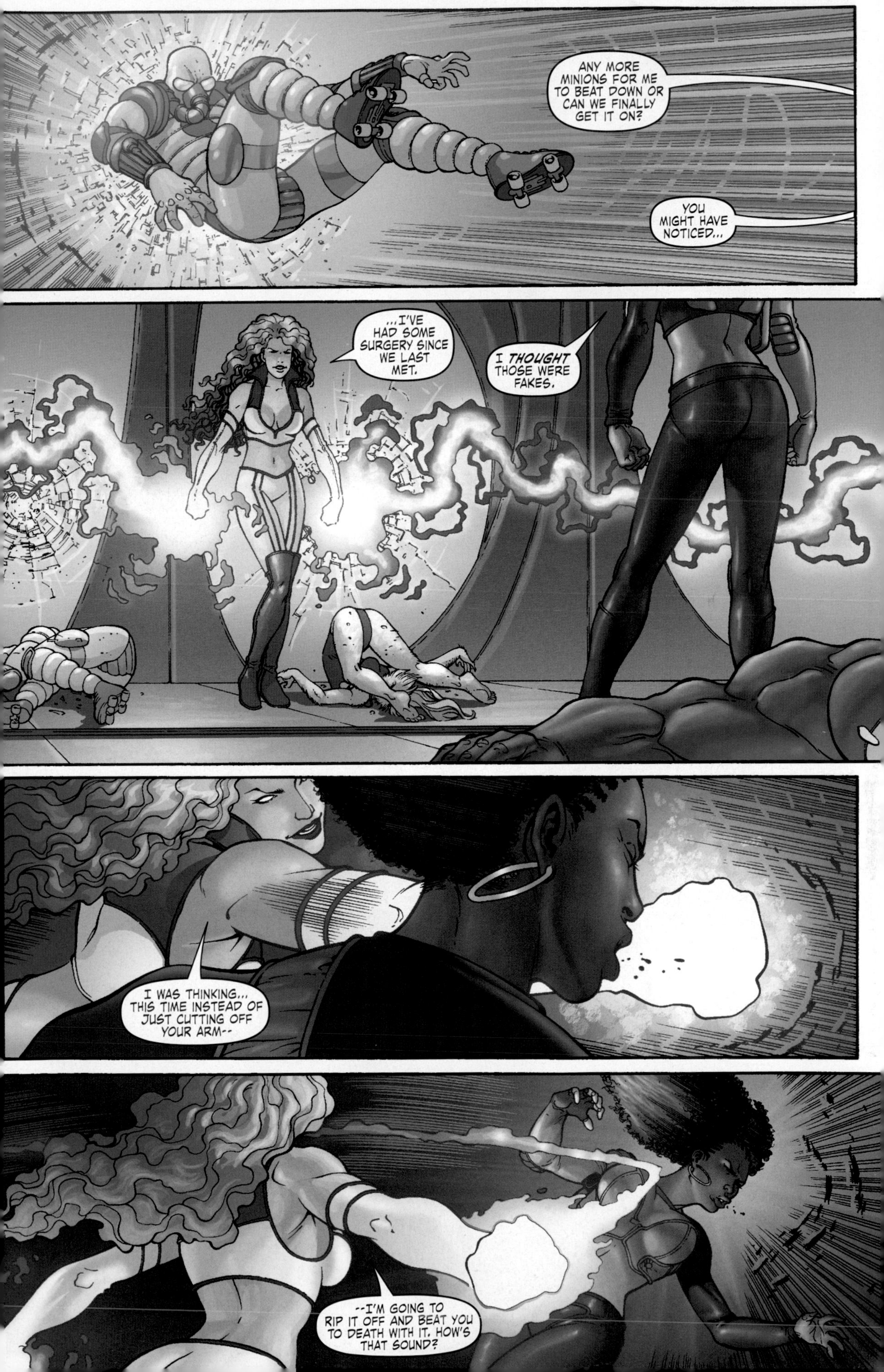
ANY MORE MINIONS FOR ME TO BEAT DOWN OR CAN WE FINALLY GET IT ON?
YOU MIGHT HAVE NOTICED...
...I'VE HAD SOME SURGERY SINCE WE LAST MET.
I *THOUGHT* THOSE WERE FAKES.
I WAS THINKING... THIS TIME INSTEAD OF JUST CUTTING OFF YOUR ARM--
--I'M GOING TO RIP IT OFF AND BEAT YOU TO DEATH WITH IT. HOW'S THAT SOUND?

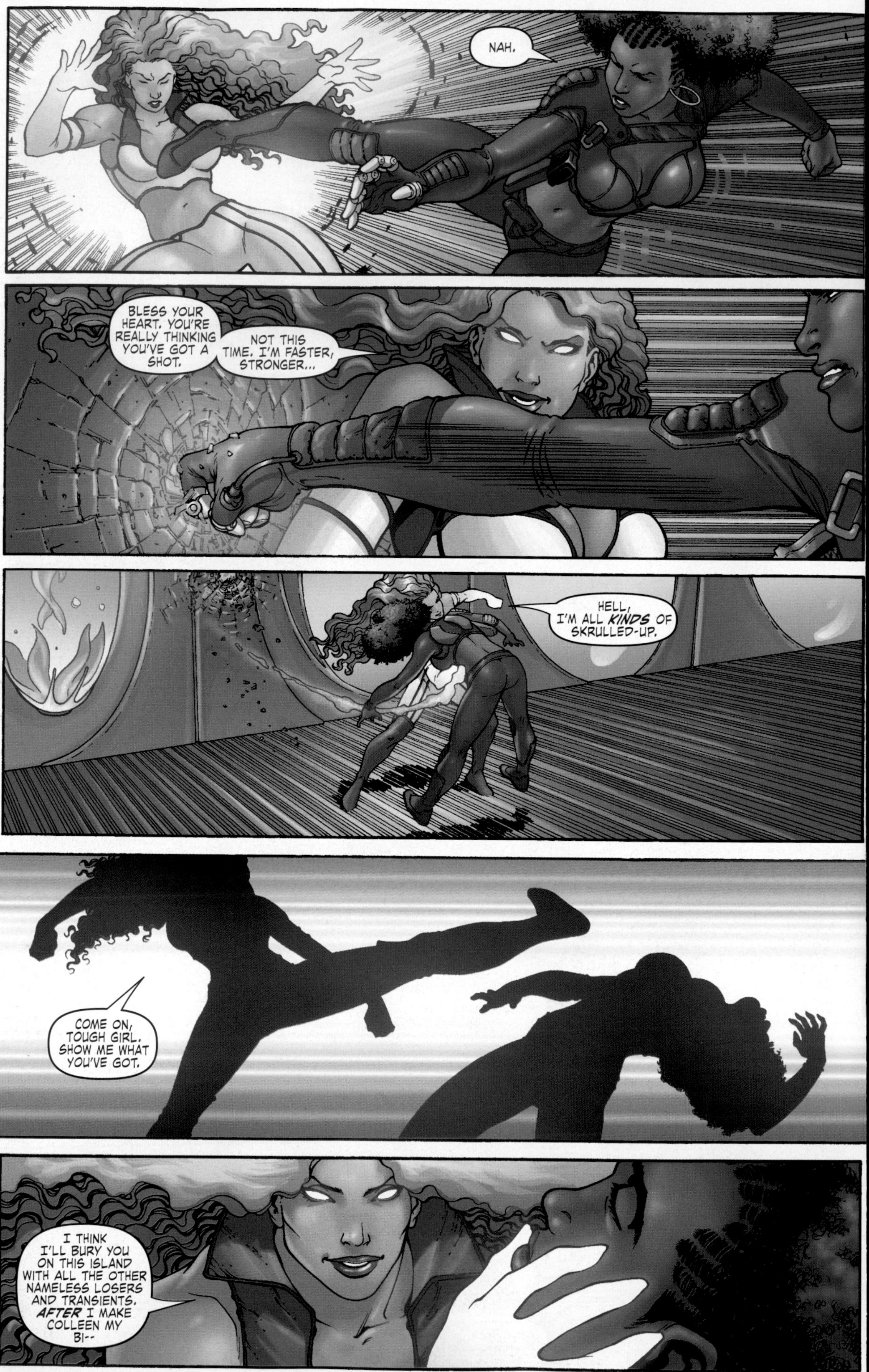
NAH.
BLESS YOUR HEART. YOU'RE REALLY THINKING YOU'VE GOT A SHOT.
NOT THIS TIME. I'M FASTER, STRONGER...
HELL, I'M ALL *KINDS* OF SKRULLED-UP.
COME ON, TOUGH GIRL. SHOW ME WHAT YOU'VE GOT.
I THINK I'LL BURY YOU ON THIS ISLAND WITH ALL THE OTHER NAMELESS LOSERS AND TRANSIENTS. *AFTER* I MAKE COLLEEN MY BI--

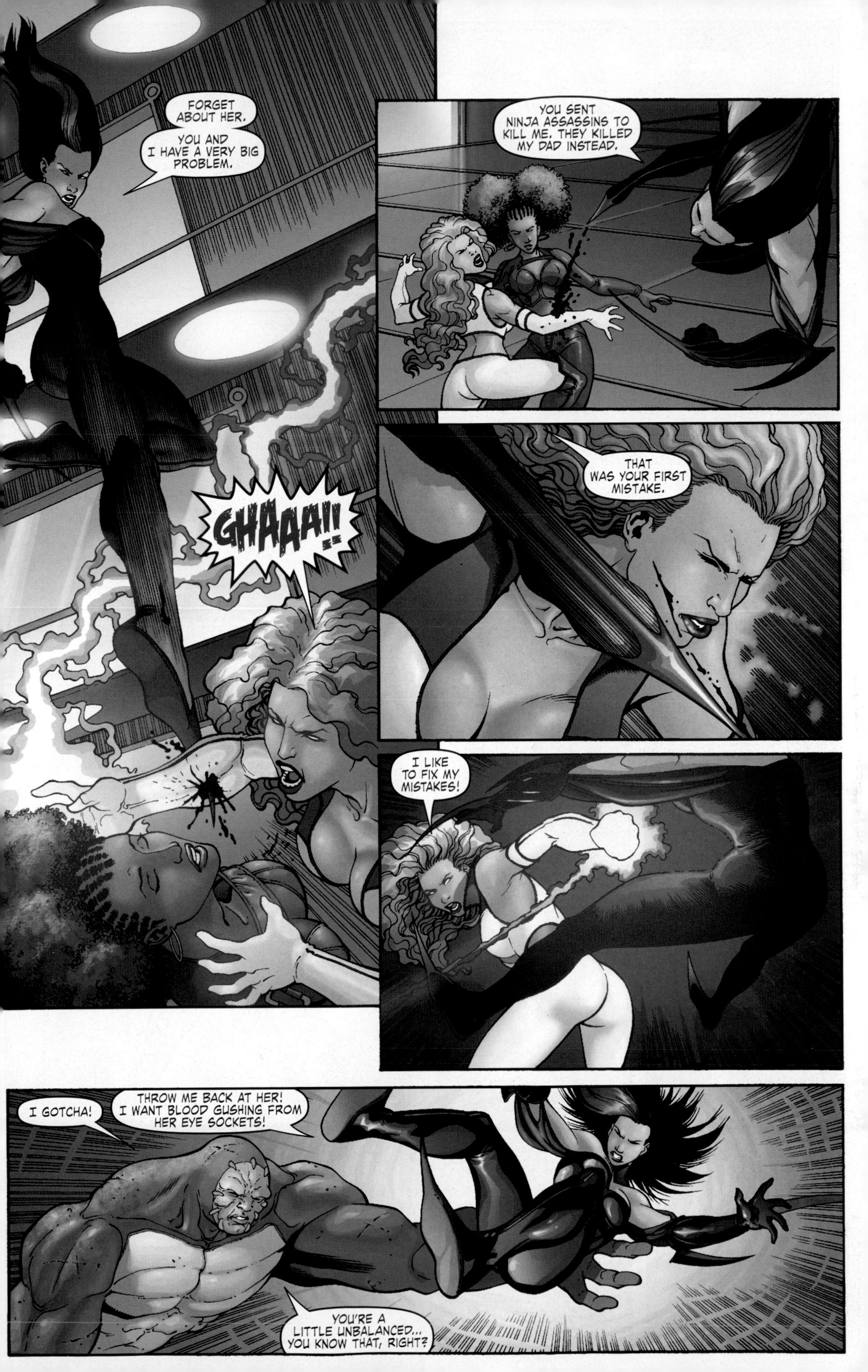
FORGET ABOUT HER.
YOU AND I HAVE A VERY BIG PROBLEM.
GHAAA!!
YOU SENT NINJA ASSASSINS TO KILL ME. THEY KILLED MY DAD INSTEAD.
THAT WAS YOUR FIRST MISTAKE.
I LIKE TO FIX MY MISTAKES!
I GOTCHA!
THROW ME BACK AT HER! I WANT BLOOD GUSHING FROM HER EYE SOCKETS!
YOU'RE A LITTLE UNBALANCED... YOU KNOW THAT, RIGHT?

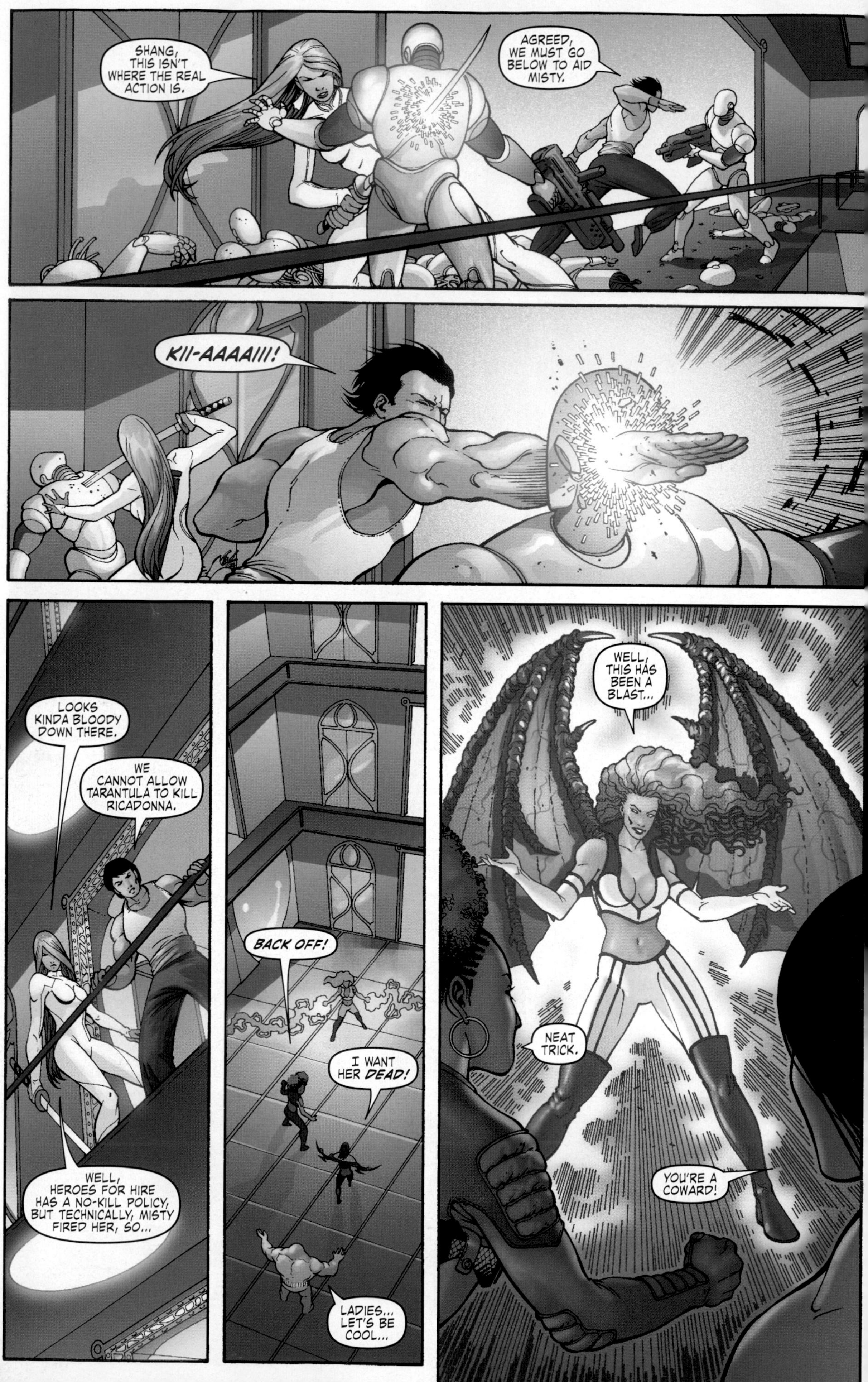
SHANG, THIS ISN'T WHERE THE REAL ACTION IS.
AGREED, WE MUST GO BELOW TO AID MISTY.
KII-AAAAIII!
LOOKS KINDA BLOODY DOWN THERE.
WE CANNOT ALLOW TARANTULA TO KILL RICADONNA.
WELL, HEROES FOR HIRE HAS A NO-KILL POLICY, BUT TECHNICALLY, MISTY FIRED HER, SO...
BACK OFF!
I WANT HER DEAD!
LADIES... LET'S BE COOL...
WELL, THIS HAS BEEN A BLAST...
NEAT TRICK.
YOU'RE A COWARD!

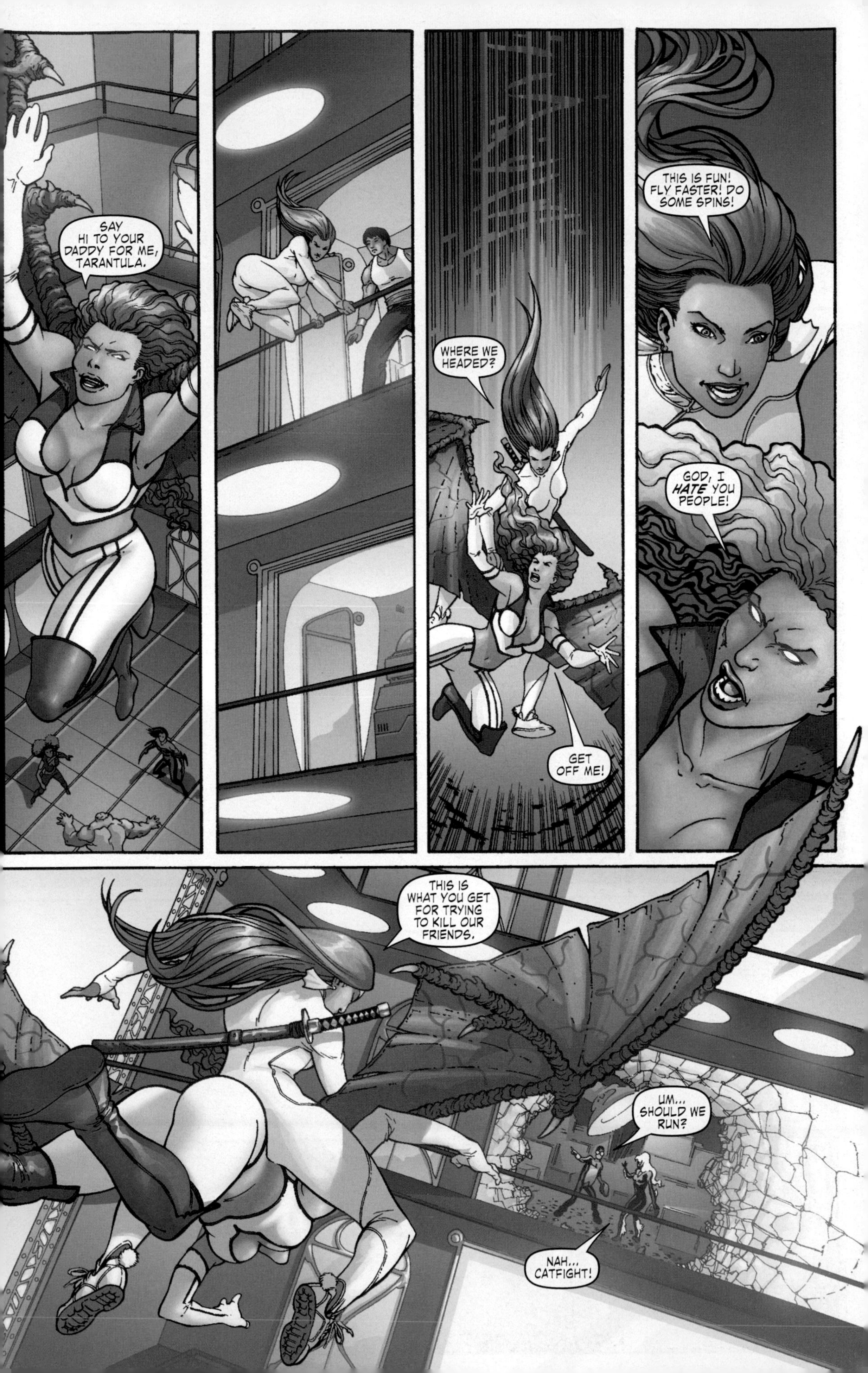
SAY HI TO YOUR DADDY FOR ME, TARANTULA.
WHERE WE HEADED?
GET OFF ME!
THIS IS FUN! FLY FASTER! DO SOME SPINS!
GOD, I *HATE* YOU PEOPLE!
THIS IS WHAT YOU GET FOR TRYING TO KILL OUR FRIENDS.
UM... SHOULD WE RUN?
NAH... CATFIGHT!

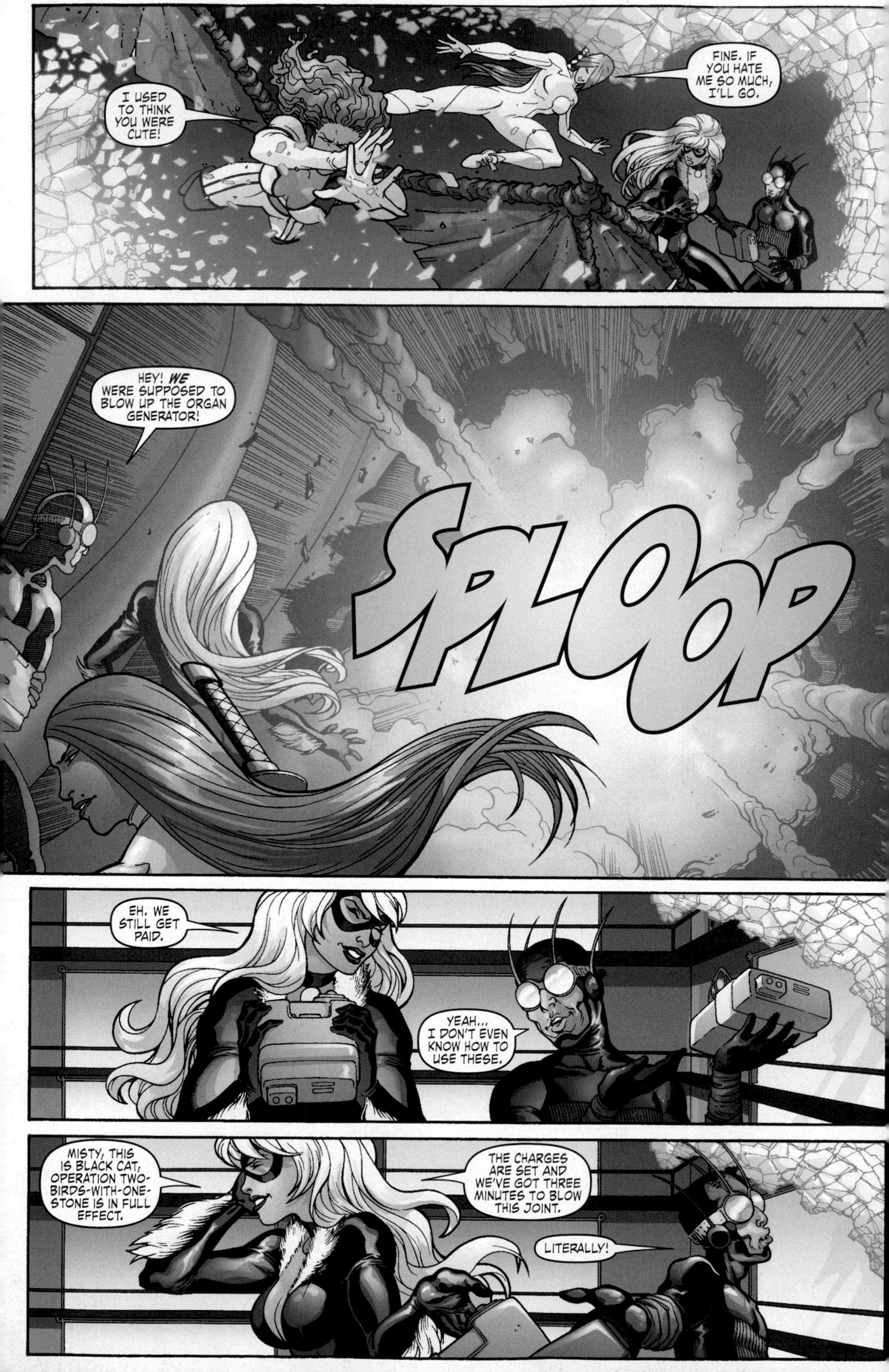
I USED TO THINK YOU WERE CUTE!
FINE. IF YOU HATE ME SO MUCH, I'LL GO.
HEY! WE WERE SUPPOSED TO BLOW UP THE ORGAN GENERATOR!
SPLOOP
EH. WE STILL GET PAID.
YEAH... I DON'T EVEN KNOW HOW TO USE THESE.
MISTY, THIS IS BLACK CAT, OPERATION TWO-BIRDS-WITH-ONE-STONE IS IN FULL EFFECT.
THE CHARGES ARE SET AND WE'VE GOT THREE MINUTES TO BLOW THIS JOINT.
LITERALLY!

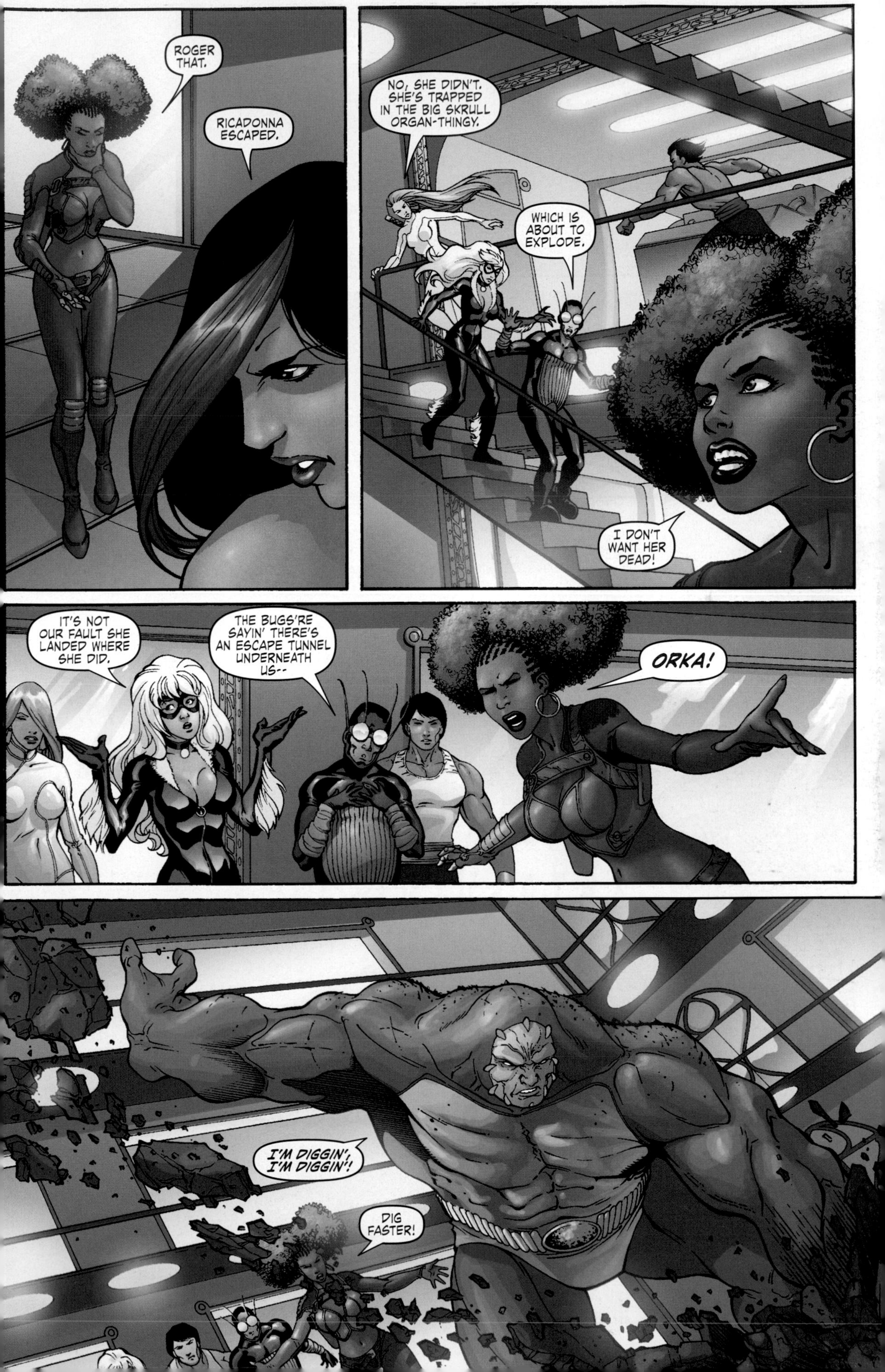
ROGER THAT.
RICADONNA ESCAPED.
NO, SHE DIDN'T. SHE'S TRAPPED IN THE BIG SKRULL ORGAN-THINGY.
WHICH IS ABOUT TO EXPLODE.
I DON'T WANT HER DEAD!
IT'S NOT OUR FAULT SHE LANDED WHERE SHE DID.
THE BUGS'RE SAYIN' THERE'S AN ESCAPE TUNNEL UNDERNEATH US--
ORKA!
I'M DIGGIN', I'M DIGGIN'!
DIG FASTER!

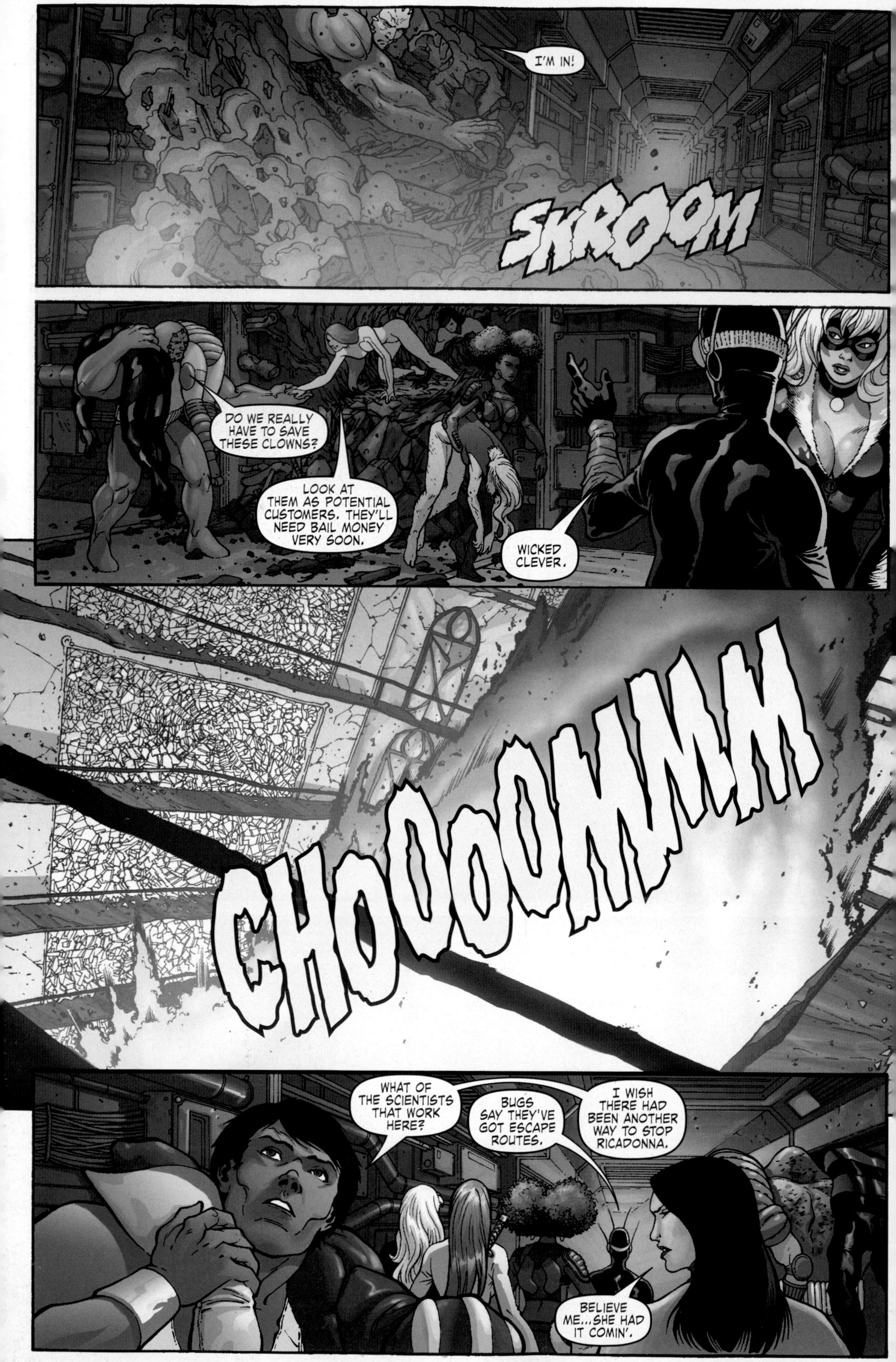
I'M IN!
SKROOM
DO WE REALLY HAVE TO SAVE THESE CLOWNS?
LOOK AT THEM AS POTENTIAL CUSTOMERS. THEY'LL NEED BAIL MONEY VERY SOON.
WICKED CLEVER.
CHOOOOMMM
WHAT OF THE SCIENTISTS THAT WORK HERE?
BUGS SAY THEY'VE GOT ESCAPE ROUTES.
I WISH THERE HAD BEEN ANOTHER WAY TO STOP RICADONNA.
BELIEVE ME...SHE HAD IT COMIN'.

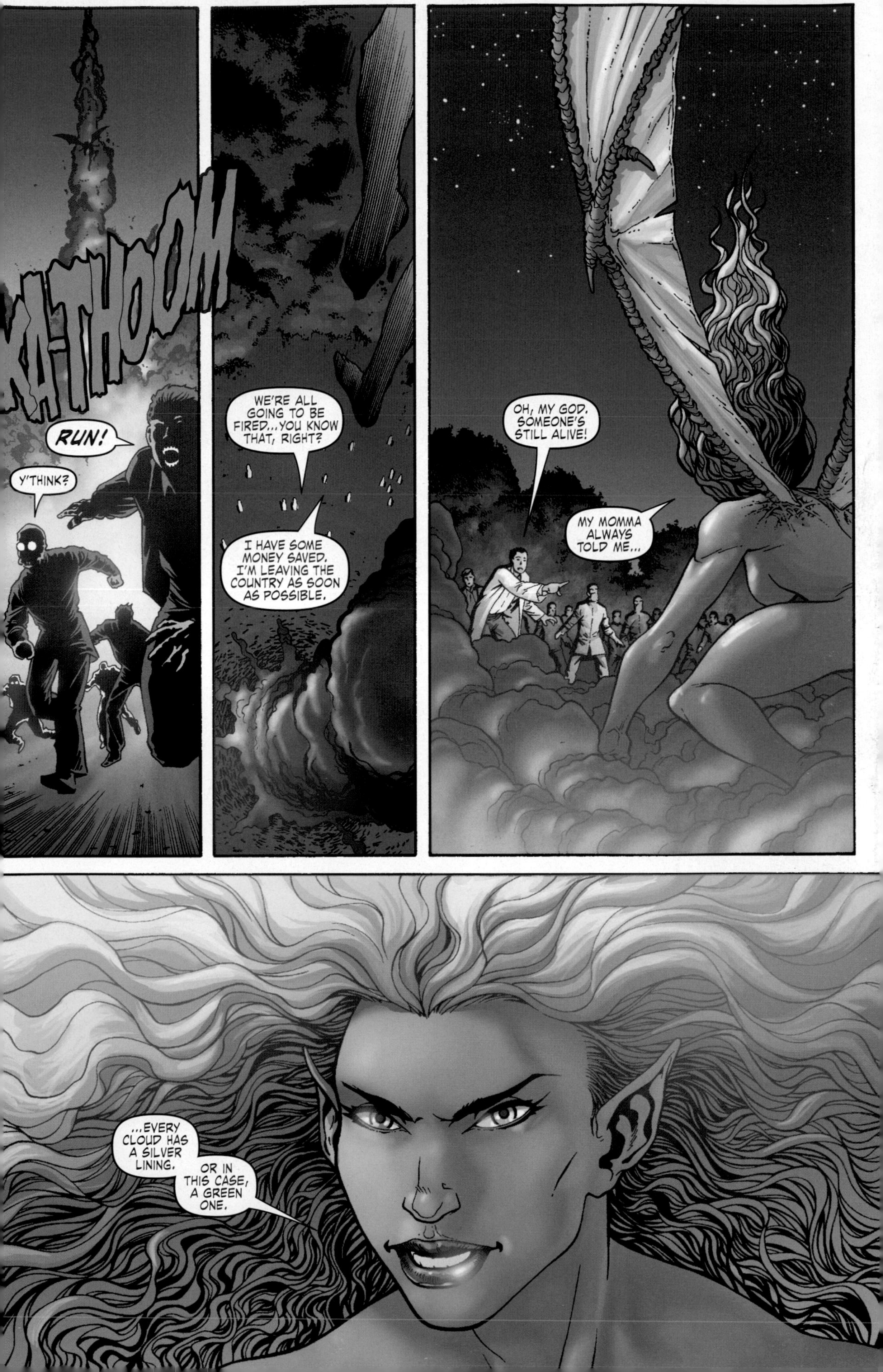
KA-THOOM
RUN!
Y'THINK?
WE'RE ALL GOING TO BE FIRED...YOU KNOW THAT, RIGHT?
I HAVE SOME MONEY SAVED. I'M LEAVING THE COUNTRY AS SOON AS POSSIBLE.
OH, MY GOD. SOMEONE'S STILL ALIVE!
MY MOMMA ALWAYS TOLD ME...
...EVERY CLOUD HAS A SILVER LINING.
OR IN THIS CASE, A GREEN ONE.

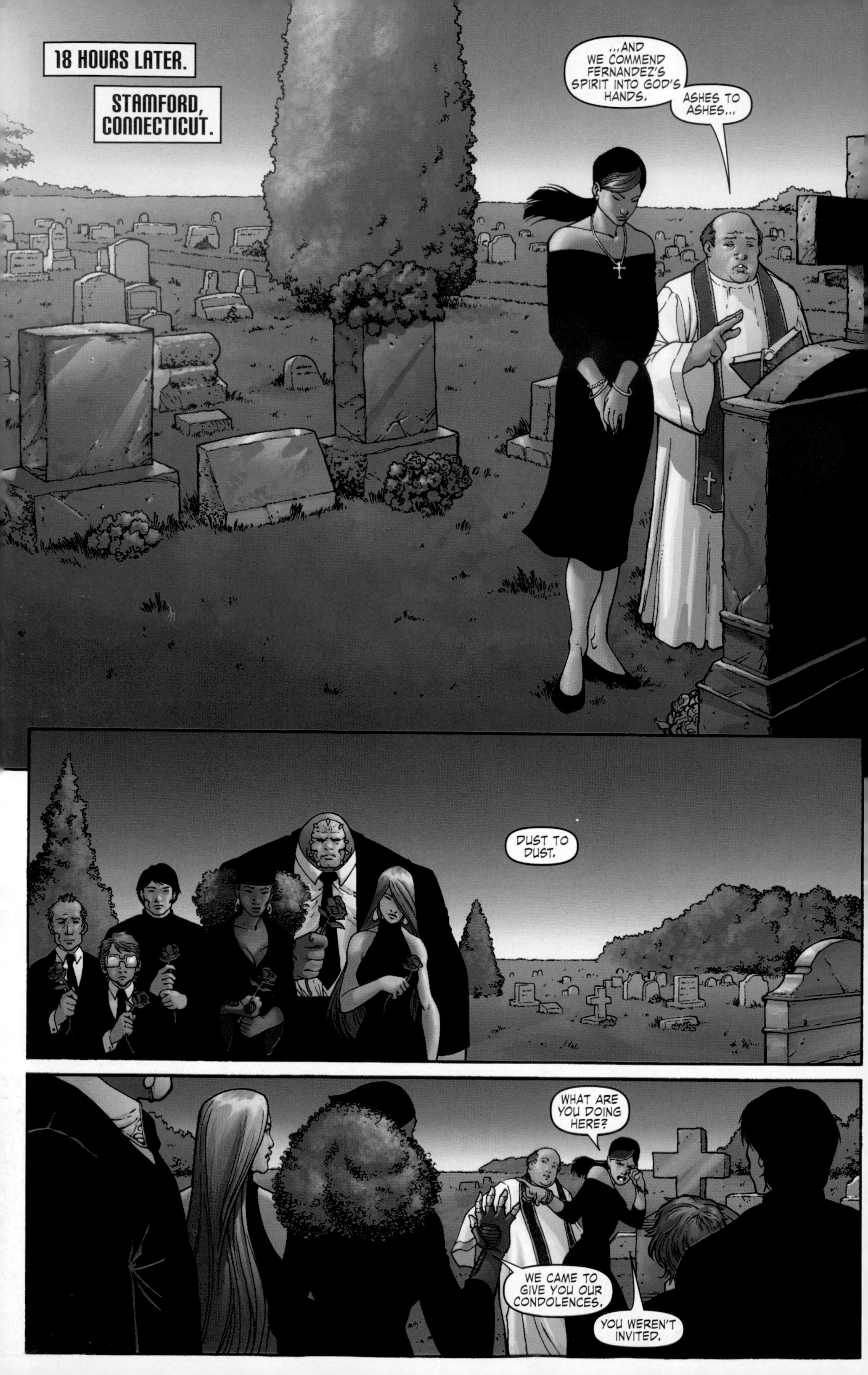
18 HOURS LATER.
STAMFORD, CONNECTICUT.
...AND WE COMMEND FERNANDEZ'S SPIRIT INTO GOD'S HANDS.
ASHES TO ASHES...
DUST TO DUST.
WHAT ARE YOU DOING HERE?
WE CAME TO GIVE YOU OUR CONDOLENCES.
YOU WEREN'T INVITED.

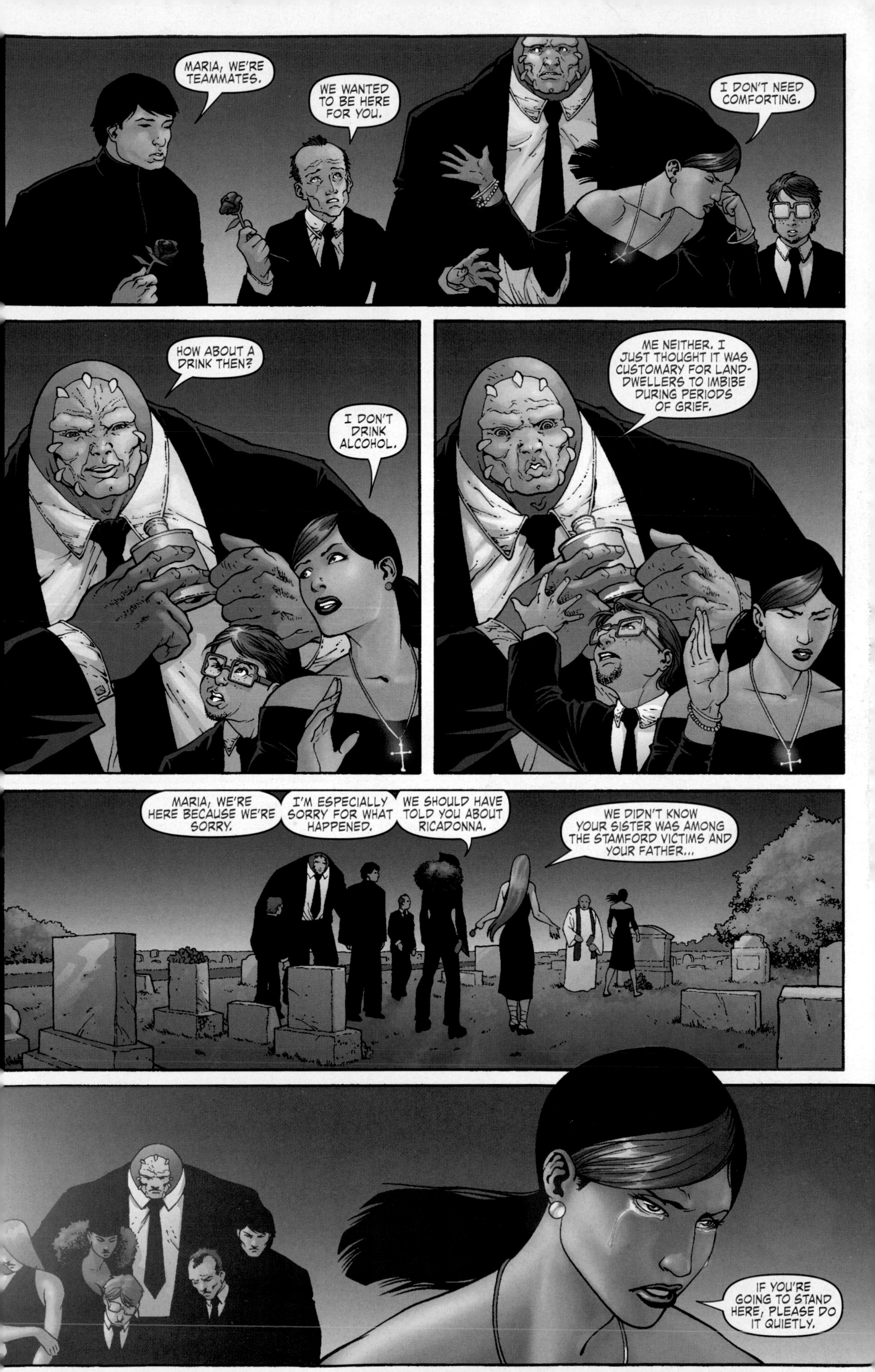
MARIA, WE'RE TEAMMATES.
WE WANTED TO BE HERE FOR YOU.
I DON'T NEED COMFORTING.
HOW ABOUT A DRINK THEN?
I DON'T DRINK ALCOHOL.
ME NEITHER. I JUST THOUGHT IT WAS CUSTOMARY FOR LAND-DWELLERS TO IMBIBE DURING PERIODS OF GRIEF.
MARIA, WE'RE HERE BECAUSE WE'RE SORRY.
I'M ESPECIALLY SORRY FOR WHAT HAPPENED.
WE SHOULD HAVE TOLD YOU ABOUT RICADONNA.
WE DIDN'T KNOW YOUR SISTER WAS AMONG THE STAMFORD VICTIMS AND YOUR FATHER...
IF YOU'RE GOING TO STAND HERE, PLEASE DO IT QUIETLY.

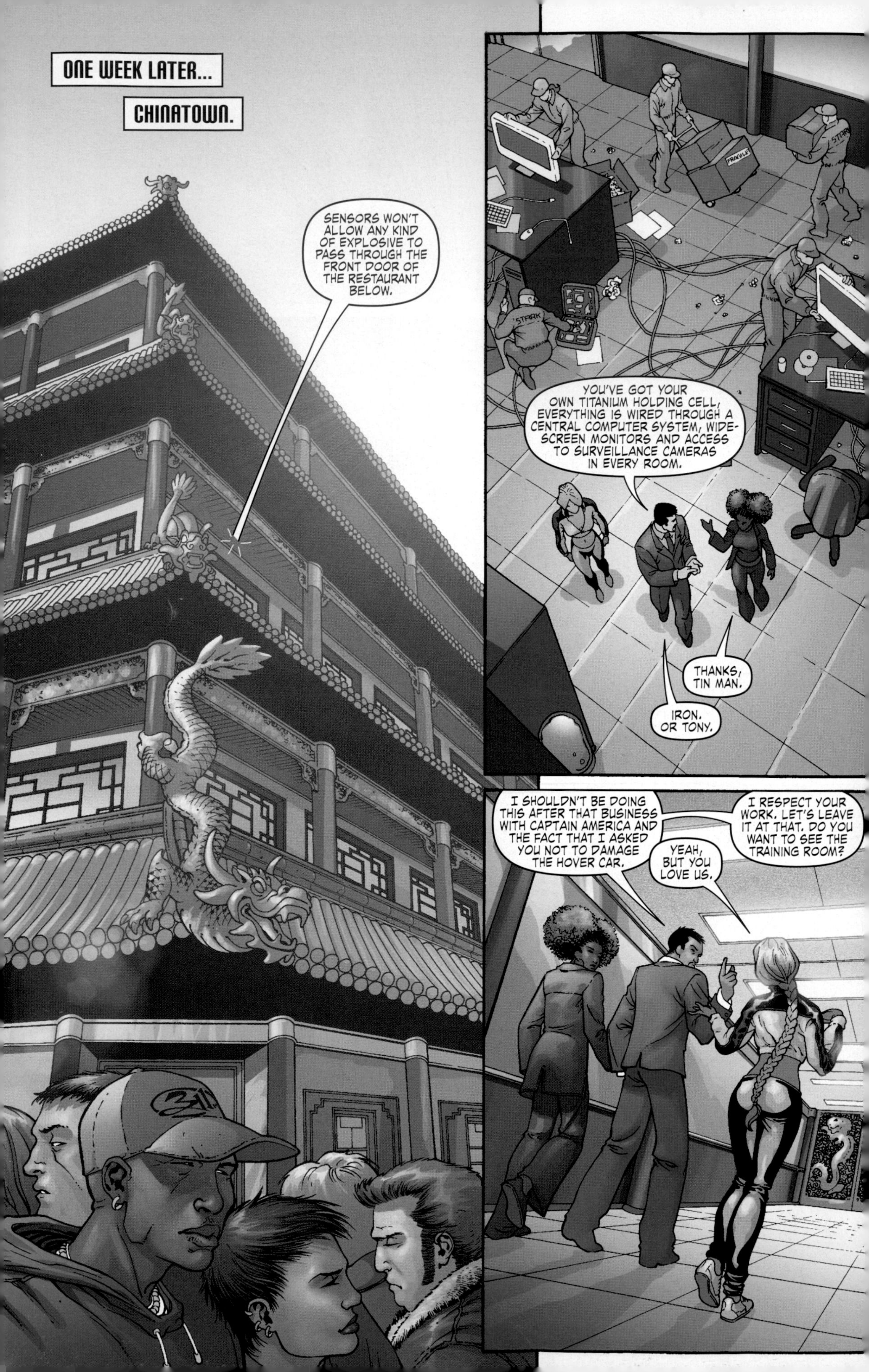
ONE WEEK LATER...
CHINATOWN.
SENSORS WON'T ALLOW ANY KIND OF EXPLOSIVE TO PASS THROUGH THE FRONT DOOR OF THE RESTAURANT BELOW.
FRAGILE
STARK
STARK
YOU'VE GOT YOUR OWN TITANIUM HOLDING CELL, EVERYTHING IS WIRED THROUGH A CENTRAL COMPUTER SYSTEM, WIDE-SCREEN MONITORS AND ACCESS TO SURVEILLANCE CAMERAS IN EVERY ROOM.
THANKS, TIN MAN.
IRON. OR TONY.
I SHOULDN'T BE DOING THIS AFTER THAT BUSINESS WITH CAPTAIN AMERICA AND THE FACT THAT I ASKED YOU NOT TO DAMAGE THE HOVER CAR.
YEAH, BUT YOU LOVE US.
I RESPECT YOUR WORK. LET'S LEAVE IT AT THAT. DO YOU WANT TO SEE THE TRAINING ROOM?

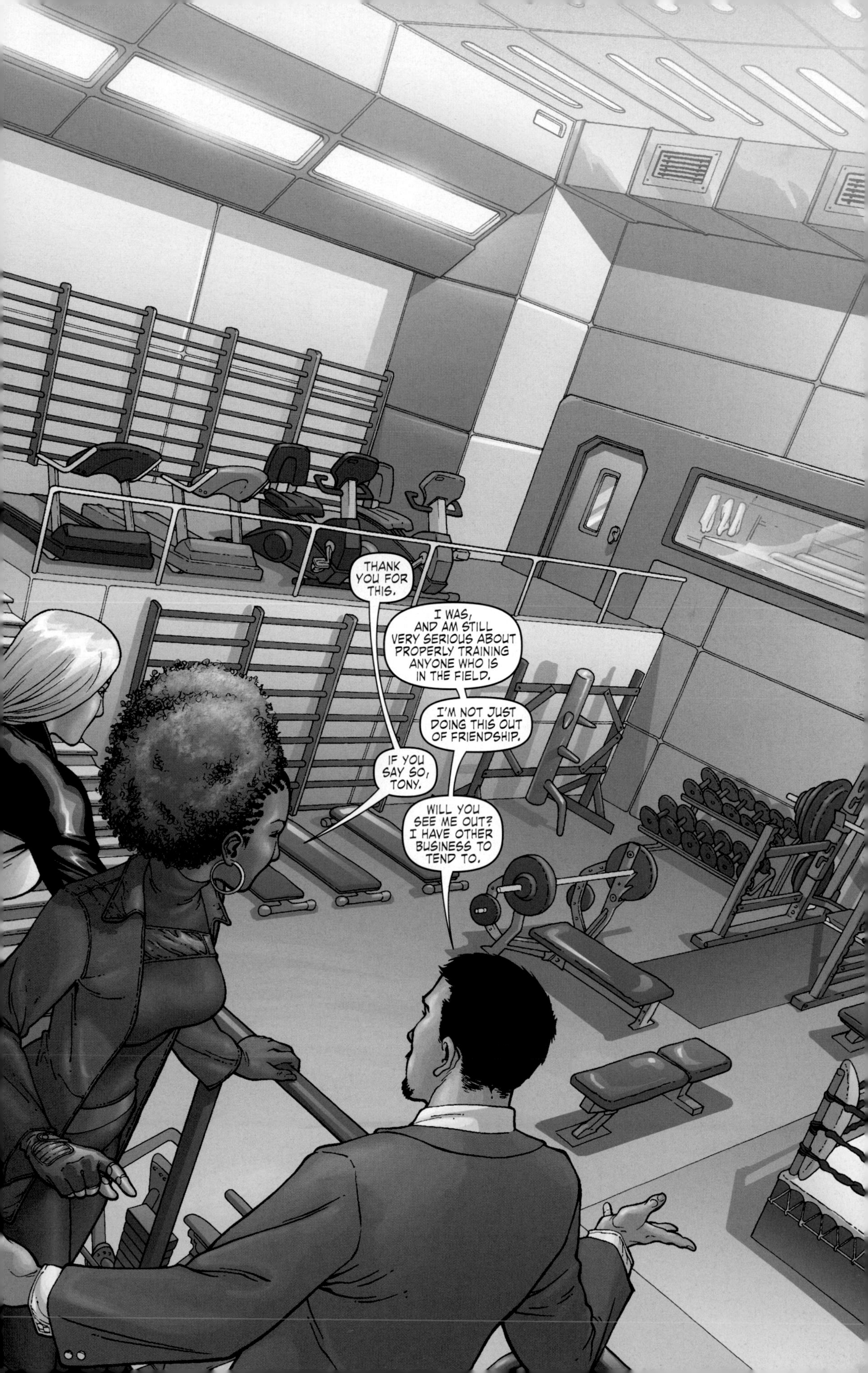
THANK YOU FOR THIS.
I WAS, AND AM STILL VERY SERIOUS ABOUT PROPERLY TRAINING ANYONE WHO IS IN THE FIELD.
I'M NOT JUST DOING THIS OUT OF FRIENDSHIP.
IF YOU SAY SO, TONY.
WILL YOU SEE ME OUT? I HAVE OTHER BUSINESS TO TEND TO.

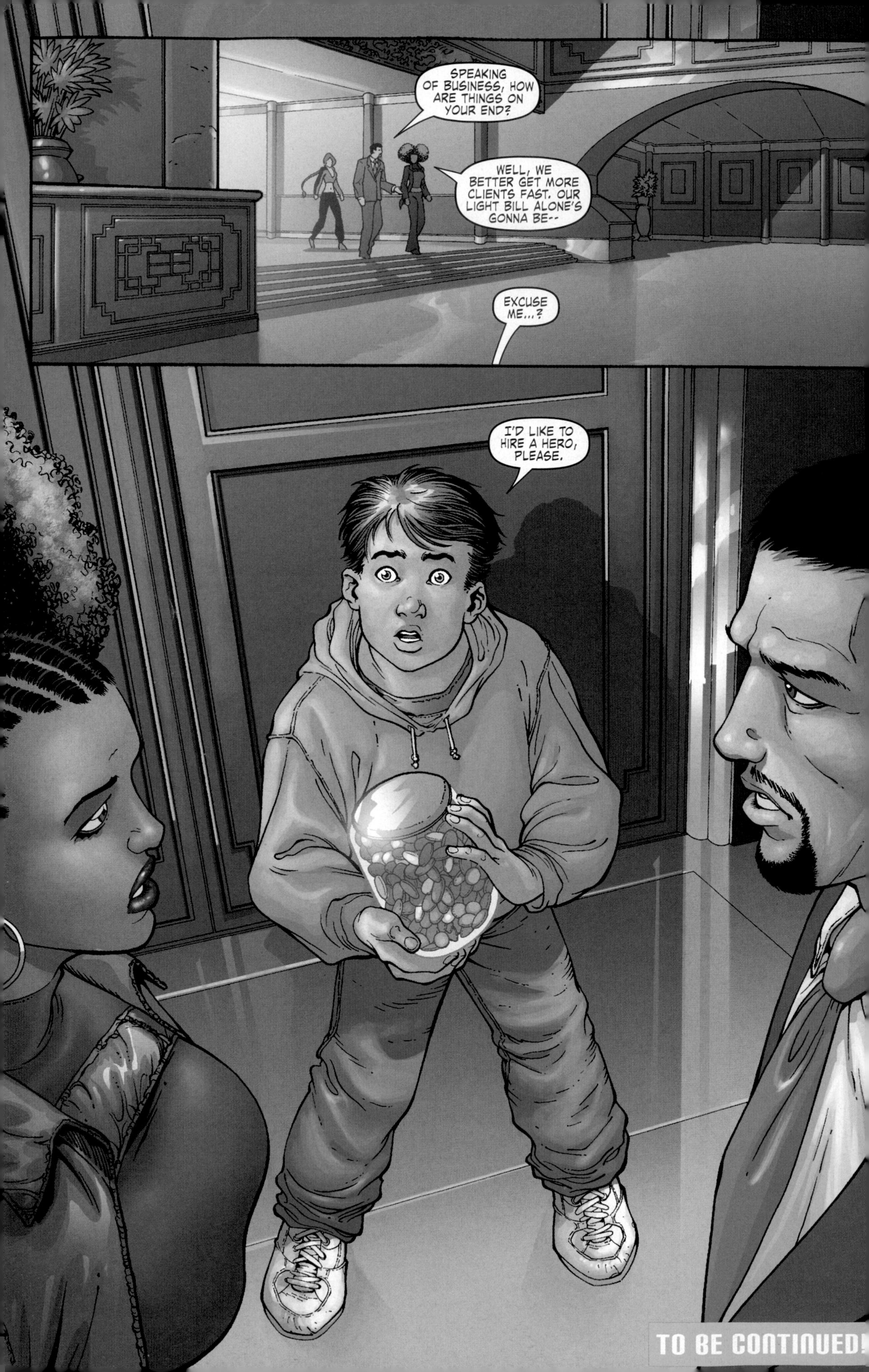
SPEAKING OF BUSINESS, HOW ARE THINGS ON YOUR END?
WELL, WE BETTER GET MORE CLIENTS FAST. OUR LIGHT BILL ALONE'S GONNA BE--
EXCUSE ME...?
I'D LIKE TO HIRE A HERO, PLEASE.
TO BE CONTINUED!

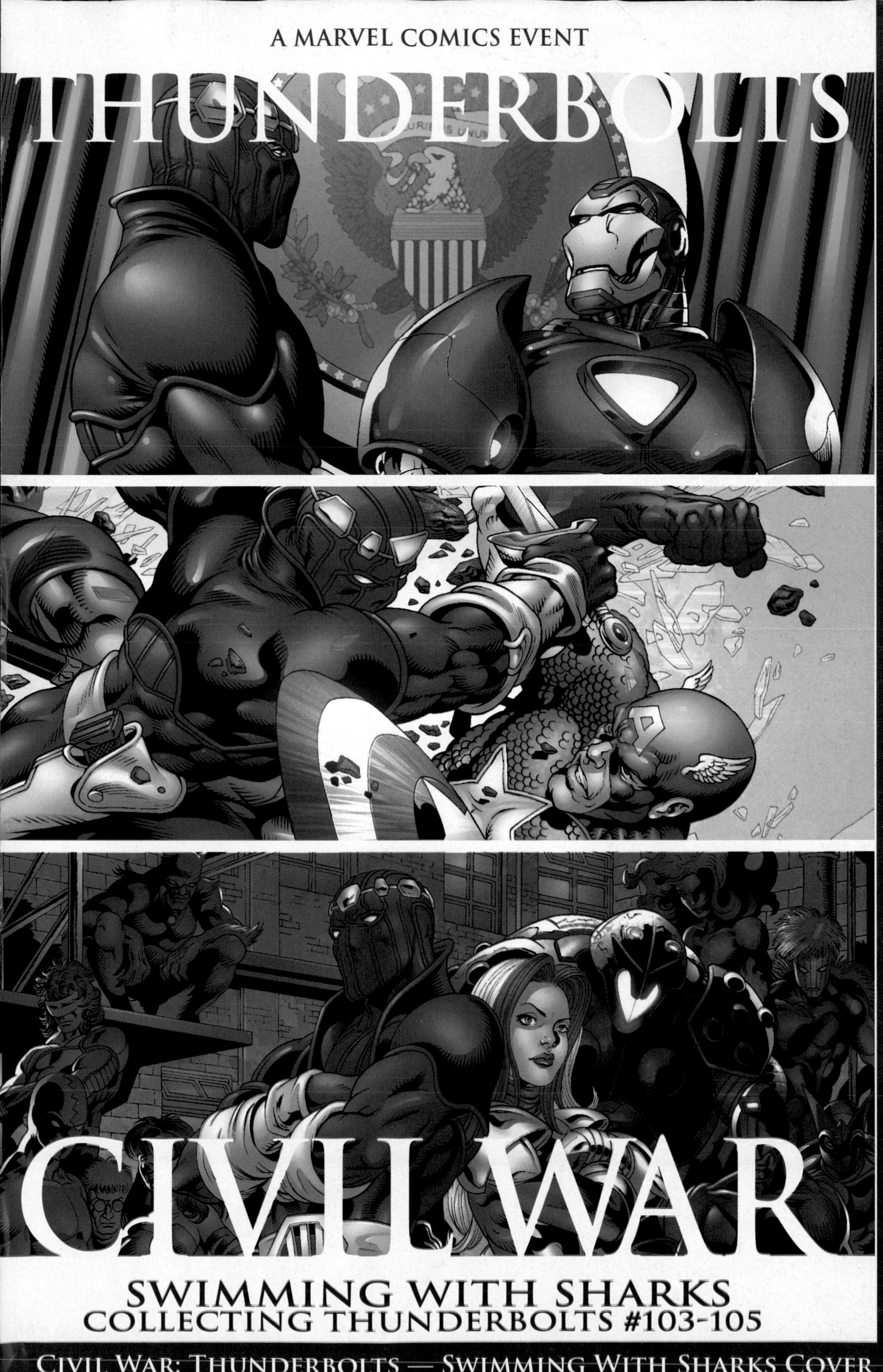
A MARVEL COMICS EVENT
THUNDERBOLTS
CIVIL WAR
SWIMMING WITH SHARKS
COLLECTING THUNDERBOLTS #103-105

CIVIL WAR: THUNDERBOLTS — SWIMMING WITH SHARKS COVER

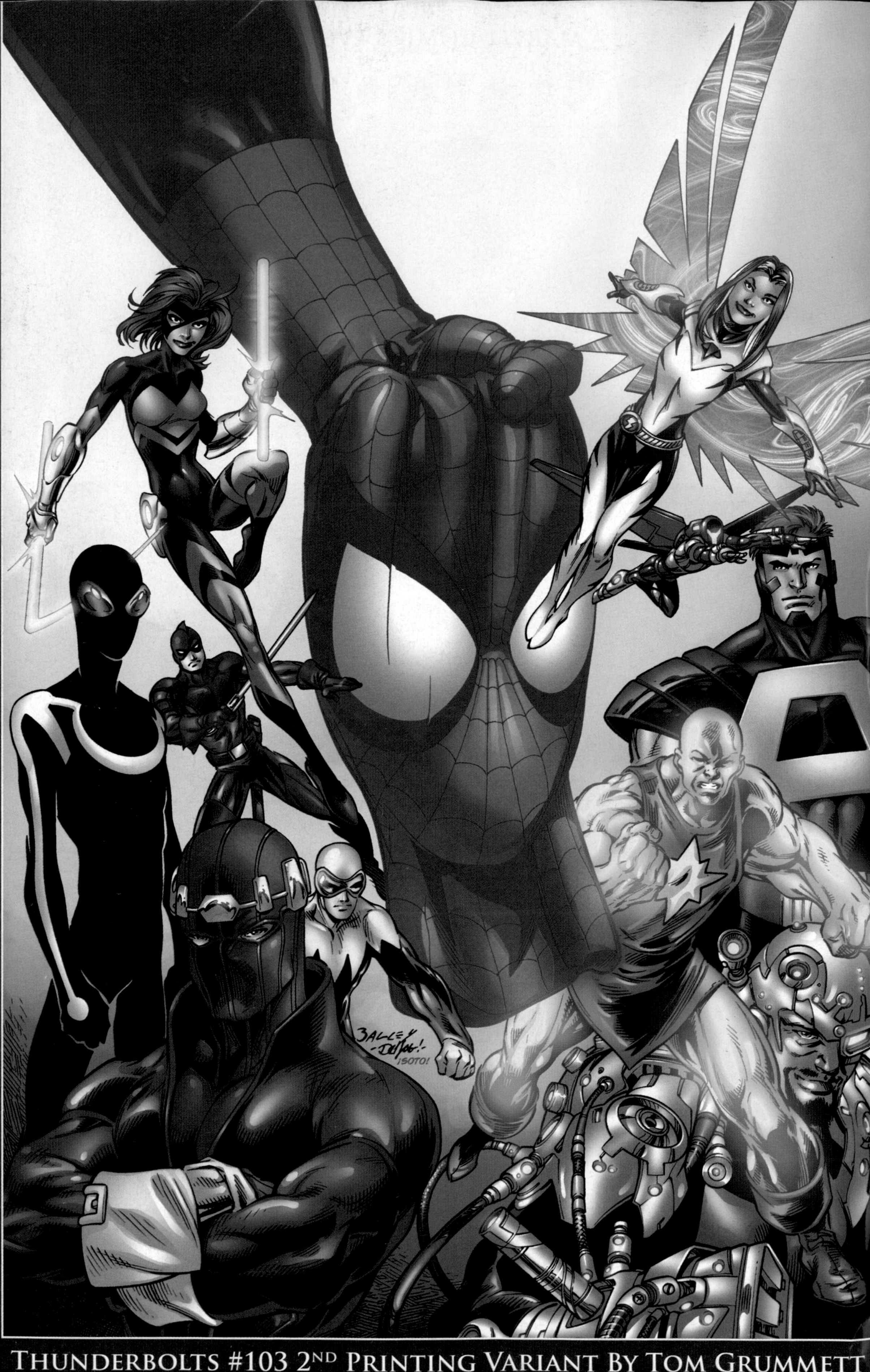

THUNDERBOLTS #103 2ND PRINTING VARIANT BY TOM GRUMMETT

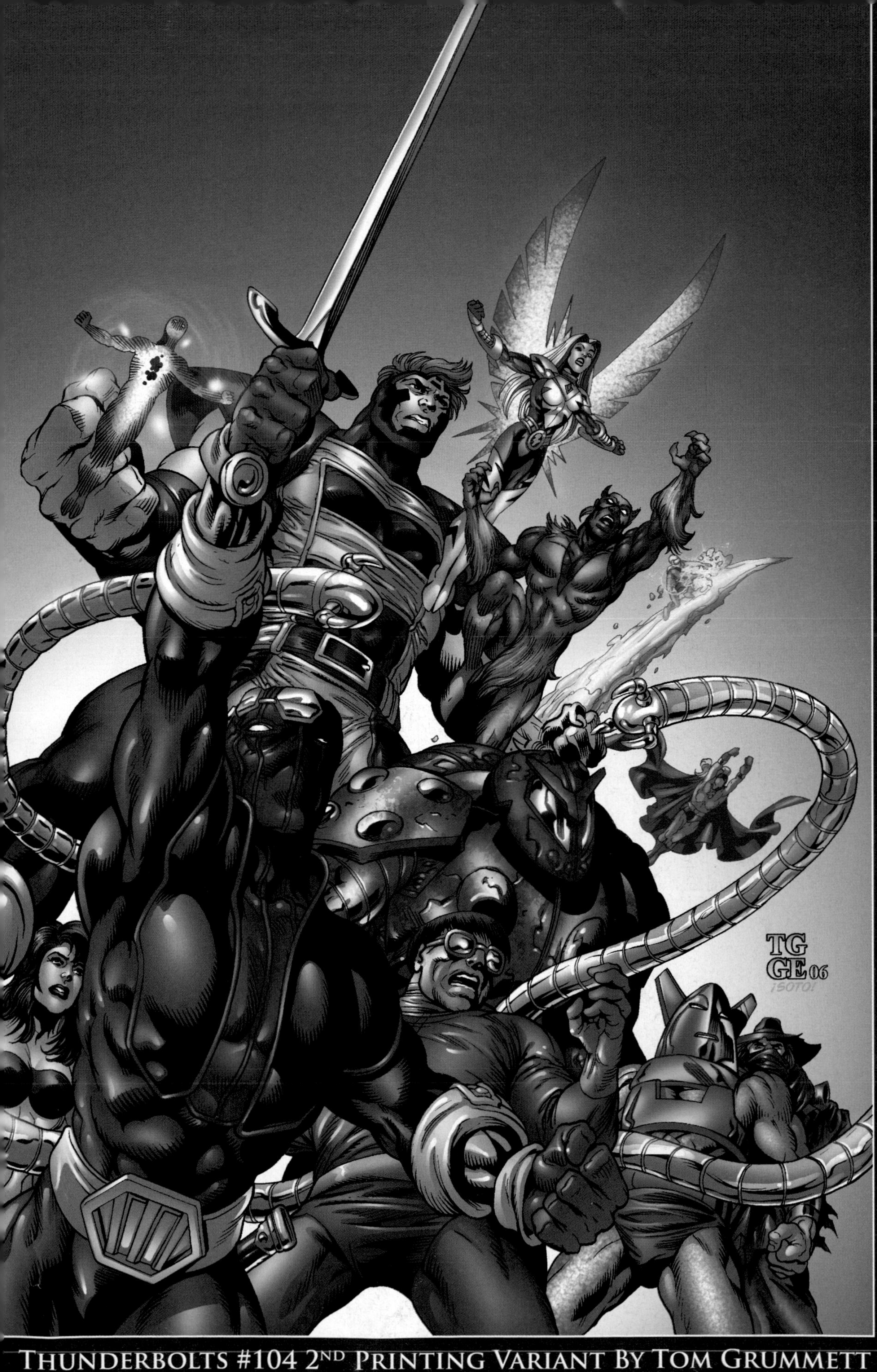
TG
GE 06
¡SOTO!

THUNDERBOLTS #104 2ND PRINTING VARIANT BY TOM GRUMMETT

# HUMBUG

**HISTORY:** Former Empire State University (ESU) senior entomology professor Buck Mitty is an eccentric scientist and inventor with an unusual fondness for insects. When the ESU regents cut off his funding to validate his thesis that "insects are our friends," Mitty turned to crime to continue his research. Wearing an amateur costume with gadgetry capable of various tricks via the amplification of insect noises, he tried to rob an armored car. Spider-Man foiled the bumbling attempt, forcing Humbug to turn his weaponry upon himself. Humbug was arrested, but the judge commuted his sentence to "time served."

Mitty immediately resumed his inept criminal tendencies, targeting ESU directly by stealing rare paintings on loan to the Art Department. When that attempt failed, he shifted sights to expensive super conductive ceramics in the Physics Building. Spider-Man captured Humbug after threatening a cruel end to a jar full of roaches. Humbug returned once again to harass the ESU faculty; this time, the obnoxious mercenary Deadpool was hired to kill the troublesome professor. Humbug deafened Deadpool with a hemorrhage around his ear drum, but the mercenary retaliated, covering Humbug with honey and South American fire ants. Humbug was left for dead, apparently eaten alive. While the outer layer of skin was being consumed, Humbug communicated with the ants, brokering a deal to exchange his life for a few younger and tastier victims. After Humbug kept his part of the bargain, Rodney, the leader of the fire ants, decided to stay with Humbug. Teaming with villains 8-Ball, Freezer Burn, and Whirlwind, Humbug robbed the wealthy publisher Ricadonna, unaware that she was an emerging crime-lord and that they stole a microchip with a computer virus that could destabilize the world economy. Unable to sell the stolen goods and with each of his colleagues murdered, Humbug turned himself over to bounty hunter Misty Knight. Ricadonna attacked Misty, severing her bionic arm holding the chip. Humbug summoned a massive swarm of insects against Ricadonna, who fled with the chip. After using his bug network to locate Ricadonna's auction for the microchip, Misty's partner Colleen Wing had Humbug arrested again.

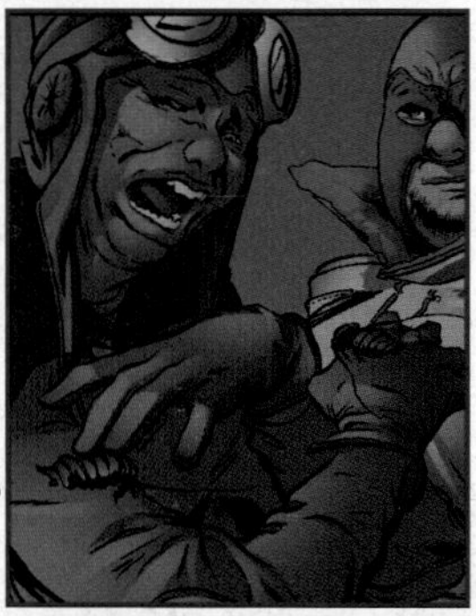

*Art by Khari Evans*

5'6"
130 lbs.

Hazel
Brown

Humbug's amplification helmet and sonic bandoliers transform the sounds various insects emanate into sophisticated weaponry. These include, but are not limited to, amplified sounds from eye-potted budmoths, imbricated snout beetles, cow-pea weevils, short-nosed cattle lice, salt-marsh mosquitoes, meadow spittlebugs, saw toothed grain beetles, buffalo tree-hoppers, bloodsucking cone noses, and plaster bagworms. Most generate sonic force blasts of various intensities and degrees of precision. Sounds from oblique-banded leaf rollers cause uncontrollable laughter. He can also communicate with insects using his helmet.

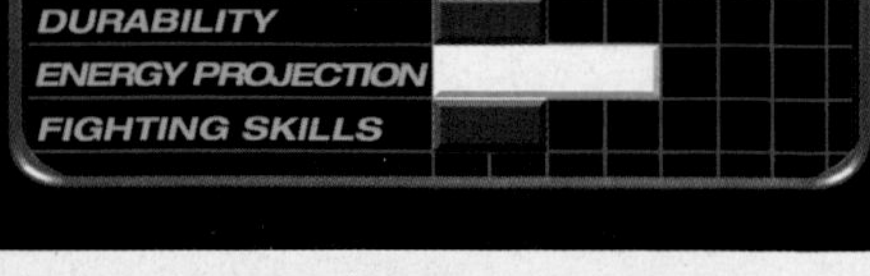
POWER GRID
1 2 3 4 5 6 7
INTELLIGENCE
STRENGTH
SPEED
DURABILITY
ENERGY PROJECTION
FIGHTING SKILLS

**REAL NAME:** Buck Mitty
**ALIASES:** The Bug-Man of Alcatraz, Red Baron
**IDENTITY:** Known to authorities
**OCCUPATION:** Criminal, scientist; former entomology professor
**CITIZENSHIP:** U.S.A. with a criminal record
**PLACE OF BIRTH:** Lodi, New Jersey
**KNOWN RELATIVES:** None
**GROUP AFFILIATION:** Unnamed villain team; formerly Empire State University
**EDUCATION:** Ph.D. in entomology
**FIRST APPEARANCE:** Web of Spider-Man#19 (1986)

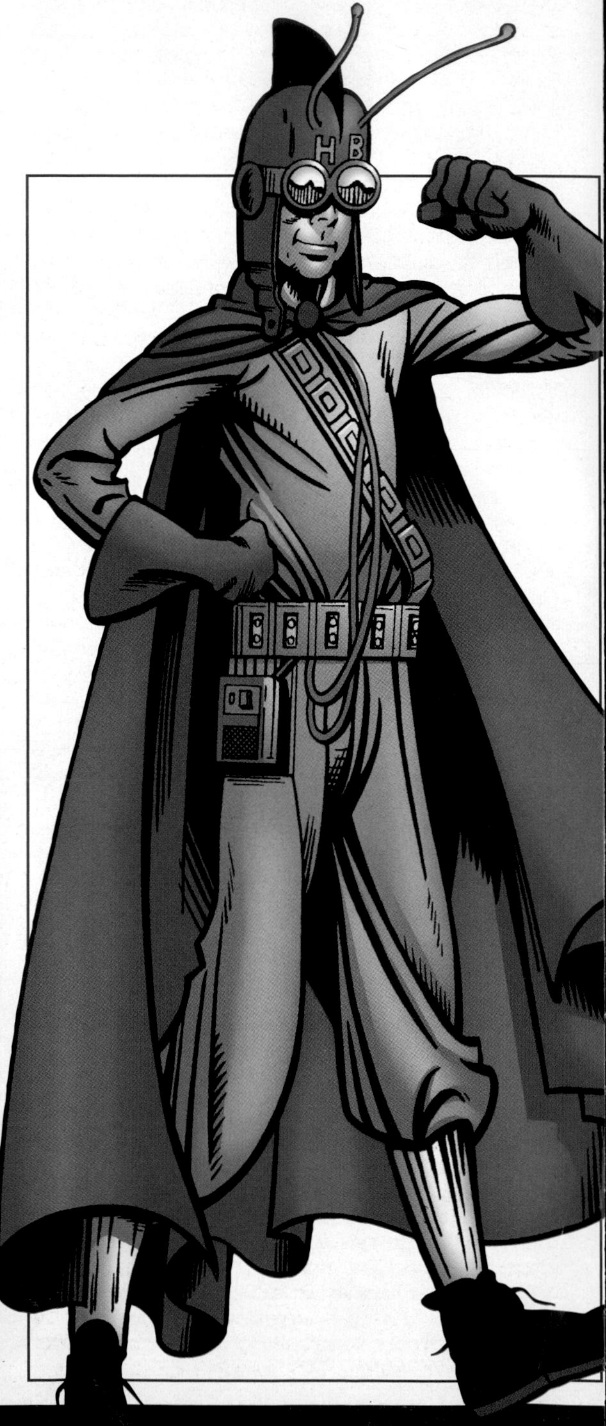

*Art by Mike Zeck*

**HISTORY:** The Squadron Sinister is a primarily criminal alliance of super-beings assembled in the Earth-616 reality in imitation of the Squadron Supreme, the leading heroes in the alternate Earth-712 reality. Over the years, both Squadrons have had similarly-powered, similarly-costumed members operating under costumed identities which originated with four of the Squadron Supreme's founders: the seemingly extraterrestrial strongman Hyperion (actually the last known survivor of Earth-712's Eternals), the nocturnal vigilante Nighthawk (Earth-712's Kyle Richmond), the super-swift Whizzer (Stan Stewart) and Doctor Spectrum (Joe Ledger), who wielded an energy-manipulating crystal prism given to him by the alien Skrull Skymax (later the Skrullian Skymaster).

Over a decade ago, Earth-712 was visited by reality-616's Grandmaster, an Elder of the Universe and cosmic-powered compulsive gamesman. Grandmaster used Earth-712's Squadron Supreme as his pawns in a game played with that reality's Scarlet Centurion, pitting the Squadron against the Centurion's super-criminal Institute of Evil. The Squadron Supreme triumphed, and an impressed Grandmaster hoped to employ them as his permanent champions, but they were unwilling, and the Grandmaster departed without them.

Later, Grandmaster visited the alternate future kingdom of Kang the Conqueror (a divergent counterpart of the Scarlet Centurion) and challenged him to a contest of champions: the Game of the Galaxies. If Kang won, he would be granted the power over life and death, which he needed to revive his near-dead love Ravonna. If Grandmaster won, Kang and Earth would be destroyed. Seeking champions, Kang recruited his old foes the Avengers, the leading superheroes of Earth-616's modern era. Remembering his success with the Squadron Supreme, Grandmaster decided to create his own Earth-616 version of the Squadron Supreme to battle the Avengers.

Traveling into Earth-616's recent past, the Grandmaster empowered chemist James Sanders and millionaire playboy Kyle Richmond as the new Whizzer and Nighthawk, doing so by tapping into the "Universal Wellspring," a mysterious and seemingly limitless source of alchemical power. Grandmaster also created a new Hyperion, an artificial being who believed himself to be the sole survivor of an atom-sized alien world which had been accidentally destroyed by human scientists, giving him a bitter grudge against humanity. Finally, Grandmaster sought out Krimonn, a treasonous Skrull who had been trapped in the form of a sentient crystal prism and set adrift in space after trying to overthrow the Skrullian emperor; Grandmaster guided the prism to Earth and into the hands of African supremacist Dr. Kinji Obatu, the influential, ruthless and power-hungry economics minister of an oil-rich emerging African nation. Forming a symbiotic bond with each other which allowed them to channel vast energies through the prism, Obatu and Krimonn became the new Dr. Spectrum under Grandmaster's guidance. Together, these new incarnations of Dr. Spectrum, Hyperion, Nighthawk and Whizzer formed the Squadron Sinister, serving the Grandmaster in exchange for their powers.

As participants in the Game of the Galaxies, the Squadron Sinister fought Avengers at the sites of various celebrated monuments. Captain America thwarted Nighthawk's attempt to steal or destroy the Statue of Liberty; Iron Man (Tony Stark) defeated Dr. Spectrum at the Taj Mahal after discovering that Spectrum's power prism was vulnerable to ultraviolet radiation, which existed on a wavelength beyond the prism's range of energy manipulation; Thor shrunk Hyperion down to tiny size and trapped him in a glass bubble outside the Sphinx; and Goliath (Clint Barton) battled Whizzer below the Big Ben clock tower in London until local hero Black Knight (Dane Whitman) intervened, taking down Whizzer by surprise. The Avengers had won, but Black Knight's interference led to that round of the game being declared a draw; in a second round, the Avengers defeated Grandmaster's backup pawns, Earth-616's World War II heroes the Invaders (1940s incarnations of Captain America,

**CURRENT MEMBERS:** Doctor Spectrum (Alice Nugent), Hyperion (Zhib Ran), Nighthawk (Kyle Richmond), Speed Demon (James Sanders)
**FORMER MEMBERS:** Doctor Spectrum (Kinji Obatu), Doctor Spectrum (Billy Roberts), Hyperion construct
**BASE OF OPERATIONS:** Manhattan penthouse apartment; formerly Nugent Technologies, Old Tappan, New Jersey; Crayton Observatory
**FIRST APPEARANCE:** Avengers #69 (1969)

---

Human Torch and Sub-Mariner). Kang won the Game, but was awarded only a partial victory due to the Knight spoiling the first round, forcing him to choose between the power of life or death rather than receiving both. His hatred for the Avengers outweighing his love for Ravonna, Kang opted for the power of death and would have killed the Avengers had he not been felled by the Black Knight. The Grandmaster departed, taking Kang's fleeting power with him, and released the Squadron Sinister from his service.

Resuming his Dr. Spectrum identity, Obatu came into further conflict with Iron Man, but Spectrum was hindered by a near-constant struggle for dominance between the rival personalities of Obatu and Krimonn. At one point, the prism deserted Obatu and took possession of Iron Man (actually Iron Man stand-in Eddie March), but the prism-possessed March was overpowered by Thor and gravely injured. The prism then re-bonded with Obatu, but Spectrum was defeated by the real Iron Man (Stark), who smashed the prism to bits. Obatu boasted that his influential

KINJI OBATU

HYPERION (ZHIB RAN)

NIGHTHAWK

DOCTOR SPECTRUM (ALICE NUGENT)

SPEED DEMON

BILLY ROBERTS

*Art by Tom Grummett with George Tuska & George Pérez (insets)*

foreign position would prevent him from facing any punishment for Spectrum's crimes, but his country's tyrannical president locked him up upon his return to Africa. Meanwhile, the power prism's fragments slowly reintegrated until the gem was whole again. Detroit sanitation worker Bob Farmer found it, but the good-hearted Farmer was apparently immune to its corrupting influence. He donated the gem to celebrity evangelist Billy Roberts, who quickly bonded with the prism and became the new Dr. Spectrum.

Meanwhile, Grandmaster's departure from Earth had somehow swept the shrunken Hyperion up into outer space, where he was eventually rescued and restored to normal by alien prospector Nebulon. Seeing a chance for revenge, Hyperion offered to sell Nebulon the Earth for mining purposes, even though Nebulon insisted Earth would have to be flooded for his people to function there. Whizzer and Spectrum (who credited Nebulon with helping him render Krimonn's consciousness within the prism largely dormant) agreed to assist in this project, confident that Nebulon could transport them to other suitable worlds if Earth became unlivable. Regrouping in secret at Crayton Observatory, the Squadron coerced their reluctant fourth member, Nighthawk, into aiding in the construction of a giant laser cannon that would melt the polar icecaps and flood the Earth. Nighthawk helped the heroic Defenders ruin the Squadron's scheme, which seemingly destroyed Nebulon and the Squadron when their cannon exploded. A reformed Nighthawk became a longtime member of the Defenders thereafter.

Nebulon and the Squadron were actually hurled into the other-dimensional realm of Zaar, home of the enlightened Ludberdites, whose advanced technology enabled Nebulon to send the Squadron back to Earth when they decided not to stay in this new world. Regrouping at Crayton Observatory with an energy-draining weapon derived from Ludberdite technology, the Squadron were unexpectedly attacked by the Defenders, who had tracked them down after mistakenly theorizing that the Squadron were responsible for the recent near-murder of Nighthawk; the true culprit in that crime had actually been criminal scientist Egghead, who was quickly apprehended by his old foe Yellowjacket (Hank Pym). The Squadron captured the Defenders after their Ludberdite weapon reduced the Hulk to human form, but Yellowjacket soon freed the heroes, who arrived in time to save the hospitalized Nighthawk from an actual Squadron attempt on his life. The Defenders defeated the Squadron Sinister, and Spectrum's prism shattered again during the battle.

Since the Squadron were not wanted criminals and could not be jailed by the authorities, Defenders leader Doctor Strange magically erased the three Squadron members' memories of their special powers and criminal careers, allowing them to pursue various civilian roles. Roberts returned to his evangelism, Sanders found work as a chemist, and Hyperion worked at a health club as "Mister Kant." Meanwhile, Obatu escaped prison and partnered with witch doctor W'Sulli, who controlled a vampiric zombie he called his zuvembie. Aided by the zuvembie, Obatu returned to America, where he abducted the African warrior monarch Black Panther (T'Challa) and various prominent African Americans, bringing them back to his native country as a peace offering to his president. The scheme was foiled through the combined efforts of Brother Voodoo, the Thing and Black Panther; the zuvembie seemingly slew W'Sulli and Obatu after they lost control of it during the conflict.

When Hank Pym restored the seemingly inert power prism as a gift for his wife the Wasp, Krimonn's consciousness possessed Wasp through the gem and attacked the Avengers as Dr. Spectrum. To treat her condition, the Avengers sought out previous prism host Roberts, though doing so meant breaking Strange's spell and restoring all of the Squadron's lost memories. Hyperion attacked the Avengers and Ms. Marvel alongside his new friend Thundra until Vision talked Hyperion into reconsidering his vendetta against humanity and ceasing hostilities. Meanwhile, Whizzer

also attacked the Avengers, who swiftly defeated him. As for Roberts, he claimed he had been an unwilling pawn of the prism and offered to help the Avengers cure Wasp, but he really wanted the prism for himself. Re-bonding with the gem, Roberts attacked the Avengers as Dr. Spectrum, but the prism abandoned him for Thor, whom Krimonn had long sought as a host body. Merging with Thor's hammer Mjolnir and controlling him through it, the prism continued attacking the Avengers until Thor was separated from his hammer, which soon transformed into the walking stick of Thor's mortal alter ego due to Odin's then-active enchantment. As a result of this transformation, the prism faded away into nothingness, taking Krimonn's consciousness with it.

For years thereafter, the Squadron remained disbanded. Nighthawk continued fighting crime; Whizzer continued his criminal career in a new guise as Speed Demon, eventually joining the team of reformed villains known as the Thunderbolts, albeit as one of their less reformed members; and Hyperion died battling his Earth-712 counterpart. Recently, however, there has been new activity relating to the Universal Wellspring that first empowered the Squadron Sinister. The Church of the Universal Wellspring, a super-powered cult devoted to its worship and protection, has been sighted tapping pockets of Wellspring energy around the world. A newly formed power prism also mysteriously appeared, bonding with divorced Des Moines factory worker Martha Gomes, who used it to become the latest criminal Dr. Spectrum. After battling the Thunderbolts as a pawn of the mind-controlling Purple Man, the new Spectrum fought them again when they interfered with her own robbery spree; however, the prism apparently rejected Gomes during the battle, going dormant and allowing her to be captured. Gomes was taken into custody for examination by the CSA (Commission on Superhuman Activities), who called in brilliant telecommunications specialist Alice Nugent to help them attempt communication with the new power prism. Both a lab assistant and an employer to Hank Pym in the past, Nugent had long coveted super-powers for herself, and the prism soon bonded with her as the newest Dr. Spectrum, a process Nugent later attributed to the Grandmaster. Around the same time, a new Hyperion (Zhib Ran) appeared on Earth, allegedly the sole survivor of a "Microverse" world unwittingly destroyed by cosmic-powered Thunderbolts member Photon (Genis-Vell). Meanwhile, the Wellspring-empowered Nighthawk and Speed Demon found their powers increasing significantly.

Claiming he must master the Wellspring for the sake of the world and the universe, and predicting that this gambit would bring his forces into conflict with the Thunderbolts, the Grandmaster convinced Nugent and the new Hyperion to help him reassemble the Squadron Sinister to this end. Nighthawk and Speed Demon refused to rejoin at first, and fought off the Squadron's attempts at forcible recruitment with the aid of the Thunderbolts; however, Speed Demon soon reconsidered, rejoining the Squadron after the Thunderbolts fired him for misconduct. Nighthawk briefly joined the Thunderbolts himself as Speed Demon's replacement, but he quit the team in part because he did not trust their new leader, infamous ex-criminal mastermind Baron Zemo. Regarding Grandmaster as the lesser of two evils in the battle for control of the Wellspring, Nighthawk reluctantly rejoined the Squadron for the duration of the conflict, which ended with the Squadron's defeat and the seeming demise of the Grandmaster.

*FURTHER READING: More details regarding the individual exploits of Earth-616's Kyle Richmond, James Sanders and the various Hyperions can be found in the Handbook profiles for Nighthawk, Speed Demon and Hyperion.*

***NOTE:** Aspiring to become the future benevolent rulers of the planet, Nugent and Hyperion prefer to call their alliance Supreme Power, though most others continue referring to the group as the Squadron Sinister.*